THE SOVIET UNION

THE
SOVIET
UNION

◆

A Guide for Travelers

◆

Eugenie and Jeffrey Gross

HARPER & ROW, PUBLISHERS
New York, Hagerstown, San Francisco,
London

This book is fondly dedicated to
Helen Pal and Cynthia Merman

THE SOVIET UNION: A GUIDE FOR TRAVELERS. Copyright © 1977 by
Eugenie Harris Gross and Jeffrey Kent Gross. All rights reserved.
Printed in the United States of America. No part of this book may
be used or reproduced in any manner whatsoever without written
permission except in the case of brief quotations embodied in criti-
cal articles and reviews. For information address Harper & Row,
Publishers, Inc., 10 East 53rd Street, New York, N.Y. 10022. Published simultaneously in Canada by Fitzhenry & Whiteside Limited, Toronto.

Maps by Jean Paul Tremblay

Library of Congress Cataloging in Publication Data

Gross, Eugenie Harris.
  The Soviet Union.
  Includes index.
    1. Russia—Description and travel—1970–
—Guide-books. I. Gross, Jeffrey, joint author.
II. Title.
DK16.G76 1976   914.7'04'85   73–14263
ISBN 0–06–011609–9 pbk.

77 78 79 80 10 9 8 7 6 5 4 3 2

CONTENTS

PREFACE   ix

INTRODUCTION   1

MOSCOW   35

LENINGRAD   83

KIEV   131

OTHER CITIES IN EUROPEAN RUSSIA   156

    Novgorod   156
    Yaroslavl   161
    Rostov   162
    Smolensk   164
    Orel   171
    Kharkov   173
    Volgograd   176

THE BLACK SEA   180

ODESSA   182

SOCHI AND SOCHI OUTLYING AREAS   193

SUKHUMI AND BATUMI   211

THE CRIMEA   218

THE GREATER YALTA AREA   221

SIMFEROPOL   229

CITIES AND TOWNS OF THE CAUCASUS   231

    Rostov-on-Don   231
    Pyatigorsk   234
    Nalchik   236
    Ordzhonikidze   236

TBILISI 238

YEREVAN 251

BAKU 260

THE MEDIEVAL TOWNS 266

Vladimir 267
Suzdal 281
Kideksha 300
Bogolyubovo 301
Yuryev-Polskoi 306

TALLINN 309

RIGA 324

VILNIUS 337

MINSK 344

LVOV 353

KISHINEV 369

CITIES ALONG THE WESTERN FRONTIER 374

Brest 374
Uzhgorod 376
Chop 378
Chernovtsy 378

SOVIET CENTRAL ASIA 381

Tashkent 381
Samarkand 390

OTHER CITIES OF CENTRAL ASIA 405

Alma Ata 405
Ashkhabad 410
Bukhara 414
Dushanbe 418
Frunze 421

INDEX 425

MAPS

The Soviet Union and Auto Routes   x
Central Moscow   42–45
Moscow Metro   68
Leningrad   84–86
Kiev   134–135

CHARTS

The Russian Alphabet   6
Temperature Chart   28

PREFACE

Over the last few years we have made several trips to the Soviet Union and found the areas visited interesting and enjoyable. The inconveniences were minor in contrast to the overall pleasure of seeing the Soviet Union and meeting its citizens firsthand. The peoples of the Soviet Republics are among the kindest human beings in the world. Each area visited has something special to offer in terms of history and culture. We hope our readers will come to share our enthusiasm.

We gratefully acknowledge the services of Intourist, the Travel-Go-Round Agency, and Aeroflot Soviet Airlines. A special area of gratitude is reserved for Mrs. Mildred Gross for her invaluable secretarial services.

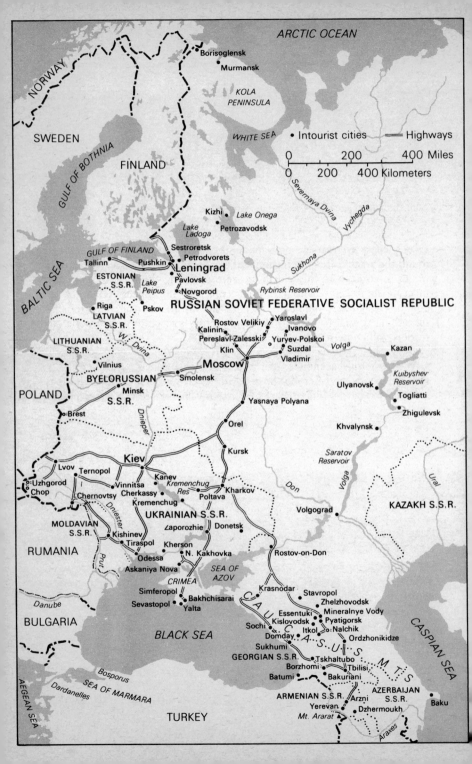

INTRODUCTION

ARRANGEMENTS FOR TRAVEL TO THE SOVIET UNION

Documents: Essential for travel to the Soviet Union are a *passport, visa,* and, if entering the U.S.S.R. from Asia, an *International Vaccination Certificate.* Passports can be obtained at various government agencies throughout the country, including certain post offices. Your travel agent can advise you of the most convenient location.

Visa: A visa for entry into the Soviet Union may be obtained only from the Consular Division of the U.S.S.R. Embassy, 1609 Decatur Street, N.W., Washington, D.C.; telephone: (202) 882–5829. The visa application may be obtained directly from the embassy or from your travel agent. A fee of $2 is required for each application requested to cover postage and other expenses. If your travel agent handles the visa correspondence there will be a small charge. Visas are generally negotiated over a period of one or two months, although extenuating circumstances and emergencies can foreshorten this period. During peak travel periods it is wise to allow a minimum of six weeks for receipt of visas from time of application.

International Vaccination Certificate: This may be acquired from your local Board of Health or your private physician. If your itinerary includes cities in Asian Russia, it is wise to have cholera and typhoid inoculations as well as a smallpox vaccination.

International Driver's License: This document is required for travelers planning to drive an automobile in the Soviet Union. An International Driver's License is available to licensed drivers through the International

AAA at a nominal fee or from Intourist at the border.

Travel Agencies: There are any number of travel agencies in the United States authorized by Intourist, the U.S.S.R. Agency for Foreign Travel, to arrange for travel to the Soviet Union. A partial listing appears on pp. 7–15. Your own travel agent may purchase your tour through one of these agencies if you prefer. Your final travel documents for entry into the Soviet Union must include a confirmation of all travel arrangements, a copy of your voucher, and a letter from a travel agent accredited by Intourist. It is strongly recommended that arrangements be made by a reputable agency. For further preliminary information regarding travel arrangements, contact Intourist, 45 East 49th Street, New York, N.Y. 10017; telephone: (212) 371–6953. A list of Soviet cities open to foreign tourists appears on pp. 17–18.

Transportation to and from the Soviet Union: It is best to avoid double-entry visas into the Soviet Union. They are difficult to obtain and frequently denied. If at all possible, plan a visit that will involve one entry and one exit, even if you intend to tour several countries on an extended itinerary. The Soviet Union is accessible by air, rail, steamship, and private car.

Soviet Union Entry and Exit Points:

By Air: Moscow, Leningrad, Kiev, Minsk, Vilnius, Irkutsk, Khabarovsk, Yerevan, Tashkent

By Rail: Luzhaika, Lososna, Brest, Mostiska, Chop, Vadul-Seret, Ungeny, Akhurian, Dzhulfa, Naushki, Zabaikalsk, Nakhodka

By Steamship: Via the Atlantic Ocean and Baltic Sea: Leningrad, Tallinn
Via the Mediterranean and Black seas: Odessa, Yalta, Sochi, Sukhumi
Via the Caspian Sea: Baku
Via the Danube River: Yalta
Via the Sea of Japan: Nakhodka
Via the Arctic Ocean: Murmansk

By Car: From Finland: Torfianovka
From Poland: Brest, Mostiska
From Czechoslovakia: Uzhgorod
From Hungary: Chop
From Rumania: Porubnoye, Leusheny
From Bulgaria: Izmail
From Turkey: Akhurya

Types of Tours

Visitors to the Soviet Union travel either independently or in groups, and travel arrangements are made accordingly. There is much to be gained from either method, depending on one's interests, finances, and time allotment. In general, accommodations and arrangements for group travel are preferred by the Soviet Union. However, those who travel independently will find a greater degree of freedom despite an occasional inconvenience. In many instances, the independent traveler may join a group for meals or a tour of a particular city. Permission will generally be granted by the tour leader, and the independent traveler will find the arrangement somewhat more convenient, especially during peak seasons when individuals are apt to receive secondary consideration.

Special-Interest Tours: Arrangements are frequently made for groups, and occasionally for individuals, with special interests. Among the various specialized tours are those arranged particularly for technical, professional, mountain climbing, camping, fishing, hunting, health treatment, and cultural interests. Intourist provides especially low rates for school children between the ages of thirteen and nineteen, in groups of twenty-five or more. Higher rates are charged for groups of college students. Representatives of commercial, financial, and industrial organizations engaged in business with the Soviet Union may find special accommodations and services at rates slightly lower than those for individual tourists. Groups desiring other types of tours for special interests should contact Intourist in New York.

Classes of Service

INDEPENDENT TRAVEL

Deluxe Suite. Available in Moscow and Leningrad only. It includes a three- or four-room suite with bath, breakfast (dining room or room service at the guest's option), chauffeured car for all transportation within the city limits from 8 A.M. until midnight, private guide and interpreter for eight hours daily, entrance fees to all museums, arrival and departure transfers, including porters' services.

Deluxe. Available in most Intourist cities. Included are a one-and-a-half- to two-room suite with bath, breakfast only or full board (as originally purchased) at the hotel dining room, chauffeured car for travel within the city limits for any three hours between 9 A.M. and 6 P.M., private guide and interpreter for six hours daily, entrance fees to museums, arrival and departure transfers, including porters' services.

First Class. Available in all Intourist cities except Ivanovo, Piarnu, Simferopol, Tiraspol, Urgench, and Viliandi. Included are a room and bath, breakfast or full board (as originally purchased), a three-hour guided sightseeing tour by bus or car, arrival and departure transfers plus porters' services.

Tourist Class. The *only* class of service available in Bukhara, Ivanovo, Piarnu, Simferopol, Tiraspol, Urgench, and Viliandi. Tourist class is *not* available in the following cities: Abakan, Ashkabad, Bratsk, Gori, Dushanbe, Kiev, Passanauri, Samarkand, Tashkent, Uzhgorod, Novosibirsk,

Ulianovsk, and from April 28–May 3, all of July and August, and from November 4–10 in Moscow and Leningrad. Included are a room with washbasin, bathroom facilities on the same floor, breakfast or full board (as originally purchased), one three-hour guided sightseeing tour by bus or car, arrival and departure transfers including porters' services.

GROUP TRAVEL

Intourist Fixed Starting Date Tours. This method of travel is arranged by Intourist. Individuals, working with Intourist-accredited agencies, arrive in Moscow independently and join a group of twenty to twenty-five people with similar arrangements. The tours provide varying itineraries with assorted starting dates and range from eight to twenty-three days. Only First Class service is provided and includes room with bath, full board (three meals), excursions, museum entrance fees, arrival and departure transfers with porters' services, and all air transportation within the Soviet Union. Additional fees are charged for concerts, ballets, and theater performances.

United States Travel Agency Tours. These tours are offered by Intourist-accredited travel agencies and offer a variety of itineraries within the Soviet Union, often in combination with visits to other countries. Generally First Class, but may occasionally be Deluxe or Tourist.

Prices and Methods of Payment

As the world currency market fluctuates and inflation accelerates, the price of travel follows suit. Generally speaking, travel and accommodations within the Soviet Union are average to high by world travel standards. Food and hotel rooms are costly, but transportation within the Soviet Union is a bargain. All transportation costs are approximately the same, whether one travels by air, land, or sea. The price is calculated according to distance, not according to conveyance. Costs also fluctuate depending on the length of the visit and the season. International transportation decreases in price as the length of time abroad increases. Seasonal rates in the Soviet Union can make a large difference in the cost of accommodations.

Off-Season is the least expensive. In Moscow, Kiev, and Leningrad, off-season is January 1–April 24; October 1–December 31. In all other cities it is January 1–April 30; October 1–December 31.

Season is medium-priced. In Moscow, Kiev, and Leningrad, season is April 25–June 30; September 1–30. In all other cities it is May 1–September 30.

High Season is the most expensive and pertains only to Moscow, Kiev, and Leningrad. High season is from July 1 to August 31. In general, tourists must book a minimum of two nights in Moscow, Kiev, or Leningrad during high season.

In general, all payment for travel and accommodations, including meals,

Laundry detergent, travel clothesline and clothespins.

Giveaway items, such as retractable ballpoint pens, souvenir pins, and postcards, especially ones representative of one's own geographical region, cosmetic gift items, American books and records, non-Russian cigarettes, chewing gum, disposable lighters and other uniquely Western European or American trinkets.

Carefully selected personal reading matter.

Russian dictionary or pocket phrase book.

What Not to Take to the Soviet Union

Religious articles in excess of customs regulations.

Firearms and other weapons, except for approved hunting and/or camping expeditions.

Magazines with an emphasis on anti-Soviet points of view or which have nude or suggestively sexual photos or content.

Books that feature "Western decadence."

Excessively high-fashioned clothing.

Soviet currency.

Narcotics, hashish, marijuana, etc.

Intourist-Accredited Travel Agencies (Partial Listing)

AAA World-Wide Travel, Inc., 1712 G St., N.W., Washington, D.C. 20006 (and all branch offices) (202)638–4000

Afton Tours Inc., 1776 Broadway, New York, N.Y. 10019 (212)757–9595

Allied Travel, Inc., 530 Fifth Ave., New York, N.Y. 10036 (212)661–6550

American Express Co., 65 Broadway, New York, N.Y. 10006 (and all branch offices) (212)944–2000

American Grand Circle, 555 Madison Ave., New York, N.Y. 10022 (212) 688–5910

American Travel Abroad, Inc., 250 West 57th St., New York, N.Y. 10019 (212)586–5230

American Travel Association, 1000 Vermont Ave., N.W., Washington, D.C. 20005 (202)638–0555

Anniversary Tours, Inc., 250 West 57th St., New York, N.Y. 10019 (212) 245–7501

Argus Travel Company, 342 Madison Ave., New York, N.Y. 10017 (212) 687–1291

Ask Mr. Foster Travel Service, Inc., 1 Park Ave., New York, N.Y. 10016 (and all branch offices) (212)683–2010

Bendel International, Inc., 913 Joseph Vance Bldg., Seattle, Wash. 98101 (206)623–1193

Bennett Tours, Inc., 270 Madison Ave., New York, N.Y. 10016 (and all branch offices) (212)532–5060

Caravel Tours & Cruises, Inc., 8 West 40th St., New York, N.Y. 10018 (212)239-4500

Chuck Hall & Associates, Inc., 975 Arthur Godfrey Rd., Miami Beach, Fla. 33140 (305)531-1195

CIT Travel Service, Inc., 11 West 42nd St., New York, N.Y. 10036 (and all branch offices) (212)564-3840

Club Tours, Inc., 25 West 43rd St., New York, N.Y. 10036 (212)354-1480

Coloyan Travel Service, 379 Trapelo Rd., Belmont, Mass. 02178 (617) 489-1860

Thos. Cook & Son, Inc., 587 Fifth Ave., New York, N.Y. 10017 (and all branch offices) (212)688-4000

Cosmos Travel, Inc., 488 Madison Ave., New York, N.Y. 10022 (212) 832-7550

Educational Travel Co., 316 Old National Bank Bldg., Spokane, Wash. 99201 (509)836-1417

Embassy World Holidays, Inc., 505 Fifth Ave., New York, N.Y. 10017 (212)682-3500

Exprinter Tour Operators, 500 Fifth Ave., New York, N.Y. 10017 (212) 244-7856

Foremost International Tours, Inc., 1600 Kapiolani Blvd., Suite 1214, Honolulu, Hawaii 96814 (808)946-6909

Garber Travel Service, Inc., 1406 Beacon St., Brookline, Mass. 02146 (617)566-2100

General Tours Inc., 49 West 57th St., New York, N.Y. 10019 (212) 751-1440

Gordon Travel Service, Inc., Prudential Plaza, Chicago, Ill. 60601 (312) 644-3003

Harvard Travel Service, Inc., 1310 Massachusetts Ave., Cambridge, Mass. 01238 (617)868-8080

Hemphill Travel Service, Inc., 1201 West 4th St., Los Angeles, Calif. 90017 (213)482-8420

Heron Travel & Tours, Inc., 9171 Wilshire Blvd., Beverly Hills, Calif. 90210 (213)275-6169

Kowbasniuk Agency, 286 East 10th St., New York, N.Y. 10009 (212) 254-8779

Lindblad Travel, Inc., 133 East 55th St., New York, N.Y. 10022 (212) 751-2300

Lissone-Lindeman, USA, Inc., 500 Fifth Ave., New York, N.Y. 10036 (and all branch offices) (212)279-7100

Maupintour, Inc., 711 West 23rd St., Lawrence, Kan. 66044 (and all branch offices) (913)843-1212

Music City Tours, 1501 North Vine St., Hollywood, Calif. 90028 (213) 461-4801

Paul Tausig & Son, Inc., 29 West 46th St., New York, N.Y. 10036 (212) 582-4611

Percival Tours Inc., 5820 Wilshire Blvd, Los Angeles, Calif. 90036 (and all branch offices) (213)936–2171

Russian Adventure Tours Inc., 20 East 46th St., New York, N.Y. 10017 (212)986–1500

Sanders World Travel Inc., 925 Shoreham Bldg., 806 15th St., N.W., Washington, D.C. 20005 (202)783–8718

Shipka Travel Agency Inc., 5434 State Rd., Cleveland, Ohio 44134 (216) 351–1700

Trans-Atlantic Travel Service, 393 W. Broadway, So. Boston, Mass. 02127 (617)268–8764

Travcoa Travel Corp., 111 North Wabash Ave., Chicago, Ill. 60602 (312) 332–0950

Travel Arrangements, 381 Bush St., San Francisco, Calif. 94104 (415) 433–1340

Travel-Go-Round, 516 Fifth Ave., New York, N.Y. 10036 (212)867–3835

Travelworld Inc., 6922 Hollywood Blvd., Los Angeles, Calif. 90028 (213) 466–5411

Union Tours, Inc., 1 East 36th St., New York, N.Y. 10016 (212)679–7879

University Travel Co., 44 Brattle St., Cambridge, Mass. 02138 (617) 864–7800

Vega International Travel Service, Inc., 201 North Wells St., Chicago, Ill. 60606 (312)332–7211

Wegiel Travel Service, Inc., 1985 Main St., Springfield, Mass. 01103 (413)734–8223

World Travel Tours, Inc., 620 North Main St., Santa Ana, Calif. 92700 (714)547–5986

Zonntours, Inc., 445 Sutter St., Suite 201, San Francisco, Calif. 94108 (415)982–1353

Intourist-Accredited Travel Agencies Abroad

AFGHANISTAN:
Afghan Tourist Organization, Helman Valley Building, Kabul

ARGENTINA:
Compagnie Internationale des Wagons-Lits, Délégation du Service Commercial, 685 Avenida Cordoba, Buenos Aires

Eurotur, Cordoba 351, Buenos Aires

Turismo Mundial, 25 de Mayo 611–1 P.Of.2, Buenos Aires

Viajes Costa, Santiago del Estero 1768, Mar del Plata

AUSTRALIA:
Orbit Travel Services Pty., Ltd., 116 King St., Sydney

World Travel Service Pty., Ltd., Western House, National Bank Building, 85–89 William St., Melbourne C1

World Travel Headquarters, Kindersley House, 33–35 Bligh St., Sydney

AUSTRIA:
Capri-Reisebüro, Wien 1., Graben 10
Osterreichisches Verkehrsbüro, Wien 1., Friedrichstrasse 7
Reisebüro "RUEFA," Wien 1., Teinfalstrasse-Lowelstrasse 18
Reisebüro COSMOS, Wien 1., Karntner Ring 15
Reisebüro "Austriatours," Wien 15., Mariahilferstrasse 140
Reisebüro "Austrobus," Wien 1., Dr. Karl-Lueger-Ring 8
Reisebüro "Adria," Wien 7., Burggasse 23

BELGIUM:
Belgatourist, 17 Rue des Paroissiens, Bruxelles
Generalcar, 10 Rue de la Montagne, Bruxelles
Havas Exprinter, 13–17 Blvd. Adolphe Max, Bruxelles
Voyages J. Dumoulin, 77 Blvd. Adolphe Max, Bruxelles
Voyages Wirtz S.A., 44 Avenue de Keyser, Anvers
Voyages Wirtz, 66 Rue Ravenstein, Bruxelles
Voyages Brook, 48 Rue d'Arenbourg, Bruxelles
West Belgium Coach Company, 14 Koningstraat, Ostende

BRAZIL:
International Travel Promotion, P.O. Box 4976, São Paulo
Siga-Tops Agencia de Viagens e Turismo, Rua São José, 90 Grupo 710, Rio
de Janeiro
Wagons-Lits/Cook, Av. Pres. Wilson 164b, Rio de Janeiro

BULGARIA:
"Balkantourist," Lenin Square 16, Sofia
"Rodina," Lenin Square 16, Sofia

BURMA:
Tourist-Burma, Ltd., Red Cross Building, 34 Strand Rd. P.O. Box 1543,
Rangoon

CANADA:
Allan's Travel Ltd., 63 Sparks St., Ottawa, Ontario
Globe Tours, 613 Selkirk Ave., Winnipeg, Manitoba
Hagen's Travel Service Ltd., 4841 Victoria Dr., Vancouver, B.C.
O.K. Johnson & Co., 697 Bay St., Toronto, Ontario
Kennedy Travel Bureau, 296 Queen St. West, Toronto, Ontario
P. Lawson Travel Ltd., 10168–102 St., Edmonton, Alberta
A. Nirenberg Travel Bureau Ltd., 1255 University St., Suite 105, Montreal,
P.Q.
Overseas Travel Ltd., 1052 Eglinton West, Toronto, Ontario
Treasure Tours, Inc., 304 Dominion Square Bldg., Montreal, P.Q.
Voyages Clause Michel Inc., 100 Rue d'Youville, Quebec, P.Q.

CEYLON:
Ceylon Carriers Ltd., 45, Alvis Place, Colpetty Colombo 3, P.O.B. 230,
Ceylon

CHINESE PEOPLE'S REPUBLIC:
China International Travel Service, "Luxingshe," Sidan, Peking

CHILE:
Via Mundi, Agustinas 828, Local 157, Santiago
COLOMBIA:
Exprinter S.A., Apartado Aereo 6127, Carrera 6-a No. 14–64, Bogotá
Wagons-Lits/Cook, Av. Jimenes 6–29, Bogotá
CUBA:
ACTI, Hotel Habana Libre, 23 y L Vedado, Havana
CZECHOSLOVAKIA:
"Cedok," Prikope 18, Praha 1
CYPRUS:
Francoudi & Stephanou Ltd., P.O.B. 31, Famagusta
DENMARK:
Danske Statsbaner Reisebureautjenesten, Solvgade 40, Copenhagen K
Folketurist A/s, Aboulevard 84, Copenhagen N
Forenede Danske Motoregere, Frederiksborggade 18, Copenhagen
Frederiksberg Rejsebureau A.S., Falkonercentret, Falkoneraile 7, Copen-
    hagen F
Jorgensens Resebureau, Jernbanegade 7, Copenhagen V
Nordisk Rustrafic A/S, Giro 34623, Tjaereborg
Scandinavian Student Travel Service, 51 Studiestrade, Copenhagen V
Trumf-Rejser, Vesterbrogade 180, Copenhagen V
Ungdommens Rejsenbureau, 7 Kultorvet, Copenhagen V
Wilson & Co., Bredgade 28, Copenhagen K
ETHIOPIA:
Ethiopian Travel & Tourist Agency, P.O.B. 1136, Addis Ababa
FEDERAL REPUBLIC OF GERMANY:
Allgemeiner-Deutscher Automobil-Club-ADAC, München 22, Königin-
    strasse 9–11a
Deutsches Reisebüro, und sämtlich Filialen, Frankfurt/Main, Escher-
    sheimer Landstrasse 25–27
Hapag-Lloyd Reisebüro, und sämtliche Filialen, Hamburg 1, Gallindamm
    25
Hotelplan, Internationale Reiseorganisation, Frankfurt/Main, Kornmarkt
    14 und Filiale in allen Stadten der Bundesrepublik
Hummel-Reise, 3 Hannover, Leinehaus Goethestrasse 18–20
Nord und Ost-Verkehr G.m.b.H., Hamburg 1, Spitalerstrasse 11
Osttourist-Reisebüro, Köln, Schildergasse 111
Reisebüro "Helios," Wiesbaden, Kaiser-Friedrich Ring 38
Reisebüro "Klinger," Würzburg, Bahnhofsplatz und Dominikanerplatz 3c
Reisedienst "Haas," Frankfurt/Main-West, Adalbertstrasse 60
Reisebüro "Die Welt," Hamburg 1, Bergstrasse 22
Reisebüro "Frohlich," Hannover, Ernst-August-Platz
Reisebüro "Lindex," München, Rauchstrasse 5
Scheffler Travel Service, Garmisch, Madl Hotel

FINLAND:
Finland Travel Bureau Ltd., Keskuskatu 1, Helsinki
Lomamatka Oy., Yrjonkatu 31, Helsinki
Matkatoimisto Kaleva Oy., Snellmaninkatu 13, Helsinki
VR Matkatoimisto, Asematalo, Helsinki
Suomen Turistiauto Oy., Annankatu 31–33 C., Helsinki
Turistimatkat Oy., Teatteritalo, Tampere

FRANCE:
Banque Commerciale pour L'Europe du Nord, 21 Rue de l'Arcade, Paris
Circuits Transcontinentaux, 2 Rue du Vingt-Neuf, Juillet, Paris
C.G.T.T., 2 Square de l'Opera, Paris
Compass Tours, 5 Square de l'Opera, Paris
Havas Exprinter, 26 Avenue de l'Opera, Paris
Monit, 4 Place de l'Opera, Paris
Riss & Cie, 68 Champs-Elysées, Paris
Touring Club de France, 65 Avenue Grande-Armée, Paris
Le Touriste, 12 Avenue Felix-Faure, Nice
Transtours, 49 Avenue de l'Opera, Paris
Transport et Voyages, 8 Rue Auber, Paris

GERMAN DEMOCRATIC REPUBLIC:
Reisebüro der DDR, Friedrichstrasse 110–112, Berlin N4

GHANA:
Akuaba Tourist Travel Agency, Republic House, P.O.B. 2059, Accra,
Ghana

GREECE:
Carayanides Travel Office, 58 Stadium Street, Athens
Hermès en Grèce, 4 Stadium Street, Athens
Pomonis Travel Service, 28 Avenue Alexandras, Athens

GUINEA:
Ministère d'Information et de Tourisme de la République de Guinée,
Conakry

HONG KONG:
Ermina Travel Center, 202 Shell House, Hong Kong
Mytravel International Ltd., Regional Office for Asia, 17th Floor Union
House, P.O. Box 235, Hong Kong

HUNGARY:
"Ibusz," Felszabadulas ter 5., Budapest V

ICELAND:
Ferdaskrifstofan Sunna Tourist Bureau, Smidjustig 4, Reykjavik

INDIA:
Jeena & Co., 10 Veer Nariman Rd., P.O.B. 849, Bombay 1
Mercury Travels Private Ltd., Oberoi Grand Hotel, Calcutta 13
The Orient Express Co. Private Ltd., 70 Janpath, New Delhi 1
Trade Wings Private Ltd., 60 Janpath, New Delhi

INDONESIA:
"Nitour" Inc. National & International Tourist Bureau, 2, Dj1, Madjapa-hit, Djarkarta

IRAN:
Gulf Agency Co. Ltd., 499 Takhte Djamshid, Bahar Square, P.O.B. 1472, Teheran
Perse Tourist, 210 Pahlavi Ave., Teheran

IRAQ:
Abultimman Travel Bureau, 2/A/8/1 Sa'addoon St., Baghdad

ITALY:
Augustea, 35–36 Piazza Augusto Imperatore, Roma
Autostradale, 1 Piazza Castello, Milano
Avai, 241 Via del Corso, Roma
Camst Viaggi, 10-a Piazza Martiri, Bologna
Chiari Sommariva, 8 Via Dante, Milano
CIMA, 13 Via della Liberta, Napoli
C I T, 68 Piazza della Republica, Roma
Gondrand, 32 Piazza della Republica, Milano
I Grandi Viaggi, 2 Piazza Diaz, Milano
Italian Express, 4 Via N-Tommaseo, Napoli
Italturist, 112 Via IV Novembre, Roma
Malan Viaggi, 1 Via Accademie delle Scienze, Torino
Mondialtur, 34 Via Valverde, Verona
Organisacion Polvani, 16 Via Ludovisi, Roma
Pierbusseti, 4 Via Dante, Milano
Sagital, 1a Via di Sottoripa, Genova
Tourist Romea, 5 Piazza del Cinquecento, Roma
Viatour, 2–4r Piazza Fontane Maroze, Genova

JAPAN:
Japan Travel Bureau, Overseas Travel Dept., 4,2-chome, Chiyoda-ku, On-temachi, Tokyo
Japan-Soviet Tourist Bureau Inc., N 11,3-chome, Sendagya, Shibuya-ku, Tokyo
Nikkai Travel Company Ltd., N 6,1-chome, Kojimachi, Chiyodaku, Tokyo
Nippon Express Co., Ltd., Head Office, Nittsu Building, N 11, 1-chome, Kanda-Hatagocho, Chiyoda-ku, Tokyo

KOREAN PEOPLE'S DEMOCRATIC REPUBLIC:
"Rehenso," Semundon St., Phenian

LEBANON:
Karnak Tourist & Transport Co. (SAL), Allenby St., P.O.B. 1460, Beirut
Transas Co. Sea & Air Travel Tourism, Arabia Bldg., Phoenicia St., P.O.B. 1372, Beirut

LIBERIA:
Mensah Travel Bureau, Ducor Hotel, P.O. Box 86, Monrovia

LUXEMBOURG:
Derulle-Wigreux & Fils, 59 Blvd. Royal, Luxembourg

MEXICO:
Garza Travel Service, S.A., Londres 106, Mexico 6, D.F.
Melia S.A., Calle Madrid 21, Mexico, D.F.
Mexamerica, S.A., Paseo de la Reforma 92, Mezzanine, Mexico 6, D.F.
Mundis Tours de Mexico S.A. de C.V., V. Carranza N 39–101, P. Box
    9170, Mexico 1, D.F.
Viajes Internacionales, Pesago, S.A., Londres 25, Mexico 6, D.F.
VIMSA, Paseo de la Reforma N 369, Mexico 6, D.F.

MONGOLIAN PEOPLE'S REPUBLIC:
"Zulcsin," Hotel Ulan Bator, Ulan Bator

MOROCCO:
Voyages Sirtam, 97 Blvd. Mohammed V, B.P. 986, Casablanca

NETHERLANDS:
Notel-Plan, Haag, Laan v. Meerdervoot 26–30
Lissone. Lindeman N.V., Haag, Pletterrijkade 50
Wm. H. Müller & Co., Amsterdam C, Damrak 90
Vernu-Reizen N.V., Amsterdam, Utrechtsestraat 48

NEW ZEALAND:
New Zealand Travel Service Ltd., Stafford St., Timaru

NORWAY:
Bennett's Travel Bureau, 35 Karl Johansgt, Oslo
Norsk Folke-Ferie, Torgatten 17, Oslo

PAKISTAN:
Universal Express Ltd., Bankukwala Bldg., McLeod Road, Karachi

POLAND:
Orbis, Bracka 16, Warsawa

PORTUGAL:
Europeia, 231 Avenida da Libertade 235, Lisbon
Turismo Santa Maria, 60–62 Rua Nova do Almada, Lisbon
Turexpresso, 44 Avenue Duque de Loule, Lisbon

RUMANIA:
"Carpaci," Bulevard Masery, 7 Bucuresti

SENEGAL:
Société Sénégalaise de Voyages et de Tourisme, 77 Avenue W. Ponty,
    Boîte Postale 1661, Dakar

SOMALI:
E.T.A.S. Ente Turistico, Alberghiero Somalo, Mogadiscio

SPAIN:
Melia, 12 Paseo del Rey, Madrid
Viajes Marsans S.A., 19 Carrera San Jeronimo, Madrid

SWEDEN:
AB Folk-Turist, Vallingaten 37, Stockholm
A/B Linjebuss, Sveavagen 22, Stockholm

A/B Nyman & Schultz, Vasagatan 19, Stockholm
Reso, Klara N. Kyrkogata 31, Stockholm
Motormannens Riksforbunol, Sturegatan 32, Stockholm
Kungl Automobil Klubben, Sodra Blasieholmshamnen 6, Stockholm
Royal Board of the Swedish State Railways, Travel Bureaux Department,
   Master Samuelsgatan 70, Stockholm

SWITZERLAND:
Cosmos A.G., 57 Missionstrasse, Basel
Cosmos S.A., 15 Cours de Rive, Genève
Danzas A.G., Bahnhoffplatz, Po.B. VIII, 3818, Zurich
Fert Tours International, 2 Rue Fendt, Genève

SYRIA:
Karnak Tourist & Transport Co. S.A.A., 114/116 Port Said, Damascus

TUNISIA:
Société Hôtelière et Touristique de Tunisie, Avenue Mohammed V, Tunis

TURKEY:
SUAD TOKAY, Galata, Persembe, Pazar Hazar Han, Istanbul
Turist Seyahat Anonim Sirkety, "Turist" Travel Company, Cumhuriyet
   Cad. 8, Taksim-Istanbul

UNITED KINGDOM:
Ashton & Mitchell Travel Ltd., 2 Old Bond St., London W1
Australian Travel Service Ltd., 11 Mayfair Place, London W1
Challis & Benson Ltd., 133 New Bond St., Mayfair, London W1
Contours Ltd., 72 Newman St., London W1
Cooperative Travel Service, 4/10 Regency St., London SW1
European Motorways Ltd., 47/48 Piccadilly, London W1
Excelsior European Motorways Ltd., 89 Holdenhurst Rd., Bournemouth
Frames' Tours Ltd., 2531 Tavistock Place, London WC1
Glabal Tours Ltd., 301/307 Oxford St., London W1
International Travel Service Ltd., 7 Haymarket, London SW1
Milbanke Travel Ltd., Milbanke House, 104 New Bond St., London W1
L. W. Morland & Co. Ltd., 27 St. Thomas St., London SE1
Poly Travel Ltd., 40 Edgware Rd., London W2
Progressive Tours Ltd., 100 Rochester Row, London SW1
Sir Henry Lunn Ltd., Marble Arch House, 36 Edgware Road, London W2
Thos. Cook & Son Ltd., Berkeley St., Piccadilly, London W1
Wakefield Fortune Ltd., 52 Haymarket, London SW1
Wayfarers Travel Agency Ltd., 20 Russell Square, London WC1
WTA Ltd., Eccleston Court, Gillingham St., London SW1

UNITED ARAB REPUBLIC:
Mena Travel & Tourist Agency, 14 Talaat Harb Street, Cairo, UAR

URUGUAY:
COT, Calle Sarandi 699, Montevideo

THE TERRITORY OF THE SOVIET UNION

Republic	Population (in millions)	Area (sq. km.)	Area (sq. mi.)	Capital
Armenian S.S.R.	2	29,800	11,500	Yerevan
Azerbaijan S.S.R.	4	85,700	33,100	Baku
Byelorussian (White Russia S.S.R.)	8.5	207,500	80,100	Minsk
Estonian S.S.R.	1	45,000	17,400	Tallinn
Georgian S.S.R.	4.5	76,100	29,400	Tbilisi
Kazakh S.S.R.	11.5	2,749,500	1,061,600	Alma Ata
Kirghiz S.S.R.	2	197,100	76,100	Frunze
Latvian S.S.R.	2	63,700	24,600	Riga
Lithuanian S.S.R.	3	65,300	25,200	Vilnius
Moldavian S.S.R.	3.25	33,900	13,100	Kishinev
Russian Soviet Federated Socialist Republic	125	16,838,900	6,501,500	Moscow
Tajik S.S.R.	2	142,200	54,900	Dushanbe
Turkmen S.S.R.	2	484,800	187,200	Ashkhabad
Ukrainian S.S.R.	45	571,400	220,600	Kiev
Uzbek S.S.R.	10	407,700	157,400	Tashkent
Total	224.40	21,996,630	8,493,700	

AUTONOMOUS SOVIET SOCIALIST REPUBLICS

Note: Autonomous Republics are located within the Russian Federation unless otherwise specified.

Abkhazian A.S.S.R.
Adjar A.S.S.R. (Azerbaijan S.S.R.)
Bashkir A.S.S.R.
Buryat A.S.S.R.
Chechen-Ingush A.S.S.R.
Chuvash A.S.S.R.
Daghestan A.S.S.R.
Kabardin-Balkar A.S.S.R.
Kalmyk A.S.S.R.
Kara-Kalpak A.S.S.R. (Georgian S.S.R.)

Karelian A.S.S.R.
Komi A.S.S.R.
Mari A.S.S.R.
Mordvinian A.S.S.R.
Nakhichevan A.S.S.R.
North-Ossetian A.S.S.R.
Tatar A.S.S.R.
Tuva A.S.S.R.
Udmurt A.S.S.R.
Yakut A.S.S.R.
Yakutsk A.S.S.R. (Uzbek S.S.R.)

AUTONOMOUS REGIONS

Note: Autonomous Regions are all within the Russian Federation unless otherwise specified.

Adygei A.R.
Gorno-Altai A.R.
Gorno-Badakhshan A.R.
Jewish A.R.
Karachai-Cherkess A.R.
  (Azerbaijan S.S.R.)

Khakass A.R.
Nagorno-Karabakh A.R.
  (Georgian S.S.R.)
South-Ossetian A.R. (Tajik S.S.R.)

NATIONAL AREAS (within the Russian Federation)

Agin N.A.
Chukchi N.A.
Evenki N.A.
Khanty-Mansi N.A.
Komi-Permyak N.A.

Koryak N.A.
Nenets N.A.
Taimyr N.A.
Ust-Ordyn N.A.
Yamalo-Nenets N.A.

SOVIET CITIES OPEN TO FOREIGN TOURISTS

Cities in the Soviet Union with Intourist Services and Overnight Accommodations

Alma Ata
Ashkhabad
Askania-Nova
Baku
Batumi
Beltsi
Bratsk
Bukhara
Cherkassy
Chernovtsy
Donetsk
Dushanbe
Essentuki
Fergana
Frunze
Gelendzhik

Gori
Irkutsk
Itkol
Ivanovo
Kalinin
Khabarovsk
Kharkov
Kherson
Kiev
Kishinev
Kislovodsk
Krasnodar
Kursk
Leningrad
Lvov
Minsk

Moscow
Novaya Kakhovka
Novgorod
Novosibirsk
Odessa
Ordzhonikidze
Orel
Passanauri
Petrozavodsk
Pitsunda
Poltava
Pskov
Pyarnu
Pyatigorsk
Repino
Riga

Rovno
Rostov-on-Don
Samarkland
Sestroretsk
Simferopol
Smolensk
Sochi
Stavropol
Sukhumi
Tallinn

Tashkent
Tbilisi
Teberda
Ternopol
Tiraspol
Tskhaltubo
Ulyanovsk
Urgench
Uzhgorod

Vilnius
Vinnitsa
Vladimir
Volgograd
Yalta
Yaroslavl
Yerevan
Zaporozhye
Zheleznovodsk

Cities in the Soviet Union Open for Day Trips Only

Abramtsevo
Arkhangelskoye
Bakhchisarai
Belgorod-Dnestrovsky
Beltsi
Bendery
Dzhizak
Gorki-Leninskye
Gulistan
Kanev
Khamsaabad
Khiva
Kizhi
Klin

Kobuletti
Kobystan
Kolomenskoye
Kuskovo
Kutaisi
Lomonosov
Margelan
Novocherkassk
Novorossiisk
Palekh
Pavlovsk
Pendzhikent
Pereslavl-Zalessky
Petrodvorets

Pushkin
Pyarnu
Rostov the Great
Siguldia
Sumgait
Suzdal
Tartu
Telavi
Tsakhadzor
Viljandi
Yagorsk
Yangi-Er
Yasnaya Polyana
Yurmala

ARRIVALS IN THE SOVIET UNION

Soviet Customs

Whether you travel by air, sea, or land, you will be presented with a customs declaration form shortly before arrival. Later you will hand the completed form to a customs official who may or may not speak any language other than Russian. Make generous use of sign language and be willing to show everything. Foreign tourists are treated more casually and politely than returning Soviet citizens or foreigners visiting relatives in the Soviet Union.

Items Permitted into the Soviet Union

1. Foreign currency and travelers checks.
2. Personal jewelry.
3. Two watches, but only one of gold.
4. One radio.

5. One carton of cigarettes.
6. One bottle of liquor.
7. One portable typewriter.
8. One record player and twenty records; the same quantity applies to tape-decks and cartridges.
9. One musical instrument.
10. One bicycle.
11. One still and one movie camera.
12. One religious article (Bible, crucifix, or other).

Items Not Allowed into the Soviet Union

1. Soviet currency, bonds, lottery tickets.
2. Firearms (except by special certificate).
3. Pornographic materials.
4. Printed matter, tapes, films, manuscripts, or other material antithetical to Soviet political or economic policies.
5. Organic matter or animals (except by special certificate).
6. Narcotics.

Customs Declaration Form

After passing the customs inspection, the stamped declaration form will be returned to you. It must be retained along with pertinent documents. The customs declaration form is necessary for all currency exchanges at Soviet Bank Offices. Upon leaving the Soviet Union, the form will be reviewed and retained by the customs official.

Items Permitted to Leave the Soviet Union

1. Foreign currency and travelers checks.
2. One each of the following souvenirs: fur coat, muff, scarf, camera, dinnerware service, coffee or tea service, gold watch, other watch, wedding ring, item of jewelry set in gold or with precious gems.
3. 400 grams of caviar.
4. Unlimited quantities of other types of souvenirs, including amber jewelry, books, records, liquors and wines, tea, dolls, etc.

Items Not Allowed to Leave the Soviet Union*

1. Objects of art.
2. Antiquities.
3. Icons.

*Except for Item 11, permission may be granted and duty fees paid for removing the above items from the Soviet Union. Through Intourist arrangements will be made for permission from the appropriate Soviet governmental agency. Smuggling contraband out of the Soviet Union is foolish and dangerous, and can result in detention, heavy fines, and/or imprisonment.

4. Archaeological relics.
5. Rugs and tapestries.
6. Organic matter and pets.
7. Automobiles (except those driven into the U.S.S.R.).
8. Firearms.
9. Manuscripts.
10. Postage stamps except those packaged as souvenirs.
11. Soviet currency, bonds, stock certificates.

Procedures from Point of Entry and Customs

After clearing the visa and customs procedures, which generally takes about an hour, you should look for the Intourist Office at the terminal. It is usually clearly marked. However, since Intourist knows of all foreign visitors' arrivals, and the names of those expected, you should not be surprised to be approached by an Intourist representative who speaks several languages. Do not try to hail a taxi or take public transportation from the terminal. Intourist will show you to your conveyance, as it has been prepaid and arranged. Have all documents ready to show the Intourist representative.

Hotel Transfers

You do not know in advance the hotel at which you will be staying, even if you have requested a particular hotel through your travel agent. Intourist places visitors in hotels according to class of service purchased and according to the tight scheduling of large groups and individual tourists traveling in the Soviet Union. Your name will be on a list for a particular hotel, and that is all there is to it. If you are not satisfied with the hotel, you may request a change at the Service Bureau of your assigned hotel, but chances of receiving a change are virtually nil. From the terminal you will be taken to your hotel. Russian drivers are generally in a hurry, and those who drive for Intourist are jet-propelled. They usually speak only Russian. You do not pay or tip the driver, as he has been paid already and is unlikely to accept a tip graciously. You might offer one of your "giveaways."

Hotel/Motel/Campsite Registration

Go directly to the Service Bureau, which is clearly marked in several languages. The porter will follow you with your luggage and wait until you have completed the registration procedures. First you will surrender your passport and visa. These will be retained for at least twenty-four hours, if not for the duration of your stay at the hotel. You will not need either passport or visa while in a particular city, only while traveling. You will then present your vouchers for that city. They will be removed from the packet and exchanged for meal and excursion coupons. If you have not purchased full board, but breakfast only, you should exchange money at the hotel bank. Should it be closed, you may pay for your meal in foreign currency or ask the Service Bureau to send a note to the restaurant stating you will pay in rubles in the morning. The Service Bureau will direct you to the Room Assignment Office, and you will then receive your room number written on a form. This form entitles you to a room key, which you will receive from the room manager on the floor to which you have been assigned. The key is generally returned to the room manager each time you leave the room and is reissued as you reenter the room. The porter with your luggage will accompany you to your room. Porters are generally elderly men who will accept tips only in Russian currency. Do not overtip: 20 kopecks is appropriate per piece of luggage. Porters become hurt and insulted if you try to carry your own baggage.

Motel and campsite registration procedures are identical to hotel registration, except that in campsites there are no porters, and one must seek out the matron somewhere on the premises to receive towels and bed linen. Usually someone from the Service Bureau will accompany you to your tent or cabin and find the matron for you. There are currency exchanges at all motels and at most campsites.

Motorists are advised to ask specific parking instructions at hotels, motels, and campsites. Parking regulations vary greatly, and there are special lots for hotel guests which may or may not be adjacent to the hotel. Leave blinkers on while registering to avoid receiving a traffic ticket. Do not leave personal property inside your automobile. Although thefts are rare in most places in the Soviet Union, the larger, more tourist-frequented cities are beginning to have problems. Keep your vehicle locked when vacant.

Should you arrive at your accommodation after the Service Bureau has closed, there will be someone to register you and collect your passport and visa. However, you may not be able to proceed with vouchers and coupons until the Service Bureau reopens.

Exchanging Currency

Soviet money is not "free currency," that is, it is not exchangeable on the world currency market. It is valid only within the U.S.S.R. The rate of exchange between Soviet and foreign currencies fluctuates periodically, and there is no way of telling whether it will rise of fall in your favor. For some time, however, exchange rates have been falling in favor of the ruble. But, with the growing strength of the American dollar, this may reverse itself.

There is only one legal place to exchange foreign currency for rubles, and that is at any office or currency exchange of the State Bank of the U.S.S.R. There are usually bank offices or currency exchanges in the lobbies of hotels to which foreign tourists are assigned. Official exchange facilities may also be found at international air, rail, and steamship terminals. Each time foreign currency is exchanged for rubles, you must present your customs declaration form. The transaction will be listed on the form and the form returned to you.

Soviet currency is measured in *rubles* and *kopecks*. One hundred kopecks make one ruble. Rubles occur in paper denominations of 1, 3, 5, 10, 25, 50, and 100-ruble notes as well as single-ruble coins. Kopecks occur in coin denominations of 1, 2, 3, 5, 10, 15, and 50-kopeck pieces.

Illegal exchanges of currency are dangerous and bear heavy penalties for both Soviet citizens and foreigners. It is becoming more and more common for foreigners to be approached by Soviets for illegal currency transactions. As expected, the rate of exchange is far more favorable than the official one. You may experience a barrage of propositions for currency exchange by Soviet citizens, especially in the larger cities. One reason for this is that Soviets save up foreign currency for travel abroad or to make purchases in foreign-currency shops. The appeals for barter are often very attractive or very annoying, as the case may be, but a firm "no thank you" will be accepted. In addition to appeals for currency exchange, Soviets will often ask you if you have anything to sell for Russian money. Items requested will range from clothing and jewelry to sunglasses and wristwatches. This type of transaction may be offered as an exchange of your goods for an icon or "church souvenir." Again, a polite but firm refusal is advised. Finally, you may be requested to purchase an item in a foreign-currency shop for the Soviet citizen who can pay in foreign money but is afraid to enter the shop. It is illegal for Soviets to make purchases in these shops, so negotiating this type of transaction is equally precarious. In any event, use your own best judgment. It is always permissible to give a *gift* to a Soviet citizen, including some small item purchased in a foreign-currency shop.

Automobile Rental

You may prearrange for a rented car or transact a rental while on tour. Hertz and Avis have the Intourist-accredited franchise in the Soviet Union. Automobiles may be rented on a self-drive or chauffeur-driven basis. Hertz and Avis offices are clearly marked in hotel lobbies or adjacent to Intourist hotels. Your hotel Service Bureau can direct you. All rented cars, self-drive or chauffeur-driven, are Russian-made and provide excellent service. All are standard shift.

Self-Drive Cars: The models available are Volga (5 seats), Moskvich, and Lada (4 seats). These may be rented one-way or round-trip in the following cities: Brest, Kiev, Kishinev, Kharkov, Leningrad, Lvov, Minsk, Moscow, Odessa, Sochi, Sukhumi, Tbilisi, Yalta, Yerevan. *Gas Coupons* are purchased at the time of rental on the basis of the estimated mileage. These are similar to meal coupons, in that they are presented at gas stations along the road in lieu of cash payment. All Soviet gas stations are *self-service.* Gas coupons can be purchased also at Service Bureaus and Intourist offices, if the traveler runs short. Extra coupons can be redeemed as credit toward the final rental payment at your destination. This negotiation is not always pleasant, but perseverance makes for success. Self-drive cars can be rented on a *daily basis* with *mileage charges added* or for a minimum of *seven days with unlimited mileage charges included.* Rental rates vary according to the car model, but all rates include servicing and repairs, collision and liability insurance.

Chauffeur-Driven Cars: The models available are Chaika (6 seats), Volga (4 seats), and Moskvich (3 seats). Chaika is available in Moscow, Leningrad, and Kiev within the city limits only. Volga and Moskvich are available in Batumi, Brest, Kiev, Kishinev, Kharkov, Leningrad, Lvov, Minsk, Moscow, Odessa, Riga, Sochi, Sukhumi, Tallinn, Tashkent, Tbilisi, Vilnius, Yalta, and Yerevan. Chauffeur-driven cars may also be rented round-trip or one-way. Rates vary according to the size of the automobile. Included in the rates are gas, servicing and repairs, car washes, a maximum of ten hours per day of chauffeur services, and a total distance of 240 kilometers (144 miles) per day. Additional fees apply to chauffeur's services in excess of ten hours daily and extra mileage.

WHILE VISITING THE SOVIET UNION

Appropriate Clothing

Although consumer-goods consciousness is rising among Soviet peoples, their own economic policies have placed greater emphasis on nonconsumer goods and services since the Revolution. Therefore, by Western standards, Soviets do not dress in what we would consider high fashion. Among the younger generation and Soviet citizens who have traveled abroad there is a high level of appreciation for Western styles. In general, however, classic clothing is the better choice for visiting the Soviet Union. *For women* it is wise to avoid extremes of fashion, but rather to stay with near-the-knee-length dresses and skirts. Pants and pants suits are appropriate. Shorts of any length are not worn in the cities, but may be acceptable for camping and beachwear. Sleepwear that covers sensitive areas is advisable because bed linen is of a fairly coarse texture, frequently mended. *For men* it is also advisable to avoid extremes of fashion. Except among diplomats suits are worn only for formal occasions. Comfortable slacks, sport coats, and sweaters are most common. Very wide neckties and bowties are seldom worn. Bikini-style bathing attire is generally not acceptable for the beach.

Food

Most hotel restaurants begin serving breakfast at 8 A.M. and stop serving dinner at 10 P.M. All restaurants close at 11 P.M. All restaurants have certain two-hour periods of the day during which they are closed so that tables can be reset and the staff can rest and eat. You will experience very little variety in menu offerings in the Russian Federation. If you travel to several republics you will have a more varied sampling of national and regional cuisines. In general, the mainstay of the Russian diet is standard Russian black bread—almost a meal in itself. There is also plenty of white bread, but butter has to be purchased or requested separately. The second and third principal foods are potatoes and cabbage. Proteins, such as eggs, meat, fish, and cheese, are expensive but available. Meats and poultry are not as rigidly classified as in the West, and tend to be tough. Standard specialties such as "beef Stroganoff" and "chicken Kiev" are safer choices than "beefsteak" and "fried chicken" because the preparation of these dishes tenderizes the meat. In the summer tomatoes and cucumbers abound. Onions, beets, cabbage, and potatoes are always in season. Occasionally, carrots and peas are available. Fruits are also scarce, mainly because they are grown domestically for export or are imported in small quantities. Watermelons are especially abundant during the summer, along with apples and pears. Russians do not generally eat the types of sweet desserts to which Americans are accustomed. The only exception is ice cream. It is the ubiquitous Russian favorite, served by vendors on the street and in cafés and restaurants. Russian ice cream is delicious.

The typical menu in the Soviet Union lists more dishes than are actually available on a given day. Only foods where the prices are written in are available. Exceptions are frequent. You may find that an item may not be available even though the price is listed, either because there is no more left or because the item was erroneously listed. Most Intourist hotels and restaurants have multilanguage menus. Frequently, there is more variety available in the Russian-language section than in the foreign-language section. Order from the Russian section if you can read Russian or have an interpreter.

Visitors traveling in groups will generally be served meals which have been preordered. That means minimal choices and substitutions. The bill of fare is quite extensive and the service is much better for groups. Independent travelers may find it difficult to be seated in a hotel restaurant because of the preference for groups, although many restaurants have special areas for nongroup guests. If all pleas and lamentations fail, talk to the Service Bureau or go and sit with a group. Explain to the group leader exactly what the problem is. Most individual travelers with meal coupons find that their meal exceeds the value of the coupon. A general guideline is that breakfast coupons are worth one ruble, and all other meal coupons are worth two rubles. One can always add rubles to the coupons.

Except for tea and coffee, beverages in the Soviet Union are served at room temperature. Russian soft drinks are strange mixtures of fruit syrups such as strawberry, peach, pineapple, etc., mixed with soda water. The taste is excessively sweet. Fruit juices are heavily watered down, but more palatable. Local water, except in major cities of the western Soviet Union, should be avoided or treated with purification tablets. Soviet vodka, champagne, brandy, and table wines are by far the best buys in beverages, except for tea and coffee. One can also order bottled mineral water, which is standard fare and very inexpensive. The mineral content varies, but usually the beverage is safe to drink and thirst-quenching even at room temperature. In general, restaurant service is very slow. Plan two or three hours for any meal but breakfast.

Shopping

The visitor is welcome to shop at state-owned department and specialty stores where Soviet currency is the only legal tender and at "Beriozka" or "Kashtan" shops where any "free" foreign currency is acceptable. Most stores are open from 8 A.M. until 8 P.M. every day except Monday. The exact time of the one-hour lunch break during which the store is closed varies considerably. Each republic offers special types of souvenirs, but standard Soviet souvenirs, such as liquors, caviar, amber, hand-painted enamels and wood pieces, are available everywhere. Contrary to the general idea that shopping where the "people" shop will be cheaper, in the Soviet Union citizens are taxed about 100 percent on consumer goods, the quality of which is below Western standards. Certain items such as Russian-style fur hats, liquor, jewelry, and clothing cost less in the foreign-currency shops because the taxes are minimal. When making purchases by travelers checks, you will be charged a small "commission" which is actually a tax on the credit extended to the institution issuing the check. State-owned phonograph record and bookshops offer merchandise at prices equal to those charged by foreign-currency shops. This is because these types of purchases are encouraged by the government, and the prices are kept low. Books and records are among the best buys in the Soviet Union, along with vodka, brandy, and wine. Amber and furs are becoming more and more expensive. Any product purchased in the Soviet Union can be shipped to the visitor's home but the procedure is costly and complicated. Be sure to save all receipts for the outgoing customs inspection.

Tipping

As a general rule tipping is not an acceptable custom in the Soviet Union. In cases where you would usually offer a tip, one of the many "giveaways" suggested earlier is much more respected and appreciated, because it is considered a personal gift. Exceptions to the nontipping policy are waiters and waitresses. The visitor may have small change coming after paying for a meal in bills. When change is not returned it means that the waiter or waitress has kept it as a gratuity. No more than 10 percent of the bill should ever be offered. Should the visitor feel obligated to a guide or interpreter for special service, a tip would be considered an insult. A nonmonetary gift or even an invitation to lunch or dinner is more appropriate. Most Intourist guides and interpreters are very nationalistic and rather sensitive about their privileged position as only a selected few are trained to host foreigners. It is advisable to study the situation carefully before offering any gratuity. In some instances it is preferable to send a gift from home. Simply ask what item would be preferred. A modest answer, but a specific one, will generally follow.

Intourist

As the government agency responsible for foreign tourists in the Soviet Union, Intourist selects its personnel with a maximum of care. The standard characteristics of Intourist personnel are loyalty and dedication to the Soviet government and way of life, a greater degree of sophistication in contrast to average Soviet citizens, and the ability to speak and read several languages. Intourist is at your service, but not at your beck and call. Arguing with Intourist can be frustrating and fruitless. Save your energy for a real crisis, not an inconvenience. If matters should seem to be serious, the best thing to do is call your consulate in Moscow, Intourist in Moscow, or your travel agent at home. In the long run these procedures are less costly and time-consuming than an argument with the local Intourist office.

Night Life

If after a daily round of touring and shopping and a dinner that may last between two and four hours and generally includes dancing and music you have any energy left, there is practically nothing to do. If you attend the theater or ballet (for which tickets should be purchased in advance) you will usually find the performance over between 10 and 10:30 P.M. It is wise to have a small meal around 5 P.M. because restaurants and cafés generally do not seat or serve new customers after 9:30 P.M. Cinemas close at 11 P.M. along with all other public places except foreign-currency bars and night-clubs located in hotels for foreigners. Nightclub tickets must be purchased in advance. There is ordinarily a cover charge. Foreign currency is the only legal tender here so as to discourage patronage by Soviet citizens. These bars and nightclubs close anywhere from 1:00 to 4:00 A.M.

Weather

European areas of the Soviet Union have a continental climate north of the Crimea and a Mediterranean climate south of the Crimea. Northern European areas of the Soviet Union tend to have a climate resembling that of Scandinavia. As one progresses north and east from Moscow, the climate becomes colder, especially in the winter. Areas of Central Asia have a climate similar to that of the Middle East or U.S. Southwest. If you are planning to spend part of the winter in the colder European or Asian areas of the Soviet Union, bring appropriately insulated clothing. In summer, if you plan to be in the south, particularly in the Central Asian areas, bring clothing that protects all parts of the body from the merciless heat and scorching sun. It is also wise to bring salt tablets to these areas. Foreigners, unaccustomed to and unprepared for this extreme climate, frequently spend their vacations in the hospital.

Medical and Dental Care

Medical care and dental care are excellent and free of charge for tourists (there may be nominal fees for special medicines and special treatment in hospitals). If you are taken ill, simply notify the Service Bureau in the Intourist office and a doctor will be summoned. Be sure to request an interpreter if you are not fluent in Russian. Dental treatment is usually administered at a clinic. Arrangements can be made for transportation to the clinic through the Service Bureau.

Note: Intourist offers special health-treatment tours to specific areas of the U.S.S.R. Information can be obtained through your travel agent or the nearest Intourist office.

Rules for Taking Photographs

Restrictions on photographing in the U.S.S.R. are relatively few and simple to understand.

It is strictly forbidden to film, photograph, or sketch seaports, military facilities, railroad junctions, tunnels and tracks, highway bridges, large hydro-technical structures, research institutes, power stations, radio stations and towers, and telephone and telegraph stations. Reproduction in the form of photograph or sketch is also forbidden from within aircraft flying over Soviet territory and in the 25 kilometer (15.6 miles) frontier zone.

Photographs and sketches are permitted in factories engaged in the manufacture of civilian products, state and collective farms, governmental

Temperatures (Fahrenheit)

All temperatures shown are averages. Days of rain are averages per month.

CITY	JAN. HIGH	LOW	RAIN	FEB. HIGH	LOW	RAIN	MAR. HIGH	LOW	RAIN	APR. HIGH	LOW	RAIN	MAY HIGH	LOW	RAIN	JUNE HIGH	LOW	RAIN	JULY HIGH	LOW	RAIN	AUG. HIGH	LOW	RAIN	SEPT. HIGH	LOW	RAIN	OCT. HIGH	LOW	RAIN	NOV. HIGH	LOW	RAIN	DEC. HIGH	LOW	RAIN
Alma Ata	24	14	5	27	17	5	35	24	6	56	46	5	66	56	4	74	64	4	79	69	2	77	67	3	67	57	4	54	44	4	35	25	4	30	20	4
Brest	49	39	11	50	38	8	53	40	9	58	44	10	63	48	10	68	53	11	71	56	12	72	57	12	69	54	13	61	49	11	55	44	10	50	41	11
Dushanbe	38	25	4	42	30	4	54	44	5	65	53	6	75	63	3	83	72	2	87	74	1	83	70	1	73	60	2	62	50	2	52	40	2	43	41	3
Erevan	29	15	3	34	18	5	50	30	7	66	42	9	76	50	11	87	57	2	95	63	1	92	64	3	83	55	1	69	45	4	50	34	6	38	26	7
Irkutsk	0	11	3	7	-6	3	21	8	5	36	27	4	52	41	8	67	52	7	70	58	9	66	54	11	52	40	8	38	26	4	3	-9	4	4	-8	4
Khabarovsk	13	0	3	23	6	6	33	19	5	46	34	7	54	43	10	63	52	13	70	60	13	76	64	12	68	55	10	55	42	6	36	24	4	20	8	3
Kharkov	28	17	10	31	19	8	38	26	7	51	39	9	65	53	8	70	58	9	74	62	11	72	60	10	63	51	7	52	41	7	39	28	9	32	20	7
Kiev	27	16	10	30	18	8	37	25	6	50	38	9	64	52	8	69	57	9	73	61	10	71	59	10	62	50	7	51	40	7	39	27	9	32	20	7
Leningrad	23	12	8	24	12	8	33	18	6	45	31	7	58	42	8	66	51	9	71	57	10	66	53	13	57	45	10	45	37	10	34	27	10	26	18	10
Moscow	14	5	11	19	8	9	29	15	8	43	29	9	60	42	9	67	50	10	71	54	12	68	51	12	56	42	9	44	33	11	28	21	10	17	10	9
Odessa	36	17	7	38	19	4	45	32	5	56	40	6	69	54	6	77	60	7	81	66	6	80	66	5	72	53	4	61	42	5	50	31	5	42	21	6
Rostov	23	10	7	25	13	4	32	19	6	45	32	6	52	45	5	64	53	5	68	58	6	66	53	5	57	45	4	44	34	5	34	22	5	27	14	6
Sochi	44	34	7	45	35	8	48	36	6	56	44	5	68	56	5	76	63	3	81	69	1	80	68	1	73	61	5	64	54	6	57	44	8	48	36	8
Sukhumi	45	35	7	46	37	8	49	37	6	57	45	5	68	58	5	77	63	3	82	70	1	81	68	1	74	61	5	65	55	6	57	45	8	48	37	8
Tashkent	36	24	4	40	28	5	52	40	7	64	52	4	74	62	3	82	70	2	86	74	1	83	70	1	72	60	2	60	49	2	51	39	2	42	40	3
Tbilisi	32	16	7	35	18	5	53	33	7	67	43	9	78	51	8	88	58	2	96	64	3	93	65	3	84	55	1	69	45	4	51	35	6	38	26	7
Volgograd	20	9	7	23	11	4	30	18	6	43	31	6	51	45	5	62	50	6	66	55	6	64	52	5	55	43	4	43	33	5	32	20	5	25	13	6
Yalta	39	30	9	41	32	5	45	36	7	54	42	6	65	52	4	74	60	5	78	65	4	79	64	4	71	57	4	63	50	6	50	39	7	43	35	11

institutions, and educational institutions only after securing the permission of the administrator of the institution.

Aside from the above restrictions, you are completely free to use photographic equipment as you wish. There is no problem with recording any of the sights (and sites) that you come to see. Of course, common sense and judgment should always be used when photographing street scenes; when photographing people at close range, it is a simple matter of courtesy to ask their permission.

Note: It is forbidden to enter the Lenin Mausoleum in Moscow with any equipment whatsoever. Checking facilities are available and all hand-held apparatus should be checked before getting on line to enter the mausoleum.

It is also important to note that developing processes for color film in the U.S.S.R. are suitable only for Agfa color film and not for Kodacolor or Kodachrome. Unless immediate developing is absolutely essential, it is advisable to have the film developed upon returning home.

Traffic Regulations

1. Any person driving a motor vehicle in the Soviet Union, be it his own or one rented through Intourist, must possess an international driver's license or an insertion in the license of his own country translated into Russian. (Available for a small fee at entry points to the U.S.S.R.)

2. The motor vehicle, be it car or bus, must carry a registered national license number and the symbol of the country of its origin in accordance with the rules of the International Traffic Convention (this pertains to vehicles brought into the U.S.S.R.; vehicles rented through Intourist are all provided with proper licensing).

3. Traffic in the U.S.S.R. is on the right-hand side of the streets and roads. Where more than one lane is available in the same direction, it is forbidden to drive in the left-hand lane if the right-hand lane is free.

4. Before making a left or a right turn or any maneuver that may alter the position of the vehicle in the lane, the driver must signal his intention not less than five seconds before he executes the maneuver.

5. It is forbidden to use the horn within city limits. Exceptions are made in the case of an emergency or if visibility is hampered by fog.

6. It is forbidden to pass a car by driving in the lanes of oncoming traffic, at road and street crossings, pedestrian crossings, on bridges, and before warning signs.

7. It is forbidden to stop the vehicle on the left-hand side of the street or road; the only exception to this is on narrow streets where traffic from both directions passes along a single lane.

8. Unless otherwise directed by a traffic policeman, the traffic on the main street always has the right of way. At street or road junctions, the car approaching from the right has the right of way.

9. At street junctions in the towns and cities, trams always have the right of way regardless of their direction of travel.

10. Pedestrians are supposed to have the right of way.

11. If a traffic light has an additional turning signal, the vehicle must wait at the "STOP" line until the green arrow lights up allowing for the turn to be made.

12. Drivers should always be aware of special service vehicles; police cars, fire engines, and ambulances always have the right of way.

13. There is no set speed limit in the Soviet Union. Drivers must use their judgment according to the conditions of the road, visibility, and intensity of traffic. It is incumbent upon the driver to slow down immediately and/or come to a full stop at any sign of an emergency or for an emergency vehicle. It is advisable for tourists who are not familiar with Soviet roads to stay at a consistent moderate speed.

14. Drivers must observe all traffic lights, signals, and road signs. One is also required to comply with any orders or instructions issued by traffic inspectors, whether in uniform or not (those not in uniform will bear an armband on their left arm and will usually carry a traffic regulation baton).

15. The driver is responsible for the condition of his vehicle, particularly the brakes, tires, steering mechanism, lights, and signals. This applies especially to drivers with foreign cars—spare parts for these cars will not be readily available in the U.S.S.R.

Insurance

Insurance in the U.S.S.R. is strictly voluntary. Many forms of insurance are available through the Soviet State Insurance Company—Ingosstrakh. Policies may be taken out against accident, luggage loss, vehicle damage, and civil claims which may be brought against a driver for damage or injury inflicted while operating his vehicle.

Premiums may be paid in rubles or in any convertible foreign currency. Payment of insurance claims is issued by Ingosstrakh in the same currency in which the premiums were paid.

Insurance may be taken out in advance of arrival if Ingosstrakh receives the proper information in time. For example, if you wish to buy insurance against damage to your car or a civil claim against you, you must inform the agency of the make of the car, the engine type, the registration number, the amount of insurance desired and the date and term of insurance. With this information, policies can be forwarded to any address (this arrangement can be made through the travel agency handling the details of your visit to the U.S.S.R.).

Insurance policies can also be taken out at representative offices of Ingosstrakh in Moscow (head office), Brest, Kishinev, Leningrad, Lvov, Odessa, Uzhgorod, and Vyborg.

TRANSPORTATION AND COMMUNICATIONS

Aeroflot Soviet Airlines

With its scheduled services to the capitals and major cities of more than sixty countries of Europe, Asia, Africa, and America, and with its extensive network of domestic flight connections (more than 3,500 cities and areas of the U.S.S.R.), Aeroflot Soviet Airlines is by far the largest airline in the world.

International flights aboard Aeroflot are quite comfortable and the service is excellent in terms of food and stewardess availability. Flights within the Soviet Union are not quite the same. Seats are generally set closer together and leg room may be a problem. On short flights (one to four hours) food is usually not served. Rather, a piece of hard candy is offered by the stewardess just before takeoff and landing and unless the stewardess is specifically summoned, she generally "disappears" for the duration of the flight. (Unlike American and European airlines, it is not the stewardess's responsibility to be at the beck and call of every passenger throughout the entire flight.) Longer domestic flights (four to twelve hours) offer meals but here, too, the stewardess is responsible only for basic services and safety.

The pilots, co-pilots, and flight navigators of Aeroflot are all highly trained and skilled and are generally used to flying in weather conditions worse than those experienced by crews of other airlines.

Check-in time at airports is usually at least one hour in advance for domestic flights and two hours in advance for international flights.

Trains

Train travel in the Soviet Union is interesting and can be a lot of fun. The service is excellent and the trains generally depart exactly on time and leave without warning or "All Aboard." Therefore, it is essential that passengers be at the station early and be aboard the train about fifteen minutes before the scheduled departure.

There are four classes of services available on Soviet trains. The most expensive is the *Deluxe,* which offers "soft seat" accommodations.(this simply means that the sleeping facility is a berth that is spring-cushioned rather than hard) and a private washroom.

First Class is known as "soft seat" and is part of a two- or four-berth compartment. Washrooms are at each end of the car. *Second Class,* or "hard seat," offers a cushion on a wooden berth and generally has two, three, or four berths to a compartment. Washrooms are at each end of the car. *Third Class* is simply wooden berths without any compartment. This class of service is usually confined to local rail service and is usually not available to foreigners. Do not be surprised if a member of the opposite sex is sharing your compartment—accommodations are not arranged on the basis of sex.

Dining cars are available on trains that are scheduled for long-distance runs. The food is quite good and the service is better than in the restaurants in the cities. If you do not wish to eat in the dining car, porters come through the cars with snack carts. Tea is almost always available at between three and five kopecks a glass.

Note: Train tickets are merely pieces of paper which contain necessary information concerning destination, car number, compartment number, and berth number. Tickets are referred to as coupons and come stapled within a cover. *Do not remove the coupon from the cover!* Coupons without covers are invalid.

Cruises

A cruise aboard a Soviet steamer is perhaps the most enjoyable and certainly the most relaxing means of transportation within the U.S.S.R.

There are usually three classes of service available to tourists—*First Class,* which offers a cushioned bunk in a two-bunk cabin, a small washbasin, a small storage area for clothing and luggage, and a reading lamp; *Second Class,* which provides a matted bunk in a four-bunk cabin; and *Third Class,* which has little more than a wooden bunk with rented mattress, four to eight to a cabin.

While steamer service is available in almost every region of the U.S.S.R., the most popular cruises (especially during the summer months) are those on the Black and Caspian seas (some Black Sea liners offer the equivalent of Deluxe Class service). Black Sea cruises service the very popular tourist cities of Odessa, Yalta, Sochi, Sukhumi, and Batumi. There is also a cruise to the Black Sea via the Danube River.

Other popular tourist cruises include those on the Volga from Kazan, Ulyanovsk, Togliatti, Khvalynsk, and Volgograd to Rostov via the Volga-Don Canal.

Dining aboard ship is enjoyable and the food is quite good. Passengers are usually assigned to a breakfast, lunch, and dinner shift and each shift eats at an announced time (to avoid overcrowding in the dining room).

Recreational facilities are available on all ships—swimming pools, ping-pong tables, etc.

Due to the constant changes in schedules and fares, it would be wise to plan your cruise well in advance (four to six weeks if possible) with the agent arranging your visit to the U.S.S.R.

Telephone, Telegraph, Post Office

Telephone service in the Soviet Union is very inexpensive. Local calls can be made from telephone booths for 2 kopecks; calls may be dialed direct. Most hotel rooms have telephones in them and, here too, local calls may be dialed direct. If you wish to call other areas of the Soviet Union or overseas, arrangements can be made at the Service Bureau of the Intourist office (usually in the hotel). The overseas operator will try to comply with the time requested for the call to be placed, but it may take from three to twelve hours for the call to come through.

Wire service is also available through the Service Bureau and any post office but a word of warning is in order here. Chances are you will be told that the message will reach its destination within twenty-four hours. However, it has been known to take as long as several days. If the message is urgent, a telephone call, although more expensive, is advised.

Postal service is fairly efficient and correspondence overseas will reach its destination within a reasonable time. Most cities have several post offices (larger cities have many) but stamps are usually available at the hotel. All hotels have mail boxes and some have entire postal units in them (large packages must be weighed and mailed at a post office). Current overseas postage rates are 14 kopecks for airmail postcards and 16 kopecks for airmail letters.

Foreign Airline Offices in Moscow

Air Canada, Hotel Metropole, Room 383   Tel: 225–60–83; 225–63–83
Air France, Hotel Metropole, Room 305   Tel: 225–63–05; 155–70–06
Air India, Hotel Metropole, Room 413   Tel: 225–61–00; 225–64–13
Alitalia, Hotel Metropole, Room 205   Tel: 225–62–05; 225–60–27
Austrian Airlines, Hotel Tsentralnaya, Room 203   Tel: 292–53–63
British Airways, Hotel Metropole, Room 375   Tel: 225–61–90; 225–63–75
Czechoslovakia Airlines (CEA), Hotel Peking, Room 903   Tel: 253–81–34; 253–83–90
Finnair, Hotel Ukraina, Room 444   Tel: 243–24–44
Iran Airlines, Hotel Ukraina, Room 486   Tel: 243–24–86
Japan Airlines (JAL), Hotel Ukraina, Room 843   Tel: 243–20–98; 243–28–43
KLM Royal Dutch Airlines, Hotel Tsentralnaya, Room 215   Tel: 229–02–85; 229–07–29
LOT Polish Airlines, Hotel Metropole, Room 161   Tel: 241–56–00
Malev Hungarian Airlines, 6 Hudozsesztvennij Proezd   Tel: 292–04–34
Pakistan Air (PIA), Hotel Ukraina, Room 601   Tel: 243–26–01
Pan American Airways, Hotel Metropole, Room 239   Tel: 223–51–83; 225–64–06

Sabena Belgian World Airlines, Hotel Metropole, Room 386   Tel: 225–63–86; 225–64–28

Scandinavian Airlines System (SAS), Hotel National, Room 206   Tel: 292–00–34; 229–99–17

Swissair, Hotel National, Room 226   Tel: 229–77–14

Yugoslavian Air, Hotel Ukraina, Room 401   Tel: 243–24–01

MOSCOW

GENERAL INFORMATION

Moscow, the capital of the Soviet Union, is also the capital of the largest Soviet republic, the Russian Soviet Federative Socialist Republic (R.S.F.S.R.). With a population of over six million, the city is spread over an area of 907 square kilometers (350 square miles). Not only is Moscow the political center of the Soviet Union, it is also the major cultural, industrial, and transportation center. Ringed by the Circular Highway *(Moskovskaya Koltsevaya)*, Moscow is located on the Russian Plateau, which is at different points between 530 and 800 feet above sea level. The climate varies greatly with the seasons, but Moscow is notoriously cold and snow-covered in winter and comfortably continental in spring, summer, and autumn. (See temperature chart, p. 28.)

The tourist's initial impression of Moscow is influenced by its massive architectural style. Russians seldom, if ever, build anything small, and Moscow provides endless examples of the Russian penchant for capaciousness. The main thoroughfares are six to eight lanes wide. To cross them, pedestrians are required to use underground passageways located at various intersections. Most of the buildings are monolithic, although there are a few new steel and glass multistory structures. Moscovites en masse may seem more serious and hurried than the citizens of other Soviet cities. This aura of severity can be attributed to the fact that Moscow is the seat of government, and the citizens sense the awesome functions and activities carried out daily by their political leaders. Another prominent feature of the

Moscow populace is its variety. Many of the 120 nationalities in the Soviet Union are represented in the population of Moscow: Russians, Ukrainians, Tatars, Jews, Mordvinians, Byelorussians, Georgians, Poles, Letts, Chuvashes, Lithuanians, and Estonians.

Moscow is primarily a worker's city; about three-fifths of the population are wage earners, engaged in the vast industrial activity of the city and its environs. The major industries are heavy machinery and tools, automobiles, electronic equipment, chemicals, watches, clothing, shoes, and perfumes. The life of the city is busiest from 7 A.M. to 7 P.M. Workers have a one-hour break for lunch, usually sometime between noon and 3 P.M. Grocery and department stores are busiest at this interval and just before closing time, usually 8 P.M. Evenings are leisurely and most restaurants, cafés, and cinemas close by 11 P.M. Radio and television programs also usually terminate at this time.

HISTORY IN BRIEF

The history of Moscow dates back to the mid-twelfth century when Prince Yuri Dolgoruky constructed a series of fortifications along the left bank of the Moskva River at its junction with the Neglinnaya. These original structures comprise the initial site of the Kremlin, although its construction did not occur until the fourteenth century. The small, wall-enclosed settlement was included in the principality of Muscovy, founded in the thirteenth century by Daniel Nevsky, son of Prince Alexander Nevsky, the grand duke of Vladimir. From that time, Moscow grew, somewhat erratically, as the nucleus of the vast empire. In 1538 a brick wall, 0.9 kilometer (1/2 miles) long, was erected to enclose the Kitai-Gorod, a settlement of craftsmen adjoining the Kremlin on the east side. At the end of the sixteenth century another wall slightly more than 3.3 kilometers (2 miles) long was constructed to enclose the Kremlin, Kitai-Gorod, and Bely-Gorod (White City). In addition to this wall with its thirty towers, the city was encircled by an earthen fortification reinforced by a wooden wall with more towers and a moat in front. This line of protection crossed the Moskva River to the right bank. The contours of these early fortifications provided the route for the present circular boulevard ringing this ancient sector.

Moscow continued to expand in concentric circles; however, the history of Muscovy (the ancient Moscow) is not one of uninterrupted expansion. Long periods of stagnation were caused by foreign invasion and domestic hardships. The first and most profound foreign invasion was by the Mongolian Tatars, who occupied Russia for about two hundred years, during which time the rest of Europe was undergoing the great changes of the late Middle Ages and the Renaissance. In 1480 Ivan the Great unseated the

Tatar despots and proclaimed himself tsar, sovereign of Russia. A period of growth followed during which foreign architects were invited to Moscow. These men, mostly Italians, initiated the construction of many stone palaces and cathedrals. The "Time of Troubles" curtailed this wave of expansion, and in 1610 Polish troops under Sigismund III occupied Moscow. In spite of drought, epidemic, and famine, the Muscovites recaptured their city in 1612 with the strong support of the Orthodox Church, and in 1613 a national assembly comprised of churchmen, nobles, and soldiers elected a new tsar, Mikhail Romanov. The Romanov dynasty ruled Russia until the February Revolution of 1917.

The middle of the eighteenth century saw the construction of an earthen rampart, about 40 kilometers (25 miles long), which became the customs boundary. In many places this route has become the site of the Okruzhnaya Circular Railroad. From the circular walls of the central fortifications, many streets radiated outward, forming trade and communication routes. Eventually these became highways leading from Moscow to distant areas of Russia and beyond. Very few original structures of the old Moscow remain today. These were destroyed by the fire of 1812, set deliberately by the Russians as a deterrent to Napoleon's occupation troops. However, Russian craftsmen, working under the supervision of French and Italian architects, were able to repair much of the damage.

For more than two hundred years (1712–1918) Moscow ceased to be the capital of Russia. Peter the Great moved his court to St. Petersburg (present Leningrad), thus making it the seat of Russian government until it was moved back to Moscow by the Soviet government in March 1918. Nevertheless, Moscow has always been a major cultural and industrial center. It was connected by rail during the nineteenth century with most Russian cities. In 1905 the uprising of Moscow's workers made the city an important part of the first revolution. In November 1917 Moscow again became the site of revolutionary activity when the Kremlin was stormed and captured by Red Guards. In August 1941 the Battle of Moscow took place between the Nazis and the Russians. The Russians were victorious. The title of Hero City was conferred upon Moscow in 1965 and is symbolized by the Gold Star and Second Order of Lenin on the city's banner.

ARRIVALS

By Air

There are four airports in Moscow, but most tourists will arrive from abroad or from other Soviet cities at Sheremetyevo Airport, located on the outskirts of the city on the Leningrad highway. Upon arrival you will be

met by representatives of Intourist who will wait until customs inspection
has been completed and confirm your hotel reservation. After the formali-
ties, you are ushered to a waiting car and driven to your hotel. The automobile is in the employ of Intourist and no fare is required, since it has been
paid in advance. It is also inappropriate to tip the driver. The driver is
required only to place the luggage in the trunk and remove it at its destination.

By Rail

There are nine railway stations in Moscow:

Byelorussia Station	Byelorussia Station Square
Kazan Station	Komsomolskaya Square
Kiev Station	Kiev Station Square
Kursk Station	Kursk Station Square
Leningrad Station	Komsomolskaya Square
Pavletsky Station	Pavletsky Station Square
Riga Station	Riga Station Square
Savelovsky Station	Savelovsky Station Square
Yaroslavl Station	Komsomolskaya Square

All tourists' intineraries are on file with Intourist, and if you are ar-
riving by train, especially from outside the U.S.S.R., you will be met by
a representative (there are Intourist offices at all international terminals). If, however, you are traveling domestically, you may not be met.
The wise move in this case is to hail a taxi and proceed to the main
Intourist office at 16 Marx Prospect, connected to the National Hotel.
There a copy of your itinerary is on file for the duration of your stay in
the Soviet Union. You will be informed as to the hotel to which you
have been assigned.

By Automobile

Moscow is the main junction of all the auto routes open to tourists
throughout the Soviet Union. Moscow also connects with all auto routes
originating outside Russia. (See map facing p.1.) Routes 1, 4, 8, 9, and 10
enter Moscow directly, connecting with the Moscow Circular Highway.
Once on this highway, it can be arduous and frustrating to find the correct
street to take to your destination in center city. This is because Moscow
street signs are attached to the sides of buildings, rather than displayed on
poles at street corners. Even in traffic paced generally at 40 kph (25 mph)
it is not easy to decipher one's whereabouts. Some cities have signs displayed at main streets and intersections directing tourists to the Intourist
office. Moscow, unfortunately, does not.

There are several ways to cope with the problem. First, ask a policeman for directions to Intourist, Marx Prospect. He will be courteous, although most policemen do not speak English. Second, try a taxi driver. Many understand some English and some may answer in English as well. You should have a map of Moscow handy (usually obtainable at any Intourist Service Bureau in a guest hotel) so that whoever you question can point out your present whereabouts as well as the way to your destination. Be certain that the automobile has an ample supply of gasoline (*benzin* in Russian), as you may have to do considerable driving before reaching the Intourist office, and there are only a few, hard-to-find gas stations in center city. The best solution is to have a map marked in advance of entry into Moscow by an Intourist representative. The closer to center city one gets, the denser the system of boulevards and tunnels becomes. The main routes off the Moscow Circular Highway are as follows (counter clockwise, starting at ten o'clock):

1. Volokolamsk Highway—Leningrad Prospect-Gorky Street—Marx Prospect.
2. Moscow-Minsk Highway—Kutuzov Prospect—Kalinin Prospect—turn left on Marx Prospect.
3. Vernad(sky) Prospect—Komsomolsky Prospect—Metrostroyevsk Street—turn left around Pushkin Museum to Volkhonka Street—turn left onto Marx Prospect.
4. Lenin Prospect to Oktyabrskaya Square—turn right at Peking Hotel on Zhitnaya Street—turn left on Bolshaya Polyanka Street and bear right onto Marx Prospect.
5. Kalvga Highway—turn left at Yuzhnaya Hotel onto Lomonosov Prospect and right on Lenin Prospect. Now consult #4 for directions.
6. Warsaw Highway—B. Tulsk Street—Lyusinovskaya Street—bear left on Dobryminskaya Square at the Burevestnik Building—Bolshaya Polyanka Street and bear right on Marx Prospect.
7. Volgograd Prospect—bear left at first intersection, continue straight at second intersection, turn left onto Zatsepsky Val Street—Valovaya Street—bear right at Bolshaya Polyanka Street—turn right on Marx Prospect.
8. Entusiasts' Highway—bear left onto Ulyanovskaya Street at Lomonosov Monument—turn left at Chkalov Street—follow the same road which becomes Zatsepsky Val Street—Valovaya Street—turn left onto Bolshaya Polyanka Street at Dobryninskaya Square—turn right onto Marx Prospect.
9. Shchelkovo Highway—Bolshaya Cherkizovskaya Street—Stromynka Street—Rusakovskaya Street—to Komsomolskaya Square, past Kazan, Leningrad, and Yaroslavl railway stations and Leningradskaya Hotel to Orlikov Pereulok, to Kirov Street. Turn right at Griboyedov statue onto a circular boulevard which changes names several times,

but eliminates Red Square traffic problems. Names of the boulevard from point of entry are consecutively Sreten, Rozhdestvensky, Petrovsky. At Tsentralny Cinema and Pushkin statue (Pushkin Square), turn left on Gorky Street, just past Hotel Intourist, and make a right onto Marx Prospect.

10. Yaroslavl Highway—Mir Prospect—Sretenka Street to Rozhdestvensky Boulevard (described in #9). Turn left and follow directions for #9.

11. Dmitrov Highway—Butyrskaya Street—Novoslobdskaya Street—Kalyayev Street. Turn left on Sadovaya—Triumohalnaya Street and right on Gorky Street at Tchaikovsky Concert Hall and the Worker and Collective Farm Woman monument. Follow Gorky Street to Hotel Intourist and turn right on Marx Prospect.

12. Leningrad Highway—bear left at Leningrad Prospect (divided highway)—Gorky Street to Hotel Intourist. Turn right on Marx Prospect.

PARKING

Each hotel has its own policy regarding tourist parking, depending on its facilities and location. You may generally park in front of the hotel while registering unless no-parking signs appear. Inquire about parking at each hotel at the registration desk.

HOTELS

There are thirty-one hotels in Moscow, varying in class and price, two motels, and one campsite. At the following times only deluxe and first-class accommodations are available: (high season) April 23–May 3; all of July and August; November 4–10. Motels are open all year long, and camping facilities are available from June 1 to September 1. At other times (low season), four classes of service are available at Moscow hotels, two classes of service at the motels and campsite. All Moscow hotels offer dry cleaners, shoe and clothing repair shops, ticket offices for railways and airlines, laundries, long-distance telephones, post and telegraph offices, souvenir stands, and newspaper stands.

Independent travelers pay full rates for each class of service and groups pay slightly lower rates which vary with the tour and the time of travel. Since prices and rates are fixed throughout the Soviet Union, varying only slightly in smaller, less traveled areas, the prospective tourist may gauge his fees according to distance charts. The following is a list of accommodations available in Moscow. (Only the major Intourist hotels are reviewed in detail.)

Deluxe and First Class Hotels

INTOURIST 5 GORKY STREET

This is the newest hotel in Moscow, conveniently located at the foot of Gorky Street near the corner of Marx Prospect. It is a short walk from here to Red Square and to all shopping. The hotel is clean and comfortable. There are two large restaurants as well as a nightclub and bar. The Intourist offers excellent service and few problems.

NATIONAL 14 MARX PROSPECT

This is one of the older and more famous hotels in Moscow, conveniently located in center city near Red Square and all shopping. It has two restaurants, a bar, and a coffee shop. The National, in addition to its old-world charm, offers some of the best food in Moscow. The main restaurant, on the second floor, is quite small, and cannot accommodate all the patrons desiring service. Be prepared to wait at least an hour before being seated for the evening meal. The service is also a bit slower than average. The elevators, which are few in number, tend to be slow and cranky. The rooms are clean and comfortable.

METROPOLE 1 MARX PROSPECT AT SVERDLOV SQUARE

A grand old hotel in imperial style, the Metropole is convenient to most Moscow activities. There are two restaurants, a bar, and a sizable Beriozka shop on the second floor. The rooms are spacious, clean, and comfortable. The quality of food served in its restaurants is high but the service is slow.

ROSSIYA 1362 OTELYATANO (SOUTHEAST OF RED SQUARE)

This is the largest hotel in Europe, covering four square blocks and accommodating over six thousand guests. There are nine restaurants and two bars. The Rossiya is the second newest hotel in Moscow and boasts such luxuries as a swimming pool and sauna bath in addition to its two Service Bureaus. The food is of excellent quality and variety in the restaurant on the 21st floor. This restaurant is open for luncheon and dinner, with reservations required for the evening meal. It is the only one which does not serve tour groups. The other restaurants serve good food with a limited variety.

The Rossiya does present a few problems to the tourist. The distances from one's room to a restaurant or Service Bureau are vast. Also, there can be some difficulty getting from one section of the hotel to another. From the lower floors, a considerable walk outdoors is required and from the extreme upper floors, a walk is necessary. Another somewhat disconcerting

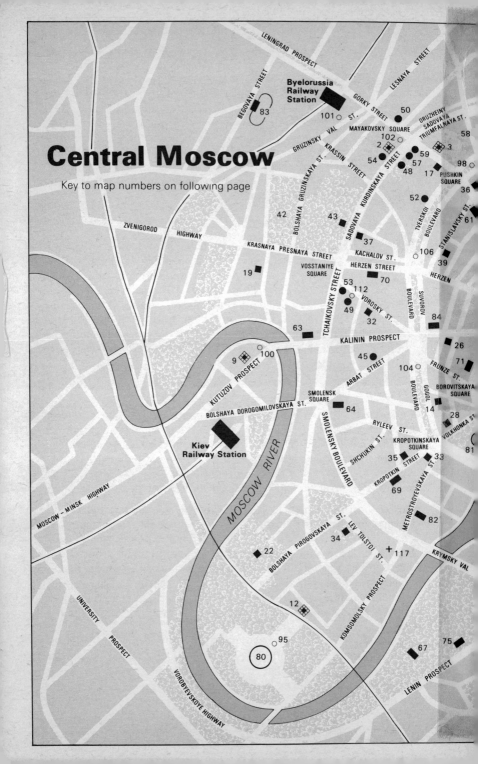

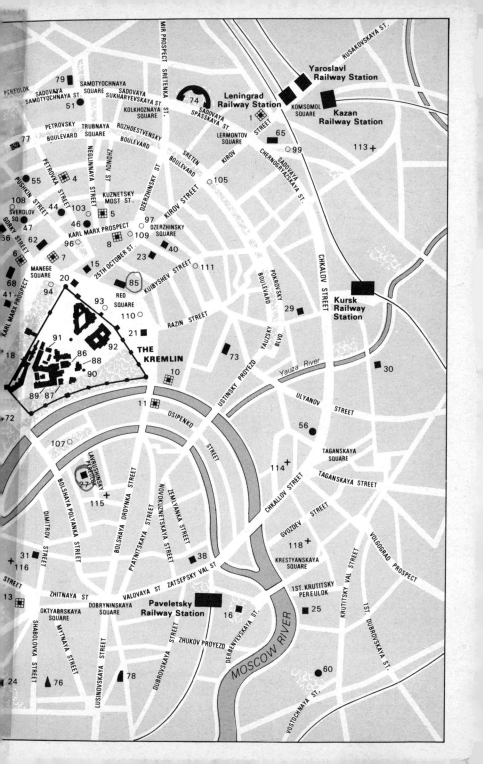

KEY TO FIGURES ON MOSCOW MAP

HOTELS

1. Leningradskaya
2. Peking
3. Minsk
4. Budapest
5. Berlin
6. National
7. Moskva
8. Metropole
9. Ukraina
10. Rossiya
11. Bucharest
12. Yunost
13. Warsaw

MUSEUMS

14. K. Marx and F. Engels Museum
15. Central Lenin Museum
16. Lenin Mourning Train Museum at the Paveletsky Railway Station
17. Museum of Revolution of the USSR
18. Mikhail Kalinin Museum
19. "Krasnaya Presnya" Museum of the History of the Revolution
20. History Museum
21. Pokrovsky Museum (St. Basil's Cathedral)
22. Novodevichy Convent, Branch of the History Museum
23. Museum of History and Reconstruction of Moscow
24. Museum of Architecture. Former Donskoi Monastery (built in 16th-17th centuries)
25. "Krutitskoye Podvoriye," Ensemble of Architectural Monuments of 15th-17th centuries
26. A. Shechusev Museum of Russian Architecture
27. Tretyakov Art Gallery
28. A. Pushkin Fine Arts Museum
29. Oriental Arts Museum
30. Andrei Rublyov Museum of Ancient Russian Art
31. Museum of Literature
32. Alexei Gorky Museum
33. Lev Tolstoi Museum
34. Lev Tolstoi Estate-Museum
35. Alexander Pushkin Museum
36. Nikolai Ostrovsky Apartment Museum
37. Anton Chekhov House Museum
38. A. Bakhrushin Theatrical Museum
39. K. Stanislavsky House-Museum
40. Polytechnic Museum
41. Central Exhibition Hall (former Manège)
42. Zoo
43. Moscow Planetarium

THEATERS

44. Bolshoi Theater
45. Yevgeny Vakhtangov Theater
46. Maly Theater
47. Maxim Gorky Art Theater
48. Mossoviet Theater
49. Pyotr Tchaikovsky Conservatoire
50. Central Puppet Theater
51. Moscow Circus
52. A. Pushkin Drama Theater
53. Vladimir Mayakovsky Theater
54. "Sovremennik" Theater-Studio
55. "Romen" Gipsy Theater
56. Drama and Comedy Theater
57. Moscow Satire Theater
58. Lenin Komsomol Theater
59. Pyotr Tchaikovsky Hall
60. Palace of Culture of the Likhachev Auto Works

INTERESTING SIGHTS

61. Moscow Soviet of Working People's Deputies
62. USSR Council of Ministers Building
63. Council of Mutual Economic Aid (CMEA)
64. Ministry of Foreign Affairs.
65. Ministry of Railway Transport.
66. Central Telegraph
67. USSR Academy of Sciences
68. M. Lomonosov Moscow State Univ.
69. Academy of Art of the USSR
70. Union of Soviet Writers
71. V.I. Lenin State Library
72. All-Union Book Chamber
73. USSR Academy of Medical Science
74. Sklifasovsky Emergency Hospital
75. City Clinical Hospital n° 1
76. Moscow Television Centre
77. "Rossiya" Cinema
78. "Pravda" Cinema
79. "Mir" Panorama Cinema
80. V. Lenin Central Stadium
81. "Moskva" Swimming Pool
82. "Chaika" Swimming Pool
83. Hippodrome
84. House of Friendship with the Peoples of Foreign Countries
85. State Department Store (GUM)

THE KREMLIN

86. Cathedral of the Assumption
87. Cathedral of the Archangel
88. Ivan the Great Bell-Tower
89. Great Kremlin Palace
90. Tsar Bell

91. Kremlin Palace of Congresses
92. Kremlin Theater
93. Vladimir Lenin Mausoleum
94. Obelisk to Revolutionary Thinkers

MEMORIALS

95. Vladimir Lenin
96. Karl Marx
97. Felix Dzerzhinsky
98. Alexander Pushkin
99. Mikhail Lermontov
100. Taras Shevchenko
101. Maxim Gorky
102. Vladimir Mayakovsky
103. Alexander Ostrovsky
104. Nikolai Gogol

105. Alexander Griboyedov
106. Klimenty Timiryazev
107. Ilya Repin
108. Yuri Dolgoruky
109. Ivan Fyodorov, first printer
110. Kuzma Minin and Dmitry Pozharsky
111. Grenadiers who fell in battle near Plevna
112. Pyotr Tchaikovsky

CHURCHES, MONASTERIES, CATHEDRALS

113. Cathedral of Christ's Appearance in Yelokhovo
114. Church of the Assumption in Gonchary
115. Church of All the Pious

116. Church of St. John the Warrior
117. St. Nicholas Church in Khamovniki
118. Former Novospassky Monastery

feature of the Rossiya is the eating facilities for individual tourists. Most, and occasionally all, restaurants except the one on the 21st floor are restricted to special groups. Without an identifying badge from a group, you will seldom get past the door guard. There are, however, self-service buffets on the 4th, 6th, and 10th floors which are open from 8 A.M. to 8 P.M. These serve a variety of beverages, fresh fruits, bread, eggs, cheese, cold fish, cold meats, and pastries.

The Rossiya is clean, comfortable, and impressive, but also unwieldy and disorganized.

UKRAINA 10 KUTUZOV PROSPECT

Until the building of the Rossiya, the Ukraina was the largest hotel in the Soviet Union. The service is slow and there are far too few elevators. However, the well-known restaurant serves excellent Ukrainian food. The Ukraina's location is convenient to shopping, the Lenin Central Stadium, and Moscow State University. The rooms are very large, clean, and comfortable.

Additional Deluxe and First Class Hotels

Aeroflot, Leningrad Highway (near Sheremetyevo Airport)
Berlin, 3 Zhandova Street
Budapest, 2/8 Petrovskiye Linii
Leningradskaya, 21/40 Kalanchevskaya Street (near the Leningrad, Yaroslavl, and Kazan railway stations)
Minsk, 22 Gorky Street, near Mayakovsky Square
Moskva, 7 Marx Prospect, near Red Square
Peking, 1/7 Bolshaya Sadovaya, near Mayakovsky Square
Sovietskaya, 32 Leningrad Prospect
Warsaw, 2/1 Oktyabrskaya Square (near Gorky Recreation Park)

Tourist Class Hotels

Altai, 12 Gostinichnaya Street
Armenia, 4 Neglinnaya Street
Balchug, 1/15 Sadovnicheskaya Naberezhnaya
Bucharest, 1 Balchug Street
Kievskaya, 2/16 Kiev Street (near Kiev Railway Station)
Ostankino, 29 Botanicheskaya Street (near the National Economic Achievements Exhibition, Botanical Gardens, Academy of Science, and Ostankino Palace–Museum)
Severnaya, 50 Sushchovsky Val (near Ostankino Palace–Museum)
Tourist, 17/2 Selshokhozyaistvennaya Street
Tsentralny, 10 Gorky Street

Ural–Building No. 1, 10 Pushkin Street
Ural–Building No. 2, 18 Stoleshnikov Pereulok
Vostok, 8 Gostinichny Proyezd
Yaroslavskaya, 4 Vtoraya Yaroslavskaya Street
Yunost, 36 Fruzensky Val
Yuzhnaya, 87 Lenin Prospect
Zarya, 5 Gostinichny Proyezd
Zolotoi Kolos, 3 Vtoraya Yaroslavskaya Street

Motels

Both of the motels are on the outskirts of Moscow. Each has a Service Bureau as well as a restaurant.

MOTEL PEKING

17 kilometers (10.6 miles) west of Moscow at the intersection of the Moscow Ring Road and the Minsk Highway (Motor Route #1)

MOTEL VARSHAVA

21 kilometers (13.1 miles) south of Moscow on the Simferopol Highway (Motor Route #1)

Camping

BUTOVO CAMPSITE

56 Pushkin Street, Butovo Village, 24 kilometers (15 miles) south of Moscow on the Simferopol Highway (Motor Route #4)

RESTAURANTS

Moscow's restaurants provide a generous sampling of regular Russian cuisine as well as the specialty foods of various nationalities within the Soviet Union. Russian food is similar to that of other Eastern European countries. Some of the specialties that characterize the Russian menu are particularly enjoyable.

Little need be said about Russian caviar. It is generally served with bread and butter or as a garnish with hard-cooked eggs. It is not, how-ever, as inexpensive as the tourist might suppose. An average serving costs about two rubles. Other appetizers in abundance are cold smoked sturgeon, salmon, herring, and a variety of jellied fish dishes garnished with chopped onions or beets. Typical Russian soups are varieties of *borshch* (hot or cold) and *solyanka*. The former are basic vegetable soups, and the latter are meat or fish soups with vegetables, potatoes, and rice. *Rassolnik rybny* (noodle soup) and *trikadelkami* (pickled cucumber soup with fish balls) are particularly interesting. Entrees, such as chicken Kiev, beef Stroganov, and pork cutlet Pozharsky are very popular. Side dishes of *blini* (pancakes), *oladyl* (yeast pancakes), and *blinchiki* (fritters filled with cottage cheese, meat, or apples) are recommended. Salads are most commonly made of cucumber, tomato, and onion garnished with sour cream. Russian food is generally simple and filling, and not highly seasoned.

Snacking is a favorite pastime of Soviet citizens, and in Moscow, near shopping areas, one will find many vendors of ice cream, *pirozhki* (meat pies), fresh fruits, and *kvass* (a soft drink similar to apple cider but made from black bread soaked in water). Vodka and champagne are also sold at kiosks on the streets.

The beverages served in Moscow restaurants are varied. Vodka, of course, is the standard drink throughout the Soviet Union, along with champagne and cognac. Russian beer differs in each republic. In Moscow the choice of beers is limited and the brews are quite weak. Georgian and Ukrainian wines are the best buys at table. Mineral water is a standard beverage, along with a variety of carbonated fruit drinks served under the generic name of lemonade.

Unless you have a fair amount of time to spend in Moscow, you will probably eat at your hotel. The food at Intourist hotels and restaurants is reputedly better than elsewhere, such as local cafés and small restaurants. It is also a bit fancier and more expensive. In Moscow there are many small cafés where a light and modest meal can be obtained. Bear in mind, however, that only Intourist restaurants have menus printed in foreign languages. Another general feature of the gastronomic experience in the Soviet Union is the slow service. In Moscow it is average: one hour for breakfast, two to three hours for luncheon or dinner. The price of meals in Moscow is also average: breakfast costs about one ruble per person and consists of juice, eggs, cheese, bread, coffee or tea; the inclusion of butter or marmalade depends on the restaurant. Luncheon and dinner are generally large meals, consisting of an appetizer, soup, entree, bread, and beverage. Exclusive of caviar and liquor, the average price of these meals is five rubles per person. Dessert is not a standard course and, when available, consists mainly of a cookie or ice cream with or without jam topping. Desserts, as we know them, are generally a midafternoon treat, taken as a break from work.

The following restaurants are recommended:

Aragvi, 6 Gorky Street. Georgian cuisine. Specialties include shashlik, chicken sastavi, broiled sturgeon, sulguni cheese, vinegared greens, chicken tabaka, Georgian bread. The best of the Georgian wines are also available: red #4, #5; white #1, #8, #12.

Ararat, 4 Neglinnaya Street. Armenian cuisine. Specialties include solyanka (soup), Yerevan bozbash, trout in various styles, lamb and pilaf with raisins, cheburek (deep-fried meat pies). Armenian cognacs are also served here: Yubileiny, Armenia, Yerevan, Dvin; also try the Armenian muscatels and sherry.

Arbat, Kalinin Prospect and Sadovaya Street. Russian cuisine.

Baku, 24 Gorky Street. Azerbaijan cuisine. Specialties include twenty varities of pilaf, piti (soup), dovta (sour-milk soup with meat or nut soup with chicken), shashlik, chopped meat and rice rolled in grape leaves, roast meat with pomegranates. Some excellent Azerbaijan wines are Matrassa and Shamkhor (red), and Akstafa (sweet white).

Berlin, 6 Pushechnaya Street. German cuisine.

Budapest, 2/18 Petrovskiye Linii (Hotel Budapest). Hungarian cuisine.

Kristall, 88 Lenin Prospect. Russian cuisine.

Metropole, 1 Marx Prospect (Hotel Metropole). Russian cuisine.

Minsk, 22 Gorky Street (Hotel Minsk). Byelorussian cuisine. The food is similar to Russian with variations of borshch and solyanka.

Moskva, 7 Marx Prospect. Russian cuisine.

National, 14 Marx Prospect (Hotel National). Russian cuisine. This restaurant is reputedly one of the best in Moscow and the tourist can count on being able to have an almost American-style steak if he is willing to endure the slow service and pay the high price charged for this cut of meat.

Peking, 1/7 Bolshaya Sadovaya (Hotel Peking). Chinese cuisine. The food here bears little resemblance to American-Chinese dishes but is closer to more authentic Chinese cookery with a Russian influence. The noodle and dumpling dishes are especially recommended.

Praga, 2 Arbat Street. Czech cuisine.

Sofia, 32 Gorky Street. Bulgarian cuisine. Interesting if one is looking for variety.

Sovietsky, 32 Leningrad Prospect (Hotel Sovietskaya). Russian cuisine.

Tsentralny, 10 Gorky Street. Russian cuisine.

Ukraina, 10/9 Kutuzov Prospect (Hotel Ukraina). Ukrainian cuisine. The food is very similar to Russian except for the dessert dumplings and borshch variations.

Uzbekistan, 29 Neglinnaya Prospect. Uzbek cuisine. Specialties include *Tkhum-dulma* (a fried meat patty with a hard-boiled egg in the center), *mastava* (rice soup with meat), *logman* (spicy meat stew with noodles), *maniar* (hotly spiced broth with meat, egg, and noodles), Uzbek-style shashlik (broiled pickled meat). Uzbek wines are generally sweet. Two well-known ones are Aleatiko and Uzbekiston.

Varshava, 2/1 Krymsky Val Street. Polish cuisine.

Cafés

Ararat, 4 Neglinnaya Street
Artisticheskoye, 6 Proyezd Khudozhestvennogo Teatra
Arfa, 9 Stoleshnikov Pereulok
Aelita, 45 Oruzheiny Pereulok
Cosmos, 4 Gorky Street
Druzhba, 5 Petrovka
Druzhba, 7/9 Kuznetsky Most Street
Kholodok, 10/34 Strastnoi Boulevard
Khrustalnoye, 17 Kutuzov Prospect
Krasny Mak (Red Poppy), 20 Stoleshnikov Pereulok
Landysh (Lily of the Valley), 29/3 Kirov Street
Leningradskoye, 38 Arbat Street
Lira, 17 Gorky Street
Mars, 5/6 Gorky Street
Molodyozhnoye (Youth), 41 Gorky Street
Moskovskoye, 8 Gorky Street
National, 1 Gorky Street
Ogni Moskvy (Lights of Moscow), 7 Marx Prospect
Otdykh, 6 Gorky Street
Praga, 2 Arbat Street
Prokhlada (Cool), 3 Marx Prospect
Raketa (Rocket), 6 Gorky Street
Record, Luzhniki (Lenin Central Stadium)
Riga, 79 Mir Prospect
Romantiky (Romantics), 40 Komsomolsky Prospect
Russky Chai (Russian Tea), 13 Kirov Street
Sardinka (Sardine), 7/5 Pushechnaya Street
Sever (North), 17 Gorky Street
Snezhinka (Snow Flake), 60/2 Lenin Prospect
Sokol (Falcon), 61 Leningrad Prospect
Sputnik, 78 Lenin Prospect
Timur, 27 Komsomolsky Prospect
Uyut (Cozy), 34 Lenin Prospect
Yunost (Youth), 40 Mir Prospect

PLACES OF INTEREST

The Kremlin

The Kremlin attracts virtually every tourist in Moscow. The center of today's Soviet regime, the Kremlin has an interesting history as the ancient nucleus of the Moscow principality.

In 1156 Prince Yuri Dolgoruky ordered a wooden fortress built atop Borovitsky Hill (now Kremlin Hill). During the Tatar invasion of 1238 the fortress was burned to the ground and in the years 1326–39 oaken walls were erected. At about the same time, two stone cathedrals—the Arckhangelsky and the Uspensky—were built, forerunners of the present Kremlin cathedrals. It was during this time that the Kremlin became the residence of the grand dukes and the metropolitans of Moscow. In 1367–68 the oaken walls were replaced by white stone walls and towers, and Moscow became known as the "white stone city." The current appearance of the Kremlin began to take shape during the reign of Ivan III, when the grounds were extended to their present area and the white stone walls were replaced (1485–95) by new brick walls and towers which are still standing today.

History was once more cruel to the great fortress when in 1737 fire destroyed all the wooden buildings then still standing. Again, in 1812, when the inhabitants and the Russian army abandoned Moscow, Napoleon's armies inflicted great damage to the Kremlin. After the War of 1812, all the historical monuments were restored and new structures were added: the Grand Palace and the new premises for the Oruzheinaya Palata (the Armory).

When the Soviet government moved from Petrograd to Moscow on March 11, 1918, Moscow became the capital and here Lenin signed the decree ordering the protection of all historical and artistic monuments of the past. Restoration of the Kremlin began almost immediately. In 1937 massive ruby-colored stars were mounted on the five highest Kremlin towers where once were the double-eagle symbols of the tsar.

Immediately at the end of World War II, restoration work in the Kremlin began on a large scale. Sections of the walls and towers that were weakening and beginning to crumble were restored. By 1955 the cathedrals and the Granovitaya Palata (the name Granovitaya comes from the many small, faceted stones in the palace façade) had been fully restored, as had the ancient stone pavement of Cathedral Square.

The Kremlin has been open to the public since July 1955. The best and most convenient way to tour it will depend on how much time you can allot from your itinerary. From the outside, you can walk along the walls stretching for 2,234 meters (7,331 feet). Or you can begin with a view of the Kremlin as seen from the Maurice Thorez Embankment, the Moskvoretsky Bridge, or the Bolshoi Kammeny Bridge. You can also have a good view from Red Square or Manège Square. Of course, the Kremlin should be seen from within and, time permitting, two days should be devoted to it.

Upon entering the grounds, the first structure you pass is the white-stone Kutafya Tower, built at the beginning of the sixteenth century to serve as a bridgehead watchtower.

The Trinity (Troitskaya) Tower, directly in front of the Kutafya, was erected in 1495. Because of its six-story height and deep two-story basements, ammunition for defending the Kremlin was stored there. In the sixteenth and seventeenth centuries these basements were used as prisons. Through the gates of Troitskaya Tower the tsar and military commanders returning from campaigns rode into the Kremlin. It was also through these gates that Napoleon's troops entered and later fled the Kremlin. The Troitskaya is the tallest tower in the Kremlin, standing 80 meters (262.4 feet) to the top of the ruby-red star above it.

To the right of Troitskaya Tower, on the far side of the Kremlin Wall, is the Palace of Congresses, built in 1961. The palace has an overall volume of 400,000 cubic meters (1,312,000 cubic feet) and in order to keep the building from towering above the rest of the Kremlin structures, it was sunk 15 meters (49.2 feet) into the ground. It contains 800 rooms on five floors that are connected by wide stairways and fourteen escalators.

You enter into a glass hall in the lower lobby. Adjacent to the auditorium, the lobby is decorated with the emblems of the fifteen Soviet Socialist Republics.

The tremendous auditorium is 50 meters (164 feet) deep, 20 meters (65.6 feet) high and 35 meters (114.8 ft.) wide with a seating capacity of 6,000. The Palace of Congresses is used for opera and stage productions (including the Bolshoi Ballet), as well as for meetings of the Soviet Communist Party and Trade Union Congresses.

Continuing the tour of the Kremlin, to the left of the Troitskaya Tower along the Kremlin Wall is the two-story location of the former Arsenal. The Arsenal is a good example of early-eighteenth-century architecture. Of historical interest, along the façade of the Arsenal are 875 guns captured by Russian troops from Napoleon's army in 1812.

Opposite the Arsenal, beyond a small square, is a three-story building, the site of the former Senate. Designed in Russian classical style and completed in 1788, its eastern façade is visible from Red Square. The seat of the Soviet government since March 1918, it is where Lenin lived and worked. His study and apartment on the third floor are now a museum. Also on this floor is a hall for meetings of the U.S.S.R. Council of Ministers.

Upon leaving this building, one sees, to the right of the Palace of Congresses, the small five-dome Cathedral of the Twelve Apostles and the Palace of the Patriarch built in 1635–56. These now contain a museum of applied art and seventeenth-century life. Included in the more than seven hundred works are tin and silver articles, fabric, and jewelry, as well as a display of rare books. In front of the Cathedral of the Twelve Apostles is the Tsar Cannon, the largest caliber gun in the world.

From in front of the Tsar Cannon you have a beautiful view of the southeastern part of the Kremlin grounds. From here you can see the Tainitsky Garden, located in the angle formed by the junction of the eastern and southern Kremlin walls. From the garden you have a good view of the Saviour's (Spasskaya) Tower, the gates of which open onto Red Square.

Tsar's (Tsarskaya) Tower, built in 1680 and topped by a pyramidal structure, can be seen immediately to the right of Spasskaya Tower. In fabled days, a wooden tower stood in its place, from where, legend tells, Ivan the Terrible watched executions. Hence the name Tsarskaya, or Tsar's Tower.

Moskvoretskaya Tower, formerly called the Beklemishevskaya, is to the right of the Tsarskaya and is of historical importance because it was the first structure to bear the onslaught of the Tatar hordes advancing on the Kremlin.

A word should be said about the walls of the great fortress. The Kremlin walls and their nineteen towers served as a great defense against enemy invaders. Varying in places, they are 4.9 to 18.9 meters (16 to 62 feet) high and from 3.4 to 6.4 meters (11 to 21 feet) thick. The narrow, slit-shaped loopholes were used to fire at enemy forces. At one time the walls had wooden roofing that sheltered the defenders in bad weather but fire destroyed it in the eighteenth century and it was never restored.

One of the most beautiful structures of the sixteenth century, standing in the center of the Kremlin, is the Bell Tower of Ivan the Great. Its design is that of a three-story pillar in the shape of elongated octagons, one on top of the other, becoming progressively smaller in diameter. Twenty-one bells hang in the arches of the octagons. While work on this tower began in 1505, the belfry was not added until 1532-43, and the structure was not complete until it was added to and crowned with a gilded cupola in 1600 during the reign of Tsar Boris Godunov.

At the foot of the tower, on a stone pedestal, stands the Tsar Bell, the largest bell in the world. Next to it stands a small fragment weighing 11.5 tons which split off during a great fire in 1737. The bell, cast in 1733-35, is decorated with a delicate design bearing the images of Tsar Alexei and Tsarina Anna and also five icons and two inscriptions telling of the bell's history.

The Bell Tower unites all the ancient cathedrals in the Moscow Kremlin. The edifices face Cathedral Square, the oldest square in the Soviet capital. As the Kremlin's main square, it dates from the fourteenth century and was the site of ceremonial processions when tsars were invested, emperors crowned, and foreign ambassadors received.

On the northern side of Cathedral Square is the five-dome Assumption (Uspensky) Cathedral, built in 1475-79 under the supervision of the Italian architect Aristotle Fioravanti. The walls are made of white stone, and the arches and the cupola supports of brick. The architectural proportions are considered to be perfect. It is 38 meters (124.5 feet) high, 2.6 meters (8.7 feet) wide, and 35 meters (116.4 feet) long. The interior is decorative and festive. The first murals were painted by Russian artists in 1514. Most of the frescoes and temperas are the work of fourteenth- to seventeenth-century Russian artists. Among the treasures is the twelfth-century

"Georgy" Icon and the thirteenth- to fourteenth-century "Troitsa." One of the cathedral's oldest relics is the "Vladimirskaya Bogomater" Icon, an example of eleventh-century Byzantine painting, now on display in the Tretyakov Art Gallery.

The southern doors are plated with black-lacquered copper sheets with twenty scenes of biblical themes wrought in gold. Near this entrance stands the throne of Ivan the Terrible, the first Russian tsar. Made in 1551, it is a rare monument of the craftsmanship of Russian wood-carvers. Of great beauty are the twelve seventeenth- and nineteenth-century church chandeliers, eleven made of gilded bronze and the center one of silver and bronze. It is interesting to note that the silver used to make the central chandeliers was recaptured in 1812 from Napoleon's troops. When Napoleon seized the Kremlin, he converted the Uspensky Cathedral into a stable. The French soldiers ransacked it and stole some 300 kilograms (661 pounds) of gold and more than 5 tons of silver.

Next to the Uspensky Cathedral is a single-dome temple called the Church of the Ordination of the Priests (Rizopolzhenie). Built in 1484–86, it was the private church of the patriarchs. Of great artistic value is the iconostasis, attributed to the painter Nazary Istomin (1627).

To the left of the church stands the Granovitaya Palata, one of the oldest civil edifices in Moscow. It was built in 1487–91 by Russian craftsmen working under the direction of Italian architects Marco Ruffo and Pietro Solari. The interior consists of one large hall with arches resting on the central pillar. In the second half of the sixteenth century the walls and arches were covered with paintings on church and biblical themes. Work on these murals was resumed in 1668 by the Russian painter Simon Ushakov. The most recent restorations of the murals were in 1949.

In the past, official ceremonies and government receptions were held in the Granovitaya Palata. It is also the site where Tsar Ivan the Terrible celebrated the conquest of Kazan in 1552 and where Emperor Peter I marked the victory of the Russian troops at Poltava in 1709. Today it is the meeting place of the Council of Elders of both chambers of the U.S.S.R. Supreme Soviet.

On the same side of Cathedral Square stands another monument of fifteenth-century architecture—Annunciation (Blagoveshchensky) Cathedral. The cathedral, with nine cupolas, was erected in 1484–89. Fire destroyed much of it in 1547 but it was restored in two years during the reign of Ivan the Terrible. During the restoration a porch was added to it (on the southeastern side) which is called the porch of Ivan the Terrible (Groznensky). This cathedral was the private church of Russian princes and tsars.

The frescoes in the Blagoveshchensky Cathedral were first executed in 1508. They were repainted many times throughout the centuries and even covered with oil paintings. For a time it was thought that the ancient frescoes had been irretrievably lost, but in 1947 Soviet artists completely cleaned the murals, bringing to light the ancient frescoes, which are for the most part themes from the Apocalypse. Near the porch of Ivan the Terrible, on the pilasters of the walls in the gallery, are portraits of Moscow princes as well as philosophers and poets of ancient Greece and Rome.

Blagoveshchensky Cathedral faces a third Kremlin temple—the Archangel (Arkhangelsky) Cathedral. Five cupolas crown this white stone edifice which was built in 1505–09. Shortly after erection the walls were covered with murals but in 1652 the paintings were removed together with the plaster. The present murals date from 1652–66. A gilded iconostasis, 10 meters (32.8 feet) high, separates the central part of the cathedral from the altar. It is completely covered with icons—magnificent relics of fifteenth- to seventeenth-century Russian painting. Of particular interest and beauty is the icon "Archangel Mikhail," credited to the fifteenth-century artist Andrei Rublev.

The Arkhangelsky Cathedral contains the burial vaults of the Moscow tsars and grand dukes (not be confused with the Russian tsars who, with the exception of one, are buried in the Peter and Paul Cathedral in Leningrad). There are forty-six tombs with white tombstones bearing inscriptions in old Slavic script. Ivan the Terrible and his sons are buried in this cathedral. The oldest tomb is that of Prince Kalita, who died in 1341.

After completing the tour of Arkhangelsky Cathedral, you can see immediately beyond the Blagoveshchensky Cathedral the sprawling structure of the Great Kremlin Palace, erected in 1838–49. From outside the Kremlin, the best view of this palace is from the Maurice Thorez Embankment across the Moskva River. The building is 125 meters (410 feet) long and the tallest central part is crowned by a gilded balustrade and a flagstaff. Sessions of the Supreme Soviet of the U.S.S.R. and the R.S.F.S.R. are held in the Great Kremlin Palace.

There are several large halls in the palace, the most well known being St. George Hall (Georgievsky). This hall is 61 meters (199 feet) long, 17 meters (57.4 feet) high, and 20 meters (67.2 feet) wide. It is ornamented with stucco moldings and has eighteen spiral columns topped by sculptured figures with laurel wreaths. All decorations commemorate victories of Russian armies in the fifteenth to eighteenth centuries. The St. George Hall is used for state receptions and official ceremonies.

Next to St. George Hall is the circular St. Vladimir (Vladimirsky) Hall which leads into the Terem Palace, the Tsarina's Golden Hall (Zolotaya Tsaritsina Palace), and the Granovitaya Palata. The Terem Palace was built in 1635–36. The Terems are rooms with low, vaulted ceilings; the walls and ceilings were covered with paintings in 1837; the windows are glazed with colored sheets of mica and tiled stoves sit in the corners. These rooms were at one time the private chambers of Russian tsars.

Of interest is the Throne Hall (Prestolnaya Palata), which was the tsar's study in the seventeenth century. The middle window of this hall was called the "petition" window: a box would be lowered from this window and anyone could submit a petition in writing to the tsar. Among the common people this box was called the *dolgy* (one in which things were shelved), for a petition could lie around for long periods of time without being read by anyone.

The Armory Palace (Oruzheinaya Palata), built in 1851, stands next to the Great Kremlin Palace. The Armory dates back to the sixteenth century, when it consisted of shops where armor and weapons were made and kept. Later, military trophies of the tsars were kept there. In 1720, by order of Peter I, the shops were made into a museum. The Armory's exhibits include rare relics of Russian and foreign applied art, royal regalia, collections of thirteenth- to eighteenth-century arms and accouterments. There is also a collection of fourteenth- to nineteenth-century fabrics and clothing as well as highly artistic gold and silver articles from the twelfth to nineteenth centuries.

Upon leaving the Kremlin, one sees two more towers crowned with ruby-colored stars. One is the Water-Drawing Tower (Vodovzvodnaya), a beautiful, well-proportioned tower, rising 61 meters (200 feet). First erected in 1805, it was wrecked by French troops in 1812 and was restored in 1819 according to the design of architect Osip Bove. The second is the Borovitskaya Tower (from the Russian word *bor*, meaning grove), erected in 1490. It is pyramidal in shape and was structurally conceived as three stepped, tapering tetrahedrons, one on top of the other, crowned by a tall stone steeple.

The tour of the Kremlin is now complete and you can leave through the exit not far from the Borovitskiye Gate. The Lenin Library Metro Station can be reached by walking along Alexandrovsky Garden, which runs parallel to the Kremlin Wall.

Red Square

Spreading out along the northeastern wall of the Kremlin, Red Square covers an area of over 971,280 square feet. It is 695 meters (2,280 feet) long and has an average width of 130 meters (426 feet). First mentioned in the annals of the fifteenth century, Red Square has seen many momentous events.

In 1671 Stepan Razin, the leader of a peasant uprising, was put to death on Red Square by the tsar's executioners. It was here, too, that Peter I in 1698 executed the *streltsy* (irregular troops in Russia before the regular army was created by Peter I) who had mutinied against him in favor of his older sister, Princess Sophia. In October 1917 fierce fighting broke out on the square. On March 12, 1918, at Lenin's orders, the red banner was raised over the Kremlin; and red became the color of the national flag of the

Soviet Union. On June 24, 1945, a triumphant victory parade was held on Red Square to mark the defeat of Germany.

Every May 1 and November 7 military parades and processions are held on Red Square. It is also on Red Square that Soviet heroes are welcomed.

The architectural ensemble facing Red Square was erected gradually, reaching completion at the end of the nineteenth century. The most outstanding edifice is St. Basil's (Pokrovsky) Cathedral on the south side of Red Square. It was erected in 1555–61 by order of Ivan the Terrible to commemorate Russia's annexation of the khanates of Kazan and Astrakhan. Ivan, according to legend, blinded the architect after the completion of St. Basil's so that he could never design anything more beautiful.

St. Basil's Cathedral is a temple formed of nine pillar-shaped chapels, the tallest of which is 41 meters (154 feet) and topped by a bright spire-shaped structure. A tenth chapel, very small in size, was erected over the grave of Yurodivy Vasily (God's fool Vasily) in 1588. Since then Pokrovsky Cathedral has been called the Temple of Vasily the Blissful.

The interiors of the ten chapels reveal beautiful sixteenth-century frescoes. One has an icon, "Entering Jerusalem," considered one of the finest sixteenth-century Russian icons. The cathedral also has one of the oldest works of Russian applied art that has been preserved: the iconostasis in Trinity Church (the Church of Troitsa).

As restoration continues, many treasures of ancient Russian art, hidden for ages under much later layers of oil paintings, have been restored to their original appearance. A branch of the Museum of History has been opened in the cathedral with exhibits tracing the history of the creation of St. Basil's and Ivan the Terrible's campaign against the khanate of Kazan.

Just outside the fence surrounding the temple is a monument to Minin and Pozharsky. It is the first civilian monument to be erected in Moscow and until 1930 it stood in the center of Red Square, opposite the Kremlin Wall. The statue, executed by Ivan Martos, depicts the meeting of Kuzma Minin, a Nizhny-Novgorod merchant, with Prince Dmitry Pozharsky. It was under the leadership of these two men that the people's volunteer corps, in 1612, drove Polish invaders out of Moscow. The inscription on the pedestal reads "To citizen Minin and prince Pozharsky from a grateful Russia, summer, 1818."

To the right of St. Basil's Cathedral is the main Kremlin tower, the Spasskaya, erected in 1491 under the supervision of Italian architect Pietro Solari. Its present appearance was acquired in 1624–25 when the Russian architect Bazhen Ogurtsov erected the octagonal multistory superstructure that now tops it. Tsars, emperors, and foreign ambassadors entered the Kremlin through the Spasskaya Tower gate. It was customarily forbidden to pass through with covered head and even the tsars removed their headdress.

In 1491 the first clock was mounted on the Spasskaya Tower. The face of the clock is 6.4 meters (21 feet) in diameter. Each figure is 0.7 meter (2.36 feet) long with the hour hand measuring 3 meters (9.74 feet) and the minute hand 3.2 meters (10.76 feet). The clock weighs 25 tons. During the storming of the Kremlin in 1917, the clock was damaged by artillery fire. It was restored the following year on the instructions of Lenin. The "Kremlin Chimes"—ten bells cast in the seventeenth and eighteenth centuries —were installed in 1851–52. The beautiful ringing of these bells can be heard every fifteen minutes.

In 1937 the Spasskaya Tower was one of the five towers to be topped with ruby-colored stars. The span between the spires of the star on the Spasskaya is 4 meters (12.3 feet) and its weight is about 1.5 tons. However, it is on a special ball-bearing mounting and can turn freely with the wind.

Near St. Basil's Cathedral is the Lobnoye Mesto, an elevated platform made of white stone. More than four hundred years old, it is where tsars proclaimed imperial edicts and was also the place for public executions.

On the northwestern side of Red Square is a red brick building, the State History Museum, established in 1883. The building was erected in 1878–83 on the site of the former Moscow University. The museum boasts over 300,000 exhibits concerning the history of Russia from the Stone Age up to the end of the nineteenth century. The exhibits include a unique collection of coins and medals, collections of precious ornaments and household articles, a valuable collection of old manuscripts and books, and many original copies of historical documents. Also on display are the clothes worn by Ivan the Terrible and the bed abandoned by Napoleon during his flight from Russia.

To the left of the History Museum is the three-story Nikolskaya Tower, designed by Pietro Solari and built in 1491. It was through this tower that the people's volunteer corps led by Minin and Pozharsky fought their way into the Kremlin in 1612 to oust the Polish interventionists. Also through this gate, in 1917, revolutionary forces broke into the Kremlin and put down the resistance of the White Guards.

Of architectural interest is the Gothic superstructure atop Nikolskaya Tower. The tall spire, designed by Ruska and erected at the beginning of the nineteenth century, was damaged in 1812 by Napoleon's troops. It was restored in 1816 under the supervision of architect Osip Bove. Including its star, the Nikolskaya Tower is 70 meters (230.9 feet) high.

The Lenin Mausoleum, in the center of Red Square, is a good example of Soviet architecture. Alexei Shchusev designed it and it was constructed of red granite and black labradorite. Designed in one night and built in two and a half days, in January 1924, the mausoleum originally was made of wood. It was reconstructed in May 1924 and remained that way until 1930 when it was replaced by the granite mausoleum. The interior is faced with polished black and gray labradorite, crossed by a bright red zigzag band of labradorite. A large oblong monolith over the main portal bears the name "Lenin" encrusted in dark purple. An honor guard stands at the entrance and the ceremonial changing attracts many onlookers.

The wait to enter the mausoleum is often hours long, but the foreign tourist can enter immediately through a special entrance upon presentation of his passport to a guard or policeman. All hand-carried baggage (handbags, briefcases, etc.) must be checked as well as all photographic equipment.

Directly behind the Lenin Mausoleum and along the Kremlin Wall are the common graves of workers and soldiers who died fighting for Soviet power in October 1917. Sculptured portraits of Yakov Sverdlov, Felix Dzerzhinsky, Mikhail Frunze, Mikhail Kalinin, and Andrei Zhdanov stand on granite pedestals before their respective tombs. Here, too, Joseph Stalin's grave is in view and is easily recognized by the statue marking it. Urns with the ashes of Maxim Gorky, Sergei Kirov, Nadezhda Krupskaya (Lenin's wife), and Georgy (Sergo) Ordzhonikidze are immured in the Kremlin Wall.

GUM, the largest department store in Moscow, stretches along the entire length of Red Square opposite the Kremlin. It was erected in 1890–93 and was formerly a great trade center. Until the Revolution, it had up to two hundred stalls. The building was remodeled in 1953. A great novelty for foreign visitors, GUM, with its 2.4 kilometers (1.5 miles) of counters and 5 kilometers (3.1 miles) of storage shelves, handles as many as 85 million customers a year.

On the corner of Red Square between GUM and the History Museum is a building, erected at the beginning of the eighteenth century, which used to house the former Provincial Administration. At that time there was a "pit"—a debtors' prison—in the yard where Alexander Radishchev, a well-known Russian writer and revolutionary, was confined in 1790 on his way to exile in Siberia.

A walk on Red Square after dinner is quite pleasant and refreshing. After dark the square resembles a scene from a fairytale book with the illuminated St. Basil's Cathedral in the forefront. One can walk on the square and watch the changing of the guard at the Lenin Mausoleum. The square does not close (hours of guard change vary depending on season).

Revolution and Sverdlov Squares

Not far from Red Square are two other squares of particular interest—Revolution Square and Sverdlov Square.

For tourists taking the Metro, both squares have a common surface station with signs "Ploshchad Sverdlova" and "Ploshchad Revolutsii" indicating the respective underground stations. The squares themselves also merge at the entrance to the Metro. Upon stepping from the station into the street, Revolution Square is to the left and Sverdlov Square is straight ahead and to the right.

To the left of the Metro station, on Revolution Square, one sees a large brick building topped by silvery tentlike structures. Erected about 1895, it housed the City Council (Duma) until the 1917 Revolution. Today this is the main branch of the Central Lenin Museum, opened in May 1936.

The museum's more than twenty halls contain numerous photographs of Lenin and his family, newspapers, leaflets, maps, and fine works of Soviet painters and sculptors. Also on display are copies of first editions of Lenin's works, photographs of his manuscripts, letters, and documents. Some of Lenin's personal belongings and other items reflecting his life and works are on view, including an exact reproduction of his study in the Kremlin. Documentary films about Lenin are shown in the conference hall. The Lenin Museum has branches in Leningrad, Ulyanovsk, Kiev, Lvov, Tbilisi, and Baku.

The entire opposite side of Revolution Square was occupied by an old five-story building, the Grand Hotel, once part of the adjacent Hotel Moskva. Before the Revolution, the Grand boasted of such frequent visitors as composers Nikolai Rimsky-Korsakov and Pyotr Tchaikovsky, writers Anton Chekhov, Vladimir Korolenko, and Maxim Gorky, and the painter Ilya Repin.

To the right of the Metro station, a public garden has been laid out near a dark red medieval brick wall. This wall extends over half the southern side of Sverdlov Square and joins with a massive tower on Karl Marx Prospect. The wall and tower are the remains of a line of fortifications that embraced Kitai-Gorod, which adjoined the Kremlin on the east, and that were built in 1535–38 under the direction of Petrok Maly.

From any point on Sverdlov Square one can see the tall, massive white columns of a building surmounted by four steeds harnessed to the chariot of Apollo. This is the building of the U.S.S.R. State Academic Bolshoi Theater, which was opened in 1780 and burned down in 1805. A new theater was built on the same site about twenty years later under the supervision of architects Osip Bove and Andrei Mikhailov. This building subsequently suffered the same fate. The walls and portico that remained standing after the fire formed the framework of the new, remodeled theater built in 1856 and designed by Albert Kavos.

Before the Kremlin Palace of Congresses was built, Russia's finest theatrical and concert-stage companies frequently performed at the Bolshoi Theater. In the first few years after the Revolution, party congresses were held there. Today the red and gold auditorium is a six-tier hall with a seating capacity of over two thousand, used primarily for dramatic productions.

To the left of the Bolshoi Theater is the Central Children's Theater, and to the right is the Maly Theater, built in 1821. A monument to the playwright Alexander Ostrovsky, unveiled in May 1929, stands at the entrance of the Maly Theater. The theater stages plays and dramatizations of works by Soviet and foreign writers.

There are two public gardens on Sverdlov Square. The one in front of the Bolshoi Theater has a beautiful fountain in the center, spouting 70 liters (18 gallons) of water a second. The other public garden, covering a greater area, occupies the center of Sverdlov Square. Here, too, is a beautiful fountain, erected in 1835 and designed by sculptor Ivan Vitaly.

On May 1, 1920, Vladimir Lenin arrived on Sverdlov Square to take part in the ceremony of laying the cornerstone for a monument to Karl Marx. The monument was unveiled on this spot in October 1961. It is carved out of a monolith of gray granite.

If you walk up Karl Marx Prospect toward Dzerzhinsky Square, next to the Metropole Hotel, you will see the familiar Kitai-Gorod wall. Somewhat farther, in a public garden, is a monument to Ivan Fyodorov, the first book printer in Russia. The monument was erected in 1909 and restored in 1957. The name "Ivan Fyodorov" is carved on the front of the stone pedestal, and below this appears a reproduction of his colophon and the date when he began the printing of the first book printed in Russia: April 19, 1563.

Tretyakov Art Gallery

The Tretyakov Art Gallery was originally located on Lavrushinsky Pereulok, a street distant from the center of Moscow. The building was refaced at the beginning of the twentieth century and the facing of the main peak was embellished with the old emblem of Moscow: Georgy Pobedonosets (St. George) slaying a reptile with a lance. However, due to the increasing interest in the gallery, the original premises could not handle the large crowds. The new home of the Tretyakov Art Gallery is now on the Krymskaya Embankment opposite the main entrance to Gorky Central Recreation Park.

Pavel Tretyakov began building this famous art collection in 1856 when he acquired two pictures, one of which was the famous *Seduction* by Nikolai Shilder. A special gallery for paintings was built by Pavel and his brother Sergei in the early 1870s. In bequeathing the gallery of art treasures to Moscow as a gift twenty years later, he wrote,

[I wish] to help organize useful institutions in the city so dear to me, to further the flourishing of art in Russia, and, at the same time, to preserve for all time the collection I have built up. . . .

In 1918 the Tretyakov Art Gallery, by virtue of a decree signed by Lenin, was transformed from a city institution into a national gallery. Great additions were acquired by the Tretyakov in 1925 when pictures in the former Rumyantsev Museum and those in several private collections—paintings dating from the eleventh to seventeenth centuries—were turned over to the gallery.

The first halls of the museum contain works of ancient Russian art. A beautiful work on display is the mosaic called *Dmitry Solunsky*. It came from a Kiev monastery and is a good example of Kievan art of the eleventh and twelfth centuries. Another great work is the fifteenth-century *Trinity icon* by Andrei Rublev. Here, too, are works by Dionysus, a painter who carried on the tradition of Rublev.

In the section devoted to eighteenth-century Russian art, the theme of the paintings has changed from religious to secular. Portraiture has become the principal genre, and among the exhibits are portraits of Peter III and Izmailova by Alexei Antropov; the masterpiece *Unknown Woman in Pink* by Fyodor Rokotov; and *Demidov* by Dmitry Levitsky.

Included in the section of early-nineteenth-century paintings are portraits by Orest Kiprensky, Karl Bryullov—the portraits of Kryiov and Kukolnik, *The Horsewoman*, and a *Self-Portrait*, and especially Alexander Ivanov's *Christ Appears Before the People*.

The first exhibition organized by Mobile Art Shows opened in 1871. The painters belonging to this association, which lasted for fifty years, were called *Peredvizhniki* (Itinerants), and strove for realism in art. Among the great paintings of members of the association, Vasily Perov's *At the Last Pub*, *Troika*, *Drowned Woman*, and *Funeral of a Peasant* leave lasting impressions.

Ilya Repin was considered to be the finest Russian painter of his time (b. 1844, d. 1930). Among his great works on display at the Tretyakov are *Barge Haulers on the Volga*, *Zaporozhye Cossacks*, *Sending Off a Recruit*, *Refusal to Confess*, *Arrest of a Propagandist*, *Not Expected*, and *Religious Procession in Kursk Province*. The most famous of Repin's paintings is *Ivan the Terrible and His Son Ivan, November 16, 1581*.

The museum's exhibits also include canvases by the portrait painter Valentin Serov, Repin's pupil. Landscape painting is represented by the works of Ivan Shishkin, Alexei Savrasov, Arkhip Kuindji, Ivan Aivazovsky, Isaac Levitan, and others.

When Pavel Tretyakov bequeathed his gallery to Moscow, it contained 1,200 paintings and 500 drawings. During 1927–35 an annex with sixteen halls was added to the original building, almost doubling the exhibition space. Today the Tretyakov Art Gallery has over 5,000 canvases, more than 3,000 works of ancient Russian art, which comprise one of the world's greatest icon collections, 900 sculptures, and upwards of 30,000 drawings and engravings.

Kropotkinskaya Square and Vicinity

Kropotkinskaya Square and its surrounding area offer a complete day of recreation and sight-seeing. One of the attractions is the open-air Moskva

Swimming Pool which was opened to the public in 1960 and functions all year round (the water is heated). The pool is located directly opposite the Kropotkinskaya Metro Station.

Volkhonka Street runs to the left of the observation platform overlooking the pool. On this street is a building designed in ancient Greek style and erected in 1898–1912 as the new premises for the museum called The Fine Arts Study. The Fine Arts Study was founded in the last third of the nineteenth century by Professor Tsvetayev of Moscow. Since 1937 the building has been known as the Pushkin Fine Arts Museum.

The museum displays one of the world's finest collections of Egyptian antiquities. It includes papyri, symbols and objects of worship, objects of applied art, reliefs, and painted sarcophagi. The department of antique art also has ancient Greek and Etruscan terra-cottas, vases, and sculptures. Replicas of the most famous works of ancient Greek and Roman sculpture, Pompeian frescoes and paintings from catacombs are also on display.

In the picture gallery, are outstanding works by Italian Renaissance artists, artists of the Dutch school (fifteenth and sixteenth centuries), the German, English, and Spanish schools (fifteenth to nineteenth centuries), and the Flemish school (seventeenth century). The largest representative collection is that of French painters of the seventeenth to twentieth centuries, among them Nicolas Poussin, Jean Baptiste Chardin, François Lemoyne, Ferdinand Victor Eugène Delacroix, Jean Baptiste Camille Corot, Gustave Courbet, and Paul Cézanne. Also represented are French landscape painters belonging to the Barbizon school and works of the Impressionists Pierre Auguste Renoir, Claude Monet, Camille Pissarro, and Hilaire Germain Edgar Degas.

The narrow street off Volkhonka Street to the left of the Pushkin Fine Arts Museum is Marx-Engels Street. Here you will find the Karl Marx and Friedrich Engels Museum. The exhibits deal primarily with the revolutionary activities of Marx and Engels in relation to the international labor and communist movements. On display are manuscripts and first editions of their works, photographs, and a collection of their personal belongings. The museum was established by the joint efforts of communist and workers' parties of several nations.

Walking back toward the Metro, on the corner opposite the station, is a three-story building with a small signboard. This is the home of the Russian Language Institute of the U.S.S.R. Academy of Sciences. Before the Revolution, it was the secondary school where the playwright Alexander Ostrovsky studied.

At the Kropotkinskaya Metro Station, two streets can be seen off to the right: Kropotkin and Metrostroyevskaya. The more interesting is Kropotkin Street because it leads to a district of old Moscow where, after the fire of 1812, the city's aristocracy built estates and mansions, many of which are still standing.

Also on this street is an old estate with a manor house, now preserved by the government. Built in 1814, the building has housed the Pushkin Museum since 1961. Among the exhibits are manuscripts, works of art, and personal belongings of the great Russian writer and poet. There is a concert hall in the building where you can hear live recitations or tape recordings of Pushkin's works, or see films based on his life.

On the left side of Kropotkin Street is the Lev Tolstoi Museum, a wooden structure with an imitation stone finish. It was built in 1822 and designed by Afanasy Grigoryev, the same architect who designed the Alexander Pushkin Museum. Organized in 1911 on the first anniversary of the writer's death, it began as a small exhibition of materials having to do with Tolstoi's life; in 1939 the Soviet government made it a museum. Today more than 160,000 manuscript pages and about 10,000 of his letters are exhibited. Recordings of Tolstoi's voice and moving pictures made of him are quite interesting as well as the works of art—painted and sculptured portraits of the writer made during his lifetime by Ilya Repin, Ivan Kramskoi, Nikolai Gae, and other artists.

National Economic Achievements Exhibition

The largest "museum" in the Soviet Union is the National Economic Achievements Exhibition (Vystavka Dostizheny Narodnovo Khosyaistva). First opened in 1959, and occupying an area of 220 hectares (550 acres), the exhibition has 100,000 displays that are renewed annually in order to show the most recent level of achievement in industry, agriculture, transportation, and science in the U.S.S.R.

In 1958 the Metro was expanded as far as the exhibition (the stop is VDNKh). To the right of the station is the silvery shaft of an obelisk, rising to a height of nearly 91 meters (300 feet). The monument (architects—Mikhail Barshch and Alexander Kolchin; sculptor—Andrei Faidysh-Krandievsky), unveiled in 1964, is in commemoration of the beginning of the exploration of space.

The main entrance to the exhibition is marked by a huge portico with the sculptured figures of a man and woman collective farmer with a sheaf of grain above their heads. The admission fee, giving the visitor the right to enter all the pavilions, is 30 kopecks. The exhibition begins with the *Central Pavilion* located down a lane with a double row of lampposts in the shape of ears of wheat. There is a 35 meter (115-foot) spire topped by a star and ears of wheat above the building. Another exhibit, the *Engineering Pavilion*, displays machines and machine tools and gives an idea of the present level of Soviet engineering, including the automobile industry.

The most popular and most crowded pavilions are those of the U.S.S.R. Academy of Sciences (Space, Atomic Energy for Peaceful Purposes, and

Public Education in the U.S.S.R.), the Soviet Schools of Higher Education, and Radio Electronics and Communications.

The most recent Soviet achievements in various fields of natural and technical sciences are exhibited in the U.S.S.R. Academy of Sciences *Space Pavilion*. Here you will become acquainted with the work of Soviet scientists and engineers in the exploration of outer space and controlled thermonuclear reactions. There is a special section devoted to the world's first Sputniks, the Lunik space rockets, and the *Vostok* and *Voskhod* spaceships. Also shown in the pavilion are instruments used for studying roentgen and ultraviolet radiation of the sun, and a model of a silicon battery with a cosmic-ray counter. Several halls are devoted to the flights of Soviet cosmonauts, including Yury Gagarin, Valentina Tereshkova, and Alexei Leonov. Exhibits provide information on the training of the cosmonauts and the construction of the *Vostok* spaceship.

In the hall called *Atomic Energy for Peaceful Purposes* you can see a scale model of the first atomic icebreaker, the *Lenin*. A section called *Safety Precautions and Protection Against Radioactivity* exhibits the work being done to protect the health of persons working with radioactive substances.

In the industry and transportation pavilions more than 5,000 machines, machine tools, instruments, and apparatus are on display. Also on view are some 18,000 products of light industry.

The exhibition grounds are a wonderful place for recreation and relaxation. There are theaters, open-air concerts (at scheduled times), a motion picture theater, a dance hall, restaurants, and many cafés. Of interest are two fascinating fountains located beyond the Central Pavilion: the *People's Friendship Fountain*, displaying figures of young women representing the nationalities of the U.S.S.R., and the *Stone Flower Fountain*, which is particularly beautiful at night, when its many-colored rocks light up.

Merging with the Main Botanical Gardens of the U.S.S.R. Academy of Sciences on the north and Dzerzhinsky Recreation Park on the west are the gardens of the National Economic Achievements Exhibition. On the grounds of the park you will find the beautiful *Ostankino Palace*. It belonged to Count Sheremetyev and was erected in 1792–97 by serfs. Built completely of wood in the Russian classical style, its façade is adorned with a six-columned portico topped by a rotunda. The interior, consisting of the foyer, halls, and galleries, is lavishly furnished, with parquet mosaic floors of different species of wood, and a collection of cut-glass and bronze chandeliers. Everything in the house is the work of serf craftsmen, including paintings by the Argunovs, serf artists. The Ostankino estate was nationalized in 1917 and the palace was turned into a museum of serf art.

Moscow State University

Standing on Lenin Hills is Moscow State University, originally named after Mikhail V. Lomonosov in 1755, one of Russia's great encyclopedists. The university consists of several buildings that extend for some distance. The main building, a 32-story structure, was erected in 1949–53 and is crowned by a 60 meter (196-foot) spire.

The Assembly Hall is quite attractive. One gets to the hall through a beautiful lobby finished in marble of different colors with mosaic portraits of great world scientists on the walls. At the entrance to the Assembly Hall are statues of Dmitry Mendeleyev, Ivan Pavlov, Ivan Michurin, and Nikolai Zhukovsky.

Of special interest is the famous Geography Museum, occuping seven floors. The exhibits are divided into three sections: the history of the natural and exact sciences in Moscow University and the history of geography; the history of the development of the Earth; the nature of the U.S.S.R.

On the other side of the main building, near the students' summer sports center, is an observatory and a meteorological station. The Institute of Theoretical Astronomy has a laboratory in the observatory on Lenin Hills. Telegrams with the cable address "Moscow. Cosmos." are sent from hundreds of stations in Russia and around the world reporting visual and photographic observations of Soviet Sputniks and spaceships. These telegrams are immediately processed, and then sent on to the computer center for data storage.

Today Moscow State University has fourteen departments and a total enrollment of nearly 32,000 (including correspondence students).

Names and Addresses of Museums and Exhibitions

ART AND ARCHITECTURE

Museum of Eastern Cultures, 16 Obukh Street
Oruzheinaya Palata, the Kremlin
Ostankino Serf Art Museum, Ostankino, 5 Akademika Korolyova Street
Pushkin Fine Arts Museum, 12 Volkhonka Street
Shchusev State Architectural Research Museum, 5 Kalinin Prospect
Annex of the Shchusev State Architectural Research Museum, 1 Donskaya
    Square
Tretyakov Art Gallery, Krymskaya Embankment opposite the main entrance to the Gorky Central Recreation Park

HISTORY

Battle of Borodino Panorama Museum, 38 Kutuzov Prospect
Central Lenin Museum, 2 Revolyutsii Square

Central Soviet Army Museum, 2 Kommuny Square
Frunze Central House of Aviation and Cosmonautics, 14 Krasnoarmeis-
    kaya Street
History Museum, 1/2 Krasnaya Square
Kalinin Museum, 21 Marx Prospect
Karl Marx and Friedrich Engels Museum, 5 Marx-Engels Street
Kolomenskoye 16th-17th Century Estate Museum, Kolomenskoye
Kutuzov Peasant Hut, annex of the Battle of Borodino Panorama Museum,
    38 Kutuzov Prospect
Museum of the History and Reconstruction of Moscow, 12 Novaya Square
Museum of the Revolution, 21 Gorky Street
Pavilion-Museum with the Lenin Funeral Train at the Paveletsky Railway
    Terminal, 1 Kozhevnichesky Skver
Pokrovsky Cathedral Museum (St. Basil's Cathedral), Krasnaya Square

LITERATURE

Chekhov Museum, 6 Sadovaya Kudrinskaya Street
Dostoyevsky Museum, 2 Dostoyevsky Street
Gorky Museum, 25a Vorovskogo Street
Lev Tolstoi Estate-Museum, 21 Lev Tolstoi Street
Lev Tolstoi Museum, 11 Kropotkin Street
Mayakovsky Library and Museum, 15/13 Pereulok Mayakovskogo
Museum of Literature, 38 Dimitrov Street
Nikolai Ostrovsky Museum, 14 Gorky Street
Pushkin Museum, 12/2 Kropotkin Street

SCIENCE

Darwin Museum, 1 Malaya Pirogovskaya Street
Main Botanical Gardens of the U.S.S.R. Academy of Sciences, Ostankino,
    4 Botanicheskaya Street
Moscow State University Museum of Geography, Leninskiye Gory
Planetarium, 5 Sadovaya Kudrinskaya Street
The Zoo, 1 Bolshaya Gruzinskaya Street

Getting Around Moscow

GUIDED TOURS

Sight-seeing excursions are generally arranged through the Service Bureau of the hotel to which the tourist has been assigned. Deluxe-class
tourists are provided with a private car and guide for six hours a day. The
fee has been included in the price of accommodations. First-class and
tourist-class visitors are provided with coupons which entitle them to one

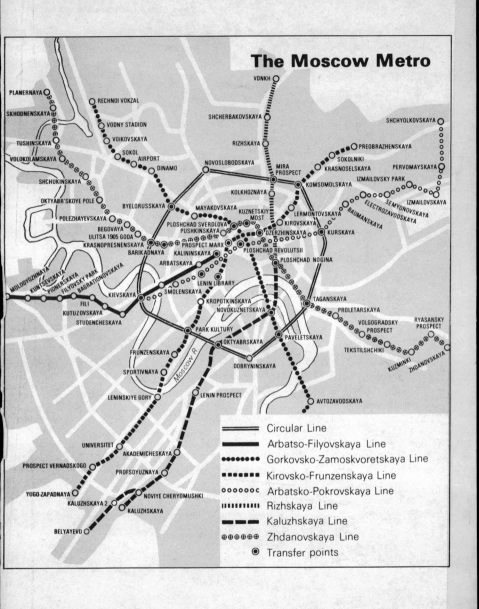

The Moscow Metro

Circular Line
Arbatso-Filyovskaya Line
Gorkovsko-Zamoskvoretskaya Line
Kirovsko-Frunzenskaya Line
Arbatsko-Pokrovskaya Line
Rizhskaya Line
Kaluzhskaya Line
Zhdanovskaya Line
Transfer points

three-hour guided bus tour per day. These run from 10 A.M. until 1 P.M. and from 2 P.M. to 5 P.M. You must sign up for the tour a day in advance at your hotel Service Bureau. Occasionally arrangements can be made for same-day excursions early in the morning. First- and tourist-class visitors may change from group to private tours by paying a fee of 3 rubles per person in addition to the coupon. The private tour by car will be arranged for a convenient time and will last for three hours. All excursions make stops for photographing and walking around major places of interest.

GENERAL TRANSPORTATION

Metro: 6 A.M. to 12:30 A.M. Fare: 5 kopecks, including transfers (see Metro map, p. 68.)

Trolley Bus: 6 A.M. to 12:30 A.M. Fare: 4 kopecks

Motorbus: 6 A.M. to 12:30 A.M. Fare: 5 kopecks

Streetcar: 5:30 A.M. to 12:30 A.M. Fare: 3 kopecks. Except for the Metro, most mass-transit conveyances operate without fare collectors. Passengers drop coins into cash boxes and tear off their tickets. It is advisable to have kopeck coins (1, 2, 3, and 5-kopeck denominations) since the boxes do not make change.

Taxis: Cabs are recognized by the checkered enclosure of the letter "T" on each side as well as the back and hood. A green light in the windshield indicates that the cab is available. Taxis are available at stands as well as by hailing them on the street. They may also be called at the hotel or reserved through the Service Bureau. The fare is metered and rates are 10 kopecks per kilometer (.6 mile) plus a 10-kopeck service charge. Waiting time is 1 ruble per hour.

Minibus and Fixed-Route Taxis: These vehicles operate between certain main squares of Moscow and run during busy hours at ten-minute intervals. They stop only at specific places en route to take on and discharge passengers. The fare is 10 kopecks.

Car Rental: There is a Hertz-Avis office in the lobby of the Hotel Intourist, 5 Gorky Street. Here cars may be rented for a few hours or for longer periods. The rates, always subject to change without notice, are as follows:

Self-Driven	1–10 Days	11–20 Days	21 Days and over	Km.
Moskvich	$5.00	$4.50	$4.00	5¢
Volga 21	$6.00	$5.50	$5.00	6¢
Volga 22	$7.00	$6.50	$6.00	6¢

Gasoline is not included in the rates. An International Driving Permit, obtainable through the AAA, is required for renting as well as a minimum age of twenty-one. Insurance costs 1.50 rubles per day for liability and collision. Special weekly rates are available with unlimited mileage. Under this plan, however, automobiles may not be taken beyond the city limits.

HOW TO REACH KEY POINTS IN MOSCOW BY PUBLIC TRANSPORTATION

Arbatskaya Square: Metro; trolley buses 2, 15, 31, 39; motorbuses 39, 89.

Byelorussian Railway Terminal: Metro; trolley buses 1, 12, 18, 20; motorbuses 10, 12, 27, 38, 63, 82, 116, 149, 263; streetcars A, 5, 29.

Dzerzhinsky Square: Metro; trolley buses 2, 9, 19, 25, 41, 42, 45, 48; motorbuses 3, 18, 24, 43, 55, 74, 89, 98, 107.

Gorky Central Recreation Park: Park Kultury in Otdykha or Oktyabrskaya Metro Stations; trolley buses B, 10, 17, 28, 31; motorbuses 8, 108.

Kiev Railway Terminal: Metro; trolley buses 7, 34, 39, 46; motorbuses 45, 69, 70, 91, 119, 132, 139, 267.

Komsomol Square: Metro; trolley buses 14, 22, 41; motorbuses 40, 85, 152; streetcars 7, 32, 37, 50.

Kropotkinskaya Square: Metro; trolley buses 11, 15, 31; motorbus 8.

Kursk Railway Terminal: Metro; trolley buses B, 10; motorbuses 40, 78, 81; streetcars 2, 20, 24.

Kuznetsky Most: Dzerzhinskaya and Marx Prospect Metro stations; trolley buses 2, 9, 13, 23, 42; motorbus 24.

Lenin Hills: Metro; trolley buses 7, 28.

Lenin Library: Metro; trolley buses 1, 2, 4, 8, 11; motorbuses 3, 5, 6.

Manège Square: Metro; trolley buses 1, 2, 5, 8, 11, 12, 20; motorbuses 3, 5, 89, 111.

Mayakovsky Square: Metro; trolley buses B, 1, 10, 12, 20, 29.

National Economic Achievements Exhibition: Metro; trolley buses 9, 13, 14, 36, 48; motorbuses 9, 33, 56, 61, 83, 93, 117, 136, 151, 265; streetcars 5, 10, 11, 25.

Noviye Cheryomushki: Metro; motorbuses 37, 41, 42, 49, 101, 103, 113, 156.

Ostankino: VDNKh (National Economic Achievements Exhibition) Metro Station; trolley buses 9, 13, 36; motorbuses 24, 76, 85; streetcars 7, 10.

Pushkin Square: trolley buses 1, 3, 12, 15, 20, 23, 31; motorbuses 5, 18, 87, 107.

Red Square: Revolutsii Square and Marx Prospect Metro stations; trolley buses 1, 2, 3, 4, 5, 9, 11, 12, 13, 20, 25; motorbuses 3, 5, 18, 24, 25, 28, 87, 107, 111, 213.

Revolution Square: Metro; trolley buses 1, 2, 3, 5, 9, 11, 12, 13, 20, 23; motorbuses 3, 5, 18, 24, 87, 107, 213.

Smolensk Square: Metro; trolley buses 5, 10, 39; motorbuses 64, 132.

Sokolniki: Metro; trolley buses 14, 32, 41; motorbuses 40, 52, 71, 75, 78,
   80, 140, 152, 216; streetcars 4, 7, 10, 13, 45.
Sverdlov Square: see Revolution Square
Trubnaya Square: trolley buses 13, 15, 31, 42; motorbus 24; streetcars A,
   1, 18, 25.
Vosstaniye Square: Krasnopresnenskaya Metro Station; trolley buses B, 5,
   8, 10; motorbuses 4, 6, 39, 48, 64, 69, 107, 116.

Places of Interest Near Moscow

ARKHANGELSKOYE

On the Volokolamsk Highway, about 16.6 kilometers (10 miles) from
Moscow, is the Arkhangelskoye Estate. It is located on the Petrovo-Dalneye
Road along the banks of the Moskva River. The estate, consisting of a
palace, park, theater, and service structures, belonged to Prince Yusupov,
who acquired the property in 1810. The orchards were designed at the
beginning of the seventeenth century, but the main work was supervised
and accomplished during Yusupov's proprietorship.

The outstanding structure is the palace, a monument to Russian classical
style of the eighteenth and nineteenth centuries. Osip Bove and other
Russian architects are responsible for the design. Credit for the actual
construction goes to Yusupov's serf architects, Strizhakov and Borunov,
and many talented serf craftsmen. The courtyard of the estate is framed
by colonnades which line the central portion of the palace. The halls of the
palace are sumptuously decorated with antique porcelain, sculpture, and
tapestries. The interior decor is enhanced by carved furniture, cut-glass
chandeliers, mirrors, murals, and variegated parquet flooring. A magnificent
park surrounds the palace with lanes decorated by colonnades, sculpture,
decorative staircases, and arbors. A triumphal arch, erected in 1817, leads
to the estate, which was a gathering place for Moscow aristocrats before
the 1917 Revolution.

Arkhangelskoye serves today as a museum and is unique as the best-
proportioned and most complete estate ensemble in the vicinity of Moscow. Part of the permanent exhibition is the Serf Theater, built in 1817.
As Yusupov was the director of the imperial theaters and the Hermitage
Museum, his estate became the repository for many valuable works of fine
and applied art on view at Arkhangelskoye today.

BORODINO

Located 124 kilometers (77 miles) west of Moscow on the Minsk Highway (Motor Route #1) is the village of Borodino. It was here, on Borodino
Field, that the Russian Army, under the command of Gen. Mikhail Kutuzov, fought a decisive battle against Napoleon's troops on August 26, 1812.

The Russians lost, but the struggle so weakened Napoleon that it ensured his eventual defeat in Russia. At the centennial celebration of the Battle of Borodino most of the monuments now on the site of the battle were erected with funds contributed by members of the Russian units who fought there. Additional funds were contributed by the French to honor their 58,000 dead from the battle.

There are thirty-five monuments commemorating the events at Borodino. An obelisk of gray granite with a bronze eagle on top is located about 152.4 meters (500 feet) from the Shevarddinsky entrenchment where, two days before the battle, a major encounter took place between French and Russian troops. This monument was erected with the combined funds of both countries. Several monuments are located on the site of the Bagration entrenchment. These are set off by an obelisk of black granite in honor of commander Lt. Gen. Dmitri Neverovsky of the 27th Division, whose grave lies below. Other monuments commemorate the site of the Raevsky battery, the chief Russian defense line. You may easily survey the whole of Borodino Battlefield from here. Northeast of this site the village of Gorki can be seen. On this vantage point there is a monument to Gen. Mikhail Kutuzov, made of gray granite and topped with a bronze eagle. On the face of the monument is a bas-relief of the general. Near here is a monument to the 3rd Division led by General Konovnitsin.

In addition to the monuments, there are markers indicating the sites of old fortifications. There is also a chapel that was commissioned in 1820 by the widow of Lt. Gen. Nikolai Tuchkov, killed in action at the Bagration entrenchment. An important place at Borodino Battlefield is the Borodino State Military History Museum. Here one can view various exhibits pertaining to the War of 1812: military clothing, weapons, and documents. There is also a collection of General Kutuzov's personal effects. A famous feature of the museum is an electrified model of the Battle of Borodino. There is also an exhibit of sketches by Frantz Rubo that were made for the Panorama of the Battle of Borodino now on display in Moscow.

LENINSKYE-GORKI

About 35 kilometers (21.9 miles) south of Moscow on the Simferopol Highway (Motor Route #4) is a county estate called *Gorki*. Lenin came to relax here during the years 1918–24, and to spend the last months of his life, from March 1923 to January 1924. On the 25th anniversary of his death, the Lenin Memorial Museum was opened on the Gorki Estate. The mansion stands on a hilltop amid tall trees in the estate's park. Lenin's rooms have been preserved exactly as they were during his lifetime. It was here that a delegation of textile workers presented him with a red calico shirt and eighteen cherry tree saplings in November 1923. Lenin also received many famous guests from home and abroad at the estate, including

Maxim Gorky, Romain Rolland, Martin Andersen Nexö, and Henri Barbusse.

PODOLSK

Thirty-eight kilometers (23.8 miles) south of Moscow along the Simferopol Highway (Motor Route #4) is the town of Podolsk. After 1784, when it had ceased to be a cloistral village, Podolsk became the main town of several small Russian limestone-mining villages along the Pakhra River. Now heavily industrialized, Podolsk retains importance as a historical site because it was the home of Lenin, his mother, brother, and sisters in 1900. After the tsar's decree exiling Lenin, the revolutionary leader visited the town on three occasions. The Ulyanov (Lenin's real last name) house, located near the entrance to the town on Moskovskaya Street, is now a branch of the Lenin Central Museum. Despite the modesty and simplicity of the structure and its accouterments, the house was a center for political activity; the place where revolutionary meetings were held, and where Lenin worked on the revolutionary newspaper *Iskra* (The Spark).

MELIKHOVO

Farther south on the Simferopol Highway, about 125 kilometers (78 miles) from Moscow, is a small town called Chekhov. The town's original name was Lopasnya, but this was changed in 1954 to commemorate the 50th anniversary of the death of Anton Chekhov. Driving south through the center of the town you come to a railway station on the left. Clustered around it are vegetable and fruit kiosks as well as stores selling beverages, meats, bread, and dairy products. There is a clearing where buses are frequently parked. The road leading past this commercial area to the right continues for about 13 kilometers (8 miles) after crossing the railroad tracks to the left of the fork. At the end of the road is the Chekhov Estate-Museum in the midst of a quaint and timeless village from which the estate takes its name—Melikhovo.

Chekhov purchased the estate in 1892 after a trip to Sakhalin. He lived at Melikhovo until 1898, whereupon he moved to Yalta because of ill health. The Estate-Museum consists of two small houses and several gardens. The main house contains all of the original furnishings of Chekhov's family as well as many of his personal effects. You may view the room in which he wrote *Uncle Vanya, The Sea Gull, Ward Number 6, The Muzhiks, Gooseberries,* and other works.

Chekhov moved to the country because, as a practicing physician, he felt that he should devote his medical services to the needy. He also felt, as a writer, that he should live among the common people, as they were the substance of reality. The smaller house on the estate consists of three rooms which Chekhov used as a treatment center for the Melikhovo villagers who were starving and victimized by a cholera epidemic. He also aided in the construction of schools for the village children. As his own health grew worse, Chekhov removed himself to the smaller of the two houses so as not to disturb or contaminate his family. To this day the residents of Melikhovo speak of Chekhov as their beloved benefactor.

TULA

Continuing south on the Simferopol Highway some 143 kilometers (89.4 miles) from Moscow, you come to the city of Tula. Famous for its samovars, gunsmiths, accordions, and filigree work, Tula is one of the oldest Russian cities, having become part of the Moscow state in 1503. Prior to joining the Moscow state, Tula was the home of an ancient Slavonic tribe, the Vyatichy, who in the tenth century came under the domination of the Kiev princes. In 1380 the Kulikovo Battle, which drove the Tatar-Mongols from the Russian territory, took place in Tula. In 1521 a wooden fortress, the Tula Kremlin, was erected as a defense against foreign invaders. This structure has survived to the present time. Within the Tula Kremlin is the Cathedral of the Assumption, built in 1762–64. It is typical of the architecture of the period with its five cupolas. The frescoes, painted by Yaroslavl masters, are the last remaining examples of frescoes copied from ancient Russian churches.

Tula has had an intense history for such a small town. In 1552 the Tula Kremlin was attacked by the Crimean Khan, Devlet Girei. In 1602 the same structure became the bastion of Ivan Bolotnikov, a rebel peasant leader. After four months of siege by the tsar's troops, the rebels would not yield until they were flooded out by the damming up of the river. During the sixteenth century the blacksmith trade began to develop and later ironworks were built. Early in the eighteenth century a decree by Peter the Great led to the founding of a state rifle plant. A second decree, forbidding old and damaged firearms to be recast, led to the founding of the Museum of Arms, which became a state museum after the 1917 Revolution. The museum contains an extensive collection of arms, including models of lances and spears used in the Kulikovo Battle. There are also exhibits of arms for ceremonial use, many of which are inlaid with precious stones and metals or have delicate designs of chased gold and silver.

The life-style of Tula, typical of industrial Russia during the brief rise of capitalism, has been depicted in the writings of Gleb Upensky and Vikenty Veresayev, both born in Tula. Today the city is heavily industrialized and it is also a cultural center. There are the polytechnical and pedagogical institutes, and other institutions of higher learning, as well as three museums, three theaters, a regional philharmonic society, and a regional library. Tula is interesting, not only for its history and its cultural centers, but because it is highly representative of modern nonurban industrial Soviet life.

YASNAYA POLYANA

Eighteen kilometers (11 miles) south of Tula to the east of the highway is Yasnaya Polyana, the estate of Leo Tolstoi. Born in 1828, Tolstoi lived here for sixty of his eighty years. The entrance to the estate is marked by two stone towers, and a wide road leads to the museum. In front of the porch of the main building is a large old elm tree under which local peasants consulted with Tolstoi about their problems. The elm has been named "Tree of the Poor." Unlike many estates of tsarist Russia, Yasnaya Polyana is not sumptuous or lavish. Furnishings were kept modest, in accordance with Tolstoi's beliefs. The largest room in the main house was used as a reception hall for many visitors, including Ivan Turgenev, Anton Chekhov, Maxim Gorky, and Ilya Repin. The hall also served for concerts given by Russian composers at the piano which Tolstoi also enjoyed playing. Here the famous writer read selections of his works to members of the family and selected friends.

The drawing room was used mainly by Tolstoi's wife, Sofia, for copying her husband's manuscripts. It opens onto Tolstoi's study, which houses the walnut writing table where *Anna Karenina* and *War and Peace* were created. Behind the writing table is an old leather sofa where his brothers, sister, and children were born. Next to the study is the author's bedroom. Sofia's bedroom is located nearby. It was here that she composed a diary, published during the Soviet period, of all the events connected with her husband's life. The second floor of the house contains Tolstoi's library and two rooms which were used by secretaries toward the end of the writer's life. In these rooms the vast correspondence was handled, with replies written by Tolstoi, his secretaries, or members of his family. There is also a tiny room under the eaves where Tolstoi wrote his later works, one of which was *Resurrection*.

Another building on the estate which is now the Writer's Literary Museum was once used as a school for the peasant children of Yasnaya Polyana. Greatly distressed by Tolstoi's radical political views, the tsarist government had the school closed. The six rooms which are now used as the museum contain many exhibits pertinent to the epoch of Tolstoi. These include photocopies of his manuscripts, paintings and photographs of the people the writer knew, and illustrations to his works. Most people familiar with Tolstoi's works will feel at home in various parts of Yasnaya Polyana which are frequently described in his writing. From the house a path leads to the estate's park. Back the other way, past the Tree of the Poor by the porch of the main house, a path leads to the ravine where Tolstoi went swimming. Along this path, called the "Bathing Road," is a small hill that is strewn with flowers in summer and pine branches in winter. This is Tolstoi's grave, a simple, unadorned mound which he selected as his final resting place before his death.

ZAGORSK

Northeast of Moscow, 58 kilometers (36 miles) along the Yaroslavl Highway (Motor Route #9), is the ancient town of Zagorsk, formerly called Sergiev. The town's growth was the result of the founding of the Troitse-Sergiev Monastery in 1337. The monastery was instrumental in the political and economic development of northeastern Russia and gave full support to the unification policies promulgated by the grand dukes. The monastery was also important as a bulwark of defense against foreign invaders. The Tatar siege from 1540 to 1550 resulted in the replacement of the burned wooden walls with brick. In 1608–09 a Polish invasion led by Sapega and Lisowski left cannonball marks which are still visible. From the fourteenth to the seventeenth century the monastery was a cultural center of ancient Russia. Books were written, transcribed, and collected, icons painted, and much wood carving and silverwork carried on. During these centuries paintings by Rublev and Dionysus were acquired along with miniature sculptures by Amvrosy, the celebrated sculptor and jeweler.

The architectural ensemble of the monastery grew most notably during the fifteenth and sixteenth centuries. In 1422–23 the white stone Trinity Cathedral (Troitsky Sobor) was built. Its pilasters and frieze-adorned façade, crowned by a massive cupola, are typical of Moscow architecture of the period. The murals and iconostasis paintings are the work of Andrei Rublev and other artists of the same school. The Dukhovnaya Church, built in 1476–77, is another important work of architecture. The two-story dome has a belfry in the lower area and an observation platform on top. By decree of Ivan the Terrible, the five-dome Uspensky Cathedral was erected, fashioned after the cathedral of the same name in the Moscow Kremlin. Inside you can still see the seventeenth-century frescoes and eighteenth-century iconostasis which have been preserved.

In 1920 the Soviet government decreed the transformation of the monastery and its grounds into the Zagorsk Museum of History and Arts. Here are some of the best icons, frescoes, and samples of decorative and folk art from the twelfth to nineteenth centuries. There are various exhibits of eighteenth-century paintings, older woodcuts, embroidery, carved bone and stone, handwoven textiles, papier-mâché objects, and handmade toys. The population of the town is now 100,000, with many schools, including the Moscow Ecclesiastical Academy and Seminary.

KLIN

Sixty-eight kilometers (42.5 miles) northwest of Moscow, on the Leningrad Highway (Motor Route #10), is the town of Klin, situated on the

Sestra River, a tributary of the Volga. The fame of Klin rests on Pyotr Ilych Tchaikovsky, whose house, now a state museum, is located at 48 Tchaikovsky Street. The composer lived in Klin from 1885 to 1893, but the museum building was his home only for the last year of his residence in the town. The house has been kept exactly as it was in his lifetime. This was initially the work of a servant, A. Sofronov, who bought the house in order to preserve it as a museum following the composer's death. The house was then passed on to the Russian Musical Society, and in 1921 the Soviet government became its sole custodian.

On exhibit in the museum is the grand piano on which Tchaikovsky composed many of his works. Twice yearly, by special invitation, Soviet musicians play this famous piano, an honor also bestowed upon the American pianist Van Cliburn in 1958. Although the museum was devastated by the Germans during World War II, it has been completely restored. The reopening of the museum occurred on May 7, 1945, the 105th anniversary of Tchaikovsky's birth.

Moscow Entertainment

There are many forms of entertainment available to the visitor in Moscow. Those who do not understand Russian will find a variety of ballet, opera, circus, and concert performances available during the theatrical season, which runs from September through May. Those with a knowledge of the language may enjoy theater and cinema as well. Except for cinema admissions, tickets to other performances can be acquired through the Service Bureau of one's hotel. At least one day in advance is usually required for reservations. Occasionally one may acquire same-day tickets, as Service Bureaus usually have access to last-minute cancellations.

It is advisable to plan meals so that they do not conflict with performance hours, which begin at 7 or 7:30 P.M., depending on the type of entertainment. It is sometimes possible to have a late meal afterward, as restaurants are open until 11 P.M. However, many do not seat patrons after 10:30 P.M.

The easiest way to get from the hotel to a theater is to have the Service Bureau reserve a taxi. There is a charge of 30 kopecks for this service, in addition to the regular fare. It is a worthwhile service, as it will alleviate the problem of hailing a taxi during the busiest hours as well as eliminate the need for the non-Russian-speaking tourist to explain his destination to the driver. Deluxe-class tourists have prepaid chauffeur service to and from all performances, but should remember to inform the Service Bureau of the time the car is desired.

Among tourists, the most frequented entertainments are the opera, ballet, and circus. The Bolshoi Ballet, while the best known, is matched by other companies that frequently reach Moscow while on tour. These troupes should not be disregarded if tickets to the Bolshoi are not available. By American standards the prices of tickets are reasonable for all entertainment: opera and ballet, $4.50; drama, circus, and concerts, $2.00–$4.00. (Theater prices tend to remain stable—these are top-price tickets as of time of writing.)

The following is a list of theaters, concert halls, and cinemas in Moscow.

THEATERS

Bolshoi Opera and Ballet Theater, 2/7 Sverdlov Square
Central Children's Theater, 2/7 Sverdlov Square
Central Puppet Theater, 32a Gorky Street
Central Soviet Army Theater, 2 Kommuny Square
The Circus, 13 Tsvetnoi Boulevard
Drama Theater, 2 Malaya Bronnaya
Gogol Theater, 8a Kazakova Street
Kremlin Palace of Congresses, the Kremlin
Kremlin Theater, the Kremlin
Lenin Komsomol Theater, 6 Chekhov Street
Light Opera Theater, 6 Pushkin Street
Maly Theater, 1/6 Sverdlov Square
Mayakovsky Theater, 19 Herzen Street
Miniature Theater, 3 Karetny Ryad
Moscow Art Theater, 3 Proyezd Khudozhestvennogo Teatra
Moscow Drama and Comedy Theater, 76 Chkalov Street
Mossoviet Drama Theater, 16 Bolshaya Sadovaya
Open Air Theater at the Gorky Central Recreation Park, 9 Krymsky Val
Open Air Theater at the National Economic Achievements Exhibition, Mir Prospect
Open Air Theater at the Sokolniki Recreation Park, 62 Russakovskaya Street
Pushkin Drama Theater, 23 Tverskoi Boulevard
Romain Gypsy Theater, 26 Pushkin Street
Sovremennik Theater, 1/29 Mayakovsky Square
Stanislavsky Drama Theater, 23 Gorky Street
Stanislavsky and Nemirovich-Danchenko Musical Theater, 17 Pushkin Street
Summer Drama Theater at the Sokolniki Recreation Park, 62 Russakovskaya Street
Summer Mass Theater in the Garden of the Frunze Central House of the Soviet Army, 2 Kommuny Square
Summer Variety Theater at the Gorky Central Recreation Park, 9 Krymsky Val
Theater of Satire, 18 Bolshaya Sadovaya
Vakhtangov Theater, 26 Arbat Street
Variety Theater in the Hermitage Gardens, 3 Karetny Ryad

Variety Theater at the National Economic Achievements Exhibition, Mir
    Prospect
Yermolova Theater, 5 Gorky Street
Zerkalny Theater in the Hermitage Gardens, 3 Karetny Ryad

CONCERT HALLS

Concert Hall at the Central Railwaymen's Club, 4 Komsomol Square
Concert Hall at Scientists' Club, 16 Kropotkin Street
Concert Hall at Sovietskaya Hotel, 32/2 Leningrad Prospect
The Hall of Columns of Trade Union House, 1 Pushkin Street
Large Hall of the Moscow Tchaikovsky Conservatoire, 13 Herzen Street
Small Hall of the Moscow Tchaikovsky Conservatoire, 13 Herzen Street
The October Hall at Trade Union House, 1 Pushkin Street
Sports Palace, Luzhniki
Tchaikovsky Concert Hall, 31 Gorky Street

MOTION PICTURE THEATERS

Barrikady (children's theater), 21 Barrikadnaya Street
Circorama, at the South Entrance of the National Economic Achieve-
    ments Exhibition, Mir Prospect
Cosmos, 109 Mir Prospect
Dynamo (at the Dynamo Stadium), Leningrad Prospect
Forum, 14 Sadovaya-Sukharevskaya
Gorky Central Recreation Park (summer theater), 9 Krymsky Val
Hermitage, 3 Karetny Ryad
Khudozhestvenny, 14 Arbatskaya Square
Kiev, 30/32 Kutuzov Prospect
Kolizei, 19a Christoprudny Boulevard
Leningrad, 12 Novopeschanaya Street
Leto, Izmailovo Recreation Park, 17 Narodny Prospect
Metropole, 1 Marx Prospect
Mir, 11 Tsvetnoi Boulevard
Moskva, 2/2 Mayakovsky Square
Mossoviet, 25 Bakhrushina Street
Ogonyok, 99 Mir Prospect
Otdykh, 12 Frunzenskaya Embankment
Patriot, 4 Salyam Adil Boulevard
Pioneer (children's theater), 25 Kutuzovsky Prospect
Plamya, 1 Vosstaniye Square
Povtornogo Filma (revivals of old films), 23/9 Herzen Street
Prizyv, 29 Kutuzovsky Prospect
Progress, 17 Lomonosovsky Prospect
Raketa, 12 Grimau Street

Record (Lenin Sports Complex), Luzhniki
Rossiya, Pushkin Square
Sokol, 71 Leningrad Prospect
Sport, 53/55 Bolshaya Pirogovskaya Street
Start, 56/2 Frunzenskaya Embankment
Stereokino, 3/3 Sverdlov Square
Strela, 23/25 Smolensky Boulevard
Udarnik, 2 Serafimovicha Street
Ukraina, 9 Barklaya Street
VDNKh (summer), on the grounds of the National Economic Achieve-
    ments Exhibition, Mir Prospect
Vstrecha, 5/9 Sadovaya-Chernogryazskaya
Zenit, 40/42 Taganskaya Street

Shopping in Moscow

In Moscow you can purchase almost anything desired as necessities
and souvenirs, except for highly specialized items restricted to specific
locales. The tourist may shop with Russian currency everywhere except
at Beriozka stores, where only foreign currency and traveler's checks are
accepted. The advantage of shopping in Beriozka stores is fourfold: (1)
sales personnel speak foreign languages; (2) purchases will be wrapped
realistically for travel; (3) prices are generally lower because there is less
tax on goods sold for foreign currency; (4) there is a wider selection of
goods than elsewhere.

Beriozka stores carry imported liquor and tobacco as well as Russian-
made items, which is not the case in other Soviet government stores. Be
sure to retain all receipts as they will be vital for customs clearance. In
Moscow there is a large variety of goods, and the prices are average. (In
the less tourist-traveled cities the prices will be slightly lower.) The best
buys in Moscow are: amber jewelry, records, furs, Khokhloma red, black,
and gold-painted bowls, spoons and trays, bone carvings, *matryoshki* dolls,
marble and alabaster figurines, wines, and vodka. Reproductions of native
costumes are rather costly but quite attractive. Hand-painted designs of
mythology and folk life on lacquered Palekh boxes are stunning, but these
items are very expensive.

There are Beriozka shops or counters in most large hotels in addition to
two very large stores: *Hotel Rossiya—South Promenade;* open daily from
9 A.M. until 8 P.M. (closed daily between 1 and 3 P.M.); closed Sundays. And
24 Kutuzov Prospect; open daily from 9 A.M. until 7 P.M. (closed daily
between 1 and 3 P.M.); closed Sundays.

DEPARTMENT STORES

Shopping in a Russian department store is unlike most other experiences one will have in Russia. If you are in a hurry or pressed for time, forget it. Consumer goods are highly desired by the citizens and fairly expensive. Nevertheless, the Russian people will endure almost any amount of waiting to purchase clothing, jewelry, notions, shoes, electrical equipment, and so forth, all of which are available in department stores that look like Macy's on the day before Christmas. Soviet stores are not air-conditioned or well ventilated in summer nor are they well heated in winter. There are no elevators and only occasional escalators. Most department stores are a block square and one to four stories high. There are no rest rooms. There are, however, redeeming features. These stores carry everything from basic groceries and delicacy foods to electric sockets and small plumbing fixtures. They are generally open from 9 A.M. until 8 P.M. with no midday closings, unlike Beriozka stores and some specialty shops in Moscow.

There are two major department stores in downtown Moscow: *GUM* (State Department Store), Red Square (east side), and *TSUM* (Central Department Store), 2 Petrovka Street. There are others scattered throughout the downtown section and the outlying areas. The two most accessible and of interest to tourists are *Detsky Mir* (Children's World Department Store) at 2 Marx Prospect, and *Central Military Department Store* at 10 Kalinin Prospect.

SPECIALTY STORES

The following is a list of the addresses of stores which carry items that may be of particular interest to visitors.

Antiques: 19 Arbat Street; 31 Sretenka

Art objects: 12 Petrovka Street; 15 Gorky Street; 46 Gorky Street; 24 Kutuzov Prospect; 8 Dvadtsat Pyatogo Oktyabrya Street

Books in foreign languages: 15 Gorky Street; 18 Kuznetsky Most

Books in Russian: 8 Gorky Street; 6 Proyezd Khudozhestvennogo Teatra; 4 Arbat Street; 5/7 Pushkin Street; Dom Knigi (Book House) in the grounds of the National Economic Achievements Exhibition (VDNKh); 18 Kuznetsky Most; 6 Kirov Street

Second-hand bookshops: 3 Proyezd Khudozhestvennogo Teatra; 10 Arbat Street; 31 Arbat Street; 13 Kirov Street; 24 Herzen Street (this store buys and sells books in foreign languages)

Cameras and accessories: 44 Komsomolsky Prospect; 19/21 Dvadtsat Pyatogo Oktyabrya Street; 25 Gorky Street; 15 Petrovka Street; 16 Kutuzov Prospect

Cut glass: 15 Gorky Street; 8/2 Kirov Street

Gifts: 12 Gorky Street; 4 Gorky Street; 13/15 Stoleshnikov Pereulok; 10 Petrovka Street; 24 Kutuzov Prospect; 8 Dvadtsat Pyatogo Oktyabrya Street

Jewelry: Yantar, 13 Stoleshnikov Pereulok (specializes in amber wares); 11 Arbat Street; 120 Mir Prospect

Perfumes: 7 Marx Prospect; 12 Pushkin Street; 6 Gorky Street

Porcelain and earthenware: 5/20 Stoleshnikov Pereulok; 8/2 Kirov Street; 4 Gorky Street

Records: 17 Kirov Street; 6/2 Arbat Street

Rugs: 9 Gorky Street

Toys: Dom Igrushki (Toy House), 14 Kutuzov Prospect

Wines: 4 Gorky Street; 7 Stoleshnikov Pereulok

LENINGRAD

GENERAL INFORMATION

Leningrad is one of the most rewarding cities to visit in the Soviet Union. Famous for its historical and cultural influence, it is equally noted for its physical beauty. Frequently called the "Venice of the North," Leningrad is constructed on 101 islands in the Neva River linked by numerous bridges and canals. One's first impression of Leningrad might be that of a fairytale city, pastel-colored buildings adorned with white confectionerylike trim, the criss-cross pattern of bridges and canals. Poetic legends of "white nights" mingled with dramatic historical events create a mood which is still very much part of the true spirit of the former capital of Imperial Russia.

The city is a vibrant metropolis of industrial, cultural, and commercial life inhabited by almost four million people. It is the second largest city in the Soviet Union, occupying 13 kilometers (8 miles) along the 74 kilometers (46 miles) of the Neva River. Modern Leningrad is a vital Soviet seaport. Industrially it produces machinery, technical instruments, electrical equipment, chemicals, textiles, footwear, and food products. There are 50 museums, 2,000 libraries, 180 research centers, 40 higher educational institutions, a university, and a conservatory.

The atmosphere of Leningrad is cosmopolitan, with more of a Western European tone than perhaps found elsewhere in the Soviet Union. The undeclared rivalry between Moscow and Leningrad is quite apparent here in the subtle but distinct feeling of superiority which Leningraders display toward the postrevolutionary capital. Despite the atrocities the Germans

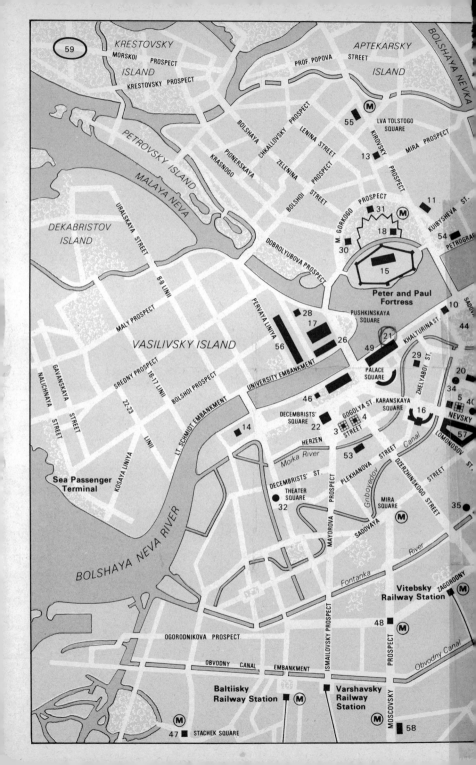

Central Leningrad

(M) Metro stations

Key to map numbers on following page

KARLA MARXA PROSPECT

LESNOI PROSPECT

AKADEMIKA LEBEDEVA ST.

KONDRATIEVSKY PROSPECT

ZHUKOVA STREET

PISKAREVSKY PROSPECT

REVOLUTSII HIGHWAY

BOLSHEOKHOTINSKY PROSPECT

SREDNEOKHOTINSKY PROSPECT

PIROGOVSKAYA EMBANKMENT

Finland Railway Station

(M)

KOMSOMOLA ST.

1

EMB.

12

LENIN SQUARE

42

ARSENALNAYA EMBANKMENT

NEVA RIVER

KUTUZOVA EMBANKMENT

ROBESPIERRE EMBANKMENT

TSCHAIKOVSKOGO STREET

50

43

Smolny

2

24

(M)

SALTYKOVA-SHCHEDRINA STREET

19

PESTELYA ST.

STREET

51

27

39

LITEINY PROSPECT

MAYAKOVSKOGO

VOSSTANIYA STREET

41

NEKRASOVA STREET

PROSPECT

MOISEENKO STREET

EMBANKMENT

SINOPSKAYA

MALOOKHTINSKY PROSPECT

NOVOCHERKASSKY PROSPECT

BELINSKOGO ST.

SQUARE OF ARTS

37

36

ZHUKOVSKOGO STREET

SUVOROVSKY PROSPECT

MYTNINSKAYA STREET

PROSPECT

33

52

6

(M)

38

7

8

Moscow

25

Moscow Railway Station

VOSSTANIYA SQUARE

BAKUNINA PROSPECT

KHERSONSKAYA ST.

NEVSKY PROSPECT

23

ZANEVSKY PROSPECT

RUBINSTEINA ST.

PROSPECT

MARATA STREET

LIGOVSKY STREET

ZASLONOVA

ALEXANDER NEVSKY SQUARE

NEVA RIVER

BOROVAYA ST.

9

RASSTANNAYA STREET

THE RIGHT BANK OF THE NEVA

PROEZD OBUKHOVSKOI OBORON

KEY TO FIGURES ON LENINGRAD MAP

HOTELS

1. Leningrad
2. Neva
3. Astoria
4. Leningradskaya
5. Yevropeiskaya
6. Severnaya
7. Moskovskaya
8. Oktyabrskaya
9. Yuzhnaya

MUSEUMS

10. The Leningrad Branch of the Central Lenin Museum
11. Museum of the Great October Socialist Revolution
12. The Cruiser Aurora Museum
13. S.M. Kirov Museum
14. History of Leningrad Museum
15. Petropavlovskaya Krepost (Peter and Paul Fortress)
16. Museum of History of Religion and Atheism (Cathedral of the Holy Virgin of Kazan)
17. Central Naval Museum
18. History of Artillery and Engineer Troops Museum
19. Suvorov Museum
20. The Russian Museum — *10–6¹⁵ Th 10–8¹⁵*
21. The State Hermitage Museum
22. St. Isaac's Cathedral
23. Alexander Nevsky Monastery. The Museum of Urban Sculpture
24. The Summer Palace of Peter the Great
25. Arctic and Antarctic Museum
26. Peter I Museum of Anthropology and Ethnography — *Hermitage 10³⁰–6 30k*
27. Ethnography Museum of the People's of the USSR
28. Pushkin's House Literature Museum
29. Pushkin's apartment
30. Zoo
31. Planetarium

THEATERS

32. Kirov Opera and Ballet Theater
33. Pushkin Drama Theater
34. Maly Opera Theater
35. Gorky Drama Theater
36. Comedy Theater
37. Komissarzhevskaya Drama Theater
38. Lensoviet Theater
39. Circus
40. Leningrad Philharmonic Concert Hall
41. Puppet Theater

PALACES AND MONUMENTS

42. V. I. Lenin Monument
43. Smolny and V. I. Lenin Monument
44. The Field of Mars. Monument to the Heroes of the Revolution and the Civil War
45. Memorial Ensemble on Piskaryov Cemetery
46. The Bronze Horseman, a monument to Peter the Great
47. Narva Arch of Triumph
48. Moscow Arch of Triumph
49. Winter Palace
50. Tavrichesky Palace
51. Engineers' Castle
52. Pioneer's Palace (former Anichkov Palace)
53. City Council Building (former Marlinsky Palace)
54. Peter the Great's Cottage
55. Kirov Palace of Culture
56. University
57. Gostiny Dvor
58. Fur Auction Palace
59. Kirov Stadium
60. The Necropolis "Literatorskiye Mostki"

inflicted upon the city during World War II, a gaiety is felt all over Leningrad, even though the older citizens painfully remember bad years. The old-world charm and grandeur has been preserved by the faithful rebuilding of the city according to previous lines. One can feel the intensity of life along Nevsky Prospect, in the hotels, restaurants, shops, and cafés. The people are very much interested in the West, and the younger generation in particular emulates a surprising number of Western, especially American, mannerisms of dress and style. In Leningrad, more than elsewhere, tourists are aggressively approached to trade Western goods for rubles. A good deal of diplomacy and prudence in these situations is advisable.

HISTORY IN BRIEF

In 1703 Tsar Peter the Great founded St. Petersburg. On the estuary of the Neva River, near its north bank, he built a fortress and buried a casket containing relics of St. Andrew and a few coins. A stone was placed over the grave, blessed and sprinkled with holy water, as Peter proclaimed, "Here shall be a town."

Peter had long dreamed of building a city on the site of this wet, swampy marshland; and in realizing this dream he revealed his love for things European. To work out the plan of the city, he chose Domenico Trezzini, an Italian architect. The building of St. Petersburg on the estuary of the Neva is indeed an interesting story. Because of its proximity to the Gulf of Finland it was not uncommon for floods to inundate the city. After almost drowning on the new Nevsky Prospect in 1705, the tsar ordered that everyone entering the city bring stones for building dikes. Workmen sank logs to assure firm ground. Progress was at first slow but finally Peter involved the entire country in building his city.

He raised national taxes to finance certain construction projects, and brought tens of thousands of workmen to the building site. The royal family and the entire court soon moved there from Moscow. Peter forced noblemen who owned thirty or more families of serfs to contribute to his project by financing the construction of at least one house. So zealous was Peter in building his new city that he outlawed the use of stone for any other purpose in Russia to assure that all needed supplies and masons would be available for the building of Petersburg. In 1710 Peter built a magnificent palace to be used as his summer residence on the south side of the Neva. In 1711 a "winter" palace was built—the first of many winter palaces to be constructed on the same site; the following year Peter proclaimed St. Petersburg his "window to the West," the new capital of Russia.

Peter himself worked feverishly to improve the life-style of Russia, particularly in St. Petersburg. In order to gain a firmer grasp on disorganized national administration, he divided the country into fifty separate provinces, each dealing with its internal problems on a local rather than a national level. He also simplified the alphabet, improved the roads, and set forth major educational programs. His plans called for compulsory education, and he favored a school system that would concern itself primarily with the training of much needed specialists. He founded the Academy of Sciences as well as an art museum, a newspaper, and the first public theater.

Today Leningrad is a thriving city and one of the major tourist centers. The visitor who is interested in architectural beauty as well as a rich history should place Leningrad high on his list of priorities, for it is an architectural gem and the scene of much of Russia's history, both past and present.

MUSEUMS AND PLACES OF INTEREST

Fortress of St. Peter and St. Paul (Petropavlovskaya Krepost)

It is indeed fitting that the first site on one's itinerary in Leningrad be the Fortress of St. Peter and St. Paul (commonly known as the Peter and Paul Fortress). Located on Zayachy Island (Hare Island) which lies near the north bank of the Neva River, the fortress was the first structure to be erected in the new city of St. Petersburg. The walls were originally made of earth, then wood, and were rebuilt in stone in 1706. The idea for the fortress was conceived and planned by Peter I (the Great) and work began on it in 1703 and continued until 1728. After the walls were constructed, barracks were added as well as storerooms and a prison area whose cells were to house some of the great names of Russian history.

Work on the fortress was so extensive that Peter I decided to call in an architect from outside Russia to supervise the project—Domenico Trezzini. Peter wanted his new city to develop from the northern bank of the Neva and, accordingly, Trezzini designed and supervised the building of the Cathedral of St. Peter and St. Paul in 1712. The church was erected in the center of the fortress and is easily recognized from afar by the tall golden spire topped with the figure of a cross-bearing angel.

Designed in the early Baroque style, the cathedral stands 122.5 meters (402 feet) high. The exterior is fairly simple and modest but the interior is breathtaking. Gold moldings and pulpit immediately catch the eye as do the painted ceilings. Opposite the altar is the red velvet throne used by the reigning tsar. An iconostasis, designed by A. Merkuryev and carved by I. Telegin and T. Ivanov of Moscow, presents a holy background for the white marble sarcophagi of the tsars and royal families. The most beautiful tombs of red jasper and green quartz are those of Alexander II and his wife. The other tombs are made of gray granite. Peter I's tomb lies to the left of the entrance of the cathedral and is situated near the high altar. Peter had planned the cathedral as the final resting place for himself and all his royal successors. Thus the tsars, the tsarinas, the grand dukes and the grand duchesses of the house of Romanov with the exception of Nicholas II and his family lie buried there.

Perhaps the Fortress of St. Peter and St. Paul is better known for its function as a prison than for the cathedral which stands in its center. Among those imprisoned in the fortress cells was Alexis, the son of Peter I. Alexis died in his cell in 1719, the victim of torture and beatings. A century later, members of the revolutionary circle known as the Decembrists were sentenced to time in the fortress's cells. The so-called Alexis Ravelin cell-block area of the fortress was the one used for those considered the most dangerous prisoners. Probably the most renowned figure imprisoned in the Alexis Ravelin was Fyodor Dostoyevsky, who occupied Cell No. 9. It is said that he found there a strange contentment and was able to accomplish great amounts of writing.

Others who suffered the dreaded fate of imprisonment in the fortress were Mikhail Bakunin, the anarchist revolutionary; Nikolai Chernyshevsky who, like Dostoyevsky, did much writing while imprisoned; and Dmitry Pisarev, who wrote brilliant philosophical essays including one on Darwin's *Origin of the Species.* Pisarev was arrested for his attack on the tsar in the pamphlet *Schedo-Ferroti.* Dmitry Karakozov, who said, "I have decided to destroy the evil Tsar and die for my beloved people," was arrested after an assassination attempt on the life of Alexander II. He was later executed. Another revolutionary, Pyotr Tkachev, encouraged the idea of tsarist assassination by a group of well-organized and trained terrorists rather than by one man. While a student at the University of St. Petersburg, he was arrested for being involved in student protests and was thrown into a cell. The master of revolutionary terrorism, Sergey Nechayev, was sentenced and imprisoned in the fortress in 1872 and spent the last years of his life chained to a wall in Cell No. 1, where he was simply left to rot. Most tourists visit the cell of Maxim Gorky, the most famous prisoner of the Peter and Paul Fortress, after Dostoyevsky.

The fortress also played a role in the plans of the Bolsheviks. Because it directly faced the Winter Palace they felt that it would be an advantage to have its guns trained on the palace at the time of the "storming." Moreover, the arsenals of the fortress contained over 100,000 rifles and other military equipment the Bolsheviks needed. The only problem was the fact that many of the soldiers and guards in the fortress were loyal to the Provisional Government. On November 5, Leon Trotsky slipped into the fortress and addressed the soldiers in a manner so convincing that they arrested their commanding officer and proclaimed complete support for Trotsky and the revolution.

The Peter and Paul Fortress did not play a role of major importance when the advance on the Winter Palace came two days later. The removal of the Provisional Government came more in the form of an almost blood-less coup than a revolution. The fortress was, however, in the hands of the Bolsheviks and they immediately made use of it. Officials of the deposed Provisional Government were imprisoned there. Vladimir Mitrovanovich Purishkevich, a member of the State Duma who took part in the plot to kill Rasputin, was arrested by the Bolsheviks and put into a cell in the dreaded Alexis Ravelin.

By 1922 the number of state prisoners had grown so vast as to render the fortress useless as a prison (it could accommodate thirty to forty prisoners and held more only during the aftermath of the Decembrist rebellion when some two hundred persons were crammed into the cells). Transforming the building of a life insurance company in Moscow into a state prison for the excess of inmates, the Soviet government designated the Fortress of St. Peter and St. Paul as a museum.

Alexander Nevsky Monastery

Located on the Alexander Nevsky Square is the Alexander Nevsky Monastery. According to legend, it is built on the site where Grand Duke Alexander defeated the Swedish army in 1240. Following the victory he was given the surname Nevsky, meaning "of the Neva."

In 1713 Peter I erected a church on the site and the remains of St. Alexander (he was canonized by the Russian Orthodox Church) were brought to St. Petersburg from Vladimir. The St. Petersburg Mint made a silver sarcophagus in 1750 for the ashes and it was placed in the Trinity Cathedral. The cathedral, designed by Domenico Trezzini with the help of Schwertfeger, Yeropkin, and Zemstov, is easily recognized by its large dome and deep red color. The sarcophagus was moved to the Hermitage Museum in 1922.

Most of the Alexander Nevsky Monastery was designed by Domenico Trezzini and was built in 1710–16. It contained eleven churches, four cemeteries, and an ecclesiastical academy and seminary. At the height of its activity, it was the second largest monastery in Russia after the Monastery of the Caves in Kiev.

Cathedral of the Annunciation (Blagoveshchensky Sobor)

Designed by Trezzini in 1720, the Cathedral of the Annunciation is the oldest surviving cathedral in the Alexander Nevsky Monastery. Alexander Suvorov, a Russian military leader and favorite of Catherine the Great, was buried here. Today, the cathedral is part of the Museum of Urban Sculpture.

Holy Trinity Cathedral (Troitsky Sobor)

Designed by architect I. Starov in 1790, the Holy Trinity Cathedral is presently the principal cathedral in the monastery and is still a functioning Russian Orthodox Church.

Lazarevskoye Cemetery

The Lazarevskoye is the oldest cemetery in the city and was used as a burial site for many of St. Petersburg's aristocratic families and prominent figures. Among those buried here are the architects Andrei Voronikhin, Hadrian Zakharov, Thomas de Thomon, Carlo Rossi, sculptor M. Kozlovsky, and the scientist Mikhail Lomonosov.

Tikhvinskoye Cemetery

Well-known figures buried in this cemetery of the monastery include the writers Fyodor Dostoyevsky, Basil Zhukovsky, Nikolai Karamzin, Ivan Krylov, composers Alexander Dargomyzhsky, Modest Moussorgsky, Nikolai Rimsky-Korsakov, Anton Rubinstein, Pyotr Tchaikovsky, painters Ivan Kramskoi, A. Kuingi, and sculptors P. Klodt and B. Orlovsky.

Cathedral of the Holy Virgin of Kazan

One of the two remaining structures from the ill-fated reign of Paul I is the Kazan Cathedral (the other surviving building is "Engineer's Castle"). Designed by architect Andrei Voronikhin, the cathedral was built in 1801–11 on the site of the former Church of the Nativity. The design of the structure is that of an elongated Latin cross with three entrances (north, south, and west), each having a six-column portico. The façade, which faces Nevsky Prospect, has a semicircular colonnade with 136 columns. The building stands on a raised granite base and is 79 meters (259 feet) in height, 72 meters (236 feet) long, and 55 meters (180 feet) wide.

To the right of the entrance is the tomb of Field-Marshal Mikhail Kutuzov, commander of the Russian army in the 1812 war against Napoleon. Statues of Kutuzov and Barclay de Tolly (commander of the Russian army at the beginning of the war) stand in the square in front of the cathedral and were designed by sculptor Boris Orlovsky in 1837.

Today the Kazan Cathedral houses the Museum of the History of Religion and Atheism of the U.S.S.R. Academy of Sciences. The Cathedral/Museum is located at 2 Karanskaya Square and is open daily from 12 P.M. to 6 P.M.; Sundays from 11 A.M. to 6 P.M.; closed on Wednesdays.

St. Isaac's Cathedral (Isaakievsky Sobor)

As famous as the Cathedral of St. Peter and St. Paul is St. Isaac's Cathedral, located between Decembrists Square and St. Isaac's Square. The cathedral was built by some 440,000 workers over a period of forty years, 1818–58. At the time of the completion of the project, five architects had worked on it: August Montferrand, V. Stasov, A. Mikhailov, A. Melnikov, and Carlo Rossi.

The beautifully colored cathedral has 144 columns and is the third highest domed building in the world, 102 meters (335 feet). The structure is 111.2 meters (365 feet) long and 97.6 meters (320 feet) wide. The cathedral is graced by 382 sculptures, paintings, and mosaics. Of great interest is the 98-meter (321-foot) Foucault's pendulum that is suspended from the central cupola and is engineered to demonstrate the earth's rotation on its axis.

St. Isaac's Cathedral is remembered most by the city's older citizens for the magnificent pageantry of the Easter midnight mass. The cathedral became a state museum in 1931 and is open daily from 10 A.M. to 5 P.M.; closed on Tuesdays.

Church of the Resurrection

Also known as the Cathedral of Our Savior-on-the-Blood *(Spas-na-Krovi)*, the Church of the Resurrection is located on the north side of Nevsky Prospect, near Griboyedov Canal. Designed by the architect Parland, the church was built in 1883–1907. The site is of historical interest for it was here that Tsar Alexander II was assassinated in 1881.

The Hermitage

Located on one of the oldest, and perhaps the most famous spot in Leningrad, the State Hermitage Museum occupies a major portion of Palace Square. At present, the museum consists of five buildings, four of which house exhibits, while the fifth is used as a lecture hall and museum theater. All the structures were at one time linked by covered passageways and thus formed a single unit. The buildings which comprise the museum are the Winter Palace, the Hermitage, the Hermitage Theater, the Gallery, and the New Hermitage.

HISTORY OF THE BUILDINGS

The oldest of these structures is the Winter Palace, designed by Bartholomeo Rastrelli, and erected between 1754 and 1762. Its inherent architectural beauty is enhanced by the historical drama that surrounds it as well as by its reputation as one of the world's leading museums. A fire in 1837 destroyed the original walls and inner decor. Restored in 1840 by architects Stasov and Bryullov, the Winter Palace retains only a few touches of the Rastrelli style; the edifice now reflects the prevailing tastes of nineteenth-century Imperial Russia. The building originally known as the Hermitage, and later called the Small Hermitage, was designed by Vallin de la Mothe and Yuri Felten. Construction was begun in 1764. The purpose of this building adjacent to the Winter Palace was twofold. First, it was intended as a palace museum with a very limited admittance; second, it was used by Catherine II, the Great, as a refuge from affairs of state. Hence the name "Hermitage." Two other buildings were added at about the same time. The Hermitage Theater, designed by Giacomo Quarenghi in 1783, was completed in 1787. It was connected to the Hermitage by an arch over the Winter Canal. The theater was intended for the exclusive use of the imperial court. It is now the lecture theater of the State Hermitage Museum and seats about five hundred people in the original amphitheater.

The second building constructed at that time was the Gallery. Designed by Quarenghi, and built between 1783 and 1792, this building overlooking the Winter Canal is an exact replica of the Raphael Loggias of the Vatican. The fifth building of the museum is known as the New Hermitage or the Imperial Hermitage, erected between 1839 and 1851, according to the design of Leo Klenze, a Munich architect. Supervision of the actual construction was delegated to Stasov and Yefimov, eminent Russian architects of the period. After the Revolution, the Winter Palace was converted to a public museum and made part of the State Hermitage Museum complex.

BRIEF HISTORY AND DESCRIPTION OF THE COLLECTION

Although an assortment of objects acquired by Peter I from different countries was the original nucleus of the museum collection, the purchase of 225 pictures from Gotzkowsky, a Prussian merchant, made by Catherine II in 1764, was the actual foundation of the Hermitage collection. Peter's acquisitions, which included antique statues, ancient gold buckles from Siberia, and some seascapes, were selectively reduced for incorporation into the museum. Between 1764 and 1785, 2,658 paintings had been acquired along with prints, cameos, medals, drawings, and coins. The massive purchase of entire collections at Western European art sales was highly characteristic of eighteenth-century acquisitions. Among these purchases were Count Brühl's collection (Dresden, 1769), the Crozat gallery (Paris, 1772), and Lord Walpole's gallery (London, 1779). In addition to purchasing works by European masters, the Russian court also commissioned works from Western European painters. During the nineteenth century a more moderate purchasing policy was exercised. The most noteworthy acquisitions of this period were the Malmaison Gallery of Empress Josephine (1814), the Coesvelt collection (London, 1814), and an outstanding group of Titians from the Barbarigo Palace in Venice shortly thereafter. During the early part of the nineteenth century excavations in southern Russia yielded enough material to result in the formation of a new department specializing in Greek and Roman antiquities. At the same time a collection of sculpture acquired during the eighteenth century was moved from the Tauris Palace to the Hermitage to augment the new Graeco-Roman department. In 1885 the Basilevsky collection of twelfth- through sixteenth-century applied art was acquired by the Hermitage. At the turn of the century, and for the decade that followed, 730 Dutch and Flemish masterpieces from the Semyonov-Tianshansky collection were acquired.

Following the Revolution many works chosen by Hermitage administrators from newly nationalized private collections were added. A systematic program was instituted at the same time for distributing art treasures among all state museums, and particularly for filling the gaps in the Hermitage collections. Other postrevolutionary innovations included the addition of three new departments: History of Primitive Culture, History of Culture and Art of Peoples of the East, and History of Russian Culture. The continued growth of the collections led to a regular increase of exhibit space until the State Hermitage Museum gradually occupied its present buildings.

Over 2,500,000 items dating from 500,000 B.C. to contemporary works comprise the museum's vast and varied collection. More than three hundred rooms are open to the general public from 10 A.M. to 5 P.M. every day but Monday. All items on display are original and each has been carefully arranged according to place of origin, school, and date. The museum is dedicated to the task of illustrating every major art period from prehistoric to contemporary times. There are over forty permanent exhibitions plus many others on loan from other Soviet or foreign museums. The major departments of the Hermitage are: History of Western European Art, History of Russian Culture, History of Culture and Art of Peoples of the East, History of Primitive Culture, History of Culture and Art of the Antique World, Numismatics, Conservation, Education, and the Library. As one of the Soviet Union's vital centers of art study, the museum maintains a staff of about two hundred historians and art historians whose functions include research, collection preservation, and the publication of numerous books, pamphlets, and articles aimed not only at professionals but also at laymen as part of a program to popularize fine and applied art. A postgraduate school, established at the Hermitage in 1949, provides sponsorship and guidance for students writing theses.

The following brief summary of the museum's collections should provide the visitor with a basic concept of the vast exhibit material to be seen at the Hermitage. The Western European paintings cover a span of seven centuries, thirteenth to twentieth, and consist of works by Leonardo da Vinci, Raphael, Titian, El Greco, Velázquez, Murillo, Rembrandt, van

Dyck, Rubens, the Impressionists and Post-Impressionists, and many other artists from the Continent and Great Britain. The collection of Western European sculpture includes works by Michelangelo, Canova, Falconet, Houdon, and Rodin. The Oriental collection, representing the Near and Far East, is best seen in the exhibits from Byzantium, Iran, India, China, and Japan. Works of Scythian, Greek, and Roman antiquity are particularly noteworthy, as well as objects unearthed from the burial mounds at Altai. The museum has an extensive collection of works from the cultures of Central Asia, the Caucasus, and Russia. In addition to some 600,000 drawings and prints, the museum possesses one of the world's largest collections of applied art. This includes tapestries, furniture, porcelain, jewelry, enamel, ivory, lace, arms, and armor. The numismatic collection, another famed asset of the Hermitage, consists of more than one million coins.

Research is another vital function of the museum, and to this end archaeological expeditions are organized each year, sponsored by the museum independently or jointly with other scientific institutions. Among the most notable expeditions are those to Karmir-Blur near Yerevan, those to Tadzhik, Pskov, Altai, and others to the Crimea, where ancient Greek towns have been uncovered. The Central Library of the Hermitage contains about 500,000 books, and each department of the museum has a subsidiary library of specialized literature. Foreign and domestic exchange policies facilitate the dissemination of information among researchers and students in the field of art. Another important museum function is that of conservation, for which there is a separate department. In addition to the preservation of the museum's exhibits, this department is also responsible for restoration and analysis of all collected material.

GENERAL INFORMATION FOR VISITORS

Most visitors to Leningrad will wish to spend some time at the Hermitage. Group tours will find an excursion to the museum is part of their planned itinerary. In most cases, the tour guide will have prearranged the visit, and a museum staff member will accompany the group through the exhibits to provide information. Individual tourists will make their own arrangements, and in this case the Service Bureau of the hotel can arrange for a taxi or give directions for public transportation as well as reserve a guided tour of the collections.

It is quite pleasant to visit the Hermitage unaccompanied by official personnel. But not the first time—lines to get in are long and it's so enormous you can't find your way around. Go first with a guide—then go back on your own. A short walk westbound on Nevsky Prospect from the center of the city will take the visitor to Herzen Street. From there, turn right and proceed to Palace Square. There is no mistaking the location.

From Herzen Street, pass under the Triumphal Arch into the breathtakingly beautiful square surrounded by pastel-colored buildings decorated with white trim. In the center of Palace Square is a huge column monument to Alexander I commemorating the Russian defeat of Napoleon in the War of 1812. The entrance to the Winter Palace is on the Neva embankment. Proceed left around the column, straight along the walk between the Admiralty Building and the Winter Palace, turn right along the river promenade, and enter directly opposite the embankment.

Upon entering the Winter Palace, you will be instructed to take all coats, handbags, briefcases, and other parcels downstairs to the checkrooms. Cameras are permitted, but it is advisable to ask a guard before using flash equipment. On the same level as the checkrooms are rest rooms, smoking areas, and cafeterias which serve lunches and small snacks. Upon returning upstairs and reentering the lobby, you will be asked to purchase admission tickets for a very nominal sum. In the lobby area and the mezzanine just above it are counters where books, postcards, and souvenirs may be purchased. From this point on, you may proceed through the collections at your own pace. Should you lose track of time, a bell will sound several times in succession before the museum is to be closed. Attendants are on hand in every room, more to keep order than to provide information, since most of them speak only Russian. Any specific information regarding photographing, sketching, note taking, etc., should be gained beforehand from personnel in the main offices.

HIGHLIGHTS OF THE HERMITAGE COLLECTIONS

The Main Staircase is one of the most imposing and impressive features of the Winter Palace. The style of the eighteenth century has been maintained in the lavishly appointed marble banisters, huge mirrors, and gilded moldings. Originally this was the Ambassadors' Staircase and was used for official functions. The polished granite columns at the top were added in the nineteenth century.

The State Rooms (189–198)

The Small Throne Room (194), also known as the Peter Room, was created in memory of Peter I in 1833 according to the design of Montferrand. After the 1837 fire the room was reconstructed by Stasov. The main feature is a silver-gilt throne chair made in 1731 by Clausen, a silversmith from London. The throne chair was occupied by Russian rulers during official receptions at the Winter Palace. Next to the Small Throne Room is *Emblem Hall* (195), the name derived from plaques attached to the many chandeliers. Each plaque bears the coat of arms of a different province of Imperial Russia.

The Gallery of 1812 (197), designed by the architect Carlo Rossi in 1826, commemorates the Russian victory over Napoleon; 332 portraits, one of each general involved in the campaign, adorn the walls. The portraits were executed between 1819 and 1829 by two Russian painters, Polyakov and Golike, and an Englishman, George Dawe. The majority were painted from life. You will note a few empty frames upholstered with green silk. These indicate that the general was deceased and there existed no likeness of him from which to paint a portrait. There are also four portraits by Dawe of soldiers who participated in the Napoleonic campaign.

The Large Throne Room (Georgievsky Room) (198) is as immense in size (800 square meters; 2,625 square feet) as it is overpowering in appearance. The awesome spectacle is created by the two single materials used in its decor: white Carrara marble and gilded bronze. The ceiling is adorned with ornamental castings of gilded bronze. The floor repeats the pattern of the ceiling and is comprised of sixteen types of rare wood. The throne was moved to the Peter Room, and in its place is a map of the Soviet Union, made by stonecarvers in 1937. The map is made of 45,000 pieces of stone, some of which are precious and semiprecious gems, including jasper, rhodonite, lapis lazuli, topaz, rubies, alexandrite, and emeralds. The map has been on display at the Hermitage since 1948. Prior to that it was exhibited at the worlds fairs in Paris (1937) and New York (1939).

The Malachite Room (189) was designed in 1839 by Bryullov, assisted by two of his pupils, Gornostayev and Lvov. Two tons of malachite, a beautiful but rare multitoned green marble quarried primarily in Russia, were used for the room's decoration. The technique used by the stonecarvers in creating the columns, pilasters, mantelpieces, tabletops, lamps, and accessories is called "Russian mosaic." The Provisional Government of July 1917 held official meetings in the Malachite Room and used it also as a place of refuge under protection of the cadets in October of the same year. They were finally arrested during the storming of the Winter Palace in the *Small Dining Room* (188) next door.

State rooms facing the Neva embankment (190–192) form a suite terminating in the Malachite Room. The *Concert Room* (190) now houses the exhibit of Russian silver. The *Large Hall*, formerly the *Ball Room* (191), and the *Antechamber* (192) are used for temporary and loan exhibitions.

DEPARTMENTAL EXHIBITS

HISTORY OF PRIMITIVE CULTURE (ground floor, 11–33) This department was organized after the Revolution. Its purpose has been to display artifacts gathered by Russian archaeologists which characterize the art and culture of primitive communal systems in territories now part of the Soviet Union. The items date from the Old Stone Age, about 500,000–300,000 B.C., to the twelfth century A.D. The most ancient pieces in the collection are stone implements belonging to the Stone Age (11). These were found in Armenia, the site of Satani-Dar, during an expedition in 1947–49. The Neolithic period (12) is noted for the visible progression of primitive man toward art. Several stones bearing designs found on the Onega Lake embankment and sculptured animal figures discovered near Sverdlovsk dating from the second millennium B.C. are displayed here. The Bronze Age exhibit (14) contains objects dating from the end of the third to the beginning of the second millennium B.C. Particularly interesting are the artifacts excavated from the Maikop burial mound in the north Caucasus. Both stone and bronze implements were found together. These provide important evidence concerning the transition from one prehistoric period to the next as well as the differentiation among primitive societies. Bronze axes, gold ornaments, and pieces from the Koban burial mounds dating from the first millennium B.C. are among the most valuable in the exhibit.

Scythian Collection (15–21) This particular group of artifacts is known throughout the world. The items date from the seventh to the third centuries B.C. during which time several tribes known as the Scythians inhabited the steppes north of the Black Sea coast and the Caucasus Mountains. An important excavation from the Kuban burial mounds revealed cultural ties between the Oriental peoples and the Scythians. Different aspects of Scythian art are to be found in the artifacts excavated from the Solokha and Chertomlyk burial mounds of the Ukraine. These items, dating from the fifth to fourth centuries B.C., show a close cultural relationship between the Scythians and the Greeks.

Pazyryk Burial Mounds (25, 26) Excavations in the Altai Mountains have yielded many objects of applied art dating from the fifth and fourth centuries B.C. Because of permafrost formations inside the burial mounds, many items of wood and textile, which would otherwise have disintegrated, have been preserved. A remarkably large find of such objects in 1949 led to the exhibits housed in these two rooms, particularly a log coffin in which the mummified body of a chieftain was found. Among the textile artifacts found were a felt carpet and a cut woolen rug, among the earliest in recorded history. Also on display are a wooden funeral chariot, harnesses, saddle blankets, and horse masks. The burial mounds of the Altai steppes, excavated during the time of Peter I, date from the fourth to second centuries B.C. Items of Siberian origin, such as bracelets, buckles, and gold neckrings, are on display. These pieces are part of the original collection of the museum. The Siberian artifacts, found between the Ob and Irtysk rivers, coincide with the dates of objects found in the Pazyryk mounds and those of the Scythian mounds in the Ukraine. Items of the Sarmatian and other tribes of the steppes of southern Russia are to be found in room 33. These date from the third century B.C. to the twelfth century A.D.

HISTORY OF CULTURE AND ART OF EASTERN PEOPLES (ground floor, 34–96; second floor, 351–397) This department was created in 1920 from a collection of seven thousand items which were scattered among various collections. At present, the exhibit is concentrated in two specific divisions, one devoted to Eastern Soviet peoples, and the other to foreign peoples of the East. The collection now totals close to 150,000 pieces. Among the outstanding exhibits are Coptic and Chinese textiles, Sassanian silver, Daghestan bronzes and reliefs, Byzantine art, and artifacts from the Graeco-Bactrian and Uratu civilizations.

Soviet Eastern Art (ground floor, 34–40, 46–54) This section contains materials illustrating the cultural and artistic history of Soviet Central Asia from the fourth millennium B.C. to the nineteenth century A.D. This lengthy period was fraught with many transitions in power and, hence, cultural changes which influenced the artistic traditions. You will notice the prolific admixture of local and foreign influences among the items in the collection. Central Asia was part of Archaemenian Persia from the sixth to the fourth century B.C. Then it fell under the aegis of Alexander the Great from the fourth century B.C. until the rise of the Graeco-Bactrian rulers in the third century B.C. From then until the first century B.C. the territories of Central Asia were generally consolidated in the Kushan Empire until its collapse in the fourth century A.D. At this time warring nomadic tribes invaded Central Asia and for two centuries the territory was dominated by the Turks. In the eighth century the Arabs became the rulers and were succeeded in the thirteenth century by the Mongols of the Golden Horde. In the latter half of the fourteenth century Tamerlane conquered the Mongols and became the ruler of Central Asia. Local consolidation occurred during the eighteenth and nineteenth centuries, at which time the Bokhara, Kokand, and Chiva khanates were formed.

The rich interlacing of cultural influences is one of the outstanding features of the collection. The visitor will be able to observe them in the architectural fragments, wall paintings, silver and bronzeware, tiles, coins, jewelry, weapons, and textiles. Not only are these items beautiful and interesting to see, but they also serve as vital sources of data for scientists and historians. Room 35 contains the Graeco-Bactrian coins of the third and second centuries B.C.; third- and fourth-century A.D. clay sculptures from Khorezm (Uzbek); and several paintings from wall fragments, a wood frieze, and another of clay depicting fantastic creatures from Pyandjikent (Tajik) of the seventh and eighth centuries A.D. There is a magnificent stone frieze from a building in Aïrtam (Tajik) from the first century A.D. in room 34. In room 36 are several Pyandjikent murals of the seventh and eighth centuries A.D. and other murals from the "Red Hall" of the Bokhara rulers' palace also of the same era. Room 48 contains a huge bronze cauldron commissioned by Tamerlane in 1399, and brought from a mosque in Turkestan (Kazakh).

The Caucasian collection is housed in rooms 55–66. The objects on display date from the Bronze Age to the eighteenth century A.D., and show evidence of the close cultural ties between the peoples of the Caucasus and those of Iran and the Roman Empire. The exhibit consists primarily of bronzework, pottery, textiles, and jewelry. A noted collection of archaeological materials is located in room 56. These were found during the Karmir-Blur excavations near Yerevan and date from the seventh and sixth centuries B.C. during the existence of the ancient Uuratu State. Another important collection is that of thirteenth- to fourteenth-century stone reliefs from the Daghestan village of Kubachi. Included in the exhibit are Daghestan bronze cauldrons of the twelfth and thirteenth centuries.

Non-Soviet Eastern Art (ground floor, 41–45, 55–96; second floor, 351–396) The ground-floor rooms of this collection house the Egyptian, Palmyran, Babylonian, and Assyrian exhibits. The Babylonian and Assyrian pieces date from the fourth through first millennia B.C.; the Palmyran items are from the second and third centuries A.D. Exhibits of these three cultures are on display in rooms 92–96. The remainder of the ground-floor rooms in this section (41–45, 55–91) contain Egyptian antiquities representing the primitive communal system of the Old Kingdom (3000–2400 B.C.), the Middle Kingdom (2100–1788 B.C.), the New Kingdom (1580–1050 B.C.), and the Late Period (1050–332 B.C.), the period of conquest by Alexander the Great, the Hellenistic, Roman, and Coptic periods. The larger portion of the collection is comprised of objects used for funeral purposes. There are also a few pieces of Egyptian monumental sculpture. A notable section of the exhibit is devoted to papyri, with the world-famous papyrus "Tale of a Ship-wrecked Man" (twentieth century B.C.), among them. Coptic textiles (fourth and fifth centuries A.D.) are abundantly represented. Two granite sarcophagi of Queen Nakht-Bastot-ru and her son, General Ahmose, are among the sixth-century B.C. pieces. Several Faiyum portraits and a bronze statue of Takhara, first ruler of the Ethiopian dynasty in Egypt, are among the seventh-century B.C. items.

Byzantine Collection (381, 381–A, 382) An unparalleled exhibit which represents all the categories of Byzantine art from the fourth to the fifteenth centuries. The collection of Byzantine silver, for example, is the richest in the world. Included is a group of plates found in the Ukraine and the Ural district. The ivories are especially lovely. Among them are several diptychs, one of which dates back to about 500 A.D., and depicts scenes from a circus. Another outstanding exhibit is the collection of icons of the eleventh and twelfth centuries. These specimens are extremely rare, because they belong to the period immediately following the iconoclast movement.

Near East: Syria, Iran, Iraq, Turkey, Egypt (383–397) Although the collection is somewhat irregularly distributed among these cultures, the exhibit as a whole provides a valuable representation of the prominent characteristics of Near Eastern art. Without a doubt, the most important group of items is the silver from the Sassanian dynasty of Iran, dating from the third to seventh centuries A.D. (383). Many Sassanian silver objects (mainly jugs and feasting vessels) were found in northern Russia along the ancient trade routes. Among the Sassanian treasures is a collection of gems which have been engraved with portraits of the nobility. Twelfth- to eighteenth-century Iranian exhibits are largely works executed in bronze or ceramic (385–387 and 391–394). Some of the twelfth- and thirteenth-century tiles contain inscriptions of Cufic writing which is highly ornamental in style. There is also a variety of pottery from Kashan, Kerman, Jezd, and Isfahan of the sixteenth and seventeenth centuries (391–392). From Persia, of the sixteenth to eighteenth centuries, are some intriguing textiles, among them numerous carpets and a velvet cloth with silk embroidery representing Mejnun in the desert (391). Syria and Iraq of the thirteenth and fourteenth centuries (388) are represented by various fascinating items of bronze and glass. Egyptian pieces from the seventh to sixteenth centuries (389–390) include rock crystal carvings, ceramics, carved wood, and woven fabrics. Particularly impressive are several glass hanging lamps from Egyptian mosques of the fourteenth and fifteenth centuries. Turkish items of the fifteenth to nineteenth centuries (395–397) consist of ceramics, jewelry, weapons, armor, and textiles.

Chinese Collection (351–364) This exhibit contains works dating from the second millenium B.C. to the mid-twentieth century. Among the wealth of archaeological materials is a group of murals and funeral sculptures excavated from the cave monastery familiarly known as "The Cave of the Thousand Buddhas," dating from the sixth to ninth centuries A.D. There are numerous icons, paintings, and drawings worked on paper, canvas, and silk dating from the tenth to the thirteenth centuries A.D. These were discovered by the Russian scientist Kozlov during the excavation of the town of I-Ching (Khara-Khoto). Other pieces represented in the Chinese collection are stone carvings, embroideries, porcelains, enamels, and lacquers. Two well-known modern Chinese painters, Hsü Pei-hung and Ch'i Pai-shih, are generously represented among several late-nineteenth- and early-twentieth-century artists whose works in applied art together with prints and drawings round out the exhibit.

The Mongolian Collection, representing the thirteenth, fifteenth, and sixteenth centuries (365–366), contains a marvelous sampling of icons, palace and temple ornaments, stone and bronze sculpture, and dress armor. Of especially great value are the silk textiles and embroideries excavated from the burial mounds of the Huns, dating back to the first century A.D. (367). Completing the exhibit of Far Eastern art is an exhibit from Japan (375–376). Represented are prints and paintings from the seventeenth to the twentieth century. Considered among the most valuable are prints by such noted eighteenth- and nineteenth-century artists as Hokusai, Harunkobu, Utamara, and Hiroshige.

The Indian Collection (368–371) represents seventeenth- to twentieth-century contemporary art. Both fine and applied art are on display. Of major interest is the steelwork of the seventeenth and eighteenth centuries. Illustrated in the items on display is a rather complete range of ornamental technique, such as damascene, gold and silver inlay, chiselwork, lace carving, and piercing. These processes were used primarily in the making of decorative armor, which is abundantly displayed. The textile collection is considered outstanding for the remarkable Kashmir textiles, Delhi and Madura embroideries and carpets. One will also find an excellent exhibit of seventeenth- and eighteenth-century miniatures representative of the Rajput and Moghul schools. In addition, numerous modern and contemporary paintings give evidence to a recent broadening of subject matter as well as the introduction of oils and pastels heretofore not used by Indian artists.

HISTORY OF ART AND CULTURE OF THE ANTIQUE WORLD (ground floor, 100–102; 106–121; 127–131) The ground floor of the New Hermitage contains twenty-four rooms devoted to Greek and Roman antiquities, dating from the ninth century B.C. to the fourth century A.D. The collection is divided into separate Greek and Roman sections: Greece (eighth to second centuries B.C.) and Greek settlements of the Black Sea coast (sixth century B.C. to third century A.D.), rooms 100, 109–121; Ancient Italy (tenth to second centuries B.C.) and Rome (first century B.C. to fourth century A.D.), rooms 101, 102, 106–108, 127–131. The first item acquired in the collection was the Tauris Venus statue. It was purchased by Peter I and housed in the Tauris (Tavrichesky) Palace until the mid-nineteenth century. The bulk of the collection, however, was formed during the eighteenth and nineteenth centuries. Russian archaeological excavations since the early nineteenth century have yielded many items originating from Greek settlements on the northern coast of the Black Sea.

Greek Antiquities. The earliest specimens of Greek art, representing the archaic and early classical periods, are on exhibit in room 111. Eighth-century B.C. clay pottery and figures of deities and sixth-century B.C. Corinthian vases are among the oldest objects on display. Fifth-century B.C. bronze ornaments and figurines are also located here. Antique marble pieces, some of which are Graeco-Roman, are on display in room 112. The oldest pieces in this exhibit are two fifth-century B.C. tombstone reliefs. In the same room are several important fifth-century B.C. sculptures. Among them is a basalt head, a copy from a statue of Doryphorus, executed by the Greek sculptor Polyclitus. Another of the same era is of Athena by an unknown sculptor of the Phidian school. Room 114 houses other works of Graeco-Roman sculpture, such as the torso of Aphrodite, Hercules wrestling the lion, a bust of Socrates, and the resting satyr. These date from the fourth century B.C. Greek decorative sculpture, including the Tauris Venus and the Hermitage Venus (Aphrodite), is in rooms 108 and 109. Third-century B.C. statuettes of terra-cotta are on display in room 121.

A separate group of artifacts from the Greek settlements of the Black Sea coast is in rooms 100, 115, 116, 117, 120, and 121. Represented here is a unique civilization combining Greek culture with the peoples of the Crimea, Taman Peninsula, and the northwestern coast of the Black Sea. One of the unusual features of the exhibit is the remarkable degree of preservation of the items which date as far back as the fifth century B.C. Pieces from the ancient Bosporan Kingdom in the Crimea are displayed in rooms 115, 116, 117, and 121, items from Nymphaeum in room 120, and those from Olbia and Chersonese in room 100. The outstanding feature of the department, a collection of Greek jewelry from the Crimea and Taman Peninsula, is on exhibit in the Gold Room. Greek vases are on display throughout the rooms assigned to the entire collection but are concentrated in rooms 111 and 118. Ancient Greek gems, including the Gonzaga Cameo, are displayed in room 121. Hellenistic pieces are in room 127.

Ancient Italian and Roman Antiquities. Etruscan objects of the seventh to fifth centuries B.C. highlight the collections of Ancient Italy (130, 131). Clay and bronze pieces are the most numerous, followed by assorted objects of other materials used for funeral purposes. Also in room 130 are Italian vases from other territories of the period. Perhaps the most famous exhibit of the museum is the collection of over one hundred Roman busts covering the period from the first century B.C. to the fourth century A.D. (room 127). Rooms 106 and 107 contain carved marble heads from the second-century Roman Forum. In room 107 are some works of monumental sculpture, including a large statue of Jupiter of the first century A.D. There are also some marble reliefs which form the sides of second- and third-century sarcophagi. Room 129 houses an extremely interesting collection of Roman ceramics, mosaics, bronzes, and glass objects.

HISTORY OF RUSSIAN CULTURE (first floor, 143–198) This department, an outgrowth of the Revolution, was officially created in 1941. Occupying over fifty rooms in the Winter Palace, it is devoted to the history of Russian culture, rather than fine arts per se. The collections are intended to demonstrate the development of Russian culture from the sixth to nineteenth centuries A.D. The items pertaining to the exhibit consist mainly of archaeological material, specimens of applied art, paintings, engravings, and other memorial pieces.

The earliest period represented, the sixth to fifteenth centuries (143–150), contains many objects excavated from the civilizations of the ancient Slavs who occupied territory as far north as Lake Ladoga, and as far south as Kiev. Among the handicrafts and agricultural implements are some noteworthy specimens of fine art. Several icons of the thirteenth to fifteenth centuries are shown in room 149. Room 148 houses a stone tablet called the "Tmutarkan Stone," upon which it is written that the Kerch

Straits were measured in 1068 upon orders of Prince Gleb. A rich exhibit of Russian jewelry dating from the twelfth century is displayed in rooms 147–150.

Rooms 151–152 house materials from the fifteenth through seventeenth centuries. This period is particularly interesting because of the consolidation of the Russian state by the Moscow princes. The objects representing this period are based on the theme of consolidation. Among them are several fifteenth-century icons, manuscripts, printed books, and the wood-carved Holy Gates from the Church of Kulikovo Field.

The eighteenth-century exhibit is divided into two sections: rooms 153–161 contain objects from the first quarter of the century; rooms 162–174 and 190, items representative of the remainder of the century. The obvious division point, 1725, marks the year of Peter I's death. Works of the first quarter century are in keeping with the reforms of Peter I: the accelerated development of science, industry, and handcrafts, and the more subtle changes in manners, morals, and artistic preference. Several pieces in the collection are personal belongings of Peter I. Among the most outstanding objects on display is a bronze bust of Peter I, made in 1723 by C. B. Rastrelli, father of the architect Bartolomeo Rastrelli. Among the emperor's personal effects is a rather sizable desk, suited to his height of approximately 2 meters, 4 centimeters (7 feet). There is also a collection of lathes designed for his personal workshop by Nártov, a noted mechanic of the period. Several engravings contemporaneous with the early development of St. Petersburg enhance this exhibit. Additional material in this section is from a memorial museum founded after the emperor's death by the Academy of Sciences. Certain rare items have also been acquired from various scientific institutions, thus rounding out a representation of early-eighteenth-century Russian scientific culture.

The latter three-quarters of the century consists generally of objects of fine and applied art as well as scientific exhibits. Here are some of the finest landscape, portrait, and architectural paintings in oil and watercolor, and books and manuscripts pertaining to the social history of the period. Among the most noted sections is the one devoted to glass mosaics from the Lomonsov workshop, including a mosaic portrait of Peter I made by Mikhail Lomonsov himself (163). Along with the mosaic revival came the discovery of porcelain making in Russia, independent of Oriental or European methods, by Vinogradov. Examples of his work, in particular a cup (1749) and snuffbox (1752) are on display in room 167. Many fine specimens of applied art, such as the Tula steelwork and samovars, the collection of glass and enamel pieces, stoneware, ivories, textiles, and embroideries are quite rewarding to the visitor. An outstanding piece of craftsmanship is the Kulibin watch. The famous watch, made in the shape of an egg, in 1765–69, consists of about four hundred separate details, and contains not only a musical mechanism, but a menagerie of moving silver figures. Room 190 is reserved for the collection of Russian silver. The major work of the exhibit is the tomb of Alexander Nevsky. The tomb was made in 1750–53 in St. Petersburg as a memorial to the military commander. The side of the sarcophagus facing visitors depicts three important battle scenes in Nevsky's life: the defeat of the Swedes on the Neva River banks (1240), the liberation of Pskov (1240), and the defeat of the Teutonic Knights at Chudskoye Lake (1242). These scenes are worked in silver in bas-relief embossing. The background of the sarcophagus consists of a decorative pyramid flanked by two candlesticks and two groups of arms and armor.

Nineteenth-century Russian objects are located in several areas of the museum: rooms 128, 172–198, 237–239, 245. There are also several entire rooms which pertain to the nineteenth century, as previously mentioned. Finally, current exchanges with other museums, excavations, and purchases cause the location of nineteenth-century objects to be rearranged from time to time, as the extension of this department is a major ongoing museum project. Pieces from the first quarter of the century consist largely of applied art similar to works of the latter portion of the previous century. Dramatic historical events, such as the War of 1812 and the Decembrist uprising of 1825, have contributed numerous documents, prints, drawings, and paintings. There is also a great deal of material about the literature of the period, particularly material relating to Pushkin. Outstanding artistic works of the Russian School are represented by numerous paintings, engravings, and sculptures. Among them the works of Bryullov, Kirpensky, Venetsianov, and Tropinin are prominent. The State Rooms of the Winter Palace pertaining to the War of 1812 are part of this exhibit. The collection of eighteenth- and nineteenth-century tables, lamps, and vases is dispersed throughout the various rooms of the museum. Rooms 237–239 and 245 house concentrated displays of nineteenth-century occasional furniture and accessories. The Georgievsky Room (Large Throne Room) and the Malachite Room are also part of the Russian Cultural Department.

HISTORY OF WESTERN EUROPEAN ART (first floor, 200–208; second floor, 314–380) The collections of this department are by far the most famous of the entire museum. The sublimity of the works displayed is acknowledged by art enthusiasts throughout the world. As it is an exceedingly large and complex department, the collections have been arranged for maximum convenience to the visitor. The following summary is intended merely to clarify the organization of the exhibits, as only a firsthand visit can do justice to the items described.

Medieval European Applied Art (259) This exhibit is fully representative of the period dating from the eleventh through fifteenth centuries. Works of copper, bronze, silver, ivory, enamel, ceramic, textile, as well as medieval arms and armor, make up the display. From the twelfth century are carvings of period life and legends. A figure of the seated Virgin is an outstanding thirteenth-century specimen. French polyptychs of the fourteenth century are especially lovely. There are a number of interesting personal objects, among which is a casket carved with motifs from the legend of Tristan and Isolde. Twelfth-century metalwork should be seen, particularly a Limoges casket worked in *champlevé* depicting scenes from the life of St. Valeria. The thirteenth-century French processional cross of an unknown silversmith and the silver church relic made in 1474 by Hans Rissenberg are just two of the many extraordinary silver objects. Fourteenth-century vessels of Hispano-Moresque origin highlight the ceramics display, along with Valencia luster-paint vases of the fifteenth and sixteenth centuries.

Italian School (207–238) Paintings, engravings, sculpture, and applied art of the thirteenth to eighteenth centuries are displayed in this section. The best-known paintings of the collection, if not of the museum itself, are the works of Leonardo da Vinci, Raphael, Giorgione, Titian, and Tintoretto. The exhibit in its entirety is outstanding because of the almost complete representation of Italian art from the thirteenth through eighteenth centuries. Room 207 contains the earliest pieces, frequently medieval-style painted panels. Among the late-thirteenth- and fourteenth-century masters represented are Tedici, Arteno, Gerini, and da Firenze; of exceptional note is the Simone Martini "Madonna." Rooms 209–221 contain works of fifteenth- and sixteenth-century painters such as Fra Filippo Lippi, Filippino Lippi, Fra Angelico, Perugino, Francia, Costa, del Sellajo, Lotto, da Conegliano, and Il Vecchio. Leonardo's two famous works "Madonna Litta" and "Madonna Benois" are displayed in room 214. Leonardo's pupils, such as Luini, da Sesto, and Melzi, are represented in room 215, along with the "Madonna and Child with the Saints" by Andrea del Sarto. Two Raphael paintings owned by the museum, "Madonna Contestabile" and "The Holy Family," are located in room 229 along with works by some of his pupils. The single work by Michelangelo owned by the Hermitage, "The Crouching Boy" in carved marble, is in room 230.

The Venetian School is in rooms 217–222; 231–238. Beginning with the fifteenth-century Bellini School, followed by the Vivarini group, the works continue through the paintings of Veronese, Tintoretto, Bassano, Tiepolo, Canaletto, Guardi, Giorgione, and Titian. Italian Mannerism, represented by painters such as Rosso, Pontormo, Parmigianino, and Tibaldi, is included in this section, along with the School of Bologna, with works by Carracci, Guercino, Domenichino, Reni, and Albani. Caravaggio and his pupils—Manfredi, Saraceni, Borgiani, Novelli, Poeti, Rosa, and Fetti—are here also. The late Venetian School of the seventeenth and eighteenth centuries, with works by Canaletto, Guardi, and Tiepolo, is in rooms 236 and 238. Italian sculpture, although displayed with the paintings, is concentrated in room 241, and includes pieces by Rosselino, da Settignano, the della Robbias, Collini, da Bologna, Bernini, and Canova. Applied art, such as textiles, furniture, glasswork, enamels, and earthenware, will be found distributed throughout the Italian collection. One should give special consideration to the fifteenth- through eighteenth-century majolicas from various Italian locales, including Tuscany, Siena, Gubbio, Deruta, Faenza, Urbino, and Castel Durante. Equally impressive is the seventeenth- and eighteenth-century glazed earthenware from Savona, Genoa, and Castelli.

Spanish School (239, 240) Consisting primarily of seventeenth-century paintings, the small but representative Spanish collection also includes works of the sixteenth, nineteenth, and twentieth centuries. Among the most prominent items are paintings by El Greco, Ribera, Zubarán, Velázquez, and Murillo. Although none of Goya's paintings is at the Hermitage, the Spanish collection displays numerous original prints representative of Goya's graphics. The collection includes canvases by many less-known Spaniards of the period, such as Morales, de la Cruz, Ribalta, Carducho, Mazo, Pareja, Puga, and Pereda. In addition to paintings, one will also find noteworthy specimens of seventeenth- and eighteenth-century Spanish furniture and glassware.

Netherlands School (258, 260–262) Representing the fifteenth and sixteenth centuries are paintings and objects of applied art. Early paintings of note are two altar panels by Maître de Flemalle, "Madonna and Child" and "The Trinity." Also on display are works by Rogier van der Weyden, Hugo van der Goes, and Lucas van Leyden. Netherlands portraiture, influential in the Low Countries in later centuries, is best represented by Pourbus the Elder, van Cleve, and Jacobsz. Genre paintings include works by Reymerswaele, Aersten, Beuckelaer, and Pieter Brueghel the Younger. Numerous landscapes include works by Van Coninxloo, Savery, and Hondecoeter. A separate exhibit of landscapes by Jan Brueghel the Elder is displayed in room 238.

Flemish School (245–248) Among the outstanding possessions of the Hermitage is the collection of forty-two paintings by Peter Paul Rubens, on display in room 247. Included are such famous works as "Perseus and Andromeda," "Descent from the Cross," "Union of Earth and Water," "Bacchus," "Christ in the House of Simon the Pharisee," and several smaller paintings, including "Venus and Adonis," "Statue of Ceres," "Expulsion of Hagar," and "Pastoral Scene." Among Rubens's landscapes are "The Carters" and "Rainbow Landscape." In addition to the master's paintings, the Hermitage owns several sketch designs rendered in oil, many of which were preliminary concepts of paintings for which he was commissioned by European royalty.

Van Dyck is represented by twenty-six paintings which are on display in room 246. Room 245 contains fourteen canvases by Frans Snyders, representing both his larger and smaller works. Jacob Jordaens's painting "The Bean King" is among the major attractions of the collection. Several canvases by Bronwer and his outstanding pupil David Teniers the Younger are also on display. Numerous prints and drawings demonstrating other elements of Flemish art round out this section.

Dutch School (249–257) The Rembrandt collection of twenty-six paintings is the outstanding feature of this section. The majority of the 730 canvases of the Dutch School are representative of the seventeenth century. Included are portraits, landscapes, works depicting morals and manners of the period, animals, still lifes, and genre pieces. Portraiture is best represented by the works of Mierevelt, Ravesteyn, Eliasz, Cuyp, de Keyser, de Bray, Van der Vliet, and Frans Hals. Among the distinguished genre painters are Dirck Hals, Adrian van Ostade, Isaak van Ostade, Jan Steen, Pieter de Hooch, Mieris, Metsu, and Terborch. Animal paintings by Cuyp and Potter deserve special mention, as do landscapes by Goyen, Isaak van Ostade, van Ruisdael, and van der Neer. Of equal importance are the seascapes by Willaerts, Cuyp, Porcellis, Vlieger, and van de Velge.

The Rembrandts are in room 254. In addition to the twenty-six paintings, almost all of his etchings are represented, most of them first imprints. The collection includes representative works from all the phases of Rembrandt's career. Works by Rembrandt's teacher, Pieter Lastman, and his pupils, Aert de Gelder, Ferdinand Bol, and Salomon Coninck, his follower, are displayed in rooms 249–253.

German School (263–268, 338–340) This collection represents German fine and applied art from the fifteenth through early twentieth centuries. It includes paintings, sculpture, prints, engravings, silver from Augsburg and Nuremburg, and porcelain from Meissen and Berlin. The earliest period of the German School is represented by the engravings of Dürer along with several prints and paintings of the period by other artists. Among the sixteenth-century works is a collection of canvases by Lucas Cranach the Elder, on display in room 264. Several woodcuts by Hans Holbein the Younger and a painting by his brother Ambrosius are excellent examples of German Renaissance portraiture. Late-sixteenth- and seventeenth-century paintings include canvases by Elsheimer, Amberger, Bruyn the Elder, Neufchatel, Paudiss, von Achen, Schönfeldt, Eismann, and Heiss. A sizable portion of the German School is devoted to eighteenth- and early-nineteenth-century works by such artists as Denner, Seybold, Pesne, Graff, Tischbein, Hackert, and Mechau. German classicism is best represented by Angelika Kaufmann and Anton Raphael Mengs. The Romantic School, in particular the canvases of Caspar David Friedrich, is housed in room 338. Other nineteenth-century trends, such as the Düsseldorf and Nazarean schools, are represented by works of Rethel, Overbeck, Hess, and Lessing. Among the nineteenth-century works are prints by Adolph Menzel, Feuerbach, Lenbach, Leibl, and Liebermann, displayed in room 339. Room 340 contains works by artists of the early twentieth century, particularly those whose subject matter depicts proletariat life. Included are paintings by Kollwitz, Ehmsen, Nagel, and Grundig.

British School (298–302) The collection encompasses seventeenth- to nineteenth-century fine and applied art, but concentrates particularly on the portraiture, landscape, and satirical paintings and prints of the eighteenth century. Among the rare seventeenth-century paintings are several outstanding portraits by Robert Walker, Godfrey Kneller, and Peter Lely. Prints, but unfortunately no paintings, by William Hogarth are displayed in room 299. In the same room are four canvases by Joshua Reynolds painted during the 1780s. One of these, "Infant Hercules Strangling the Serpents," was commissioned by Catherine II. Two others, "Continence of Scipio Africanus" and "Venus and Cupid," were sent by the artist to Russia. Other famous portrait painters of the period, Gainsborough, Opie, Raeburn, Hoppner, and Russell, are in room 300. Another highlight of the British collection in the field of applied art is a 1774 dinner service by Wedgwood. It consists of 952 pieces depicting 1,244 scenes of England. The service was ordered by Catherine II for Chesman Palace, located in a district which had been nicknamed the "frog marsh." The Wedgwood service contains a tiny green frog painted on each piece and has thus come to be called the "Green Frog Service." The last portion of the eighteenth-century collection is devoted to canvases which depict themes from the industrial revolution. Among the nineteenth-century works are paintings by Bonington, Wilkie, Lawrence, and Dawe, and prints by Smith, Green, and Bartolozzi. An excellent set of caricatures rounds out the collection.

French School (273–297, 314–332, 343–350) This section covers French fine and applied art from the fifteenth through twentieth centuries and occupies over forty rooms. The collection is sufficiently complete to detail the principal phases, trends, and styles of French art over five centuries. Beginning with late medieval and early Renaissance specimens, the exhibit begins in rooms 273 and 274 with a display of rare fifteenth-century paintings, clay vessels from Saint Porchaire, Palissy's glazed earthenware and figurines, several exceptional Limoges enamels, and crayon portraits by Clouet, Dumoustier, and Lagnot.

The seventeenth-century collection contains works by several notable painters, but the outstanding representation is the work of Nicolas Poussin. On display in room 279 are ten canvases painted over several periods of his career. The various subjects of the paintings include landscape, literature, religion, and mythology. Among the seventeenth-century landscapes are the classical concepts of Claude, among which are his famous cycle "Four Times of the Day" (280). The Academic School is displayed in rooms 278, 281, and 283. Included are the works of Bourdon, Lesueur, de la Hyre, Mignard; the society portraits of Rigaud, Largillière, and Vivien; and several battle scenes of van der Meulen and Courtois.

Eight canvases of Antoine Watteau highlight the early-eighteenth-century collection, displayed in room 284. The same room also contains the works of Watteau's competitors, such as Lafosse, de Troy, and Restout, as well as canvases by his followers, such as Lanret and Pater. Room 285 contains paintings of the mid-eighteenth century. The special feature of this period is the decorative emphasis of such painters as Coypel, Lemoyne, Nattier, and Tocqué. The collection also contains a large exhibit of the works of François Boucher, whose repertoire of subject matter was prolific, ranging from the pastoral and religious to the more decorative. Room 286 contains the rich collection of eighteenth-century sculpture, particularly the works of Etienne-Maurice Falconet and Jean-Antoine Houdon. The singular masterpiece of Houdon is his sculptural portrait of Voltaire. Commissioned by Catherine II, the marble statue depicting the philosopher seated in an armchair was originally housed in Tsarskoye Selo with the empress's private collection. It is now displayed in room 287 along with several of Houdon's other works, which include sculptural portraits of Buffon, Saltykov, Catherine II, and Lise. Works by other sculptors of the period, such as Caffieri and Defernex, are in rooms 285 and 286.

Eighteenth-century French realism is represented by the paintings exhibited in room 287. The works of Jean-Baptiste-Simeon Chardin are particularly important. Other realistic canvases in the same room include works by Perronneau, Oudry, and Desportes. Late-eighteenth-century paintings are also exhibited in rooms 287–289, among them works by Fragonard, Vernet, and Robert. The Vernet collection of twenty-six landscapes is located in room 287; the fifty-four landscapes of Robert are in room 289.

Applied art of the seventeenth and eighteenth centuries in France will be found in rooms 282, 290–297, and 303. Especially noteworthy is the silver collection, which includes rare Louis XIV items as well as several important eighteenth-century pieces. Among these is a centerpiece, the work of Claude Ballin; the "Paris Service" by François-Thomas Germain, commissioned by Empress Elizabeth; and the "Orlov Service," commissioned by Catherine II as a gift for Count Orlov. The silver collection is shown in room 282 along with numerous watches and snuffboxes of the period. Gobelins and other tapestries are generously displayed in rooms 292, 293, 296, and 303. Rooms 289 and 293 contain examples of period furniture. Startlingly lovely are a carved ebony cabinet designed by Antoine Lepôrte; a wardrobe decorated with marquetry by Charles Boull; a secretary by Riesener; and numerous pieces by David Roentgen. French porcelain is divided between the French section, rooms 294 and 296, and the section devoted to Western European porcelain, room 271. Distributed throughout the French exhibit one will find many works of applied art, such as textiles, ceramics, ormulu pieces, and metalwork.

Nineteenth- and early-twentieth-century French painting is very well represented. Early and mid-century works of the Restoration are exhibited in room 331. Included are canvases by David, Gros, Boilly, Delacroix, and Ingres. Rooms 320–322, 325, 328, and 329 contain paintings from the Barbizon School. Included are works by Rousseau, Dupré, Daubigny, Corot, Jacque, Troyon, Millet, and Courbet. Among the Impressionist paint-ings in rooms 317–319 are canvases by Monet, Sisley, Pissarro, Renoir, and Degas as well as sculptures by Rodin. Eleven canvases by Cézanne begin the Post-Impressionist exhibit in room 316. Room 317 contains four of the canvases painted at Arles by Van Gogh. Fifteen paintings from Gauguin's Tahiti period are in room 343. Thirty-five paintings by Matisse are located in rooms 344 and 345. Picasso canvases are displayed in rooms 346 and 347. Room 349 contains several landscapes by Marquet as well as paintings by Vuillard, Derain, Rousseau, and Signac. In addition to the painting and sculpture of French artists, there are numerous prints and drawings repre-senting Callot, Daumier, Gavarni, Lautrec, and Steinlen. These will be found by period in the rooms assigned to the French section.

ART OF WESTERN EUROPE AND NORTH AMERICA (334–342) Here one will find representative paintings from Canada, the United States, Finland, Sweden, Belgium, Poland, Hungary, Czechoslovakia, and Rumania, as well as Italy and Germany continued. The principle behind this grouping is to display the development of trends in modern and contemporary art since the end of the nineteenth century.

NUMISMATIC DEPARTMENT (second floor, 398–400) Displayed in a trio of rooms overlooking the Neva embankment are over a million coins, medals, and orders of Russian and foreign origin. Containing one of the largest numismatic collections in the world, the department is important to the museum's historical function. It will be of value to the numismatist, but should not be missed even by the casual observer. Of special interest is the famous "Konstantin Ruble" coin, valued at $60,000–$100,000.

St. Nicholas' Cathedral

St. Nicholas' Cathedral, or Nikolsky Morskoi Sobor, located at 1/3 Kommunarov Square, was built by Chevakinsky in 1753–62. It is the largest of the functioning churches in Leningrad.

State Russian Museum

The Russian Museum consists of two buildings, the first of which is the former Mikhailovsky Palace built in 1819–25. Designed by architect Carlo Rossi, the building stands in the central court separated from the Square of Arts by a wrought-iron railing. The main façade has an eight-column Corinthian portico above an arcade. The interior, also designed by Rossi, is quite beautiful and houses exhibits of prerevolutionary Russian art.

The second building of the museum was designed by Alexander Benois and Ovsyannikov and built in 1916. Having suffered extensive damage during World War II, it was rebuilt in 1948. Postrevolutionary Soviet art can be seen here.

In all, the Russian Museum has one hundred halls and exhibit rooms containing about 250,000 works of art, including a large and valuable collection of icons. The museum is at 4/2 Inzhenernaya Street and is open daily from 11 A.M. to 6 P.M.; closed on Tuesdays.

Museum of Ethnography of the Peoples of the U.S.S.R.

The building that houses the Museum of Ethnography of the Peoples of the U.S.S.R. was designed by architect B. Svinyin and built in 1895. One of the most interesting museums in Leningrad, it is separated into sections, each representing a republic or nationality of the Soviet Union. Exhibits deal with the history, traditions, and customs of the peoples of the U.S.S.R. in very extensive and thorough fashion.

The museum is located at 4/1 Inzhenernaya Street and is open daily from 11 A.M. to 6 P.M.; closed on Mondays.

Leningrad Branch of the Central Lenin Museum

Like all branches of the Central Lenin Museum, the one in Leningrad offers exhibits dealing with the life and work of Vladimir Lenin. The museum is housed in the former Marble Palace (Mramorny Dvorets), designed by architect Antonio Rinaldi and built in 1768–85. The structure is unusual in that it is the only building in Leningrad whose walls are faced with marble on the inside as well as the outside. Thirty-two kinds of marble were used in the construction of the palace. The armored car from which Lenin called for a socialist revolution, in 1917, stands outside the building.

The Lenin Museum is located at 5 Khalturina Street and is open daily from 11 A.M. to 7 P.M.; Sundays from 10 A.M. to 5 P.M.; closed on Saturdays.

State Museum of the Great October Socialist Revolution

This museum presents exhibits dealing with the events leading up to and through the socialist revolution. It is housed in the former mansion of ballet dancer Matilda Kshesinskaya. It was on the balcony of this mansion that Lenin addressed revolutionary workers upon his return to Russia in April 1917. The museum is located at 4 Kuibysheva Street.

Peter I Museum of Anthropology and Ethnography

This is one of the largest anthropological and ethnographic museums in the Soviet Union. Originally known as the Kunstkammer, it was founded by Peter the Great and was the first museum in Russia.

The Museum of Anthropology and Ethnography is located at 3 University Embankment and is open on Thursdays and Sundays from 11 A.M. to 5 P.M.; on Fridays from 11 A.M. to 4 P.M.

Alexander S. Pushkin Memorial Museum

At 12 Moiki Embankment is the house in which Alexander Pushkin spent the last years of his life, and where he died in 1837. Today it is a museum, where visitors can see many of the poet's personal effects. The house is open daily from 11 A.M. to 5 P.M.; closed on Thursdays.

Literary Museum

Located at 4 Makarova Embankment, the Literary Museum is housed in what was formerly the Customs House and is sometimes referred to as Pushkin's House. In 1905 the museum acquired Pushkin's library and many of his manuscripts. Exhibits include Pushkin's study as well as rooms devoted to Dostoyevsky, Tolstoy, Chekhov, and other Russian literary figures. The museum is open daily 11 A.M. to 6 P.M.; Saturday 11 A.M. to 4 P.M., closed Tuesdays.

Museum of the History of Leningrad

The Museum of the History of Leningrad offers an extensive collection concerning the city from its earliest beginnings to the present. Located at 44 Krasnogo Flota Embankment, the museum is open on Mondays, Thursdays, Saturdays, and Sundays from 11 A.M. to 7 P.M., on Tuesdays and Fridays from 1 P.M. to 9 P.M.; closed on Wednesdays.

Central Naval Museum

Housed in what was formerly the Stock Exchange building is the Central Naval Museum. The structure was designed by architect Thomas de Thomon and built in 1805–10. The building is encircled by forty-four columns which almost conceal the walls. Above the main entrance is a powerful piece of sculpture entitled "Neptune Emerging from the Waves." On the opposite side is a sculpture of a woman wearing a crown, surrounded by two rivers and the god Mercury. The woman represents Neva.

The museum offers interesting and extensive exhibits depicting the history of the Russian and Soviet navy. The collection was moved to the museum from the Admiralty building in 1939.

The Central Naval Museum is located at 4 Pushkinskaya Square and is open daily from 12 noon to 7 P.M.; on Sundays from 11 A.M. to 7 P.M.; closed on Tuesdays.

Cruiser Aurora Museum

The cruiser *Aurora* is one of the most famous treasures of the history of the socialist revolution. On the night of November 1, 1917 (new calendar) the *Aurora* fired a blank shot that signaled the Bolshevik revolutionaries to advance on the Winter Palace. The ship became a training vessel after the Revolution. Seeing action again in World War II, the *Aurora* shelled German troops in the region of Crow Hill and Pulkovo Heights as it stood in the port of the town of Lomonosov.

The cruiser was permanently anchored at the Petrograd Embankment on the Bolshaya Nevka opposite the Nakhimov Naval School on November 17, 1948. In 1956 it became a branch of the Central Naval Museum.

Zoological Museum

Standing to the left of the former Stock Exchange where the University Embankment begins is the Zoological Museum. Once used as a warehouse, the museum has 100,000 exhibits. If time is limited, the Hall of Mammoths (Zal Mamontov) is highly recommended as a first priority.

Finland Railway Station

When Lenin secretly returned to Russia on April 16, 1917, he arrived at the Finland Station in Petrograd. It was here that he addressed revolutionary workers and soldiers proclaiming that the bourgeois revolution of February 1917 was complete and that the next stage, the socialist revolution, must begin with the overthrow of the Provisional Government. Using the slogan "all power to the Soviets," Lenin set forth a program demanding peace (withdrawal of Russia from World War I), seizure of land by the peasants, and factory control by workers' committees. This scene is depicted by a statue of Lenin near the Finland Station. The monument was built in 1926 by sculptor S. Yevseev and architects V. Shchuko and V. Gelfreich.

The site of the station itself is a modern building topped by a 13-meter (43-foot) tower with a spire. The building was erected by architects I. Ashastin, N. Baranov, Ya. Lukin, and engineer I. Rybin in 1960. Behind the station, in a glass pavilion, is the locomotive in which Lenin fled Russia to escape the police of the Provisional Government and it was in the same locomotive that he returned to Petrograd. This historic piece was presented to the Soviet Union by the government of Finland in 1957.

Smolny

The Smolny area consists of an ensemble of structures and monuments and is located on a beautiful bank of the Neva River.

The Swedish fort "Sabina" once stood here. After the founding of St. Petersburg the area was used for the storage of tar for the city's shipbuilding industry. The present name comes from *smolny dvor* (tar yard). Tar storage was moved to another site in 1723 and a summer palace was built here for

Elizabeth, daughter of Peter I. After fire completely destroyed the palace, Elizabeth decided to build a convent for orphans in its place.

In 1748 the architect Bartolomeo Rastrelli designed the Resurrection (Voskresensky) Cathedral in the Baroque style with five domes, the central one of which is 80 meters (300 feet) high. Later, a house for widows, designed in the classical style by Giacomo Quarenghi, was added to the complex. This building, known as the Smolny Institute (first building), later became the building of the Society for the Education of Young Ladies of Noble Birth which was established by Catherine II. After the society was founded, widows were housed in the convent building.

The most important building in the ensemble is the Smolny Institute (second building), designed and built in the classical style by Giacomo Quarenghi in 1805–09 near the convent. This building was the headquarters of the Bolsheviks during the Revolution. In the Assembly Hall of this building Soviet power was proclaimed and the Soviet government was formed with Lenin at its head.

Lenin and his wife, Nadezhda Krupskaya, lived and worked in the Smolny Institute from the end of October 1917 to March 1918. Their room is now a museum.

The other buildings in the Smolny ensemble are the former "Kikin's Chambers," an early-eighteenth-century structure that now serves as a district Young Pioneer Palace, and the Tauride Palace. The Tauride Palace was designed in the classical style by the architect I. Starov and was built in 1789 for Prince Potemkin-Tavrichesky.

The main building is flanked on each side by winglike structures and has a six-column portico. While the exterior is rather plain and free of ornaments, the interior is decorated with stuccowork and wall paintings.

After the monarchy was overthrown, the Tauride Palace became the headquarters of the Petrograd Soviet of Workers' and Soldiers' Deputies. It was here that Lenin delivered his "April Theses" speech in 1917.

Cottage of Peter I

Located at 5 Petrograd Embankment is Peter I's summer cottage. Built in 1703 in three days, the structure had no stone foundation and because it was for summer use, no heating facilities. When the Summer Palace was completed across the river, Peter no longer used the cottage. A stone casing was built around the cottage for protection in 1784.

Leningrad State University

Originally designed by Domenico Trezzini to house Peter the Great's Twelve Colleges, this building was built in 1722–42 and is divided into twelve identical, but independent, sections. Around 1830 it was taken over by St. Petersburg University and it was here that Lenin completed his study of law as an external student in 1891. Other prominent figures who worked and studied at the university include the scientists Dmitri Mendeleev, Ivan Sechenov, Alexander Popov, and writers Nikolai Chernyshevsky, Ivan Turgenev, and Nicholas Nekrasov. Today 17,000 students study in the university's thirteen departments.

Nevsky Prospect

This is the main thoroughfare of Leningrad, dating back to the time of Peter I, who envisioned it as a connecting road with the route north from Novgorod. Originating at the Admiralty Building, it extends a total of 4.5 kilometers (3 miles) and terminates at the Alexander Nevsky Monastery. This lively, sophisticated avenue was once such a dangerous swamp that Peter himself almost drowned in it. The incident led to his edict that all visitors to the new city bring at least one stone for fill. When completed, Nevsky Prospect became the site of the finest shops, banks, and palaces of the nobility. Among these was the Stroganov Palace built in 1752–54 by Bartolomeo Rastrelli. The white-columned building remains one of the best examples of Russian Baroque architectural style. Another building, number 22–24, formerly the Evangelistic Church, was built in 1833–38 in Romanesque style by Bryullov. Number 32–34, formerly the Roman Catholic Church, was built in 1763–64 by de la Mothe in the form of a Latin cross. Number 29–31, built by Giacomo Quarenghi in 1784, was the former Silversmiths' Row. Quarenghi also designed the neighboring city hall to which a tower was added by Ferrari in 1802. The tower was used for firewatching as well as for a mirror telegraph between the Winter Palace and Tsarskoye Selo. Number 35 was the famous Merchants' Yard (Gostiny Dvor), designed by de la Mothe and built between 1761–85. Today, Nevsky Prospect is a bustling commercial avenue in the daytime and a well-lit, exciting place in the evenings.

Beginning at the Admiralty Building, you will enjoy the mixture of old and new buildings. Walking east, past Herzen and Zhelyabov streets, one sees on the left the former Lutheran Church of St. Peter and St. Paul, built in 1838 by Bryullov. At Karanskaya Square, also to the left, is the former Cathedral of the Holy Virgin of Kazan, now the Museum of the History of Religion and Atheism. To the left of the square is a major bus depot and taxi stand. On the right of Nevsky Prospect, past the museum, is Bank Bridge (Bankovsky Most) which spans the Griboyedev Canal. This bridge is noted for the gilded griffins which adorn each side. Next along the way, on the left at number 28, is Leningrad's largest bookstore, the House of Books. The building was originally constructed by the Russian architect Susor for the Singer Company of the United States. This shop contains three stories of books, maps, posters, and postcards. The book inventory is vast, ranging from technology to art in many languages.

Continuing along, one arrives at the Square of Arts (Ploshchad Iskusstv). The ensemble to the left of Nevsky Prospect, which comprises this square, was designed by Carlo Rossi. To the right of the square is Gostiny Dvor, located at number 35. The former Merchants' Yard forms a square itself and is 1 kilometer (.6 mile) around. Today it is called the Leningrad Department Store.

Behind the Gostiny Dvor to the right of Nevsky Prospect are Ostrovsky and Lomonosov squares. Facing Nevsky Prospect on the same side of the street is the State Public Library, dedicated to Mikhail Saltykov. The original building was constructed in 1801 by the architect Sokolov. A new building designed by Rossi was added to the old one in 1828–32. The façade, consisting of eighteen columns, is richly decorated with sculpture. It overlooks Ostrovsky Square. A third structure, designed by Vorotilov, was added in 1896–1901. Next to the library is a monument to Catherine II, designed by Mikeshin and carved by the sculptors Chizhov and Onekushin. The building next to the monument is the Comedy Theater. Adjacent to the theater is the Young Pioneer Palace. Overlooking the Fontanka River, this building was once the Anichkov Palace. Several architects, including Zemstov, Bartolomeo Rastrelli, Carlo Rossi, and Sokolov, worked on the structure, which was rebuilt a number of times. The Anichkov Bridge, decorated by delicately sculptured horses, spans the Fontanka River on the side of the Young Pioneer Palace.

Behind the monument to Catherine II, also facing Nevsky Prospect, is the Academic Drama Theater, named the Pushkin Theater in 1832. The main façade is a portico of six columns. Between them, in the niches, are statues of the Muses. Atop the building is a statue of the chariot of Apollo, patron of the arts. All sides of the building are decorated with garlands and friezes of tragic masks. Directly behind the Pushkin Theater is Rossi Street, which leads to Lomonosov Square. Along this square, which faces the Fontanka River, are the Press Building and the Gorky Academic Bolshoi Drama Theater. Continuing along Nevsky Prospect, one passes Uprising Square and the Moscow Railway Station. Nevsky Prospect terminates at the Metro station and becomes Alexander Nevsky Square, leading directly to the main entrance of Alexander Nevsky Monastery.

Palace Square (Dvortsovaya Ploshchad)

To the north of Nevsky Prospect, just past the Admiralty Building, is Palace Square, the oldest and most important square in Leningrad. It has been the site of many revolutionary events, two of the most memorable having occurred in the twentieth century. The first of these was "Bloody Sunday," January 9, 1905, when a peaceful demonstration led by Father Gapon was fired upon by the troops of Nicholas II. The second was the storming of the Winter Palace by revolutionaries in October 1917. Since that time Palace Square has been used for parades and demonstrations.

ALEXANDER'S COLUMN (AT THE CENTER OF PALACE SQUARE)

Designed in 1834 by August Montferrand to celebrate Russia's victory over Napoleon in 1812, the column stands 47.5 meters (156 feet) high, and is made of polished monolith red granite from Finland. The stone was hauled across the Gulf of Finland in 1832 by a specially built barge. Twenty-two hundred soldiers were needed to operate the pulleys which raised it into position. The column rests freely upon its pedestal by virtue of its own weight. Atop the column is an angel holding a cross while trampling a snake underfoot. Boris Orlovsky was the sculptor for the statue.

WINTER PALACE

Now known as the State Hermitage Museum (see pages 92–93), the Winter Palace was designed by Bartolomeo Rastrelli in 1754. It stands on the north side of Palace Square and is considered to be Rastrelli's best architectural work.

FOREIGN MINISTRY AND GENERAL STAFF HEADQUARTERS

Directly opposite the Winter Palace stands a semicircular building which formerly housed the Ministry of Foreign Affairs and the General Staff Headquarters of the tsar. Linking the two wings is a triumphal arch. Designed by Carlo Rossi, the architectural ensemble was built in 1811–29. Atop the arch is a victory chariot carved by the sculptors Pimenov and Demut-Malinovsky, in commemoration of the Russian defeat of Napoleon in 1812. The façade of the entire building which overlooks Palace Square is 639 meters (1,919 feet) long.

GUARDS CORPS HEADQUARTERS

This building on the east side of Palace Square facing the Admiralty formerly housed the Imperial Guards Corps. The structure, designed by Alexander Bryullov, was built in 1840–48.

THE ADMIRALTY (LOCATED ON THE WESTERN SIDE OF PALACE SQUARE)

Originally constructed in 1704 as one of the earliest buildings in Peter's new city, it served as a shipyard. It now houses the Dzerzhinsky Naval College. The present structure, designed by Andrei Zakharov, was built in 1806–23. The Admiralty is richly decorated with fifty-six sculptures and eleven large relief carvings based on mythology. The highly polished gilded spire rises 90 meters (273 feet) high and can be seen from almost anywhere in the city.

Decembrists' Square (Ploshchad Dekabristov)

South of Nevsky Prospect on the opposite side of the Admiralty Building is Decembrists' Square. Formerly Senate Square, the name was changed in honor of the uprising of the Imperial Guard against serfdom and autocracy which occurred on December 14, 1825. The entire architectural ensemble of the square took a century to complete.

PETER I MONUMENT

Known as the "Bronze Horseman," this huge statue of Peter I was completed by Etienne Falconet in 1782. The tsar, dressed in a classical toga, is mounted on a rearing horse which is trampling a snake underfoot. The base of the statue is a rolling wave. The statue faces the Neva, with Peter's right arm raised toward the west.

SENATE AND SYNOD BUILDINGS

Designed by Carlo Rossi, these structures were completed in 1834 and represent the last major work of the great architect. The buildings are independent but joined by an archway. They are ornately adorned with sculptures and loggias. Today these buildings house archives.

GODDESS OF GLORY COLUMNS

Created by the sculptor Christian Rauch, these twin granite columns to the left of the Senate and Synod Buildings were a gift of the Austrian emperor in 1845. Atop each 10-meter (33-foot) column is a statue of the Goddess of Glory.

HORSE GUARDS RIDING SCHOOL

Designed by Giacomo Quarenghi in 1804, this building stands to the left of the Goddess of Glory Columns and faces St. Isaac's Cathedral. The main façade features a classical Greek portico with its imposing columns. Marble sculptures of the sons of Zeus and Leda, known for their mastery of horses, adorn the building which is now used as an exhibition hall.

MAXIM GORKY GARDEN

This decorative piece of landscaping runs along two sides of the Admiralty building. On the side facing Admiralty Prospect is a statue of Przhevalsky, erected in 1892.

St. Isaac's Square

St. Isaac's Cathedral separates Decembrists' and St. Isaac's squares. The cathedral, now a museum, is the focal point of the square. In the center of the architectural ensemble is a monument to Nicholas I created by Peter Klodt in 1859. Behind the monument is the Blue Bridge (Siny Most) which spans the Moika River and is the widest bridge in Leningrad (99 meters, 390 feet). Herzen Street cuts across the square. At the corner of Herzen Street nearest to the cathedral are the Leningradskaya and Astoria hotels. It was at the latter that Hitler planned to hold his victory celebration over Leningrad, going so far as to have invitations printed. Across Herzen Street, facing the square, is the Institute of Plant Protection of the U.S.S.R. Academy of Sciences. Directly across the square is the Institute of Plant Breeding. Both buildings were designed by Yefimov and were completed in 1853.

POST OFFICE

This building is across Herzen Street from the Institute of Plant Breeding. Originally built in 1789 from a design by Lvov, the structure has been rebuilt numerous times. It is one of the largest post offices in the U.S.S.R. Mounted on the gallery façade in 1962 is a clock which has two faces arranged one within the other. The outer clock shows Moscow time, while the inner one tells the time in all other Soviet time zones.

MARYINSKY PALACE

Directly opposite St. Isaac's is the former Maryinsky Palace, erected in 1844 according to the design of Andrei Stakenschneider. Since 1945 the former palace has been the home of the Executive Committee of the Leningrad City Soviet. The exterior of the building displays models of the emblems awarded to Leningrad as a Hero City. Inside, securely guarded, are the actual awards: the Red Banner with the Hero City Golden Star, two Orders of Lenin, Order of the October Revolution, and Order of the Red Banner.

Theater Square

Located between the Moika River and the Griboyedev Canal, this square is located to the southwest of the principal squares of Leningrad. Although it dates back to the 1730s, its present appearance began to be formed during the latter portion of the nineteenth century.

EDUCATIONAL WORKERS' PALACE OF CULTURE

At the intersection of Glinka and Decembrists' streets is the former Yusupov Palace, designed by Giacomo Quarenghi. It is here that Grigory Rasputin was murdered.

RIMSKY-KORSAKOV STATE CONSERVATORY

Across Decembrists' Street from the former Yusupov Palace is the State Conservatory named for Rimsky-Korsakov. The building was designed by Nicole in 1862. In addition to the musician honored by the building's name, many other well-known Russian composers studied here. Among them were Tchaikovsky, Shostakovich, and Prokofiev. In 1952 a statue of Rimsky-Korsakov was placed in front of the conservatory. The sculptors were Bogolyubov and Ingal.

KIROV OPERA AND BALLET THEATER (FORMER MARYINSKY THEATER)

Directly opposite the Conservatory is the major opera and ballet theater of Leningrad. It was designed by Albert Cavos and completed in 1860. Many well-known Russian classical operas were premiered here and it has seen some of the world's greatest performers on its stage. Today it is the home of the Kirov opera and ballet companies.

NEW HOLLAND ARCH

Designed by de la Mothe, this arch was constructed during the 1760s. It is located at the far end of Theater Square by the Moika River. The name of the arch is derived from an island formed by the Moika River and the Admiralty Canal. The island was previously used as a storage area for shipbuilding timbers which were kept in low warehouses along the island. The function of the arch was to link these structures.

NAVAL CATHEDRAL OF ST. NICHOLAS

Located at the edge of Theater Square bordered by the Griboyedev Canal, the cathedral was designed by Chevakinsky and was completed in 1762. Although it bears the five domes associated with traditional Russian church architecture, the structure more closely resembles a secular palace. The cathedral contains both a lower and upper church, the latter elegantly decorated with stuccowork. The iconostasis is considered to be one of the finest examples of eighteenth-century Russian decorative art.

Strelka of Vasilievsky Island

Covering an area of 243 hectares (600 acres), Vasilievsky Island, located on the right bank of the Neva River, is the largest of the islands comprising the city of Leningrad. The island's eastern point, near the University of Leningrad, is called the "Strelka," which means "tip" or "point."

Rostral Columns

These two dramatic pillars standing in front of the former Stock Exchange were designed by Thomas de Thomon and built in 1810. They are 32 meters (105 feet) high and are decorated with ships' figureheads. At the base of each column are allegorical figures of Russia's commercial waterways: the Neva, Volga, Dnieper, and Volkhov rivers. The original oil cups at the tops of the columns were lit at dusk to guide ships into port. These were replaced by gas jets which are lit on national holidays.

Field of Mars (Marsovo Polye)

This 10-hectare (25-acre) square, one of the oldest in Leningrad, is located at the end of Sadovaya Street between the Moika and Neva rivers. During the reign of Peter I it was the site of military victory celebrations and popular festivals. Following the tsar's death, the square became a favorite gathering place for the nobility and acquired the nickname "Tsarina's Meadow." By the end of the eighteenth century the area was again used for military drills, reviews, and parades.

MONUMENT TO THE HEROES OF THE REVOLUTION AND CIVIL WAR

At the very center of the square is a semicomplete rectangle formed by memorial plates inside of which an eternal flame burns. This monument, designed by Lev Rudnev, was erected in 1920. To the north of the monument is the Kirov Bridge. En route to the bridge is the Suvorov Monument, designed by Kozlovsky and erected in 1801. This monument commemorates the triumph of Generalissimo Alexander Suvorov, responsible for crushing the Polish uprising of 1794-95.

SUMMER GARDEN (LETNY SAD)

To the east of the Field of Mars is the luxurious 14-hectare (35-acre) Summer Garden laid out by Alexandre Leblond in 1704-12. Leblond was a former pupil of Le Notre, designer of the park at Versailles. The garden abounds with 15,000 trees. Fountains draw from the Fontanka River to the east. During the time of Peter I exotic animals and birds were maintained in the park. Large numbers of statues were imported from Italy, Holland,

and England. Owing to Peter's mania for learning, which he wished to impose on visitors to the garden, more statues were erected to represent subjects from Aesop's Fables. They were destroyed by a flood in 1777. However, in 1855 a monument designed by Peter Klodt was erected which illustrates in high relief on granite the most popular fables of the Russian writer Ivan Krylov. The wrought-iron gate, remarkable for the black and gold railings, was designed by Russian architects Felten and Yegorov and built from 1770 to 1784.

SUMMER PALACE (LETNY DVORETS)

To the east of the main entrance to the Summer Garden is the Summer Palace of Peter I. Designed by Domenico Trezzini, construction was begun in 1713. This somewhat modest building is known for its beautiful entrance hall, symmetrical windows, and stolid Dutch-style interior. The reliefs on the exterior were designed by Andreas Schlueter.

COFFEE HOUSE

This classically styled pavilion is located south of the Summer Palace. Completed in 1826, it is the work of Carlo Rossi. Nearby is the Tea House, designed by Charlemagne, and completed in 1827.

ENGINEER'S CASTLE (PAUL'S CASTLE)

Dominating the southern portion of the Summer Garden is the Engineer's Castle, former residence of Emperor Paul I. Designed by Brenna and Bazhenov, it was built in 1800. Paul ordered that the building be isolated from the town by a maze of canals and moats and guarded by cannons. The castle is built on a square plan with an octagonal inner courtyard. The original name was changed when in 1819 a school for military engineers was installed on the premises. Today the building is used as a naval library. In front of the main entrance is a statue of Peter I created by Bartolomeo Rastrelli.

LENENEGRO BUILDING

At the western edge of the Field of Mars is a large building designed by Stasov in 1817. It is the former barracks of the Pavlovsky Regiment, famous for its activity in the war against Napoleon.

MARBLE PALACE

To the immediate north of the Lenenegro Building is the former Marble Palace, now the Leningrad Branch of the Central Lenin Museum (see page 112).

The Country Palaces

PETERHOF (PEDRODVORETS)

Located 34 kilometers (21 miles) northwest of Leningrad, this country estate makes for a most pleasant excursion. Peterhof, as it was called originally, began as a modest summer house at Strelna, near Kronstadt Island, on the Gulf of Finland. Peter's desire for something more elaborate is said to have been influenced partially by the opulent palace of Prince Menshikov at Oranienbaum and by Peter's visit to Versailles. Thus, the original designs of both the house and the grounds were expanded from 1708 until 1803 during the reign of Elizabeth. Peter first consulted Leblond, and in 1715 a plan was presented which was grandiose enough to satisfy even the tsar. It included a large, two-story house at the summit of a steep incline, behind it a formal garden, and in front a terrace of sculptured fountains. The project required four thousand workers. Water was brought in through wooden pipes from Ropshinsky Heights, a distance of 20.8 kilometers (thirteen miles). The gardens were also embellished with smaller structures. Among these was Marky, a small white pavilion nestled at the edge of a pond; the Hermitage, an even smaller building inside a miniature moat; and Monplaisir, a row of one-story brick buildings set among the trees. Leblond died and was replaced by Michetti, Yeropkin, and Zemstov in 1718. Peter's death in 1725 made it incumbent on his daughter, Elizabeth, to complete the work. The new empress engaged Rastrelli, who quadrupled the size of the palace, improved the cascades, and added more statues. Peterhof was finally completed by Veronikhin in 1803, and for the next century it remained a favorite resort of the monarchy. After the Revolution, Peterhof was renamed Petrodvorets, and the former preserve of the tsars became a national museum.

Among the most notable sights at Petrodvorets is the Grand Cascade with the gilded statue of Samson shooting water 18.3 meters (60 feet) high. This forms the starting point of the Avenue of the Fountains which bisects the park and terminates at the shoreline of the Gulf of Finland. There are the Chessboard Fountain, the Roman Fountain with its seemingly transparent spray, the Pyramid Fountain with more than five hundred water jets, and the Hill of Gold and Menagerniye fountains with hollow sprays. Perhaps the most amusing feature of the park is the Jester Fountains hidden among the trees. These, along with the Parasol, Oak Tree, and Little Mushroom fountains, are timed to spray the unwary visitor. Thus, it is advisable to bring a raincoat to Pedrodvorets.

PUSHKIN (TSARSKOYE SELO)

Twenty-four kilometers (15 miles) southwest of Leningrad is the former Tsar's Village (Tsarskoye Selo), renamed in 1937 for Alexander Pushkin, who was educated here. It is said that Catherine had the first structures built in 1708 as a surprise for her husband, Peter I. The stone house, wooden churches, arbored garden, and linden-tree-lined path were designed by Johann Forster. The enlarged manor house was created by S. F. Braunstein, who also added a number of outbuildings in the shape of a horseshoe. Catherine bequeathed the estate to Elizabeth, who is responsible for the extravagantly beautiful and most sumptuous of the imperial country estates. Initially the empress intended only for alterations to be made. These were assigned to Zemstov. In 1743, as her fortune increased, Elizabeth engaged Domenico Trezzini for the addition of two wings designed by Kvasov and Chevakinsky. After seven years of building, the project was discarded in favor of a more grandiose design by Rastrelli. Initially called the Great Palace, its name was later changed to Ekaterininsky Palace for Catherine II. The result of Rastrelli's enthusiasm was a three-story monolith having a façade nearly 304.9 meters (1,000 feet) long. Eighty enormous French windows adorned with wrought-iron balconies and interspersed with columns supported by huge caryatids adorn the main façade. The landscaping was improved as well. After the sixth remodeling Elizabeth was satisfied with her estate, which contained not only the palace, outbuildings, and gardens, but a toboggan slide, shooting galleries, picnic arbors, fishing ponds, and a miniature zoo.

Today the visitor to Pushkin will be impressed by the restored luxury of the estate. In addition to Ekaterininsky Palace, still one of the most sumptuous relics of Imperial Russia, there are numerous other buildings which attract attention. The Grotto Pavilion, for example, was used by Alexander I as a ritual after-breakfast bird-feeding station. The Concert Hall on the island, the Upper and Lower Bath Houses, and the Ruined Kitchen are quite interesting. Catherine's Park, impressively overshadowed by the Hermitage, is beautifully laid out in formal eighteenth-century style. Alexander's Park is especially noteworthy because of the Chinese-style Summer House and Village, as well as the Grand Caprice, a bridge dividing the two parks. Among the famous monuments are the fountain statue "The Girl With the Broken Pitcher," designed by Sokolov in 1810, and the monument to Pushkin designed by Bakh in 1900. One can also visit the lyceum, "Vlycée," now a museum, where Alexander Pushkin was once a student.

PAVLOVSK

About 3 kilometers (2 miles) south of Pushkin is Pavlovsk, the estate that Catherine II built for her son, Paul, and his wife, Maria Feodorovna. As the empress and her son were irreconcilably hostile to each other, the motivation for building the estate was essentially to provide Paul with a suitable domicile as far away from his mother as propriety would permit. Catherine chose Cameron, her favorite architect, in 1781 to begin designing the estate. Despite continual wrangling with Paul, most of the original designs were retained. However, various alterations were completed by other architects, including Carlo Rossi, Brenna, Voronikhin, Gonzaga, and Giacomo Quarenghi.

In accordance with the request of Paul and his wife, simplicity and nobility are the key features of the estate. The Grand Palace, essentially the work of Quarenghi, is a square building topped by a flat dome, similar to that of the Pantheon. A large square hall under the dome was once Paul's throne room. Exhibited here is a meticulously re-created banquet table set for one hundred guests. The appurtenances of both the public rooms and private quarters retain their original positions, except for those items lost or destroyed during World War II. Many pieces of furniture have been re-created from original sketches and photographs.

The details of Pavlovsk are as magnificent as those of either the Peterhof or Tsarskoye Selo estate, although the setting is less spectacular. Set above the Salyanka River, which forms a lake here, the Palace Park is divided into two sections. The western portion is called Big Star and the eastern portion White Birch. Via the numerous pathways through the park one will see the lovely structures which make Pavlovsk memorable. Among these are Cameron's works which include the Apollo Colonnade, Temple of Friendship, and the Pavilion of the Three Graces. Thomon's decorative Mausoleum of Paul I, although not his burial place, built in 1807, is located in the Old and New Silvia sections, which were designed by Brenna. Here, too, are the Grand Circles which contain the statues "Justice" and "Peace." Specially designated lawns mark the graves of World War II soldiers from many nations.

GATCHINA

Approximately 48 kilometers (30 miles) south of Leningrad is the town where Catherine the Great commissioned Rinaldi in 1776 to build a palace for Count Orlov. It is a simply designed, somewhat Teutonic edifice containing seven hundred rooms. The stone terrace contained in the mammoth park at one time boasted an underground gallery and Roman bath. The palace underwent several alterations in its early years. When Paul was banished to Gatchina, the palace was transformed into a fortress. Subsequently it was redesigned by Brenna as a medieval castle.

Among the noteworthy features of the palace grounds are the Octagonal Well and Cesme Obelisk, designed by Rinaldi in 1780. Located at White Lake, the obelisk is constructed of several varieties of marble. Nearby lies the Island of Love, the site of the Pavilion of Venus. At Black Lake is the Priory, designed by Lvov in 1797 for a friend of Paul's. The Admiralty Gate, designed by Brenna in 1796, is one of the decorative highlights of the estate. The last addition of note is the Aviary, created in 1800 by Zakharov, who also designed the Admiralty building in Leningrad. The Aviary, used as a preserve for game birds, stands beside the Kolpanka River, which makes its way through the property.

LOMONOSOV

Formerly Oranienbaum, this was the first country palace of the Leningrad area. It is located south of the city just past Gatchina. Although it was not a royal estate, its owner, Prince Menshikov, was known for his imperial tastes and aspirations. Peter I gave the lands to his friend and generalissimo, Alexander Menshikov, who commissioned Gottfried Schaedel to design the palace and gardens. Constructed in 1710–25, Oranienbaum became a symbol of opulence reputed to have been the envy of the tsar himself. The palace is a two-story building balanced by low galleries on each side which terminate in domed pavilions. Terraces descend to a canal which feeds into the Gulf of Finland. In 1743 Catherine II's husband, Peter III, gained title to the estate, and he commissioned Rastrelli to design the Stone Hall. Rinaldi was engaged for the building of the Opera House and the Small Palace of Peter III. The Small Palace was decorated in Chinese rococo style. For Catherine, Rinaldi designed the Chinese Palace, completed in 1768. It was here at her husband's favorite retreat that Catherine had Peter III arrested in 1762. Among the interior decorations are some small mosaics created by Mikhail Lomonosov, the eighteenth-century scientist, scholar, and craftsman.

USEFUL INFORMATION

Hotels

Astoria, 39 Herzen Street
Baltiiskaya, 57 Nevsky Prospect
Leningradskaya, 10/24 Mayorova Prospect
Leningrad, 7 Petrograd Embankment
Moskovskaya, 43/45 Ligovsky Prospect
Oktyabrskaya, 118 Nevsky Prospect
Rossia, 163 Moskovsky Prospect
Sovietskaya, 43 Lermontovsky Prospect
Sputnik, 34 Morisa Toreza Prospect
Yevropeiskaya (European), 1/7 Brodskogo Street

Restaurants

Albatross (floating restaurant), Lieutenant Schmidt Bridge
Astoria, 39 Herzen Street
Baku, 12 Sadovaya Street
Baltiisky, 57 Nevsky Prospect
Baltika, 4/1 Mira Square
Chaika, 14 Griboyedeva Canal Embankment
Deflin (floating restaurant), Admiralty Embankment
Kavkazsky, 25 Nevsky Prospect
Metropol, 22 Sadovaya Street
Moskva, 49 Nevsky Prospect
Moskovsky, 43/45 Ligovsky Prospect
Narva, 75 Stachek Prospect
Neva, 46 Nevsky Prospect
Oktyabrsky, 118 Nevsky Prospect
Parus (floating restaurant), Reki Zhdanovki Embankment
Sadko, 1/7 Brodskogo Street
Sputnik, 34 Morisa Toreza Prospect
Yevropeysky, 1/7 Brodskogo Street

Cafés

Aurora, 60 Nevsky Prospect
Belye Nochi, 41 Mayorova Prospect
Druzba, 15 Nevsky Prospect
Lakoma, 22 Sadovaya Street
Leningrad, 96 Nevsky Prospect
Ogonyok, 24 Nevsky Prospect
Sever, 46 Nevsky Prospect
Ulybka, 79 Nevsky Prospect

Museums

Peter and Paul Fortress, Revolutsii Square
State Hermitage Museum, 34/36 Decembrists' Embankment
Leningrad Branch of the Central Lenin Museum, 5 Khalturina Street
State Museum of the Great October Socialist Revolution, 4 Kuibysheva Street
Museum of the History of Leningrad, 44 Krasnogo Flota Embankment
State Russian Museum, 4/2 Inzhenernaya Street
Museum of the History of Religion and Atheism, 2 Karanskaya Square
Museum of Ethnography of the Peoples of the U.S.S.R., 4/1 Inzhenernaya Street

Peter I Museum of Anthropology and Ethnography, 3 University Embankment
Central Naval Museum, 4 Pushkinskaya Square
Cruiser Aurora Museum, Petrograd Embankment
St. Isaac's Cathedral Museum, St. Isaac's Square
Pushkin Memorial Museum, 12 Moiki Embankment
Literary Museum, 4 Makarova Embankment
Alexander Nevsky Monastery, Alexander Nevsky Square
Smolny, Proletarskoi Diktatury Square

Theaters and Concert Halls

Kirov Academic Theater of Opera and Ballet, 1 Theater Square
Pushkin Academic Drama Theater, Ostrovsky Square
Academic Maly Theater of Opera and Ballet, 1 Square of Arts
M. Gorky Academic Bolshoi Drama Theater, 65 Reki Fontanki Embankment
Comedy Theater, 56 Nevsky Prospect
Lensoviet Theater, 12 Vladimirsky Prospect
Lenin Komsomol Theater, 4 Park Lenina
Komissarzhevskaya Drama Theater, 19 Rakova Street
Musical Comedy Theater, 13 Rakova Street
Variety Theater, 27 Zhelyabova Street
Drama and Comedy Theater, 51 Liteiny Prospect
Maly Drama Theater, 18 Rebensteina Street
Young Spectators' Theater, 1 Pionerskaya Street
Bolshoi Puppet Theater, 10 Nekrasova Street
Circus, 3 Reki Fontanki Embankment
Philharmonic Society (Grand Hall), 2 Brodskogo Street
Rimsky-Korsakov Conservatory, 1 Theater Square
Oktyabrsky Grand Concert Hall, 6 Ligovsky Prospect
Yubileiny Palace of Sports, 18 Dobrolyubova Prospect

Stores and Souvenir Shops

Kirov Department Store, 9 Stachek Prospect
Moskovsky Department Store, 191 Moskovsky Prospect
Gostiny Dvor, 25 Nevsky Prospect
Passage, 48 Nevsky Prospect
Beriozka (foreign currency shop), 7 Nevsky Prospect
Yakhont (jewelry), 24 Herzen Street
Cut glass and porcelainware, 64 Nevsky Prospect
Gifts and souvenirs, 26 and 54 Nevsky Prospect
Musical instruments, 69 Nevsky Prospect
Record store, 34 Nevsky Prospect

Antiques, 54 and 102 Nevsky Prospect
Dom Knigi (Central Book House), 28 Nevsky Prospect
Mir (bookstore), 13 Nevsky Prospect

Transportation and Communications

Aeroflot Office, 54 Nevsky Prospect
Central Post Office, 9 Soyuza Svyazi Street
Telegraph Office, 15 Soyuza Svyazi Street

KIEV

GENERAL INFORMATION

Kiev is one of the leading industrial centers of the Soviet Union and is known for its production of excavators, electric measuring apparatuses, cameras, gas equipment, and motorcycles. It also has plants for the chemical, wood-working, printing, building, textile, shoe, confectionery, meat, milk, and wine-making industries.

A major transportation center, Kiev has air, rail, waterway, and highway connections with other cities of the U.S.S.R. and Eastern Europe. Aeroflot Soviet Airlines provides air service between Kiev and other republics and regional centers of the Ukraine as well as Berlin, Budapest, Bucharest, Prague, Sofia, Vienna, and Warsaw. The city's railway network links Kiev with thirty-one cities, including Moscow, Leningrad, Lvov, Riga, and Sevastopol.

In prerevolutionary Kiev, there were seven institutions of higher education with 15,000 students. Today 100,000 students attend eighteen advanced education establishments. More than 9,000 teachers are employed in 222 secondary schools with a daily attendance of more than 170,000 pupils. As a center for scientific learning and research, Kiev ranks as a leading city in the U.S.S.R. The Academy of Sciences of the Ukrainian S.S.R. is in Kiev.

Kiev is rich in institutions of performing arts. Visitors can enjoy performances given by the Shevchenko Opera and Ballet Theater of the Ukrainian S.S.R., the Ivan Franko Drama Theater, the Lesya Ukrainka Russian

Drama Theater, the Dance Ensemble of the Ukrainian S.S.R., the Ve-
ryovka Ukrainian Folk Choir, the Bandore Players, the "Dunka" Choir,
and the Symphony Orchestra of the Ukrainian S.S.R. Kiev has three film
studios: the Alexander Dovzhenko Studio of Feature Films, the Studio of
Popular Science Films, and the Studio of Documentary Films, as well as
a Philharmonic Society, a circus, and a radio and television center.

HISTORY IN BRIEF

The story of the founding of Kiev is told in the following legend: Three
brothers, Kij, Shchek, and Khoriv, and their younger sister, Lybed, settled
on the heights above the Dnieper and founded a city on one of the hills.
The city was called Kiev in honor of the oldest brother. To honor the other
siblings, a second hill was named Shchekavitsa, a third named Khorevitsa,
and the river was called Lybed.

While the legend is exaggerated, excavations have proved that there is
some truth in it. On the site of what is now Kiev, there once did exist the
small town of Kij. It is believed that the prince of the Polyane tribe was
Kij and that he lived at the end of the sixth and beginning of the seventh
centuries A.D. It was probably at this time that the foundations of a stronghold, later known as Kiev, were laid on Mount Staro-Kievskaya (Old Kiev
Mountain).

The three hills in the legend still exist: Mount Staro-Kievskaya, Mount
Shchekavitsa, and Mount Kiselyovka.

Ancient Kiev was situated on the important waterway known as "the
route from the Varangians to the Greeks"; the route also included the
entire length of the Dnieper. This greatly helped to promote trade and Kiev
was a large commercial center of the East Slavs where Byzantine, Varangian, and Arab merchants brought their wares. The economic growth of
Kiev flourished and by the end of the ninth century it had become a
political, administrative, and cultural center of Kiev Rus, an ancient Russian state that developed after the unification of the East Slavs.

The formation of a unified Russian state is depicted in a chronicle of 882
according to which Prince Oleg of Novgorod sailed down the Dnieper with
his men-at-arms, and with his men remaining behind in their boats, he
entered the town as a merchant. The story continues that, having tricked
Askold and Dir, the princes of Kiev, out of the stronghold, he ordered their
execution. After seizing Kiev, Oleg proclaimed: "This will be the mother
of all Russian towns!" The Novgorod principality was united with Kiev, and
the town was made the capital of a unified Russian state.

Kiev Rus held within its territory what were to be three fraternal peoples:
the Russian, the Ukrainian, and the Byelorussian. As Kiev Rus gained in
strength, so did its capital. Kiev became one of the largest and most

powerful towns of medieval Europe, reaching its zenith at the end of the tenth and beginning of the eleventh centuries under the rule of Prince Vladimir Svyatoslavich.

Kiev Rus gained in power and fame under Prince Vladimir's son, Yaroslav the Wise, and kings and princes of many European states established dynastic ties with the princes of Kiev. The daughters of Yaroslav were married to the kings of France and Norway and one of his sons, Vsevolod, married a Byzantine princess. As Kiev continued to grow in wealth and power, it was fortified with walls and defenses. The main gateway to the town was the famous Golden Gate which is said to have been taken from Chersonesus by Prince Vladimir.

After almost three centuries as the capital of Kiev Rus, internal strife greatly weakened the position of Kiev. Rivalries among individual princes undermined the authority of the grand duke of Kiev, which in turn shattered Kiev Rus and led to its disintegration into separate principalities.

Kiev made rapid progress during the centuries that followed. Brick houses were built and a wooden bridge was constructed over the Dnieper. The eighteenth century saw the building of the Marlinsky Palace and St. Andrew's Church. In addition, the Belfry and other parts of the Kiev-Pechersky Monastery were erected.

The decade of the 1790s was one of great significance for Kiev, for in 1793 the two parts of the Ukraine that were situated along the left and right banks of the Dnieper united within the Russian state and in 1797 Kiev became the capital of the general governorship and the center of the Kiev, Volynia, and Podolia provinces.

Of importance to the town's history was the foundation of the Kiev Academy at the beginning of the eighteenth century. Some of the famous men who were students at the academy include Mikhail Lomonosov, the scholar and scientist; Grigory Skovoroda, the philosopher; the historian Dmitry Bantish-Kamensky; and the architect Ivan Grigorovich-Barsky.

In the nineteenth century Kiev continued to grow as the center of Ukrainian culture, economy, and political life. The first theater was opened in 1805, and in 1836 a newspaper known as the *Kievskie Gubernskiye Vedomosti* (Kiev Provincial Gazette) was published. The educational quality of the capital city was greatly advanced when, in 1834, Kiev University was opened.

Kiev became the capital of the Ukrainian Soviet Socialist Republic in 1934 and an extensive plan was drawn up to develop the city further. Industrialization grew at a more rapid pace than ever before as a result of the first five-year plans. Several administrative buildings were constructed, among them the buildings of the Supreme Soviet, the Council of Ministers of the Ukrainian S.S.R., and the Central Committee of the Communist Party of the Ukraine. Transportation systems in Kiev were greatly improved as new tram and trolleybus lines were put into operation. New museums,

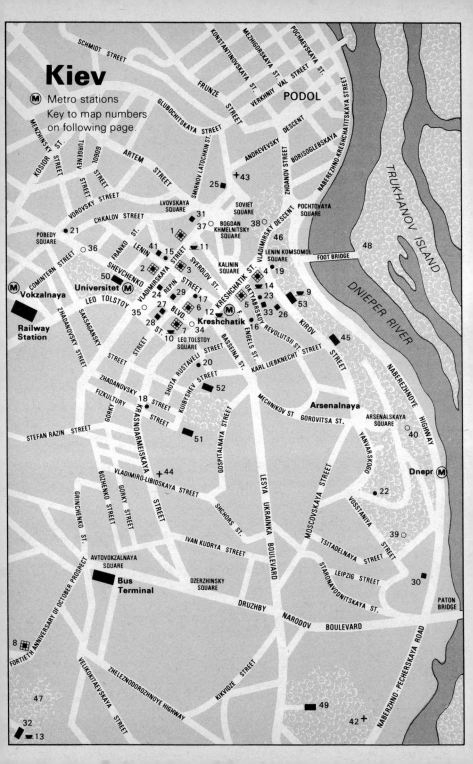

KEY TO FIGURES ON KIEV MAP
HOTELS

1. Kiev
2. Teatralnaya
3. Intourist
4. Dnipro
5. Moskva
6. Leningradskaya
7. Ukraina
8. Mir

LARGE RESTAURANTS

9. Dynamo
10. Kavkaz
11. Leipzig
12. Metro
13. Praga
14. Stolichny

There are restaurants at all hotels

THEATERS

15. Shevchenko Opera and Ballet Theater
16. Ivan Franko Ukrainian Drama Theater
17. Lesya Ukrainka Russian Drama Theater
18. Musical Comedy Theater
19. Philharmonic Society
20. Puppet Theater
21. Circus
22. Young Pioneers Palace
23. Oktyabrsky Palace of Culture

MUSEUMS, EXHIBITIONS, PRESERVES

24. Branch of the Central Lenin Museum
25. State Museum of History
26. Museum of Ukrainian Art
27. Museum of Russian Art
28. Museum of Western and Oriental Art
29. Taras Shevchenko Museum
30. Kiev-Pechersky Monastery Preserve (Lavra); Museum of Ukrainian Decorative Folk Art
31. St. Sophia's Preserve
32. Exhibition of Advanced Methods in Ukrainian Industry and Agriculture
33. Art Exhibition Pavilion

MONUMENTS

34. Lenin
35. Taras Shevchenko
36. Nikolai Shchors
37. Bogdan Khmelnitsky
38. Prince Vladimir
39. Obelisk beside the Tomb of the Unknown Soldier
40. Askold's Grave

ARCHITECTURAL MONUMENTS

41. The Golden Gate
42. Vydubetsky Monastery
43. Church of St. Andrew
44. Former Catholic Cathedral
45. Former tsarist (Mariinsky) Palace

PARKS AND STADIUMS

46. Central Recreation Park
47. Maxim Rylsky Goloseyevsky Recreation Park
48. Dnieper Recreation Park
49. Central Botanical Gardens of the Academy of Sciences
50. The Fomin Botanical Gardens
51. Central Stadium
52. Sports Palace
53. Dynamo Stadium

libraries, and movie theaters were opened and the population increased rapidly as the city boundaries expanded.

After World War II reconstruction was carried out under the General Reconstruction Plan for Kiev. Many Soviet towns and cities participated in the rebuilding of the Ukrainian capital by sending equipment, building and raw materials, construction workers, and engineers. Within a period of five years, factories, science installations, educational and cultural establishments, and homes were rebuilt.

Multistoried apartment houses were built in the city and the Kiev suburbs underwent great changes. Buildings were constructed here and an excellent system of transportation was established to link the suburbs with the city. Today the suburban areas enjoy excellent facilities for medical care and education as well as for entertainment. Good restaurants are numerous, as are schools, libraries, and movie theaters.

The construction of homes and administrative buildings was not the only postwar project in Kiev. New bridges were built spanning the Dnieper, and the pavilions of the Exhibition of Progressive Methods in Ukrainian Industry and Agriculture were erected. The Sports Palace, the Young Pioneers' Palace, the river station, the bus station, and Borispol airport were constructed as well as the Moscow, Dnieper, Mir, and Druzhba hotels. Also, a hydroelectric power station was built on the Dnieper, north of Kiev.

Kiev is now one of the largest cities in the Soviet Union. Its territory stretches 50 kilometers (31 miles) along the Dnieper and is 45 kilometers (28 miles) across, occupying 770 square kilometers (481 square miles). The population is approximately 1,470,000.

MUSEUMS AND PLACES OF INTEREST

State Museum of History

The State Museum of History was founded in 1899 as the State Museum of Antiquities. Located at 2 Vladimirskaya Street, it is now one of the largest scientific establishments in the Ukraine. Twenty-nine halls are used to hold its more than half a million exhibits.

The first section deals with the history of primitive tribes that inhabited the area of present-day Kiev and other areas along the Dnieper. An impressive collection of flint and bone tools is on exhibit as well as ornamented mammoth tusks and other items dating back to the twenty-fifth millennium B.C. Archaeologist Vikenty Khvoiko made these finds at the end of the nineteenth century in what was then Kirillovskaya Street (now Frunze Street). It is believed to be the earliest settlement within the city limits and became known as the Kirillovka settlement.

The gradual development of primitive culture is shown with the first man-made tools. Man began to use iron in the first millennium B.C. and the Ukrainian area was, at that time, inhabited by the Scythian tribes. The culture of these tribes and the ancient towns of the Black Sea area are the primary subjects of the second hall. On display are agricultural implements used by the Scythians and local tribes of the Western Ukraine. Of particular interest is a primitive iron plow, an invention that helped start the development of crop farming.

Other displays show leather items, bone ornaments, and weapons as well as the pottery for which the Scythians were famous.

The third and fourth halls are devoted to exhibits dealing with the state of Kiev Rus. While Kiev Rus traces its beginnings to the ninth century, finds from a much earlier period are exhibited. Pottery found in the Kiev suburb of Korchevaty has been dated to two thousand years B.C. A collection of later jewelry, silverware, coins, and other articles extends the pre-Christian-era collection.

The next few halls are dedicated to the history of the Zaporozhskaya Sech (fortified Cossack camp) and the role it played in opposing foreign invaders: the Polish *szlachta* and Lithuanian, Moldavian, and Hungarian feudal lords. The museum has an excellent collection of Cossack arms and articles of everyday use.

At the end of the sixteenth and throughout the first half of the seventeenth centuries, there were peasant and Cossack uprisings in the Ukraine. As the uprisings gained in intensity and number, the movement came to be known as the Ukrainian people's war of liberation. Its leader was Hetman Bogdan Khmelnitsky and his personal belongings as well as the arms used by the peasants and Cossacks are on display.

The last hall in the exhibition of the state of Kiev Rus before the second half of the nineteenth century is "The Ukraine During Feudalism." In this half exhibits deal with the early and mid-nineteenth-century revolutionary movements and groups such as the Decembrists and the "Cyril and Methodius" Society.

The five halls that follow are devoted to the Ukraine during the development of capitalism from the middle of the nineteenth century through the early part of the twentieth century. The period following the abolition of serfdom saw an increase in the growth of factories and industrial enterprises. Some of the displays portray the difficult labor conditions of the time such as the conditions at the Greter and Krivanek Engineering Works.

A very interesting exhibit is devoted to the numerous scientists and writers that have come from that area. Visitors are introduced to the efforts of Daniil Zabolotny to combat plague in Mongolia and China. The personal belongings of the surgeon Nikolai Pirogov have been preserved and are on display along with those of other Ukrainian scientists. Ivan Franko, Lesya Ukrainka, Mikhail Kotsulimsky, Maria Zankovetskaya, Mark Kropivnitsky, and Nikolai Lisenko are among the writers and artists represented.

The twentieth-century exhibition hall follows and on display are works of Lenin and documents on the Kiev uprising of field engineers led by Lieutenant Zhadanovski. An extensive exhibition is that of the October Revolution and the establishment of Soviet power in the Ukraine. Accounts of those days are given by photographs, documents, and personal belongings of some of the heroes of the Revolution and the Civil War, among them Nikolai Shschors, Yuri Kotsubinsky, and Vitali Primakov.

Exhibits show fifty years of Soviet power from the first five-year plans through the years of World War II, and the postwar reconstruction. The museum's last exhibit shows the economic, scientific, and cultural achievements of the Ukrainian people.

The State Museum of History is open from 10 A.M. to 5 P.M.; Tuesdays from 10 A.M. to 4 P.M.; Thursdays from 11:30 A.M. to 6:30 P.M.; closed Wednesdays. Trolley buses: 2, 4, 12, 16, 18; Buses: 20, 38, 68, 71.

Kiev Branch of the Lenin Museum

The Kiev branch of the Central Lenin Museum is located in a white, three-story house at 57 Vladimirskaya Street.

The building, constructed in 1911–13 by architect P. Aleshin, housed the Pedagogical Museum before the Revolution. In 1938 the structure was extended and remodeled as a branch of the Central Lenin Museum. After the city was liberated from the Germans restoration began and the museum was opened on April 22, 1945, the anniversary of Lenin's birth.

There is a circular entrance hall and seventeen galleries containing six thousand items. The life and revolutionary activities of Lenin are depicted in exhibits of historical documents, photographic essays, photocopies of manuscripts as well as first editions of his books, and models of houses and rooms in which he lived.

An exact replica of Lenin's study in the Kremlin is on view. Here one can see copies of his personal documents such as his party card, notebook, his credentials to Party Congresses, and questionnaires answered in his handwriting.

For the art enthusiast there are many paintings and sculptures of Lenin by Nikolai Andreyev, Sergei Merkurov, and Matvei Manizer, and others.

The cinema hall offers a film on Lenin with stills taken during his lifetime. Recordings of his speeches are also available.

The Kiev Branch of the Central Lenin Museum is open daily from 10 A.M. to 6 P.M.; Thursdays from 12 noon to 8 P.M.; closed Mondays. Trolley buses: 2, 7, 8, 9, 10, 12, 17; Buses: 2, 9, 20, 24, 38.

Museum of Ukrainian Art

The Museum of Ukrainian Art, located at 6 Kirov Street, was built at the end of the nineteenth century by architect G. Boitsov and civil engineer

V. Gorodetsky under the supervision of V. Nikolayev. Formerly the Museum of Science and Industrial Art, it was opened in 1936 and its galleries house one of the finest collections of art from the fifteenth century on. Works by classical and Ukrainian artists such as Taras Shevchenko, Vladimir Orlovsky, Konstantin Trutovsky, Sergei Vasilkovsky, Nikolai Murashko, and Nikolai Pimonenko are on display.

Works of the postrevolutionary period make up an extensive collection of paintings and sculptures. Painters and sculptors such as Ivan Izhakevich, Nikolai Samokish, Alexei Shovkunenko, Vasily Kasiyan, Tatiana Yablonskaya, and Mikhail Deregus are represented.

The Museum of Ukrainian Art is open from 11 A.M. to 6 P.M.; Thursdays from 11 A.M. to 5 P.M.; closed Fridays. Trolley buses: 1, 7, 8, 11, 13, 20; Buses: 62, 71; Tram: 16 to Lenin Komsomol Square.

Museum of Russian Art

The Museum of Russian Art, at 9 Repin Street, has more than thirty galleries containing collections of Russian art from the thirteenth century to the present.

One of the most interesting parts of the museum is the one devoted to ancient Russian art and its collection of thirteenth- to seventeenth-century icons.

The most extensive collection in the museum is from the nineteenth century. From the first half of the nineteenth century are works by Orest Kiprensky, Karl Bryullov, Alexander Ivanov, Vasily Tropinin, and Pavel Fedotov. Among the well-known artists of the second half of the century are Vasily Perov, Ivan Kramskoy, Vasily Makovsky, Nikolai Gue, Ilya Repin, Vereshchagin, Ivan Shishkin, and Mikhail Vrubel.

The museum is rich not only in paintings but has an extensive collection of fine sculpture. Included are works of Mark Antokolsky, Vasily Demut-Malinovsky, Feodosy Shchedrin, Karl Klodt, Stepan Pimenov, and Evgeny Lansere.

There are also outstanding exhibits of wood engravings by Vladimir Favorsky, watercolors by Kukriniski, and lithographs by Evgeny Kibrik and Boris Prorokov. Pre- and postrevolutionary porcelain, glass, and crystal also make for an interesting display.

The Museum of Russian Art is open from 11 A.M. to 5 P.M.; Wednesdays from 11 A.M. to 4 P.M.; closed Thursdays. Trolley buses: 9, 10, 12, 17; Buses: 2, 9, 20, 24, 38.

Museum of Western and Oriental Art

At 15 Repin Street is the Museum of Western and Oriental Art which was established in the 1870s with a private collection of Khanenko. The museum has two sections: Western European art (this section has a department of antique art) and Oriental art.

The collection of antique treasures includes Greek and Roman art from ancient towns of the Black Sea area. There is a fine exhibit of Roman copies of Greek sculpture and a collection of terra-cotta statuettes dated fifth to first centuries B.C. Also on display are black and red ceramics as well as medieval Byzantine icons and stained glass panels, grooved enamels, and carved ivory.

Renaissance and Baroque art of the Italian school of painting is represented by Giovanni, Bellini, Pietro Perugino, Jacopo del Cellaio, Luca Giordano, and Giovanni Battista Tiepolo.

The gallery of paintings from the Netherlands, Flemish, and Dutch schools of the fifteenth to eighteenth centuries provides an opportunity to view some of the greatest works of such masters as Pieter Brueghel the Elder, Peter Paul Rubens, Jacob Jordaens, and Frans Hals.

The Golden Age of Spanish art has a place in the museum and works by the realistic painters are on display. Diego, Velázquez, Francisco de Zurbarán, Juan Carreño de Miranda, and Goya are represented.

Eighteenth-century French art is represented by works by François Boucher, Jean Baptiste Greuze, and Jacques Louis David.

Traditional Chinese scroll paintings and carvings in ivory, stone, and wood are displayed in the Oriental section of the museum. Also exhibited are samples of Tibetan painting and sculpture and Japanese color engravings, paintings on silk, and Japanese arms of the fifteenth through nineteenth centuries. Ceramic pieces from Central Asia, Bokhara miniature paintings, and rugs from the Azerbaijan Republic of the U.S.S.R. are all quite beautiful, as are pieces of Buddhist sculpture of Thailand and Nepal and multicolored Turkish pottery.

The Museum of Western and Oriental Art is open from 11 A.M. to 6 P.M.; Thursdays from 11 A.M. to 5 P.M.; closed Wednesdays. Trolley buses: 9, 10, 12, 17; Buses: 2, 9, 20, 24, 28.

Shevchenko Museum

The Taras Shevchenko State Museum of the Ukrainian S.S.R. Academy of Sciences is located at 12 Shevchenko Boulevard. Established in 1949, it has twenty-four halls and more than four thousand exhibits which include over eight hundred works of the Ukrainian poet and painter.

The first thirteen halls of the museum are devoted to Shevchenko's personal life and work. The exhibits help the visitor learn and understand the social and political conditions in Russia and the Ukraine at the end of the eighteenth and the beginning of the nineteenth centuries. The living conditions of the people and of Shevchenko's father, the serf Grigory, are shown in these halls.

In 1831, at the age of sixteen, Taras moved to St. Petersburg and became associated with I. Soshenko, a student of the Academy of Arts. With the help of the St. Petersburg Society for the Encouragement of Painters, Shevchenko took a serious interest in art. On display in the museum are several drawings dating from the period of his association with Soshenko. The collection includes copies of engravings, drawings of plaster casts, and sculptures on themes from ancient Greece and Rome. There are also several portrait paintings that are quite good in view of the fact that Shevchenko had not yet had any formal art education.

Shevchenko's talent was recognized by several Russian critics and they decided to help him pursue a course of formal study. There was, however, one obstacle: Shevchenko was a serf and his owner, Engelgardt, demanded 2,500 rubles for his freedom. To raise the necessary funds, Karl Bryullov painted a portrait of the poet Vasily Zhukovsky and sold it at an auction. The proceeds were used to purchase Shevchenko's freedom on April 22, 1838. The Bryullov painting is on display in one of the halls.

Shevchenko graduated from the Academy of Arts in 1845 and left for the Ukraine, where he worked as an artist for the Kiev Archaeological Commission.

Arrested in April 1847 for belonging to the "Cyril and Methodius" secret society, Shevchenko was assigned to the Orenburg army corps and was forbidden, by order of the tsar, to write or paint. Despite the restriction, Shevchenko continued his work and the museum has on display a series of drawings and watercolors from this period.

Shevchenko was transferred to the Novo-Petrovsk Fort for disobeying the tsar's orders but through the efforts of his friends he was allowed to return from exile in 1857. In the summer of 1859 he was given permission to return to the Ukraine and many of the landscapes and portraits that were painted by Shevchenko in his native land are exhibited.

In 1860 a series of his etchings was exhibited at the Academy in St. Petersburg and he was awarded the title of Academician of Engraving. A copy of the diploma and the etchings are on display in the museum.

The remaining galleries of the museum present exhibits based on the theme "Shevchenko and Our Time." On display are copies of monuments that have been erected in Shevchenko's honor in the Soviet Union and abroad and collections of his writings.

The Taras Shevchenko State Museum is open from 10 A.M. to 5 P.M.; Tuesdays from 10 A.M. to 4 P.M.; Fridays from 10 A.M. to 3 P.M.; closed Mondays. Trolley buses: 9, 10, 12, 17; Buses: 2, 9, 20, 38.

Shevchenko Memorial Museum

The Shevchenko Memorial Museum is housed in a small seven-room house at 8 Pereulok Shevchenko. Unlike the State Museum, which portrays the entire life and times of the painter and poet, this small structure is devoted to "Shevchenko and Kiev."

The house opened as the Shevchenko Memorial Museum in 1928. Many of the landscape paintings of the artist are on display here, as well as valuable collections of sculpture, ceramic work, and rare publications of texts and documents.

The most popular room is the small attic in which he lived in 1846. Many of his personal belongings are on view, among them his easel, pencils and brushes, and clothing.

The Shevchenko Memorial Museum is open from 10 A.M. to 5 P.M.; Thursdays from 10 A.M. to 4 P.M.; closed on Fridays. Trolley buses: 1, 4, 7, 8, 11, 13, 16, 18, 20; Buses: 68, 71.

The Golden Gate

The fortifications surrounding Kiev had several entrances into the city. The main one was through the Golden Gate, built in 1037. The remains of the gate can be seen on the corner of Vladimirskaya and Bolshaya Podvalnaya streets.

In its complete state the gate was a heavily fortified structure with a double-tiered construction. The lower part consisted of a stone wall with an entrance arch bordering on the rampart; the top of the wall was the Annunciation (Blagoveschenskaya) Church, which is said to have been used as a watchtower. With the passing of time, the Golden Gate gradually lost its defensive status and was used as a means of entrance to the city on important occasions.

By the middle of the eighteenth century the Golden Gate was forgotten as it lay buried under layers of earth and rubble. Archaeologist K. Lokhvitsky discovered the remains in 1832 and arrangements were made to construct brick counterforts and metal reinforcements to protect the gate against further destruction.

St. Sophia's Cathedral

A gateway from Vladimirskaya Street opens onto the site of one of the most treasured and beautiful monuments in Kiev—St. Sophia's Cathedral. Like the Golden Gate, St. Sophia's Cathedral was built in 1037 during the reign of Yaroslav the Wise, as a symbol of the victory over the Pechenegs in 1036.

Reconstructions of the cathedral over long periods of time have to some extent changed its appearance. The original design had the structure surrounded on three sides by open arcades. The cathedral had thirteen cupolas with the central highest cupola above the wide nave and four aisles supporting three cupolas each. A second story was added at a later date and the southwestern tower was added. This occurred sometime during the reign of Yaroslav the Wise.

Work on the interior as well as the exterior continued as the walls of the cathedral were decorated with magnificent frescoes and mosaics.

The eleventh century saw the addition of the northwestern tower and the construction of a tomb for Vsevolod, the son of Yaroslav. During the twelfth and thirteenth centuries the stone walls were covered over with plaster.

Fresco paintings cover a major part of the interior and investigations have shown that the lower walls of the outer façade were once covered with fresco paintings. Unfortunately many ancient frescoes were destroyed during periods of reconstruction. There is, however, a beautiful collection of twelfth and thirteenth century frescoes covering the walls, ceilings, arches, pillars, and pilasters. Visitors are especially attracted to the portrayal of the family of Yaroslav. The likenesses of the four younger daughters of Prince Yaroslav are on the southern wall with Anna, the future queen of France, in the foreground; on the northern wall are the four sons; and Yaroslav, the Grand Princess Irma, their elder daughter and future queen of Norway, Elizaveta, and their elder son, Vladimir, were painted on the western wall.

Many of the more interesting paintings are on secular subjects: hunting scenes, animals and birds, as well as games and dances. These frescoes are on the walls of the spiral staircases and are the only surviving paintings showing everyday life in Kiev Rus.

Other arts are well represented in the cathedral, such as the fine examples of stonecarving and sculpture. On view is the unique marble sarcophagus of Yaroslav the Wise, covered with carved ornamentation.

One of the most important additions to the reconstructed exterior of the cathedral was the St. Sophia's Belfry. Built during the years 1699–1707, the belfry has fortunately been well preserved. It was originally constructed as a three-story structure, with the addition of a fourth story and a large gilded cupola in 1851–52. A two-story refectory was built between 1722 and 1730 in a typical Baroque style. On the initiative of A. Melensky, the chief architect of Kiev, it was converted into a winter church. Later additions to the cathedral include the former seminary building (eighteenth century) and a two-story structure, situated to the left, which housed the monastic cells.

St. Sophia's Cathedral played an important cultural as well as religious role in the life of the state. While the cathedral was originally looked upon as a symbol of Christianity and the power of the princes of ancient Rus, it was also a major center for the writing of manuscripts. The first Russian library was organized under its auspices and it was also the site for the reception of foreign ambassadors and the enthronement of princes.

St. Sophia's is open from 10 A.M. to 5 P.M.; Wednesdays from 10 A.M. to 4 P.M.; closed Thursdays. Trolley buses: 2, 4, 12, 16, 18; Buses: 20, 24, 38, 71.

Kiev-Pechersky Monastery

The Kiev-Pechersky Monastery, built in the middle of the eleventh century, covers a territory of 22 hectares (66 acres) consisting of two large hills and the valley between them. Kiev-Pechersky was the first Russian monastery and its name comes from the Russian word *peshchera*, meaning cave. The Higher Monastery (Lavra) is situated on the highest hill; the Near Caves occupy the valley with several buildings of various kinds; and the smaller hill is the site of the Far Caves with their churches and other facilities.

The Pechersky Monastery was built during a time when the Kiev princes, needing the support of the church because its backing lent divine authority to the existing feudal order, showered valuable gifts, including land, on the monastery. The beginnings of ancient Russian culture and the foundations of the cultures of the Russians, Ukrainians, and Byelorussians were laid during this time. Inside the monastery trades and arts developed, including the production of colored smalt used for mosaic work in ecclesiastical structures.

The first buildings of the monastery were constructed on what is now the Far Caves, including the Church of the Assumption of the Virgin, the first church of the monastery. Later, other cells were built on the site of the Near Caves.

The Church of the Trinity, built in 1108, has been extremely well preserved to this day. The structure was built above the central gates and functioned as a lookout post as well as a church. The interior is adorned with carved iconostasis and frescoes, the work of eighteenth-century Ukrainian craftsmen.

Another ecclesiastical structure is the Church of the Savior "at the village of Berestovo," situated on the outer side of the monastery walls. The village of Berestovo was once the domain of the Kiev princes. Prince Vladimir Monomach built the church at the turn of the eleventh century and in 1157 the body of his son, Yuri Dolgoruky, the founder of Moscow, was interred there. The interior is considered to be one of the last examples of Byzantine art and was decorated in the seventeenth century by Greek craftsmen from Aphon. In 1947, the eight-hundredth anniversary of the founding of Moscow, a granite tomb was erected over the grave of Yuri Dolgoruky.

With the invasion of the Mongol-Tatars in the thirteenth century, the power of Kiev was greatly weakened and the monastery was neglected. It was not until the fifteenth century, a time of great economic and political revival for Kiev, that the monastery underwent restoration and reconstruction.

As Kiev continued to advance at a rapid pace, the Pechersky Monastery grew wealthier and its lands increased. So rich did the monastery become that by the eighteenth century it was operating as a large-scale enterprise with 56,000 serfs and it owned thirteen monasteries, seven settlements, 189 villages, and three glassworks. This wealth aided in the construction of new ecclesiastical buildings within the borders of the monastery. Among them were All-Saints Church, over the Economic Gates (1696–98), the Church and Tower of St. Onuphri (1698–1701), and the Church and Tower of Ivan Kushchnik (1698–1701). New monastic cells were built at the end of the seventeenth century and churches were constructed on the sites of the Far Caves in 1696 and the Near Caves in 1700.

A structure that quickly catches the eye is the Belfry of the Higher Monastery, built in 1731–45. Reaching a height of 96 meters (314 feet) it was at one time the tallest building in Russia. Designed by the famous St. Petersburg architect Johann Shedel, the belfry follows an octagonal ground plan and has four proportioned tiers. Each of the tiers has a particular characteristic. The first tier is built of hewn stone slabs; the second is encircled by thirty-two Roman-Doric columns grouped in fours; and the third tier is surrounded by sixteen Ionic columns in groups of two. Eight Corinthian columns grace the fourth tier in groups of two while the cupolas are plated with gilded copper.

In the eastern part of the monastery grounds stands the Kovnir Building, designed by Stepan Kovnir, an architect and serf of the monastery. The building is one of the first civic structures of eighteenth-century Kiev. The south wing was used as a bakery. Later, a symmetrical building was added to house the monastery's bookshop. In addition to the building, there is also a Kovnir Belfry, built during the years 1754–61.

The Kiev-Pechersky Monastery Preserve is open from 10 A.M. to 5 P.M.; Mondays from 10 A.M. to 4 P.M.; closed Tuesdays. Trolley bus: 20; Bus: 62; Trams: 3, 27, 30; Metro: Station Arsenalnaya.

St. Vladimir's Cathedral

St. Vladimir's Cathedral is located opposite the Fomin Botanical Gardens on Shevchenko Boulevard. The cathedral was built to commemorate the nine-hundredth anniversary of the conversion to Christianity in Kiev Rus. Work began on the cathedral in 1862 and took thirty-four years to complete due to errors in architectural calculations. In 1866 these errors led to serious defects in the structure, including dangerous cracks in the walls, and for ten years work was at a standstill. Finally the building was completed in 1896.

I. Storm was the original architect of St. Vladimir's and P. Sparro later collaborated with him. The entire concept was later remodeled by A. Beretti. The interior was designed and decorated by several well-known scholars and artists from the Ukraine, among them A. Prakhov, V. Kotarbinsky, M. Nesterov, N. Pimonenko, P. Svedomsky, and V. Vasnetsov.

Vasnetsov's portrayal of the Madonna with Child set against a golden background is quite beautiful. Portraits of ancient Rus princes decorate the supporting pillars of the central nave and the northern and southern walls are braced with the *Last Supper, Christ Before Pilate,* and *Crucifixion* by Kotarbinsky and Svedomsky.

Trolley buses: 2, 6, 7, 8, 9, 10, 17; Buses: 2, 9, 38; Metro: Station Universitet.

Kiev University

The buildings of Kiev University occupy a square between Leo Tolstoy Street and Shevchenko Boulevard on one side and Vladimirskaya and Komintern streets on the other, with the main building in the center.

When the university was opened in the summer of 1834 it consisted only of a faculty of philosophy with two departments: history and philology, and physics and mathematics. Later the schools of law and medicine were introduced. During the university's first years there was no permanent building and classes were held in rented quarters in the Pechersk district.

Planning a permanent residence for the university, the Academy of Arts announced a competition for its design and the award went to an Academician of Architecture, Professor Vikenty Beretti, who began construction of the building in 1837. It was completed by his son, Andrei Beretti, in 1842.

The main building is in the typical Russian classical style. The central façade is 146 meters (479 feet) long and is ornamented by an eight-column portico in Ionic style. The construction of the building led to the building up of the immediate area.

Today the arts faculties are housed at 14 Shevchenko Boulevard, a three-story building constructed by Andrei Beretti in the 1850s.

The university saw its worst moments during World War II when, in the face of invading German troops, it was forced to evacuate to Kizil-Orda in the Kazakh S.S.R. Here, together with Kharkov University, it formed the Joint Ukrainian State University. In Kiev, most of the university equipment was plundered and rare volumes from the library as well as apparatus from the astronomical observatory were transported to Germany. During the German retreat from Kiev, the university building was blown up. It was reconstructed in 1950 by architect P. Aleshin.

Today the university serves 17,000 students in day, evening, and correspondence divisions. It has expanded to fourteen faculties: mechanics and mathematics, physics, radiophysics, chemistry, geology, biology, geography, history, philosophy, economics, law, philology, journalism, and foreign languages, and houses an observatory and a computer center. The university also has a botanical gardens, a scientific and research institute of animal physiology, experimental biology centers, museums of zoology, geology, paleontology, and archaeology as well as a publishing house for scientific literature and textbooks and a scientific library which contains over a million volumes.

In recognition for its outstanding achievements in the sciences, Kiev University was awarded the Order of Lenin in 1959.

Exhibition of Advanced Methods in Ukrainian Industry and Agriculture

The exhibition was opened on July 6, 1958, to mark the fortieth anniversary of the Ukrainian Communist Party. Covering an area of 337 hectares (832 acres), it has over three hundred buildings among which are the Central Pavilion, fourteen pavilions devoted to various areas of industry, the "Science" and "The Wealth of the Sea for Man" pavilions, and a center of agricultural meteorology. Advances in methods of crop growing and cattle breeding are shown through exhibits in more than thirty buildings. Models of new machinery and equipment are displayed in open-air exhibition areas.

The achievements of the Ukrainian people and prospects for the future are presented in the Central Pavilion's nine halls: Introductory, Industry, Agriculture, Science, Higher and Specialized Secondary Education, Culture, Art, Health, and People's Welfare.

The Hall of Industry gives a detailed account of all industrial operations in the republic. Exhibits show the development of industry as well as the growth of output and labor productivity. On display are models of industrial machinery and instruments.

The Hall of Agriculture is devoted to the work and achievements of Ukrainian farmers. Samples of grain are on display, as are many of the tools that are vital to successful farm production. The Hall of Science provides information concerning recent discoveries and research being carried out by Ukrainian scientists.

In the Halls of Culture, Health, and People's Welfare, visitors learn of the new schools, medical establishments, theaters, and cinemas built in the Ukraine. Along with these halls, the Hall of Higher and Specialized Education shows the work being done by the higher and secondary technical schools in the Ukraine.

The Hall of Art presents an excellent exhibition of painting, sculpture, and applied art from various periods of Ukrainian history.

A highly recommended pavilion on the exhibition grounds is the Pavilion of Mining and Metallurgy. At the entrance a large electric chart shows important mineral deposit areas and enterprises of the mining industry. An exhibit of mineral samples includes various ores, coal, and clays. Of great interest are working models of mines, quarries, blast furnaces, and one of the Inguhetsk ore-dressing works.

The Coal Industry Pavilion is one in which visitors can truly participate. On display are machines used for coal mining and coal loading and, to see them at work, visitors are invited to take a ride into a mine which is a replica of a highly mechanized coal-mining enterprise.

The Pavilion of Machine-Building and Instrument-Making Industries is quite interesting. The sections of the pavilion have exhibits on chemical engineering, heavy engineering, power engineering, agricultural engineering, machine-tool construction, automobile construction, instrument making, and automation equipment. Outside the pavilion are samples of mini-cars manufactured by the Zaporozhye "Communar" automobile works, buses made at the Lvov plants, tractors from Kharkov, and heavyweight trucks from the Kremenchug motor plant.

The Chemical Industry Pavilion presents various exhibits on the most recent achievements in the industry. One section shows the application of chemistry in agriculture. Methods of production of simple and compound mineral fertilizers, herbicides, and growth stimulators are illustrated.

Information on soil quality and the climatic zones of the Ukraine can be obtained in the Farming Pavilion, where interesting dioramas of the steppe and forest-steppe regions, the Polesye (Woodlands), and the Carpathians can be seen. Information is also available concerning the methods used to raise crop yield in the Ukraine.

One of the most popular pavilions is Vegetable Growing, Gardening, and Vine Growing. Standing in a huge orchard, the pavilion shows the work of hundreds of state farms in the vicinity of Kiev, Kharkov, and Donetsk. Exhibits show the latest advances in vine growing and wine making as well as information on the canning industry of the republic, which produces more than two hundred kinds of canned fruits and vegetables.

The Stock Breeding Pavilion always attracts many visitors to its livestock shows. The pavilion deals with areas such as cattle breeding, pig breeding, sheep and rabbit breeding, poultry raising, group maintenance, and mechanical cow milking.

The Hall of Science has exhibits that inform the visitor of achievements and advances made by Ukrainian scientists in areas of cybernetics, electrodynamics, mechanics, medicine, nuclear physics, and related areas. The Pavilion of "The Wealth of the Sea for Man" is visited by almost everyone who goes to the exhibition grounds. Exhibits in the pavilion give an excellent presentation and detailed account of marine life from microscopic fauna to the great mammals of the sea.

The Exhibition is on Fortieth Anniversary of October Prospect and is open daily from 9 A.M. to 9 P.M. in summer and from 9 A.M. to 5 P.M. in winter. Trolley buses: 11, 12; Buses: 1, 14, 23, 24, 56, 60, 61.

THEATERS

Ivan Franko Ukrainian Drama Theater

In 1920 Gnat Yura and Amvrosy Buchma, artists of the Ukrainian stage, founded the Ivan Franko Ukrainian Drama Theater in Vinnitsa. Using the Moscow Art Theater and the Maly Theater as its models, the company of the Ivan Franko Theater brought to the people the theatrical art of the Ukraine. Today the theater presents works of Ukrainian, Russian, and West European classical drama. The Ivan Franko Ukrainian Drama Theater is located at 3 Ivan Franko Square. Trolley buses: 1, 4, 7, 8 11, 13, 16, 18, 20; Buses: 68, 71 to Kalinin Square; Metro: Station Kreshchatik, north exit.

Taras Shevchenko State Opera and Ballet Theater

The Shevchenko Opera and Ballet Theater is located at 50 Vladimirskaya Street, in a small square on the site of the prerevolutionary municipal theater which was burned down in 1896.

The Ukrainian Opera and Ballet Theater was founded in 1926, and in 1936 it was awarded the Order of Lenin for its development of opera in the Ukraine. The theater was named after Taras Shevchenko in 1939 to commemorate the one hundred twenty-fifth anniversary of the poet's birth. The theater performs classical works by Ukrainian, Russian, and foreign composers as well as modern productions of Soviet artists.

Trolley buses: 2, 7, 8, 9, 12, 17; Buses: 20, 38.

Philharmonic Society

Located at 2 Vladimirsky Descent in the Hall of Columns is the State Philharmonic Society. The building, opposite Vladimirskaya Hill, on the other side of the Vladimirsky Descent, was built by architect V. Nikolayev in 1882. The Hall of Columns is the former meeting place of the prerevolutionary Merchants' Assembly. The hall is now dedicated to Nikolai Lisenko, a well-known and very popular Ukrainian composer.

The society, founded in 1929, gives regular symphony concerts as well as performances by soloists, choirs, and chamber orchestras. Artists from other Soviet republics and from other nations are often invited to perform in Kiev.

Trolley buses: 1, 4, 7, 8, 11, 13, 16, 18, 20; Buses: 62, 68, 71 to Lenin Komsomol Square; Tram: 16.

Musical Comedy Theater

The Musical Comedy Theater is at 51a Krasnoarmeiskaya Street. Formerly the People's House (Troitsky Narodny Dom), performances have been given here since 1903 when actors of the Ukrainian Drama Theater played for Kiev audiences. Not only has the building been used for drama, it was also the site of many prerevolutionary workers' meetings and it witnessed many a heated debate.

Trolley buses: 1, 10, 11, 12, 13; Bus: 41; Trams: 23, 24, 30.

PARKS AND RECREATIONAL AREAS

Fomin Botanical Gardens

The Fomin Botanical Gardens are connected with Kiev University and occupy 22 hectares (55 acres) of land. The first plots were laid out in 1841 when plants were brought from the Kremenetsk school for scientific research. The gardens are named for botanist Alexander Fomin, who in the 1920s conducted extensive research there.

Over two thousand species of plants from all over the Soviet Union and the world are represented, including the flora of the Caucasus, the Ukraine, and Siberia. There are species of tropical and subtropical plants as well as rare species such as the ginkgo, the tulip tree, the Indian ficus, the black pepper, and the cinchona tree. There are also forty species of palm trees and a large collection of cacti.

The Gardens are located at 1 Komintern Street. Trolley buses: 2, 6, 7, 8, 9, 10, 17; Buses: 2, 9, 38; Metro: Station Universitet.

Vladimirskaya Hill

Vladimirskaya Hill (Vladimirskaya Gorka) is one of the great attractions of Kiev. From the hill you have a beautiful view of Podol and the land on the other side of the Dnieper River. You can also admire the many bridges that span the river and the beach whose sands cover a large part of Trukhanov Island.

In the years 1830–40 a park was laid out on the slopes of the hill in the form of terraces and ash trees, maples, Canadian poplar, and chestnut trees add to its beauty. Visitors enjoy taking leisurely walks along the lanes lined with hedges of yellow acacia. The main area of the park is on the slopes of the right bank of the Dnieper.

In 1853 a monument to Prince Vladimir of Kiev was erected on the hill's summit, thus the name Vladimirskaya Gorka. The monument was designed by Vasily Demut-Malinovsky of the Academy of Arts of St. Petersburg and the work was executed by sculptor Pyotr Klodt. The statue of Prince Vladimir is of bronze and stands on an eight-sided brick base (designed by architect Konstantine Ton) which rests on a square slab with hewn steps and is covered with cast-iron plating. Dressed as an ancient Russian warrior, he is holding a cross in his right hand. The statue stands 4.5 meters high (14.8 feet) and weighs almost six tons. The height of the entire monument is 20.4 meters (70 feet) and it can be seen from a great distance because of its position on the hill.

Vladimirskaya Hill is part of a complex known as the Central Recreation Park, which also includes Pioneer Garden, Pervomaisky and Sovetsky parks, and Askold's Grave.

Trolley buses: 1, 4, 7, 8, 11, 13, 16, 18, 20; Buses: 62, 71; Trams: 3, 16, 27, 30.

Trukhanov Island

One of the most popular recreational areas in Kiev is Trukhanov Island. The beach on the island is easily reached by crossing the Park Bridge. A beautiful park with excellent sports and recreation facilities has been laid out and tennis courts, volley-ball nets, billiard halls, and table tennis equipment are available. There are, of course, fine swimming facilities. In winter the island is converted into a skiing and skating center and equipment may be rented.

Maxim Rilsky Goloseyevsky Forest-Park

The Goloseyevsky Forest-Park, located within the city limits of Kiev on the southern outskirts, was once part of a large forest that encircled Kiev hundreds of years ago. As Kiev grew and expanded, housing developments reached the forest area and today the park is still abundant with oaks, hornbeams, and lindens. After much work, the forest-park is now a pleasant and convenient place to visit. The park offers pavilions, shows, sports and game facilities, as well as an open-air theater which is used for concerts and lectures. There are also boating and fishing facilities and several restaurants and cafés.

The park is located at 87 Fortieth Anniversary of October Prospect. Trolley buses: 1, 11, 12; Buses: 1, 14, 24, 38; Trams: 9, 10, 24.

Pushche-Voditsa

Located 20 kilometers (12.5 miles) to the north of the center of Kiev is Pushche-Voditsa, one of the largest tracts of land in the city. The area is beautiful and peaceful with a very mild mean temperature. With various levels of turpentine, ozone, iodides, bromides, and chlorides in the atmosphere, Pushche-Voditsa is the site of treatment centers for cardiovascular ailments and diseases of the respiratory and nervous systems. Health facilities are open all year, the largest being the Pervoye Maya neurological sanitorium which can accommodate fifteen hundred patients.

A large and well-equipped recreation center is available with an assembly hall seating eight hundred, game rooms, a dance hall, and a winter garden. A tourist center is also available to help plan itineraries of Kiev and its surrounding areas.

USEFUL INFORMATION

Hotels

Dnipro, 1 Lenin Komsomol Square
Intourist, 26 Lenin Street
Kiev, 36 Vladimirskaya Street
Leningradskaya, 4 Shevchenko Boulevard
Lybid, Pobeda Square
Mir, 70 Fortieth Anniversary of October Prospect
Moskva, 4 Oktyabrskoy Revolutsii Street
Teatralnaya, 17 Lenin Street
Ukraina, 5 Shevchenko Boulevard
Zolotoi Kolos, 95 Fortieth Anniversary of October Prospect
Motel and Campsite Prolisok, Sviatoshino 5th Proceka

Restaurants and Cafés

LARGER RESTAURANTS

Dynamo, 3 Kirov Street
Kavkaz (Caucasian cuisine), 22 Krasnoarmeiskaya Street
Leipzig (German cuisine), 29/39 Sverdlov Street
Metro, 19 Kreshchatik Street
Praga (Czechoslovak cuisine), Fortieth Anniversary of October Prospect, Exhibition of Advanced Methods
Stolichny (Ukrainian cuisine), 5 Kreshchatik Street

SMALLER RESTAURANTS AND CAFES

Druzhba, Bulvar Druzhbi Narodov
Galushki, 6 Kreshchatik Street
Krasny Mak, 8 Kreshchatik Street
Kukushka (open-air), 16 Petrovskaya Alleya
Riviera (open-air), Petrovskaya Alleya

Varenichnaya, 44 Kreshchatik Street

Zakarpatskaya Troyanda (Ukrainian wines), 12 Krasnoarmeiskaya Street

There are also restaurants at all hotels.

Museums, Preserves, and Exhibitions

Branch of the Central Lenin Museum, 57 Vladimirskaya Street. Open from 10 A.M. to 6 P.M.; Thursdays from 12 noon to 8 P.M.; closed Mondays. Trolley buses: 2, 7, 8, 9, 10, 12, 17; Buses: 2, 9, 20, 24, 28.

State Museum of History, 2 Vladimirskaya Street. Open from 10 A.M. to 5 P.M.; Tuesdays from 10 A.M. to 4 P.M.; Thursdays from 11:30 A.M. to 6:30 P.M.; closed Wednesdays. Trolley buses: 2, 4, 12, 16, 18; Buses: 20, 38, 68, 71.

Museum of Ukrainian Art, 6 Kirov Street. Open from 11 A.M. to 6 P.M.; Thursdays from 11 A.M. to 5 P.M.; closed Fridays. Trolley buses: 1, 7, 8, 11, 13, 20; Buses: 62, 71; Tram: 16 to Lenin Komsomol Square.

Museum of Russian Art, 9 Repin Street. Open from 11 A.M. to 5 P.M.; Wednesdays from 11 A.M. to 4 P.M.; closed Thursdays. Trolley buses: 9, 10, 12, 17; Buses: 2, 9, 20, 38.

Museum of Western and Oriental Art, 15 Repin Street. Open from 11 A.M. to 6 P.M.; Thursdays from 11 A.M. to 5 P.M.; closed Wednesdays. Trolley buses: 9, 10, 12, 17; Buses: 2, 9, 20, 24, 38.

Shevchenko Museum, 12 Shevchenko Boulevard. Open from 10 A.M. to 5 P.M.; Tuesdays from 10 A.M. to 4 P.M.; Fridays from 10 A.M. to 3 P.M.; closed Mondays. Trolley buses: 9, 10, 12, 17; Buses: 2, 9, 20, 38.

Shevchenko Memorial Museum, 8 Pereulok Shevchenko. Open from 10 A.M. to 5 P.M.; Thursdays from 10 A.M. to 4 P.M.; closed on Fridays. Trolley buses: 1, 4, 7, 8, 11, 13, 16, 18, 20; Buses: 68, 71.

Lesya Ukrainka Memorial Museum, 97 Saksagansky Street. Open from 10 A.M. to 5 P.M.; Tuesdays and Fridays from 12 noon to 7 P.M.; closed Thursdays. Trams: 9, 10, 23, 30.

Museum of Theatrical, Musical and Cinema Art, 21 (block 6) Yanvarskogo Vosstaniya Street. Open from 10 A.M. to 5 P.M.; Mondays from 10 A.M. to 3 P.M.; closed Tuesdays. Trolley bus: 20; Bus 62; Metro: Station Arsenalnaya; Trams: 3, 27, 30.

Museum of Ukrainian Decorative Folk Art, 21 Yanvarskogo Vosstaniya Street. Open from 10 A.M. to 5 P.M.; Mondays from 10 A.M. to 4 P.M.; closed Tuesdays. Trolley bus 20; Bus 62; Metro: Station Arsenalnaya; Trams: 3, 27, 30.

Kiev-Pechersky Monastery Preserve, 21 Yanvarskogo Vosstaniya Street. Open from 10 A.M. to 5 P.M.; Mondays from 10 A.M. to 4 P.M.; closed Tuesdays. Trolley bus 20; Bus 62; Metro: Station Arsenalnaya; Trams: 3, 27, 30.

St. Sophia's Preserve, 24 Vladimirskaya Street. Open from 10 A.M. to 5

P.M.; Wednesdays from 10 A.M. to 4 P.M.; closed Thursdays. Trolley buses: 2, 4, 12, 16, 18; Buses: 20, 24, 38, 71.

Exhibition of Advanced Methods in Ukrainian Industry and Agriculture, Fortieth Anniversary of October Prospect. Open daily from 9 A.M. to 9 P.M. in summer and from 9 A.M. to 5 P.M. in winter. Trolley buses: 11, 12; Buses: 1, 14, 23, 24, 56, 60, 61.

Exhibition Hall of Union of Ukrainian Artists, 12 Krasnoarmeiskaya Street. Open from 12 noon to 7 P.M.; closed Tuesdays. Trolley buses: 1, 3, 10, 11, 12, 13, 20; Buses: 2, 9, 41.

Theaters, Concert Halls, Circus

Shevchenko Opera and Ballet Theater, 50 Vladimirskaya Street. Trolley buses: 2, 7, 8, 9, 12, 17; Buses: 20, 38.

Ivan Franko Ukrainian Drama Theater, 3 Ivan Franko Square. Trolley buses: 1, 4, 7, 8, 11, 13, 16, 18, 20; Buses: 68, 71 to Kalinin Square; Metro: Station Kreshchatik, north exit.

Musical Comedy Theater, 51a Krasnoarmeiskaya Street. Trolley buses: 1, 10, 11, 12, 13; Bus 41; Trams: 23, 24, 30.

Lesya Ukrainka Russian Drama Theater, 5 Lenin Street. Trolley buses: 1, 7, 9, 11, 13, 17, 20; Metro: Station Kreshchatik.

Puppet Theater, 13 Shota Rustaveli Street. Trolley buses: 1, 10, 11, 12, 13, 20 to Leo Tolstoy Square; Buses: 2, 9, 41; Trams: 3, 23, 24, 27, 30.

Philharmonic Society, 2 Vladimirsky Descent. Trolley buses: 1, 4, 7, 8, 11, 13, 16, 18, 20; Buses: 62, 68, 71 to Lenin Komsomal Square; Tram: 16.

Circus, Pobeda Square. Trolley buses: 6, 7, 8, 9, 17; Buses: 2, 9, 53, 71; Trams: 2, 6, 9, 13, 23, 25.

Cinemas

Dnepr, 1 Kirov Street
Druzhba, 25 Kreshchatik Street
Imeni Vatutina, 65 Krasnoarmeiskaya Street
Kiev, 19 Krasnoarmeiskaya Street
Kinopanorama (Cinerama), 19 Shota Rustaveli Street
Kommunar, 95 Artem Street
Komsomolets Ukraini, 17 Sverdlov Street
Pobeda, 79 Chkalov Street
Sputnik, 14 Iskrovskaya Street
Stereo Kino (stereo cinema), 29 Kreshchatik Street
Ukraina, 5 Karl Marx Street

Shops

Ukraina Department Store, Pobeda Square
Central Department Store, 2 Lenin Street
Podarki (gift shop), 9 Karl Marx Street
Detsky Mir (shop for children), 15 Kreshchatik Street
Kashtan (jewelry shop—foreign currency), 2 Shevchenko Boulevard
Perlina (jewelry shop), 19 Kreshchatik Street
Jupiter (photographic equipment), 3/5 Kalinin Square
Pottery and china, 34 Kreshchatik Street
Records, 24/2 Druzhby Narodov Boulevard
Irkusstvo (canvases, paintings, posters), 24 Kreshchatik Street
Dom Knigi (bookshop), 44 Kreshchatik Street
Central Food Store, 40 Kreshchatik Street
Confectionary, 4 Karl Marx Street
Crimean wines, 10 Kreshchatik Street
Trans Carpathian wines, 12 Krasnoarmeiskaya Street
Tobacco Shop, 12 Lenin Street

Transportation and Communication

Aeroflot Office, 66 Shevchenko Boulevard, Tel: 24–25–26
Train Inquiry Office, Tel: 21–90–96
Advance Railway Booking Office, 14 Pushkinskaya Street, Tel: 23–47–71
    (open daily from 9 A.M. to 8 P.M.)
Central Post Office, 22 Kreshchatik Street
Central Telegraph Office, 10 Vladimirskaya Street
Lost and Found Offices:
    For trolley buses, trams, and Metro, Tel: 36–90–13, Ext. 6
    For taxis, Tel: 46–17–36; 97–42–24
    For railways, Tel: 23–30–50

OTHER CITIES
IN EUROPEAN RUSSIA

Novgorod, Yaroslavl, Rostov, Smolensk, Orel, Kharkov, Volgograd

NOVGOROD—General Information and History in Brief

Novgorod is the administrative center of the Novgorod Region and is located 189 kilometers (113 miles) south of Leningrad along the Leningrad-Moscow Highway (Motor Road #10). This well-known historical city, which is over eleven hundred years old, played an important part in the founding of the Russian state, especially during the Middle Ages and early Renaissance. Owing to its location on the banks of the Volkhov River near Lake Ilmen, Novgorod was well situated at a major crossing of the Eastern European trade routes. Today Novgorod is an important industrial and cultural center in one of the best-developed areas in northwestern Russia. One will find here an intricate blending of the old and new. During World War II, the city was severely damaged and was designated as one of the fifteen principal cities to be reconstructed immediately after its liberation from enemy troops. Since the city's restoration large-scale housing construction has taken place, and the population has swelled to 90,000. The principal industries of Novgorod are machine building, timber and food processing, and chemical refining. Among the scientific and cultural institutions is the Novgorod Teacher Training Institute, well known throughout this area of Russia.

Novgorod was founded during the ninth century by the Ilmen Slavs. When Prince Oleg of Novgorod conquered Kiev he transferred the seat of government to his city. In 989 Christianity was adopted. For three centuries the political life of Novgorod was controlled by the princes. However, in 1136 numerous riots occurred which resulted in the seizure of all of the city's possessions by the bishop and the nobles. The Veche-Novgorodian People's Assembly was formed, and it was only by special invitation from the Veche that Kiev princes could visit the city. Moreover, the princes could come only as military leaders accompanied by professional soldiers to lead the Novgorodian army. Other rights and duties of princes were also specified. Thus, in the middle of the twelfth century, Novgorod became an independent city-state of merchants and nobles.

In comparison to other areas of Russia, Novgorod was virtually unaffected by the Tatar invasions of the early thirteenth century. This was mainly due to impassable swamplands and very bad roads. However, during the mid-thirteenth century, Novgorod succumbed to the Tatars because a new threat to northwest Russia occurred simultaneously. This was the combination of Teutonic Knights and the Order of Sword-Bearers who approached via Germany and Sweden. The Swedes attacked Russia during the summer of 1240. Prince Alexander Yaroslavich of Novgorod, aided by the joint forces of soldiers and armed citizens, defeated the Swedes on the banks of the Neva River. Henceforth, Prince Alexander was surnamed Nevsky. In 1242 he defeated the Teutonic Knights in a historic battle on the ice of Lake Chudskoye.

From the thirteenth to fifteenth centuries the importance of Novgorod increased because of its military prowess and location on the principal trade route between the Baltic and Black seas. During this period, the city was called "Lord Novgorod the Great." In 1478 Grand Duke Ivan III of Moscow defeated the Novgorod boyars, and Novgorod was joined to the Moscow principality. In 1570 Ivan IV (the Terrible), suspecting the Novgorod merchants of disloyalty, ordered several thousand people of the city to be executed. By the mid-seventeenth century, the population had been reduced from 50,000 to about 8,000. When St. Petersburg was founded in 1703, the city of Novgorod ceased to flourish. However, in its prime it had been one of the best-planned and best-built cities of Europe. Novgorod streets were paved five hundred years before those of London and two hundred years before those of Paris. The reconstruction of Novgorod, a project of the past three decades, was designed by Shchusyev, a prominent Soviet architect. The restoration of ancient historical monuments, combined with the construction of modern facilities, has resulted in the creation of a magnificent organic architectural ensemble.

Museums and Places of Interest

NOVGOROD KREMLIN

The principal feature of Old Novgorod is the kremlin or citadel which is located along the embankment of the Volkhov River. Today there are twenty-three points of interest within the kremlin, of which nine are watchtowers, four are churches, five are residential structures reserved for church officials, two are bell towers, and the remainder include a belfry, government offices, and a monument commemorating the Russian millennium. The original Novgorod citadel was built during the ninth century and consisted of wooden structures. The first stone walls were constructed in 1044, but have not survived. The walls one sees today, as well as the remaining structures, are products of the fifteenth century.

Of the eleven towers existing in the fifteenth century, nine remain, each with a name and specific characteristic. Palace (Dvortsovaya) Tower is located at the southeastern part of the kremlin. Savior's (Spasskaya) Tower served as a gate tower. Prince's (Knyazhaya) Tower is similar in structure and function to Dvortsovaya. Kokui Tower was built near the end of the seventeenth century with an upper platform for cannons. Intercession (Pokrovskaya) Tower is unique among the kremlin towers in that the upper tier is formed by an overhang perforated with gun holes for firing down upon the enemy. It was named for the Church of the Intercession, built in the Novgorod kremlin in 1389. Before being converted to use as a gun tower it was used as a gate tower. Zlato-Ustovskaya Tower was converted into a torture chamber during the sixteenth century. It was previously called Prison (Tyuremnaya) or Devil's (Chortova) Tower. The new name was derived in the seventeenth century from the nearby Church of John the Golden-Tongued (Ioann Zlatoust). Metropolitan Tower and Fyodorovskaya Tower, adjacent to each other, were erected in the fifteenth century. Vladimirskaya Tower, named for Prince Vladimir's Gate Church, was a gate tower built in 1311. Numerous hidden chambers and secret passageways leading from structure to structure have also been discovered in the kremlin walls.

The most prominent feature of the Novgorod kremlin is the Cathedral of St. Sophia, thought to be the shrine of ancient Novgorod. The cathedral, the oldest in Novgorod, was built between 1045 and 1052 by architects brought from Kiev. After 1136, when control of the government was transferred to the archbishop and the nobles, the cathedral became the political center of Novgorod life. The central dome of St. Sophia is a reproduction of an ancient Russian warrior's helmet. At the top are a cross and a dove. A local legend states that Novgorod will stand until the dove departs. At the western entrance to the cathedral are the Sigtuna Doors. These were designed and built in Magdeburg between 1152 and 1154 by Riquinius and Wiasmut. It is believed that the doors were originally commissioned by the Bishop of Plotzk and were captured in 1187 from the ancient Scandinavian capital of Sigtuna, where they had been the town gates. The doors, made of oak, are overlaid with forty-eight bronze plates in high and low relief depicting scenes from allegory, myth, and the Old and New Testaments. Only a few of the frescoes inside the cathedral are visible today, the best of them along the south wall, painted during the eleventh century. The remains of the eleventh-century mosaics have been moved to local museums. The cathedral's tower at one time held the church treasure in assorted secret repositories. The Pskov Chronicle relates that when Ivan the Terrible came to Novgorod in 1547 he ordered the torture of the St. Sophia sexton and sacristan so that they would divulge the location of the treasure. Loyal to Prince Vladimir, the churchmen revealed nothing. Taking an educated guess, the tsar commanded that the wall to the right of the staircase be broken open. This accomplished, the treasure spilled out onto the floor. It was promptly loaded into carts and taken to Moscow.

Other examples of medieval Russian secular and church architecture are also located within the kremlin. One of these is Archbishop's Court (Vladychny Dvor), the fifteenth-century structure which housed the archbishops of Novgorod. This is located just behind St. Sophia's Cathedral. In the middle of Vladychny Dvor is the Faceted Chamber (Granovitaya Palata). The Palata is what remains of an earlier ensemble built in 1433. It was here that the Soviet Gospod (Council of Lords) convened under the chairmanship of the archbishop. The building underwent subsequent changes, but there are many rooms in which the original design has been preserved. During World War II, the Palata was used by the Germans as an officers' casino. For this reason it was the only structure in the kremlin to be left unharmed. Today the Palata contains exhibits of articles from St. Sophia and other churches. The Clock Tower (Yevfimiyevskaya Chasozvonya) was erected in 1443 as a watchtower, but a clock was later installed, thus changing its function and name. The tower collapsed at the end of the seventeenth century but was rebuilt. Other structures of interest to the visitor are the Church of Sergei Radonezhsky, the St. Sophia Belfry, Archbishop's Palace, Church of Andrei Stratilatis, Church of the Intercession, Church of the Entrance into Jerusalem, Likhudov's Quarters, Nikitsky Quarters, and the Monument to the Russian Millennium. There is also the Novgorod Art and History Museum within the kremlin. Here one will find over 30,000 items including archaeological discoveries, ancient Russian art treasures, and a gallery of paintings representing modern Russian and Soviet artists.

Across the Volkhov River from the kremlin was the Marketplace (Torgovaya Storona). The visitor will see in this area four important churches. Ioann-na-Opokakh Church, built in 1127–30, was partially reconstructed in 1453. It is located on Herzen Street. On Lenin Prospect is Uspenya-na-Torgu Church, built in 1135–44. Gheorghiya-na-Lubyanitse Church, on Pervomaiskaya Street, was constructed during the seventeenth century, just before the decline of Novgorod. St. Supraxia's Church (Paraskeva Pyatnitsa) was built in 1207 by Novgorod merchants involved in overseas commerce. The church, located near Yaroslav's Court, was reconstructed in 1345. Yaroslav's Court (Yaroslavovo Dvorishche) served as the pagan burial grounds and sacrificial site up to the adoption of Christianity by the

Novgorodians in 989. From the end of the eleventh to the early twelfth century, the area was the residence of Prince Yaroslav the Wise. After that time it became the place for popular assemblies which served as the legislative body of the city. In Yaroslavovo Dvorishche is St. Nicholas Cathedral (Nikolo-Dvorishchensky). It is the second oldest church in Novgorod. Built in 1113, it served as the court church of the Novgorod princes. Two other churches are also located here. These are the Prokopiya Church, built in 1529 in the style of Moscow architecture, and the Church of Zhen-Mironosits, built in 1510. This church was dedicated to the women who brought herbs for embalming the body of Christ. On Torgovaya Storona one will also find the Coaching Palace (Putyevoy Dvorets). Built in the eighteenth century, presumably by Vassily Bazhenov, the small palace was for the use of the imperial family during travels through Novgorod. Located on Herzen Street, it is now designated as a House of Culture.

South of Novgorod about 1 kilometer (.6 mile) along the Volkhov is a hill called Gorodishche. Primitive tribes, essentially hunters and fishermen, dwelled there. During the twelfth century the Novgorod princes resided at Gorodishche following the changes in government which limited their rights and privileges and forced them to leave the kremlin. The tsars also stayed at Gorodishche. At the end of the seventeenth century Gorodishche was given as a gift by Peter I to his favorite prince, Alexander Menshikov. During World War II, all of the buildings on the estate were destroyed. The nearby Church of Our Saviour-on-Nereditse (Spasa-na-Nereditse), built in 1198, was also razed, but has since been restored.

USEFUL INFORMATION

Hotels and Campsite

Hotel Sadko, 20 Gagarina Prospect
Hotel Volkhov, 24 Nekrasova Street
Campsite Novgorod, Vishersky Canal Embankment, 11 kilometers (6.6 miles) south of Novgorod on the Leningrad-Moscow Highway (Motor Road #10)

Restaurants

Sadko, Hotel Sadko, 20 Gagarina Prospect
Volkhov, Hotel Volkhov, 24 Nekrasova Street
Self-Service Buffet, Campsite Novgorod

YAROSLAVL AND ENVIRONS—General Information and History in Brief

Yaroslavl is an ancient town located 260 kilometers (156 miles) northwest of Moscow along Motor Route #9. It was founded in the ninth and tenth centuries, during which time the Medvezhi Ugol village was settled. During this era, Rostov the Great was the center of northeast Russia. In 1010 Prince Yaroslav the Wise of Rostov conquered the villagers of Medvezhi Ugol and founded a fortress which was named for him. Yaroslavl developed rapidly because of its favorable location along the Volga trade route. In 1218 it became the capital of the independent feudal Yaroslavl principality. In 1463 the principality merged with the Moscow state. During the seventeenth century Yaroslavl became a port of entry into Russia, and by 1634 the city had advanced to third place after Moscow and Kazan as a center of trade. The Poles invaded Moscow in 1612, and the capital of Russia was temporarily moved to Yaroslavl. It was here that the Home Guard was formed which subsequently expelled the Polish forces. With the establishment of St. Petersburg as a port during the eighteenth century, Yaroslavl's position as a foreign trade depot ceased to be as vital as it had been. Nevertheless, the city retained its importance as an economic and cultural center. The first Russian theater was established in Yaroslavl by Fyodor Volkov in 1750, and the first Russian provincial magazine had its origins here in 1786. By the twentieth century the city had numerous thriving enterprises, such as textiles, food processing, paint, lacquer, and timber processing.

Since the advent of Soviet power, new industries have appeared in Yaroslavl. Of major importance was a synthetic rubber plant, established in 1932, which by 1940 produced almost all of the automobile tires in the Soviet Union as well as one-third of all synthetic paints, lacquer, and rubber. The economic upsurge has been especially dynamic since the end of World War II. One major factor was the establishment of the Novo-Yaroslavsky Oil Refinery, to which oil was piped from the Tatar Republic. This led to the production of diesel engines, electric motors, and other industrial machinery and equipment. Today Yaroslavl is an important railway junction and river port as well as an industrial and cultural center in northwestern Russia. The population has reached the half-million mark. Bisected by the Volga River, Yaroslavl encompasses an area of 265 square kilometers (102 square miles).

MUSEUMS AND PLACES OF INTEREST

A walk through the Old City will provide the visitor with an opportunity to see the major points of interest in Yaroslavl. Among the oldest monuments of the past are three churches: the Church of Our Lady's Assumption, constructed of brick in 1215; the Church of the Savior, built in 1216; and the Church of the Transfiguration and Transfiguration Monastery, built in 1218. Near these churches are the remains of the old earthen ramparts and brick towers which enclosed the Old City. An outstanding monument of twelfth-century architecture is the Spasso-Preobrazhensky Monastery. The next major phase of Yaroslavl architecture can be seen in the seventeenth-century churches, including the Church of John the Golden-Tongued, Church of John the Baptist, Church of Mikola Mokry, and Church of Elijah the Prophet. The paintings and frescoes of these churches mark a major change in the evolution of Russian religious art. Innovations can be seen in the use of bright colors and the humanization of religious subjects. While in Yaroslavl, it is advantageous to visit the Nakrasov Estate Museum and the Museum Reserve, where numerous archaeological items as well as valuable specimens of fine and applied art can be seen. One should also visit the Museum of National History.

ROSTOV

En route back to Moscow is Rostov, a well-known ancient Russian town. It is located 57 kilometers (34 miles) south of Yaroslavl along Motor Route #9. Today Rostov is the district center of the Yaroslavl Region. At the height of its fame, the town was called Rostov the Great. Rostov was the stronghold of the Russian state as far back as the ninth century. In the eleventh century it was designated as the chief city of the Rostov-Suzdal principality. In 1207 it became the capital of the Rostov principality but merged with Moscow in 1474. Nevertheless, Rostov developed as an economic, religious, and cultural center because of its favorable location on the northern Russia trade route. A shift in routes brought about a decline of the town's development, and by the late nineteenth century Rostov was no more than a fading provincial town with a population dwindled to 15,000. Today Rostov is a small, quaint place with only about 10,000 permanent residents. Its principal attractions are the marvelously well preserved architectural monuments of the fifteenth, sixteenth, and seventeenth centuries.

One of the most interesting sites of Rostov is the ensemble of the Metropolitan House, or Rostov Kremlin. Built for Metropolitan Iona

Sisoyevich in 1670–83, it consists of a large square which contains the Metropolitan's Residence and the White Chamber, which was used for official receptions. Surrounding these structures is a stone wall atop which are numerous towers. The gateways in the wall have large churches built above them. Adjacent to the kremlin is the Assumption Cathedral, built during the fifteenth century. Next to the cathedral is a tall belfry, erected in 1680. Another imposing structure is the Cathedral of the St. Abraham Monastery, built in 1554. Ascension Church nearby was designed by the architect Andrei Maly and built in 1566. One of the rare nineteenth-century structures of Rostov is the Dmitri Cathedral of the Spasso-Yakolevsky Monastery. This was the work of serf architects who built the cathedral in 1802–04. Just outside Rostov is a magnificent monument of sixteenth-century architecture—the ensemble of the Monastery of St. Boris and St. Gleb.

Pereslavl-Zaleski

On the shores of Lake Pleshcheevo at the mouth of the Trubezh River, 66 kilometers (37 miles) south of Rostov, is Pereslavl-Zaleski. This town was founded by Prince Yuri Dolgoruky as a defensive stronghold for the Rostov-Suzdal lands. This history of the town is intimately connected with the development of Russia, particularly with the activities of Alexander Nevsky, Ivan the Terrible, and Peter the Great. In 1174 Pereslavl-Zaleski was the administrative center of the Pereyaslav principality which became part of the Moscow state in 1302. During the fourteenth and fifteenth centuries the town was besieged by the Tatars, and in the seventeenth century by the Poles. Thus the architecture of all structures, even the churches, was oriented toward fortification and defense.

Lake Pleshcheevo, the largest lake in Central Russia, is noted for its plentiful fish. Pereslavl herring *(ryapushka)* became famous during the fifteenth century as a delicacy and is still considered one of the best fish served in Soviet restaurants. Lake Pleshcheevo is also the birthplace of the Russian navy. It was here that Peter I built his first flotilla between 1688–93, and this became the first Russian naval school.

Many of the old churches remain in Pereslavl-Zaleski and are considered valuable monuments of Russian history. The oldest of these is the Savior of the Transfiguration Cathedral, built in 1152–57 in the time of Prince Yuri Dolgoruky. It is a small single-domed church of majestic simplicity, one of the earliest specimens of the Vladimir-Suzdal school of architecture. A particularly interesting structure is the Church of Peter the Metropolitan, built in 1585. One of the largest architectural ensembles is the Nikitsky Monastery, which was built over a period of years spanning the sixteenth and seventeenth centuries. The Nikitsky Monastery complex includes fortress walls and towers, a cathedral, refectory, belfry, and the Annunciation

Church. Another ensemble is the Danilov Monastery, of which the belfry and refectory are noteworthy. A special historical monument is Trinity Cathedral, built in 1532 by architect Grigori Borisov. The decorations were executed by the Kostroma artists under the tutelage of Guri Nikitin and Sila Savvin. The Holy Gates of the cathedral, built during the seventeenth century, are notable artistic works. Pereslavl-Zaleski has two branches of the Museum of Regional Studies. They are the Alexander Nevsky and the Ivan the Terrible museums and offer valuable data relating to the lives and times of those Russian rulers.

USEFUL INFORMATION

Hotels, Restaurants, and Cafés

Hotel Yaroslavl, 40/2 Ushinskogo Street
Medved (Bear) Restaurant, Hotel Yaroslavl, 40/2 Ushinskogo Street
Cafés: Yaroslavl, Rostov, and Pereslavl-Zaleski have cafés which serve hot
　　　and cold buffet-style foods.

SMOLENSK—General Information and History in Brief

Smolensk is located 377 kilometers (226 miles) due west of Moscow via Motor Route #1. It is accessible by car and train. Smolensk is one of the oldest Russian cities, dating as far back as Kiev and Novgorod. Most people associate the city with historical events, particularly military and revolutionary situations. Because of its location, Smolensk has suffered many invaders en route to Moscow. As the administrative center of the Smolensk Region, the city occupies a vital geographical position on the surface and inland water routes of western Russia. The Dnieper River flows through the city. World War II left Smolensk in ruins. The postwar period has been one of successful renovation and reconstruction. Today, with a population nearing 250,000, Smolensk is a highly industrialized educational and cultural center. Among the numerous factories are those specializing in motor vehicle parts, automatic machinery, radio engineering equipment, electric light bulbs, woodwork products, knitted goods, shoes, fine linens, and diamond polishing. Among the higher educational establishments in Smolensk are institutes of medicine, pedagogy, physical culture, and engineering. There are four specialized technical schools, three vocational schools, two theaters, six cinemas, and a major museum.

The ancient lands of Smolensk were inhabited by Slavic tribes of the Gnezdovskaya-Timuli group. The date of settlement goes back to the sixth century. Over three thousand tombs from these tribes have been found by archaeologists. The year 863 has come to be considered the date of its founding. Smolensk's growth and importance were due to its advantageous situation along the Great Waterway. In the ninth century Smolensk became the chief town of the Slav tribe known as Krivichi. In the eleventh century it was incorporated into Kiev Rus, the ancient Kievan state during the reign of Vladimir Monomach. In 1229 trade agreements were made between Smolensk and several towns in Western Europe and Scandinavia, thus fortifying its already prominent trading situation. At the same time it became the capital of an independent feudal principality. Old Smolensk was typical of the feudal capitals of its day. On the elevated left bank of the Dnieper stood the fortress, known as the Detinets (Kremlin). At the center of the fortress was the Monomach Cathedral, which no longer remains. On the right bank of the Dnieper was the *posad*, a settlement of merchants and artisans. At the center of the posad was the St. Peter and Paul Cathedral. Smolensk princes resided on the banks of the Smiadin River among their own fortified palaces and churches. Of these, the most notable was the St. Boris and St. Gleb Temple, erected in 1145–46.

Hard times were brought upon Smolensk by foreign invaders. The Tatar-Mongols and the Lithuanians arrived in the later part of the fourteenth century. The plague of 1388 weakened the population and allowed the Lithuanians to gain control in 1395. They were expelled in 1401 but returned in 1404 under Lithuanian Prince Vitovt. Again the Lithuanians were routed by a popular uprising in 1440, and again they returned. During the early part of the sixteenth century the Moscow state sent aid to Smolensk and the city was liberated from its captors. However, in August 1609 Polish King Sigismund and his regiments attacked and successfully occupied Smolensk after a two-year siege. A series of wars was fought for Smolensk by the Moscow state which succeeded in expelling the Poles in 1654. In 1709 Peter I recognized the strategic importance of the city and proclaimed Smolensk a provincial capital. During the Northern War (1700–1721), Smolensk became the prize target of King Karl XII of Sweden, but the plan to seize the town failed after a bloody battle. Peter I ordered the refortification of the town with an elaborate and virtually impenetrable defense system. For almost a century Smolensk was inviolate.

During the War of 1812 Napoleon planned to capture Smolensk on his way to Moscow. For three days French troops failed to take the town. On the fourth day they found it abandoned and in flames. Smolensk was a turning point in the war, for the way both to and from Moscow lay along the Smolensk road and was marked with heavy losses for Napoleon. On the return trip, however, he ordered the destruction of the structures still standing, including the Smolensk Kremlin, which the Russians had deliberately spared.

It was several years before the traces of destruction were removed from Smolensk. Industry and commerce revived slowly over the following decades, but the building of the railroads during the mid-nineteenth century proved the strongest impetus for redevelopment. By 1870 Smolensk had become a major railway junction on both the north-south and east-west routes. In 1903–05 a transportation-technical office for the Russian Socialist Democratic Labor Party (RSDLP) was located in Smolensk. During the Civil War Smolensk was a frontline town with Western Front Headquarters and the RSDLP Northwest Regional Committee stationed there. The October Revolution greatly changed the life of the town. By 1940 the industrial, educational, and municipal facilities had increased.

World War II was a disaster for Smolensk, which was among the first towns in Russia to be bombed. During 1940–42 continuous assaults were made on the area, but in 1942 the liberation of the Smolensk Region began and was completed in 1943. Again, Moscow had been spared by the defensive position of Smolensk, which lay in ruins. Shortly after the war, eight common graves were uncovered containing the remains of 135,000 people. Once again, Smolensk was rebuilt. Today it is a thriving industrial and cultural city with grim memories and a bright future.

PLACES OF INTEREST

Smolensk Regional Museum of Local Lore is the only museum in Smolensk. It is divided into three sections, all of which have separate locations. The first is the Natural History Department, located at 7 Soborny Dvor. This is devoted primarily to the natural resources of the entire Smolensk Region and features their economic utilization as a principal theme for exhibits. The second section is the Historical Department, located at 9 Lenin Street. The range of exhibits covers the history of the Smolensk Region from ancient times to the postwar period. The oldest items on exhibit are from the archaeological expeditions into the burial mounds of Gnezdovsky-Tumili, the tribal settlements of ancient Smolensk. Among the displays are samples of messages, written on birchbark, concerning trade between Smolensk and Novgorod during the thirteenth century. Several exhibits are devoted to the role of Smolensk against foreign invasions, particularly during the seventeenth century against the Poles, the eighteenth century against the Swedes, and the nineteenth century against Napoleon. Another exhibit is centered around the revolutionary movement of the Smolensk Region. The section on Soviet history begins with the October Revolution and displays the photographs and personal effects of Smolensk participants in the storming of the Winter Palace and the Civil War. Other exhibits deal with prominent Soviet leaders who have visited Smolensk. An extensive section is devoted to World War II. Finally there is a special exhibit concerning Yuri Gagarin, an honorary citizen of Smolensk. On display are photographs, personal effects, and gifts sent to the cosmonaut.

The third section of the museum is the Picture Gallery, located at 7 Krupskoy Street. It features a collection of European, Russian, and Soviet pictorial art and sculpture, arranged chronologically. The Western European collection was started by Maria Tenisheva, an artist and patron of art of the nineteenth century who also founded the Smolensk Art Museum. Represented in this display are fifteenth- to nineteenth-century works from Italian, Dutch, Spanish, French, German, and Flemish artists. The Russian exhibit is represented by eighteenth-, nineteenth-, and twentieth-century painters, with special emphasis on Russian classicism of the eighteenth century. Soviet art is also strongly represented, with emphasis on works by artists of the Smolensk region.

Talashkino

The Smolensk Museum of Local Lore has a branch in the village of Talashkino, which is 13 kilometers (8 miles) south of Smolensk along the Roslavsky Highway. Talashkino is located on the Sozh River and is famous for its magnificent old oak groves. Atop the village hill is a two-story wooden house decorated with brightly painted fretwork. The house is situated on the former estate of Maria Tenisheva. It was here that she provided studio space for such noted Russian artists as Ilya Repin, Victor Vasnetsov, Vasily Polenov, and Mikhail Vrubel. The log walls of the upper story are decorated with carved plates and cornices painted with illustrations from Russian folk and fairy tales. The house was designed by the artist Sergei Malyutin, whose specialty was Russian antiquities. The illustrations on the house were painted by Mikhail Vrubel and Maria Tenisheva. In the house is an excellent collection of local folk art. Included in the exhibits are embroideries and lacework, carvings, and paintings.

Ioann Bogoslav Church

This is the oldest structure remaining in Smolensk. Built between 1160 and 1180, it is located on the left bank of the Dnieper. The church is a four-pillared building with three semicircular apses. The façades, separated by pilaster strips, are decorated with relief work in the shape of Byzantine crosses. The upper parts of the walls contain narrow slit-windows. Burial vaults were placed on three sides of the base of the church. Alterations carried out during the eighteenth century distorted the original lines of the building, but recent restoration work has brought it into conformity with its earlier design.

Petropavlovskaya Church

The second-oldest structure in Smolensk, this church was built almost simultaneously with Ioann Bogoslav Church; on the right bank of the Dnieper, it is located near the Smolensk Railway Station. The building was given a cruciform shape supported by four pillars. The western side is occupied by the choir box, accessible by a spiral staircase within the wall. The roof of the vault-shaped main body of the church is adorned with a row of small arches with *kokoshniks* at the top. The interior of Petropavlovskaya Church was decorated with polychromatic frescoes of the Kiev style. Only fragments of the frescoes remain. Adjoining the church on the west is the former episcopal palace with its private Church of St. Barbara. There is also a belfry on the western side. The adjacent buildings are products of the eighteenth century.

Michael Archangel Church on Smyadin (Svirskaya Church)

Erected in 1191–94, this church was ordered to be built by Prince David Rostislavovich near his residence at the northern end of Smolensk. The church is better known as Svirskaya because of its location where all roads from the northern lands (Svirsk) converged. Svirskaya is essentially a cruciform structure, supported by four pillars. The external decor consists of corner pilasters and splayed portals. The roof consists of a dominant central tower topped by a *baraban* (the crowning cylindrical or octagonal structure) with a low cupola. The corners of the church stand lower than the rest of the building and are crowned with domes standing at right angles which give the walls an unusual appearance.

Smolensk Kremlin

A towering structure on the left bank of the Dnieper, the Smolensk Kremlin was built between 1595 and 1601 to replace the crumbling remains of the old fortifications. The work was ordered by Tsar Fyodor Ivanovich, supervised by his brother-in-law, Boris Godunov, and built by people selected from all over the Moscow state. The architect Fyodor Kon is credited with the major structural plan. The walls were fortified with thirty-eight towers of which nine had gates. A large portion of the kremlin wall and fifteen towers remain. The tallest of the towers was Dneprovskaya, which had five tiers of loopholes instead of the three tiers built into the others. The tower was crowned with a turret and dome atop of which was a double-headed eagle poised for flight. The gate was made of oak reinforced with iron fittings. Beneath the gate was a moat. Makhovaya Tower, located between Smirnov Square and Shein Bastion, is tetragonal in design. Nikolskaya Tower guards the wall along Krasnogvardskaya Street in which a breach was cut in 1898 for traffic. The next grouping, along Timiryazev

Street, consists of Orel Tower, Pozdniakov Tower, and Veselukha Tower at the sharp turn of the kremlin wall. Between the Dnieper embankment and Sobolev Street are two towers and two gates. The most outstanding of these is Kostarevskaya Tower, round in shape, and constructed of red brick in 1835 to replace the previous one which had decayed with age and stress. Three other towers, Gromovaya, Bubleinik, and Kopytinskaya, are located in a section that is now the town park. The Royal Bastion, an earthen rampart built by the defenders of Smolensk during the Polish siege led by King Sigismund, whose troops had managed to penetrate the wall, is nearby. The Royal Bastion was later improved and fortified with underground cellars for storing ammunition and weapons. The last fragment of the kremlin wall, along with Donets Tower, is located in the Kutuzov Garden.

Assumption Cathedral

Located on Soborny Hill, the architectural center of Old Smolensk, is Assumption Cathedral. It was built to commemorate the defense of Smolensk against the Poles in 1609–11. According to the town records, the project was begun in 1677 but was not completed for nearly a century. The architect who designed the cathedral was Aleksei Korolov from Moscow, but completion of the structure was supervised by architect Gotfrid Schedel. The cruciform shape is achieved by the construction of three naves supported by four pillars. The eastern nave extends into three hemispherical apses. The exterior walls are divided into three sections by rectangular pilasters. The upper portion of the cathedral is encircled by a wide, multilevel cornice culminating in three column heads at the top of the pilasters. Seven cupolas originally crowned the cathedral, but only five remain. The helmet-shaped roof arrangement consists of *barabans* topped by onion-shaped domes.

The interior of Assumption Cathedral is noted for the iconostasis, with its spectacular fretwork. It is a hand-carved composition of wood comprised of columns that are separated by tiers of cornices. Between the columns carved panels frame the paintings. The murals of the iconostasis have been distorted during numerous restorative efforts. Only two retain their original appearance: "Great Archpriest" and "Holy Mother." The belfry of the cathedral was built in the late seventeenth century in a well-defined style of Russian Baroque. It was reconstructed in 1767, more in the Petersburg style. The belfry is small and quite decorative. A consistory was erected in 1790 in Russian classical style. It now serves as the repository of regional archives. The last structure in the Assumption Cathedral ensemble is Epiphany Cathedral. Built in 1794 to replace a wooden cathedral of 1712, it complements the grouping with its graceful, elegant lines. Pilasters and cornices adorn the façades, and surrounding the entire structure is a gallery enclosed by an iron grille. A stairway links the gallery with Bolshaya Sovetskaya Street and also leads to the Assumption Cathedral.

USEFUL INFORMATION

Hotels and Campsite

Hotel Rossiya, 2/1 Karl Marx Street
Hotel Smolensk, 11/30 Glinky Street
Campsite, 8 kilometers (5 miles) west of Smolensk along the Brest-Minsk-
    Moscow Highway (Motor Route #1)

Restaurants

Dnepr, Hotel Smolensk, 11/30 Glinky Street
Rossiya, Hotel Rossiya, 2/1 Karl Marx Street

Cafés

Sputnik, Nikolayeva Street
Zarya, Konenkova Street

Museums

Regional Museum of Local Lore:
    Natural History Department, 7 Soborny Dvor
    Historical Department, 9 Lenin Street
    Picture Gallery, 7 Krupskoy Street
    Talashkino Branch, 13 kilometers (8 miles) south of Smolensk on the
        Roslavsky Highway

Theaters and Concert Halls

Smolensk Drama Theater, 4 Karl Marx Street
Smolensk Puppet Theater, 5a Lenin Street
Philharmonic Society, 12/1 Bolshaya Sovetskaya Street

Department Stores and Shops

Main Department Store, 1 Gagarina Prospect
Smolensk Souvenir Shop, 1/6 Lenin Street

Transportation and Communications

Railway Station Inquiries, Tel: 2–15–20; 2–22–85
International Telephone Office, 6 Oktyabrskoy Revolutsyi Street, Tel: 3–
    06–00
General Post Office, 6 Oktyabrskoy Revolutsyi Street

OREL—General Information and History in Brief

Orel, located 350 kilometers (218 miles) south of Moscow, is one of the Soviet Union's major industrial and construction sites. The city, which got its name from the Orel River (today the Orlik River), was built by decree of Ivan IV in 1566. The purpose was to have Orel serve as a stronghold against the invasions of the Tatar-Mongols. Fifty years after these raids, Orel was destroyed by Polish invaders on their drive toward Moscow. The city was again raided by Crimean Tatars in the seventeenth century and in 1673 was almost totally destroyed by fire. After the fire, the city was moved to its present location.

Orel was an important center of trade in the eighteenth and nineteenth centuries. It was geographically advantageous because it was situated at the junction of important trade routes. After the construction of the railway to the south, the city lost its trade significance and the early part of the twentieth century saw Orel become a simple provincial town.

Today Orel plays an important role in the industrial makeup of the Soviet Union. Since World War II, almost one hundred enterprises have been set up here. Among the leading industries are textile machinery production and metalworking plants.

PLACES OF INTEREST

Many of the great masters of Russian literature were born in or near Orel, among them Ivan Turgenev, Nikolai Leskov, Ivan Bunin, Dmitry Pisarev, and Leonid Andreev. Two of Orel's largest museums are dedicated to these artists.

Turgenev State Literary and Memorial Museum

The Turgenev Museum offers reproductions of some of the rooms in Turgenev's house in Spasskoye-Lutovinovo. On display are portraits of the writer's relatives and paintings of mythical subjects as well as tables and chairs made of Karelian birch. Visitors can see the writing table at which Turgenev worked during his stay at Spasskoye.

The museum's library owns volumes annotated by Turgenev, books written by Turgenev that were published in Europe, Asia, and America, and rare Russian and foreign publications owned by the writer. Of the library's possessions, perhaps the most valuable is a large book collection of the famous Russian critic Vissarion Belinsky. Turgenev bought the collection after Belinsky's death.

The Turgenev Museum is located at 11 Turgenev Street and is open to the public daily, except Fridays, from 10:30 A.M. until 6 P.M.

Museum of Writers Born in Orel

In January 1957 a museum was opened at 24 November 7th Street. Dedicated to the lives and works of writers born in Orel, its location is the birthplace of the well-known historian Timofey Granovsky. Exhibited are the personal belongings as well as books, manuscripts, photographs, and documents portraying the lives and works of Granovsky, Nikolai Leskov, Dmitry Pisarev, Ivan Bunin, Leonid Andreev, and others.

The museum is open to the public daily, except Fridays, from 10:30 A.M. to 6:00 P.M.

Regional Museum

The Regional Museum is located at 1/3 Moscow Street and occupies the second floor of the Trade Rows building. The history of the Orel Region, its culture and nature are the primary core of the museum's exhibits.

Aside from a widely representative display of archaeological finds, there is an interesting collection of seventeenth- and eighteenth-century articles used in everyday life. Included are embroidered holiday clothes worn by peasant women and luxurious table settings from the estates of Orel landlords—the Kurakins, the Romanovs, and others. The area of the museum concerned with recent history offers exhibits portraying the Soviet Union's role in World War II.

The Regional Museum is open daily, except Tuesdays, from 9 A.M. until 5 P.M.

There are many monuments in Orel, among them one to Lenin, one to the aviation designer Nikolai Polikarpov, and one to Major General Gurtyev, who died in the fight to retake Orel from German forces. The city park now houses on display the first tank that entered the city during the liberation drive.

Located on Lenin Square are the House of Soviets, the House of Communications, the Young Pioneers' Palace, an art gallery, and the Rossiya Hotel.

USEFUL INFORMATION

Intourist Office, 37 Gorky Street, Tel: 7–46–96

Hotels

Orel, 5 Pushkin Street
Rossia, 37 Gorky Street

Restaurants

Oka, 18/20 Lenin Street, Tel: 20–96
Orel, 5 Pushkin Street
Orlik, 228 Komsomol Street, Tel: 28–52
Rossiya, 37 Gorky Street, Tel: 7–46–91
Tzon, Krymskoye Shosse, Agricultural Exhibition, Tel: 39–14

Museums and Theaters

Museum of Writers Born in Orel, 24 November 7th Street. Open daily, except Fridays, from 10:30 A.M. until 6 P.M. Tel: 34–65.
Regional Museum, 1/3 Moscow Street. Open daily, except Tuesdays, from 9 A.M. until 5 P.M. Tel: 27–79.
Turgenev Museum, 11 Turgenev Street. Open daily, except Fridays, from 10:30 A.M. until 6 P.M. Tel: 27–59.
Philharmonic Society, 1 Sacco i Vanzetti Street, Tel: 24–76.
Puppet Theater, 5 Cooperativny Pereulok, Tel: 57–65.
Turgenev Drama Theater, Theater Square, Tel: 23–10.

Communications

Central Post Office, 43 Lenin Street, Tel: 30–38.

KHARKOV—General Information and History in Brief

Kharkov is located 722 kilometers (433 miles) south of Moscow at the junction of Motor Routes 4 and 13. Travelers by automobile will find Kharkov a pleasant stopover on the way north to Moscow, west to Kiev, southwest to Yalta, or southeast to Rostov-on-Don en route to the Caucasus. Kharkov is also a major railway junction. Formerly the capital of the Soviet Ukraine (1917–34), Kharkov is now an important industrial, cultural, and research center. There are about sixty research institutes in the city, along with twenty-two higher education facilities and the Maxim

Gorky University, founded in 1805. Principal industrial products include diesel engines, turbines, electric generators, lathes, tractors, and consumer goods. The visitor to Kharkov will find it typical of Ukrainian cities in its hospitality, gentle life-style, and attractive physical appearance, consisting of wide streets, carefully tended parks and gardens, and well-kept public buildings.

Kharkov was founded during the seventeenth century by Ukrainian immigrants from the Pridnieper territories. Originally it served as a military settlement for the liberation movement of the Ukrainians against the Polish nobility. During the early part of the eighteenth century, Peter I ordered that Kharkov's fortifications be extended and reinforced so that southern Russia and the Ukraine would be protected from the intrusion of the Swedes. During the same period Kharkov was rapidly becoming an important trade center, inhabited by merchants, craftsmen, and artisans. By the end of the nineteenth century sizable industries had developed in the city. The construction of the railroad connected Kharkov with the major areas of Russia and the Ukraine. Thus the city became vital as a transportation as well as a trade center. Kharkov was the place of assembly for the First All-Ukranian Congress of Soviets which proclaimed the Ukraine a Soviet Republic. The end of the October Revolution and Civil War brought about a new phase of economic development in Kharkov. Old industrial establishments were drastically reorganized and reconstructed to accommodate modern machinery and technology. New industries were similarly equipped and administered. The severe damage wrought upon the city, its enterprises, monuments, and housing has been repaired.

MUSEUMS AND PLACES OF INTEREST

State History Museum, 10 University Street

This museum contains exhibits pertaining to the history of Kharkov and the Ukraine. The principal themes of the items on display are the struggle of the Ukrainians against the Polish feudal nobility and the development of revolutionary activities in Kharkov. The museum is open from 10 A.M. to 6 P.M. every day except Tuesday.

State Museum of Fine Arts, 11 Sovnarkomovskaya

Open daily from 10 A.M. to 6 P.M., except Friday, this museum houses a collection of several thousand paintings and sculptural works of Russian and Ukrainian classical masters as well as Soviet artists. Represented here are Karl Bryullov, Ivan Shishkin, Vassily Surikov, Ilya Repin, Ivan Aivasovsky, and Isaak Levitan.

Cathedral of the Assumption (Uspensky Sobor) and Cathedral of the Intercession (Pokrovsky Sobor)

Both cathedrals are in center city on either side of Klochkovskaya Street. The Cathedral of the Assumption was erected during the seventeenth century and is of a simple but well-defined Baroque style. The bell tower of the cathedral was added at the beginning of the nineteenth century in commemoration of Napoleon's defeat by Russian troops. The Cathedral of the Intercession was constructed during the eighteenth century and displays features characteristic of Russian and Ukrainian classical architecture.

Dzerzhinsky Square

At the northern end of Klochkovskaya Street is Dzerzhinsky Square, one of the largest squares in any Soviet city, occupying an area of over 100,000 square meters (6 square miles). The square was designed during the 1930s. Included in the architectural complex are a state industrial building, administrative offices, organizations of science, culture, and design, the Maxim Gorky State University, and the Kharkov Hotel. At the center of the square is a monument to Lenin.

Sumskaya Street

Leading into Dzerzhinsky Square from the south is Sumskaya Street, the major thoroughfare of Kharkov. Between Sumskaya Street and the square is a public garden in which stands a monument to Taras Shevchenko, beloved poet of the Ukrainian people. Sumskaya Street has been the site of many public gatherings and revolutionary events.

At Number 13 is a house which bears a plaque commemorating the inception of the Ukrainian Government of Workers and Peasants, dated December 18, 1917. The Shevchenko Academic Ukrainian Drama Theater is located at Number 9. Next door, at Number 10, is the Kharkov Philharmonic Society. From Sumskaya Street it is pleasant to stroll the streets of Kharkov and enjoy the numerous monuments, parks, gardens, and restaurants.

USEFUL INFORMATION

Hotels and Campsite

Hotel Intourist, 21 Lenin Prospect
Hotel Kharkov, 2 Trinklera Street
Campsite Merefa, 18 kilometers (11 miles) south of Kharkov on the Moscow-Yalta Highway (Motor Route 4)

Restaurants

Dynamo, 3 Dynamoskaya Street
Kharkov, Hotel Kharkov, 2 Trinklera Street
Intourist, Hotel Intourist, 21 Lenin Prospect
Lux, 3 Sumskaya Street
Moskva, 14 Sverdlov Street
Teatralnyi, 2 Sumskaya Street
Tsentralny, 20 Rosa Luxemburg Square

Museums

State Museum of Fine Arts, 11 Sovnarkomovskaya Street
State History Museum, 10 University Street

Theaters and Concert Halls

Circus, 17 Millitsionera Square
Krupskaya Puppet Theater, 3 Krassina Street
Lysenko Academic Opera and Ballet Theater, 21 Rymarskaya Street
Musical Comedy Theater, 28 Karl Marx Street
Philharmonic Society, 10 Sumskaya Street
Pushkin Russian Drama Theater, 11 Chernyshevskaya Street
Shevchenko Academic Ukrainian Drama Theater, 9 Sumskaya Street
Young Spectators' Theater, 3 Krassina Street

Transportation and Communications

Railway Terminal, Sverdlov Street, due west of center city
Central Post and Telegraph, 15 Feyerbakha Square

VOLGOGRAD—General Information and History in Brief

Volgograd, formerly Stalingrad, is located 920 kilometers (552 miles) southeast of Moscow on the Volga River. The city has been rebuilt from the ruins of war into a major industrial and transportation center with a population now nearing three-quarters of a million. The visitor to Volgograd will find an impressively planned urban community of industrial, cultural, recreational, and residential areas interlaced with dramatic war memorials. Around the city a green belt has been planted to protect it from dry regional winds. The concentration of heavy industry in Volgograd has been the result of its location along the principal inland waterways, the Volga River and the Volga-Don Canal. The Volgograd shipyards play a vital role in the water transportation industry. Another major facet of

Volgograd industry is the Volga Hydroelectric Power Station, one of the largest in the Soviet Union. Among the many items produced by Volgograd enterprises are tractors, mining timbers, tankers, refined oil, steel, aluminum, and medical equipment. As a cultural center of the Volga region, the city has six institutes which include polytechnics, pedagogy, municipal engineering, agriculture, medicine, and physical culture. There are three theaters, several museums, libraries, cinemas, and a planetarium.

Originally called Tsaritsyn, Volgograd was founded in 1589, when a fortress was built southeast of the Moscow state to prevent attacks by Volga nomads. The defensive purpose of Tsaritsyn remained unchanged until the middle of the eighteenth century when it developed into a provincial town. With the building of the railroads and the increase of steamboat traffic on the Volga, Tsaritsyn developed into a trade and transportation junction during the latter part of the nineteenth century. In the early part of the twentieth century, iron and steel mills and processing plants for raw agricultural products were built in the town which was developing into a major industrial and commercial center of the Volga region. During the Revolution and Civil War, Tsaritsyn was an important stronghold against the White Army troops led by General Peter Wrangel and General Krasnov. In 1925 the city's name was changed to Stalingrad. The postwar five-year plans accelerated industrial development and Stalingrad became the site of the first Soviet tractor factory in 1930. The major achievement, however, was the construction of the Krasny Oktyabr Iron and Steel Mill. The legendary Battle of Stalingrad began in the summer of 1942 and lasted for two hundred days. Over two million people were involved in the several stages of military maneuvers which ultimately routed the Germans and turned the tide for the Soviets during World War II. Stalingrad was designated as a Hero City of the Soviet Union as the result of this encounter.

MUSEUMS AND PLACES OF INTEREST

Mamayev Hill

Among the most solemn and impressive World War II monuments is Mamayev Hill. Accessible from Lenin Avenue, Volgograd's principal thoroughfare, it is the highest point in the city. Here the visitor will find a magnificent architectural complex designed by Yakov Belopolsky and sculpted by Yevgeni Vuchetich. Mamayev Hill was the site of one of the most important and violent battles in the Stalingrad area—a battle that raged for five months. After the war, each square foot of ground was reputed to contain over twelve hundred fragments of ammunition. Today one ascends a spacious staircase leading to the hill of the complex. Along the walls are carvings which depict people of different ages and nationalities. The path leading to the summit ends at the monument of a soldier. He stands poised as the focal point of the Square of Those Who Stood Up to Death. Behind this square are the remains of walls on which bas-relief sculpture portrays episodes of the Battle of Stalingrad. The next section is the Square of the Fallen Heroes, in which six monuments stand around a pond. The final ascent leads to the Pantheon, an architectural composition called "Grief of the Motherland," and the final statue, of a woman holding a sword raised above her head. In the center of the Pantheon is a hand, seeming to emerge from the ground, in which burns an eternal flame.

Lenin Avenue

Returning from Mamayev Hill along Lenin Avenue, on the left, is an entrance to the Central Stadium, the principal sports complex of Volgograd. Continuing toward the center of the city, one comes to the monument to Lenin, erected in 1960 by Yevgeni Vuchetich. A left turn on Tambovskaya Street brings the visitor first to Pavlov's House, which was defended from total destruction for fifty-eight days during the war. The second structure of major importance is the Ruined Mill, a grisly memento of the war which stands, as it was left, shelled and gutted. During the war it was used as a Soviet army command post. Returning to Lenin Avenue one makes a right turn on Gagarin Street and finds at the corner of Peace Street the Volgograd Planetarium. The building was a gift to Volgograd from the German Democratic Republic.Farther along Lenin Avenue, one approaches the center of the city. The Central Department Store is on the right side of the street. Intersecting Lenin Avenue is a tree-lined walkway called the Alley of Heroes. It leads from the Volga River embankment to the Square of Fallen Heroes. At the center of the square is a gray granite obelisk commemorating the fifty-four defenders of the Revolution executed in Tsaritsyn by the White Guard. Next to the obelisk is the common grave of Stalingrad defenders who perished during World War II. The Gorky Drama Theater, where Soviet power was announced in 1917, is on this square, and other buildings include the Hotel Volgograd, Central Post Office, and Medical Institute.

Museum of the Defense of Stalingrad

From the Square of Fallen Heroes one should proceed to Gogol Street, which connects the square with Railway Station Square. The two prominent buildings here are the Volgograd Railway Terminal and the Museum of the Defense of Stalingrad. Here are exhibits pertaining to the October Revolution. During 1917–18 the museum served as defense headquarters for the Tsaritsyn Soviet, comprised of Cossacks, peasants, soldiers, and workers. The exhibits of this period include photographs, weapons, documents, and personal effects of those involved in the revolutionary movement. The next section concerns the Battle of Stalingrad and other strategic sites along the Volga during World War II. A third section of the museum displays the many gifts sent to the citizens of Volgograd as a tribute to their heroism.

USEFUL INFORMATION

Hotels

Hotel Intourist, 14 Mira Street
Hotel Volgograd, 12 Mira Street

Restaurants

Intourist, Hotel Intourist, 14 Mira Street
Volgograd, Hotel Volgograd, 12 Mira Street

Museums

Museum of the Defense of Stalingrad, Railway Station Square
Mamayev Hill, Outdoor Museum and memorial complex at the extension
    of Lenin Avenue
Pavlov's House, Tambovskaya Street

Transportation and Communications

Railway Terminal, Railway Station Square
River Port Terminal, Volga embankment at the foot of the Alley of Heroes
Central Post and Telegraph Office, Square of Fallen Heroes, center city

THE BLACK SEA

Eight thousand years ago, according to radio-isotopic research, the Mediterranean spilled through the Bosporus, into a freshwater basin at the bottom of the Black Sea. This phenomenon made the Black Sea unique among all the seas in the world by creating a two-layered body of salt water. The lower portion is devoid of organic life, while the upper level, ten fathoms deep, abounds with it. The Black Sea has been connected three times with the Caspian Sea and twice with the Mediterranean during its multimillion-year history. Called Pontos Axenos (Inhospitable Sea) by the ancient Greeks, the present name seems to derive from the contrast between its darker, sometimes blue-black water and the turquoise hue of the Mediterranean.

The Black Sea is rather young, and its present shape is only about five thousand years old. Fifty years ago the cause of the sulfurated hydrogen deposits in the Black Sea was discovered by Nikolai Zelinsky, a Russian chemist. The bodies of dead and dying marine plants and animals sink to the bottom, where they are dissolved by bacteria into simpler chemical compounds. Sea salts, acting on these compounds, release free sulfurated hydrogen. Geologists believe that the conditions which prevail on the floor of the Black Sea are the same as those in other bodies of water where there is little or no oxygen in the depths. It is believed also that these conditions led to the formation of oil deposits during the earth's geological history, and that perhaps the Black Sea will become a source of oil in the future.

The Black Sea covers an area of 416,000 square kilometers (160,000 square miles) and has a maximum depth of 2,134 meters (7,000 feet). The salt content is much lower than that of an ocean or other seas. Because of the narrows and shallows of the Bosporus, Dardanelles, and Strait of Gibraltar, ocean tides do not reach the Black Sea. Nevertheless, its tides are quite strong owing to powerful coastal winds. While severe storms are rare, coastal tides are notoriously rough, and numerous breakwaters have been built to preserve the coastline and beaches.

Although the lower portion of the Black Sea contains no organic life except for bacteria, over 250 varieties of algae and 100 types of fish exist in the surface layer. The forms of animal life abundant in the Black Sea range from the microscopic plankton to the giant squid. Edible fish include oysters, mussels, sea scallops, and lobsters, along with the high-priced beluga, many varieties of sturgeon, herring, anchovy, mackerel, mullet, salmon, and tuna. Two other important animals found in the Black Sea and along its coastlines are dolphins and seals. In 1966 the U.S.S.R. Ministry of Fisheries abolished dolphin hunting, as the species was threatened with extermination. Rich in birdlife, the Black Sea boasts numerous varieties of gulls and roseate terns, in addition to stormy petrels, cormorants, and pelicans.

Literature concerning the Black Sea has been abundant. From Homer and Ovid down through the ages, this body of water has been celebrated in prose and poetry. Many of Alexander Pushkin's poems are dedicated to the Black Sea and the reminiscences of Soviet writer Konstantin Paustovsky contain many references to it.

ODESSA

GENERAL INFORMATION

Odessa, with a population of 800,000, covers an area of 303 kilometers (155 square miles) on a plateau 46 meters (150 feet) above sea level. The climate is similar to that of Paris and Vienna, with an average annual temperature of 11 degrees C. (51.8 degrees F.). The city boasts 250 sunny days per year, indicating a low annual rainfall of about 431.3 mm (17 inches). Winters are cool and summers are quite warm. More than a seaside resort, Odessa is an important industrial, trade, and tourist city. In addition to the production of steel, agricultural equipment, linoleum, fur coats and trimming, refrigerators, footwear, clothing, and computers, Odessa is the largest ship repair yard on the Black Sea. The city is also an important educational and cultural center, housing Mechnikov State University and several other institutes of higher education.

The most distinctive feature of Odessa is the Black Sea and its lagoons. Not only do they add beauty to the setting, but they provide various properties and substances useful in health treatments. Thus, Odessa has become one of the largest climatotherapeutic resorts in the Soviet Union. As early as 1928 the potential of Odessa as a health center was recognized, and the Ukrainian Health Resort Institute was established. Today several hundred thousand people receive treatment at the many sanitaria and resort clinics in the area. These stretch along the coastline among the lagoons from Luzanovka to Carolino-Bugaz.

The three most famous lagoons are the Kuyalnitsky, Hadjibeevsky, and

Dry lagoons which produce curative mud and mineral waters. The district known as Great Fountain (Bolshoi Fontan) has ten sanitaria, thirteen holiday homes, and more than thirty Young Pioneer camps. Among the most famous of the treatment centers near Odessa is the Molodaya Gvardia, a sanitarium for children, located in Luzanovka. Here both medical and educational facilities are provided. The climate of Odessa attracts large numbers of tourists who come each year to enjoy the sights and holiday facilities.

HISTORY IN BRIEF

Ancient relics found in and around Odessa indicate that this area of the northern Black Sea coast was inhabited thousands of years ago. Recorded history begins with the settlement of Kotsubievo in the thirteenth century. Destroyed by the Tatars in 1540, it was restored by the Turks, who named it Hadjibei. In 1764 a fortress was built beside the city and called New World (Eni Dunya). During the Russo-Turkish War of 1787 Russian troops, accompanied by Ukrainian Cossacks, conquered Hadjibei. Following the war, the city was renamed Novorossia. On the site of the old fortress of Eni Dunya, a seaport was constructed at the order of the empress, Catherine II.

Thus it was that Odessa was born on August 22, 1794, when the first foundation stones were laid and the first piles driven into the water for the pier. The name Odessa was chosen because it was believed that Odessus, an ancient Greek settlement, was originally on this site (later it was discovered that Odessus was actually near the Bulgarian city of Varna). Odessa was planned by the leading architects of Russia, and the city grew rapidly. A unique feature of the times was the austerity of the architecture and overall city plan. The romance of a seaport plus a mild climate attracted many newcomers. When Catherine II died in 1796, her son, Pavel I, succeeded to the Russian throne. He negated his mother's program for Odessa, halting the construction of the city. Merchants, feeling threatened by the possible loss of such a valuable port, made an appeal to Pavel by sending him three thousand imported oranges and requesting a loan of 250,000 rubles to complete the construction of the port. Appeased and amused, Pavel granted the loan. Building resumed with great rapidity, and the work brought many skilled laborers to Odessa. The city became known as the "southern winds to Europe" as its foreign trade began to grow.

During the first half of the nineteenth century the city's formation was completed. For nearly one hundred years Odessa had no serious trade competitors on the Black Sea because it was a duty-free port until 1859. Trade was not the only factor in the growth of the city; its cultural influence in southern Russia led to additional renown. By the turn of the century

Odessa was second only to St. Petersburg in foreign trade. Because of the expanding industries in and around Odessa, the city attracted a large working-class population. During the 1870s, Odessa was the center of revolutionary and working-class activity in the south. Study groups were set up by progressives and funds raised to found the first Russian working-class organization, the Southern Russia Workers' Union, in 1875.

The first social democratic organization was started in 1893. By 1901, Lenin's underground newspaper *Iskra* had had enough influence to motivate the founding of the South Revolutionary Group of Social Democrats. This organization was headed by Lenin's brother, Dmitri Ulyanov, who worked as a doctor in the Usatov hospital near Odessa. Later, Rozalia Zemlyachka replaced Dmitri Ulyanov at Lenin's own directive. Lenin's election to the Third Party Congress held in London was largely the work of Odessa social democrats. On June 14, 1905, the battleship *Potemkin* dropped anchor in the port.

Odessa won the title of Hero City during World War II for its staunch land, sea, and air resistance. The occupation of Odessa lasted for 907 days during which time all commodities and supplies were cut off; even drinking water was rationed. Civilians and military personnel were forced to perform superhuman tasks in order to survive while an enemy of 300,000 besieged the city. The Odessa catacombs provided a unique hiding place for Soviet military and political intelligence forces until their location was discovered and the enemy attempted to suffocate them with noxious gases and burning oil. Many legends have grown out of the grim truths of Odessa's heroic struggle during World War II. On April 10, 1944, the city was liberated by troops of the Third Ukrainian Command under the leadership of Rodion Malinovsky.

MUSEUMS AND PLACES OF INTEREST

Archaeological Museum, 4 Lastochkin Street

Next door to the Town Soviet in Commune Square is the Archaeological Museum, founded in 1825. There are over 150,000 exhibits here relating to the ancient Slav tribes who at one time inhabited the northern Black Sea coast. (There are several exhibits concerned with the invasion of the Greeks into Panticapaeum, Scythia, and Sarmatia. The best representation of the ancient cities is that of Olvia.) The noteworthy numismatic collection contains over 50,000 rare coins from various nations. A section devoted to ancient Egypt has a fine assortment of bronze and earthenware vessels, literary relics, sarcophagi, and grain specimens that are 3,000 years old.

Maritime Museum, 6 Lastochkin Street

Opposite the Archaeological Museum is the U.S.S.R. Merchant Marine Museum. One of the most interesting features is the large exhibit devoted to the development of the whaling industry, which is still a vital part of Soviet maritime activity. Since so much of Odessa's history is connected with sea trade, this museum is very popular among residents as well as tourists. One will find models and pictures along with lengthy explanations in text concerning the old trading vessels dating back to the earliest maritime activities of Hadjibei.

Museum of Western and Oriental Art, 9 Pushkin Street

Built in 1856 and designed by A. Otton, a St. Petersburg architect, this museum exhibits a stimulating array of paintings, sculpture, drawings, and works of applied art. In recent years two major discoveries have greatly enriched the collection. First, a portrait of an unnamed woman by an uncertain artist was verified as a portrait of Marie Louise d'Orléans, queen of Spain, painted by Carreño de Miranda, a noted follower of Velázquez. Second was the discovery that the presumed copy of Caravaggio's "Treachery of Judas" was the original canvas of the late-sixteenth-century master. Numerous works by sixteenth- to eighteenth-century artists, such as Michelangelo, van Leyden, Magnasco, and Hals are also on display. The nineteenth-century section displays the art of fourteen different nations. Oriental art features the works of Japanese, Iranian, and other Eastern artists and craftsmen. Greek vases, terra-cotta figurines, Roman glass, and casts of sculpture dating from the fifth century B.C. to the third century A.D. can be found in the museum's halls of ancient art.

Museum of History and Regional Studies, 4 Khalturin Street

Although the building was erected in 1876, it was not a museum until eighty years later. There are three different departments of this museum, located at different places in Odessa, but each within walking distance of the others. The Division of History, located here, contains fourteen exhibition rooms concerned with Odessa's colorful past. The main theme of these exhibits is dedicated to Soviet history, particularly those events which depict armed conflict between revolutionary workers and White Guards and the dramatic struggle during World War II. There are photographs of partisan life in the catacombs, Odessa in ruins after the war, and contrasting pictures of postwar repairs and rebuilding.

The Nature Study Department is located at 24 Lastochkin Street. The street was named for Nikolai Lastochkin, a Bolshevik leader who was tortured and killed by White Guards in 1919. This department of the museum houses the exhibits of regional resources, flora, and fauna.

Pushkin House, 13 Pushkin Street, is the Literary Department. This small house was the residence of Alexander Pushkin from July 1823 to August 1824. Pushkin while in exile in Odessa for his rebellious poetry conceived and wrote the first two chapters of *Eugene Onegin*. He wrote many new poems during this period and completed *Fountain of Bakhchisarai* before he left Odessa. Before its official designation as a museum in 1961, Pushkin House had been the home of the Odessa chapter of the Writers' Union of the Ukraine. The museum now features exhibits of manuscripts and photographs of some of the most important Russian and Soviet writers connected with Odessa. These include Valentin Kataev, Konstantin Paustovsky, Isaac Babel, and Ilya Ilf.

Art Gallery, 5 Korolenko Street

This museum is housed in a large palace of Russian classical style built by an unknown architect ten years after the founding of Odessa. The palace originally belonged to Count Potocki. In 1889 a picture gallery was opened here by the Odessa Society of Fine Arts. Over 3,000 works represent seventeenth- to twentieth-century Russian and Soviet painting. This collection is considered to be one of the best in the Ukraine. Its varied schools of painting throughout the four centuries provide a very interesting and worthwhile visit.

Potemkin Stairs, Seaside Boulevard

As is the Eiffel Tower to Paris and the Empire State Building to New York, the Potemkin Stairs are the emblematic landmark of Odessa. The insurgent sailors of the battleship *Prince Potemkin Taurichevsky*, storming up the stairs in 1905, made the site famous. People around the world have seen these stairs in Sergei Eisenstein's film *Potemkin*. The stairway was designed by the architect Beaufort and constructed between 1837 and 1841. The ten flights are comprised of 192 steps. The total length of the stairway is 42.7 meters (140 feet), and its height is 30.5 meters (100 feet). Owing to the design of the stairs, only the steps are visible from below, and only the landings from above.

Seaside Boulevard

At the top of the Potemkin Stairs is the beautiful and historic seaside thoroughfare along which many of Odessa's best-known landmarks are located. The first of these to capture the eye is the bronze statue of Duc de Richelieu, first governor of Odessa and Novorossia, from 1803 to 1814. Although he was a French statesman, Richelieu was in the paid service of the tsar for twenty years. This valuable and dedicated administrator worked diligently to develop Odessa and the surrounding region. The Richelieu monument was designed by Abram Melnikov, a St. Petersburg architect, and Ivan Martos, rector of the St. Petersburg Academy of Arts. Directly opposite the monument are two semicircular buildings also designed by Melnikov. At 8 Seaside Boulevard is the booking office for boat excursions. This building was formerly the St. Petersburg Hotel. Next door, at Number 7, is the Odessa Gorky Scientific Library. Originally founded as a library in 1830, it was converted to a tsarist courthouse and was used as such until the completion of Soviet power in Odessa. At 11 Seaside Boulevard is the Hotel Intourist. Continuing along, one approaches two very important buildings, both designed by Beaufort. First is the Sailors' Palace of Culture, built in 1830. Next is the Town Soviet, built during 1829–34, and used originally as the stock exchange. The choice of this building as the home of the Town Soviet was based on the historic decision made there in 1918 by representatives of the workers, sailors, and soldiers to transfer the power of government to the Soviets. Just in front of this building is a monument to Alexander Pushkin. In 1888 the citizens of Odessa contributed their own personal funds for the monument to commemorate the fiftieth anniversary of Pushkin's death. Next to the monument is a cast-iron gun, taken from the English frigate *Tiger,* which is dedicated to a small group of Russian soldiers who defended Odessa against a fleet of English and French ships in 1854 during the Crimean War.

Opera and Ballet Theater, Theater Square

Along Seaside Boulevard, past Commune Square, is Theater Square, where one of Odessa's most noted landmarks is to be found. The Opera and Ballet Theater ranks among the world's finest theater buildings. It was designed by Viennese architects, Felner and Gelmer, along with Gonsiorovsky, an Odessa engineer. Between 1884 and 1887, Ukrainian and Russian workers completed the construction. The exterior of the edifice is decorated with figures representing the theater arts. The main façade contains a two-story portico topped with the figure of Melpomene, the Greek Muse of tragedy. On the semicircular façade are the figures of Terpsichore, Muse of the dance, and Orpheus, the legendary musician. Below these figures are sculptural ensembles representing tragedy and comedy. In the various niches are busts of prominent contributors to Russian culture: Alexander Pushkin, Alexander Griboedov, Mikhail Glinka, and Nikolai Gogol.

The interior of the theater is resplendent with dramatically arranged foyers and marble staircases. The lower vestibule is decorated with imposing arches, columns, and pilasters, and the upper vestibule with stucco molding. The ceiling, painted by the Viennese artist Teffler, depicts colorful scenes from Shakespeare's plays. The hall itself seats

1,700. At intermission, the audience can view the sea from the exterior balconies. Among the famed composers who have conducted at the Odessa Opera and Ballet Theater are Tchaikovsky, Rimsky-Korsakov, and Glazunov. Visitors to Odessa may obtain the schedule of performances as well as tickets from the Service Bureau of their hotel or directly from the box office.

Odessa Regional Philharmonic Society, corner of Pushkin Street and Rosa Luxemburg Street

At the turn of the century this building was constructed under the direction of architect Yuri Bernardasti for the exclusive use of the executive board of the Odessa stock exchange. Hence the motif of the six pictures in the frieze under the ceiling which depict the development of commerce from primitive barter to modern capitalism. As no expense was spared in its design and construction, the building is among the most notable structures in Odessa. The façade, marble window sashes, arched loges, and rostral columns add great luxury to the interior. The loges are decorated with designs in colored stone, both inlaid and carved in relief, while the ceiling was designed and painted by Karazin. The concert hall features national and international soloists and ensembles, orchestras, and choral groups. During the summer the resident philharmonic orchestra presents outdoor concerts in the City Garden located on Deribassovskaya Street or at the Green Theater in the Central Park. The International Club for foreign seamen visiting Odessa is located in the Philharmonic Society building. Established in 1926, the club presents lectures, tours, meetings, and film showings for foreign seamen as well as providing them with a place to stay in Odessa.

October Revolution Square, next to the Railway Station at the juncture of Pirogov and Sverdlov streets

This is the main square of Odessa where on national holidays parades and patriotic demonstrations are held. During the years of the Revolution and Civil War, many battles were held here. Today trees of friendship grow along the square and bouquets of flowers are constantly brought to the site by Odessa citizens. A monument to Lenin and another to the soldiers of the Revolution have been placed here. Along the sides of the square are eighteenth and nineteenth century dwellings, preserved in their original state, as well as several new buildings. Among the newer structures are the Spartak Stadium, two schools, and a maternity hospital. At the southern edge of the square is a five-story building, constructed in 1958, which houses the Regional Committee of the Ukrainian Communist Party.

Deribassovskaya Street, running parallel to Seaside Boulevard several blocks inland and crossing Lenin and Marx streets

Named for Admiral Deribas, who drew up the plan for Odessa, this street is the site of most of the commercial life of Odessa. One would expect this to be the case, not only because almost every building houses a department store, hotel, café, or restaurant, but also because it is here that Mechnikov Novorassiisk University is located. The Odessa Richelieu Lyceum was opened at 16 Deribassovskaya Street in 1817. The Polish poet Adam Mickiewicz lived at that address in 1825, and the famous Russian chemist Dmitry Mendeleev was a teacher at the Lyceum in 1855-56. Nikolai Pirogov, a Russian surgeon as well as pedagogical specialist, initiated the procedures for making the lyceum over into the university in 1865.

To the right of Deribassovskaya Street is the City Garden. Near the City Garden, to the left of Deribassovskaya Street, is Martynovsky Square. To the left is Karl Liebknecht Street, home of the Ivanov Russian Drama Theater and the Musical Comedy Theater. Both theaters maintain resident and touring repertory companies, and both theaters produce both Russian and foreign works. Just past the theaters are Soviet Army Square and Soviet Army Street. In the middle of the square is a statue of Count Mikhail Voronstov who was governor of Novorossiisk and led the battle of Craonne in 1814 against Napoleon.

Arcadia and Shevchenko Central Recreation Parks, New Boulevard

Near the Port of Odessa is a large green plateau on which are situated the city's main recreational facilities: libraries, recreation halls, an open-air theater, and the Avangard Stadium, which seats 50,000 spectators. There is an ancient stone wall near the stadium with turrets and bay openings facing the sea. This is what remains of the fortress built in 1793 by General Alexander Suvorov to protect Russia from the Turks. Near the fortress is a towering granite obelisk, the Monument to the Unknown Sailor, at the foot of which burns an eternal flame. Four bas-relief motifs decorate the obelisk and commemorate the Crimean War, the *Potemkin*, the 1918 January uprising, and the liberation of Odessa in World War II. The memorial, designed by Odessa architects Gopuz and Tormilin, and carved by Naruzetsky, was dedicated in 1960.

The Avenue of Glory runs next to the monument. Here is the burial ground for Odessa patriots. Slightly beyond this section is the Astronomical Observatory of Mechnikov State University founded in 1871. The park surrounding the observatory contains a monument to the Ukrainian poet and philosopher Taras Shevchenko.

Filatov Research Institute of Ophthalmic Diseases and Tissue Therapy, 33 Proletarian Boulevard

Through the Central Recreation Park, via Lermontov Lane and Belinsky Street, one arrives at Proletarian Boulevard where Filatov Institute, founded by Vladimir Filatov, an ophthalmic surgeon, is located. Here thousands of patients from many different countries have regained their vision through the work of Filatov and his staff. There are seven clinical departments connected with the institute, which is now under the directorship of Nadezhda Puchkovskaya, a former student of Filatov.

Arcadia Resort, Proletarian Boulevard

This well-known complex of sanitaria, hotels, and holiday homes is situated on the outskirts of Odessa in a section called Arcadia. Among the more famous health resorts is the Rossia, the largest trade union sanitarium for the treatment of cardiovascular and neurological diseases. Almost all of the therapeutic and vacation facilities located in Arcadia have parks in the front which slope down to the beaches of the Black Sea. Odessa University's Botanical Garden, with specimens of tropical plants from all over the world, is also located on Proletarian Boulevard. The dendrarium displays 320 types of trees, the rosarium has over 250 varieties of roses, and the impressive peach orchard contains 200 different types of peach trees.

Tairov Research Institute of Viticulture and Wine-making, Karl Liebknecht Collective Farm, Chernomorka

Reached by an excursion launch from Arcadia, this section of the Odessa beach area is famous for the Tairov Institute, founded in 1931 and named after Vasily Tairov, a prominent Russian scientist whose specialty was viticulture. In 1905 he established the first wine-making laboratory among Russian vintners. The first laboratory occupied two small rooms and was tended by two employees. In 1911 new and larger premises were built at Sukhai Liman, and an experimental vineyard was planted. Since the establishment of the institute, scientists have devoted their efforts to developing new varieties of grapes, improving older ones, the mechanization of production, and the chemical control of processed wine.

Port of Odessa, Seaside Boulevard

No visit to Odessa would be complete without a tour of the port. Today ships from nearly seventy countries dock here regularly. At least one-third of Odessa's residents earn a living connected with the sea. Since the advent of Soviet power the handling of cargo has been almost entirely mechanized. Gantry cranes and automatic loaders and stackers work the area from warehouse to ship. These functions previously required the labor of hundreds of men. The annual cargo tonnage handled in the port has increased 300-fold since the Revolution. Odessa is also the permanent base of the Soviet Ukrainian whaling fleet. Because of the immense flow of passengers and cargo through the port of Odessa it has been nicknamed the "sea gates of the Ukraine."

USEFUL INFORMATION

Intourist Office, Hotel Krasnaya, 15 Pushkin Street, Tel: 2–39–34, 5–01–05

Hotels

Krasnaya, 15 Pushkin Street
Odessa, 11 Seaside Boulevard
Arkadiya, 24 Shevchenko Prospect

Motels and Campsites

Delfin Campsite, Kotovsky Road near Luzanovka Beach
Chernoye More Motel, near Zolotoi Beach

Restaurants

Odessa, Hotel Odessa, 11 Seaside Boulevard
Krasnaya, Hotel Krasnaya, 15 Pushkin Street
Delfin, Delfin Campsite, Kotovsky Road near Luzanovka Beach

Theaters

State Academic Opera and Ballet Theater, 1 Lenin Street
Ukrainian October Revolution Drama Theater, 15 Pasteur Street
Russian Drama Theater, 46 Karl Liebknecht Street
Musical Comedy Theater, 48 Karl Liebknecht Street
Circus, 25 Podbelsky Street
Philharmonic Society, 15 Rosa Luxemburg Street

Cinemas

Rodina (wide screen), 104 Mechnikova Street
Ukraina, 9 Lenin Street
Frunze (wide screen), 27 Karl Marx Street

Bookshops

Bookshop No. 1, 27 Deribassovskaya Street, has foreign, musical, and technical literature departments.

Druzhba, 23 Soviet Army Street, specializes in political works.

Post and Telegraph

Central Post Office, 7 Sadovaya Street

Aeroflot Office, 17 Karl Marx Street

Telephone Numbers

Railway Station, 94–42–42
Seaport, 2–32–11
Airport, 5–04–14
Bus Terminal, 5–04–96

SOCHI

GENERAL INFORMATION

Sochi, nicknamed the "Russian Riviera," is the most famous resort on the Black Sea coast. It is a city of parks, beaches, hotels, and sanitaria. Now known as Greater Sochi, the city includes four districts: Adler, Khosta, Lararevskoye, and Central. Greater Sochi extends along 144 kilometers (90 miles) of coastal land. A recently adopted plan for expansion will link by monorail the resort areas of Magri, Golovinka, Loo, Dagomys, and Ashe. Hotels, motels, and camping facilities for 14,000 tourists are projected.

The *trompe l'oeil* effect of Sochi's geographical location is the result of what appears to be an uninterrupted descent of greenery directly from snow-capped mountains to the sparkling blue-black sea. Sochi is indeed favored by nature with its protective mountain range to block cold, northerly winds and its cooling sea breezes which control summer heat. The yearly average temperature is 15 degrees C. (59 degrees F.), seldom exceeding 23 degrees C. (74 degrees F.) in summer. Subtropical vegetation heightens the beauty of Sochi's natural surroundings. In addition to beauty and climate, Sochi boasts another natural wonder: hydrogen sulfide springs, useful in the curative treatment of various ailments. Of the two million visitors annually, at least one-third are there for reasons of health. The area of Greater Sochi is dense in hotels and shopping facilities as well as sanitaria and medical treatment centers.

Park Riviera, the original center of Sochi, is located on the northern bank of the Sochi River. In 1909 a Moscow merchant named Tarnopolsky opened Kavkazskaya Riviera, a private hotel, complete with restaurant, theater, and health treatment facilities. In 1921 the hotel was converted to a sanitarium open to all Soviet citizens. Additional medical facilities were installed as time went on, and in 1962 the Riviera merged with a neighboring sanitarium, Lazurny Bereg (Côte d'Azur), a treatment center for foreigners. The 10 hectare (25-acre) park next to the sanitaria was named for the original hotel. Today, Park Riviera is a major attraction. It is the center for outdoor festivals and sporting events, and has many facilities such as a planetarium, lecture hall, open-air theater, band shell, dance pavilion, library, and a special area for chess and other table games. There are numerous refreshment areas, both indoor and outdoor. The park also has playgrounds for children. Various cultural exhibits are displayed from time to time in addition to permanent objects such as busts of noted Russian authors along Writers' Alley and a large relief map of the Krasnodar Territory along the side of the central walkway.

From Park Riviera stretches Sochi's main street, Kurortny Prospect. Two glass and concrete buildings highlight the square at the beginning of Kurortny Prospect. These are the Sputnik Cinema and the main post and telegraph building. Plane Tree Alley forms a tunnel of greenery from the square to the heavily trafficked street. At the other end of Plane Tree Alley is the Oktyabrsky Garden, noted for its large fountain. Nearby is the Fish restaurant, famous for its seafood prepared in the Eastern European style. Behind Oktyabrsky Garden, Kurortny Prospect climbs steeply to an area of small shops. Leading out from Kurortny Prospect is Gorky Street, which terminates at Railway Station Square. The modernistic railway station was designed by Alexei Dushkin and completed in 1952. The open porticos, arcades, and flowerbeds of the station building are in keeping with the tropical atmosphere of Sochi. The station restaurant has an open veranda for its clientele. About ten minutes' walk from Railway Station Square, on the banks of the Sochi River, is the famous roofed market which is open all year, specializing in both domestic and imported foodstuffs ranging from fresh fish and poultry to exotic fruits and vegetables.

Kurortny Prospect, which winds through the city, can be picked up again along the riverbank. Following along this street, you will eventually come to the port of Sochi on the other side of the city. In addition to the natural glamor of the Black Sea, there are many other worthwhile points of interest in this sector of Sochi. The most noticeable structure in the seaside area is the seaport building with its 35 meter (114-foot) spire, topped with a star that can be seen from miles out at sea. Designed by Soviet architect Karo Alabyan, the exterior of the building is faced with Caucasian limestone slabs, and the interior with majolica and marble. To the left of the building a wide staircase leads down to the beach. Farther to the left is another staircase leading up to several parks. Close by is a lighthouse near which a grove of trees encloses the monument of a Soviet soldier. Clustered around the statue are the graves of World War II soldiers.

Connected to the seaport building is a large pier where deep-sea vessels are moored. Until 1950 Sochi could not accommodate these large ships, but by 1963 even the largest ocean liner could dock here. There are smaller mooring areas for hydrofoils and other vessels as well. The seaport area provides a pleasant place for strolling, day or night. Smaller piers also dot the Sochi beach area. These are used for sunbathing by the general public and for swimming and diving instruction by the children's camps.

The public bathing beaches are to the south of the center city. You may arrange transportation to these areas at the Service Bureau of your hotel. Most hotels not directly on the beach provide free half-hourly bus service every day from 9 A.M. until 7 P.M. By showing your hotel receipt to the beach attendant, you are entitled to a private dressing room, towels, and a beach chair. Refreshments are also available at the beach, but no eating is permitted on the sundeck or on the beach proper. Tourists are advised to wear lightweight rubber bathing shoes, as the Sochi beaches are stony and rocky. What little sand there is provides more decoration than comfort. A swim in the Black Sea is a most exhilarating experience owing to the high salt content and cool temperature of the water.

Just off Kurortny Prospect is a large square which is the home of the Sochi Theater, erected in 1937. The theater seats 1,100 and, as the main entertainment hall of Sochi, it is frequently filled to capacity. Designed by Konstantin Chernopyatov, the theater is situated within a glade of roses and other flowers. Sculptress Vera Mukhina created the decor of the front façade.

Continuing along Kurortny Prospect, you will again pass Gorky Street. From here the central department store of Sochi is accessible. Off to the right is Voikov Street, where Grocery No. 1 is located, one of the largest grocery establishments in Sochi. Along Voikov Street you will also find a souvenir shop, barber, hairdresser, and confectionery store. Another prominent place is the Sochi Art Shop, where wood and ceramic items, crafted by local artists, are for sale.

If you walk over to Gorky Street from here, you come to a large tobacco shop and the main chemist shop. Next to these is the Emerald (Izumrud), a shop specializing in crystal, gold, silver, Ural stones, watches, and women's jewelry. To the left is the Gorka restaurant. On the right is the Sochi Art Exhibition Hall, and just behind it is the Kaskad restaurant. At the summit of the hill is the children's music school, next to which is the Palace of Young Pioneers. The Sochi newspaper office and the Hotel Sochi complete the block.

Back again on Kurortny Prospect, on the right, is the Sochi Cinema. Next along the way is a large public garden with a monument to Lenin. On the left side of Kurortny Prospect is a vertical white slab commemorating the author Nikolai Ostrovsky in haut-relief. Bus stop Svetlana looms ahead, always crowded with shoppers. Farther along is the newest hotel, Kavkaz. From here, Kurortny Prospect becomes an avenue of sanitaria. Along this row of specialized health facilities is a stairway which leads to the Hotel Intourist. At the end of the Prospect is a Sputnik International Youth Camp, one of five scattered throughout the Soviet Union. These camps offer facilities to young people from many foreign countries and extend various privileges such as reduced air and rail fares, along with simplified visa procedures.

HISTORY IN BRIEF

The word "Sochi" is believed to have been adapted from the Circassian "Sshatche," the name of an Ubykhi tribe living in the Sochi area during the early nineteenth century. The Ubykhi had a culture and language akin to that of the Adighes and Abkhazians. These, like other tribes of the Western Caucasus, were mountaineers who fell under conquest by the Turkish sultanate during the latter part of the sixteenth century. In 1829 the Treaty of Adrianople returned the Black Sea coast, from the mouth of the Kuban River to Poti, to Russia. However, it was not until several years later, after a long, drawn-out war, that the remainder of the Caucasus was conquered by Russia. Between 1830 and 1842, the Russians erected seventeen fortifications along the coast of the Black Sea.

In June 1837 Russian sailors landed at Cape Adler to build the Fort of the Holy Spirit near where the Mzymta River flows into the Black Sea. In July and August they built the forts of Lazarevskoye and Golovinskoye. In April 1838, a fort was erected at the mouth of the Sochi River. A church and lighthouse were constructed later and survive to the present time. The original name, Alexandria (in honor of the tsar), was later changed to Navaginskoye to commemorate the regiment which had shown heroism in war. These forts along the coast were constantly besieged by mountaineers who refused to obey the tsar's edict to surrender arms. In 1854, during the Crimean War, Russian troops were ordered to abandon and/or destroy most Black Sea forts.

Ten years later, when the Treaty of the Caucasus was signed, the old fortress in the Sochi area was restored. Renamed Outpost of Dakhovsky, the fortress became a settlement. During the famine of 1891–92 the government initiated the construction of a road linking Novorossiisk with Sukhumi, nicknamed the "Hungry Highway" because its construction attracted those driven from their homes by lack of food. Unfortunately, these migrant laborers found the subtropical area as hostile as their original homes due to the heat, humidity, disease, and exhausting work. In 1896 Dakhovsky was renamed Sochi and continued with the status of settlement until the Revolution of 1917.

Just after the turn of the century a wealthy Muscovite named Khludov bought 1,080 hectares (2,700 acres) of land near Sochi. His example was followed by numerous businessmen. The government established a land-reclamation project in the area, making purchases attractive to wealthy people and granting other plots as gifts to veterans of the Caucasus wars. Peasant farmers were forced to take to the mountains when the seashore became populated by a bourgeois class that owned villas and summer estates. The development of the area was continued by industrialists and horticulturists who envisioned a promising future. In 1893 a scientist named Frederick Struve, examining a grotto in Matsesta, concluded on the basis of his climate and mineral studies that a treatment resort would have no better future anywhere in the world. The government invited the Parisian speleologist Martel, to examine the caves around Matsesta to support Struve's theory. Almost simultaneously, Sochi was visited by a foreign architect who had designed structures for French and Italian Riviera resorts as well as some in the Tyrol. He proclaimed Sochi a more favorable climate than other Mediterranean areas whose summers were too hot and autumns too rainy and cold. These enthusiastic observations caused a boom in land speculation. However, in the early 1900s, Sochi had no sewer system. The lack of a first-rate commercial pier was sorely felt by tourists and townspeople until well into the twentieth century. Surface transportation was equally poor until after the Revolution.

The years 1905–18 saw the growth and emergence of Sochi as a major health treatment and vacation resort. The official birth year of Sochi is 1909, when the first health center, named the Caucasian Riviera, was opened. A joint-stock company had begun the development of the Matsesta sulfur springs in 1910, but the outbreak of World War I in 1914 interrupted and ultimately ended this project. The much-needed railway between Tuapse and Sochi was finished hurriedly when German warships sailed through the Bosporous shelling the Sochi coastline. The railway stimulated the area's growth and finally made supplies easily available. Between 1918 and 1920 the Civil War impeded progress, but in the latter year, all private property in the Greater Sochi area was declared state-owned and designated for specific use as health and holiday resorts. The coastal railway was repaired, and by 1925 Sochi became accessible to all Soviet working people. Between 1934 and 1954 a twenty-year plan expanded Greater Sochi by means of increased surface and sea transportation facilities, sanitaria, parks, theaters, and tourist accommodations as well as such industrial improvements as bakeries, meat-packing plants, dairies, and fruit canneries.

Today, Greater Sochi has 250,000 permanent residents largely employed in the health and holiday resort industries.

MUSEUMS AND PLACES OF INTEREST

Sochi Museum of Regional Studies

The Sochi Museum of Regional Studies, established in 1920, is located in a small two-story structure and boasts several thousand exhibits in twelve showrooms. Here you are introduced to the diversity of Sochi, its history, economy, and culture.

The museum's opening section is arranged to provide general information about the resort area. A special feature is an exhibit on physical features and landscapes. The centerpiece of the exhibit, a map of the Black Sea floor, is flanked by seascape paintings and models of fish. Submarine plants are represented by dried algae, and a model of the seabed shows deep-dwelling fish, such as plaice, red mullet, and sea-ruff.

A large stand exhibits a varied collection of mineral resources found in the Sochi area. On display are pieces of colored marble-type limestone, granite, sandstone, roofing slate, mica, gypsum, marble, rock crystal, calcite, and jasper. Collections of Sochi soil samples are also exhibited.

Information on the flora and fauna in and around Sochi is available from what are called "biogroups." On display are model seabirds—eiders, grebes, colored-nosed roseate terns, and seagulls. Beautifully composed scenes of animal habitats show stuffed aurochs, chamois, Caucasian mountain goats, and hybrid European and American bison weighing 1,110 kilograms (505 pounds). Almost extinct, these animals have multiplied in the Caucasian preserve which now boasts over 400 bison, 15,000 aurochs (and the number is increasing), close to 7,000 Caucasian stags, and approximately 4,000 chamois.

For those interested in the remote past, there are several rooms of displays containing many photographs and drawings depicting the sites and life of primitive man. Fossil animals, plants, and working tools dating to the Stone Age are exhibited, as well as maps of Neolithic sites found near Sochi.

Authorities agree that several objects in the collection confirm links between the North Caucasian peoples and tribes with ancient Greek settlements north of the Black Sea. Two glass cases hold displays of ceramic bowls, fragments of black-varnish vessels, glass beads, vessels for oil, and cult figurines of clay.

The same section of the museum has many items of Adyghe culture. Displayed are such objects as clothing, cult bowls, weapons, bridle-bits and harnesses, and vessels for wine and grain. Arrows, shields, coats of mail, and other military equipment of the ancient and medieval Adyghe make for a fascinating historical exhibit.

Photographs depict the Sochi armed uprising in 1905. Other photos show parts of the Sochi resort in its earliest years with Matsesta wooden bathtubs, used at the start of the century, buffaloes wading in street puddles, and the first buildings of resort Kavkazskaya Riviera.

Of recent historical interest is the section called "Sochi Area During the Great October Socialist Revolution and the Civil War." The centerpiece of this hall is a sculptured portrait of Lenin. Documents, paintings, and photographs portray the fight of the Red Guards against the troops of Georgia's Menshevik government in 1918 and against the White Guards in 1919. Enhancing the display is a model of a guerrilla camp, weapons used by fighters, and photographs of members of the underground Communist Party organization. In another section devoted to the same period the museum offers pictures of the reestablishment of Soviet government in Sochi after the Red Army's victory.

In 1933 the Soviet government set itself the task of rebuilding the Sochi-Matsesta complex. Many sanitaria, summer and winter theaters, and consumer shops were built, as well as dairy plants and a meat-packing plant. For visitors interested in this era of rebuilding, exhibits are on display in the section called "Resort Reconstruction."

The museum offers an extensive display dedicated to Sochi's involvement in World War II. During the war years all Sochi sanitaria were converted into military hospitals. Many residents of the city participated in the defense of the Caucasus against German troops.

The postwar reconstruction of Sochi is adequately represented. Exhibits show the completion of the seaport, the construction of new health institutions, the building of the railroad station in Sochi and the airport in Adler.

Finally, a large model offers a view of the city as it was within its old boundary limits. In the center of the display is the text of the "Edict of the Presidium of the R.S.F.S.R. Supreme Soviet," dated February 10, 1961, decreeing that the coastal part of the Adler and Lazarevskoye districts were to be accepted within the city's boundaries.

The Sochi Museum of Regional Studies is located at 29 Ordzhonikidze Street. It is open daily, except Thursday, from 10 A.M. until 6 P.M. and is easily reached by buses 1, 2, 3, 3d, 4, 5, 8, 19, 21, and 23.

Nikolai Ostrovsky Museum

Two buildings located at 4 Perulok Ostrovskogo house the museum named for the Soviet writer. One of the buildings was built by the Soviet government for the author, who worked in it in 1936. The other is a pavilion consisting of four halls. Contained in these halls are exhibits featuring the life and work of Nikolai Ostrovsky.

Ostrovsky, born into a large and poor family in 1904, lived in the important railroad center of Shepetovka during the years of the Revolution and Civil War. In 1919 he joined the Young Communist League and without the knowledge of his parents left for the front. In 1920, in combat near Lvov, Ostrovsky was shell-shocked and seriously injured.

In the autumn of 1921, while working at a wood-storing center near Kiev, he contracted enteric fever and severe rheumatism. His health became gradually worse and treatment and surgery did little to alleviate the condition. Early 1927 saw Ostrovsky confined to bed with gradual stiffening of the joints. He journeyed to Sochi for the first time in 1928 in the hope that the baths of Matsesta could relieve his condition. The sharp pain subsided briefly but several inflammations of the eyes threatened total loss of sight. All operations were fruitless.

Under these conditions, bedridden for the rest of his life, almost always in a state of excruciating pain, and nearly totally blind, Nikolai Ostrovsky began work on his first book. While the book was an account of his life and his times, he insisted that the work was a novel and not an autobiography. His "autobiographical" novel, *How the Steel Was Tempered*, appeared in 1934. In December of that year, Ostrovsky started to work on *Born of the Storm*, which he did not live to complete. In October 1935, one year before his death, he was awarded the Order of Lenin.

His house in Sochi remains unchanged. Visitors to the museum first walk past his bust, the work of K. Golubev. Ostrovsky's personal effects are on public display: the overcoat he wore and the weapons he used when in the Red Army. His telephone still sits near the bedstand. Among the more interesting documents is a diagnosis report of the oculists who treated the writer's failing eye condition: "Vision in the right eye—0,0005, in the left eye—0,02."

In the exhibition pavilion of the museum is a model of the house in which Ostrovsky was born. A major part of the museum's exhibition are publications of his books in over a hundred languages, personal manuscripts and books, and other private belongings, including his membership card in the Young Communist League, dated 1919, and his membership card in the Union of Soviet Writers, signed by Maxim Gorky.

The Nikolai Ostrovsky Museum is open daily, except Wednesday, from 10 A.M. until 6 P.M.; on Tuesdays from 10 A.M. until 4 P.M.

Arboretum Park (Dendrarium)

Admirers of nature's beauty will enjoy a visit to Arboretum Park. At the end of the nineteenth century, S. Khudekov, publisher of a St. Petersburg newspaper, bought a large plot of land in Sochi to lay a park and build a conservatory. Brought from the shores of the Ligurian Sea, from the nursery gardens of the Caucasus and the Crimea, were palms, cacti, agaves, cypress, magnolias, and eucalyptus. Flanking the beautiful foliage are impressive works of sculpture.

In 1924 the park became the base for the Sochi Experimental and Research Center for Subtropical Park and Forest Management. The center's primary tasks included park improvement, pest control, forestation methods, and tree protection on the coast of the Black Sea lying within the Krasnadar Territory. A considerable amount of work was done to enrich the park's collection with new species. Today Arboretum Park has over 1,600 varieties of trees and shrubs.

The first landing, with a vase-topped marble column in the center of a flowerbed, is a good spot from which to view Italian stone pine. Higher up the walk, in the middle of a parterre, an ashen eucalyptus can be seen. Indian rhododendrons, sometimes called Indian azalea, grow in front of a columned arbor. This is an evergreen shrub usually showing red flowers.

A very interesting small tree is the Grecian laurel. This tree with its spherical crown traces its origin from the Mediterranean coasts. In ancient times laurel groves surrounded the temples of Apollo. Throughout history the leaves of this tree have had mysterious connotations. Priests chewed aromatic leaves of the laurel, convinced that it would increase their soothsaying powers. Since the laurel was believed to expiate blood spilling, Roman soldiers wiped blood from their hands with its leaves. Laurel branches have been laid on people suffering from mental illness to "exorcise evil spirits" from their souls.

Growing nearby are the medium-height English yews, often reaching a height of 20 meters (65 feet). Some specimens are four thousand years old. Visitors to the park should make a point of seeing the beautiful seventy-year-old Washington palms, native to deserts of California, Arizona, and Colorado; the hovenia from China; the cinnamon tree or camphor tree, an evergreen that contains generous amounts of camphor oil in its wood; the dawn redwood of the yew family, which is older than man; the Japanese cryptomeria; the Himalayan spruce and the Oriental spruce; the Douglas fir; the Iberian oak; and the holly oak.

Arboretum Park is always in a process of expansion, and today its area is close to 60 hectares (150 acres). The collections are being continually increased and enriched. The Sochi Experimental Research Center maintains communications with sixty-four institutions in thirty countries. The center now receives seeds from Australia, Austria, Canada, Federal Republic of Germany, France, Japan, Tunisia, Uruguay, and other countries around the world. In return, these countries receive large numbers of packages with seeds of plants native to the Soviet Union.

Arboretum Park is located at 74 Kurortny Prospect and is open daily from 10 A.M. until 6 P.M.

Tree of Friendship

The Tree of Friendship grows on the Experimental Farm for Subtropical and Thermophillic Plants. It is thirty-six years old and a little over 4 meters (12 feet) tall.

For about thirty years the Soviet selectionist Fyodor Zorin worked in the garden of the Experimental Farm. Oranges and lemons can grow on open ground in Sochi, but the citrus trees suffer from frost. The need to evolve a frost-resistant variety was recognized. In order to speed up the process (it takes a long time to grow a new kind of citrus plant), Zorin grew, in natural environments, trees whose crowns consisted of several varieties of citrus and whose underparts were made up of different rootstocks.

In 1940 the Soviet scientist Otto Schmidt asked Zorin's permission to make a graft. Schmidt got permission, as did many after him, and this is how the Tree of Friendship was so named. Branches have been grafted to the tree and the harvest from the Tree of Friendship is sent to those who made the grafts. Packages of soil have arrived at the Experimental Farm from various parts of the world and the Soviet Union. Parcels from Leningrad and Pyatigorsk brought soil from the places where the Russian poets Pushkin and Lermontov were killed in duels; the tree also rests in earth from the grave of Leo Tolstoy in Yasnaya Polyana. A true symbol of universal desire for peace, the Tree of Friendship now grows forty-five varieties of fruit and has received grafts from people from 125 countries.

Mt. Bolshoi Akhun

An interesting excursion is the trip to Mt. Bolshoi Akhun. One of highest mountains in the coastal area, it is easily recognized by its observation tower which can be seen from a considerable distance. The trip from the center of Sochi to the top of the mountain and back (22 kilometers; 14 miles) takes approximately three and a half hours by bus.

The word "Akhun" comes from the pagan god Akhyn. It is said that man often visited the mountaintop in ancient times. Today the ascent is possible thanks to a road, 12 kilometers (7.5 miles) long, built in 1935. Later, the observation deck and a restaurant were opened for visitors.

Built in 1936, the tower was designed by the architect Sergei Vorobyov. It is a five-floor structure made of limestone and marl quarried from the mountain. The tower is 30.5 meters (100 feet) high and the structure tapers to a narrow observation platform on top. The restaurant was designed by the architect D. Chisliev, and is about one kilometer (.6 mile) from the tower.

Tourists can arrange excursions to Mt. Akhun through special tourist services. For those who prefer to visit the mountain unaccompanied, there is a direct bus line (Bus 39) between the Riviera (section of the city and also the name of the bus station) and the mountaintop. One can also reach Mt. Akhun by taxi.

Yew and Boxtree Grove

On the eastern side of Mt. Akhun, about 20 kilometers (12.5 miles) from the center of Sochi, is the Yew and Boxtree Grove, part of the Caucasian National Preserve. Having a total area of 260,000 hectares (650,000 acres), the preserve was set up in 1924 to protect, study, and increase the animal population, and to restore herds of aurochs.

The preserve is part of several climatic zones, ranging from subtropical to alpine. It contains about three thousand varieties of plants including oak, beech, hornbeam, maple, and ash. The upper forest zone consists mainly of spruce, some of which are 60 meters (200 feet) in height and two meters (80 inches) in diameter.

Among the animals that were near extinction not too long ago and are now multiplying in the preserve are deer, mountain goat, gazelle, raccoon dog, and Altai squirrel. The number of wild boar, bear, roe deer, mink, and wildcat have also increased, as well as turkey, golden eagle, griffon, vulture, and lammergeyer.

The yew and the boxtree, dead in most parts of the world, live in large numbers in the preserve. For this reason, in 1930 the Soviet government made the Yew and Boxtree Grove a national preserve.

Tea Plantation

The Krasnodar Territory, of which Sochi is part, is the northernmost area of the world where tea is grown. The vicinity has four major tea plantations, located at Solokh Aul, Goitkha, Maikop, and Dagomys. The tea farm near Dagomys is the largest of these with a total area of 650 hectares (1,625 acres). The farm also has 600 hectares (1,560 acres) under orchards and vineyards. Tea specialization is primarily in Chinese, Assami (Indian), and Ceylonese varieties (a hybrid of the Chinese and Assami tea leaves).

The plum orchards of the Dagomys tea farm are quite interesting. Plums were grown here before tea, yet it wasn't until 1876 that the Russian agronomist Fyodor Geiduk introduced plum growing in the Sochi area.

The Krasnodar Territory saw its first tea plantation established during the early part of this century. It was located at the village of Solokh Aul, 15 kilometers (9 miles) north of Dagomys. The man who began tea growing in the area was Judah Koshman, a peasant from the Ukraine. Tea seeds were sown on five acres of land. It was four years before the first harvest of tea leaves could be collected.

Despite obstacles presented by local merchants who sold imported tea, Koshman's plantation was successful. Today, Krasnodar varieties are sold along with Chinese and Ceylonese brands.

Caves

There are a number of large caves in the Caucasus that can be visited by tourists. Largest of the caves near Sochi are the Vorontsovskiye and the Kudepstinskiye.

The Vorontsovskiye Caves are named for the neighboring village of Vorontsovka. Specimens of bone, stone tools, and clay pottery found in these caves show that man had lived in this area some 15,000 to 20,000 years ago. Prehistoric settlements have been found in regions near the caves. Also accommodating primitive man were the Kudepstinskiye Caves. Here archaeologists have found tools, weapons, and bones of animals.

It is recommended that excursions be taken only with an experienced guide.

SOCHI: OUTLYING AREAS

The districts that comprise the Greater Sochi area extend for 144 kilometers (90 miles) along the Black Sea coast. Visitors to Sochi proper will find convenient transportation from the Lazarevskoye District to the north all the way down to Adler in the south. Each district enriches Greater Sochi with its own particular characteristics and specialties of product, service, and historical landmarks.

ADLER

In 1961 the coastal section of Adler was designated as part of Greater Sochi. Geographically, Adler falls into the Abkhazian Autonomous Republic, which is a section of Georgia. Located 35 kilometers (22 miles) south of center Sochi, Adler provides the central airport for the entire area, with connecting flights to all major Soviet air routes.

However, Adler provides much more than a flight terminal for its visitors. Many guests remain in Adler for their holidays. The climate is somewhat different from that of Sochi. The summers are hotter, the winters colder, and the rainfall slightly less. At Adler a turbulent and only recently controlled mountain stream called Mzymta flows into the Black Sea. Its frequent flooding made Adler at one time an infamous marshland noted as a breeding ground for malaria. Since 1921 all this has changed. Now Adler is a sunny, subtropical garden of fruits, vegetables, tea, and tobacco owing to the drainage system introduced after the Revolution. Adler also supplies vast quantities of pork, poultry, and eggs to the region. Another important industry is the fish-processing plant from which pickled, salted, and smoked fish products are distributed.

The Adler District is noted for many health spas and Young Pioneer Camps. Toward the mountains are various specialized sanitaria, hotels, campgrounds, and hiking stations; closer to the beach is a motel. To the north of Adler lies a special village of summer cottages built by and for the herring trawler sailors of Murmansk. The village is equipped with restaurants, clubhouses, health facilities, and cinema.

KHOSTA

To the north of Adler District is Khosta. The two districts are separated by the Kudepsta River. Khosta District is famous for its health treatment centers and contains more of them than any other district of Greater Sochi. The town of Khosta is located 20 kilometers (13 miles) south of center Sochi and is adjacent to a small stream of the same name, which empties into the Black Sea at Tikhaya Bay. The bay, whose name means "calm," is formed by Cape Vidny. It is believed that Khosta received its name from Genoese traders during the thirteenth, fourteenth, and fifteenth centuries, who called the coastal area "Costa." There is some evidence that the region was at the earliest inhabited by cavemen. There are also remains of pagan temples, castles, and forts which indicate a later sequence of inhabitants.

Before the 1917 Revolution, Khosta was a small village of huts dotting the slopes of Mt. Maly Akhun (Small Akhun), near Cape Vidny, and on the bank of the Khosta River were private villas. After the Revolution, Khosta was developed as a popular resort. The streets were widened, gardens and parks designed, and sanitaria were constructed. The most recent addition to Khosta's health services has been the result of a deep drilling which produced a bed of hydrogen sulfate water. This has enabled patients to receive medicinal bath treatments in Khosta instead of having to go to Matsesta. The city also provides Soviet travelers with a hiking station and Soviet artists with a hotel of their own equipped with studios as well as painters' and sculptors' supplies.

LAZAREVSKOYE

Lazarevskoye District, the northernmost district of Greater Sochi, occupies 109 kilometers (68 miles) of coastal area and includes the villages of Magri, Makopse, Lazarevskoye, Golvinka, Dagomys, and Loo. The Lazarevskoye District borders on Tuapse, a district of the Krasnodar Territory of the R.F.S.S.R. There are many health resorts and sanitaria in Lazarevskoye where climate, sea bathing, physiotherapy, diet, sulfur baths, curative mud, and exercise treatment are offered. Motor tourists are offered motel accommodations in Dagomys and Lazarevskoye and campsite facilities in Dagomys. Ashe and Dagomys provide hiking stations. Bus and train services connect the villages of the Lazarevskoye District with Sochi proper.

The name of this district commemorates Admiral Mikhail Lazarev, a military leader, Antarctic explorer, and scientist. Lazarevskoye Fort is connected with another Russian hero, Alexander Odoyevsky, who participated in the Decembrist uprising of 1825. For this he received twelve years' hard labor in Siberia as well as a demotion in military rank to that of private. After his Siberian sentence, he was exiled to the Caucasus.

North of Lazarevskoye about 10 kilometers (6 miles) is Ashe, a village whose name comes from a mountain stream. Ashe is famous for its excellent beaches and mountains suitable for climbing. The Gorge of Mamed is a noted site among climbers of this section of the Caucasus called the Ashe Range. The slopes ascend in terraced steps and ledges. In the Gorge of Mamed are waterfalls and several grottoes. In another area of the Ashe Range is Mt. Lysaya (Bald) which provides a panoramic view of the Greater Caucasus.

Dagomys, named for the Dagomys River, is a village adjacent to Sochi proper. A well-known hiking center is located on the riverbank close to the beach. The facilities offered here are required by the many hikers who pass through this area which is a terminus of all the hiking routes through the Caucasian State Preserve. The slopes of Mt. Armyanka provide beautiful views of the Greater Sochi area, the Black Sea, and the Greater Caucasus. In addition to hiking and other tourist facilities, Dagomys possesses many camps for Soviet children.

Foreign tourists may reach Sochi:

By Rail: from Finland via Vyborg, Leningrad, Moscow, Kharkov, and Rostov-on-Don;

from Western Europe via Brest, Minsk, and Moscow or via Kishinev, Odessa, and Kiev;

from Hungary, Yugoslavia, and Czechoslovakia via Lvov and Kiev;

from Turkey via Yerevan and Tbilisi;

from East or Southeast Asia via Chita and Moscow or Ussuriisk and Moscow.

By Air: Sochi maintains air service with more than eighty cities of the Soviet Union.

By Automobile: via Moscow, Kharkov, and Rostov-on-Don and then along the Great Caucasian Circle motorway linking Sochi with Tbilisi, Sukhumi, Pyatigorsk, and other Soviet cities.

By Sea: via Odessa, Yalta, and Batumi or Sukhumi. Also, most Soviet cruise ships on the Black Sea call at Sochi.

USEFUL INFORMATION

Intourist, Sochi office, 91 Kurortny Prospect, Tel: 92–29–35.

Hotels

Gorizont, 24 Prosveshcheniya Street
Intourist and Camelia, 91 Kurortny Prospect
Kavkaz, 72 Kurortny Prospect
Khosta, 14 Yasenskaya Street
Leningrad, 2 Morskoy Pereulok
Primorskaya, 1 Sokolov Street
Sochi and Magnolia, 50 Kurortny Prospect
Zhemchuzhina, 5 Chenomorskaya Street

Restaurants

Akhun, Mt. Bolshoi Akhun
Dietichesky (dietetic food), 10 Voikov Street
Goluboy, 8 Voikov Street
Gorka, 22 Voikov Street
Intourist, 91 Kurortny Prospect
Kavkaz, 72 Kurortny Prospect
Khosta, Parkovaya Street in Khosta
Kuban, 5 Gagarin Street
Kurortny, 12 Chernomorskaya Street
Lazurny, 103 Kurortny Prospect
Morskoy, Harbor Station Building
Novy Sochi, at bus stop Gorbolnitsa (City Hospital)
Primorsky, 1 Sokolov Street
Sochi, 50 Kurortny Prospect
Svetlana, 10 Pushkin Street
Volna, Harbor Station in Khosta
Zheleznodorozhny, Railway Station Building

Cafés

Lakomka (Sweet Tooth), 3 Gargarin Street
Ogonyok, Privokzalnaya Square
Olyen, 105 Kurortny Prospect (bus stops at Gorny Vozdukh)
Prokhlada, Oktyabrsky Skver (bus stops at Platanovaya Alleya)
Sputnik, in the building of Cinema Sputnik, 11 Bulvarny Pereulok
Teatralnoye, 15 Theater Street

Tri Kedra, Riviersky Pereulok (at Riviera Park)
Vareniki (curd dumplings), at the city market
Yug, at Riviera Park

Museums

Arboretum Park, 74 Kurortny Prospect. Open daily from 10 A.M. until 6 P.M. Bus stops at the park or Fabritsius sanatorium on Kurortny Prospect.

Nikolai Ostrovsky Museum, 4 Pereulok Ostrovskoyo. Open daily, except Wednesday, from 10 A.M. until 6 P.M.; on Tuesdays from 10 A.M. until 4 P.M.

Sochi Museum of Regional Studies, 29 Ordzhonikidze Street. Open daily, except Tuesday, from 10 A.M. until 6 P.M.

Theaters, Cinemas, Circus

Sochi State Theater, Theater Square. Evening performances begin at 8 P.M., matinees at noon.

Summer Theater, Park imeni Frunze (bus stops at Svetlana or Frunze park).

Wide-Screen cinema Kuban, 41 Vorovskogo Street

Wide-Screen cinema Looch, Khosta

Wide-Screen cinema Sputnik, 11 Bulvarny Pereulok

Cinema Khronika (newsreel), 7 Sokolov Street

Cinema Oktyabr, Adler

Cinema Rodina, 25 Krasnoarmeiskaya Street

Cinema Smena, Pereulok Voikova

Cinema Sochi, 1 Svobodny Pereulok

Cinema Temp, Lazarevskoye

Circus, Pushkinsky Prospect. Buses 1, 2, 3, 3D, 4, 5, 8, 19, 23. Open from May to November. Performances begin at 8 P.M.; on Saturday at 4 P.M. and 8 P.M.; on Sunday at noon, 4 P.M. and 8 P.M.

Shops

Beryozka, 16a Primorskaya Street

Books, 8 Maxim Gorky Street

Department Store, 2 Liebknecht Street

Flowers, 26 Kurortny Prospect

Gastronome No. 1, 16 Voikov Street, corner of Kurortny Prospect (city's largest foodstuff store). Open daily from 8 A.M. until 11 P.M.

Gifts, 40 Maxim Gorky Street

Hunting and Fishing Gear, 55 Sovetskaya Street

Izumrud (watches, gifts, gold and silver ware, crystal), 26 Kurortny Prospect

Resort Goods, 4 Kooperativnaya Street
Souvenir Shop, 25 Kurortny Prospect
Svetlyachok (children's store), Chaikovskogo Street, opposite city market

Transportation and Communications

Aeroflot Agency, Harbor Station, Tel: 92–26–36
Airport, Adler, Tel: 92–33–11
Harbor Station, 1 Voikov Street
Helicopter Port, Plastunskaya Street, Tel: 92–38–72
Railway Station, inquiry office, Tel: 99–30–44
Central Post Office, 35 Vorovskogo Street
Interurban Telephone, 35 Vorovskogo Street, Tel: 05 and 07

SUKHUMI AND BATUMI

SUKHUMI—General Information and History in Brief

Sukhumi, lying between the mouths of the Gumits and Kelasuri rivers, is known as the "garden city." Three hundred hectares (750 acres) of this small city are covered with greenery. Palms, magnolias, cypresses, and eucalyptuses cover the streets of Sukhumi where the average temperature is 15 degrees C. (59 degrees F).

In 1888 an international congress of physicians decided that Sukhumi would be a fine climatic resort. As a result, a few wealthy persons built private resort institutions. Today, Abkhazia has dozens of sanitaria of which six are in or near Sukhumi. The famous medicinal springs Tkarcheli and Avadkhara are near Lake Ritsa. In all, the republic has about one hundred mineral springs.

Sukhumi is the capital of Abkhazia, an autonomous republic forming part of the Georgian Soviet Socialist Republic. The first century B.C. saw the landing of Roman legions at Sukhumi Bay and the driving of the Abkhazians into the mountains. The invaders built the fortress of Sebastopolis for use in defense of the town. It was during this time that the town of Tskhumi (ancient name of Sukhumi) was founded on the shores of the Besletka River.

The Romans were challenged by the Apsils and Abazgs in the third and fourth centuries A.D. For protection and defense, the Kelasuri or Great Abkhazian Wall was built. However, a new invader threatened Tskhumi, and in the eighth century A.D., the Arabs destroyed both the fortress and the town of Tskhumi. Turkish rule was established in the mid-sixteenth century and did not end until 1810 when Abkhazia, with the aid of Russia, freed itself from the hands of outside forces. On March 24, 1921, the Soviet Republic of Abkhazia was proclaimed.

PLACES OF INTEREST

Botanical Gardens

While Sukhumi seems to be a park in itself, you will find a trip to the Botanical Gardens to be most interesting. Although the Sukhumi Botanical Gardens occupy an area of only 4 hectares (10 acres) eight hundred varieties of trees and shrubs grow there.

Special note should be made of the rare and unusual specimens. Among these are the zelkova trees from the Tertiary Period, the Pitsunda pine, ancient sequoias, a gutta-percha tree, a strawberry tree, a tulip tree, and a lacquer tree.

The hothouse contains plants of the tropical variety, among them the giant cactus and the golden bamboo. Blue water lilies, water poppies, and the large-leafed Victoria regia can be seen at the reservoirs of the Botanical Gardens.

State Museum

Not far from the Sukhumi Botanical Gardens, located on Lenin Street, is the State Museum, named for the Abkhazian poet Dmitry Guliya. The museum displays exhibits depicting the life of the Abkhazian people from ancient times to the present day. The mystery of ancient Dioscuria is particularly fascinating.

The town of Dioscuria on Sukhumi Bay was built by the Greeks in the sixth to fifth centuries B.C. The town served as the center of trade between the Black Sea coast and ancient Greece. Several written sources have confirmed the existence of Dioscuria, but the town itself seemed to have disappeared without a trace. A search lasting more than twenty-five years culminated in the finding of the vanished town at the bottom of Sukhumi Bay. Archaeologists have determined that the shores of Sukhumi Bay over a period of time kept sinking until Dioscuria was completely submerged.

The State Museum displays the finds that were discovered among the ruins of the ancient town. Amphorae, weaving implements, metalworking tools, water pipes, and works of art are representative of these treasures.

Mt. Sukhumi

Mt. Sukhumi is a place for recreation. It can be reached by way of Dmitry Guliya Street (Ulitsa Dmitriya Gulia), going up the wide basaltic staircase built for pedestrians. A 32 hectare (80-acre) forest-park complements the mountain slope. Because the plants have been specially selected, the park is always in bloom.

Artistic fountains are everywhere and from the observation platform one has a beautiful view of the city and the bay from Cape Sukhumi to Cape Kororsky.

Monkey Nursery

Located on Mt. Trapetsia is one of the most frequently visited attractions in Sukhumi—the world-famous Primate Breeding Station of the Institute of Experimental Pathology and Therapy of the Academy of Medical Sciences of the U.S.S.R.

Established in 1927, the station covers an area of 25 hectares (62.5 acres). The nursery consists of laboratories and clinics, as well as the "laboratory of higher nervous activity" where experimental neurological surgery is performed on monkeys.

During the early years of the institute, monkeys were brought from other countries but were unable to adapt to the conditions of their new surroundings. Of the first fifteen monkeys brought to Sukhumi on the steamer *Pestel,* only four were alive when the shipment reached its destination, and two of the four died later. Scientists at the nursery did not know how to keep the monkeys alive during the winter since they could not stand to be in the enclosed rooms and they caught cold outside.

In 1928 two monkeys were born in the nursery and survived. A particularly hardy pair, they were able to withstand the winter and adapted to a diet of vegetables, nuts, and various forms of bread. Today there are more than 1,500 monkeys in the nursery and almost all of them were born in Sukhumi.

State Theater of Abkhazia

The State Theater, built in 1952, is located in the center of the city at 1 Pushkin Street. The building, in Georgian style, boasts fine pieces of sculpture. The busts of famous Georgian and Abkhazian artists are on display, among them Georgi Eristavi, Lado Meskhishvili, Zakhary Paleashvili, Kote Mardzhanishvili, and Samson Chanba.

The performances of the State Theater are primarily by Georgian and Abkhazian theater companies. Stagings vary from Shakespearean classics to plays by Soviet and foreign dramatists.

HISTORICAL SITES IN AND AROUND SUKHUMI

There are several sites of historical interest in Sukhumi that can be visited and examined in a relatively short period of time. In 1905 in the Roman fortress near the pier Grigori Ordzhonikidze, the man who headed the revolutionary movement in Abkhazia, was imprisoned by tsarist authorities.

A favorite with visitors to Sukhumi is the site of the ruins of the Castle of King Bagrat. The castle was built between nine and ten centuries ago and is located in the southeast area of the city. It was built on a mountain spur close to the shore of the Besletka River and served to defend the Sukhumi harbor against attack.

Four kilometers (2.5 miles) from Sukhumi, on the left shore of the Kelasuri River, is a watchtower. This tower is the beginning section of the Great Abkhazian Wall. The sixth-century wall was 160 kilometers (100 miles) long, stretching from the entire southern part of Abkhazia and reaching the sea again at the Inguri River. The wall is now in ruins, but several fortifications still remain.

The Dranda Cathedral, dating from the sixth to eighth centuries, is located about 17.6 kilometers (11 miles) from Sukhumi. Of equal interest is the Mokva Cathedral, built by Leon II of Abkhazia ten centuries ago. The cathedral stands on a plateau where the Mokva joins the Deab River. Mikhail Chachba (Shervashidze), the last ruler of Abkhazia, and his son, writer Georgi Chachba (Shervashidze), are buried here.

USEFUL INFORMATION

Intourist Office, 2 Frunze Street, Service Bureau, Tel: 52–01

Hotels

Abkhazia, 2 Frunze Street
Sinop, Tbilisi Highway
Tbilisi, 2 Dzhguburi Street

Restaurants

Abkhazia, 2 Frunze Street
Amra, Rustaveli Prospect
Amza, Sukhumskaya Gora
Dioskuria, 6 Gogol Street
Eshera, Verkhnyaya Eshera

Merkheuli, Merkheuli
Tbilisi, 2 Dzhguburi Street

Museums and Theaters

State Museum, 20 Lenin Street
State Theater of Abkhazia, 1 Pushkin Street
Summer Theater of the Philharmonic Society, 18 Lenin Street

Transportation and Communications

Aeroflot Agency, 4 Sovetskaya Street
Central Post Office, 92 Mira Prospect
Railway Station, Sukhumi Station
Seaside Station, 56 Rustaveli Prospect

BATUMI—General Information and History in Brief

Batumi is the capital of the Adjarian Autonomous Soviet Socialist Republic. Both a port and a large industrial center, it is located only 12.8 to 16 kilometers (8 to 10 miles) from the Turkish border.

In ancient times Adjaria was part of the West Georgian state of Colchis. Colchis had a reputation in the ancient world as being a very rich land, and this legend brought to its shores numerous foreign invaders. The Arabs tried to settle in Adjaria in the seventh century but did not succeed. It was not until the tenth century, when Adjaria was united with the Georgian kingdom, that Seljuk Turks were able to settle there.

By the end of the sixteenth century, the Turks captured Adjaria and Batumi. The fight against foreign invaders continued from the time of the Turkish takeover until 1878, when Adjaria became part of Russia. A small city surrounded with forests and marshes in the mid-nineteenth century, Batumi began the task of rebuilding after Georgia was annexed by Russia. The first and most important priority was the draining of the mosquito-ridden marshlands.

Soon the first industrial enterprises appeared, a water supply system was built, and the streets were paved. The only drawback to these improvements was that they were initiated in the center of the city, while in Chaoba (meaning "swamp" in Georgian), the district where most of the working people lived, conditions remained unchanged.

Batumi was greatly strengthened economically with the construction in 1883 of a railway connecting Batumi with Poti, Tbilisi, and Baku. Within a few years, Batumi ranked third among the industrial centers of Transcaucasia.

The Bolshevik Revolution saw Batumi workers unite to join the Red forces. By 1920 Abkhazia was engaged in a civil war and Georgia was in danger of an armed uprising. The Menshevik government fled the city and on March 18, 1921, Batumi became a Soviet city. Three months later, Adjaria was proclaimed an Autonomous Soviet Republic and part of the Georgian Socialist Republic.

Today Batumi, a city with a population of about 100,000, is the main exporter of Soviet oil. Once a city whose principal industry was the production of containers for transporting kerosene, Batumi now ships thousands of tons of citrus fruit, tea, and tobacco.

Places of Interest

MUSEUM OF THE REVOLUTION

If you are interested in the Revolution and its historical and sociological results, the Museum of the Revolution should not be missed. It is located at 8 Gorky Street in a Georgian-style building designed by K. Djavakhishvili.

Most of the exhibits relate to the Revolution as it took place in Batumi. Displays begin with the early strikes of Batumi laborers and continue through the success of the Revolution in Adjaria. Re-created for tourists are the revolutionary actions of Batumi workers, the activities of the Batumi social-democratic organization, the strikes and demonstrations of 1902, and the general strike of 1905.

BATUMI BOTANICAL GARDENS

The Batumi Botanical Gardens, founded in 1912 by A. Krasnov, cover an area of 100 hectares (250 acres). The land is divided into several sections: Himalayan, Australian, New Zealand, Mediterranean, North and South American, Mexican, Japanese, Chinese, and the Transcaucasian subtropical area. Soviet scientists have continued the work started by Krasnov, and today there are six hundred new kinds of plants in Adjaria.

PALACE OF CULTURE

The Palace of Culture, built in 1954 by the architect G. Yerkamaishvili, is both beautiful in design and interesting. It is located in the settlement of the Batumi oil workers. The entrance arch is decorated with bas-reliefs and it has an artistically decorated auditorium that accommodates seven hundred people. The palace also has a gymnasium, a lecture hall, and a library.

Health Institutions and Resort Areas

Batumi is a leading health and resort area with twenty-seven sanitaria and rest homes. The three best resort centers are Green Cape, Makhindjauri, located 6.4 kilometers (4 miles) from Batumi, and Tsikhis-Dziri, which is about 19.2 kilometers (12 miles) by rail. The town of Kobuleti, although only 32 kilometers (20 miles) from Batumi, is less humid and has less rainfall. At the Makhindjauri resort one can undergo various kinds of treatment. There are sulfur springs, baths, test laboratories, and consultation rooms.

Unlike the Kobuleti and Makhindjauri resorts, which are situated in the valleys, the Tsikhis-Dziri is in the mountains. Also located on a hill, the Green Cape is considered by many to be the most beautiful area in Adjaria. From the hilltop one has a vast view of the sea and the bamboo and tangerine groves.

Near Green Cape is the Chakva state farm's tea plantations which can be visited by tourists.

USEFUL INFORMATION

Intourist Office, Hotel Intourist, Service Bureau, Tel: 97–3–25

Hotels

Hotel Intourist, 11/1 Ninoshvili Street
Tourist Hostel, 37 Ninoshvili Street

Museums and Theaters

Adjaria State Museum, 4 Djincheradze Street
Museum of the Revolution, 8 Gorky Street
Komsomolets Cinema, 14 Dzhaparidze Street
Letny Summer Theater, Primorsky Park
State Drama Theater, 1 Rustaveli Street
Tbilisi Cinema, 6 Baratashvili Street

Transportation and Communications

Aeroflot Office, 39 Lenin Street
Central Post Office, 33 Oktyabrsky Prospect
Railway Station, 39 Kalinin Street

THE CRIMEA

When ice covered the entire East European plain, man discovered that the climate of the Crimea was more hospitable to his survival. This simple fact explains why two hundred of the four hundred Paleolithic camps discovered in the Soviet Union are in the Crimea.

Twenty-five kilometers (15.6 miles) east of Simferopol is the ancient cave dwelling known as the Kiyik-Koba grotto. Based on the findings of stone implements and the remains of a Neanderthal man, archaeologists believe that man lived there 100,000 years ago.

The first Crimean inhabitants that left behind traces of their civilization in written sources and surviving geographical names are the Cimmerian and Tauri tribes. Existing materials show that these tribes appeared in the Crimea during the first millennium B.C. The Scythians, a nomadic people who came to the coastal area from the Caucasus, overpowered the Cimmerian settlements during the first half of the first millennium B.C.

By the fourth to third centuries B.C., the Scythian tribes began building fortified settlements and towns in the Crimea. The first Scythian state, the kingdom of Ateas, emerged in the fourth century.

The Tauri and Scythian population maintained close economic ties with the Greek city-states. The Black Sea, previously referred to by the Greeks as Pontos Axenos (Inhospitable Sea), came to be called Pontos Euxenos (Hospitable Sea) as trade developed and flourished.

The first century B.C. saw the Greek colonies known as the Bosporan kingdom and Chersonesus come under Roman rule. Rome maintained strongholds along the Crimean coast for the next three centuries only to fall prey to Byzantium after the collapse of the empire. By the early Middle Ages, the Crimea was populated mostly by the descendants of the Tauri, Scythians, Samatians, and Alani.

The Crimea, situated at strategic crossroads of important trade routes, was continually raided by nomadic tribes coming from the inner regions of Asia. Goths, Huns, Khazars, Pechenegs, and Polovtsi were among the invaders. By the end of the sixth century the greater part of the Crimea was occupied by the Khazars.

Christianity spread from Byzantium, and by the ninth century several Christian monasteries had taken root in the area. The early Middle Ages also saw the establishment of contact with East Slavs. Prince Bravlin of Novgorod in the early ninth century and Prince Vladimir of Kiev in 988–989 conquered areas of the coastal territory of the Crimea.

The great Varangian Route, from the Baltic countries to Byzantium, was now under the control of the Novgorod and Kiev princes. The major Crimean trade centers of Chersonesus, Bosporus, and Sugdeya (known in Russian as Korsun, Korchev, and Surozh) played important roles in the economic and political relations between Rus and Byzantium and the East.

Still open to invasion, the Crimea in the thirteenth and fourteenth centuries was penetrated by Pechenegs, Polovtsi, and later Tatar-Mongols. By the end of the thirteenth century a vice-regency of the Golden Horde had established itself in the Crimea. As a result, ties between the Crimea and Rus were broken. In the mid-fourteenth century the center of the Crimean vice-regency was in Solkhat (presently Stary Krym).

During the summer of 1475 the Turks landed near Kaffa (the center of Genoese colonies in the Crimea). In little time the Turkish armies controlled the entire coast. The Tatars allied themselves with the new invaders. An immediate consequence of the takeover was the destruction of the advanced culture of the local tribes. Having enslaved the population, Turkish and Tatar feudal lords established rule over the area in the form of the Crimean khanate.

Using the Crimea as a base, Turkey launched attacks on Russia and the Ukraine. A bitter struggle ensued between the Russian and Ukrainian people and the Crimean khanate and Turkey. In 1768 Turkey was engaged in total war with Russia and after years of fighting Russia regained the lands on the Black Sea coast and secured an exit to the sea. The peace treaty of 1774, signed by Turkey, granted full independence to the Crimean khanate. In 1783 the foreign lords of the Crimea swore allegiance to the tsar, and the Crimea became part of Russia. Sevastopol, a Black Sea naval base, was founded in the same year and Simferopol, the present center of the Crimean Region, saw its founding near the Ak Mechet village on the Salgir River in 1784.

During the first half of the nineteenth century the Crimean Peninsula experienced an increase in population and trade. The growth of towns and the development of agriculture were rapid. Throughout the 1800s the Crimea prospered and the construction of a railway linking Sevastopol, Feodosia, and Kerch greatly influenced the region's economy. Between 1865 and 1890 the population of the Crimea doubled.

In June 1905 the crew of the battleship *Potemkin* mutinied. This revolt in the Black Sea navy marked the beginning of armed revolts throughout the Russian army and navy. An uprising occurred on board the cruiser *Ochakov*, in Sevastopol, in November 1905. To follow were revolts by the crews of eleven other naval vessels and among soldiers of the Sevastopol garrison. By 1906–07 revolutionary activity was common throughout many Crimean towns. Soviet rule was proclaimed in Sevastopol in January 1918.

The Crimean economy was ailing at this time as a result of the Civil War and foreign intervention during World War I, but prewar five-year plans called for the Crimea to be transformed from a totally agricultural area to a highly industrial and modern agricultural complex. Among the new industries that developed were ship repairs, oil production, and the manufacture of farm tools and machinery. Expanded were the industries of canning, wine-making, tobacco, and fishing.

A decree issued by the Soviet government in 1920, "On Utilizing the Crimea for Treating Working People," was an important step toward the establishment of the region as a great health resort and vacation center. The Crimea, during the whole of the twenty-four years before the Revolution, had only 360,000 visitors. By 1940 the area was equipped with 195 sanitaria and vacation homes with facilities for 300,000 persons per holiday season. Today the region consists of the entire peninsula and is part of the Ukrainian Soviet Socialist Republic. The eight cities that are the Crimea are Alushta, Eupatoria, Feodosia, Jankoi, Kerch, Sevastopol, Simferopol, and Yalta. The major industries are metalworking, mining, production of building products, wine-making, canning, and tobacco production.

THE GREATER YALTA AREA

YALTA—History in Brief

Yalta, known as the capital of the southern coast of the Crimea, stretches along the seashore from Baidarskiye Gates in the west to Mount Bear in the east incorporating the resorts of Alupka, Foross, Gaspra, Gurzuf, Koreiz, Livadia, Miskhor, and Simeiz.

The exact date of Yalta's founding is obscure, although it is known that there was a Greek settlement on the site in the eleventh century. It is surmised that the name Yalta was derived from the Greek word *yalos,* meaning shore.

The first guidebook on Yalta was published in Odessa, in French, in 1834. It described the city as having thirty households and a population of 224. The Nikitsky Botanical Gardens, founded in 1812, and the Magarach School of Viticulture were mentioned as being the major attractions. After the 1860s, Yalta began to develop into a fashionable resort for the aristocracy and it was not until the 1870s that Yalta undertook the building of facilities for large numbers of people. Private cottages and small hotels appeared between the Uchan Su and Derekoika rivers. The Hotel Rossiya, a three-story structure, was completed in 1875. Today it is known as Hotel Tourida.

In 1910–11 approximately 3 kilometers (1.9 miles) from the city (in Livadia) a palace was erected in the Early Renaissance style. Designed by the architect Krasnov, the Livadia Palace was the summer residence of the tsar and his family. The palace gained world recognition in February of

1945 when the heads of states of the United States, Great Britain, and the Soviet Union met there to discuss the final steps in the ultimate defeat of Germany.

Among the list of prominent names associated with Yalta are Anton Chekhov, who in 1898 came to Yalta, built a house, and lived there for five years; Nikolai Nekrasov, the Russian poet who lived in the Rossiya Hotel; and the poet Vladimir Mayakovsky, who fifty years later lived in the same room as Nekrasov.

When Soviet power was established in the Crimea in 1920, the palaces, private hotels, and guest houses belonging to the tsars and grand dukes became state property. On this foundation the area was developed as a holiday resort and medical treatment center for all the peoples of the Soviet Union. In 1921 Yalta had 18 sanitaria able to accommodate 7,000 people, and by 1941 the number of people receiving treatment for various ailments increased to 20,000. Today the Greater Yalta area has 80 sanitaria and vacation homes able to accommodate 30,000 people at a time. Over a million people each year spend all or part of their vacations in Yalta.

The climate of Yalta in comparison with other resort areas shows that its mean winter temperature is closest to that of Venice. The summer season is quite hot with a mean temperature in July of 24 degrees C (75.2 degrees F).

Chekhov Memorial Museum

Anton Chekhov was probably the most popular figure in Yalta during the time of his residence there. Aside from providing medical aid and advice, he was a member of the board of trustees of Yalta's gymnasium (secondary school) for girls (now School No. 5).

Chekhov came to Yalta for the first time during the summer of 1888. The purpose of his visit was nothing more than to satisfy an urge to travel. For three weeks during July and August of the following year, Chekhov stayed in Yalta and worked on "A Dull Story." Five years later, not realizing how seriously ill he really was, Chekhov returned to Yalta for medical treatment. In 1898, acting on the advice of his physicians, he decided to make Yalta his permanent home, bringing with him his mother and sister. Chekhov bought a small plot of land and built a two-story house which was known to his contemporaries as the White Cottage. He lived there from 1899 to 1904.

After the Civil War in the Crimea ended in the spring of 1921, the Yalta Revolutionary Military Committee decided to preserve Chekhov's house and his sister was asked to supervise the organization of a museum. Through her efforts everything in the house was kept exactly as it was on May 1, 1904, the day Chekhov left Yalta for the last time.

Visitors see the dining room, the writer's bedroom, and his study in their original state. From the dining room, looking through a windowed verandah, you can see the garden in which Chekhov planted many of the trees. Above the sofa in the drawing room hangs a photograph (taken in 1899) of the writer, under which are the three palm leaves that he received at the last performance of *The Sea Gull.*

Chekhov usually worked in his study, and on the walls of this room hang portraits and photographs of his contemporaries. These include photos of almost all the members of the Moscow Art Theater of that time. It was in this house that he wrote some of his most memorable works, including *The Three Sisters, The Cherry Orchard,* "The Lady With a Dog," "The Betrothed," "At Christmas," and "In the Ravine."

As Chekhov's health deteriorated, he worked at the little table near his bed, which is on display. The last time the writer slept here was on April 30, 1904. The following day he left for Moscow for medical consultation and never returned to Yalta. After his stay in Moscow, Chekhov went to Badenweiler in Germany, where he died on July 2, 1904.

The Chekhov Memorial Museum is open daily, except Tuesdays, from 8 A.M. until 7 P.M.

LIVADIA

Located 3 kilometers (1.9 miles) outside Yalta is Livadia, former summer residence of the tsars. Livadia was probably settled by Greek colonists and it is thought that the name originated from the Greek *livadion,* meaning "meadow."

In the 1840s, a 40-hectare (100 acre) park was laid out and the first palace buildings were constructed. The entire estate was owned by Count Patotsky. Building was increased under the supervision of architect Monigetti when, in 1860, the estate was passed over to the tsar. Two palaces, as well as conservatories and stables, were added. Also, the central part of the park was redesigned.

In 1911, on the site of an older palace, a new one designed by architect Krasnov was built. It was constructed in white Inkkerman stone in the Italian Renaissance style. The white façades of the palace are ornamented with fretwork. The interior is decorated with mosaics and wood and marble carvings.

The two patios of the palace are of Arabian and Italian design. A wrought-iron gateway and railings of intricate lace-like design characterize the Arabian Patio. The Italian one is surrounded by a large rectangular gallery with a marble floor, its columns similar to those of the main entrance. The patio is linked to a Byzantine-style palace church by a smaller gallery. The church was built in 1866 by Monigetti and nearby one can see a bell tower and a gray marble column.

The Livadia Palace was nationalized in 1920 and converted into a medical sanitarium for peasants. The first of its kind, the sanitarium was also used as a meeting place where peasants could attend lectures on scientific, agricultural, and political topics. Those who were illiterate were taught to read and write.

World War II marked a temporary end to the use of the palace as a medical facility. The invading German forces confiscated all the medical equipment, plundered the Grand Palace, and destroyed the smaller palace. The Great Hall of the structure was reconstructed and was ready to accommodate the opening of the Yalta Conference on February 4, 1945.

The present-day Livadian sanitarium is used for treating general and cardiac conditions. Accommodating approximately 1,000 people at a time, it is the largest medical facility in the Crimea. The former music room of the tsars in the Grand Palace presently serves as the sanitarium library and reading room with a stock of 12,000 volumes. Publications are available in the national languages of the U.S.S.R. as well as in foreign languages.

The beautiful Livadian Park provides a comfortable and relaxing stroll. Landscaped over 60 hectares (150 acres), it contains 400 species of trees and shrubs.

In 1960 a new sanitarium, Chernomorye (The Black Sea), was opened in Livadia. Designed by Moscow architects, it accommodates 250 patients. The structure was awarded a certificate for design at the Brussels World's Fair of 1958.

OREANDA

Oreanda, a pleasant resort area between Livadia and Cape Ai Todor, is reached by walking along the "tsar's lane," a path linking the Livadia and Oreanda royal estates and the scene of royal walks and rides. Running through dense woods, the path leads to a rotunda from which one has a beautiful view of the seashore.

Mast (Machtovaya) Rock is visible from the rotunda. A gray mass split into two parts, the rock conceals a natural grotto which archaeologists believe to have been a dwelling place of primitive man. Also of historical interest is the Krestovy (Cross) Cliff to the left. Residents of the Crimea have given it the name "bloody" because it was here that White Guards shot revolutionary workers and sailors of Sevastopol and Yalta.

At the base of the rocks once stood a palace which was severely damaged by fire in 1882. The remains were used to build a Byzantine-style church which still stands today. The mosaics that complement the interior are the work of the Venetian master L. Salviati. Also here are the buildings of the Lower Oreanda Sanitarium. This facility is well equipped for medical treatment and has a beautiful seawater swimming pool.

ALUPKA

The resort town of Alupka is one of the most beautiful in the Crimea. It is a wonderful area for vacationing throughout the entire year. The weather is generally warmer than in Yalta and the humidity rarely exceeds 70 percent. The beauty of the town is enhanced by Mt. Ai Petri, which can be seen 35 kilometers (21.9 miles) away.

The most interesting tourist attraction is the Alupka Palace in the center of the town. The palace and its surrounding park belonged to Count Mikhail Voronstov, governor-general of the Novorossiisk Territory. Obsessed with impressing people by his wealth, this owner of estates in seventeen guberniyas and 80,000 serfs spent over nine million silver rubles on the estate.

The designer of the palace was Edward Blore, court architect for King William IV and Queen Victoria of England. (He was also the designer of Buckingham Palace in London.) Work on the Alupka Palace began in 1830 and continued for eighteen years. Its construction was supervised by William Hunt, also an English architect.

The palace takes its style from a variety of influences; it is in part reminiscent of medieval castles, while the northern façade of the central building and the western wing show a modification of the Tudor style. The façade facing the sea is modeled after the Alhambra Palace in Granada.

Flowerbeds surround the palace. At the front are two marble fountains. Near the right wing is the Fountain of Flowers and farther down the slope is the marble Shell Fountain. Nearby is the Fountain of Tears.

The interior consists of 150 beautifully decorated rooms. Gothic ornamentation in wood is prevalent in the vestibule, antechamber, dining room, and billiard room. The wainscots, doors, and ceilings are made of fumed oak. The fireplaces, of polished stone, are also Gothic-style. In the dining room are four panel paintings by Hubert Robert, an eighteenth-century French artist.

Stucco moldings can be found in the blue drawing room and excellent sculpture is abundant on the terraces of the southern side, in the blue drawing room, and in the winter garden. On display are sculptural portraits of Count Voronstov's family and relatives as well as copies of statues of ancient gods and philosophers.

In the reception rooms furniture of the early nineteenth century, made of walnut, mahogany, and oak, complements the artistic work of Voronstov's carvers, plasterers, and needleworkers. Also of artistic note are bronze candelabra, vases, and items of cut glass, porcelain, and malachite.

The 40-hectare (100 acre) park surrounding the Alupka Palace was landscaped about 145 years ago by a German gardener, Karl Kebach.

Alupka Park has a collection of more than 200 species of trees and shrubs from different countries. The park is graced by ponds, cascades, and streams. The most well known pond, Swan Lake, is surrounded by ashes and bald cypresses and large white swans glide over its surface.

MASSANDRA

For those who appreciate excellent wine, a visit to Massandra is a must. Just to the east of Yalta, Massandra is the wine-making center of the Crimea. At a cost of one million rubles, the country's oldest wine vault was built in 1898. The main cellar consists of seven tunnels, each 164 meters (492 feet) in length and four to five meters (13 to 16 feet) in width.

The Massandra Winery was founded in 1936 and a new wine cellar was completed in 1957. Able to store ten million liters at a time, the winery is supplied by twelve state and six collective vineyards.

An important scientific research center is the Magarach Institute of Viticulture and Wine Making. Involved with the development of new brands of wine, the institute is especially dedicated to the problems of raising grape yields, breeding and introducing better grape varieties, and controlling pests and diseases that attack the vine.

CRIMEAN GAME PRESERVE

One of the most interesting places in the Crimea, the Crimean Game Preserve extends into the mountains from a road that branches off from the Yalta-Simferopol Highway after Massandra. The preserve begins 600 meters (183 feet) above sea level at Pear (Grushevaya) Glade. It extends into the mountains and opens onto a wide plateau. Even in summer there is sufficient chill in the area to warrant a sweater or wind-breaker. The game preserve was founded in 1923 on the site of the former royal hunting grounds. Today it covers approximately 32,000 hectares (80,000 acres) of mountain plateau and part of the northern and southern slopes of the Main Range.

The preserve has thirty-six species of mammals, the oldest being the Crimean stag, which has inhabited the mountain forests for thousands of years. It was popular hunting prey for its flesh, durable skins, and antlers, which were all invaluable to the human inhabitants in ancient times. During the Middle Ages large numbers of the stag wandered into the northern steppes. In the nineteenth century the population of the Crimean stag declined because they were hunted without restriction.

One of the most interesting animals in the preserve, the mountain ram (also known as the European moufflon), is a native of Corsica. Brought to the Crimea from the Askania-Nova Sanctuary (the largest in the Soviet Union) in 1913, it began populating the *yaila* (mountain pasture) and the mixed forests. Today the Crimea is the only region of the Soviet Union where the moufflon is found. The species prefers the upper mountain areas and goes to the valleys only in winter when hunger and snowdrifts drive it out of the mountains.

Among other species found in the Crimean Game Preserve are the stone marten, the wild boar, the fat badger, the Crimean weasel, the mountain fox, hare, and squirrel.

There are 300 species of birds (almost half of all the species found in the Soviet Union) including the woodcock, the quail, the wild pigeon, vultures and griffon vultures, eagles, falcons, and hawks.

For the visitor interested in fishing, brook and lake trout are abundant. There is a fish pond in the central part of the preserve used for breeding lake or rainbow trout.

Several areas in the preserve are especially worth visiting. The glade known as Lunny Kamen, or Moonstone, is quite beautiful. Another glade, called Kamennaya Kuznitsa (Stone Forge), is at a height of 127 meters (381 feet). Slightly lower and southward, one finds the very pleasant Red Stone Restaurant. It is advisable to have an experienced, local guide along. He will be of help in pointing out the most interesting attractions. (Guide service can be arranged through the Intourist office at your hotel or motel.)

Visitors to the Crimean Game Preserve can learn more about the wildlife of the mountain regions at the small museum in the forestry center.

NIKITSKY BOTANICAL GARDEN

Nine kilometers (5.6 miles) from Yalta is the Nikitsky Botanical Garden. Founded in 1812 as the Economo-Botanical Garden, it has done much to promote the growing of fruit, tobacco, and the cultivation of industrial and medicinal crops in the south of Russia.

The first curator, Christian Steven, was a well-known Russian botanist and a leading expert on Crimean and Caucasian flora. With the help of European botanists, Steven introduced several new plants whose climatic requirements could be provided by the Crimea. Of the specimens new to the Crimea were wisteria, holly, cedar, and stone pine.

As the garden expanded and developed, the need for botanical specialists grew. To meet the requirement, the Nikitsky School of Fruit Growing and Wine Making was established in 1868. It was from this school that the Magarach Institute of Viticulture and Wine Making was born. A tobacco-growing experimental station and a station devoted to the cultivation of essential oil-bearing and medicinal plants are also connected to the Botanical Garden.

The garden's arboretum has over 1,700 species and forms of trees and shrubs from all over the world. Over 600 flower species and 250 greenhouse plants grace the garden. Near the seashore is the world's largest rose garden with 1,600 Russian and foreign varieties. The arboretum maintains contact with over 400 research institutions in 48 countries.

Visitors to the Botanical Garden can walk through its many parks—the Upper, Lower, Seaside, and one on Cape Montodoro. Of the parks, the oldest is the Lower, which was landscaped by Christian Steven. A special attraction of this area is a pond with pink and white water lilies as well as specimens of the Caspian lotus and other water plants. The designers of the Lower Park grouped plants of the same species together. As a result of this plan, groves of cork oak, cedars of Lebanon, magnolias, and laurels were created between 1820 and 1823.

The southern end of the park offers a beautiful view of the seashore from a pavilion designed after the summer pavilion in the Mikhailov Palace in Leningrad. The attractions of the park's northern end are a lovely pond in the form of a cascade and a multitrunk pistachio tree over 1,000 years old.

At the northern entrance to the Upper Park is an administrative building, a parterre, a pond, and a summer theater. Near the parterre in front of the main building are Chinese fan palms which were planted in 1860. The park is also generously adorned with box honeysuckle, lavender, and wisteria.

Seaside Park, in the southern part of the garden, was founded over fifty years ago and, sheltered from the colder north and northeastern winds by Cape Martyan, is in an area where warmth-loving plants thrive.

Nikitsky Botanical Garden is interesting in any season. Crimean violets and white Crimean snowdrops appear in February. By the end of March the trees and shrubs are showing their new leaves and buds. May is the time of bloom and the entire park is covered with magnificently colored flowers.

SIMFEROPOL

HISTORY IN BRIEF

Simferopol, translated from Greek, means collective town, symbolically represented on its ancient coat of arms showing bees and a beehive. As the gateway to the Crimea, the city is an important junction of Soviet air and surface routes. In ancient times Simferopol was the capital of the Scythian state and was called Scythian Neapol. Destroyed by Hun invasions, it became a Tatar settlement a thousand years later. The Tatars called their city Ak-Metchet. In 1784 when the Crimea became a part of Russia, Simferopol was established near the Tatar settlement. During the Crimean War this strategically located city was used as a Russian army base. It has had many famous visitors, among them Alexander Pushkin, Leo Tolstoi, Anton Chekhov, Maxim Gorky, and Vladimir Mayakovsky. They and other notables are remembered today by memorial plaques displayed on the houses they visited.

GENERAL INFORMATION

Simferopol is the largest city in the Crimea with a population of 250,000. There are over one hundred industrial enterprises, including food-processing machinery and electrical engineering plants, canneries, clothing and furniture factories. There are three specialized institutes in Simferopol: medical, agricultural, and pedagogical. The Maxim Gorky Drama Theater and the Ukrainian Music and Drama Theater provide some of the Crimea's best entertainment. In addition to several cinemas the Simferopol Circus and the Philharmonic Society offer entertainment.

MUSEUMS

Regional Museum, 18 Pushkin Street

This museum provides a variety of features concerning the history of the Crimea. There are three departments: one for local history, another for prerevolutionary times, and the last for Soviet history. The book repository of the Taurika Library is also located in this museum and contains over 50,000 volumes concerning Crimean history. Open daily except Wednesdays from 10 A.M. to 4 P.M.

Regional Art Gallery, 35 Karl Liebknecht Street

Here one will find a rich collection of Russian paintings from the eighteenth through twentieth centuries. There is also a sizable representation of Soviet painting and sculpture. Open daily except Fridays from 10 A.M. until 5 P.M.

USEFUL INFORMATION

Intourist Office, Hotel Ukraina, 9 Rosa Luxemburg Street, Tel: 46–71

Hotels

Ukraina, 9 Rosa Luxemburg Street, Tel: 98–41
Yuzhnaya, 7 Karl Marx Street, Tel: 7–46–18
Simferopol, 17 Kirov Prospect, Tel: 7–32–12

Restaurants

Astoria, 16 Karl Marx Street
Simferopol, 2 Karl Marx Street
Yuzhny, 3 Odesskaya Street
Ukraina, 9 Rosa Luxemburg Street

Communications

Post Office, 15 Karl Marx Street
Telegraph, 11 Rosa Luxemburg Street

CITIES AND TOWNS
OF THE CAUCASUS
Rostov-on-Don, Pyatigorsk,
Nalchik, Ordzhonikidze

The Caucasus Mountain Range is located in the southeastern portion of the Soviet Union between the Black Sea and the Caspian Sea. The main Caucasian Range stretches approximately 1,500 kilometers (900 miles), spanning the Russian Federation in the north and the Georgian, Armenian, and Azerbaijanian republics in the south. Visitors to the Caucasus will find the scenery astonishingly beautiful, both the mountain retreats and the seaside resorts which lie at the foot of the snow-capped peaks. Many come to the Caucasus for the benefit of health spas and balneological baths; others purely for recreation. You can reach the Caucasus via airplane, railroad, automobile, or steamship.

ROSTOV-ON-DON—General Information and History in Brief

Located on the high right bank of the Don River, Rostov is the largest city in the North Caucasus. Frequently called the "gateway to the Caucasus," its position makes it a vital transportation, communications, and trade center. The Volga-Don Canal provides access for vessels to Leningrad, Archangel, and Murmansk via the Volga-Baltic Waterway. In addition, the canal permits passage between the Black and Caspian seas. Rostov-on-Don is also an industrial and agricultural center, with its primary industry the production of agricultural machinery. Numerous consumer goods, including footwear, musical instruments, clothing, soap, medicines, cigarettes, and candy, are also produced. One associates Rostov-on-Don with the many poems, songs, and legends engendered by the Don River and the Don Cossacks. Although the Cossacks have faded into history, the "Quiet Don" attracts many people to its beaches, shady groves, and boating facilities. While Rostov-on-Don is a busy place, it is among the most picturesque, "typically Russian" cities one can visit. The people are friendly, the food good, and the lodgings comfortable.

Before the actual town was formed, Peter I had established a settlement in 1711 called Bogaty Kolodez. In 1749 a border customs house was built near the settlement because of the intersection of important overland trade routes. At the same time the Temernitsky Port was also built near the settlement because of its location at the mouth of the Don River. In 1759 a fortress was erected and named for Metropolitan Dmitry Rostovsky. As trade increased by both land and water routes, a city evolved around the fortress and the port. In order to distinguish the new Rostov from the old one located in the Yaroslavl region, the new city was called Rostov-on-Don. The city expanded rapidly and developed into a typical mercantile and trade center with warehouses along the riverbanks and privately owned townhouses in the center of the city. By mid-nineteenth century Rostov-on-Don had become the largest river port in Russia, with wheat, wool, fish, salt, timber, coal, iron, butter, and fat as the principal items of trade. When railway communication was established with Moscow in 1870–71, the growth of industry was accelerated. After the October Revolution, Rostov-on-Don became the administrative center of the North Caucasian territory and later for the entire Rostov Region. Industrialization expanded under the five-year plans, and the population increased proportionately. World War II brought devastation to Rostov: over half of its dwelling and municipal structures as well as nearly all of the industry were destroyed. After the liberation of Rostov in 1943, all historical buildings were restored, industry rebuilt and expanded, and all other structures for housing and public services rebuilt.

MUSEUMS AND PLACES OF INTEREST

Since central Rostov-on-Don is rather compact, most of the city's major places of interest can be reached by walking. Engels Street, the main thoroughfare running east to west, parallels the flow of the Don. A convenient place to begin a walking tour of Rostov is at the Hotel Rostov, located at the western end of Engels Street where it intersects with Budyonovsky Prospect. During the nineteenth century this section of Rostov was on the outskirts and orchards and gardens were located here. As the city spread outward from the center, the section became urbanized. Engels Street, however, was called Large Garden (Bolshaya Sadovaya) Street up to the Revolution. At its northern extremity, Budyonovsky Prospect leads to

Mayakovsky Park, one of many horticultural and recreational areas of the city. Proceeding south, you come to the Rostov-on-Don Circus, a major amusement facility. Near the intersection of Engels Street and Budyonovsky Prospect, on the east side, is the Pedagogical Institute. On the west side of the intersection is a monument to Lenin.

Proceeding eastward on Engels Street you arrive at the Gorky Recreation Park. Cross Semaschko Prospect and on the north side of Engels Street you will see the Palace of Young Pioneers, and on the south side the Hotel Moskovskaya. At the juncture of Marx Prospect and Engels Street is the Institute of Finance and Economy. North on Marx Prospect are the Hotel Yuzhnaya to the east and the Trade Unions Building to the west. South on Marx Prospect on the west side are the Musical Drama Theater and the Hotel Don. Across Marx Prospect, continuing on Engels Street, is Sovietskaya Square, one of the city's largest and most beautiful squares, built on what was formerly barren land.

Just past Sovietskaya Square is the Regional Lore Museum. Among the numerous exhibits is a very large collection pertaining to ancient civilizations of the Rostov Region. Archaeological excavations at the Bosporskaya Fortress have produced some outstanding specimens of fine and applied art, such as vases, bowls, bronze statuettes, and gold ornaments. The natural history department displays the skeleton of a now-extinct variety of southern elephant. Of particular importance is a chariot dating back to 1500 B.C.

The next major intersection of Engels Street is at University Prospect. On the north you see the buildings of Rostov State University. Just past the university is Theater Square, which forms the actual center of the city and is the scene of popular demonstrations and public celebrations. The major building here is the Gorky Drama Theater. Erected in 1936, the structure was noted for its splendid architectural design. Since its destruction during World War II, the theater has been totally restored and was reopened in 1963. At the end of Engels Street, where it becomes Sovietskaya Street, is an obelisk in honor of Soviet soldiers. Farther east is another monument to the Soviet soldiers, to the north, and the Lenin Komsomol Theater, to the south. City beaches and facilities for boating and sightseeing excursions via hydrofoil on the Don River are located south of center city along the river embankment.

USEFUL INFORMATION

Hotels, Motel, and Campsite

Hotel Don, 62 Engels Street
Hotel Moskovskaya, 34 Gazetny Prospect
Hotel Rostov, 59 Budyonovsky Prospect

Hotel Yuzhnaya, Marx Prospect at Engels Street
Rostov Motor Court, Novocherkassk Road near the airport on the southern
    outskirts of the city
Campsite Kharkov, Rostov Road on the northeastern outskirts of the city

Restaurants

Don, Hotel Don, 62 Engels Street
Moskovskaya, Hotel Moskovskaya, 34 Gazetny Prospect
Rostov, Hotel Rostov, 59 Budyonovsky Prospect
Yuzhnaya, Hotel Yuzhnaya, Marx Prospect at Engels Street

Museums and Theaters

Circus, Budyonovsky Prospect at Gorky Street
Museum of Fine Arts, Gorky Street between Marx and Semaschko pros-
    pects
Museum of Regional Lore, Engels Street between Marx and University
    prospects
Gorky Drama Theater, Engels Street at Theater Square
Musical Comedy Theater, Marx Prospect at Socialistitcheskaya Street
Lenin Komsomol Theater, at the end of Sovietskaya Street, the eastern
    extension of Engels Street

Shopping

Central Department Store, Engels Street near Theater Square
Beriozka Shop (foreign currency only), Hotel Rostov, 59 Budyonovsky
    Prospect

PYATIGORSK—General Information and History in Brief

Pyatigorsk is located on the Podkumok River along the southwestern
slope of Mashuk Mountain. The town is a very popular resort because of
its natural attributes. The average elevation is approximately 561 meters
(1,840 feet) and provides not only scenic splendor but a healthful combination of mountain and steppeland climates. Mineral springs and curative
muds in the vicinity of Tambukan Lake offer assorted health benefits and
numerous health problems are treated at the medical facilities in and
around Pyatigorsk. For those interested simply in a vacation, the town has
a theater, open-air concert stage, cinemas, and ample sports facilities.

In 1780 Konstantinogorsk Fortress was founded and a settlement developed called Goryachegorsk. The name was changed in 1890 to Pyatigorsk,
the Russian translation of the Tatar "Besh Tau" meaning "Five Moun-

tains." Since the Revolution, Pyatigorsk has expanded its medical facilities, administrative buildings, schools, and hotels. Food and consumer goods are the principal industries.

MUSEUMS AND PLACES OF INTEREST

The most advantageous way to see the principal sites of Pyatigorsk is to take a leisurely stroll through the town. All landmarks are clearly designated. The Pyatigorsk Museum, near the center of town, is noted for its collections pertaining to regional and local history. Nearby is the Lermontov Museum, the house where the poet Mikhail Lermontov spent the last months of his life prior to his death in a duel in 1841. The house contains his personal possessions, etchings, drawings, and documents associated with his career. One can also see a bust of Lermontov set on an obelisk on the slope of Mashuk Mountain, marking the spot where he was killed. In Tsvetnik Park is the Lermontov Grotto, and in Lermontov Park is another monument to the poet created by the sculptor Opekushin. Another architectural site of importance is the Lermontov Baths (formerly the Nikolayev Baths), designed in Russian classical style by the architect Bernardacci in 1826–31. The Academic Gallery, a museum of regional fine art built in 1849–51, is another structure of Russian classical design. You should not miss Diana's Grotto, set in a rock, or the Aeolian Harp Arbor, a hillside sculptural ensemble. Finally, there is the Proval, a picturesque cave containing a deep lake, formed by the eruption of hot sulfur springs through the mountain rock.

USEFUL INFORMATION

Hotels and Campsite

Hotel Mashuk, 26 Kirov Prospect
Hotel Pyatigorsk, 43a Kraineva Street
Campsite Belaya Romashka, 2 Kalinin Street

Restaurants

Druzhba, near the center of town
Mashuk, Hotel Mashuk, 26 Kirov Prospect
Pyatigorsk, Hotel Pyatigorsk, 43a Kraineva Street
Tsentralny, near the center of town

NALCHIK—General Information

Nalchik is located 79 kilometers (47 miles) southeast of Pyatigorsk in the foothills of the Caucasus. The Nalchik River crosses the town. In 1818 Nalchik was established as a fortress. In 1921 the town became the administrative center of the Kabardinian-Balkar Autonomous Republic. It is now principally a resort town, but numerous industries have been introduced in recent decades. The climate is especially healthful because of the ozone-rich ionized air. Several local hot-water springs possess a high content of iodine and bromine. There is also a plentiful supply of curative mud in the vicinity. A monument in the city square commemorates the merger of Kabardia and Russia. Although there are no Intourist facilities in Nalchik, the town is significant since it marks the border between Kabardin-Balkar and the Stavropol Territory of the Russian Federation. The road from Nalchik to Ordzhonikidze levels off on a plain from which one can see the majestic five-peaked Beshtau ringed by other mountains of the Caucasian range.

ORDZHONIKIDZE—General Information

Ordzhonikidze is the last major city in the southern part of the Russian Federation before crossing into the Georgian S.S.R. It is also the capital of the North Ossetian Autonomous Republic. The city's origins date back to the founding of the Valdikavkaz Fortress, built in 1784 by the tsarist government of Russia. Today Ordzhonikidze is a major industrial center concentrating on heavy industrial machinery. Visitors will want to see the Khetagurov Recreation Park, Freedom Square, Palace of Culture, Drama Theater, Philharmonic Society, and Young Pioneers Palace, all located in the center city area. Just outside the city limits are some interesting collective farms.

The Georgian Military Highway spans the 207-kilometer (124-mile) distance through the Caucasus between Ordzhonikidze and Tbilisi. This road was described, as it existed at the time, by Strabo, the Greek geographer, and by Pliny, the Roman historian. The road gained greater importance during the eleventh and twelfth centuries as a trade route between the North and South Caucasus. During the nineteenth century, its strategic value was recognized and improvements were made. Today it serves as a major north-south surface route. While travel over the Georgian Military Highway is an experience for those who appreciate natural spectacle, it can be treacherous. There are mountain fogs, sudden hairpin curves, natural cascades which cross the asphalt and occasionally flood the road, and places where only the smallest vehicles can turn around.

USEFUL INFORMATION

Hotels and Campsite

Hotel Intourist, 19 Mir Prospect
Hotel Kavkaz, 50 Vatutina Street
Campsite Pervyi Redant, 7 kilometers (1.5 miles) south of Ordzhonikidze
    on the Georgian Military Road

Restaurants

Intourist, Hotel Intourist, 19 Mir Prospect
Kavkaz, Hotel Kavkaz, 50 Vatutina Street

TBILISI

GENERAL INFORMATION

Tbilisi, the capital of the Georgian Soviet Socialist Republic, is one of the major industrial, cultural, and scientific cities of the Soviet Union. Having celebrated its fifteen hundredth anniversary in 1958, it is among the oldest cities in the world. Tbilisi is situated in the bowl of the Trialeti and Saguramo-Ialoni mountain ranges. Surrounded on three sides by mountains and on the fourth by the Kura River, Tbilisi has an interesting tiered city plan which forms ascending rings along the mountainsides. The various elevations of different sections of the city account for relatively sharp climatic contrasts within the city limits. Other contrasts also make Tbilisi a fascinating place to visit. Like many ancient cities that have survived to the present, Tbilisi has an old city enclosed within a modern one. Numerous nationalities have left their distinct traces, and one finds elements of Arabic, Mongolian, Turkish, and Persian cultures alongside today's predominating Georgian and Russian aspects.

Tbilisi's population of 900,000 is highly heterogeneous, embracing Georgians, Russians, Armenians, Ukrainians, Azerbaijanians, Ossets, and Greeks. Almost half of the working population is engaged in the city's industries. The other half is divided among professionals and office workers. The most highly developed industries in Tbilisi are mechanical engineering, metalworking, lighting, and food processing. Tbilisi is known for its wineries, brandy distillery, and tea-weighing station, since the cultivation of wine grapes and tea is such an important facet of Georgia's agricultural economy. Tbilisi is also a major land-route junction because of its location along the Georgian Military Highway and the Transcaucasian Railway. Among the educational facilities here are the Georgian Academy of Sciences, which contains 120 research institutions, 11 schools of higher education, and 27 specialized secondary schools. Culturally Tbilisi boasts 9 theaters, 2 film studios, 19 museums, several dozen cinemas, over 100 public libraries, the State Conservatory, Academy of Arts, and Theatrical Institute.

Tbilisi is one of the friendliest of Soviet cities. The people are busy but relaxed, hospitable to a fault, eager to greet foreigners, and totally charming. Many legends concerning the longevity of the Georgians circulate worldwide. According to Soviet statistics, about .05 percent of the population are centenarians. Scientists are not certain of the reason for this longevity, but they count among the probable causes abundant natural vitamins from native foodstuffs, plenty of wine, and a great deal of outdoor physical activity. The visitor to Tbilisi will readily agree that the food, although spicy, is some of the world's best. The wines rank in the same category, having achieved numerous first-place medals in international competition. The mountain air is exhilarating, as are the native teas, brewed strong enough to be medicinal. One will find the people of Tbilisi, particularly the Georgians, extremely sentimental about their native land. They enjoy recounting folk legends and reciting pithy proverbs. They are eager to share their culture and their provisions. A visit to Tbilisi is a fascinating and heartwarming experience.

HISTORY IN BRIEF

The city of Tbilisi was established by Vakhtang Gorgasali in 458 A.D. Initially it served as a fortress vital to defense in the wars against the Persians. Legend has it that the king was hunting in a dense wood in the Kura valley. While pursuing his quarry he lost his retinue and managed to shoot a pheasant which flew out of the bushes. Dismounting to retrieve the bird, the king found it, already cooked, in a hot spring. Catching up with their ruler, the hunters found him lost in thought. Then the king announced that he would build a town in this place which would be called Tbilisi, the word *tbili* meaning "warm" in Georgian.

Tbilisi, along with the rest of Georgia, was besieged repeatedly by the Arabs during the seventh and eighth centuries. By 730 the Arabs had gained complete control and they ruled Transcaucasia until the end of the ninth century. During the tenth century new states engaged in a power struggle in Georgia. The rise of King Ashot Bagrationi established the supremacy of the principality of Tao-Klarjeti. His heir, David III, who lived from 961 to 1001, established the Union of Georgia. The year 1065 marked the beginning of prolonged conflict with the Seljuk Turks. From 1089 to 1125 David IV, known as David the Builder, consolidated the diffuse factions of Georgia and drove the Turks out of Transcaucasia. He also established a regular army and the academies of Gelati and Ikalto. His other achievements were the building of hospitals, old-age homes, bridges, canals, a reliable water supply, and numerous caravansaries for travelers. During 1184–1213 Queen Tamar ruled feudal Georgia in the same manner as David IV. Her reign marks the zenith of development during which the independent empire of Trapezund was established and its rule placed in the hands of the queen's kinsman, Alexei Komnen. Trade flourished with countries of the North and South Caucasus, the Mediterranean states, and the Near East. Political ties with Russian lands were consolidated during this period.

The thirteenth and fourteenth centuries saw the decay of the Georgian feudal state. Much of this was due to repeated attacks by the armies of Khoresm, followed by the invasion of the Mongols, to whom Georgia became enslaved for almost a century. During the fifteenth and sixteenth centuries feudal Georgia disintegrated into several kingdoms and principalities which were further subdivided into independent states called *tavads*. After the fall of Byzantium in 1453 Georgia was torn between Turkish and Persian rulers who enslaved the Georgians and forcibly converted them to the Islamic religion. During the seventeenth century even worse atrocities befell the Georgians. The Turks and Persians initiated a program of genocide in order to aid in the assimilation of all Georgian lands. In defense of the Georgians arose two heroes whose deeds of bravery gave courage and moral support to the persecuted. These men were King Teimuraz and a soldier named George Saakadze.

During 1703–24, the East Georgian kingdom under the rule of Vakhtang VI fared well domestically, and the first written code of public and private laws was established. The king, like his predecessors, was engaged in establishing ties with Russia. Fearful of such an alliance, the Turks invaded Georgia, followed by the Persians. From 1744 to 1798 the history of Georgia was strongly influenced by Irakly II, a king whose accomplishments in both war and statesmanship led to the unification of Kartly and Kakhetia as the East Georgian state. Various reforms introduced by Irakly contributed to the development of trades and crafts. In foreign affairs the major accomplishment of Irakly was the negotiation of the Treaty of Georgievsk in 1783: a document establishing the East Georgian kingdom as a protectorate of Russia.

At the beginning of the nineteenth century a peaceful era of development began for Georgia. The last king, George XII, in seeking further protection from Russia, acceded to the Manifesto of Alexander I which proclaimed the inclusion of Georgia within the Russian empire. A Russian administration was established in Georgia, leading to reinforced frontiers, rapid economic and industrial development, and a renewed cultural life. Tbilisi played a vital role during this period and benefited greatly from the expansion of Georgian economy. The most important factor was the construction of the Transcaucasian Railway providing Tbilisi with convenient access to land and sea routes. Numerous industrial enterprises were set into operation, handcraft production accelerated, and trade flourished. Tbilisi became an important cultural center through the establishment of schools, theaters, newspapers and magazines. By 1897, Tiflis, as Tbilisi was then called, had become an important center for transportation, trade, and administration.

MUSEUMS AND PLACES OF INTEREST

The Old City

This section of Tbilisi is located on the right bank of the Kura River, against the slopes of the Sololaki and Tabori mountains. Up to the end of the eighteenth century this area was surrounded by a brick wall. In prerevolutionary times most industrial and trade activities were located within the limits of the Old City. Now, however, most industry is concentrated on the left bank of the Kura. One will find the streets of the Old City narrow and winding and quite steep. Sidewalks are frequently replaced by stairways, particularly along those streets which are built into the mountainsides. Over the past several decades certain portions of the Old City have been replanned to facilitate transportation, but traces of the ancient flavor remain even in the modernized areas.

NARIKALA FORTRESS, ALONG THE LEDGES OF THE SOLOLAKI MOUNTAIN

Dating from the fourth century, this fortress was built in the narrowest part of the valley for defensive purposes. Today only the round towers and the crenellated walls remain, although the fortress was destroyed and rebuilt several times. During the fifteenth and sixteenth centuries an observation tower was added to one of the bastions.

SIONI CATHEDRAL, SHAVTELI STREET

Originally built during 575–639, this cathedral was destroyed and rebuilt so many times during various wars that it is considered to be a monument of medieval Georgian architecture, as that was the period in which it acquired its final style. The belfry was added in 1425. The St. Nino Cross, an important religious relic, is kept at the cathedral. The residence of the patriarch of Georgia is on the cathedral grounds.

ANCHISKATI CHURCH, SHAVTELI STREET

This is the oldest religious building in the Old City. Built in the early part of the sixth century by the son of Vakhtang Gorgasali, this basilican church with three naves was remodeled several times over the course of its long life. However, it still retains its original architectural lines. The church was named for the Icon of Anchi, painted in the twelfth century by Beka Opisari.

THE MAIDAN

Rising above the small square located on the level below the Narikala Fortress is a steep wall which contains the towers of the fortress. Although the Maidan has been rebuilt into a large modern square, one can still discern the outlines of the old area. The importance of the square is its location at a narrow part of the Kura River. In olden times a wooden bridge spanned the water, allowing tradesmen's caravans to cross from one side of Tbilisi to the other. In 1951 a wide suspension bridge of reinforced concrete was built. Under the bridge is an embankment which connects the Old City with the central district of Tbilisi. The old narrow street running along the embankment has given way to a modern one called Gorgasali Street.

OBELISK, GORGASALI STREET

This monument commemorates the Battle of Krtsansi in which three hundred Aragvi soldiers were killed defending Tbilisi against the Persians in 1795. An eternal flame burns at the foot of the obelisk. Inscribed on the façade of the monument is a poem by Lado Asatiani telling of the heroic deeds of the Aragvi who kept the Persians out of the city.

ORTACHALA HYDROELECTRIC POWER STATION, KURA EMBANKMENT

From Gorgasali Street one can reach the Ortachala Dam of the Hydroelectric Power Station. Built as part of the post-revolutionary electrification program, it has played an important part in the industrialization of Tbilisi.

KOMSOMOL ALLEY

This picturesque street runs along the top of Sololaki Mountain near the Narikala Fortress. Here a huge statue of Mother Georgia looks over Tbilisi. She holds in one hand a sword against enemies and in the other a bowl of hospitality for friends.

LESELIDZE STREET, NORTHWEST OF THE MAIDAN, OFF GORGASALI STREET

Before the Revolution Leselidze Street was called Shuabazari. It was a winding alley lined with shops and bazaars which sold all sorts of consumer items. During the 1930s the street was widened and the market stalls were torn down. Today, Leselidze Street is a wide thoroughfare suited to vehicular and pedestrian traffic.

TBILISI BOTANICAL GARDENS, LESELIDZE STREET

Near the foot of Narikala Fortress, in a deep gorge between the Sololaki and Tabori mountains, is the Botanical Gardens. Built in the 1840s, the property was formerly the gardens of Georgian royalty. The Botanical Gardens feature numerous plants ranging from those indigenous to Georgia to others which have exotic origins. The gardens are landscaped along the mountainsides and form an extremely appealing natural display.

Modern Tbilisi

LENIN SQUARE

At the foot of Leselidze Street is Lenin Square, the main square of Tbilisi. The square is the source of Rustaveli Avenue, the main street of Tbilisi, named for the Georgian national poet Shota Rustaveli. The avenue is lined with trees, bushes, and flowers and is noted for its beautiful buildings, both old and new. A statue of Lenin, erected in 1956, stands at its center. Facing Lenin Square is the building that houses the Executive Committee of the City Soviet. Atop the building is a clock tower adorned with the flag of the republic.

PUSHKIN SQUARE, OPPOSITE THE EXECUTIVE COMMITTEE BUILDING

This small, verdant square was dedicated to Alexander Pushkin during the 1890s at which time a monument to the poet was erected by the residents of Tbilisi. During Pushkin's residence in Tbilisi he lived in a small house adjacent to the square. The house is indicated by a plaque.

JANASHIA STATE MUSEUM, LOCATED NEAR LENIN SQUARE, AT THE BEGINNING OF RUSTAVELI AVENUE

Built in 1923 on the site of the former Museum of the Caucasus, the museum now contains a rich assortment of archaeological and ethnographic exhibits from every area of Georgia. The collections date as far back as the Stone and Bronze Ages. Among the exhibits is a particularly large and valuable numismatic collection of 80,000 coins, most of which are of Georgian origin. A special feature of the museum is the famous Ahalgori Treasure, a collection of ancient icons and jewelry excavated from the burial mounds at Trialeti, Armazi, and Vani. With permission, you may also see the collection of the works of ancient goldsmiths, kept in museum vaults.

PALACE OF YOUNG PIONEERS, RUSTAVELI AVENUE, ACROSS FROM THE STATE MUSEUM

This architectural monument of the Italian Renaissance was once the residence of the Russian viceroy of the Caucasus. The park on the palace grounds was part of the private gardens of the last Georgian king, George XII. The front of the Pioneer Palace is lined with English elms, imported for the pleasure of the building's previous residents.

GEORGIAN GOVERNMENT HOUSE, RUSTAVELI AVENUE, NEXT TO THE PALACE OF YOUNG PIONEERS

Formerly an Orthodox cathedral, this structure is adorned with tall columns faced with gold Bolnisi tuff. It is one of the most elaborate architectural monuments in downtown Tbilisi. The walkways approaching the Government House are flanked by colorful flowerbeds.

ST. GEORGE OF KASHVETI CHURCH, RUSTAVELI AVENUE, DIAGONALLY ACROSS FROM THE GEORGIAN GOVERNMENT HOUSE

This church, built in 1904–10, is designed in traditional Georgian style and possesses some of the finest stone ornamentation in the republic. It is a duplicate of the Samstavisi Temple, a monument of ancient Georgia, erected in Kartli at the beginning of the eleventh century. Inside the church you will notice the decorative painting behind the altar and along the ceiling. This project was the work of Gudiashvili, a noted modern artist of Georgia. The tomb of Orbeliani, a famous poet of the republic, is inside the church.

From here to the end of Rustaveli Avenue you will pass the State Art Gallery and then cross Jorjiashvili Street. At the corner is the Rustaveli Drama Theater. Next is the Paliashvili Opera and Ballet Theater. The pseudo-Moorish architectural style of the building is quite interesting. In the theater garden are the tombs of three famous Georgians connected with music: Paliashvili, the composer; Sarajishvili, the opera singer; and Marjanishvili, the producer. Near the theater is the Georgian branch of the Institute of Marxism-Leninism, built in 1938 according to the design of Shchusev. The monumental building with its grand colonnades is a frequent gathering place for professionals in scientific and cultural fields. The graceful, tree-lined avenue terminates in a small square where a monument to Shota Rustaveli was erected in 1937.

LENIN STREET, NORTHWEST OF RUSTAVELI SQUARE

A comparatively new street in Tbilisi, this wide thoroughfare, lined with new apartment buildings which form a single architectural ensemble, crosses the Vere River. Lenin Street runs along the Saburtalo Plain. At the fork of Lenin and Melikishvili streets is the new glass and concrete Philharmonic Hall. Melikishvili Street merges with Ilya Chavchavadze Street, a broad thoroughfare which runs through the western district of Tbilisi called Vake-Saburtalo. Divided by the Vere River, the district is comprised of Vake on the south and Saburtalo on the north. Most of Vake is of a relatively high elevation, while Saburtalo is located in the hollow that merges with the lower terraces along the Kura River. Vake-Saburtalo is a district noted for its educational and scientific institutes. Ilya Chavchavadze Avenue, cutting through the heart of these educational facilities, is lined with the buildings of Tbilisi State University. In front of the oldest building are monuments to the university's founders, Ivan Javakhishvili, Pytor Melikishvili, and Korneli Kekelidze. In addition to the university, one also finds here the institutes of agriculture, veterinary medicine, foreign languages, and physical culture.

SQUARE OF HEROES, AT THE INTERSECTION OF VAKE, SABURTALO, AND LENIN STREETS

Named for the heroes of the Soviet Union, this is one of the most picturesque spots in Tbilisi, as it nestles at the foot of the city's most scenic slopes. Adjoining the Square of Heroes is the Tbilisi Zoo, and above the zoo at the top of a small hill is the Tbilisi Circus. On another adjacent hilltop is the new campus of the Academy of Sciences and the Scientific Library. Nearby are the buildings of the Lenin Polytechnic Institute and the Medical Institute. Lenin Street continues past the Square of Heroes and merges with Ordjonikidze Square, the largest square in Tbilisi, and the site of the new Palace of Sports with a seating capacity of 11,000.

MOUNT MTATSMINDA

A visit to Tbilisi is not complete without an excursion to the Mtatsminda Plateau. One may reach this summit (727 meters; 2,385 feet) within the city via several conveyances: by a leisurely drive to the top in a private or hired automobile; by cable car from Rustaveli Square; or by the most interesting and enjoyable means, the Tbilisi funicular railway. The lower station is on Chonkadze Street. An intermediary station is located at the very foot of the mountain. The second lap of the funicular railway goes directly to the top of Mt. Mtatsminda. The mountain boasts one of Tbilisi's best parks from which to view the panorama of the city and the surrounding Caucasus Mountains.

ST. DAVID CHURCH AND PANTHEON

Just above the foot of Mt. Mtatsminda, built into the slope, is the old St. David Church and the remains of an adjacent monastery. The church forms the center of the Pantheon where many outstanding Georgian writers and public figures are buried. At the entrance to the cemetery, behind an iron grille, lie two graves notable for their monuments. The one on the right is marked by a black marble pedestal with a crucifix. A statue of a grieving woman inclines against this pedestal marking the grave of Alexander S. Griboydov, a noted poet-diplomat. The inscription on the pedestal reads, "Your deeds are immortal in the memory of the Russians, but why has my love outlived you?" The statue is a likeness of the poet's wife, Nina Chavchavadze, widowed at the age of eighteen when her husband was killed by a rioting mob in Teheran. Her grave, marked only by a plain tombstone, lies next to his. Another famous gravesite at the Pantheon is the polished granite slab bearing only the word "Akaki." This is the tomb of the best-loved poet of Georgia, Akaki Tsereteli. Joseph Dzhugashvili's ("Stalin") mother is also buried here.

NORTHERN DISTRICT, LEFT BANK OF THE KURA RIVER

This district is very large and encompasses the Didube, Nadzaladevi, Grma-Gele, and Avchala sections. The area forms the primary industrial and transportation center of Tbilisi. The major streets of the Northern District run parallel to the Kura River and the railroad. A large thoroughfare, Akaki Tsereteli Avenue, begins near the Tbilisi Railway Terminal which is adjacent to the Central Dynamo Stadium, an indoor swimming and recreational facility. Facing Akaki Tsereteli Avenue are the structures which comprise the Georgian Republic Exhibition of Economic Achievements. The central area of the Northern District adjoins the Didube and Nadzaladevi sections at the southeast. Plekhanov Avenue, the main thoroughfare, connects the Dynamo Stadium and Ordjonikidze Park, a major cultural and recreational facility. Farther along Plekhanov Avenue is Karl Marx Square. In the immediate vicinity of the square are Tbilisi's most popular cinema houses, summer parks, and clubs.

ISANI (AVLABARI) DISTRICT

Known by both names, this district lies between the central left bank area and Navtlugi, running along the banks of the Kura River. Isani is located at a higher elevation than its neighboring districts, and one will still find here some of the narrow, winding streets reminiscent of the Old City. Shaumyan Street is the main thoroughfare of the district, crossing it from northwest to southeast. Along Shaumyan Street are located industrial, transportation, educational, and residential buildings. First City Hospital, the largest medical facility in Georgia, is located here.

METEKHI FORTRESS

A rocky cliff rises from the left bank of the Kura River running almost the entire length of Isani. The fortress is located at the top of the cliff and dates back to the twelfth and thirteenth centuries. (For a brief while, the world's most renowned Georgian, Joseph Dzhugasvili ["Stalin"], was incarcerated here by the tsarist authorities.) The area around the fortress was, until the Revolution, inhabited primarily by craftsmen and small traders. From an observation platform near the fortress one can see Sachino Castle, on the right bank of the Kura River, atop the Mtambori Mountain. Built in the eighteenth century by King Irakli II, the castle was a gift for his wife, Queen Daredzhan.

NAVTLUGI

Located at the extreme southeast of Tbilisi, this district is primarily an industrial and transportation area. At the center of the district is the Navtlugi Railway Station where two rail lines diverge from the Transcaucasian Railway. One goes to the Republic of Armenia, the other to Kakheti. Navtlugi is comprised of an upper and lower terrace, each having specific industrial facilities. In recent years multistory apartment buildings have been constructed in the district adjacent to the Samgori Canal irrigation zone.

Tbilisi Suburbs

MTSKHETA

Located about 13 kilometers (8 miles) northwest of Tbilisi is Mtskheta, the ancient capital of the East-Georgian kingdom. It is in the region known as Inner Kartli, the present name of ancient Iberia. The town of Mtskheta stretches along the banks of the Kura and Aragvi rivers and is almost totally surrounded by mountains. In ancient times, numerous fortifications and settlements adjoining the town formed a reasonably large state. Mtskheta flourished from the fifth century B.C. to the fourth century A.D. After the transfer of the capital to Tbilisi in the fifth century A.D., Mtskheta remained a religious center. Today Mtskheta is primarily a museum town, consisting of valuable architectural and archaeological relics. Excavations in Mtskheta and its environs have revealed material dating from the last millennium B.C.

JVARI CHURCH

Located on a rocky promontory high above the juncture of the Kura and Aragvi rivers, the church will easily be seen by those traveling south along the Georgian Military Road before entering Mtskheta or by train approaching from the west. Jvari (meaning "cross") is one of the most splendid architectural monuments of ancient Georgia. Built during 585–604, it is the earliest central-domed structure in the republic. The monastery adjacent to the church is built into the cliff. At night the church is illuminated by floodlights and provides a spectacular sight.

SVETITSKHOVELI CATHEDRAL

Inside a crenellated stone fence at the very center of Mtskheta is the Svetitskhoveli Cathedral. Renowned for its graceful architectural composition and profusion of stone-carved ornamentation, the cathedral was designed at the beginning of the eleventh century by the noted architect Arsakidze. Arsakidze's fate was tragic. His teacher, the royal vizier, ordered the architect's right hand chopped off as a gesture of reprisal because he felt his pupil had outdone him. The teacher was especially piqued because he was engaged in building the Samtavro Church at the same time that Arsakidze was building the cathedral.

MONUMENT TO ILYA CHAVCHAVADZE

Along the Georgian Military Road, north of Mtskheta on the way to Saguramo, is an obelisk which marks the site of the assassination of Ilya Chavchavadze. Considered an enemy of the tsarist government, the poet was slain by hirelings for his espousal of political freedom. His estate in the village of Saguramo has become a museum and is 3 kilometers (1.8 miles) from the monument.

RUSTAVI

Located in the Gardabani Steppe about 20 kilometers (12 miles) southeast of Tbilisi, is Rustavi, a vital center of heavy industry. This newest town in Georgia has its roots in medieval history, tracing its origin back to the ruins of an ancient fortress city which was destroyed by Tamerlane in the fourteenth century. Aside from the various industrial facilities of Rustavi, the visitor will want to see Mikhail Mamulashvili's Garden. Known to horticulturists throughout the world, this ensemble of gardens provides an awesome exhibit of color and design. The one-time errand boy who created this spectacle is now honored by the title of Merited Art Worker of Georgia.

Another place of interest is the Dzhvari Monastery. On a hilltop above the Aragvi and Kura rivers, this sixth-century structure is among the finest surviving examples of ancient Georgian architecture. Mikhail Lermontov employed the monastery as a background for his poem "Mtsyri" (The Novice), concerning a young man's love of freedom. At the foot of the hill is the dam of the Zemoavchalskaya Hydropower Station, built during the electrification program of 1927. At the dam is a statue of Lenin, designed by the Soviet sculptor Shadr.

USEFUL INFORMATION

Hotels

Hotel Abkhazia, 12 Vazha Pshavela Avenue
Hotel Intourist, 7 Rustaveli Avenue
Hotel Iveria, Rustaveli Square
Hotel Sakartvelo, 12 Melikishvili Street
Hotel Tbilisi, 13 Rustaveli Avenue

Motels

Motel Tbilisi Sea, Tbilisi Sea, Grma-Gele area of the Samgori Steppe
Motel Digomi, Georgian Military Highway, 9 kilometers (5.6 miles) north
    of the city

Campsites

No. 1, 13 Guramishvili Street
No. 2, Georgian Military Highway, 10 kilometers (6.3 miles) north of the
    city

Restaurants

Abkhazia, Hotel Abkhazia, 12 Vazha Pshavela Avenue
Intourist, Hotel Intourist, 7 Rustaveli Avenue
Iori, Tbilisi Sea, Grma-Gele area of the Samgori Steppe
Iveria, Hotel Iveria, Rustaveli Square
Krtsanisi, right bank of the Kura Embankment
Mtatsminda, at the summit of Mount Mtatsminda
Sakartvelo, Sakartvelo Hotel, 12 Melikishvili Street
Samadlo, Davitashvili Street
Uzhba, Motel Digomi, 9 kilometers (5.6 miles) north on the Georgian
    Military Road
Vake, Vake Park

Cafés

Metro, 4 Inashvili Street
Nargizi, 22 Rustaveli Avenue
Tolia, 52 Rustaveli Avenue
Tsiskari, 52 Ilya Chavchavadze Avenue

Museums

Museum of the History and Ethnography of Tbilisi, Komsomol Alley
Janashia State Museum of Georgia, Rustaveli Avenue
State Art Gallery, Rustaveli Avenue
Lenin Museum, Herzen Street

Theaters and Concert Halls

Rustaveli Georgian Drama Theater, Rustaveli Avenue
Marjanishvili Georgian Drama Theater, Marjanishvili Street
Russian Drama Theater, Griboyedov Street
Armenian Drama Theater, Griboyedov Street
Paliashvili Opera and Ballet Theater, Rustaveli Avenue
Young Spectators' Theater, Rustaveli Avenue
Philharmonic Hall, corner of Lenin and Melikishvili streets
Musical Comedy Theater, Plekhanov Avenue

Transportation and Communications

Post and Telegraph, 12 Rustaveli Avenue, 44 Plekhanov Avenue
Railway Terminal, at the foot of Akaki Tsereteli Avenue, near the Dynamo
    Stadium

YEREVAN

GENERAL INFORMATION

Yerevan is the capital of the Armenian Soviet Socialist Republic. It is located in the eastern part of the Armenian upland called Ararat, named for the two peaks of Mount Ararat which are part of the Armenian mountain range. To the southwest of Yerevan flows the Aras River, which separates the Armenian Republic from Turkey. Yerevan is an integral part of the grand panorama of the Ararat Valley. Visitors to this thoroughly modern city will appreciate the view of the two mountain summits, Great Ararat (Masis) and Little Ararat, which are only 50 kilometers (30 miles) away. In recent years an irrigation system has been introduced within the city of Yerevan. The numerous reservoirs not only improve the city's arid climate, but provide moisture for the abundant greenery which enhances the appearance of this sunny southern capital. Another geological feature accounts for the appearance of modern Yerevan as a city of predominantly low structures. Up to recent years, it was not possible to construct buildings exceeding six stories because of the high earthquake potential created by the volcanic mountains of the Gegam Range to the east of Yerevan. Newer technology (since 1964) now permits the construction of buildings up to sixteen stories through the use of specially reinforced concrete. Thus, the overall visage of Yerevan is one of splendid sun, lush greenery, and multicolored buildings constructed from a variety of volcanic tuffs, felsites, and basalts.

Since the Revolution, Yerevan has become an important industrial, cultural, and scientific center in southwest Asia. Its population of approximately 775,000 places it among the twenty-five largest cities in the Soviet Union. Before the Revolution, the major industry in Yerevan was the distillation of brandy. Although this is still important, other industries share equally in the vigorous economy. These include machinery and instruments, transportation equipment, computers, chemicals, building materials, knitted goods, silk, and footwear. In addition to manufactured goods, Yerevan produces wine, items of Armenian marble, and canned fruits from nearby collective farms.

Yerevan, like the rest of the republic, is populated predominantly by Armenians. In fact, Armenia's national composition is the most homogeneous of all the Soviet republics. Other nationalities represented here are Azerbaijanians, Russians, Kurds, Ukrainians, Greeks, and Aisors. Armenia is basically a mountainous territory, but its population is designated as dwellers of the plains (up to 800 meters/2,400 feet above sea level) or inhabitants of the mountains (over 2,000 meters/6,000 feet above sea level). Although modern times have brought sweeping changes to the republic, the visitor will notice the strong retention of national customs in the areas of family life, traditional goods, and holiday celebrations. Throughout the republic, pagan and Christian holidays are celebrated, although most religious content has been eliminated. The visitor to Yerevan will be able to enjoy the customary national foods, such as various soured-milk dishes, *aris* (a dish made from cooked groats and chicken), *gata* and *pahlava* (pastries), *shorva* and *arganak* (soups).

Yerevan offers the visitor a wealth of cultural and recreational facilities. There are several museums with a vast array of historical, ethnographic, and artistic exhibits. There are five theaters where one can enjoy Armenian, Russian, and traditional European entertainment. One will also appreciate the architecture of the city which is world famous for its colorful beauty. Those with specialized interests may also wish to visit the state university, some of the eleven schools of higher learning, or some of the sixty scientific institutions. North of Yerevan one will find the industrial district, while south of the city one can arrange to visit the farmlands. The traveler will receive a warm welcome in this lively and hospitable city.

HISTORY IN BRIEF

The Armenian upland was one of the cradles of civilization. Archaeologists have unearthed primitive stone implements which date as far back as the Chellean era of the Paleolithic period—about half a million years ago. Stone axes and arrowheads dating from the Neolithic period have also been found. These correspond to the same epoch in which Yerevan was settled. The materials found in the Shengavit excavations show that the territory around Yerevan was originally inhabited in the sixth millennium B.C. and largely settled by the third millennium. A stone slab in Arin-Berd, the southeastern section of the city, was found bearing an Urartu cuneiform inscription. The slab is believed to have been carved in 782 B.C. The inscription tells of the founding of Yerevan:

> By the greatness of God Khaldi,
> Argishti, son of Menua, built this
> mighty fortress and named it Erebuni
> for the might of the country of Biainy
> and to dismay hostile lands . . .

Thus, the fortress gave its name to the city, Erebuni-Yerevan, as it was originally known. Urartu was a powerful state formed by the union of the Nairi tribes at the beginning of the ninth century B.C. It is the oldest state in the territory of the Soviet Union. Some five hundred Urartu cuneiform inscriptions have been left on the cliffs near Yerevan, Lakes Van and Sevan, Armavir, and other areas of the Armenian upland. In addition, numerous fortresses, canals, and bridges of the Urartu period have been excavated. It is also known that the Urartu civilization cultivated grapes and wheat, produced wine, smelted metals, and possessed a highly developed range of handcrafts.

From A.D. 63 to 428 the economy of Armenia developed rapidly owing to connecting trade routes with Persia, India, China, and ports of the Mediterranean and Black seas. Simultaneous with the burgeoning economy and town life was an upsurge of spirituality. An original Armenian culture evolved contemporaneous with that of the Greek Hellenistic period. It has been established that the two cultures had numerous features in common. Paganism was replaced in A.D. 301 by Christianity in Armenia, which thus became the first country in the world to adopt Christianity as the official state religion. Closer ties between Armenia and Rome led to conflict with Persia. In 378, the nation was divided by the two dominating influences, with the eastern portion—by far the larger—falling to Persian rule. By 428 the Arsacid dynasty had fallen and the country was entirely controlled by satraps, the name given to Persian provincial officials. However, the Armenian alphabet, invented in 396 by Mesrop Mashtotz, was a signal factor in preserving the national culture and identity of the Armenians. From the fifth to seventh centuries, a galaxy of outstanding cultural figures emerged in the fields of history, philosophy, literature, and translation. At the same time, the spread of Christianity brought about the creation of many new churches and monasteries, often, however, at the expense of old masterpieces of pagan architecture. The flowering of Armenian culture of this period culminated in the career of Anania Shirakatzi, a remarkable philosopher, mathematician, geographer, and astronomer who defended the notion of the earth's spherical shape and produced an explanation for lunar and solar eclipses.

Yerevan remained a principal city throughout the Middle Ages and at the beginning of the sixteenth century it acquired enhanced strategic military importance because of its position between the rival Persian and Ottoman empires. In 1735 it became the administrative center of the Yerevan khanate, a provincial stronghold of Persia. In 1801 Eastern Georgia and a portion of Eastern Armenia were annexed by Russia. On October 1, 1827, Russian troops, accompanied by Armenian volunteers, stormed the Persian positions in the Yerevan fortress. Shortly thereafter the Yerevan and Nakhichevan khanate became Russian territory. Meanwhile, the western section was still within the Ottoman Empire, with the exception of the Kars region, which was ceded to Russia as a result of the Russo-Turkish War (1577–78).

In Eastern Armenia in the nineteenth century industry, trade, and culture flowered. New transportation systems enabled the economy to develop at a rapid rate. A revived economy spurred the cultural revival which in turn fomented a renewed and vigorous strain of Armenian patriotism. A new class structure emerged comprised of a bourgeoisie and urban proletariat, a wealthy landowning class and landless peasantry. Revolutionary ideas filtered into Armenia and found a reception among the downtrodden.

Social Democratic Bolshevik organizations appeared in Armenia, led by such men as Stepan Shaumyan, Suren Spandaryan, and Bogdan Knunyants. From 1903 to 1907 strikes occurred among the miners, railway men, and distillery workers. These were accompanied by revolts of army units. Armenians participated in the first Russian Revolution of 1905–07. In 1917, following the October Revolution, Transcaucasia, including Eastern Armenia, was taken from Soviet Russia. In 1918 governmental power in Armenia was taken by the Dashnakzutium Party. Turkey regained its lost portion of Western Armenia and seized a section of Eastern Armenia. Uprisings against the Dashnaks in May 1920 were suppressed. The tottering government was faced not only with political strife, but with famine and a cholera epidemic which reduced the population by one-third. A second rebellion in November of the same year, supported by Bolshevik troops, was successful. On December 4, 1920, Armenia was declared a Soviet Socialist Republic with Yerevan designated as the capital. Since the Revolution the population has increased twentyfold. The city's economy has kept pace with the rapid expansion of the entire Armenian economy as the republic moves toward industrialization and modernity.

MUSEUMS AND PLACES OF INTEREST

Lenin Square

Lenin Square, at the center of the city, contains the most outstanding architectural ensemble in Yerevan. The buildings surrounding the square express a single architectural concept. They are constructed of colorful volcanic tuff, elaborately decorated with carved Armenian national ornaments. Included in the group are the Armenia Hotel, Communications House, Trade Unions Palace of Culture, Government House, and Yerevan History Museum. The museum contains a rich collection of exhibits pertaining to the city's history dating from ancient times to the present. On the western side of the square is a monument to Lenin, designed by Sergei Merkurov and constructed of forged copper. Lenin Square is encircled by the principal streets of Yerevan which link the center city with nine other districts and the suburbs.

Shaumyan Square

A short distance northwest of Lenin Square is the central square of the Shaumyan District. Here one will find the Sundukyan Armenian Academic Theater and the monument to Stepan Shaumyan. East of the square toward Lenin Avenue, is the Yerevan City Soviet Deputies' Building. Past the corner, on Lenin Avenue, is the large enclosed Central Agricultural Market.

Lenin Avenue

Along this major thoroughfare are several of the city's points of interest. Proceeding eastward, one will first encounter the monument to Ovanes Tumanyan, a favorite Armenian poet. The huge building farther on is the Spendiaryan Opera and Ballet Theater. This building, designed by Tamanyan, houses two theaters which were constructed to share a single stage. Next to the theater is a monument to Alexander Spendiaryan. At the juncture of Lenin Avenue and Moskovya Street is the Large Concert Hall of the Armenian Philharmonic. A short walk north on Moskovya Street brings one to the Ovanes Tumanyan House Museum. Returning to Lenin Avenue and continuing eastward to its termination point, one encounters the Matenadaran, the most important museum in Armenia, and one of the world's most important repositories of ancient manuscripts. Among the Matenadaran's outstanding treasures are the "Lazarevskoye Gospel" (A.D. 887), the "Echmiadzinskoye Gospel" (A.D. 989), and the eleventh-century "Mugni Gospel."

Kirov Street

From the Matenadaran, one proceeds south along Kirov Street. At the corner of Abovyan Avenue is the monument to Avetik Isaakyan, a beloved writer of the Armenian people. Farther south is the monument to Dmitri Nalbandyan, a noted Armenian painter. The large structure which appears next is the Yerevan State University. From the university one can proceed northeastward via Sayat-Nova Street to the central part of Yerevan. Along the way is the Armenian State Picture Gallery, which houses over 15,000 works of art. The Armenian department, by far the richest, has an outstanding collection of nineteenth- and twentieth-century painting and sculpture. The Armenian State Historical Museum, located in the same area, possesses a vast collection of materials from all historical epochs dating back to the Paleolithic Age. Nearby is the Museum of Natural History of the Armenian S.S.R. housing a complete collection of exhibits pertaining to the flora and fauna of the republic. Proceeding northeast on Sayat-Nova Street, the visitor will cross Moskovya Street near the Opera and Ballet Theater. Here the thoroughfare becomes Barekamutyan Street. The large building on the left is the Academy of Sciences of the Armenian S.S.R. Established in 1935 as a branch of the U.S.S.R. Academy of Sciences, the institution was reorganized in 1943 as the Armenian Academy of Sciences. The academy is divided into numerous departments where several thousand scientists are engaged in research and development projects.

South of center city are several important historical sites. Farthest southwest at the end of Erebuni Street is an ancient Urartu fortress. As you move north along Tamantsineri Street, you will arrive at Shengavit, an Eneolithic settlement of the fourth millennium B.C. Lake Yerevan is to the east. The lake flows into the Razdan River. West along Echmiadzini Street is the ancient town of Teishebaini, built during the seventh and sixth centuries B.C. Another Urartu fortress of the eighth century B.C. is located here. In contrast to the ruins of the fortress, a bold architectural structure appears on the same tract of land: the Republican Exhibition of Economic Achievements.

Yerevan Suburbs

ECHMIADZIN

Twenty kilometers (12 miles) west of Yerevan is Echmiadzin, known in the past as Vagarshapat. Historically the town has been a religious center in Armenian life. After Christianity was adopted as the state religion in A.D. 301, Echmiadzin became the center of the Armenian Gregorian Church. At that time a cathedral and monastery were built. For a brief period

Echmiadzin was the capital of the Armenian state in the second and third centuries. During the fifth century, the monastery became the residence of the Supreme Catholicos of all the Armenias, the highest ecclesiastical position in the church hierarchy. After an interval of about a thousand years, the Armenian Church was reestablished in the fifteenth century. Again its headquarters were located in Echmiadzin. Up to the establishment of Soviet power in Armenia, the town remained the central seat of clerical feudalism. Today Echmiadzin is an industrial town with a population of about 30,000. In addition to the manufacture of plastics, the town also has one of the major brandy distilleries of the Ararat plain. There are several noteworthy architectural monuments which make a visit to Echmiadzin worthwhile.

ECHMIADZIN CATHEDRAL AND MONASTERY

Established as a museum in 1955, these buildings contain exhibits of church plates, robes, tapestries, and other articles of medieval applied art. The cathedral dates from the fourth and fifth centuries, although it has been reconstructed many times. The frescoes are products of the late seventeenth and early eighteenth centuries. The monastery ensemble includes a refectory, a hotel, monks' cells, and the residence of the head of the Armenian Church. Most of the structures retain the form given to them during the seventeenth and eighteenth centuries. Armenian historians, notably those of the fourth and fifth centuries, claimed that Christian structures were built on the sites of pagan temples demolished during proseltyzing and conversion efforts and during the reconstruction of the altar of the cathedral in 1967 the remains of a pagan temple were discovered.

ST. HRIPSIME, ST. GAYANE, AND ZVARTHNOTS TEMPLES

These early Christian temples are monuments of the seventh century. St. Hripsime and St. Gayane were restored during the seventeenth century. Zvarthnots was not discovered until 1902 during an excavation project. During the tenth century the temple was demolished by an earthquake. The remains were destroyed by Arab invaders. Over the ensuing centuries the ruins were buried under layers of earth. The excavations revealed that Zvarthnots had been a departure from conventional architecture of the period, an innovation of style and construction which subsequently influenced the architecture of Armenia and neighboring countries. It is said that the Byzantine emperor, Constantine III, attended the consecration of the Zvarthnots Temple and was so impressed by the audacity of the structure that he ordered its builder to return with him to Constantinople to build a similar temple there.

GARNI

Due east of Yerevan about 30 kilometers (18 miles) is the town of Garni, where the ancient Armenian nobility spent their summers. During the first century A.D., King Tiridates I built the Garni fortress at an elevation of nearly 1,500 meters (4,921 feet) above sea level. Within the fortress are the remains of a pagan temple which was destroyed by an earthquake during the late seventeenth century. Visitors are awed by the beauty of the temple's remains, which have been well preserved. The temple and all the structures built for royal family members were the labor of slaves. Few of these outstanding relics of the past remain, having been ravaged by wars, invasions, and time.

DVIN

About 15 kilometers (9 miles) southeast of Yerevan is Dvin, the medieval capital of Armenia. Although the area was settled centuries earlier, it was not until the fourth century A.D. that the capital was moved to Dvin. Over a period of time the city became the center of the Armenian Church. Thus it developed more rapidly than other cities and became a vital center for culture, politics, and international trade. At the top of the Dvin hill are the remains of the residence of the Supreme Catholicos. Here also are the ruins of the cathedral and numerous secular buildings. The area surrounding Dvin along the upper reaches of the Vedi and Azat rivers was planted in the fourth century by King Khosrov Kodak. It is called the Khosrov Woods and is now a national preserve.

ARTASHAT

Ten kilometers (6 miles) south of Dvin is the town of Artashat, now the second largest wine-producing center of Armenia. Artashat is also known for the remarkable historical monuments located in the surrounding area. The most famous of these is Artaxata, the capital city built by King Artaxias during the second century B.C. Plutarch referred to Artaxata as the "Armenian Carthage." Indeed, the city was an important center of Hellenistic culture in southwest Asia, where arts, crafts, and trade had reached a high level of development. However, Artaxata is most renowned as the birthplace of Armenian theater. It is recorded that in 53 B.C. Euripides's *Bacchae* was performed by the royal dramatic entourage.

USEFUL INFORMATION

Hotels

Hotel Armeniya, 1 Amiryana Street
Hotel Arabkir, 5 H Komitasa Street
Hotel Yerevan, 24 Abovyan Street
Hotel Ani, Sayat-Nova Street

Restaurants

Armeniya, Hotel Armeniya, 1 Amiryana Street
Arabkir, Hotel Arabkir, 5 H Komitasa Street
Yerevan, Hotel Yerevan, 24 Abovyan Street
Ani, Hotel Ani, Sayat-Nova Street

Museums

Matenadaran, Lenin Avenue at Korov Street
Yerevan History Museum, Lenin Square
Ovanes Tumanyan House Museum, Moskovya Street
Armenian State Picture Gallery, Abovyan Street
Armenian State Historical Museum, Abovyan Street
Natural History Museum of the Armenian S.S.R., Abovyan Street

Theaters, Concert Halls, and Cinemas

Sundukyan Armenian Academic Theater, Shaumyan Square
Spendiaryan Opera and Ballet Theater, Lenin Avenue
Armenian Philharmonic Concert Hall, Lenin Avenue
Nairi Cinema, Upper Charbakh, near the Hippodrome
Moskva Cinema, Abovyan Street near Sayat-Nova Street
Aragats Cinema, Razdan River Embankment near Komitas Street

Transportation and Communications

Central Telegraph and Post Office, Lenin Square
Railway Terminal, Railway Terminal Square, Oktemberyan Avenue

BAKU

GENERAL INFORMATION

Baku is the capital of the Azerbaijan S.S.R. and is located along the southern part of the Apsheron Peninsula on the shores of the Caspian Sea. The center of the Soviet oil industry, it is the fifth largest city in the Soviet Union. In addition to oil-producing and refining industries, Baku serves as a major shipyard and ship-repair center. Other industries include electromechanics, heavy machinery, chemical products, and precision instruments. Baku is accessible to visitors from within the Soviet Union by air or rail, or by special Intourist bus from Tbilisi. Baku also serves as a point of entry into the Soviet Union from the Caspian Sea, and many travelers coming from Iran arrive by ship.

Baku is one of the most picturesque cities of the Soviet Union. It is built like an amphitheater around Baku Bay. The climate is essentially warm and arid, but modern irrigation methods have made possible the cultivation of lush vegetation throughout the city. Considered the eastern gateway to Transcaucasia, the Azerbaijan shares the Islamic cultural heritage of the Transcaucasus Region. One will enjoy a visit to the fascinating museums and ancient historical sites in and around Baku. The visitor will find the Azerbaijanis hospitable and courteous.

HISTORY IN BRIEF

Archaeological findings have revealed that Baku is an extremely old city, originating as a settlement on the Caspian shores in the seventh century A.D. During the ninth century, the settlement developed into a significant market town ruled by the Arabs. Azerbaijan feudal estates came into power during the tenth and eleventh centuries when the Arab caliphate fell into decline and eventually collapsed. Of the most powerful and wealthy feudal estates, Shirvan emerged as the ruling one. The capital of Shirvan was Shemkah, which included Baku. In the sixteenth century Azerbaijan was caught up in the power struggle between Persia and Turkey, and in the settlement between the warring states it fell to the Persians. In 1806 Baku and northern Azerbaijan were incorporated into Russia. The area remained a relatively backward province for the remainder of the nineteenth century, and Baku was a rather squalid city exploited for oil. At the beginning of the twentieth century a revolutionary movement was beginning to form throughout Transcaucasia. On April 25, 1918 Soviet power was proclaimed, but the Baku Commune was quelled by counterrevolutionary forces. By 1919 Soviet power was restored.

During the past five decades Baku has been transformed into an industrial, cultural, and scientific capital city, and a great deal of effort has gone into irrigation.

MUSEUMS AND PLACES OF INTEREST

One should begin a tour of Baku on Primorsky Boulevard which extends along the shore of Baku Bay. In addition to passing some of the city's principal sites, Primorsky Boulevard is a pleasant thoroughfare for strolling because of the numerous facilities for relaxation located along its tree-lined pavements. Here one finds shops, restaurants, cafés, teahouses, reading rooms, yacht clubs, an open-air cinema, and a sports stadium. One will also find along the shore of the bay the remains of the ancient city of Sabail, or the Bailovskye Stones. An old Azerbaijan legend tells of the magnificent city of Sabail, one of several residences of the Shirvan Shahs, which disappeared into the stormy sea. The only trace of the lost city was a road leading directly into the water. During the 1930s the level of the Caspian Sea began to fall, and receding waters revealed stone walls, towers, and slabs bearing Arabic writing. Nearly six hundred pages of a book written on stone tablets have been recovered and deciphered revealing much about the ancient life of Sabail.

Near the seashore is the twelfth-century Maiden's Tower (Kyz Kalasy).

The legend of the tower tells of the incestuous love of a Shirvan ruler for his daughter. She requested that her father build the tower to prove his love for her in the hopes that his passion would cool before the structure was completed. However, the project served only to increase his ardor. Thus, when the tower was complete, he claimed his amorous rights. The girl, unable to tolerate his advances, leapt from the tower into the sea. Visitors to the Maiden's Tower will notice the unusual key shape in which the structure was built. Numerous loopholes were designed in the construction of the walls. The general theory is that the structure served as both a defense bastion and a lighthouse. The tower rises to a height of 28 meters (92 feet) with walls that are 5 meters (16 feet) thick at the base. Inside the tower is a spiral staircase. From tier to tier are exhibits of medieval arms and armor and a variety of wooden utensils. At the top of the tower is a parapet which functions as an observatory. From this vantage point one can look down upon the Old City.

Baku Fortress and the Old City are adjacent to the Maiden's Tower. Built between the twelfth and fifteenth centuries, the fortress enclosed all of Baku. Among the prominent sites of the Old City—or Inner City, as it is occasionally called—are the remains of the Synk-Kala Minaret, built in 1078–79. Some sections of the remaining walls are 22 meters (70 feet) high. The minaret of the Djuma Mosque is another fifteenth-century monument of the old quarter.

By far the most impressive feature of Old Baku is the architectural ensemble comprising the Shirvan Shahs' Palace. A two-story building of very austere design, the palace now houses the Museum of the History of Baku. The other structures within the palace are more spectacular, and it is for these that the Shirvan Shahs' Palace is frequently noted. Among these are the Divankhane, a structure of cut stone with an impressive portal; a double-domed mosque with a highly decorative minaret; the octagonal Mausoleum of Seid Yakhya Bakuvi; the Eastern Gate; a rain cistern with attached bathing facilities. The Old City is itself a museum where one can walk for hours through the labyrinth of narrow streets along which are fascinating portals of carved stone, mosques, and caravanserai.

Nizami Square is one of the most vibrant areas of Baku, a gathering place for students and visitors attracted to the Nizami Museum of the History of Azerbaijan Literature. The square is dedicated to the thirteenth-century poet Nizami Gyandzhevi, for whom a bronze monument has been erected. The museum is the focal point of the architectural ensemble flanking the square. In addition to manuscripts and books, the museum houses a fabulous collection of fine and applied art. The most noteworthy feature of this collection is the Azerbaijan rugs. Also on display are documents and materials related to prominent national writers dating back to the twelfth century. Nearby is the Mustafayev Azerbaijanan Museum of Fine Arts. Named for the prominent Soviet stage designer Rustam Mustafayev, the museum contains over six thousand items. Painting and sculptural exhibits represent Russian, Azerbaijan, and European artists. The applied arts section contains Azerbaijan rugs, jewelry, brocades, embroideries, wood and copper pieces. In the same area is the Museum of Azerbaijan History whose collection includes archaeological and ethnographic exhibits as well as a re-creation of the Azerbaijanan quest for national independence. Among the items featured in the collection are coins, embroideries, and an especially decorative *hookah* (waterpipe) cover made by the nineteenth-century poetess Natavan.

Fizuli Square is the home of the new Azizbekov Azerbaijan Theater. For over ninety years major works by leading world playwrights have been staged by this theater organization. Baku also has a Musical Comedy Theater, the Vergun Russian Drama Theater, the Akhundov Opera and Ballet Theater, named for the founder of Azerbaijan dramaturgy, and the Magomayev Baku Philharmonic Society.

Kirov Street, another major thoroughfare of Baku, was dedicated to S. M. Kirov, a prominent Soviet statesman who served as secretary of the Central Committee of the Communist Party of Azerbaijan during the 1920s. Also named for him is the Central Kirov Park, built on terraces overlooking Baku Bay. The Azerbaijan State University was dedicated to him, too. One might wish to visit the Kirov Museum, an apartment in which the statesman lived on the street that now bears his name. A branch of the Central Lenin Museum is located nearby. Along Kirov Street, one will find the Square of the 26 Baku Commissars commemorating the execution of twenty-six Bolsheviks who were captured by the counter-revolutionaries in 1918 and taken to the Azerbaijan desert, beyond the Caspian Sea, to meet their deaths. Their remains were brought back to Baku and laid to rest in a marble mausoleum located in the square.

Any tour of Baku should include a visit to the Metro. This underground transit system was opened in 1967 on the fiftieth anniversary of the October Revolution. Each station is a work of art. Among the most beautiful are the Baku Soviet Station, which has a glass pavilion; the Shaumyan Station with halls made of marble; the Narimanov, and the Genzhlik stations. Throughout the city modernization has been accompanied by an endeavor to preserve national styles and motifs.

BAKU SUBURBS

Sumgait

Located about 75 kilometers (45 miles) northwest of Baku is the town of Sumgait. A legend accounts for its name. Once there was a monster who demanded tribute from the inhabitants. When they refused, he drained all the water from the river. A courageous young man named Sum vowed that he would free the water for the people. Setting out on his mission to the mountains, he promised to return victorious. The water did indeed flow back into the river, but it was red with blood. The townspeople went out to greet their hero, crying *"Sum gait"* (Sum, come back). When he did not return, they returned to their homes. Realizing the futility of her vigil, his betrothed threw herself into the river.

Modern history has created a similar set of circumstances which reinforce the legend. Up to the post-World War II period, the land between Sumgait and Baku was a combination of swamp and scorched saline steppe. The territory was named Dzherainbatan for the Azerbaijan word *dzherain* meaning gazelle. Many of these creatures died in the brackish marshes. In the last thirty years a systematized network of irrigation canals has been built to bring water to the Dzherainbatan Reservoir. The surrounding area has flourished with olive groves and vineyards. Sumgait has become a busy industrial center noted mainly for its chemical plant, thermal power station, and metallurgical activities. It is also a city of pure sea air and verdant avenues which make it a pleasant side trip for visitors to Baku.

Neftyanye Kamny

East of Baku, off the coast of the Caspian Sea, lies the offshore town of Nefyanye Kamny. It is but one of the many offshore oil fields of the Azerbaijan Republic. Trestles driven into the bed of the sea form a network of steel islands joined by suspension bridges. Thus a highway is provided for vehicular traffic. Neftyanye Kamny is a busy town with its own post office, hospital, schools, library, and museum.

Surakhany, Ramany, Mardakyany, and Kobystan are located south of Baku along the interior coastline of the Caspian Sea. Surakhany, about 32 kilometers (19 miles) from Baku, is noted for the Ateshga, an eighteenth-century Indian monastery and temple of fire worshipers. Ramany, 36 kilometers (22 miles) from Baku, features the ruins of an eleventh-century castle. Mardakyany, 50 kilometers (30 miles) from Baku, is known for the tower castle built during the twelfth through fourteenth centuries. Mardakyany is also important as a resort area. Kobystan, 70 kilometers (42 miles) from Baku, is considered to be one of the best-known open-air museums of Azerbaijan. Four thousand rock drawings have been left to posterity by artists of the Neolithic Age. These drawings depict customs and ceremonies as well as scenes of everyday life. Near Mt. Beyukshad is a circular plot of ground enclosed by stones. At the center is an altar where rituals were held in ancient times. Nearby, along the side of the mountain, is a Latin inscription carved on the rocks about two thousand years ago.

USEFUL INFORMATION

Hotels

Hotel Intourist, 63 Neftyanikov Prospect
Hotel Yuzhnaya, 6 Kirova Prospect

Restaurants and Cafés

Intourist, Hotel Intourist, 63 Neftyanikov Prospect
Yuzhnaya, Hotel Yuzhnaya, 6 Kirova Prospect
Café Zhemchuzhina, Primorsky Boulevard

Museums

Nizami Museum of the History of Azerbaijan Literature, Nizami Square
Branch of the Central Lenin Museum, Kirova Prospect
S. M. Kirov Flat Museum, Kirova Prospect
Museum of the History of Baku, Shirvan Shahs' Palace, Old City
Museum of the History of Azerbaijan, Kommunisticheskaya Street
Mustafayev Art Museum, Kommunisticheskaya Street

Theaters and Concert Halls

Azizbekov Azerbaijan Theater, Fizuli Square
Magomayev Baku Philharmonic, Kirova Prospect
Akhundov Opera and Ballet Theater, Neftyanikov Prospect

THE MEDIEVAL TOWNS
Vladimir, Suzdal, Bogolyubovo, Yuryev-Polskoi

Russia's medieval past is associated with the names of three historical places: Kiev, Moscow, and Vladimir. The earliest period in this era is concerned with Kiev, which was the center of the rapidly growing Russian state. By the twelfth century feudal disintegration was weakening the Russian lands, and a new locus of culture and political power developed along the northeastern boundaries in the area of Vladimir. This territory also included other townships, such as Suzdal, Rostov, Bogolyubovo, and Yuryev-Polskoi. When Vladimir and its domains began to suffer the effect of prolonged Mongol invasions, a nearby, somewhat insignificant town became a stronghold and rallying point for Russian principalities against the Mongol yoke. The town was Moscow, which within two centuries became the center of a newly emerging Russian culture and the capital of the newly centralized Russian state. Just as Vladimir had drawn its culture from the Kievan heritage, so Moscow drew upon the Vladimir period for continuity and precedent.

Many visitors to the Soviet Union take an excursion to the Vladimir region. It presents a wealth of historical sight-seeing, unique among the vast offerings available throughout the U.S.S.R. The Vladimir region abounds with relics of religious art and architecture, many of which have been taken to museums in Moscow and Leningrad. Nevertheless, what remains cannot be seen or duplicated elsewhere. The land itself, with the many fortresses, palaces, and churches bespeaks the unified aspirations of the Russian medieval church and state.

From Moscow a trip by bus can be arranged at the excursion office of

Intourist, located next door to the Intourist Hotel on Gorky Street. The visitor may also rent a car in the adjacent auto rental office. To reach Vladimir and Suzdal, follow Motor Route #8 due east of Moscow. Vladimir is 310 kilometers (168 miles) from Moscow and Suzdal is 48 kilometers (30 miles) north along the same road. In Vladimir and Suzdal there are restaurants and automobile service stations, but no hotels. Train service to both Vladimir and Suzdal is also available. Specific inquiries for schedules and ticketing should be made through the Service Bureau of your hotel.

VLADIMIR—History in Brief

The original town of Vladimir, shaped somewhat like an elongated triangle, was situated on high ground on the left bank of the Klyazma River. To the north and east of the town were the Lybed and Irpen rivers, respectively; to the west were vast pine forests. The earliest settlements, revealed by archaeological excavations, date back to the first century A.D. during which time the inhabitants were Finno-Ugrians. Slavic settlers from the Smolensk Krivichi tribes and Slovenes from the Novgorod area appeared during the tenth and eleventh centuries. The Vladimir lands seem to have attracted people for both political and economic reasons. First, the location of Vladimir on the promontory above a river offered excellent natural defenses at a time when primitive tribal society was being superseded by feudalism. Second, the Klyazma joined the Oka River, thus providing access to the main trading waterway of Eastern Europe, the Volga. Hence, the gates of Vladimir that led to the Klyazma were called the "Volga Gates."

Originally called Zalessky region ("beyond the forests"), this remote sector of the Kievan state attracted many newcomers because of its natural resources. Moreover, it soon attracted the attention of the Kiev princes, and in the eleventh century it came under the rule of Prince Vsevolod I. Several decades of infighting ensued, and in 1108 a fortress was erected by Vladimir Monomach, Vsevolod's son. Traces of the ramparts of this fortress can still be seen in the northeast corner of the old town which is now Proletarskaya Street, and in the northwest corner on Komsomolskaya Street. The town was named Vladimir in honor of its founder. His heir, Prince Dolgoruky, realizing the futility of his ambition for the throne of Kiev, built several new fortress towns in the north, among which was Moscow. In 1157 a new royal palace was erected in Vladimir along with a church dedicated to St. George, the prince's patron saint. By the middle of the twelfth century the growth of Vladimir had spread eastward toward Suzdal.

Prince Andrei Bogolyubsky, Dolgoruky's heir, moved his residence from Kiev to Vladimir. During the years 1158–65 a wave of vigorous building took place and such landmarks as the four turreted gates known as the

Volga, Wooden, Golden, and Copper gates were erected. A new royal palace was built along with a new church. Vladimir became a town of clearly defined sections. The western portion was reserved for royalty, aristocracy, and the very wealthy. The east was the home of artisans, craftsmen, and merchants. The western section was called Novy Gorod (New Town), and when the fortifications of the eastern quarter began to crumble, the section was called Vetchany Gorod (Decayed Town). The middle portion of Vladimir was called Pecherny Gorod (Cave Town or Middle Town). During this industrious period of building, Uspensky Sobor (Cathedral of the Assumption) was built in the Middle Town along with three sets of gates known as the Trading, Ivan, and Silver gates.

Between the end of the twelfth century and the beginning of the thirteenth Vsevolod III consolidated power under the title of grand prince. Political awareness had come to the citizens of Vladimir resulting in riots and uprisings which endangered the royal sector. Thus Vsevolod decided to transfer his residence to the Middle Town where, between 1194 and 1197, he built a grandiose stone palace along with the Cathedral of St. Dmitri. This area became known as Detinets (Inner Citadel) because of the stonewall fortifications protecting the royal residence at the innermost core of the city. An outer citadel was formed by the Monastery of the Nativity and its cathedral, built in 1192–95. The Vladimir marketplace was moved to the northern part of the Middle Town at this time. Prince Konstantin, who succeeded Vsevolod III, erected the Church of the Exaltation of the Cross in 1218 on the plot where the old market had been. Vsevolod's widow, Princess Maria, had added the Convent of the Assumption (known also as the Princess's Convent), which was built in the northwest corner of the New Town in 1200–01.

In 1212, after the death of Vsevolod III, the unity of the Vladimir lands was destroyed by feudal disintegration. This left the area weak and vulnerable to the Mongol invasion in 1238. The Mongols departed after looting and burning the town. In spite of the disaster Vladimir was still considered to be the political and religious citadel of northeastern Russia. At the end of the thirteenth century the Metropolitan of the Russian Church was placed here. The rulers of Moscow and Tver continued to contest the Grand Duchy of Vladimir with the result that many of the actual treasures as well as traditions of Vladimir were transferred to Moscow for political and practical purposes. The eventual political decline of Vladimir dates from 1486–1536, after which time it ceased to be the capital of the northeast and became merely one of the towns of Muscovy, famous for relics and memories.

Vladimir was primarily a town of merchants, artisans, and petty government officials. The industrialization of Russia passed by the ancient town, and little effort was exerted to maintain what was left of the historical sites. Apartment houses were constructed along with small private homes. In

1861 the railroad from Moscow to Nizhny Novgorod reached the foot of the southern slopes of Vladimir. Until the completion of the Revolution and Civil War, Vladimir's history was neglected. Since then, however, a systematic process of restoration has been carried out with the result that today Vladimir more closely resembles its golden age than at any time since the sixteenth century.

PLACES OF INTEREST

Golden Gates

At the main entrance to the town are the Golden Gates, erected in 1158–64 by local builders whose skills implemented the intense architectural impetus of the twelfth century. The gates served not only as defense fortifications but also as triumphal arch leading to the capital's main thoroughfare and aristocratic residential quarter. This accounts for the height of the structure and the grace and splendor of the arched entrance with gilded copper over the wooden gates as well as on the dome of the church over the gateway. The construction and design of the Golden Gates reflect the desire of Prince Andrei Bogolyubsky to enhance and consolidate the importance of the capital and to prove it equal to Kiev as "the mother of Russia" and to Constantinople as the "Rome of the East."

To defend the approaches to the gates, a wooden platform was constructed on a level with the arched crosspiece which rested on joists inserted into sockets in the walls. The platform covered the entire archway and was used to dispense arrows, stones, or boiling water on the approaching enemy. The first flight of stone stairs with a spreading vault ceiling in the south wall led to this platform. The odd inscriptions and crosses scratched on the walls of the archway leading to the platform date back to the twelfth and thirteenth centuries. The upper flight of stairs leads to another defensive platform surrounded by an indented parapet on a level with the present windows. In the center of this platform was the tiny Church of the Deposition of the Robe with its single dome of gilded copper.

Both then and now, the passageway through the gates was covered by a huge semicircular vault on stilted arches supported by flat pilasters topped with functional posts. The height of the arched gateway caused defensive difficulties, but the addition of an arched crosspiece solved the problems. This crosspiece was located about halfway up the wall so that the enormous oak gates, covered with copper sheeting, fitted tightly into it. The huge iron hinges of the gates can be viewed on either side of the archway along with the deep groove into which the thick bolt shaft was placed.

The present form of the Golden Gates differs greatly from the original. The gates were first damaged in 1238 when the Mongols seized the town.

After their departure the little church above the gateway was rebuilt in 1469 by the Russian architect Vassili Yermolin. The next serious damage to the gates was caused at the beginning of the seventeenth century by the invasion of the Poles. The gates were not repaired until the end of that century when all of the town's fortifications were repaired. The final transformation of the Golden Gates occurred in 1785 when the earthen ramparts adjoining the gates on either side were replaced by buttresses added to the four corners surrounded by circular bastions. Residential dwellings were constructed between the two bastions on the north side of the gateway, and a new flight of stairs was built on the south side. The decrepit main archway was also rebuilt with a new brick church above it.

All that remains today of the original building are the two thick walls of white stone. These were constructed according to the traditional Vladimir method of erecting two parallel partitions of hewn white stone and filling the intermediate space with rubble over which a concentrated lime solution was poured to form a cement-like setting. A lighter, more porous material was used for the arches. Over the centuries the gates have settled about five feet into the ground. The previous earthen ramparts adjoining the gates were topped with protective wooden walls. Carved into the walls at the point where they joined the ramparts were deep, curving recesses. Traces of the old wooden walls can be observed above the buildings which were added later on. The ramparts were about 9 meters (30 feet) high and 23.8 meters (78 feet) wide at the base. They were protected by a moat 7.6 meters (25 feet) deep and 21.3 meters (70 feet) wide. Vestiges of the moat and ramparts can be seen south of the gates in Kozlov Val.

Church of St. Nicholas at the Galleys, Upper Kalinin Street

The twelfth-century chronicles of Vladimir indicate that at the bottom of the hill upon which this church is located there was a quay where large vessels propelled by oars arrived frequently. The ancient name for this type of vessel was "galley," or in Russian, *galeya*. Hence, the church above the quay was dedicated to the patron saint of sailors and travelers, St. Nicholas. The original wooden church was completely rebuilt in 1732–35. The style of the church is designated as refectory type or *trapeznaya*, since the main square-shaped building is adjoined at the western wall by a low refectory, which is connected to the bell tower. The church consists of gradually diminishing octagons on a square base. First appearing in the wooden architecture of Russia's medieval period, the octagonal plan was imitated in stone architecture after the seventeenth century. The main octagon of the church is especially handsome with the slender semicolumns at each corner and the opulent carvings around the windows which stand out in relief against the flat white wall surface. As the eye proceeds upward to the diminishing octagons, one notices the strong rectangular pillars of the bell tower, the bell tier of the middle section, and the tent-shaped roof. The exterior of the ensemble of St. Nicholas at the Galleys is decorated with highly glazed green tile. Near St. Nicholas, on Shchedrin Street, on a steep rise which used to be called Ascension Hill, is the Church of the Ascension. Built in 1724, it has been greatly altered by numerous additions including a bell tower. During the twelfth century the Monastery of the Ascension was located here. One will immediately notice the similarity between the Church of St. Nicholas at the Galleys and the Church of the Ascension: the *kokoshnik* which crowns the walls and the window frames. Named for the medieval headdress of Russian married women, this purely decorative, seventeenth-century architectural feature is semicircular in shape, rising to a point that is framed by elaborate molding.

Church of Our Savior, at the foot of Kozlov Val

On the former site of Andrei Bogolyubsky's palace is the Church of Our Savior. Made of white stone, it was erected in 1164 but severely damaged by the fire of 1778 and replaced by the present building at the end of the century. Although the architects attempted to imitate the original, the present structure does not fulfill the task. Of note, however, are the stylistic effects which resemble fairly closely the twelfth-century craftsmanship. Among these decorative features are the blind arcading around the outer walls, the pilaster strips which divide the walls, and the deeply recessed portals. The carved relief figures of the original building were hewn from the white stone of the church itself. The rebuilders of the eighteenth century were forced either by economy or lack of craft to imitate the relief carvings with molded plaster.

Church of St. Nicholas, at the foot of Kozlov Val next to the Church of Our Savior

During the seventeenth century, a second church was erected nearby on the same site. This one, the Church of St. Nicholas, is in the style of the period, and by virtue of its authenticity of design and construction, rather outstrips its neighbor as an architectural masterpiece. The most striking feature of the church are the rows of *kokoshnik* gables crowning all the walls and window frames. Of equal note is the rectangular bell tower decorated with arches and bands of deeply recessed rectangular niches faced with green tiles. The bell tier is formed by arches resting on rectangular pillars.

Church of St. George, Kozlov Val, near the Church of Our Savior

This stone church was added in 1157 to the site on which stood the palace of Prince Yuri Dolgoruky. The fire of 1778 demolished the church, and when it was rebuilt in 1783–84 the salvaged stone from the original building was used. However, the new Church of St. George was reconstructed in Provincial Baroque style. The original church was almost square and had a single dome supported by cruciform pillars. There were flat pilasters on the outer walls and three huge apses. The massive proportions of this church lent quite a contrast to the more modest-sized churches nearby. The Church of St. George bears a close resemblance to the Church of St. Boris and St. Gleb near Suzdal, the country residence of Dolgoruky.

Cathedral of the Assumption, at the south end of Vladimir near the Klyazma Embankment

The foundations of this cathedral were laid in 1158 during the same period in which work was begun on the defensive ramparts surrounding the town. Ancient chronicles describe the intention of Prince Andrei Bogolyubsky in ordering the cathedral to be built. Not only was it to be the main cathedral of the Vladimir bishopric, but it was a demonstration of the independence of the Vladimir Metropolitan from Kievan ecclesiastical authority. The building of the cathedral clearly announced Vladimir as the political and ecclesiastical capital of feudal Russia. The time was particularly ripe, as the separate feudal principalities, engaged in constant petty strife among themselves, required a new and powerful symbol of unified authority. This, essentially, was to be the function of the Cathedral of the Assumption. From its position on high ground at the edge of the town, it became not only the focal point of the new architectural ensemble of Vladimir but seemed to dominate the entire area. The huge golden-domed cathedral was visible at quite a distance from Vladimir and became something of a metaphorical giant warrior with a golden helmet guarding the capital.

The building which the visitor sees today dates back to two separate periods of construction. The original cathedral which Prince Andrei commissioned was destroyed beyond repair by the fire of 1185. The architects engaged by Vsevolod III decided to surround the original structure with new walls and to strengthen the old walls with pillars. The old and new walls were connected by arches, thus encasing the old cathedral with the new one. From the outside, then, it is Vsevolod III's cathedral that the visitor views today. The new building became a cluster of rising tiers starting with the vaulted roofs of the galleries, their small corner domes topped with filigree crosses of gilded copper, all yielding visually to the large golden dome on a square base with its huge golden cross on the top. In rebuilding the Cathedral of the Assumption, Vsevolod III increased its proportions as well as its elegance by adding several decorative features, among them the bands of blind arcading, the deeply recessed portals, and the elaborately molded window frames.

Although little remains today of the carved stone on the outer walls, some traces of popular medieval legendary and religious art are visible to the careful viewer. Upon close inspection of the masonry at the west end of the south wall one will see two blocks depicting people immersed in water, which is obvious from the wavy lines. The figures represent the Forty Martyrs of Sebaste. To the right of the pilaster is the faint outline of a carving which depicts Alexander the Great being borne by two winged griffins toward heaven. In the central section of the north wall above the vaulting around the corners of the windows are carved lion and lioness masks.

The interior of the Cathedral of the Assumption is very impressive. Beginning at the west gallery one is immediately confronted by the west wall of the original cathedral which is intersected by large arches. On the same level as the choir gallery is an ornamental frieze. The ornamentation consists of a band of blind arcading over which is a line of vertically set stone. There is a series of slender columns, wedge-shaped consoles, and Romanesque cubed capitals. The upper section of the wall contains window slits with indented window jambs. The northern gallery contains a frieze of similar ornamentation. Here one will find rare fragments of frescoes which were painted on the walls in 1161. Above the narrow slit window are two painted blue peacocks with spread tails. On each side of the peacocks is a foliate design. To the right and left of the columns are spaces filled with the figures of two prophets holding scrolls. The fresco band of decoration predates the subsequent ornamental strip carving. Excavations have revealed that what now are larger apertures in the middle of the north, south, and west walls were at one time deeply recessed portals which led to the main sanctuary of the cathedral. The portals were covered with sheets of gilded copper. The upper wall sections were decorated with *zakomaras*, semicircles adorning the upper sections of outer walls which covered the adjoining cylindrical vault and reflected its shape.

Entering the old cathedral one is immediately struck by the light, spacious interior and the great height of the dome. In order to reinforce the impression of height the architects designed six cruciform pillars which appear to support the vaulted roof and single dome. Light entering the cathedral's twelve-windowed dome creates the illusion that the head of Christ painted on the inside of the dome is ascending to heaven. The use of carving adds to the effect of light and height.

The interior of the old cathedral clearly indicates the division of the feudal hierarchy. The prince and his entourage entered the cathedral via a private doorway which led to their seats in the choir gallery. From here they not only had a privileged view of the congregation and the altar service but were able to be seen in their symbolically lofty position by all who came to worship. The hierarchical nature of feudal Russia was reinforced by the large fresco of the Last Judgment. This fresco was one of the most important of the strictly prescribed religious frescoes with which Russian churches were decorated. Placed directly under the choir gallery it served to remind the congregants of their dual allegiance to heavenly and earthly masters as well as of the abominable retribution meted out to sinners in the hereafter.

The rebuilding of the Cathedral of the Assumption changed the appearance of the interior of the original cathedral to a great extent. Most noticeably, the interior was darkened by the new arches which blocked a considerable amount of light from outside. The new galleries were made deliberately dark, as they were intended as burial places for princes and church dignitaries. Special arched niches to contain the sarcophagi were built into the walls. The floors of the 1189 restoration have survived. These are decorated with mosaics of majolica tiles and copper plates.

Very few of the original frescoes remain. Most of the walls are now covered with late-nineteenth-century paintings which are considered meritless. However, some important fragments of the original group may be seen here and there, such as the figures of Abraham and Artemius on the inside walls of the apertures leading to the southwest corner of the old cathedral. What exists today are sections from the Last Judgment. On the arch are figures of angels blowing trumpets to summon the dead to judgment. On the keystone is an enormous hand holding numerous tiny human figures. The motif represents the biblical saying that "the souls of the righteous are in God's hand." The figure of Christ sitting in judgment under a halo of seraphim appears on the vault. Here also is a medallion of the four beasts symbolizing the four kingdoms. Beneath the vault is pictured the judgment seat with the kneeling figures of Adam and Eve, the Virgin Mary, and John the Baptist. These are supplicants sent to intercede on behalf of human sinners. Last are the apostles Paul and Peter at the sides of the vault with the apostolic tribunal and the angelic host. On the flat surface of the north pillar under the choir gallery is an angel appearing to the prophet Daniel. A very interesting but now only faintly visible section of the composition is located on the south wall above the arch. Here the earth and sea, represented by female figures together with a ship also symbolizing the sea, are offering up their dead. Farther along the flat surface of the south pillar under the choir gallery is the final scene of the Last Judgment. The righteous are entering paradise in a procession led by the apostle Paul, continued on the south arch and the side of the southwest vault over the gallery. On the wall of the south arch are the wooden gates of paradise guarded by an angel with a fiery sword. Next to the angel is a penitent robber, the first to enter the gates. On the curve of the arch itself is a portrayal of paradise with three forefathers and smaller figures of the righteous resting in Abraham's bosom while others wait their turn. Finally, on the north arch, is the Queen of Heaven surrounded by angels.

The iconostasis on view today is the heavy, sumptuous, richly carved and gilded one made during the 1773–74 restoration of the cathedral. When this new one was made, the icons of the Renaissance iconostasis were sold to the village of Vassilyevskoye. In 1922 the icons were taken to Moscow to be restored and were then dispersed to the Tretyakov Gallery there and to the Russian Museum in Leningrad.

Cathedral of St. Dmitri, Klyazma Embankment, northeast of the Cathedral of the Assumption

Through the town park, along the ancient ramparts of Vladimir on the banks of the Klyazma River, one arrives at the periphery of the Middle Town. Although no chronicle provides the exact dates of the construction of this cathedral, it has been established by the obituary of Vsevolod III that he erected a church on the palace grounds dedicated to St. Demetrius of Salonica which he had adorned with the choicest icons and frescoes. Research dates the founding of the cathedral between 1194 and 1197. Dmitri Donskoi assumed the patronage of the cathedral after Vsevolod's death. The Cathedral of St. Dmitri clearly embodies the concept of the omnipotence of Vsevolod III, Grand Duke of Vladimir. It was constructed at the height of his influence over the northern principalities and stands out as the royal church of the strongest feudal ruler of Russia. The cathedral belongs to a type of architecturally small churches consisting of four pillars and a single dome. This type of structure was frequently found in the feudal palaces and town parishes of twelfth-century Russia.

Despite what may be considered its small size, the proportions of the building are boldly impressive, and a spirit of majesty has been captured down to the last detail. The cathedral contains three semicircular apses and is divided into three horizontal tiers. The lower tier is almost devoid of decoration. The middle tier, narrower than the one below it, begins above a band of blind arcading, and is richly adorned with decorations. The walls are vertically divided into three broad sections by restrained pilasters which blend into the *zakomara* arches. The upper section of the walls contains long, narrow windows. Around the windows are large areas of relief carving which are duplicated on the entire upper section above the blind arcading as well as on the drum of the dome. The dome, which forms the third tier, is shorter than the upper section of the walls. The gradual reduction in height of each section creates the impression of upward movement. The dome tier is decorated with slender columns next to the windows. The columns are modified by broad, horizontal cornices. The entire structure is rounded off by the curved form of the helmet-shaped dome.

The decoration of the Cathedral of St. Dmitri is a careful blending of form and function. The architects designed each decorative area according to the requirements of structure and lighting for that section. For example, the main portal located on the west side of the cathedral is decorated much more lavishly than the north or east portals. The brightly illuminated south portal is decorated primarily with a flat intertwining pattern. This contrasts sharply with the deep, rich molding of the north side where shadows are the most prevalent. These are just a sampling of the decorative features of the cathedral which result in the organic unity of the structure. In contrast to the sparseness of carving on the Cathedral of the Assumption, the Cathedral of St. Dmitri abounds with a variety of sculptural forms on its exterior. It must be borne in mind, however, that time has taken its toll on the exterior sculpture. Many of the original forms have been replaced, restored, and rearranged.

The interior of the cathedral is quite impressive, especially now because many of the age-darkened wall paintings have been stripped, so that the visitor is struck by the majestic whiteness and illusion of space. All of the interior apertures and divisions are powerfully executed and contrast dramatically with the airy lightness of the open spaces. The carvings on the interior surfaces were as intricate as those outside and were most likely painted. Few of the originals remain. Under the vaulting above the gallery are the remains of a twelfth-century fresco which originally formed part of the Last Judgment in the western end of the building. The central vault of the gallery depicts the main feature of the fresco, the twelve apostles seated on their thrones with the angelic host of warriors behind them. At the corner of the southwest vault are the righteous entering paradise, led by Peter and accompanied by angels with trumpets. Last is the panel showing paradise, with the Virgin Mary seated on a throne, and the figures of Abraham, Isaac, and Jacob standing under a foliage canopy. The style of the Last Judgment fresco denotes the work of a Greek and a Russian painter. The Greek painter's angels and apostles appear in natural poses but have severe, portraitlike faces. The Russian painter's angels are rather more simple, human, and ornamental. The pale, subdued shades of the fresco in half-tones of blue, green, mauve, and light brown render a gentle solemnity to the interior of the cathedral, and enhance its quiescent dignity.

MONASTERY AND CATHEDRAL OF THE NATIVITY, TOWN HEIGHTS, KLYAZMA EMBANKMENT, SOUTH OF THE CATHEDRAL OF ST. DMITRI

From this elevated site, located at a break in the town heights where at the end of the eighteenth century the foundation for the Provincial Administration Building was laid, the visitor has an impressive view of the Klyazma River, its water meadows and forests, and the dome of the Cathedral of the Assumption. To the left, along the curve of the hill, are the walls of the Monastery of the Nativity, erected on the earthen ramparts of the Middle Town at the beginning of the eighteenth century. The Cathedral of the Nativity that the visitor sees today is an exact copy of the original one which was built at about the same time as the Cathedral of St. Dmitri,

1192–95. It was linked with several other buildings, including the abbot's residence, and was comprised of several galleries and staircase towers. Prince Alexander Nevsky, commander of the battle against the Livonian Knights which took place on the ice-covered Lake Chudskoye, was buried in the cathedral in 1263. Disfigured by wear and tear as well as numerous alterations, the original Cathedral of the Nativity was dismantled and reconstructed in 1859–64.

The general plan of four-pillared support of a single dome is similar to the Cathedral of St. Dmitri. However, the likeness ends here. The Cathedral of the Nativity represents a totally different concept in church architecture which appeared in Vladimir at this time. Like the Cathedral of the Assumption, the Cathedral of the Nativity follows severely ascetic lines of monastic austerity. Unlike the lavish external decor of St. Dmitri, the broad outer walls of the Nativity are almost devoid of ornamentation. Instead of blind arcading there are bands of narrow triangular spikes pointing downward. The frugal carving was reserved for arches of the portals and capitals. The splendid ornamentation of St. Dmitri represents the artistic and imaginative preferences of the common people and the feudal nobility. The almost puritanical plainness of the Nativity represents the condemnation by the clerical hierarchy of what it considered the vain and sinful sumptuousness of ornamentation too clearly allied with pagan idolatry. Visitors to Suzdal and Yuryev-Polskoi will see that the decorative and artistic tendency was the one that prevailed.

Church of the Assumption of Our Lady, Street of the Third International

From the Cathedral of the Nativity along the walls of the Monastery of the Nativity proceed along the reinforced slopes of the Decayed Town, the eastern section of old Vladimir. Along Proletarskaya Street are the earthen ramparts and traces of the deep fortification moat which date back to 1108. Past the corner of the monastery wall is a large building called Bishop's House (Arkhiyereisky Dom). Through the Decayed Town along the Street of the Third International are many stone churches. Originally these structures were made of wood, but during the seventeenth and eighteenth centuries they were reconstructed in stone. One of the most beautiful is the Church of the Assumption of Our Lady, erected in 1649 under the patronage of three merchant brothers from Vladimir, Patrikei, Andrei, and Grigory Denisov, their nephews, and two artisans, Vassili Obrosimov and Semion Somovovich. The church itself, as well as chronicle descriptions of it, provides a definitive statement of the final period of early Russian art.

The Church of the Assumption of Our Lady crowns the eastern section of the town's southern façade and is strongly silhouetted against the skyline of other structures owing to its height and onion-shaped cupolas. The entire architectural ensemble consists of the church, bell tower, and refectory. The rectangular main body of the church is partitioned by flat pilaster strips and topped with cornices crowned by deeply recessed *kokoshnik* gables. Behind the gables rises another tier of more elaborate *kokoshniks*. The central section of the roof contains a tight cluster of five onion-shaped cupolas which rest on bases that are decorated with tin-plated iron *kokoshniks*. Originally the cupolas were covered with shingles arranged in a fish-scale design. Adjoining the north and west walls is a covered arcade with porches leading to the entrances. The bell tower's lower section is in the conventional rectangular shape and houses the first bell tier in its wide, semicircular, arched walls. The unconventional aspect of this bell tower is the absence of an octagonal section. Instead there is a very elongated bell tier with diagonal surfaces and arches narrowing as they radiate farther from the center.

The interior of the Church of the Assumption of Our Lady was as handsome as its exterior, although today many of its decorative and religious treasures are located elsewhere in various museums. The walls were adorned with frescoes, traces of which can be seen near the north and west doors. To the left of the west door one will find a niche of white stone in which has been carved a history of the founding of the church. The intricate decor of the interior was highlighted by stamped silver frames around the icons of the iconostasis and inlays of gold and silver on the Holy Doors and altar canopy. The hollow candles of the church, now in the Vladimir museum, stood on a stone base, and were decorated with designs rendered in colored wax. Around these hollow wax cylinders the church founders had their names inscribed in Church Slavonic. Both the interior and exterior of the church mark the degree of refinement and wealth of the rising merchant and artisan class which was gradually supplanting the feudal nobility and titled landowners. Evidence of this social trend is seen in the choice of ornamentation and design of the church which has its origins in Russian folk art, indigenous to the class from which these newly rich and powerful people originated.

Princess's Convent and Cathedral of the Assumption, Podbelsky Street

En route to the western part of the old town, one proceeds along Herzen Street where the earthen ramparts and moat of 1108 are located. Turning at Podbelsky Street, the visitor will see the site of the town market which was relocated here at the order of Vsevolod because of several riots. This area also contains the ruins of the Church of the Exaltation of the Cross, the last major building constructed before the Mongol invasion.

The Convent of the Assumption was founded at the northwestern corner of the New Town at the end of the twelfth century by Princess Maria

Shvarnovna, wife of Vsevolod III. Thus it became known as the Princess's Convent, and like the citadel and Monastery of the Nativity, was built as a small stronghold within a larger one. The Cathedral of the Assumption (not the episcopal cathedral of the same name discussed above) was erected at the center of the convent in 1200–01. The cathedral, like the convent, came to be referred to as the "Princess's." What is seen today is not the original cathedral but a reconstruction dating from the end of the fifteenth century. The reconstructed cathedral was built on the original brick foundations. Excavated blocks of the original brickwork represent a style predominantly linked with the flourishing of urban culture which demonstrated a reappraisal and change in church architectural style. Aside from the complex form of the roof, there was no exterior sculptural adornment. Traces of additional structures adjoining the cathedral have been found. Among these was a narrow gallery encircling three sides, at the eastern end of which were two chapels: on the south side the Chapel of the Annunciation, and on the north side the Chapel of the Nativity of Our Lord. These chapels became the burial grounds for Princess Maria, her sister Anne, who became Vsevolod's second wife, and Prince Alexander Nevsky's wife and sister. There is also the tomb of the legendary merchant Avraami who was put to death by the Volga Bulgars for spying in the service of the Vladimir princes in 1229. His remains were interred in the cathedral in 1230 amid great political and religious uproar which resulted in his being granted the title of martyr and his remains esteemed as sacred relics.

The exterior of the Princess's Cathedral as it is today is representative of fifteenth- and sixteenth-century Russian architecture. It is a large brick structure with four pillars, one dome, two chapels, and three formidable apses. The tiered composition of the roof (restored in 1960) consists of *zakomara* arches above which rises a rectangular base decorated with painted *kokoshniks*. The base of the dome drum is similarly decorated with smaller *kokoshniks* forming a wreath. The interior of the cathedral is closer in concept to the original structure owing to the cruciform pillars, semicircular apses, and the small burial niche located in the north wall. However, most of the detail of the interior bespeaks the period of its reconstruction. Unlike earlier structures, the walls are not interrupted by pilaster strips, so that the smooth surfaces project the impression of unified space. The arches supporting the dome are higher than the aisle vaulting, thus creating an upward-soaring sensation as well as providing better illumination through the windows of the dome drum. The frescoes which enhance the interior have been completely restored by the Soviet government with the exception of the ones on the vaulted ceilings. The frescoes were commissioned in 1647–48 by Patriarch Joseph and executed by a group of royal icon painters from Moscow headed by Mark Matveyev, who had previously decorated the Cathedral of the Assumption in the Moscow Kremlin.

The murals of the Princess's Cathedral are arranged in several tiers divided into different compositional blocks. Of the main compositions in the cathedral a few are very impressive. At the top of the central apse is a large and complex fresco interpreting the transubstantiation of the bread and wine into the body and blood of Christ. A procession of angels carries the sacraments, thus providing the title The Great Procession. On the lower left and right of the apse is The Last Supper. At the front of the altar is a large fresco of the Dormition of the Virgin, so placed because of the cathedral's dedication. Other scenes on the south wall complement this composition illustrating scenes connected with the Virgin's life. On the pillars are several paintings of the Vladimir princes, including one of Andrei Bogolyubsky. The main vaults under the dome depict the twelve primary festivals of the Russian Orthodox calendar. The corner cross vaults show interpretations of Christ, the Lord of Hosts, and Our Lady of the Sign.

The west wall is reserved for the supreme fresco of the cathedral, the Last Judgment. Just under the window is Christ sitting in judgment on a throne encircled by seraphim. On either side of Christ engulfed in swirling clouds are the apostles on their thrones and the angelic host. Kneeling at Christ's feet are Adam and Eve interceding for humanity. Below them are the angels of judgment, and just above the west door is a tiny naked human soul lost amid the powerful figures of this momentous occasion. The lower section of the wall depicts the scenes of paradise and hell. The right-hand area shows a fresco containing a vile-looking serpent who has trapped condemned sinners in its coils. Behind them is a disk within which is depicted the resurrection of the dead. In another disk in the opposite left-hand corner by the door are four beasts which symbolize the four kingdoms. A bright band of eternal flames surrounds the section depicting hell. A series of stylized medallions illustrates the eternal torments of the damned. A thin serpent ringed with white coils bearing the names of the seven deadly sins is positioned so that the congregation could read them easily. In the right-hand corner is a cluster of winged devils representing hell itself. The left half of the lower wall shows the apostle Peter leading the righteous into paradise. Above the gates of paradise in a circular frame is the Virgin seated on a throne. At the corner of this section is Abraham enfolding the righteous plus several scenes from the gardens of paradise. The entire composition, despite its complexity, has been rendered comprehensible by the many explanatory inscriptions. The sense conveyed by all the frescoes of the Princess's Cathedral is one of earthly joy.

Church of St. Nicetas the Martyr, Podbelsky Street

To the right of the Princess's Convent and Cathedral is a public garden which follows on its eastern side the line of the old defensive ramparts of the New Town originating at the Golden Gates. The dense forest which adjoined the ramparts is remembered in the names of the streets Great

Forest (Bolshiye Remenniki) and Little Forest (Malikye Remenniki). Behind the public garden is the Church of St. Nicetas the Martyr, built in 1762–65 by Semyon Lazarev, a Vladimir merchant. The building is representative of a new trend in church architecture which rendered religious structures more like Baroque palaces than rectangular refectories. Each of its three stories had its own iconostasis illuminated with light from the large windows of the side walls. The interior gave an impression more of sociability and festivity than religious solemnity. The Baroque decor of the exterior is highlighted by a slender bell tower, corner pilasters in clusters, and spiral scrollwork adorning the upper tier, lucerne windows, and the rectangular sections beneath the dome. The adjoining two-story structures that one sees today were added during the middle of the nineteenth century.

SUZDAL—History in Brief

The 30-kilometer (18.8 miles) distance between Vladimir and Suzdal is noted for its rich soil and the arable lands which fan out for miles on either side of the road. The traveler will find the journey between the two medieval towns interesting because of the historic villages which dot the highway. From Dobroye the route forks left at the Church of St. Constantine and St. Helena. The village of Sukhodol appears on the left, situated in a small hollow. Halfway from Vladimir to Suzdal is the larger village of Borisovskoye. At one time it was owned by Prince Ivan Kalita (whose name means "moneybags") and it was left to his son, Simon the Proud. Before Russian settlers appeared, the land was inhabited by Finns. A tiny stream here still bears its Finnish name Ikishka. Another village, Batiyevo, comes next on the right. It is reported in an eighteenth-century chronicle that the Mongol Khan Batu selected this spot to pitch camp en route to Suzdal. Next along the way is Pavlovskoye, probably the oldest settlement in this area. It was purchased by the wife of Alexander Nevsky, indicating that it existed in the thirteenth century and withstood the Mongol invasion. Suzdal appears quite suddenly from the summit of Poklonnaya Hill situated on an elongated stretch of high ground encircled by forests and fields.

The town of Suzdal is mentioned as early as 1024 because of a peasant uprising which occurred. A number of old settlements which formed the basis of the subsequent town were inhabited by peasants from Smolensk and Novgorod who migrated in search of arable land and a life of freedom. The imposition of a feudal order by the Kiev princes led to the great uprising which was put down by Prince Yaroslav the Wise. In 1054 the Rostov and Suzdal lands came into the possession of Yaroslav's son, Vsevolod. The political settlement of the area attracted many boyars from the south who sought economic opportunity at the expense of the formerly free and independent peasants. Similarly attracted by the political developments was the Russian Orthodox Church, which saw in the situation an opportunity to establish its authority in the previously pagan area. A bishopric was set up in Rostov under Leontius. The decade of the 1070s saw violent insurgence among the pagan peasants which cost Bishop Leontius his life. At the end of the century internal struggles occurred among the feudal princes for control of the northeast lands previously allotted to Vladimir Monomach. By this time Suzdal contained a royal residence as well as other wooden fortifications. These were burned to the ground by a fire set by Prince Oleg, who entered Suzdal by way of the Klyazma. All that survived was the visitors' dormitory and the wooden Church of St. Dmitri on the other side of the Kamenka River.

The result of these events was an acceleration of development along the banks of the Kamenka. The town was fortified thereafter by a deep moat at the riverbend where the density of population was greatest. Earthen ramparts topped with wooden walls were erected. This fortress was erected by Vladimir Monomach sometime toward the end of the eleventh century, at the same time that he commissioned the building of the brick Cathedral of the Assumption and the adjacent royal residence. Suzdal became the capital of those lands ruled by Vladimir's son, Yuri Dolgoruky.

Along the eastern ramparts of the fortress were the Ilynsky Gates. A *posad* (traders' and artisans' quarters) developed outside these gates along the Gremyachka River. The *posad* covered an area almost twice the size of the fortress. It was surrounded by earthen ramparts reinforced with tall timbers. On its northern side was a deep moat, and in 1207 the Convent of the Deposition of the Robe was erected outside the northern gates. The road to Yuri Dolgoruky's residence passed through the southern gates. The royal castle with its own stone church was erected in 1152 near the mouth of the Kamenka River in the village of Kideksha. After the murder of Prince Andrei Bogolyubsky in 1174, the townspeople supported the nobility against the boyars of Suzdal. Thus the town was refortified in 1192 during the reigns of Vsevolod III and his successor Georgi.

During the fourteenth century the capital of the principality was shifted to Nizhny Novgorod, a rich town on the Volga. Suzdal continued to expand with the construction of new buildings to its present size. The fourteenth century also marked a revival of cultural life. In 1377 Bishop Dionisi arranged for the transfer of icons and other religious treasures from Constantinople to Suzdal. In 1383 he ordered a niello-work canopy made, adorned in enamel and gold.

The decline of Suzdal-Nizhny Novgorod dates from approximately 1392 when its political role became ineffectual and ultimately inactive. In 1445 the old cathedral collapsed and remained in ruins for nearly a century. Because of its location off the main trade routes, Suzdal maintained importance only as a religious center. In order to retain power, the church authorities continuously created new saints and innovated new sacred relics. The rulers at the new Russian capital in Moscow favored the Suzdal monasteries with generous land endowments during the fifteenth and sixteenth centuries. The growing wealth of the monasteries was reflected in the revival of stone architecture. The importance of the fourteenth century bishopric, bestowed upon Suzdal, increased in the sixteenth century by the establishment of an archbishopric. A new episcopal stone church was erected in the kremlin next to the restored cathedral. The kremlin boasted fifteen towers and seven wooden churches. The *posad* had fourteen churches within its walls. Together with the numerous monasteries, the Suzdal community had a disproportionate ratio of religious structures to secular ones.

The first half of the seventeenth century dealt cruelly with Suzdal. The Polish invasion of 1608–10 reduced the number of homesteads by half. In 1634 the Crimean Tatars sacked the town. A fire in 1644 destroyed the section of the *posad* adjacent to the kremlin. A plague in 1654–55 carried off half of the population. Poverty and stagnation did not arrest a new wave of building which began in the 1630s. This was initiated by the bishopric, the only establishment with sufficient financial resources. This spate of construction saw the transition from wooden to stone architecture. Many talented architects emerged during this period to create some of the lasting structural masterpieces. Nevertheless, Suzdal remained a relatively poor town which contained only 126 more homesteads in 1711 than it had a century and a half earlier. The eighteenth century brought more depressing events, such as the fire in 1719 which again destroyed most of the homes and a recurrence of the plague, once more diminishing the populace by half. In 1767 the Spaso-Yevfimiev cemetery was converted into a prison for religious and political offenders. State reforms instituted by Peter the Great encroached seriously upon the economic and political power of the Church, and at the end of the century the bishopric was abolished. Nevertheless, the merchant class carried on with the construction of numerous churches equal to, if not more magnificent in craftsmanship than those erected two centuries earlier. These new churches were constructed on the sites of former ones so that the original architectural topography was retained. At this time the Suzdal school of iconography also flourished, thus establishing the artists as the "Suzdal God painters."

During the nineteenth century few architecturally valuable buildings were constructed. The area retained its agricultural life-style, and between 1806 and 1811 a large covered market was built.

Today the town is an outstanding architectural museum, containing more examples of period architecture than any other Russian town. Tourism here is high, not only because of the educational value of the locale, but also because Suzdal has preserved a picturesque timelessness which visitors find interesting as well as relaxing.

PLACES OF INTEREST

The Kremlin

In the heart of the old town is a group of buildings located within the old fortress of Suzdal. There is still a moat on the east side. The old earthen ramparts which provided additional protection were converted into a boulevard during the eighteenth century. Originally the main entrance tower, the Ilyinsky Gates were located here connected to wooden walls atop the earthen ramparts. On the southwest side were the Dmitriyevsky Gates, which led to the Monastery of St. Dmitri. On the southeast side were the Nikolsky Gates, which led to a bridge over the Kamenka River. Within the kremlin are several of the most important buildings of old Suzdal. One may see excavations from time to time along the street. These archaeological explorations have revealed many dwellings of bygone townspeople sunk deep below the present surface. Once inside the ramparts one will immediately notice the small stone Church of the Assumption. This was built on the site of an earlier wooden church and rebuilt in 1720. In 1958 the church was restored.

Cathedral of the Nativity

At the center of the group of old buildings stands this cathedral which was built in 1222–25 by Prince Georgi, son of Vsevolod III. It is one of the oldest surviving examples of Vladimir-Suzdal architecture. Originally this was the site of the Cathedral of the Assumption, built by Vladimir Monomach at the end of the eleventh century at the same time as the Suzdal kremlin. Special pains were taken by church authorities to maintain and decorate the structure because it represented the stronghold of religion in a newly Christianized area. Despite the meticulous care given the old structure, it partially collapsed within a century and was ordered to be dismantled by Prince Georgi with a new cathedral of white stone to be erected on the same site. The new cathedral had its problems, and has not survived intact. In 1445 the roof collapsed. In 1528 the walls were partially dismantled, and in 1530 the upper sections were rebuilt and a standard five-domed roof attached. At the close of the seventeenth century the choir gallery was destroyed and the slit windows widened. In 1750 the building gained its onion-shaped domes and the *zakomara*-styled roof was replaced with a hipped one.

The Cathedral of the Nativity is the usual town cathedral elongated by protruding apses which create an eight-pillared look from the inside. The main entrances, adjoined by narthexes on three sides, provide the cruciform appearance. Pilaster strips surrounded by a band of blind arcading divide the outer walls. The cathedral is built mainly of rough slabs of porous tufa which provide an uneven surface.

The division of the outer walls was simplified by replacing the elaborate pilasters and semicolumns with flat, narrow strips intersected by a band of ornamental carving with reliefs of lions and griffins inserted at the corners. The major architectural change here is the lack of correspondence between exterior decoration and interior structure. This new appreciation of ornament for its own sake can be seen in the elaborately detailed carving, showing a marked preference for form over function. The band of blind arcading on the south front is deeply recessed to provide a greater interplay of shadow. The capitals and round block underneath are enlarged and densely covered with carving. The lions on the south portal are graphically executed with each line given full expression.

Special attention was given to the south wall and its narthex. Richer in ornamentation than the other walls, the carved portal resembles a huge icon frame of white stone which contained panels of copper embossed with gold. The side walls of the narthex were decorated with a stunning cornice made of two strips of protuberant cut stone producing a richly shaded effect. The *zakomara* of the narthex was decorated with carved figures and a generous band of plants and birds. The reason for the lavishness of the south entrance was that here the townspeople entered the cathedral. The west wall, which faced the prince's courtyard, was second in importance. The front of the west narthex contained a broad, sumptuously carved portal with white stone facing on the archivolt. The north wall, which fronted onto the ramparts, was considerably simpler. Its portal was made of thin brick, and the molding contained neither bases nor capitals. The subject matter of the band of blind arcading was less varied and detailed.

The interior of the cathedral also represents two different periods of decoration. On the north side of the southwest pillar, 3 meters (10 feet) above the floor, is a molded cornice indicating that a choir gallery of an unusually large size rested on these pillars. The area beneath the choir gallery was utilized as a burial vault. Niches built into the bases of the cathedral walls and narthexes served as tombs for royalty and bishops. The invasion of the Mongols in 1238 interfered with the burial plans of the original dignitaries. Not until the fifteenth, sixteenth, and seventeenth centuries were the niches used for the feudal nobility of Suzdal-Nizhny Novgorod.

An altar barrier was used to divide the main body of the church from the sanctuary. The floor of the cathedral was laid with multicolor majolica tiles of yellow, dark brown, and green. Simultaneously with the installation of new flooring Bishop Kirill summoned artists from Suzdal and Rostov to decorate the walls with frescoes. Remains can still be seen on the upper portion of the south apse. Depicted here are stern-faced elders in restrained poses. They are framed by patterns of foliage and geometric ornamentation, somewhat like tapestry. Another example of this style of painting, plating, and ornamental sculpture is to be found on the "golden gates" of the cathedral's south and west portals. The doors are divided into rectangular panels by raised rolls. The gold designs which richly decorate the scenes on small panels were executed by fusing the gold onto a bronze background. The original door handles were shaped like lions' heads with rings through their jaws. The west gates were adorned with scenes from the Gospels. The Virgin Mary, considered patroness of the Vladimir lands, was depicted in the prominent upper panel in portrayal of the Intercession Festival instituted by Vladimir church authorities. The lower panels contained figures of lions and griffins surrounded by intricate foliate ornamentation. There were also medallions in which various saints were portrayed, among whom was St. Mitrophanes, patron saint of Bishop Mitrophanes of Suzdal, 1227–38. It was he who commissioned the construction of the west gates and was later burned to death by the Mongols invading the Cathedral of the Assumption at Vladimir.

The main south gates, another important feature of the cathedral, were commissioned by Prince Georgi and built in 1230–33. They contain damascene pictures of saints whose names the Vladimir rulers adopted. The primary scenes on these gates demonstrate angels in action. Other panels on the gates depict scenes from the Gospels along with others from the Old Testament showing the Creation. Inscriptions on each pictorial panel create the impression of the gates as an illustrated manuscript.

Alterations to the cathedral in 1528–30 left the walls without paintings. New frescoes were painted in 1635–36 and freshly repainted in 1775, 1818, and 1850. Among the better-preserved seventeenth-century frescoes are those on the upper sections of the walls, particularly those on the ceiling of the north narthex devoted to the exaltation of the Virgin. The same theme is developed on the south narthex in the frescoes of the lower section of the west wall. The southwest pillar under the dome contains another fragment of unadulterated seventeenth-century art. Other fragments of these frescoes are the group of the righteous from the Last Judgment on the north side of the southwest pillar, and the figures of saints contained in the medallions on the right-hand side of the central apse. Among the latter group is the stunning picture of Archdeacon Stefan clothed in white robes with green-tinted folds in a yellow-ocher medallion.

The present interior of the cathedral is the result of alterations made at the end of the seventeenth century. The choir gallery was removed along with the tombstones underneath upon orders of Metropolitan Illarion. The choir gallery entrance was barricaded and the first floor of the narthex destroyed. New architectural tastes demanded the widening of the old windows. Illarion also commissioned the present iconostasis which, strangely enough, retains the old traditions in its austere simplicity. It resembles a flat wall covered with gilded silver sheets. The severe figures of the saints are placed upon this shining background, heads reverently bowed in the direction of the center of the iconostasis which contains the icon of Christ.

New structures were added to the cathedral between the fifteenth and eighteenth centuries. The bell tower with a tent-shaped roof and a small church in its lower section were built opposite the main south wall in 1635 by Archbishop Serapion. It differs from other Suzdal structures in its severe octagonal shape with pilaster corners which appear to emerge out of the ground. At the base of the tent-shaped spire is a *politsa*, a sloping projection usually found in fortified towers. Along the old skyline of Suzdal the tall tower complemented the silhouette of the kremlin as a focal point among the proliferation of smaller surrounding structures. Near the end of the seventeenth century the bell tower was provided with a clock.

Archbishop's Palace, next to the Cathedral of the Nativity

Today's architectural ensemble consists of several buildings erected between the fifteenth and eighteenth centuries. The oldest structure is the Bishop's Palace, which dates from the end of the fifteenth century. The north wing, which faces the west portal of the cathedral, was erected on the site of an earlier structure, the Church of St. John Theologos, built in 1528. To the west of the palace is the bishop's private chapel, built in 1559 complete with a parvis and a refectory. The intersecting double-sloped roofs which form a gable on all four sides is rather unusual for Suzdal at this time; it is more in keeping with the fourteenth- and fifteenth-century architectural styles of Novgorod and Pskov. Between 1682 and 1707 the old buildings of the palace were absorbed into the larger Archbishop's Palace built for Metropolitan Illarion. The front of the main building faced the cathedral courtyard and was closely tied into the functions and architectural style of the cathedral. The palace's main entrance is directly opposite the cathedral's west portal. Leading up to the vestibule on the first floor are two broad, ceremonial staircases. Visiting dignitaries entered through this section on their way to the main reception hall known as Krestovaya Palata (Cross Chamber).

Church of St. Nicholas, west section of the Kremlin

This wooden structure was built in 1766 in the village of Glotovo, located in the Yuryev district, and was moved to Suzdal in 1960. The purpose of transferring the building was to add to the collection of architectural examples in the formation of Suzdal as an outdoor museum. The Church of St. Nicholas is one of the few surviving specimens of early wooden churches whose main bodies were fashioned after peasants' homes. The simple, rectangular structure consists of logs laid horizontally and interlocked at the corners. The church is elevated over a ground floor and surrounded on three sides by a raised gallery. Adjoining the main body of the church on the west side is a lower building which served as a refectory. On the east side is an adjoining altar apse.

Church of St. Boris and St. Gleb, along the western ramparts of the Kremlin on the right bank of the Kamenka

This stone church stands on the site once inhabited by a monastery of the same name built before the sixteenth century. The exact date of its construction is unknown, but its Baroque style provides a clear indication that it was built between 1600 and 1700. It is simple and its proportions have a powerful effect. The large dimensions, coupled with elegance of decoration, provide an expression of strength and plasticity. The cornice of the main octagon is particularly lavish. Restoration of the church was completed in 1961 by Alexei Varganov.

Church of St. Nicholas, southeast corner of the Kremlin

Built in 1720–39 this tent-shaped wooden structure was a replacement for an earlier church of the same name which was burned beyond repair in 1719. It is believed that the earlier church dated back to the origins of Suzdal because the old town gates nearby leading to a bridge over the Kamenka also had the same name. The church of today is cube-shaped with lavish portals, window frames, and a wide cornice topped with a row of kokoshniks. Although it is believed that the original structure had five domes, at present there is only one resting on a slender, elongated drum in the center of the hipped roof. Adjoining the building on the west side is a small, narthexlike refectory which links the church with the bell tower. The attractively decorated bell tower is modeled on the old-style tent-shaped wooden octagonal church resting on a square base. The uppermost corners of the square base are adorned with small tent-shaped pinnacles. The base of the tower's octagon is decorated with kokoshniks which repeat the theme above the cornice of the church itself. Above the kokoshniks is a row of square niches. Atop these is a second row of Baroque octagonal niches and a row of colored tiles. The tiles separate the octagon from the bell tier, which is extravagantly decorated with pilasters, cornices, molded arches, and a row of tiles. Small Gothic-type pinnacles crowned with crosses occur on the top of the bell tier, repeating the motif from the corners of the square base. These small crosses reinforce the impression of height. The tent-shaped spire, concave in form, was an innovation of Suzdal builders.

Church of St. Cosmas and St. Damian, across the Kamenka River to the left of the bridge

On a sandy bank at a sharp bend in the river stands the beautiful white church constructed in 1725 on the site of the Monastery of St.

Cosmas and St. Damian. The asymmetrical composition of the church indicates that its style is more in keeping with the architecture of the previous century. Adjoining the cube-shaped, single-domed body of the church is an octagonal bell tower resting on a square base. The tower stands out because of its austerity. Ogee-shaped coverings cap the arches of the bell tier. Above these coverings is a narrow, tent-shaped spire with slit windows. Atop the spire is a tiny dome. Adjoining the south wall of the church is a small chapel with a slender dome. Originally the ensemble was contained by a stone wall, with a flight of steps leading out from the center of the bell tower to the riverbank. Restoration of the Church of St. Cosmas and St. Damian was completed in 1960 under the direction of R.S. Kuznetsov.

Church of the Sign, on the left side of the Vladimir Road on the bank of the Mzhara River

This structure was built in 1749 on the steep river embankment where the Monastery of the Presentation had been founded several centuries earlier. During the seventeenth century the small village of Pinaika grew up on adjacent lands, so that the building of a new church was called for. The Church of the Sign is an interesting specimen of Suzdal architecture, containing many features which harmonize with the lives of ordinary people. A large porch supported by stocky, faceted pillars almost obscures the deeply recessed main portal of the church. A theory holds that the impressive size of the porch was intended to support a bell tower. In the south wall are large rectangular windows resembling secular more than religious architecture. The north wall, more elaborately decorated because it faced the town, contains a second portal. However, rather than with *kokoshniks,* the cornice bands are separated by a series of paintings on religious themes. On the west side are two large windows which, in combination with the other apertures in the church, render the interior particularly light. The section of the octagonal dome drum just under the dome itself is decorated with the same types of blue and white tiles used in domestic Russian stoves. The Church of the Sign was restored by Alexei Varganov in 1959.

Posad Marketplace and Central Square

Beyond the fortifications of the Suzdal kremlin is an area which was the *posad,* an outlying district reserved for merchants, traders, and artisans. This community contained a concentration of some of Suzdal's oldest and finest architectural structures, many of which still stand today. The majority of stone churches are replacements of earlier wooden ones. The stone structures were built mainly during the seventeenth and eighteenth centuries on the same sites as their predecessors. Despite the fact that so many buildings served similar purposes, architectural repetition was carefully avoided, thus giving each church an individuality of structural composition and decoration.

Church of St. John the Baptist, left-hand side of Vladimir Road at the edge of the kremlin moat

Although the Church of St. John the Baptist was built in 1720 along with the Church of St. Nicholas inside the kremlin, the two structures are vastly different in style. This *posad* church is austere yet impressive with its bell tower and narthex-type refectory. The body of the church is cube-shaped with pilaster strips on the corners. The hipped roof has no decorative cornices, and the window frames are unadorned. The base of the simple bell tower rests on two pillars which form the church porch. Small windows appear in the walls of the bell tower's square base which is perfunctorily decorated with pilaster strips in the upper section. The rather short octagonal bell tier resting on the base is adorned only with narrow half-columns. The tent-shaped steeple slopes at the sides and contains several slit windows. Only the main portal of the church contains any appreciable ornamentation. The overall impression one has of the Church of St. John the Baptist is dignified simplicity.

Churches of the Entry into Jerusalem and St. Paraskeva, southwest corner of the marketplace

As was frequently the custom in old Suzdal, these churches were deliberately paired and were surrounded by a brick wall with stone gates topped with a vaulted stone roof in the form of a *bochka* (cask) shaped like a cross. Each wall of the stone gates formed an ogee-shaped *zakomara*. The two churches shared a bell tower which had a concave tent-shaped spire. The tower was considered a masterpiece of antique Suzdal architecture. The older of the two structures, the Church of the Entry into Jerusalem, was built in 1702. It is the more architecturally intriguing with its lavish ornamentation of pilaster strips, ornate window frames, and the frieze of *kokoshniks* on top of the consoles. The Church of St. Paraskeva, built in 1772, is sometimes referred to as the Church of St. Nicholas. It is more in keeping with the trend toward eighteenth-century civic architecture, whereas its older counterpart bespeaks the previous century in concept and style.

Gostiny Dvor, west side of the posad central square

This long building occupying the entire western side of the square contains the arcades of the small shops built during 1806–11. The structure was designed by A. Vershinsky, the head architect for the Vladimir governing body. The unfortunate effect of Gostiny Dvor is that it does not blend in with the otherwise picturesque panorama of the area. Typical of nine-teenth-century Russian provincial life, the function of Gostiny Dvor was more social than commercial. The townsfolk strolled here to observe and be observed by their peers rather than to shop. The arcades provided a place to gossip, display sons and daughters of marriageable age, and parade the ostentatious fashions of the period. Across the street from Gostiny Dvor are churches marking the southern edge of the square.

Church of the Resurrection and Church of Our Lady of Kazan

These represent the focal point of the cluster of churches along the southern edge of the square. The Church of the Resurrection, built in 1720, stands on the site of a previous wooden church of the same name. The smaller Church of Our Lady of Kazan was built in 1739. Together they form an architectural ensemble recalling the earlier wooden churches. The most important element in the grouping is the bell tower of the Church of the Resurrection. Made of stone, it was designed in the same style as the old church. It is a slender octagon mounted on a square base. The sides of the octagon are decorated with deep niches running the full length of the structure. Inside the niches are glazed tiles of green and polychrome. A continuous band of tiling decorates the circumference of the bell tier base, forming a row of round red balusters and alternating green glazed tiles. The effect of these decorations is a vibrant interplay of light and color. The church itself contains very little ornamentation except for a row of tiny kokoshniks which adorn the cornice atop the clear white walls. Adjoining the Church of the Resurrection on the west side is a one-story parvis decorated with a typical Suzdal cornice of rounded balusters and rows of indented brick. The yellow and henna octagonal dome drum contains tiny pediments. The south wall of the church contains the main entrance porch adorned with round columns, pendant arches, and a pediment. The Church of Our Lady of Kazan is a modest structure decorated mainly with folk-art motifs which show best on the open metalwork along the ridge of the roof.

Church of the Emperor Constantine, northeast corner of the posad central square

Erected in 1707, this large and sumptuously built church replaced an earlier wooden group of buildings on the same site. The white stone walls are decorated with a wide cornice of small, deep-set kokoshniks shaped like horseshoes. Ornamental bands around the cornices appear to be embroi-dered on the walls. The window frames are elaborately decorated with molding at the top. The roof is crowned with five domes which are intri-cately designed. The domes rest on slender drums decorated with small columns in high relief. It is believed that the Church of the Emperor Constantine is the work of the three famous seventeenth-century architects, Mamin, Gryazanov, and Shmakov or their apprentices. The narthex is in the classical circular style. Its double-columned porticos were added to the west wall at the beginning of the nineteenth century. The sanctuary was rebuilt at the end of the eighteenth century. Nevertheless, the more recent additions blend in well with the older sections of the building. Such grandeur gave emphasis to the importance of the building in the group of churches on the square.

Church of Our Lady of the Sorrows, northeast of the Church of the Emperor Constantine

This small church, built in 1787, is connected to a tent-shaped bell tower. Many of the bell tower's features resemble those of the bell tower of the Church of St. Nicholas. The lower section of the octagon on this tower is simpler in order that it fit the design of the church itself. The elegant tent-shaped spire contains tiny octagonal windows and a needlelike dome that harmonizes with the church's domes. The spire and the octagon of the bell tower are decorated with glazed red and green baluster-shaped tiles. These tiles appear also on the cornice of the church. Restoration of the Church of Our Lady of the Sorrows was completed in 1952.

Church of St. Lazarus, right-hand side of Old Street going from the central square toward the monastery

This five-domed structure was built in 1667 to replace a fifteenth-century wooden church of the same name. The cube-shaped main body of the church contains three apses. The portals of each wall are differently designed. The cornice is decorated with horseshoe-shaped *kokoshniks* and a tile band. A repeat *kokoshnik* motif adorns the bases of the corner dome drums, which also have a band of blind arcading. An unusual feature of the Church of St. Lazarus is the windows of the dome drums. Usually churches of this style did not contain windows there. The rare two-pillared construction accounts for these windows. The pillars support two pairs of longitudinal arches on the interior of the church. The vaulted arches are suspended between the east and west walls.

Church of St. Antipus, next to the Church of St. Lazarus

Built in 1745, this church forms a pair with the Church of St. Lazarus. Its two main features are the crest of open metalwork along the roof and the bell tower at the west end. The bell tower is slender with a tent-shaped concave spire typical of Suzdal architecture. The restoration of the bell tower was completed in 1959 by Alexei Varganov. At this time the original bright colors were repainted, thus making this structure more prominent than other bell towers around Suzdal. The particular coloration of the bell tower dates back to the style of the seventeenth century and shows the desire of Suzdal architects to retain characteristics from the past as well as to innovate.

Convent of the Deposition of the Robe, at the end of Old Street

Most of the structures in the convent ensemble were built in 1688 by three architects who usually worked as a team: Ivan Mamin, Andrei Shmakov, and Ivan Gryaznov. Among the many examples of the works of this architectural trio, the Holy Gates of the convent rank with the best. The white façade of the Holy Gates has two entrances, each of a different shape and size. The arch of the small entrance is shallow, while that of the larger is semicircular. Cornices in the shape of pillars adorn the abutments. A small staircase in the wall leads to a small room above the vaulted roof. The façade of the Holy Gates is decorated with deep niches lined with colored tiles. There is also a central icon niche above the lower arch. The top of the façade is adorned with a tile band set in square frames. The cornice is indented. Similar decorative motifs are repeated on the octagonal tower bases. On the left-hand tower the windows are set in plain frames, while the right-hand tower's window frames are elaborately decorated. The right-hand tower was given greater ornamental features because of its position over the main entrance.

Immediately behind the Holy Gates is the Cathedral of the Deposition of the Robe, built during the first half of the sixteenth century. The north chapel was added in 1586. The small cathedral is among the earliest specimens of nonpillared churches in Central Russia. It is covered by a three-sectioned vaulted roof with *zakomaras* on the exterior. Large pentagonal niches framed by decorative molding form a frieze which encircles the plain windows. The dome drums repeat the motif with a series of double niches at the top. Because of the austere appearance of the cathedral by seventeenth-century standards, extravagantly decorated galleries were added to the south and west walls in 1688 by the three architects. The central wall of the west parvis contains a large portal embellished with glazed tiles of green, brown, yellow, and white. Intricately decorated pilasters flank the portal. The bell tower of the Convent of the Deposition of the Robe was built between 1813 and 1819. At the beginning of the twentieth century cement plastering was added for reinforcement. The result was a contradiction of the soaring element of the bell tower. Since that time the structure has been restored and the original yellow and white color scheme has been repainted on the surface.

Monastery of St. Alexander, north of the Convent of the Deposition of the Robe, near the Kamenka River

This monastery was founded in 1240 by Alexander Nevsky and became greatly favored by the early Muscovite princes Ivan Kalita and his son, Ivan II. Only two gravestones of the original complex remain. They belong to two Suzdal princesses: Maria, buried in 1362, and Agrippina, interred in 1393. Important monasteries such as this were given the title Bolshaya Lavra (Grand Monastery) by members of the royal family. The Holy Gates of the Monastery of St. Alexander were added in the late seventeenth century by architect Gryzanov. They are on the south side of the monastery's surrounding wall and open onto a spacious area where the large Cathedral of the Ascension stands. Built in 1695, the cathedral was funded by Tsarina Natalia, Peter the Great's mother. In the immediate neighborhood of the cathedral the visitor will see the original log houses *(izbas)* of the ordinary townspeople. The contrast between church and domestic architecture is clearly evident in the total domination of the cathedral over the insignificant dwellings. However, by the time the cathedral was built, Suzdal architects had begun to adapt certain folk motifs for church decoration. This accounts for the feeling of intimacy about the Cathedral of the Ascension, which lacks the frequently cold symmetry of other religious buildings. Many of the decorative motifs on the cathedral's exterior repeat themselves with a touch of innovation which provide freshness and originality. The corners of the square body of the cathedral are adorned with narrow pilaster strips. The apse repeats the concept with a decoration of paired half-columns. The dome drums and window frames contain small semicolumns with a bead molding. Adjoining the cathedral on the north wall are a parvis and chapel which substitute for the customary paired heated church. The bell tower is stark and undecorated, except for the ornamented bell tier and the tent-shaped, windowed spire.

Church of the Nativity and Church of the Epiphany, via the Kamenka Bridge to the right bank of the river

From the Cathedral of the Ascension, cross the water meadows of the Kamenka. On both sides of the river, bricklayers and other builders of Suzdal's landmarks labored in the claybeds and brick kilns during the eleventh, twelfth, sixteenth, and eighteenth centuries. The Church of the Nativity was built in 1739 and the Church of the Epiphany in 1781. They form a typical pair of corresponding religious structures. The earlier church is heated, while the later one is not. Both belonged to a tanners' settlement at the riverbend. (The combination of a simple, heated church with the main, unheated one emphasized the latter's importance. Unheated churches were generally larger and more aristocratic; small unheated churches basically resembled the loghouses of the peasants. The architectural purpose of the ensemble was esthetic; the symbolic purpose was to show solidarity between upper and lower classes.) The Church of the Nativity is small with plain walls and a tiny dome. At the west end of the main body of the church is a bell tower with a thin, concave, tent-shaped bell tower. The Church of the Epiphany is larger with innovative decorations. Instead of *kokoshniks,* there is a plain cornice. At the corners of the main body of the church and the narthex are two ornamental rows of masonry. The two double-sloped roofs curve upward at the base and are topped with an octagonal two-tiered dome.

Convent of the Intercession, the largest structural ensemble on the right bank of the Kamenka River

Not part of the ensemble, but close to the south wall of the convent stands the Church of St. Peter and St. Paul, built in 1694. Its eminence for a parish church seems to stem from its proximity to the convent, for it closely resembles a cathedral. The large main body of the church consists of a square vaulted roof and five domes. Horseshoe-shaped *kokoshniks* adorn the upper portion of the outer walls. These are divided by pilaster strips which also function to form part of the elaborate window frames. The rest of the church no longer remains.

The Convent of the Intercession was established in 1364. It became a virtual prison for women of noble birth who, for one reason or another, were consigned by their families to the nun's life. The convent became one of the wealthiest in all of Russia through gifts and grants of noble families who employed the institution as a depository for disfavored daughters, sisters, and wives. Personnel as well as land and money grants were donated, and by the end of the seventeenth century 7,427 serfs belonged to the convent. In order to maintain its status as a shrine, the convent authorities frequently created new saints and holy relics.

None of the original structures remains. Those seen today were partially built of stone in the sixteenth century, and by the end of the eighteenth century were completely replaced with stone. The inner portion of the walls are fortified by blind arches which support a wooden gallery on the upper section. Above this is a brick parapet containing narrow loopholes. A number of seventeenth-century tent-shaped towers along the northern side have survived for three centuries. These are plain with almost no decoration at all. Their main function was ornamental rather than defensive. Inside the outer wall is another wall which encloses a courtyard. This wall supports towers built in the eighteenth century which are octagonally shaped and elaborately decorated with horizontal bands and window niches. Along the south wall are the Holy Gates, the main entrance to the convent. At one time the Holy Gates were topped by the portals of the Church of the

Annunciation. The gates, built in 1518, were one of the endowments of Vassili III. They were restored in 1958 by Alexei Varganov and remain among the finest and most original works of sixteenth-century Suzdal architecture. The Holy Gates are decorated full-length with bands of brickwork offset by niches and molded posts of assorted sizes. To the east of this section is a gateway. Above the opening is a tiny church intended for two or three people to worship in each of its small chapels. The walls of the church are decorated with *zakomaras* and a dome rests atop a row of *zakomaras*. The roofs of the narrow parvises are lower than the walls of the main body of the church. The apses are proportionately reduced in size and seem barely discernible. Just inside the Holy Gates one sees all the principal buildings of the convent around the courtyard. The perimeter of the courtyard, surrounded by an inner wall, contained cells along with chambers set aside for storage cellars, ice chambers, and a brewery. The southwest corner of the convent contains an early-seventeenth-century brick building that was used for clerical trials. Underneath was the dungeon for political and religious prisoners. A similar structure is located in the northwest corner of the courtyard.

The principal building of the convent complex is the Cathedral of the Intercession. Built in 1510–18, the cathedral underwent many structural alterations over the centuries, and was finally restored to its original appearance by Igor Stoletov in 1962. The large body of the cathedral has four pillars and three apses which are raised a story above ground level. Underneath is the burial vault for nuns of the nobility. Small windows cut into the outer wall are the only openings of the burial vault's façade. Staircases at the northwest and southwest corners lead to the gallery whose corner arches rest on large pillars. The open arcade of the gallery provides a clear view of the cathedral's portals. The vast square body of the cathedral is sectioned by flat pilaster strips and adorned with a band of blind arcading. The three-domed roof is asymmetrically arranged. The central dome rests on a cylindrical base decorated with large *kokoshniks*. The overall impression is one of austerity, in strong contrast to the richly decorated Church of the Annunciation at the convent gateway. The cathedral interior is similarly devoid of decoration.

The tent-shaped bell tower stands opposite the southwest corner of the cathedral. Formerly the two structures were connected by a covered gallery. The lower, two-tiered section of the bell tower is powerful and plastic with its corner pilaster strips and semicolumns. The plain-arched windows are narrow slits. This section is older than the upper portion, which was built in 1515. While the lower tier contained a burial vault, the upper one houses a tiny church like the one atop the Holy Gates. In the seventeenth century the upper octagon containing the bell tier and tent-shaped spire were added. This accounts for the difference in design between the two sections. A staircase inside the lower section originally continued higher, thus suggesting that the church also contained its own bell tier. The cathedral's bell tower is an interesting specimen of early Russian architecture, particularly because the small stone church on top was among the first of the structures of its type to have its own bell tier.

To the north of the cathedral is the refectory Church of the Conception. Built in 1551 to replace a wooden church on the same site, it was restored in 1958 by Yevgeni Arkhipov. The main section consists of a large square refectory hall with a single pillar and high ceiling. The smaller rectangle which formed the worship area adjoined the east wall of the refectory. Adjoining the west wall is another building which provides architectural balance. The façade of the ensemble fronted onto the inner courtyard of the convent. The lower story of the church contained the domestic areas, such as kitchen and bakery. The upper story, housing the refectory, has two particularly distinctive features which differentiate it from the other convent buildings. One is a band of red rhomboid designs on a white background along the cornice. The second is the employment of the unusual technique of laying the walls and vaults in small brick. It is probable the architect was a Pole, since these features are common to Polish architecture of this period. During the sixteenth century a clock bell tower was added to the southwest corner of the refectory. Rather than the traditional octagon, an irregular hexagon is mounted on the high square base. On top of the hexagon is a smaller one decorated with corner semicolumns, rosettes, and niches carved on the surfaces. The bell tier above is indented with shallow arches and a short, tent-shaped spire at the top. What is architecturally important about this structure is that it represents a transition in Suzdal workmanship. The design shows that the builders were accustomed to working with wood rather than stone, and have thus lent to the brick structure an earlier spirit of wooden architecture.

Spaso-Yevfimiev Monastery, north of the Convent of the Intercession on the left bank of the Kamenka River

Founded in the mid-fourteenth century by the princes of Nizhny Novgorod and Suzdal, the monastery formed at one time the northern defensive outpost of Suzdal. Blended into the countryside, the red walls, towers, and domes of the monastery buildings impart a feeling of strength and security without gloom or menace. The result is an almost perfect example of architectural form and function. Needless to say, it was because of the generous monetary and land endowments from wealthy nobles and boyars that the Spaso-Yevfimiev Monastery could afford the expensive red stone structures.

Among the many impressive features of the ensemble is the monumental entrance tower. This enormous square building is 23 meters (75 feet) in height with low arches that appear to rest on squat posts. The tower, located strategically at an angle to the road and adjoining walls, is quite plain. The lower surface is interrupted only by two icon niches and a few circular loophole windows. The upper portion is more abundantly decorated. A row of elongated niches is followed by loopholes with ogee-shaped frames. Above is a cornice with tile-studded niches. Higher up is a row of loopholes topped by a band of blind arcading designed with small columns and pointed *kokoshniks*. The white ornamentation provides a stunning contrast to the red walls. The pyramid-shaped roof of the tower is emphasized by polygonal corner towers. These are modestly adorned with round loopholes surrounded by ogee-shaped frames on the upper platform. This tower is given prominence by its position near the center of the southern façade. It is interesting to note that the towers on the east side of the ensemble, which fronts on the road, are more sumptuously decorated than those along the west wall, which faces the open fields. The domination of Spaso-Yevfimiev Monastery over the Suzdal skyline had an important psychological purpose. Built during a period when foreign invasions had ceased to be an imminent threat, the defensive factors might seem superfluous. However, there was ample reason for seventeenth-century monasteries to symbolize force and protection. At this time restlessness among the common people threatened the structure of the feudal state. Discord was growing among the nobility. And finally, because Patriarch Nikon had decreed the supremacy of the church over the state, monasteries and cathedral palaces of the period tended to emulate the kremlins of secular authority.

Through the main entrance of the monastery is a second gate formed in the lower tier of the Church of the Annunciation, believed to have been built in the sixteenth century. The main body of the church is square with elongated apses on the east side and a parvis on the west side. The original roof had two tent-shaped towers which rose above ogee-shaped *zakomaras*, but it has since been altered. The outer walls are lavishly decorated. Underneath a broad cornice adorned with a row of round balusters are two symmetrical windows with molded frames and an icon niche in between. The parvis walls contain large windows surrounded by deeply recessed portals. The three large windows opposite the west wall of the parvis have ogee-shaped molding. An inner frame in the shape of a double arch is decorated with pendants.

Past the Church of the Annunciation via the second set of gates are the oldest structures of the monastery. These are the bell tower (right), refectory Church of the Assumption (left), and Cathedral of Transfiguration (center). Beyond these three structures are the monks' cells, domestic buildings, and lands. It is believed that the bell tower was constructed in the first decade of the sixteenth century, but subsequent alterations have greatly changed the original design. The refectory Church of the Assumption was built around 1525 and extends the unity of the inner courtyard structures. It is richly decorated with bands of ogee-shaped niches, *kokoshniks,* and a row of narrow arched windows. The tower and refectory are essentially sidepieces to the enormous five-domed Cathedral of the Transfiguration built in the middle of the sixteenth century. It is the focal point of the group.

At the southwest corner of the cathedral is a chapel erected without pillars over the grave of Abbot Yevfimi. Built in 1507–11, it is the first stone building of the monastery complex. The cathedral was built onto the chapel later in the century. The small pillarless chapel is typical of a style that emerged late in the fifteenth century in artisans' and tradesmen's communities near Moscow.

The interior of the Cathedral of the Transfiguration is very traditional, consisting of four broad pillars and deeply recessed apses. A long period of time elapsed before the inside walls contained any embellishments. An inventory of 1689 lists the numerous trappings that were gradually added. Among these were icons mounted on gold, silver, enamel, and embroidered silk. These were frequently donated by well-to-do pilgrims. The frescoes were dated to 1689 but subsequent inventories note that new ones were added in 1865 and 1877. The earliest frescoes were painted by a team of masters, Guri Nikitin and Sila Savin. Each artist had a highly individualized style as can be seen from the contrast of large spatial techniques and minute detail set in complex composition.

Among the impressive wall paintings is a group of four narrow bands portraying the acts of the apostles and scenes from the life of Christ. Lengthy descriptions were added to explicate the scenes for the congregation. Facing the altar, the surfaces of the pillars depict the founders of the Romanov dynasty. Tsars Mikhail and Alexei Romanov are featured alongside the biblical kings David and Solomon; Constantine the Great (sometimes referred to as the "Thirteenth Apostle" in the Russian church); Constantine's mother, St. Helena; and those Russian princes who were canonized: Vladimir, Boris, and Gleb. The last figure in the group is Vsevolod III. The particular emphasis on former Russian rulers depicted in the frescoes was the attempt of the church to stem the tide of popular unrest during the seventeenth century by showing the political authorities of the past as sacrosanct.

The Yevfimiev chapel contrasts sharply with the frigid decorum of the cathedral. The intimate atmosphere of the chapel's interior is due in part to its smallness, but also to its design. The chapel is covered by a cylindrical vault, at the center of which is a dome drum with four slit windows. Frescoes in the chapel were painted simultaneously with those in the cathedral in 1689. On the apse and arches are figures of the apostles and archangels. Most of the remaining frescoes are concerned with scenes from the life of Yevfimi. In the background of the Yevfimi frescoes are ornamental motifs taken from Moscow architecture of the period, indicating that the painters were not local.

Opposite the southeast corner of the monastery are three important buildings. At one time they formed part of a settlement called Skuchilikha, owned by the monastery, where craftsmen such as the monastery's masons and bricklayers lived. Two wooden churches erected during the sixteenth and seventeenth centuries were later replaced with a pair of stone churches. These are the Church of Our Lady of Smolensk, built from 1696 to 1706, and the Church of St. Simeon, built in 1749. The former is a large, unheated structure, while the latter is smaller and heated. Near the paired churches, at 134 Lenin Street, is a fine example of seventeenth-century domestic architecture. It is believed to have been the property of a Suzdal priest, Nikita Pustosvyat, an Old Believer. Despite the fact that the dwelling is made of brick, it echoes many of the features of earlier wooden architecture.

KIDEKSHA

North of the Suzdal kremlin and to the west of the *posad,* the village of Kideksha stands on the banks of the Nerl near the mouth of the Kamenka. Settled during the eleventh century, the village sprang up around a fortress built by the Suzdal princes to guard the river exit from the town. Sacred legends emanated from the construction of the fortress, enhancing not only the ecclesiastical aura of the region, but augmenting the political prestige of the Suzdal principality. The legend of greatest impact was that two Russian princes, Boris and Gleb, had sojourned in the vicinity of Kideksha during their campaign against the Kiev princes. Murdered by their brother, they were later canonized. The link between Suzdal lands and Russian saints was extremely beneficial to the development of the region.

Today Kideksha is important mainly for the outstanding surviving specimen of early Suzdal architecture, the twelfth-century Church of St. Boris and St. Gleb. Constructed in 1152, the church rests on a slope of the Nerl embankment with its apses facing the water. The striking feature of the structure is its architectural simplicity. The cube-shaped main body supports three apses and a single dome. The static serenity of the church emanates from the three massive semicircular apses and the unadorned portals, like framed entrances, in the main body. The only decorative element is a band of blind arcading and cut stone. Even the interior of the Church of St. Boris and St. Gleb is dark and static. Burial niches for the tombs of royalty are under the choir gallery. It was not until about 1180 that frescoes were added to the interior. The muted colors of the paintings of this period did not yield to brighter hues until the thirteenth century.

The church has undergone many changes over the centuries. Ravaged by the Mongols, it was repaired in 1239. After a period of neglect the dome and vaults collapsed. During the sixteenth and seventeenth centuries vigorous restoration was carried out. The new vault, dome, and hipped roof were out of context with the original design. The interior of the church was also greatly altered. In spite of the changes, the essential lines of the original structure remain.

BOGOLYUBOVO

En route from Vladimir to Bogolyubovo the tourist will travel much the same route as his medieval predecessors did on their way from the old capital to the castle of the grand prince. One will cross the small Irpen River along which were settlements bearing their ancient names until the nineteenth century. On the high ground along the river stands the village of Krasnoye which can be distinguished by the tall silhouette of its tent-shaped bell tower. Farther on is the village of Dobroye, situated on a splendid hill which demanded architectural structures in accordance with its irregular contours. Dobroye is among the oldest settlements of the Vladimir lands. Its burial mound on the eastern edge dates back to the late twelfth century. The Monastery of St. Constantine and St. Helena was founded at about the same time as a defensive outpost of Vladimir. It was located at the top of the hill where there now stands a mid-eighteenth-century church. Past Dobroye, to the right of the main road, artifacts of the oldest Stone Age settlement in the area were discovered during clay-quarrying. Beyond this, on the left bank of the Klyazma River, are vestiges of earthworks from a twelfth-century fortress built at the Slav-Merya settlement, which dates back to the ninth century. This fortress, overlooking the water meadows of the Klyazma, guarded the border of the Vladimir lands.

The large village of Bogolyubovo comes next. Situated on high hills above the Klyazma, Bogolyubovo played a very important role in twelfth-century Russian cultural history. Those buildings that have survived date from 1158–65, the early turbulent period of Prince Andrei Bogolyubsky's reign. Although the course of the Klyazma has altered southward, at that time it ran along the bottom of the Bogolyubovo hill and has since formed a swampy lake there, now called Old Klyazma. The Nerl River, flowing from the heart of the Suzdal lands, linked the Klyazma with the Volga, cutting diagonally across the fertile, prosperous lands of northeast Russia. The wealthy and powerful boyars of Suzdal and Rostov controlled the lands of the Nerl. The confluence of the Nerl and Klyazma rivers was a strategic commercial and political location. Thus, Prince Andrei's choice of a site for his sumptuous new royal palace threatened the independence of the boyars and brought about a telling struggle for dominance in this area. Church authorities took the side of Prince Andrei against the boyars and attributed the founding of Bogolyubovo to miraculous events. Various legends accumulated concerning the establishment of the village. Among them was the appearance of the Virgin Mary to Prince Andrei during his sleep and her assurance of divine protection. The impact of these numerous religious legends accounts for the naming of the new village "Bogolyubovo," meaning "a place loved by God." Thus it followed that the prince himself acquired the name "Bogolyubsky." In gratitude for divine protection, the prince commissioned a large icon of the Virgin, as beautiful and lavish as the famed Vladimir Icon. It became known as the Bogolyubskaya Icon and fragments of it have been preserved in the Vladimir Museum.

The southern portion of the royal compound is occupied by the Bogolyubov Monastery. It was founded in the thirteenth century after the desertion of the castle. The monastery attracted religious pilgrims by capitalizing on the miraculous stories connected with the establishment of Bogolyubovo. Particularly publicized were the Bogolyubskaya Icon and the murder of Prince Andrei which occurred here. As the monastery increased its revenues, it expanded. Above the Holy Gates of the monastery is a large bell tower, constructed in 1841. An impressive arch and a small church are under the bell tier. Just behind the bell tower is the enormous monastery cathedral which was built in 1866. Past the bell tower and cathedral to the left is the small monastery courtyard which was the main courtyard of the original royal compound.

There remains little of the original ensemble. On the southern edge of the courtyard wall stands the Church of the Annunciation. Built in 1683, it has been considerably disfigured by alterations made in 1804. Next to it is a seventeenth-century chapel which was built on the ruins of one of the most important structures of the old ensemble, the Cathedral of the Nativity of Our Lady.

The cathedral stood in the center of the palace complex. Only part of the north walls remained intact, supported by a passageway connecting it with the staircase tower. These remains were preserved along with the sacred spot upon which Prince Andrei was murdered. The rest of the cathedral was demolished and the present church constructed on its foundations in 1751.

Entering the western building adjoining the present church, one sees the lower portion of the 1158 cathedral's west wall with its magnificently finished attic plinth and powerful pilasters with semicolumns resting on Romanesque bases with griffins decorating the corners. Recent excavations have revealed stone carvings from the exterior of the original building. Among them are fragments of large capitals adorned with leaves. Others are female masks indicating the dedication of the cathedral to the Virgin Mary.

Upon entering the cathedral one immediately notices the excavated southern section. Here the pillars of the new structure rest upon the old circular pillars with Attic plinths. Although nothing remains of the old floor, excavations have revealed its lime base tinged with green outlines left by bronze slabs soldered together with tin. Fragments of these slabs have also been found. When the bronze was highly polished it looked very much like gold. By the southeast pillar are some surviving stones from the altar screen. In the rubble left from the demolition of the original cathedral are fragments of the frescoes which covered its walls and ceilings. These were done in subtle shades of predominating ocher, green, and blue. In the rubble from the western side are fragments of majolica tiles decorated with flowers and mythical beasts. On the west side of the north wall is the old arch from the entrance to the choir gallery. The present building contains a collection of many of the items salvaged from excavations. Among these relics is a four-headed capital from the cathedral's narthex which was mentioned in old chronicles. There is also a stone cross carved with an inscription of praise. This rare specimen of twelfth-century Russian writing originally stood at the mouth of the Nerl River as a warning of shallows and sandbars occurring at the juncture of the Klyazma.

Through the north portal is a covered passageway. On the left side of it is a portion of the old wall of the cathedral. Underneath the arch are wedge-shaped consoles on a band of blind arcading above which is the entrance to the choir gallery. Farther along is the staircase tower, restored in 1963. It was here in June 1174 that Prince Andrei, fleeing the boyars who had assailed him in his sleeping quarters, crawled while wounded to hide in the niche behind the central pillar. This spot marks the murder scene of the prince. Stone steps of the vaulted spiral staircase lead to the next floor where a sumptuously decorated triple window faces out over the Nerl. An opening in the wall leads to the choir gallery. The passageway has narrow rectangular windows and on the walls are scenes depicting Andrei's murder painted by monks from the monastery.

Bogolyubovo Palace was among the most impressive architectural feats of Prince Andrei's reign. It was the second most important political center after Vladimir. Many vital decisions affecting the Vladimir lands, as well as all of Russia, were made here. In addition to the lavish royal chambers, made of glistening white stone and gilded bronze, other dwellings rooted in traditional Russian domestic architecture were also built. These belonged primarily to wealthy families and were designed in three parts: living quarters *(izba)*, entertaining areas *(klet)*, and passageways *(seni)* connecting the two. Because of the regal nature of the settlement, all structures were built of white stone rather than the traditional wood used for domestic dwellings.

Church of the Intercession on the Nerl

On the water meadows at the juncture of the Nerl and the Klyazma, 1.6 kilometers (one mile) from Bogolyubovo Palace, this masterpiece of twelfth-century Vladimir architecture was built to commemorate the victory of Prince Andrei over the Volga Bulgars in 1164. Legend claims that the defeated enemy was forced to haul the stone overland to the building site as a form of tribute. The building of the church also commemorates the death of Andrei's son, Izyaslav, who was killed in the battle against the Volga Bulgars. The church was dedicated to the Intercession of the Virgin in honor of special protection granted to Vladimir rulers and their lands. The new festival of the Intercession was established by Prince Andrei and the Vladimir church officials without consent from either the patriarch or the metropolitan of Kiev. The assorted motives for the construction of the Church of the Intercession have a great deal to do with the choice for its location as well as with its majestically tiered design. At this spot the Nerl crossed the principality, linking its main towns with the Klyazma and the waters of the Oka and Volga rivers. Thus ships from Asia as well as the West sailed by the site and their passengers could be impressed with the image of Vladimir power. The tiered structure, similar to the Cathedral of St. Sophia in Kiev, proclaimed Vladimir's religious independence as well. Beginning with a stone hill at the base of the building and continuing with an arched gallery tier up to the main body of the church itself, the structure continues upward with a cylindrical dome drum, topped with a helmet-shaped dome and crowned, finally, by an openwork gilded cross.

All that is left of the original architectural group is the main body of the church. Its checkered history tells of the ravages of time and mankind. In 1784 the abbot of Bogolyubovo Monastery requested and received permission to demolish the church and to use the stone for the monastery's new bell tower. The only thing that prevented this catastrophe was the rejection of his paltry fee by the contractors. In 1803 the present onion-shaped dome replaced the original helmet-shaped one. In the middle of the nineteenth century a brick gateway topped with a belfry was erected on the north side of the church, but has since been removed and is now employed as a hostel for hikers. At about the same time, crude and deleterious restoration work was begun. In 1877 some of the worn stone carving was destroyed or replaced by repaired pieces. Unattractive iron bracing was banded around the building. A spherical roof was added, obscuring the rectangular base and drum.

The architects who designed the Church of the Intercession on the Nerl infused the traditional single-domed, four-pillared structure with graceful feminine lines which effect a soaring progression. The structure is barely extended on the longitudinal axis. The apses, rather than forming the usual massive semicylinders, project less sharply and are somewhat dominated by prominent pilaster corners. A calm symmetry results, in keeping with the vertical emphasis of the design. The unusual position of the band of blind arcading above the level of the choir gallery which divides the outer walls into two nearly equal sections enhances the vertical effect. The walls lean slightly inward, and this accentuates the degree of foreshortening. The impression of height is reinforced also by the multiple pilasters with semicolumns which pierce the outer walls with clusters of vertical lines. These join new vertical lines of molded *zakomaras* in the upper walls which contain elongated narrow windows above the drip mold. Rather than the wedge-shaped consoles of the period, masks and small animal figures are placed in such a way as to seem like pendants hanging from small cords. Above the *zakomaras* is the dome resting on a square base which is occluded from view by the new roof. Narrow windows framed with small semicolumns repeat the vertical motif as the dome seems to flow into the sky.

The east front presents the same impression of upward momentum. Breaking the horizontal line of the band of blind arcading, the central apse rises higher than the two that flank either side. Its window is also raised above those of the side apses. The exterior carving is simple and modest with the same pattern repeated on all three walls. The central *zakomara* depicts King David seated on his throne rendering a prophecy. On either side of the throne is a dove with two lions underneath. Adjacent to the lions are masks which, in combination with the central mask, form a frieze. These masks symbolize the Virgin. Beneath the side *zakomaras* are griffins facing the center carrying a lamb. All of the exterior carving is positioned so as to reinforce the vertical motif. The rich interplay of light and shade in the carving and molding offsets any suggestion of flat solidity in favor of movement and lightness.

The same can be said of the church interior. By placing the choir gallery lower than usual, the architects increased the height of the upper section. The opening between the walls and the cruciform pillars is very narrow, and the arches are about ten times the height of the spaces between them. The pillars taper slightly at the top, thus extending the vertical illusion. The dome of the church gives the impression of ascending into a sea of light. Unfortunately, all the frescoes were removed during the heavy-handed restoration of 1877. The same fate was shared by the flooring, which originally contained majolica tiles and valuable bronze plating similar to that of the Cathedral of Bogolyubovo. Excavations conducted in 1954 and 1955 show that the church was the center of a much larger ensemble of structures which surrounded it.

YURYEV-POLSKOI

Situated northwest of Vladimir, Yuryev-Polskoi is most easily accessible by bus. The name of Yuryev-Polskoi derives from its founder, Yuri Dolgoruky. Specifically it means "Yuri's town among the fields." The old Yuryev Highway runs through the outskirts of Vladimir through fields of exceptionally fertile "black earth," similar to that found in the Ukraine. Some of the oldest villages in the area, among the richest of the royal lands, lie along this route. About 3.2 kilometers (2 miles) from the town itself the visitor will see the Church of the Annunciation on the right-hand side of the road. It is the only remaining structure of the Snovitsky Monastery, erected in the fifteenth century. Approaching the town, one can discern the silhouette of the Monastery of the Archangel Michael and the dome of the Cathedral of St. George. The earthen ramparts which encircle the town have stood since 1152.

The main attraction of Yuryev-Polskoi is the architectural ensemble which comprises the Monastery of the Archangel Michael. From the town square, a street leads through the ancient ramparts to the monastery. Founded in the thirteenth century during the reign of Svyatoslav, the present structures of the monastery are products of the seventeenth and eighteenth centuries.

Church of John Theologos

The Holy Gates leading to the church were built in 1654, while the church itself was constructed in 1670. The entire ensemble was restored in 1963. The Holy Gates are composed of a portico with four arched entrances resting on octagonal columns which form four separate entryways —two for pedestrians and two for horse-drawn carriages. Within the archway of the Holy Gates are seats for pilgrims. Once through the dark passage one enters the central courtyard formed by the main buildings of the monastery. The plan resembles that of Suzdal's Spaso-Yevfimiev Monastery, with the cathedral opposite the entrance and the bell tower and refectory church on either side of the courtyard. Looking back at the Holy Gates one sees the gateway Church of John Theologos. It is surrounded on three sides by a parvis containing a band of arched windows and niches. The five-domed church has cornices and *kokoshniks* on the walls. The corner triple semicolumns are separated by diamond-shaped ornamentation running longitudinally.

Of the three structures in the monastery's courtyard, the bell tower is the most impressive. Built in the seventeenth century, it has a broad square base containing three symmetrically placed windows and a large octagon on the front wall. Square niches completely cover the lower tier, and niches shaped like icon grottoes adorn the second tier. The arches of the bell tier are decorated with bead molding above which is a tent-shaped spire with projecting ridges, three rows of miniature windows, and a small dome covered with green-glazed tiles.

Opposite the main entrance is the Cathedral of the Archangel Michael, built in 1792 to replace a previous one. The high body is crowned with an elaborate five-domed complex repeating the design of the gateway Church of John Theologos. A decorative band over the *kokoshniks* repeats the bell tower's motif, thus enabling the cathedral to blend harmoniously with the other courtyard structures.

The refectory Church of the Sign, located on the south side of the courtyard, was built in 1625. It contains two stories, identical in layout, with the lower one intended for domestic use. The large, square, single-pillared refectory is located on the west side of the structure. The east wall of the refectory has two broad windows and a large arch which leads to the narrow church. The west wall adjoins the cellarer's chamber, which projects into the courtyard. The main façade contains a central portal and a covered staircase made of stone which leads to the courtyard. The other walls, which front on the monastery, are plain.

Cathedral of St. George

Beyond the monastery turn right at the new brick cathedral. As one comes upon the Cathedral of St. George it is obvious that this is the most impressive building in Yuryev-Polskoi. Most striking is the odd greenish-gray coloring with yellowish-silver tinges here and there, quite unlike the dazzling white stone churches customarily seen throughout the medieval cities. The cathedral appears to be outsized because of the immense onion-shaped dome resting on a broad drum and the bulky apses spreading outward from the main body. Another unique feature is the chaotically arranged carving, which appears to be almost excessive after one has viewed the regularized sculpture on similar buildings. The pictorial motifs of the carvings are bizarre, ranging from monsters, masks, and animals to saints and angels, all of which form a puzzling stone mosaic of mammoth proportions.

The Cathedral of St. George is historically as well as architecturally interesting in that it was the last specimen produced by the Vladimir-Suzdal school. The original structure dates back to 1152 at which time a white stone Church of St. George was erected. This was replaced in 1234 because the structure had deteriorated seriously and was in danger of collapsing. In the late 1460s it too collapsed and in 1471 Vassili Yermolin, the well-known Moscow architect, was sent to restore it. There have been several subsequent alterations and additions over the past five centuries and in recent years restoration projects have succeeded in returning the cathedral to a close approximation of the original structure of 1152.

The generally bulky appearance of the cathedral disguises its actually small composition. The side walls are joined to vaulted narthexes which feature a pointed *zakomara* on the outer wall and flat pilaster strips at the corners. The west narthex, higher and larger than the two side ones, at one time contained an upper story where royalty worshiped. At the juncture of the north wall of the main body and the east wall of the north narthex, the small trinity chapel contained the burial vault of the Yuryev princes. The burial niche of Prince Svyatoslav, dated 1252, is still visible in the north wall of the cathedral. The interior of the structure creates an illusion of space. Square pillars are widely separated and the walls lack the customary pilaster strips. There is no choir gallery, and thus no division of the vertical structure that would reduce the interior height by breaking it into levels. In the west wall an archway leads to the second story of the narthex. Here the royal family worshiped, instead of in a choir gallery. The merging of the altar area with the main body of the cathedral is another method used to enlarge the interior space. Only a low screen with a carved Deesis marks off the altar area.

The carving on the building's exterior is a valuable collection of thirteenth-century sculpture. The intricate patterns contain several important motifs, among them Alexander the Great ascending to heaven, Svyatoslav's Cross, a fire-figure Deesis, and the Crucifixion. The north wall, the cathedral's main façade, is well preserved. A figure of St. George, the cathedral's patron saint, is located above the north portal. Many sections of the mosaic composition are stones which were part of the original building of 1152 and were relaid by Yermolin during his restoration work. The main sculptural compositions on the north wall embody the theme of divine protection. Above the figure of St. George is a male figure believed to represent Prince Svyatoslav. Along the archivolt of the portal are two carvings of Christ. Near one of these figures are the vertically placed letters B-A-K-U. This is believed to be the signature of Balcun (an abbreviation of Avvakum), the principal sculptor of the cathedral.

TALLINN

GENERAL INFORMATION

Tallinn is the capital of the Estonian Soviet Socialist Republic and one of the oldest cities in the Soviet Union. The city lies on the coast of the Baltic Sea, at the entrance to the Gulf of Finland. A large port, the Tallinn harbor is protected from winds by the Cape of Viimsi and the island of Aegna on the east and northeast and the islands of Naissaar and Paljassaar on the west.

Almost all areas of the Estonian economy are represented in Tallinn. Mechanical engineering, shipbuilding and repair, pulp and paper, textiles, building materials, and food are a few of the city's major industries. Tallinn also manufactures electric motors, oil equipment, boilers, chain-bucket excavators, graders, and trailers, and is the main base for Estonia's large fishing fleet.

Tallinn has also made tremendous strides in the area of higher education; the city presently houses four institutions of advanced education. The largest, founded in 1936, is the Polytechnical Institute, with students in the fields of engineering, chemistry, technology, shipbuilding, and mining. The Eduard Vilde Teachers' Training Institute, founded in 1952, specializes in training future teachers in mathematics, physics, chemistry, geography, the Estonian language, foreign languages, physical culture, and singing. In 1951 the State Arts Institute was founded. Its three faculties, Fine Arts, Architecture, and Applied Arts, enroll students who study painting, theater art, ceramics, metal, leather and textile work, and architecture. For those

who wish to devote their studies to music, the Tallinn Conservatory gradu-
ates composers, conductors, instrumentalists, opera singers, and music
critics.

HISTORY IN BRIEF

Tallinn was first referred to in writing by Abd-Allah Mohammed Idrisi,
an Arab geographer who included it on his map of the world. In the
appendix he wrote: "The towns of Astlanda include also the town of
Koluvan [it is generally agreed that Koluvan is a corruption of 'Kolyvan,'
the name for Tallinn found in old Russian chronicles]. This is a small town,
something like a large fortress. Its inhabitants are ploughmen; their income
is small, but they have many cattle."

The Estonians were destined to have a long and bitter struggle for
freedom beginning in the thirteenth century when German feudal lords
launched attacks from the south and overran part of Estonia. During this
time the armies of Russia proved to be an invaluable ally and after the
Estonian and Russian forces joined in 1217, the German invaders approached Denmark for aid. The Danish response came in the spring of
1219 when a fleet of ships appeared off the coast of Tallinn. The Danes
captured the town and thus began a period of foreign rule which lasted
several centuries.

Many attempts were made to liberate Tallinn but even with the support
of Russian troops the Estonians were unsuccessful. A peasant revolt, which
came to be known as Yuri's Night, broke out in 1343. A popular army of
ten thousand men were able to liberate the north and west of Estonia but
as they approached Tallinn, the Danes sought the help of the Livonian
Order, which was then advancing on the Russian town of Pskov. The
Estonians were defeated and forced to retreat. The king of Denmark,
probably fearing new peasant revolts, sold the Estonian lands to the Teutonic Order in 1346, which in turn sold them to the Livonian Order a year
later.

During the Middle Ages Tallinn was divided into two parts: the Lower
Town and Upper Town (Toompea). The inhabitants of the Lower Town
were primarily craftsmen and merchants while Toompea was the center of
administrative, clerical, and feudal power. Here the residence of the Tallinn
bishop, the cathedral, and the homes of the vassals were located. Also, the
Small Fortress, once the residence of the Danish viceregent, was rebuilt
here.

Tallinn declined as conflicts erupted between rich German merchants
who held important town positions and local feudal lords. The merchants
welcomed the influx of peasant labor from the villages but this meant the
loss of feudal serfs. The feudal lords were interested in selling their grain

directly to foreign merchants while the local German merchants tried to establish a monopoly in foreign trade. Conflicts also arose between the town oligarchy and the craftsmen and petty merchants. Large merchant houses were gradually forcing smaller merchants out of the market; craftsmen were demanding a larger role in the city administration and as these issues became hotter, violent clashes often broke out.

By the mid-sixteenth century this once-flourishing trading town fell into a drastic decline. The Teutonic Order began to lose power and influence and the Livonian War (1558–83) completely ended its power and that of the bishop. In 1561 new rulers, the Swedes, arrived in Tallinn.

The first decades of Swedish rule were disastrous. The times were marked by wars, hunger, and plagues and, to make matters worse, trading ties between Russia and the West were broken, badly affecting the town's role as the link between the two. Merchants who depended on trade for income and large numbers of townspeople who depended on the link for employment were very hard put.

Meanwhile, Russia was in need of an outlet to the Baltic Sea and in the summer of 1700 the Northern War broke out. Russian armies, led by Peter the Great, defeated the Swedes in the Poltava Battle in 1709. On September 29, 1710 Swedish rule over Tallinn officially ended.

Estonia joined Russia and a period of economic growth and development began. Priority was given to construction and an order by Peter the Great provided for the building of a harbor, shipyards, and workshops. As fortifications were erected to protect the harbor and the town, Tallinn became a strong sea fortress. Trade between Russia and the West not only was resumed but was widely expanded and as a result Tallinn grew in importance as a trading center. The town was developing rapidly and by the early nineteenth century it had become a major industrial center.

Efforts to improve the city continued and in 1825 a law was passed which provided that new houses were to be built according to designs approved by the guberniya authorities. Streets were lighted and as traffic increased all streets were widened and the main streets were paved.

The middle of the nineteenth century marked the end of Tallinn's role as a fortress; the city ceased to be a land fortress in 1857 and ten years later its function as a sea fortress terminated. Work to strengthen and expand the existing fortifications ceased. During these busy years the economic growth of the city continued rapidly. With the completion of the Baltic railway in 1870, which connected Tallinn and St. Petersburg, trade was stimulated and its market expanded as access to raw materials was made easier.

At the end of the nineteenth century the center of the new city began to take shape and as the old medieval town gradually merged with the new city, the fortified wall was partially removed. New buildings were built in the new city center: the Agricultural Bank, a school, and two theaters—

today's Drama Theater (1910) and Estonia Theater (1913). Later, the city center was moved to a large square, the present-day Victory Square.

Today building and reconstruction continue and according to an old legend, the work of building up Tallinn will last forever. The legend says that the Lake of Ülemiste was filled with the tears of Kalev's widow. Järvevana, its old guardian, lives at the bottom of the lake and every New Year's Eve he emerges and asks the people of Tallinn: "Is the city built or does the work continue?" If the answer comes that the work is complete, the old man will turn the waters of the lake on the city. Thus, the task of building and reconstructing will always be a part of Tallinn life.

PLACES OF INTEREST

Tallinn is a city full of historical sites. Almost all of the buildings of the old city are museums in themselves, the structures revealing the artistry of the medieval masters.

Toompea Castle

The construction of the Toompea Castle was supervised by Kamil, who was appointed by the king of Denmark after the town was captured by the Danes in 1219. Completed in 1229, the castle was then encircled by fortified walls. The area of Tallinn known as Toompea was more heavily fortified in 1347 when the town and its surrounding areas were taken over by the Livonian Order and by the end of the fourteenth century the castle was largely rebuilt. The improved structure included a chapel, sleeping quarters, and an assembly hall for the order's convention. The castle was surrounded by a deep moat with drawbridges and a large wall.

The castle underwent many periods of reconstruction, each one suited to the times and needs of the rulers. In the fifteenth century a new building was erected between the Konvendihoone (Convention Hall) and the Pikk Hermann Tower. This new building served as the Town Hall, of which only the wide windows in the western wall have survived.

Some of the most extensive alterations were done in 1767 when, under the order of Catherine II, the eastern moat was filled and part of the eastern wall demolished. In 1773, on that site, a large structure was erected, its façade designed in the Baroque style. The building was used by the guberniya administration.

Over the last two centuries the castle gradually lost the traits of a fortress. In the nineteenth century a park was laid out on the grounds of a once fortified yard and in 1894–1900 the Cathedral of Alexander Nevsky was built here. The Livonian Convention Hall had become a prison but on the day that Soviet power was established in Estonia in 1917, the inmates were released. The castle is still in use today, housing the Council of Ministers of the Estonian S.S.R. The state flag of the republic flies over the Pikk Hermann Tower.

Dom Church

The Dom Church is a late-thirteenth-century structure that was, during the Middle Ages, the main building of what was known as the Large Fortress in Tallinn. Surrounding this Gothic masterpiece were the homes of vassals. The church was originally a three-nave cathedral with a gable roof but acquired the form of a Gothic basilica after a fire in the second half of the fifteenth century necessitated extensive rebuilding. The Baroque-style tower was added in 1779.

The church served as a burial vault for centuries and visitors will find the tombstone-covered floor very interesting. Also, the walls are decorated with the coats of arms of the noble families buried there. The right to be buried in the church was also given to prominent members of the guilds.

The most interesting tomb is probably that of Pontus de la Gardie, a Swedish army leader, and his wife. It was built in the late sixteenth and early seventeenth centuries by Arent Passer, a Tallinn stonecutter, and is in the Renaissance style. Two life-size stone figures representing Gardie and his wife make up the main part of the tomb while the sides are low reliefs. One of the reliefs depicts an episode in the siege of Navara. Among the other tombs in the church are those of Olof Ryning, a Swedish knight; Samuel Greigh, a Russian admiral and hero of the Chesme Battle against the Turkish navy; and Estonian-born Admiral Ivan Krusenstern, the first Russian explorer to travel successfully around the world.

Burial tombs are not the only surviving relics of importance in the church. Of particular interest is a carved wooden altar in Baroque style dating from the seventeenth century. The altar was made by Christian Ackermann, a citizen of Tallinn, from the drawings of the Swedish artist N. Tessin (who also designed the Royal Palace in Stockholm). Many of the coats of arms and epitaphs on the walls of the church were also made by Ackermann and his students.

Fortress Wall

The wall that once surrounded the town, and of which three-quarters still stands, is one of the most interesting historical sites remaining from medieval Tallinn. The construction of the fortress began in the late thirteenth century and the wall surrounding it was continually raised and fortified by the addition of new towers.

To match the more sophisticated artillery of the fifteenth and sixteenth centuries, the fortress walls and the walls of the towers were reinforced and thickened. Two of the gun towers, Kiek in de Kök and Paks Margareeta, have survived. Kiek in de Kök, which is situated on the slope of the hill, was built about 1475 and had an original height of 46 meters (150 feet). After the Ingeri Bastion was built on Harju Hill, the two lower stories of the tower were buried. Literally translated from Estonian into Low German, the tower's name means "look down into the kitchen." The name is attributed to the height of the structure from which the kitchens of nearby houses could be seen.

Lodged in the wall of the tower are six large stones and three small iron cannonballs, memories of the siege of Tallinn during the Livonian War in 1577.

The Paks Margareeta Tower was built in the early sixteenth century and is an impressive structure. Its diameter is 24 meters (78 feet) and its thickness at the base is 4 meters (13 feet). So large is the tower that to install it at the entrance to the harbor and the town, the builders had to remove part of the wall and one of the side towers of the Sea Gates. The tower was used as a barracks at the end of the nineteenth century and after the Revolution of 1905 it was converted into a political prison.

Pikk jalg (Long Leg) Street

Long Leg Street is one of the oldest in Tallinn. Ten centuries ago this street was the only road leading from the hill. The most interesting attraction on this narrow passageway is the stone wall which was erected in 1454 as a result of the strife between the feudal lords in Toompea and the inhabitants of the Lower Town. Bad feeling and anger became so intense that the magistracy decided to surround the town with a strong wall. The gates at the end of the street were closed at 9 o'clock every night, forcing all traffic between Toompea and the Lower Town to halt.

From Long Leg Street, through the gates, one can reach Luhike jalg (Short Leg Street, a curvy street that is too narrow for a car to pass through). This street leads to the oldest part of the Lower Town.

Niguliste Church

On the corner of Harju and Niguliste streets is the Church of St. Nicholas (Niguliste Church), one of the oldest architectural monuments in the Lower Town. The northern portal is in the Roman style, which suggests that the church was probably built in the second half of the thirteenth century. Originally a three-nave church, it was rebuilt in the early fourteenth century as a Gothic basilica after being badly damaged by fire. Reconstruction went on, with a series of interruptions, for two centuries and was finally completed in 1510.

The church was destroyed in World War II but fortunately many articles of the interior were salvaged. Among the treasures are a carved wooden altar dated 1482 and built by Hermann Rode, a Lubeck artist; stone tombs decorated with reliefs; floor plates; a beautiful chandelier; and a fragment of the painting "The Dance of Death," by the Lubeck painter Bernt Notke.

Restoration of the church has been under way for several years and it will be the home of a Museum of Medieval Art when completed.

Church of the Holy Ghost

This is one of the oldest churches in Tallinn and the only one that has never undergone any changes since its completion in the fourteenth century. During the Middle Ages the church was called the Town Hall Chapel and the magistracy assembled there on public occasions.

The church has a tiled roof with stepped pediments and the structure is graced by a beautiful tower with a Baroque spire. Of the works of art that have survived, the most valuable is a carved wooden folding altar decorated with paintings, made in 1483 by Bernt Notke.

On the outside wall of the church facing Pikk Street is the oldest clock in Tallinn, decorated with paintings by Christian Ackermann. The inscription on it reads: "I strike time correctly for all, for the maidservant and for the manservant, for the master and for the mistress of the house. No one can reproach me."

Tallinn Town Hall

The Tallinn Town Hall building is one of the most fascinating structures in the Town Hall Square and another remarkable relic of medieval Tallinn. Most of the work by an unknown builder was completed in two periods, 1371–74 and 1401–04. The roof was tiled in 1436 and in 1530 a weather vane (a figure of a warrior) was placed over the spire. The popular weather vane was nicknamed "Vana Toomas" ("Old Thomas"). The Gothic spire was replaced by a Baroque one in the seventeenth century but "Vana Toomas" remained.

The Town Hall served several purposes throughout its history. It was fortified well enough to be used as a sanctuary and sometimes its premises were used as warehouses. The open gallery was once a busy marketplace but when the gallery was closed in the seventeenth century, shops were set up between the columns of the Town Hall.

The building's interior is even more interesting than the exterior. The magistrates' hall occupied a large part of the first floor and the burghers' hall was in front of it. One can walk through a door in the wall of the magistrates' hall and down a narrow staircase to the basement where torture chambers were once in use.

Attention should be brought to the carvings on the wooden benches in the magistrates' hall, eight paintings on biblical themes, and four tapestries depicting scenes from King Solomon's life, made in Flanders in 1547.

Oleviste Church

The dominating feature of this church is the tremendous tower which was built in 1433. Originally 140 meters (459 feet) high, it has been rebuilt several times and is now a little over 120 meters (393.7 feet). Those who come to Tallinn by sea can see the greenish spire of the Oleviste Church from many miles offshore.

The architectural characteristics are more Gothic in this church than in any other church in Tallinn. The loftiness of the pointed arches is obvious and from the interior one can see that the central nave under star-shaped vaults is much larger than those on the side. Also, the windows are designed to emphasize height. The altar, highly decorated, is connected with the inner rooms through narrow arched bays. The magnificent stone sculptures at the altar, the pulpit, and the carved sashes are the work of the sculptor Eksner. The paintings for the altar and the bronze reliefs were executed by L. Maidel.

One of the most interesting areas of the church is the outside wall facing Pikk Street. Built into the wall is a carved stone cenotaph, the only one of its kind in the Soviet Union. In the recess are eight reliefs depicting biblical scenes. The cenotaph was built in 1513–14 and is believed to have been done by Heinrich Brobender Beldensneider.

Great Guild Building, 17 Pikk Street

The Great Guild was formed in the early fifteenth century. Guild members consisted primarily of the town's wealthy merchants and only members could be elected to the magistracy. In 1410 the Great Guild building was erected. Originally consisting of two two-naved halls, only the second hall of the one-story building has survived. The vaults of the hall are supported by three flagstone pilasters. Of interest are the huge doors with forged nails and bronze knockers shaped as lions' heads.

The coat of arms of the Great Guild (a large gold cross on a red background) can be seen both on the façade and inside the building. This also served as the minor coat of arms of Tallinn. The medieval heating system, located in the basement, has also been preserved.

The Great Guild building was originally used by the merchants for meetings and celebrations. Today the structure houses the State Museum of the History of the Estonian S.S.R.

House of the Brotherhood of the Blackheads

The Brotherhood of the Blackheads was formed in 1399, and its membership was open to local and foreign merchants who were unmarried. The House of the Brotherhood is also on Pikk Street, not far from the Great

Guild building. The name "Blackhead" originated with St. Mauricius, a Christian Moor, who is represented on the coat of arms of the brotherhood.

The building was first rented by the brotherhood in 1495 and was later bought. It was rebuilt in 1597 under the supervision of Arent Passer. The new design was very much in conformity with the then popular Renaissance style. The Brotherhood of the Blackheads was dissolved in 1940 and the building is now the Jaan Kreuks Palace of Culture for Young People.

Guild of St. Olai

Formed in the thirteenth century, the Guild of St. Olai was probably the oldest guild in Tallinn. The guild was housed in a building next to the Brotherhood of the Blackheads on Pikk Street. Only the two-nave hall with star-shaped vaults and octagonal columns has survived. The guild, which consisted primarily of Tallinn craftsmen, terminated in 1698. Today the building is used as part of the Palace of Culture for Young People.

Convent of St. Michael

On Nooruse Street one will find a building that was once part of the Convent of St. Michael. The convent was founded in 1249 and originally consisted of several buildings around a courtyard. In the thirteenth century girls of noble birth studied here, and in 1631 the Swedes used the building as a school for boys.

After the Northern War the convent church became an Orthodox church and was renamed the Cathedral of the Transfiguration. It has a beautiful carved and painted iconostasis, the work of I. Zarudny. Today the building serves as a secondary school.

Dominican Monastery

The Dominican Monastery, located on Vene Street, was originally a simple structure without decoration, but as the monastery became wealthier, much ornamentation was added. The monastery church was destroyed by the reformists in 1524. In 1531 a fire broke out, and after restoration only some parts of the old buildings remained with any original architectural detail. The buildings were completely rebuilt in 1841–45 and taken over by the Estonian religious community who used the monastery as a hospital.

Medieval Homes

One of the most interesting aspects of Tallinn from a historical and architectural viewpoint is the great number of homes built during the

Middle Ages. Visitors can get a good idea of how the townspeople of that time lived even though all of the thick flagstone-walled buildings have undergone some alteration or reconstruction.

In the homes of the burghers the living quarters were in the lower stories while the upper stories were warehouses. The hatches in the walls were opened to receive goods upstairs and the beams over the hatches held the pulleys that were used to raise the goods. There was usually a large anteroom where the master of the house conducted his business. The door to this room opened directly onto the street. Most of the windows were secured with bars.

Medieval homes can be found at 29 and 40 Lai Street, 17 Vene Street, and 71 Pikk Street. Some of the still-standing medieval warehouses in Tallinn are located at 13 Säde Street and 6 Tolli Street.

MUSEUMS

Museum of History

The Museum of History was founded in 1940 and is the central museum of the Estonian Republic. Its collections and exhibitions are primarily concerned with the history of Estonia. The museum displays archaeological and ethnographic discoveries, as well as coins, armor, medals, works of art, and photographs.

The museum is located at 17 Pikk Street and is open daily from 11 A.M. to 6 P.M., except Wednesdays.

City Museum

The City Museum contains exhibits about the history of Tallinn from the time of the Northern War to the present.

Museum of Arts

The Museum of Arts is probably the most beautiful museum in Tallinn. Not only are the exhibits of great value, but the building that houses the museum is a work of art in itself.

Housed in the Kadriorg Palace, the Museum of Arts was founded in 1919 by the Tallinn Museum Society and taken over by the state after Soviet power was restored in 1940. Permanent exhibits of the museum deal with the history of Estonian art from the early nineteenth century to the present. Visitors can learn of the national traditions of Estonian art and the development of Estonian art in Soviet times. The museum's collections consist of over 17,000 works of art by Estonian, Russian, and West European artists.

The Kadriorg Palace is an excellent example of Baroque architecture, particularly the hall with a two-tiered dome and a painting on the ceiling, "Diana and Actaeon," by an unknown artist. Most of the other halls are of little historical value because they have been rebuilt so many times and have lost their original appearance.

The Tallinn State Museum of Arts is open daily from noon to 7 P.M., except Tuesdays.

Museum of Natural History

The Museum of Natural History was founded in 1941 on the strength of the collection on natural sciences of the Estland Literary Society and many private collections. Today the museum has a collection of over 80,000 geological, mineralogical, and zoological pieces. There are exhibits dealing with the earth's structure and the evolution of life at various geological periods. The zoological section deals with the fauna of the earth but in particular of the Estonian Republic.

The museum is located at 29 Lai Street and is open daily from 11 A.M. to 7 P.M., except Tuesdays.

Peter the Great's Cottage

Before the palace was built this small cottage in Kadriorg was where Peter the Great stayed during his visits to Tallinn. The furnishings are simple: the living room has a large oval table near the window surrounded by several chairs; the small bedroom is furnished with a canopy-covered bed, a small white cupboard, an English clock, and figures of Greek gods and goddesses on the windowsills; the anteroom exhibits some of Peter's personal effects among which are a plumed cocked hat and a jackboot said to have been made by Peter himself.

Museum of Theater and Music, 4 Voidu väljak

Displays of musical instruments, manuscripts of composers, phonographs, letters, and photographs make up the primary exhibitions dealing with music in the Museum of Theater and Music. For those interested in theater, stage scenery, costumes, posters, playbills, photographs, and documents concerning theatrical organizations are also on display.

TALLINN WEATHER VANES

One of the most charming aspects of Tallinn is the number and variety of weather vanes on the roofs of houses. Archaeological finds show that the art of the blacksmith in Estonia can be traced to ancient times. Evidence of melting metal has been found at a site of primitive settlements near Tallinn. The blacksmith was always something of a legendary figure and the Estonian word "sepp," meaning "blacksmith," came to denote a master craftsman, whatever his particular skill. The work of the old Tallinn blacksmiths can be seen today on doors, knockers, locks, signs over shops, and especially weather vanes. Old weather vanes are found not only in Tallinn but throughout Estonia, particularly in the towns of Pärnu, Tartu, Volga, and Viljandi.

While weather vanes were first mentioned in writing as early as the fifteenth century, none from this period has survived. The oldest existing Tallinn weather vanes are from the sixteenth and seventeenth centuries, of which "Vana Toomas" is the earliest. One of the most beautiful weather vanes in the city also sits over the Town Hall building's western gable. This copper weather vane, made in 1627, has a tracery surrounding the main coat of arms of the city that seems to be made of the finest copper thread.

Over the house at 16 Vene Street is a weather vane in the form of a unicorn, a common representation on the coats of arms of that time. It is believed to have been made around 1554.

The weather vane over the State Museum building is typical of the Renaissance period. A flag with a foliage ornament, it once decorated the spire of the Church of St. Charles. The weather vane was probably made in 1670, the year the church was built.

In Christian art a dragon or a winged serpent symbolized sin and the embodiment of evil. However, in medieval Tallinn, it was believed that a dragon kept evil spirits away. Over 6 Kohtu Street is a weather vane in the shape of a dragon with a crown on its head.

Many of the weather vanes made in the sixteenth century have the names of their owners on them. On 15 Pikk Street is a weather vane bearing the initials "JH" for Johann Hokes. This is the only weather vane of old Tallinn known to be made of iron. Hokes purchased the house in 1636 and the weather vane was probably made in the late 1630s.

In the seventeenth century craftsmen began indicating on weather vanes the year in which they were made. A good example of this is the lily-shaped weather vane over the staircase of 6 Kohtu Street with the year 1666 inscribed on it. There are relatively few eighteenth-century weather vanes in Tallinn, although one dated 1789 can be seen on the tower of the Dom Church. Another one, in the shape of a dragon with protruding teeth installed in 1780, is on the bell tower near the Kalamaja Cemetery. During the eighteenth century the traditional roosters on the spires of churches were replaced by crosses. For most of that century, the number of hammered designs was on the decrease as was the number of houses built. For many years the making of weather vanes was neglected, but the 1870s saw an enthusiastic revival of the art.

The new weather vanes were hammered out by blacksmiths. It is interesting to note that copper and gold were no longer used in the production of these pieces; iron was used exclusively. One of the most beautiful examples of this new variety is on 37 Pikk Street. The weather vane, whose blacksmith is unknown, was probably designed by Tamm, who used the traditional lion to support the rod of the weather vane. Another example of this period is at 2 Uus Street—the head of an old man swallowing fire.

Recently, weather vanes have been installed on Kuldjalg and Grusbeke, the restored towers of the old fortress wall. All of the modern weather vanes in Tallinn are based on traditional designs, but they are made of anodized aluminum instead of being hammered out in the old fashion.

PIRITA

Pirita is a very beautiful suburb and the most populated part of Tallinn during the summer, particularly on weekends. The sea is the main attraction here, and the swimming season in Pirita begins in May when the water temperature reaches a mere 15 degrees C (59 degrees F). The Tallinn yacht club is located in Pirita.

A bit of history can also be appreciated in Pirita. Most interesting are the ruins of the Convent of St. Brigitta on the right bank of the Pirita River (many believe that the name Pirita is a corruption of Brigitta). Brigitta was a Swedish woman who founded the convent order in Tallinn while the main convent was in Sweden. Built in 1436, the structure was originally 56 meters (184 feet) high and 24 meters (79 feet) wide. This convent structure and the Dominican Monastery in old Tallinn were the two largest buildings in the entire republic. The convent was destroyed during the Livonian War. The portions of the structure that are the most well preserved are the main portal made of flagstone, the western pediment, and the stairs of the bell tower in the southwest.

Kohviks (Cafés)

Special mention of Tallinn's cafés is made because one can certainly feel the atmosphere of the city as well as get to know the local people better by visiting a *kohvik*. It is to the *kohvik* that a person goes to have his coffee, read the newspaper, talk with friends, or simply relax. Visits to the *kohvik* are a national custom.

There are many cafés in Tallinn and some, such as the Tallinn, Moskva, and Energia, have large halls and orchestras. Others are small and cozy with only four or five tables, such as the Gnoom, Toome, and Linda.

USEFUL INFORMATION

Hotels

Kungla, 23 Kreutzwald Street
Palace, 3 Võidu väljak
Ranna, 11 Tchaikovsky Street
Tallinn, 27 Gagarin Boulevard
Toome, 7 Rataskaevu Street
Viru, in the city center

Restaurants

The cuisine in Tallinn restaurants is generally European but national dishes can be specially ordered in most.

Astoria, 5 Võidu väljak
Gloria, 2 Müürivahe
Kännu Kukk, 75 Vilde tee
Kaukaasia, 4 Vana-Tooma Street
Kevad, 2 Lomonosov Street
Kosmos, 1 Makarov Street
Palace, 3 Võidu väljak
Pirita, 1 Merivälja tee
Tallinn, 27 Gagarin Boulevard
Vana Toomas, 8 Raekoja plats

Cafés (kohviks)

Energia, 4 Lenin Boulevard
Moskva, 10 Võidu väljak
Pärl, 1 Pikk Street
Pegasus, 1 Harju Street
Solnok, 101 Vilde tee
Tallinn, 6 Harju Street
Tuljak, 26 Pirita tee
Tuluke, 124 Vilde tee

Museums

Museum of History, 17 Pikk Street. Open daily from 11 A.M. to 6 P.M., except Wednesdays.
Museum of Arts, Kadriorg Palace. Open daily from noon to 7 P.M., except Tuesdays.

City Museum, 17 Vene Street. Open daily from 11 A.M. to 6 P.M., except Tuesdays.

Museum of Natural History, 29 Lai Street. Open daily from 11 A.M. to 7 P.M., except Tuesdays.

Museum of Theater and Music, 4 Võidu väljak

Cinemas

Kaja, 118 Vilde tee
Kosmos, 45 Pärnu maantee
Oktoober, 10 Viru Street
Rahu, 696 Kalinin Street
Soprus, 8 Vana-Posti Street

Theaters and Concert Halls

Estonian Opera and Ballet Theater, 4 Estonia puiestee
House of Composers, 7 Imanta Street (At 7 P.M. on Thursdays composers and musicians take part in musicals.)
Philharmonic Society of the Estonian S.S.R., 4 Estonia puiestee
Puppet Theater, 1 Lai Street
Russian Drama Theater, 5 Võidu väljak
Viktor Kingissepp Dram Theater, 5 Pärnu maantee
Young Spectators' Theater, 12 Salme Street

Souvenir Shops

Souvenirs of ceramics, leather, silver and copper can be found at: 27 Pikk Street, 19 Viru Street, 8 Võidu väljak, and 8 Raekoja plats. Art objects can be bought at 6 Võidu väljak.

Communications

Central Post Office, 20 Suur-Karja Street. Open from 8 A.M. to 7 P.M.
Central Telegraph Office, 9 Vene Street. Open twenty-four hours daily.

RIGA

GENERAL INFORMATION

Riga, capital of the Latvian Soviet Socialist Republic, is one of the oldest and most beautiful cities on the Baltic coast. The Daugava (West Dvina) River flows through the city, emptying into Riga Bay, an arm of the Baltic Sea. Thus Riga is a vital Soviet seaport, ranking second only to Leningrad. The Daugava divides the city into Old Riga, the ancient sector, and Riga, the modern scientific, cultural, and industrial center of Latvia. With a population of nearly 700,000, Riga is a city rich in history and vibrant with contemporary life. The chief manufactured goods are washing machines, textiles, trolley and railroad cars, radios, porcelain, and artistic glasswork. The city is also an important railroad center and has been a commercial junction throughout its history. Riga houses an Academy of Sciences and the Latvian State University in addition to five other medical and polytechnical institutes. There are fourteen museums, seven theaters, a circus, a philharmonic, and a conservatory. Numerous parks and gardens contribute to the graceful and relaxed tone of the city. Many seaside resorts and health spas are located along the Baltic shore not far from Riga. The combination of historical sites, abundant cultural and recreational facilities, and the extremely pleasant temperament of the Lettish people make Riga a delightful visit on one's itinerary.

HISTORY IN BRIEF

Until recently it was believed that Riga was founded in 1201, a date still displayed on the city's emblem. A few years ago, however, while digging a foundation pit for a new house, an entire neighborhood with many artifacts completely intact was found beneath ground level. From this archaeologists have determined that the founding of Riga actually occurred in the twelfth century. Historians date the origins of Riga as far back as the tenth and eleventh centuries at which time Liv and Latvian tribes settled along the lower banks of the Daugava River. These tribes were principally engaged in fishing, cattle breeding, and beekeeping in the wooded areas. Owing to Riga's favorable position along the developing east-west trade routes, the city became a center of commerce. Toward the end of the twelfth century a cluster of houses along a now extinct tributary of the Daugava evolved into a fishing village. The development of the fishing industry led to the settling of a second fishing village nearby. In 1201 Bishop Albert and a band of German religious crusaders founded a city near these early settlements and the name given to it was Riga, derived from Ridzene, the name of a Daugava tributary. Numerous churches, monasteries, merchant hotels, and castles were erected within the ensuing century until the entire right bank of the Riga River was settled as far as the Daugava. By this time Riga had a town plan which absorbed the old fishing settlements, included a road system, and specified the various districts which now comprise Old Riga, or the Old City as it is called by the citizens of Riga.

During the thirteenth century Riga joined the Hanseatic League to protect its maritime commerce. Like most towns of this period, it was surrounded by a high stone wall atop which were thirty watchtowers. Beneath the wall were earthen ramparts and a wide moat. Fifteen gates provided access to the city. During the Middle Ages the growing population did not have room for expansion beyond the elaborate fortification system. Thus the town became crowded, the buildings more profuse, and the streets narrower.

The rule of the Teutonic Order was supplanted by the Livonian Order under the dominance of the Bishop of Livonia. The Battle of Grunewald in 1410 ended Livonian rule and Riga became an independent city. In 1581 Lithuanian-Polish rule was established under the Rech Pospolitaya. In 1621 Riga was seized by Sweden, and after 1629, the end of the Swedish-Polish war, Latvia was divided between the two nations. The Northern Wars of Peter the Great resulted in the occupation of Riga by Russian troops in 1710. The Neistad Treaty of 1721 granted the northeastern Baltic territory to Russia, and this included all of Latvia.

Lettish ties with imperial Russia remained intact until World War I, at which time German troops occupied portions of Latvia. Prior to the war, activists in the proletarian movement against Russian capitalism had begun to make their power felt. In 1899 Riga was the scene of a general strike. The Riga Revolt, as it was called, was a protest against police brutality exercised upon the striking workers of a jute factory. Another general strike in Riga in 1905 was a solidarity protest against the Bloody Sunday massacre in St. Petersburg. Thus, by the advent of World War I, Latvia already had one underground army, formed during the 1905 Revolution, and was preparing for another. These troops fought against the Kaiser until 1917, when they joined the February Revolution which deposed the tsar. Soviet power was growing in the nonoccupied portions of Latvia until February 1918, when all of Latvia fell to the Germans. Latvian revolutionists joined the Red Army during the Civil War, and at the end of 1918 Soviet power was proclaimed throughout the territory under the leadership of Peteris Stucka. This short-lived government fell to White Guards and Entente troops in 1920. For the next two decades Riga was the capital of a Latvia largely controlled by Germany.

In July 1940 Soviet power was reestablished in Latvia and Riga was renamed capital of the Latvian Soviet Socialist Republic. Despite repeated bombing during World War II, Riga managed to preserve a large portion of historic buildings and monuments. Municipal buildings, homes, and factories have been restored or rebuilt. The Old City retains its antique charm, while new Riga continues to expand into the twentieth century.

MUSEUMS AND PLACES OF INTEREST

Old Riga

The 50-hectare (125-acre) area known as the Old City is bordered by Gorky Street on the west, Padomju Boulevard on the north, 13th January Street on the east, and Komsomolskaya Esplanade on the south. The Old City is itself a museum because of the historic and architectural relics located here. The streets are winding and narrow, as one would expect of a fortified medieval town. The quaint structures, some of which have original forged-iron lanterns hanging out in front, are as well preserved as state funding and human effort can make them. Restoration work is continuously in progress.

Many changes over the centuries have reshaped the Old City and its boundaries. Up to the sixteenth century no expansion was possible because of the elaborate fortification system. As the city became overcrowded, the fortifications had to be modernized. One enlargement effort was the creation of a moat at the eastern border reinforced by watchtowers and an earthen rampart. The moat is now the City Canal. A new section was then added to the Old City to the east. At the same time a citadel was erected at the northwest corner. The eastern section gradually became the repository of warehouses and dwellings of the poor. The central area remained intact as a neighborhood of the wealthy, who lived in stone houses. Between the two areas was a strip largely occupied by wooden structures, nearly all of which were destroyed in the fire of 1689. The citadel on the northwest enclosed barracks, warehouses, parade grounds, quarters for the military commander and his guards, and the Peter and Paul Cathedral. During 1857–63 the old fortifications were dismantled. Owing to the development of industrialization and capitalism in Russia, Riga expanded as a typical commercial city of the nineteenth century. The Old City was displaced by boulevards lined with private dwellings, municipal buildings were erected along the canal, and the center of Riga shifted toward what had been its former outskirts.

As one strolls the narrow, mysterious streets of the Old City a careful look at the buildings will show that what appear to be random structures are parts of entire architectural ensembles: castles of the Teutonic and Livonian orders and their bishops, monasteries, guild halls, cathedrals, and private dwellings.

Dom Cathedral

Just south of Lenin Street is June 17 Square, the site of Riga's famous cathedral. The Dom Cathedral is as indigenous to the Riga skyline as the Leaning Tower is to that of Pisa or the Empire State Building to New York City. Construction on the cathedral began in 1211 and was completed by mid-century. Additions and reconstructions went on until the nineteenth century, and the net result is a mixture of many architectural styles. The altar is Romanesque, the thirteenth- to fifteenth-century extensions of the nave are Gothic, the spire and altar roof are Baroque, while the former library is classical. The cathedral and its adjoining cloister served the nobility of Old Riga. Up to 1773 it was the burial place of the feudal nobility. Visitors will notice intriguing epitaphs and coats of arms on the tombstones. A particularly interesting relic in the cathedral is a money barrel in which collected monies were stored. The barrel has three locks and could be opened only when all three key wardens were on hand for an unlocking of the coffer. The Dom is noted for many features including a massive red brick tower upon which a copper spire was added and topped by a weather vane. The halls, gallery, vaults, and stained glass are lovely. However, the chief attribute of the cathedral is the organ, built in 1883, which at the time was one of the largest in the world. The organ has close to 7,000 pipes and 127 registers. In 1959–62 the Dom was converted to a concert hall with seating for several thousand. Frequent organ concerts are held and are worth attending while visiting Riga.

St. Jacob's (Jekaba) Church

South of the Dom Cathedral on Vestures Street is a small church originally built outside the fortress for dwellers in that area of Old Riga. The thirteenth-century Romanesque structure has the only Gothic spire in Riga. Surprisingly, however, the Jekaba Church has no bell. Originally the spire housed a bell which was called the "Bell of Poor Sinners." Its function was to warn of fires, floods, and invasions. It was also said to ring in the presence of unfaithful wives. The bell was mysteriously removed and has never since been replaced.

Skarnu Street Churches

Southeast of the Dom Cathedral across Lenin Street runs Skarnu Street, the former road to the Riga port. Three important churches of the Old City stand close together, and near them is a convent. Of the three churches, St. Peter's (Petera) Church is the best known. Begun in 1207, it was the largest church in Riga. Except for postwar reconstruction, the church has remained unchanged since the sixteenth century. It is held to be the best example of Gothic architecture in the Baltics. The altar section, completed in 1406, was supervised by Rumeschottel, a master of architecture brought from Rostock. The unique architectural feature of St. Peter's is the 126-meter (412-foot) wooden belfry with its characteristic weathercock on top. The wooden structure, built in 1209, was destroyed by lightning in 1721 and rebuilt to maintain its status as the primary element in the Riga skyline. Destroyed again in 1941, it has since been rebuilt. An observation platform has been installed from which the panorama of Riga and its environs can be seen.

The second church in the Skarnu Street group is the Jura Church, begun in 1207. It was the chapel of the first Teutonic Order castle. During the sixteenth century it was incorporated into a warehouse and has remained unchanged since that time. It is thus difficult to differentiate it from the twenty-four other warehouse buildings on Skarnu Street.

Third, and farthest south on the street, is St. John's (Jana) Church. Formerly the chapel of the Livonian bishop's castle, a gradual enlarging by Dominican monks resulted in what is now the nucleus of the Jana Church. Dating from the very early thirteenth century, it has become a conglomeration of successive architectural styles. The nave is Gothic, while the altar section added in 1580 is distinctly Manneristic. Just north of Jana Church is Eke Convent, at one time part of the Teutonic Order castle. Around 1598 it became an asylum for poor widows, founded by Nieka, a Riga burgher. Renovated late in the Renaissance, it became the largest warehouse in Old Riga.

St. Catherine's (Katrinas) Church

Located in a courtyard between Laipu and Skunu streets, is a small seventeenth-century building discovered in 1964 to be part of the Katrinas Church and cloister ensemble. During restoration work several buildings nearby revealed characteristics of pre-Reformation church architecture, such as Gothic windows and semicircular arches. It is now believed that Katrinas Church was the original Dom property which subsequently became a Franciscan monastery attached to Katrinas Church.

Reformed Church

Situated at the corner of Marstalu and Sarkanas streets is one of the latest churches to be built within the confines of the Old City. Permission was granted by Peter I for Riga merchants to build a Reformed Church, which was then constructed in 1720–30. The Baroque façade contains a stone portal which was made in Bremen and shipped to Riga. The church looks very much like the private homes in the vicinity except for the spire which differentiates it. Due to lack of space in the crowded city, the worship area was moved to the second floor during the nineteenth century so that the ground floor could function as a warehouse.

Riga Castle

In the northwest corner of the Old City, bordering on Gorky Street and Young Pioneer Square, is the imposing fourteenth-century Riga Castle. The four corner towers which enclose its original section have remained basically unchanged for six centuries. Formerly the stronghold of the Livonian Order, it was built after 1330 because the first Livonian castle on Skarnu Street had been destroyed by battles between the order and the Riga citizens. A bitter feud between the order and the municipal council broke out, culminating in a citizens' attack on the castle in 1484. The order and its allies subdued the city thereafter, and by 1515 the castle was completely restored. Its thick dolomite walls concealed a system of gangways used for defense. Sections of the old walls and some iron-barred windows belonging to the castle are now part of the museums housed in the old structure. The former castle garden is now the site of an al fresco sculpture exhibit, and a summer café is located on the terrace overlooking the Daugava which once served as a horn bastion.

Swedish Gates

Running the length of the northeast corner of the old city was the Riga fortification wall, some of which remains standing. At the western end is a small house which is the Latvian Architects Union (11 Torna Street). Beneath the upper stories is an archway which contains the Swedish Gates, built in 1698, the only city gates left in Riga. At the eastern end is the Powder (Pulvera) Tower, occasionally referred to as Sand (Smilsu) Tower. Although it is presently fused with the building which houses the Revolution Museum, at one time the tower stood apart and dwarfed the little houses on Noise (Troksna) Street. It was one of the most important towers in the fortification system of Old Riga and guarded the Sand Gate on the Sand Road. During the sixteenth century gunpowder was stored there, and thus it acquired its present name.

Guild Halls

Southwest of the Powder Tower, between Lenin and Sand streets, is a courtyard where two guild halls are located. Formerly these buildings were protected by the city wall. The Large and Small Guilds were referred to as Minstera and Soesta Chambers. The main section of the Large Guild Hall consisted of an assembly hall and an adjacent "bridal chamber." The large fireplace, still in existence, was a Renaissance addition (1633) to these otherwise Gothic structures. Today the Large Guild Hall is part of the State Philharmonic. The former assembly hall is the foyer, reconstructed in 1965, and the "bridal chamber" is the artists' room. On the other side of the courtyard is the former Small Guild Hall, which is now the Central Republican Trade Union House of Culture.

Russian Courtyard

This intimate architectural ensemble from the Middle Ages is enclosed by Brewers' (Aldaru), Little Noise (Troksna), and Komsomol (Komjaunatnes) streets, just south of the Swedish Gates. The structures included St. Nicholas Russian Orthodox Church, the guild hall of Russian merchants, warehouses, and several private homes. After 1580 nothing more was known of the ensemble until 1967, when restoration work was begun at 11 Aldaru Street. It was then that a Gothic pediment and other structures were revealed to lie buried under centuries of neglect.

Castle of Peter I

To the west of the Dom Cathedral along Komsomol Esplanade is Palasta Street. The house known as Peter's Castle was originally built during the early eighteenth century. Peter was a frequent visitor to Riga and was personally involved in helping to extinguish the fire of 1721 which nearly destroyed Petera Church. The castle was subsequently rebuilt and enlarged. The part of the original structure which remains intact is a garden located on the fortifications overlooking the Daugava. It was here that the tsar watched the maneuvers of his naval fleet.

City Hall Square

South of Peter's Castle across Lenin Street is what was once the ancient center of Old Riga, destroyed during World War II. Only photographs remain of the erstwhile buildings, which have been replaced by the Museum of Latvian Red Riflemen and the area known as Latvian Red Riflemen Square. At its center is a monument to the riflemen. The periphery consists of the Riga Polytechnical Institute and new residential houses of contemporary architectural design.

Residential Structures

The names of the streets of the Old City reflect the character of its medieval population. Merchants and artisans lent trade titles to streets: Merchants (Tirgonu), Blacksmiths (Kaleju), Butchers (Miesnieku), Coopers (Mucenieku), Cobblers (Kurpnieku), Painters (Gleznotaju). There are still a few carefully preserved specimens of medieval and Renaissance housing in the Old City. In the northern section, just behind Jekaba Church, is Maza Pils (Little Castle) Street. Located at numbers 17, 19, and 21 are fourteenth- and fifteenth-century houses which have come to be called *Three Brothers* (Tris Brali). Almost fused, the three houses are typical of the trades' and artisans' center of the medieval period. Pediments facing the street, the façades are speckled with miniature windows and Gothic niches. The rear of the houses at one time opened onto gardens, orchards, and outbuildings used for barns and coaches. As crowding gradually reduced space in the Old City, the outbuildings and yards were abolished. During the Renaissance a new style in housing developed among the well-to-do. Two remaining specimens of the later period are the Dannenstern House and the Reutern House located respectively at 21 and 24 Marstalu Street just south of Latvian Red Riflemen Square. These delightful models of Baroque architecture have stone façades and are three stories high. They are richly decorated with pilasters and cornices. Beyond the fortification walls were the homes of the poorer classes, whose ranks swelled even faster than the wealthy. Houses seemed to sprout wherever available land could be negotiated. Typical of these sixteenth- and seventeenth-century dwellings are the buildings north of the Swedish Gates along Masters (Meistaru) and Tower (Torna) streets. Steep, slanting roofs and smooth façades with narrow doorways characterize them.

Warehouses

As a major port and center of trade Old Riga attached much importance to the style and structure of its warehouses. The principal warehouse district is located at the southernmost boundary of the Old City. Adjacent to

13th January Street are Red Guard and Old City streets, which represent the heart of the Old Riga warehouse district. Rather quiet and deserted these days, the streets are still home to some of the tall buildings, once warehouses, with tightly shuttered windows, hatchways, and winches swinging above the doors. Today about twenty-four of the old warehouses remain unaltered. The best specimens are clustered along Miesnieku and Aldaru streets, along the western edge of the Old City.

Forest Park (Mezapark)

Located in the northern part of Riga, this 370-hectare (925-acre) park along the wooded shores of Lake Kish (Kiso Ezers) is a favorite spot. The park was opened in 1949 and has abundant facilities for culture, entertainment, and recreation. Among the major attractions is the Exhibition of Latvian Economic Achievements which contains numerous halls and pavilions with exhibits pertaining to Latvia's economic and industrial progress. Another interesting area is an amphitheater constructed especially for the Latvian Song and Dance Festival, held every fifth year since 1873. Sports facilities include a yacht basin, parachute tower, swimming pools, and ball fields. A children's railway runs through the park, and Riga schoolchildren under professional supervision operate three of the stations. There is a large restaurant, café, and cinema, as well as many lovely, scenic paths for strolling. The visitor will not want to miss the zoo or the botanical gardens here. A more solemn feature of the park is the Common Cemetery, the burial place of Latvian soldiers who fought in both world wars. The exhibition of commemorative sculptural monuments is striking. Near the Common Cemetery is the Janis Rainis Cemetery, named for the Latvian poet. This is a special burial ground for Communist Party leaders and Soviet Army senior officers.

Riga History and Navigation Museum, 4 Palasta Street

As the name implies, the museum is dedicated to exhibits pertaining to the origin and history of Riga. The four departments include navigation, history, archaeology, and socialist progress, and a special section on the post-World War II period. The museum building is the former Dom Monastery. It is open to the public every day except Monday and Tuesday. An extension of the museum is located at the Dom Cathedral, open Monday, Tuesday, Thursday, and Friday.

Latvian S.S.R. History Museum; State Museum of Foreign Art; Janis Rainis Literature and Art History Museum, all located at Riga Castle, 3 Pionieru Square

The Latvian S.S.R. History Museum is devoted primarily to the economic and cultural development of Latvia, with a special section containing archaeological specimens found in the republic. It is closed on Monday and Tuesday. The State Museum of Foreign Art includes art treasures from around the world with special sections for Oriental and ancient exhibits dating as far back as the fourth millennium B.C. It is closed on Tuesday and Wednesday. The Janis Rainis Museum is dedicated to exhibits showing the history of the development of the arts in Latvia, particularly biographical data and samples of the works of the best-known Lettish cultural figures. It is closed on Sunday and Monday.

Latvian Ethnography Open-Air Museum, Balozi, on the banks of Jugla Lake, northeast of Riga

This unique museum is situated in the pine forests bordering the city on 76 hectares (190 acres) of ground. It is an open-air exhibit of folk architecture established in 1932. There are fifty structures, ranging from eighty to four hundred years old, grouped according to geographical and ethnic origin and consisting of dwellings and farm buildings representing communities throughout the republic and preserved in their original form. The interiors contain the original furnishings, accessories, clothing, tools, and utensils. The museum is open every day from May to November.

Revolution Museum of the Latvian S.S.R., 20 Smilsu Street

Opened in 1940, the museum contains exhibits pertaining to the Latvian revolutionary movement. Special exhibits feature the role of Latvian revolutionaries during the October Revolution, Civil War, and World War II. A separate section is devoted to the development of Riga in the postwar years. The museum is closed on Friday and Saturday. Affiliated with this museum is the Memorial of Latvian Red Riflemen, founded in 1970, and located at Latvian Red Riflemen Square. It is closed only on Monday.

State Museum of Arts, 10a Gorky Street

Here are the finest works of Lettish and Russian painting and sculpture. One will also find an excellent collection of applied folk art. Since the opening of the museum in 1873 over eleven thousand items have been added to the exhibit. A special feature of the museum is the section devoted to contemporary painting, sculpture, and graphics. The museum is closed on Monday and Tuesday.

Paula Stradina Museum of the History of Medicine, 1 L. Paegles Street

Established in 1957, the museum is dedicated to Paula Stradina, a noted Latvian academician and surgeon. Many of the exhibits were originally private collections of Stradina and other medical scientists and practitioners. The focus of the exhibits is on the history of medicine from prehistoric times to the present. In addition to exhibits featuring antique medical implements, there are many works of art with medicine as the main theme. The museum functions also as a center for the dissemination of medical information. It is closed on Monday and Tuesday.

V. I. Lenin Memorial Museum, 17 Cesu Street

V. I. Lenin Memorial Flat, 18 Kirov Street

In 1900 Lenin visited Riga for the purpose of contacting Latvian revolutionaries and to discuss the publication of *Iskra* in Riga. The house in which he stayed and the flat in which the meetings took place are now museums. They are open daily.

Nature Museum of the Latvian S.S.R., 14 K. Barona Street

The purpose of this museum is to display the natural wealth of Latvia and to foster a love of nature in an age of technology. There are extensive mineral and insect exhibits as well as an abundant array of stuffed rare birds from all over the world. Of particular interest is the collection of amber, for which Latvia is famous. During the spring, summer, and autumn the museum exhibits an astounding variety of fresh flowers and mushrooms. The museum is closed on Friday and Saturday.

Central Collective Farm Market, south of 13th January Street on the banks of the City Canal

On Saturday and Sunday this huge open-air market is alive with workers from nearby collective farms and shoppers from Riga and its environs. The farmers occupy hundreds of stalls where they sell handcrafts, clothing, fresh fruits and vegetables, meats, fish, poultry, cheeses, and varieties of prepared foods. It is a marvelous place to stroll, observe, and make an occasional purchase. Prices are not always clearly indicated, and even where they are, bartering and bargaining are still very much in style.

RIGA SUBURBS

Salaspils, 20 kilometers (12 miles) east of Riga

This is the location of a former Nazi concentration camp where over 100,000 Soviet prisoners along with many others from other European countries were executed. Today a dramatic sculptural ensemble has been erected as a memorial to those who perished here. The high concrete wall, built where the prison gate stood, is symbolic of the border between good and evil. At intervals along the field in front of the wall stand massive concrete figures representing prisoners arising from the dead. Each has been given a symbolic name, such as "Solidarity," "Humility," "Unsubdued," to memorialize the determination of the prisoners not to surrender their ideals.

Sigulda, 45 kilometers (27 miles) northeast of Riga

This is an archaeological preserve in the wooded hills leading to the Gauja River. Among the footpaths lie the remains of Turaid Castle, built during the Middle Ages by German crusaders. Portions of the castle which have been restored function as a museum of regional exhibits. An observation tower is situated at the top of the narrow staircase from which a panorama of the Gauja Valley can be fully appreciated. Nearby is the Gutmanis Cave famous for its walls and vaults which bear inscriptions dating back to the seventeenth century. The cave is also noted for its water spring. A cable car traverses the valley, taking tourists to such intriguing sites as the castle of Prince Kropotkin and Artists' Hill.

Jurmala, 39 kilometers (23 miles) west of Riga

More popular than any other Latvian seaside resort, Jurmala offers a variety of pleasures. Located between the Gulf of Riga and the Lielupe River, the town provides broad, sandy beaches and forest parks, resulting in a particularly salutary climate. Because of this natural feature, many health resorts are located in Jurmala, where patients can utilize the ozone-rich air mixed with sea salts and pine resin. In addition to sanitaria, there are numerous campsites, hostels, and summer cottages. There is an open-air concert hall where Soviet and foreign performers are regularly scheduled. Two famous Latvian restaurants, Lido and Juras Perle, are also located at Jurmala.

USEFUL INFORMATION

Hotels

Hotel Baltica, 33 Raina Boulevard
Hotel Riga, 22 Padomju Boulevard

Restaurants and Café

Astoria, Lenin Street
Baltica, Hotel Baltica, 33 Raina Boulevard
Riga, Hotel Riga, 22 Padomju Boulevard
Café Luna, 18 Padomju Boulevard

Museums

Dom Museum, Dom Concert Hall, 17th of June Square
Janis Rainis Literature and Art History Museum, Riga Castle, 3 Pionieru
   Square
Latvian Ethnography Open-Air Museum, Balozi, Jugla Lake
Latvian S.S.R. History Museum, Riga Castle, 3 Pionieru Square
V. I. Lenin Memorial Museum, 17 Cesu Street
V. I. Lenin Memorial Flat, 18 Kirov Street
Museum of Latvian Red Riflemen, Latvian Red Riflemen Square
Museum of the Latvian Underground Press, 22 Kraslavas Street
Nature Museum of the Latvian S.S.R., 14 Barona Street
Paula Stradina Museum of the History of Medicine, 1 L. Paegles Street
Revolution Museum of the Latvian S.S.R., 20 Smilsu Street
Riga History and Navigation Museum, 4 Palasta Street
State Museum of Arts, 10a Gorky Street
State Museum of Foreign Art, Riga Castle, 3 Pionieru Square

Theaters and Concert Halls

Dom Concert Hall, 17th of June Square
Latvian Academic Drama Theater, 2 Kronvalda Boulevard
State Philharmonic of the Latvian S.S.R., 6 Amatu Street
State Opera and Ballet House, 3 Padomju Street

Stores and Shops

Collective Farm Market, Market Square between 13th of January Street
   and Maskavas Street
Foreign Currency Shop, 14 Lenin Street
Maksla Shops, 52 Lenin Street, 25 Valnu Street
Sakta Souvenir Shop, 32 Lenin Street

Transportation and Communications

Central Railway Station, Suvorova Street
General Post Office, Suvorova Street
Steamship Passenger Terminal, Komjaunatnes Krastmala

VILNIUS

GENERAL INFORMATION

Vilnius is the capital of the Lithuanian Soviet Socialist Republic. It is located on the banks of the Neris River and has a population of nearly 320,000. Rich in historical sites, the old part of the city dates back to the twelfth century. The Gothic and Renaissance structures contrast dramatically with the plethora of modern buildings constructed in this century, particularly since the end of World War II. Vilnius is the center of Lithuanian industry and culture. The Lithuanian Academy of Sciences is located here, along with numerous research institutes, six schools of higher education, and three hundred libraries. As in Tallinn and Riga, regular national song and dance festivals are held in Vilnius. Among the thriving industries the most prominent are machinery, metalwork, tools and dies, instruments, processed foods, and electrical parts. There are eleven museums in Vilnius, an Opera and Ballet Theater, Russian Drama Theater, Conservatory, and Lithuanian Drama Theater. Vilnius is a pleasant city to visit for its fascinating past, productive present, and for the timeless warmth and charm of the Lithuanian people.

HISTORY IN BRIEF

Archaeological research has revealed that the area along the Baltic coast which is now Lithuania was inhabited as far back as the ninth millennium

B.C. Recorded history of the region dates back to the tenth and eleventh centuries A.D. at which time feuding principalities engaged in constant battles throughout the Lithuanian territories. After Latvia was conquered by the Livonian Order during the thirteenth century and the Teutonic Order had settled into the lands west of Lithuania, the Lithuanian feudal lords felt that their only protection would be through political unification. The result was that Prince Mindaugus, after subduing his rivals for leadership, declared himself grand prince of Lithuania in 1240, and established a forceful feudal state. Continued rivalry from within and onslaughts from without weakened the Lithuanian state. Mindaugus was assassinated and no successful authority was established until 1316, the year that Grand Prince Gediminas achieved solidarity among the feudal lords and proclaimed hereditary succession to the Lithuanian throne.

Among the many popular myths and legends surrounding Prince Gediminas is one concerning his choice of Vilnius as the Lithuanian capital. On a hunting expedition to the valley where the Vilnia River joins the Neris, the virtuous prince fell asleep and dreamed that a gigantic wolf was howling from a mountaintop. The prince requested an interpretation from Lizdeika, the chief priest. The priest advised him that the dream was a sign from the gods that a city should be erected at the place in the valley where the dream had occurred. Thus it was that a castle and surrounding town were built and in 1323 the town was established as Vilnius.

The date of the founding of Vilnius marks the ascent to power of Lithuania as a political and commercial stronghold. Expansion into fragmented Slav principalities followed. Under Gediminas's heirs, Prince Algirdas and Prince Kestutis, Lithuanian power worked its way as far north as Smolensk and as far south as the Black Sea. While the Lithuanians pushed eastward, joining the Russians in their battles against the Mongols, the lands to the west were encroached upon by German crusaders. The Poles, fearing for the integrity of the Western Slav lands, hoped to unite with the powerful Lithuanians by offering the throne to Lithuanian Grand Prince Jogaila. The treaty of union was signed in 1385, and in 1389 Lithuania adopted Christianity, being the last pagan European nation to do so.

In 1410 Lithuania and Poland were joined by Russian, Tatar, and Czechoslovakian troops to defeat the Teutonic Order at Grunewald. Klaipeda, a vital port on the Baltic Sea, remained in German hands until the twentieth century. Relations between Poland and Lithuania deteriorated steadily. Lithuania preferred independence, while Poland pushed for a single state. In 1569, when there were no more Lithuanian heirs to the throne, a treaty called the Lublin Unia joined the two states into a single entity named Rzecz Pospolita. Wars with Russia and Sweden during the late sixteenth and early seventeenth centuries weakened Rzecz Pospolita. Famine and plague worsened the living conditions and morale of the people. At the beginning of the Northern War of 1700 Lithuania was occupied by Sweden for a period of nine years. Thereafter, from 1709 to 1795, Rzecz Pospolita was partitioned by Russia, Prussia, and Austria with the final annexation of Lithuania to Russia occurring in 1795.

The War of 1812 was ruinous for the Lithuanian economy; but after the abolition of serfdom in 1861 industry grew and Lithuanian towns expanded with a working-class population. The revolutionary movement gathered force toward the end of the nineteenth century when working-class political parties were established in Lithuania. Vilnius and Kaunas were two principal cities from which Lenin's newspaper *Iskra* was smuggled into central Russia. During World War I, German troops again occupied Lithuania. Soviet power was declared in Vilnius in December 1918. By the early months of 1919 several other Lithuanian cities followed suit with declarations of Soviet government. The summer of 1919, however, saw the demise of Soviet power and its replacement by an independent system of government. That same year Vilnius was awarded to Poland by the League of Nations. Twenty years later Vilnius was again declared a Soviet city. As troops moved in to prepare for war against Germany the Communist underground surfaced. By August 1940 Lithuania had joined the Union of Soviet Socialist Republics. During World War II Lithuania was occupied by the Germans and 600,000 persons were executed. In July 1944 Vilnius was liberated, and by July 1945 all of Lithuania had been freed of enemy troops. The devastated cities and towns have been gradually rebuilt over the years and the Lithuanian national culture has been strongly revived.

MUSEUMS AND PLACES OF INTEREST

The Old City

This is the area of Vilnius which includes Muziejaus, Gorky, Traku, and B. Sruogos streets. Originally this area was a trading settlement located along the crossroads which led to Riga, Novgorod, Krakow, and Moscow. Three castles situated on mountaintops overlooked the settlement, one of which is still in existence.

Gediminas Square, at the foot of Castle Hill

This wide and spacious square rests on the ruins of the Lower Castle, built in the fourteenth century. Formerly the duke's residence, the castle and its contingent palace structures were surrounded by walls and towers. A series of fires from 1399 to 1419 destroyed the castle ensemble, but later in the fifteenth century repairs were made. Numerous wars ravaged the walls and they were gradually dismantled, the stones being used for constructing the city. Many alterations to the castle ensemble were made during the fifteenth and sixteenth centuries. By the beginning of the nineteenth century the only remaining structure of the original architecture was a tower. It stands now in Gediminas Square, on an even older stone structure, considered to be the oldest piece of architecture in Lithuania. The upper portion of the tower contains a clock which was installed during the eighteenth century. Its chimes were designed to play music as well as to signal the passing hours.

Art Gallery

This dazzling white classical cathedral is the focal point of Gediminas Square. The original cathedral building was erected in 1389, the year that Lithuania adopted Christianity. Formerly the site had been an altar to the pagan god of thunder, Perkunas. Numerous alterations were carried out over the centuries. At the end of the eighteenth century, the Lithuanian architect L. Stuoka-Gucevicius provided the design which has been retained to the present time. The cathedral ensemble, representing Baroque and classical styles, includes a main building, king's chapel, and belfry. The front and side façades of the Art Gallery are set off by columns. The pediment and niches are decorated with sculptural representations of biblical scenes and heroes. A special feature of the building is the subterranean mausoleum where wall niches contain the remains of Polish and Lithuanian royalty. The exhibits of the Art Gallery include works by Lithuanian and Western European artists of the sixteenth through nineteenth centuries and also an exceptionally fine pipe organ. Regular concerts are held on Sundays.

St. Anna Church and Bernadine Church, Tiesa Street

It is believed that these two structures were originally part of a single architectural ensemble. Both churches are representative of Gothic style. St. Anna Church is small and extremely narrow. In spite of its size (22 meters [74 feet] by 10 meters [33 feet]) the elaborate construction makes it a hallmark of Gothic beauty. The decorations, all of which are made out of thirty-three different forms of brick, include pilasters, pinnacles, and ropework. The church, a symphony of graceful contours rising to the heavens, is unique among the architectural monuments of Eastern Europe. The Bernadine Church, which stands next to St. Anna Church, is noted for its especially beautiful belfry. Constructed as an octagonal tower with lancet arches, it fulfills the customary skyward aspiration of Gothic architecture. It is said that Napoleon was so impressed with the ensemble, particularly St. Anna, that he wished to transport it to Paris.

St. Mikhail Church, opposite St. Anna and Bernadine churches

This church, built during the sixteenth century, is representative of Renaissance style. Its features are moderate and serious, and it is to these characteristics that it owes its quiet beauty. Today the church is the home of the Republican Construction Exhibition.

Peter and Paul Cathedral, Gorky Street

Of the numerous Baroque churches on Gorky Street, the cathedral, built during 1668–76, is the most dramatic. The exterior resembles the neighboring churches, all of which feature the extravagances of Baroque architecture. However, the interior of the cathedral is unparalleled among the world's architectural masterpieces. More than two hundred craftsmen labored under the direction of the Italian sculptors Perti and Galli to create the sculptural ornamentation. More than two thousand human images of mythological, religious, and historical origins are depicted. The most impressive feature of the cathedral's interior is the huge cupola which crowns it and appears to be free floating. The cathedral's splendor does not impair the realism of its architectural purpose, and in all aspects it is considered to be the Baroque masterpiece of Vilnius.

Other Baroque structures along Gorky Street include Kazimiero Church, St. John's Church, St. Theresa Cathedral and Convent, and Holy Ghost Church.

Vilnius State University, Gorky Street

Founded in the sixteenth century, the university is the oldest in the Soviet Union. Its numerous buildings comprise an architectural monument representing styles ranging from Gothic through classical. Throughout the vaulted corridors and quaint courtyards are echoes of famous Lithuanian personalities. Among these are the Polish poet Adam Mickiewicz, the architect Stuoka-Gucevicius, and the artist Smuglevicius. The library of the university is supplied with over two million volumes. Another feature is the very old astronomical observatory. Near the university is an important historical site: the Skornia Print Shop where book printing was begun in 1525. This is the earliest print shop known to exist in the present Soviet Union.

Piles Street and Piles Square, behind Gorky Street

One must look carefully for this area, but it will become apparent because there is no vehicular traffic at all. Every structure is under state protection as an architectural monument. Plaques on each building provide the essential information. Taken as a whole, Piles Street is a Baroque museum. Each house is adorned with its original armorial bearings, gates, and street lamps. Frequently artists come to sketch the relics. Among the famous personalities who once inhabited the houses are the poet Mickiewicz and the painter Vienozinskis. Along Piles Square is St. Stanislav's Basilica, a cathedral built in 1777–1801; the Aushros Vartai Gates, which are attached to an old city wall and chapel, built over three centuries, from 1502 to 1824; the Officer's House, converted from a fourteenth-century bishop's palace by Stuoka-Gucevicius in 1792.

Museum of Revolution of the Lithuanian S.S.R., Karolio Pozelos Street

The exhibits here document the progress of socialism and the revolutionary events and personalities from the middle of the nineteenth century.

Museum of History and Ethnography, Trakai Palace

This museum has the largest existing collection of Lithuanian art, separated into three departments: folk art, fine art, and applied art.

Pushkin Literary Museum

In this former apartment of Pushkin's son one will see many of the furnishings and personal effects of the Pushkin family. Several items were stolen by German forces and have not yet been recovered.

Lithuanian Academy of Sciences

The Academy, founded in 1941, is the leading facility for all research work carried out in the republic. There are departments of physics, chemistry, technical, natural, and social sciences. Its library contains about one and a half million books, including a special collection of rare volumes dating from the fifteenth century.

Paneriai

On the outskirts of Vilnius stands this memorial complex commemorating the 100,000 people of Vilnius who were executed during World War II. Today at the edge of the pine forest an obelisk is placed at the spot that was formerly the center of the prison camp. A memorial museum here also exhibits photographs and personal effects of the victims.

Vilnius Suburbs

Trakai, 28 kilometers (16 miles) west of Vilnius, the fourteenth- and fifteenth-century capital of Lithuania. Trakai is an ancient town, established during the thirteenth century, on an island surrounded by numerous lakes. Trakai Castle is located here, the former residence of Lithuanian grand dukes, and the only island fortress of the republic. Today the castle houses a museum where artifacts of Lithuanian craftsmanship are on display.

Kaunas, 100 kilometers (60 miles) northwest of Vilnius, the second largest city in Lithuania. It was founded three centuries before Vilnius, in 1030. Among the historical structures in Kaunas are the Castle ruins (sixteenth century), the Vitautas Church (fifteenth century), Town Hall (fifteenth century), and the Kaunas Basilica (fifteenth century). Today there are many interesting places to see in Kaunas aside from the architectural monuments. These include the History Museum, Ciurlenis Art Museum, Literary Museum, and Zoological Gardens.

Pirciupis, 44 kilometers (26 miles) southwest of Vilnius, once a small village in the picturesque Dzukin area of southern Lithuania. Its fate was similar to that of Lidice, the Czechoslovakian village razed by the Germans as an object lesson for those who participated in the Resistance. At Pirciupis on June 3, 1944 fifty-eight men and sixty-one women were burned alive. Today a monument stands in the place where the village previously flourished. The monument is in the shape of a Lithuanian woman posed in mourning, mounted on a granite pedestal.

USEFUL INFORMATION

Hotel Neringa, 23 Lenin Prospect
Hotel Vilnius, 20 Lenin Prospect
Hotel Gintaras, 14 Sodu Street
Intourist Office, 20 Lenin Prospect

MINSK

GENERAL INFORMATION

Minsk is the largest city as well as the capital of the Byelorussian Soviet Socialist Republic. It is located 690 kilometers (431 miles) southwest of Moscow on the southern plateau of the Minsk Hills, and is bisected by the Svisloch River. The population is close to 750,000. The capital serves as more than a political center for the republic; it is also the leading cultural, scientific, and industrial city of Byelorussia. Lighting and food products are the chief output, although textiles and finished clothing are rapidly gaining ground as competitors. In the areas of education and science, Minsk boasts twelve institutions of higher learning plus the Lenin State University, twenty-two specialized secondary schools, eight medical research facilities, and the prestigious Byelorussian Academy of Sciences which consists of twenty-nine scientific institutes. Minsk is also considered to be the capital of Byelorussian art, having the best theaters, concert halls, museums, galleries, and libraries. The Byelorussian State Theater of Opera and Ballet produces numerous Russian, Byelorussian, and foreign programs. Of particular note are the specialized Byelorussian Folk Choir and Folk Orchestra which have gained widespread popularity.

Minsk is a totally modern city. Indeed, the Minsk of today is only thirty years old. It was under siege by the German forces during World War II for 1,100 days and was completely demolished. Since the end of the war everything has been rebuilt and restored. This herculean effort involved assistance from many other Soviet Republics, particularly the Russian Federation, Baltic, Central Asian, and Ukrainian. Although much construction continues in Minsk, the city's effort to rebuild itself was recognized by the presentation of the Order of Lenin in December 1966.

HISTORY IN BRIEF

The area of Byelorussia was first populated during the early Stone Age by Eastern Slavic tribes. Engaged primarily in farming, cattle breeding, and handicrafts, they lived in fortified settlements along shores of lakes and rivers. From the sixth to ninth centuries A.D. a feudal system evolved among the tribes, bringing with it the emergence of a class structure which lent itself to the formation of Eastern Slavic principalities. Eventually these tribes merged into a single nationality during the formation of the Kiev-Rus state at the beginning of the ninth century. The peoples comprising Kiev Rus were the Russians, Byelorussians, and Ukrainians. The capital of the ancient state was Kiev. Between the ninth and twelfth centuries internal warfare among the feudal lords resulted in the fragmentation of Kiev Rus. Various areas separated from the previous union and the area of Byelorussia became known as Belaya Rus, or White Russia, as it is referred to in the old chronicles.

In 1101, under Gleb Vseslavovich, Minsk became an independent principality. The city developed culturally and economically under his rule. Its growth was enhanced by its advantageous situation at the juncture of the Svisloch and Nemiga rivers. The disintegration of feudal power weakened Byelorussia as a whole during the fourteenth century. The territory was seized by the Lithuanians. Minsk was invaded by the Tatar-Mongols several times. From the late fourteenth century to the fifteenth, Minsk became a fortified town surrounded by earthen ramparts, watchtowers, and a defensive moat. A treaty known as the Lublin Union between the Lithuanians and the Poles was signed in 1569, which resulted in Byelorussian bondage to the Poles for two centuries. However, these years also saw the development of a strong national culture among the Byelorussians.

Polish rule ended late in the eighteenth century at which time Byelorussia was united with Russia. This led to a degree of industrialization for the Byelorussians. Minsk expanded its geographical boundaries and the population grew. Byelorussia joined the Russians in the war against Napoleon, after which Minsk was rebuilt according to a formal city plan. After the abolition of serfdom in 1861 industrial and agricultural capitalism flourished. One of the primary achievements under this system was the construction of the Moscow-Brest and Libava-Ramensk railways in 1871–73. These railroads connected Minsk with other industrial and agricultural areas of Russia with the result of even greater industrial and commercial focus on Minsk.

Byelorussian participation was heavy during the Revolution of 1905–07. During World War I, Minsk became the center of revolutionary activity led by Mikhail Frunze and Alexander Myasnikov, who had been sent by the Central Committee. Simultaneous with the October Revolution in St. Petersburg in 1917, the Minsk Soviet gained power. In January 1919 Minsk was proclaimed the capital of Soviet Byelorussia. The next month Polish troops supported by the Entente seized the western region of Byelorussia and did not release it until 1939. Since December 1922 Byelorussia has belonged to the Union of Soviet Socialist Republics.

PLACES OF INTEREST

Lenin Prospect

Beginning at the Byelorussian Government House, Lenin Prospect runs northeast the length of the city as far as the Moscow Highway; 50 meters (164 feet) wide, the avenue is lined with double rows of linden trees. The architecture of the buildings along Lenin Prospect is typically Byelorussian, which is to say, stolid, but lacking in the massive appearance of Russian architecture.

Lenin Square

At the beginning of Lenin Prospect is Lenin Square, noted for two important structures. The first is the Byelorussian Government House, a gigantic building, one of the few to survive World War II. The second structure is the monument to Lenin, which stands directly in front of the Government House. The monument, designed by Matvei Manizer, depicts the revolutionary standing at a lectern looking out at the crowd. Beneath the lectern on the supporting base are sculptured scenes from the October Revolution.

Central Square

Proceeding northeast along Lenin Prospect, one will pass two large buildings on the left. The first is the Hotel Minsk, the second the Central Department Store. At Central Square one can see almost all of Minsk. Central Square opens onto the public gardens at the southern end. Facing the square from this direction are the Yanka Kupala Byelorussian Drama Theater, named for the Byelorussian poet, and the Lenin State Library. The large building on the opposite side of the square is the Trade Union Palace of Culture. Here one can examine displays of Byelorussian trade union history and contemporary activities. Continuing east along Lenin

Prospect away from Central Square, you come to a large building on the right with a silver dome. This is the Minsk Circus.

Victory Square

As Lenin Prospect continues eastward, it is intersected by the Svisloch River. After crossing the bridge one arrives at Victory Square, the third largest square in Minsk. In the very center is the World War II memorial to Soviet soldiers and patriots of Byelorussia. The monument is a granite obelisk, 37 meters (123 feet) high. At the top is a red star which is electrically illuminated at night. On the left (northwest) side of Victory Square is a small wooden house, the Museum of the First Congress of the Russian Social Democratic Labor Party (see p. 348).

As Lenin Prospect continues eastward past Victory Square, there are many new buildings which form a complex nicknamed "clinical town" because they comprise the center of Byelorussian medical study and practice. On the right side of Lenin Prospect is a large structure with columns along the main façade. This is the Byelorussian State Philharmonic Building which houses a symphony orchestra, choir, folk orchestra, and folk chorus. On the left side of the avenue is Yakub Kolas Square, named for a famous Byelorussian poet. Here are located the buildings which house the printing facilities for Byelorussian books and periodicals. Diagonally opposite is the Minsk Department Store. East of Yakub Kolas Square on the same side of Lenin Prospect is a large, impressive building, the Byelorussian State Polytechnic Institute. The tiny square which one approaches next is Kalinin Square. Across from it is the massive complex of the Byelorussian Academy of Sciences which contains twenty-nine separate institutes for research and development.

Chelyuskintsky Park

Toward the easternmost end of Lenin Prospect is Chelyuskintsky Park of Culture and Recreation which occupies 56 hectares (140 acres). In this century-old pine forest are numerous flower gardens, many sports facilities, and in the summer an open-air theater. The park also houses the Central Station of the Children's Railway. Commissioned in 1955, the railway trains are operated by schoolchildren, who conduct passengers between the Park and Pine Wood stations, a distance of 4.8 kilometers (3 miles). At the northern edge of the park is the Belarusfilm Studio, which produces commercial films distributed throughout the Soviet Union. South of the park are the Botanical Gardens of the Academy of Sciences. Since the damage to the gardens incurred during the war was so great, most of the plants have been replaced. The gardens have also been enlarged. At present they occupy 106 hectares (260 acres) and contain about 400,000 plants belonging to 3,000 species.

Geophysical Observatory

Located at the eastern terminus of Lenin Prospect near the Moscow Highway is the well-known Observatory, built in 1930, and fortunately preserved during the war. In addition to investigative research connected with solar radiation and atmospheric electricity, the scientists here spend a great deal of research time on problems connected with national economy.

Zamchishe

A few blocks north of Lenin Prospect from the Central Department Store is Zamchishe, the only remaining historical sector of Minsk. Along Bakunin Street are the Orthodox Cathedral, built in 1611; the seventeenth-century Bernadine Convent; the Freemason House of the eighteenth century; and the nineteenth-century Kalvariisky Cemetery Gate.

MUSEUMS

Museum of the First Congress of the Russian Social Democratic Labor Party, on the northwest side of Victory Square

This small wooden house is the birthplace of the most revolutionary organization of the twentieth century. The first congress was held in March 1898 in the apartment of Pytor Rumianstev, a railway official sympathetic to the goals of the RSDLP who offered his quarters as a meeting place. In 1923 on the twenty-fifth anniversary of the congress, the building became a museum. Rumianstev himself aided in the selection of furniture and documents for display. During World War II the building was ruined, but it has been meticulously rebuilt and restored. There are two departments of the museum. One consists of exhibits pertaining to the socioeconomic situation of Russia in the late nineteenth century and the efforts of Lenin to establish a Marxist organization. The other department of the museum is the quarters of Rumianstev which housed the actual meetings of 1898.

Byelorussian State Museum of the History of the Great Patriotic War, 25a Lenin Prospect

This museum houses exhibits pertaining to Byelorussian participation in World War II. To many citizens of the city as well as the republic, it is especially important, since the memory of the war still lingers mixed with pride and bitterness. It is recalled that nearly 400,000 people perished in Minsk and its environs. The exhibits in this museum show both sides of the conflict. There are vivid photographs of the people engaged and dying in the struggle. Also on display are German and Soviet weapons, uniforms, documents, propaganda leaflets, partisan banners, and the personal effects of Byelorussian heroes. One of the first Soviet tanks to arrive now rests on a pedestal at the corner of Karl Marx and Krasnoarmeyskaya streets.

Yanka Kupala Memorial Museum, 4 Yanka Kupaly Street

This ten-room house was the dwelling place of Yanka Kupala, a poet and folk hero of Byelorussia. Reconstructed since the war, the museum contains a thousand documents associated with the poet whose partisan affiliations have rendered him the title "People's Poet."

State Art Museum, 20 Lenin Street

Exhibited here is a wealth of painting, sculpture, and applied art. One will find both academic and folk traditions representing Byelorussian and Soviet artists of the prerevolutionary and postrevolutionary periods. Included in the Russian collection are paintings by Repin, Levitan, Vrubel, Korovin, and Nesterov. Byelorussian painting is highlighted by the works of Zhukovsky and Byalynitsky-Birulya.

EXCURSIONS

Mound of Glory

Twenty-one kilometers (13 miles) east of Minsk along the Minsk-Moscow Highway is a dramatic memorial to the Soviet Army in honor of the liberation of Byelorussia. A metal sculptural ensemble marks the top of a small hill which is called the Mound of Glory. A multinational delegation representing all of the Soviet Republics brought handfuls of earth from the major Byelorussian battlefields to create the hill.

Khatyn

Sixty kilometers (37 miles) from Minsk on the Logoisk Highway is the memorial complex at Khatyn, the site of a former village which was decimated by the Germans. On March 22, 1943 a ground force attacked the village and herded the residents into a shed. Setting fire to it, they killed 149 people, including 76 children. All 26 farmsteads were burned to the ground. Khatyn was just one of 9,200 villages similarly destroyed along with 209 towns and settlements in Byelorussia. Khatyn was chosen for the exemplary memorial. At the site of the former village, in a glen encircled by birch trees, is the bronze sculpture of a man holding a dead boy in his arms. The original model for this sculpture, created by Gennady Selikhanov, was a Byelorussian peasant named Iosif Kaminsky. He was the only survivor of Khatyn, found the day after the massacre, burned and wounded, lying beside his dead son.

USEFUL INFORMATION

Hotels

Hotel Airport, 91 Chkalov Street
Belarus, 13 Kirov Street
Minsk, 11 Lenin Prospect
Pervaya Sovietskaya (1st building), 13 Komsomolskya Street
Pervaya Sovietskaya (2nd building), 11 Internatsionalnaya Street
Sputnik, 30 Brilevskaya Street
Vtoraya Sovietskaya, 6 Volodarskogo Street
Yubileinaya, Parkovaya Magistral

Restaurants

Belarus, 13 Kirov Street, Tel: 29–26–97
Chaika, 3 Tolbukhina Street, Tel: 6–24–03
Kolos, 2 Klumova Street, Tel: 4–20–04
Kosmos, 26 Boulevard Shevchenko, Tel: 7–06–41
Leto, 18 Pervomaiskaya Street, Tel: 22–55–92
Minsk, 11 Lenin Prospect, Tel: 29–23–96
Nieman, 22 Lenin Prospect, Tel: 22–17–91
Raduga, 1 Kirov Street, Tel: 22–25–56
Sputnik, 2 Brilevskaya Street, Tel: 25–88–39
Yubileiny, Parkovaya Magistral, Tel: 22–08–16
Zarya, 2 Lenin Street, Tel: 22–76–12

Cafés

Belarus, 11 Kirov Street, Tel: 22–61–91
Beryozka, 40 Lenin Prospect, Tel: 3–47–71
Bulbyana, 53 Lenin Prospect, Tel: 3–51–52
Druzhba, 33 Volgogradskaya Street, Tel: 6–13–53
Minsk, 11 Lenin Prospect, Tel: 29–23–96
Molochnoye, 17/30 Yanka Kupaly Street, Tel: 22–76–14
Molodyozhnoye, 1 Bogdana Khmelnitskogo Street, Tel: 6–27–94
Otdykh, 11 Internatsionalnaya Street, Tel: 22–01–06
Planeta, Boulevard Lunacharskogo, Tel: 3–66–07
Vesna, 18 Lenin Propect, Tel: 22–63–27
Yubileiny, Parkovaya Magistral, Tel: 22–08–16
Zhuravinka, Yanka Kupaly Street, Tel: 22–45–96

Museums

State Museum of Art, 20 Lenin Street
State Museum of the History of the Great Patriotic War, 25a Lenin Prospect
State Museum of the Byelorussian Soviet Socialist Republic, 12 Karl Marx Street
Literary Museum of Yanka Kupala, 4 Yanka Kupaly Street
Literary Museum of Yakub Kolas, 66a Lenin Prospect
House Museum of the 1st Congress of the RSDLP, 31a Lenin Prospect

Cinemas

Belarus, Yubileinaya Square
Letni, Gorky Park
Mir, 4 Kozlov Street
Novosti Dnya, 12 Engels Street
Partizan, Boulevard Tolbukhina
Pioneer, 20 Engels Street
Pobeda, 21 Internatsionalnaya Street
Raketa, 3 Rabochi Pereulok
Rodina, 16 Lizy Chaikinoi Street
Spartak, 2 Daumana Street
Tsentralny, 13 Lenin Prospect

Theaters and Concert Halls

Bolshoi Opera and Ballet Theater of Byelorussia, 23 Parizhskoi Kommuny Square
Maxim Gorky State Russian Drama Theater, 5 Volodarsky Street
Yanka Kupala State Academic Theater, 7 Engels Street
Young Spectators' Theater, 24 Engels Street
Puppet Show, 20 Engels Street
Byelorussian State Philharmonic Society, 50 Lenin Prospect

Circus

Byelorussian State Circus, 32 Lenin Prospect

Department Stores and Shops

GUM (State Department Store), 21 Lenin Prospect
Minsk Department Store, 54 Lenin Prospect
Alesya Department Store, 3 Parkovaya Magistral
Beryozka Shop (goods sold for foreign currency only), 3 Sverdlov Street

Pavlinka (art shop), 19 Lenin Prospect
Lyanok (linen fabrics), 46 Lenin Prospect
Priroda (nature), 89 Lenin Prospect
Central Bookshop, 19 Lenin Prospect
Druzhba Bookshop, 43 Lenin Prospect
Salon Chassy (watches and clocks), 72a Lenin Prospect
Kristall (earthenware, cut glass, and porcelain), 39 Lenin Prospect
Music Shop, 4 Lenin Street
Sporting Goods, 16 Lenin Prospect

Transportation and Communications

Aeroflot, 28 Karl Marx Street, Tel: 22–18–22, 22–62–11
General Post Office, 10 Lenin Prospect, Tel: 22–27–23
Central Telegraph Office, 6 Engels Street, Tel: 22–19–67

LVOV

GENERAL INFORMATION

Lvov lies north of the eastern slope of the Carpathian Mountains. Its climate is fairly continental with an average January temperature of −4 degrees C. (25 degrees F.) and a July average of 18 degrees C (64 degrees F.). Average rainfall is quite high with 61–71 centimeters (24 to 28 inches) a year and reaching as high as 1 meter (40 inches) in the mountains.

Lvov occupies an area of 111 square kilometers and has a population of over half a million, of which 70 percent are Ukrainians. The entire Lvov Region of the Ukraine occupies an area of 21,000 square kilometers and has a population of 2.2 million (86 percent are Ukrainians).

Lvov has always been an economically oriented city but until 1939 it was primarily involved with small enterprises and industries dealing with metalwork, jewelry, watchmaking, tinned foods, and confectionary. Drastic changes have taken place in the economic makeup of Lvov and today industrial plants can produce in fifteen days the equivalent of the entire industrial output of 1940.

HISTORY IN BRIEF

Lvov was founded by Daniil Romanovich, prince of Galicia and Volhynia, and named in honor of his son, Lev. Lvov fell under constant attack during the last half of the thirteenth and the beginning of the fourteenth centuries. Tatar-Mongols as well as Polish, Hungarian, and Lithuanian invaders struck the town until, at the end of the fourteenth century, it became a stronghold of the Polish feudal lords who controlled Eastern Galicia. The Poles dominated the area until 1772, when it fell to the Austrians following the partition of Poland.

Due to the relentless invasions, the center of the town was a fortress surrounded by a wall as well as many ramparts and moats. A high watch-tower was the town's dominant structure. The prince's palace was well protected by a fortified wall. Merchants, craftsmen, and the poor lived on scattered settlements to the west, north, and south.

Lvov was able to gain strength and develop as an important commercial center because it stood on the crossroads between Kiev and Western Europe. Unfortunately, the founders and builders of Lvov were not able to rule their own land, for when Yuri II Boleslav, the last ruling Romano-vich, died in 1340, King Casimir III of Poland, taking advantage of internal problems, won two victories over the town. After plundering the prince's castle and making away with two gold crowns, a gold-plated throne, the prince's mantle, and several valuable crosses, Casimir burned the castle to the ground. He ordered a new stone fortress built and named it the High Castle.

Numerous attempts to seize the castle failed and it was virtually impreg-nable until 1648, when the entire Ukraine was raging with a national war of liberation under the leadership of Hetman Bogdan Khmelnitsky. As the war continued, it spread to Galicia and the Ukrainian peasants and urban poor turned to the Cossacks for help. Prepared with arms and internal organization, the people of Lvov were ready to aide Khmelnitsky when he marched into the town. It was in late September 1648 that the High Castle came under siege by Khmelnitsky's troops. The first attempts to gain control failed but success finally came on October 14 when a detachment under the leadership of "first colonel" Maxim Krivonos, with a following of Ukrainians, Moldavians, and Don Cossacks, seized the castle.

The once invincible castle was taken by the Turks in 1672 and by the beginning of the eighteenth century it had fallen into such a state of decay that it could no longer be used as a stronghold. With virtually no resistance, Carl XII, king of the Swedes, gained control of the castle. Several decades later it lay in ruins. The only thing that remains of the High Castle today is a house, at 3 Lenin Street, built of stones from the castle walls. The hill on which the structure once stood is now the site of a park.

As part of the Austrian Empire, the town was renamed Lemberg but Poland regained possession in November 1918. Under the terms of the Molotov-Ribbentrop treaty, Lvov was occupied by the Soviet army in September 1939 and while Germany later occupied the city, the Soviet Union confirmed its possession in 1945.

Not a single structure from Lvov's ancient past has been preserved and only through the evidence of archaeological finds do we have a picture of days gone by. Investigations show that the first stone fortifications on Castle Hill were built at the beginning of the fourteenth century. Several stone churches were also built at this time and excavations on nearby Prince's Hill found two thirteenth-century fragments of white stone columns with bas-reliefs depicting figures, plants, and birds (these are on display in the Lvov Historical Museum).

MUSEUMS AND PLACES OF INTEREST

Lvov Branch of the Central Lenin Museum

Located at 20 Lenin Prospect, the Lvov Branch of the Central Lenin Museum was opened on April 22, 1950, to commemorate the eightieth anniversary of Lenin's birth. Designed by architect V. Marconi, it was built in 1904 and served as the Art Gallery. Its façade was graced with sculptured works by Peter Voitovich and the stucco molding was executed by the sculptor Mikjail Parashchuk.

The museum, a popular tourist attraction, has five thousand exhibits including rare documents and photographs, books, newspapers, and works of art that portray the life and work of Lenin. Copies of *Iskra* and the Bolshevik newspapers *Vperyod, Proletariy,* and *Sotsial-Demokrat* are on display. Other exhibits show Lenin's involvement with the peoples of East Galicia as well as details of his stay in Cracow and Poronino and the visit of his sister to Lvov in 1915.

The museum is open daily, except Monday, from 11 A.M. to 7 P.M.

Museum of History

The Lvov Museum of History is housed in two buildings, at 4 and 6 Rynok Square. The building at Number 4 is known in literature as the Black Palace or Anchovsky House after one of its owners, Marczin Nikanor Anchovsky. The foundation for the palace which now stands was laid by architect Pietro Krasowsky in 1577. At the beginning of the seventeenth century a third story was added. New pieces of sculpture were added to the façade and the interior redesigned in the 1670s by architect Maryan Gradowski. Final changes were made in 1884 when the attic was converted into a fourth story. The architectural design of the Black Palace is very much like that of most of the structures in the Market Place (the center of old Lvov). According to the laws of the sixteenth century, structures were allowed a maximum of three windows across the façade (additional windows could be put into the design only with permission and the payment of a special tax).

The other structure of the Museum of History, 6 Rynok Square, is also a Renaissance palace known as Kornyakt House or Sobiesky House. The structure is in the Renaissance style. Passing through a narrow hallway, one enters an Italian courtyard. Three sides of the house are tiered with a closed balcony and semicircular arches are supported by columns. The Black Palace and the Kornyakt or Sobiesky House are themselves to be considered exhibits of the Museum of History.

Other structures that contain Museum of History exhibits are the houses at Numbers 2 and 24. The museum is one of the best endowed in the Ukraine and has over 200,000 exhibits and displays of archaeological finds, photographs, documents, paintings, drawings, works of sculpture, and historical relics.

The Lvov Museum of History is open daily, except Wednesdays, from 10 A.M. to 6 P.M.

Ukrainian Art Museum

The Lvov Ukrainian Art Museum, located at 42 Dragomanova Street, has one of the richest and most complete collections of national art in the Ukraine. The museum was founded in 1905 and is most famous for its collection of fourteenth- to eighteenth-century Galician icons and wood engravings.

The section of Ukrainian fine arts of the nineteenth and early twentieth centuries is diversified, showing paintings, drawings, and engravings by prominent artists such as Taras Shevchenko, Sergei Vasilevsky, Konstantin Trutovsky, Kornila Ustiyanovich, Alexander Murashko, Sergei Svyatoslavsky, Kiriak Konstandi, Ivan Trush, Osip Kurilas, Alexei Novakovsky, and Modest Sosenko.

The crafts section has fine exhibits of Ukrainian ceramics, glass, embroidery, clothes, textiles, rugs, wood engraving, and metalwork. The museum also has over six thousand manuscripts and old books.

The House Museum of Ivan Trush (Dom Muzei Ivana Trusha) is a branch of the Museum of Ukrainian Art and is located on Ivan Trush Street. Trush, a well-known Ukrainian painter, was instrumental in developing progressive trends in West Ukrainian fine arts. He is most famous for his landscapes and genre paintings depicting the life of the Gustul peasants. The house where he lived, worked, and died has been preserved and visitors can see the furnishings of his studio as well as many paintings, sketches, and personal belongings.

The Museum of Ukrainian Art is open daily, except Fridays, from 11 A.M. to 6 P.M.; Thursdays until 5 P.M.

Museum of Ethnography and Crafts

The Museum of Ethnography and Crafts, at 15 Lenin Prospect, is extremely interesting for those who wish to learn about Ukrainian culture as well as local customs and traditions. This museum is the only one of its kind in the Ukraine and its collection includes works of woodcarving, ceramic, embroidery, carpet weaving, glass blowing, and metalworking by craftsmen of Lvov, the Gustul region, and other parts of the Western Ukraine. Other exhibits tell of the life and work of Ukrainian farmers and workers and collections of porcelain, furniture, and watches are displayed.

The museum is open daily, except Mondays, from 11 A.M. to 6 P.M.

Lvov Art Gallery

The Lvov Art Gallery, one of the largest art museums in the U.S.S.R., is at 3 Stefanika Street. The gallery opened its doors in 1907 and today it has over ten thousand works of art (paintings, sculptures, and drawings) dating back to the sixteenth century.

There is a fine section of Western European art which includes works by Goya, Rubens, Titian, Diaz Menier, and Rockwell Kent. There are several exhibits representing the works of Dutch, Italian, French, Spanish, and Austrian painters.

Artists of the socialist countries are well represented with works of several Czech and Hungarian painters on display. The gallery also has the nation's largest collection of Polish fine arts dating from the sixteenth to the twentieth century. Among the Polish painters whose works are on display are Anatoli Brodowski, Peter Mikhajlowski, Jan Matejko, Henrick Rodakowski, Julius Kossak, Arthur Grottger, Julian Falat, Alexander Kotsis, Jan Stanislawski, Jaczek Malczewski, and Zigmund Walishewski.

Of course, there is an extensive collection of works by prerevolutionary Russian painters as well as modern Soviet artists. Among them are Ilya Repin, Isaac Levitan, Mikhail Vrubel, Ivan Shishkin, Sergei Konenkov, Sergei Gerasimov, Martiros Saryan, Alexander Keineka, and Vladimir Favorski.

The Lvov Art Gallery is open daily, except Mondays and the last day of each month, from 11 A.M. to 6 P.M.; Tuesdays from 12 noon to 6 P.M.

Ivan Franko Memorial Museum

At 152 Ivan Franko Street (formerly Poninsky Street) is the house where the Ukrainian writer spent the last fourteen years of his life. There are many places in Lvov that bear memorial plaques or that are named for Franko, and in 1940, after the Ukraine's reunification with the Soviet Union, his house was opened to the public as the Ivan Franko Memorial Museum.

The museum's exhibits portray the life and work of the writer from his childhood in the very poor settlement of Naguevichi to his death. Documents, photographs, paintings, and works of sculpture tell the story of Franko, his friends, and his time. Through the exhibits the visitor becomes acquainted with the personality of Franko the poet, fiction writer, playwright, philologist, linguist, historian, economist, ethnographer, and connoisseur of music, theater, and the fine arts.

On display are many of the writer's personal belongings as well as books from his library and an exact replica of his study. A bust of Franko, executed by Grigory Pivovarov, stands in front of the house.

The Ivan Franko Memorial Museum is open daily, except Tuesdays, from 11 A.M. to 7 P.M.; Mondays from 11 A.M. to 3 P.M.

Armenian Cathedral (Armyansky Sobor)

Armenians had settled in Lvov from the time of Prince Daniil Romanovich and it became one of the largest centers of the Armenian people outside of their own country. The Armenian Cathedral, built in 1363–70, stands on Armenian Street and is one of the most magnificent structures in Lvov. In order to appreciate fully the visual and historical beauty of the Armenian religious complex, one must descend into a courtyard. Once in the yard you will be overpowered by the cathedral, the cemetery with tombs dating from the fourteenth to eighteenth centuries and bearing Armenian inscriptions and bas-reliefs, the building of the former monastery of the Armenian Benedictines, and the palace of the Armenian archbishop.

Although the cathedral has undergone a history of rebuilding and remodeling from the fourteenth to the twentieth century, the essential features have been retained. Its style is a workable combination of Byzantine, Old Russian, and, foremost, the Armenian national architectural style of the fourteenth century (the cathedral is the only structure of fourteenth-century Armenian style in all of the Ukraine).

The ground plan, in the shape of a Greek cross, formed the base of a decahedronal drum topped by a dome. The cathedral is supported by four pillars and the dome is constructed with masonry of baked clay. This is typical of medieval (twelfth- to fifteenth-century) Simenian architecture; however, its three-apsed structure, Eastern Byzantine in character, shows the influence of Old Russian features. It is believed that the original architect was an Armenian from Ani or from the Crimea. Credit for the technical guidance of the construction has been awarded to a German from Silesia named Doring.

The cathedral began to acquire new architectural traits with the advent of the Renaissance. An open arcade was added to the south wall in 1437 and was to be used as a burial ground. In 1571 architect Pietro Krasowsky built an octagonal belfry topped by an onion-shaped cupola. It was destroyed by fire in 1788 and took on a different design after restoration. The premises for the Armenian archbishops were built in the sixteenth century, a time when the Armenian Gregorian Church in Galicia was forced into a union with the Vatican and lost its independence. The Catholic influence on later remodeling can easily be observed.

The cathedral underwent extensive changes in 1630 when the central façade with the portal was replaced by an elongated nave, the design of sculptor Albert Kelar. A new carved wooden ceiling was added and in 1723 the whole interior was redesigned in the Baroque style. An altar was built in the courtyard, also in Baroque style, and a column bearing a statue of St. Christopher was erected.

At this point the cathedral had still not undergone complete remodeling, for in 1908, under the guidance of architect F. Menchinsky, the western façade was added. The interior of the dome was ornamented with mosaic in 1926, the work of Polish painter Yusef Mekhkhoffer, and the walls were decorated with modern murals, the work of Jan Rozen.

Today those who visit this ancient monument can see treasures of Galician icon painting and wooden sculptures, now the property of the Lvov Museum of Ukrainian Art.

Gothic Cathedral (Latinsky Sobor)

The Gothic Cathedral stands on the site between Theater and Galicia streets at the entrance to the marketplace.

The cathedral occupies the site where, during the reign of the Galician princes, stood one of the remote churches of Lvov—the Church of the Assumption. The church was torn down by order of Casimir III and in 1360 he laid the cornerstone for the cathedral that was to become the primary symbol and sanctuary of the Catholic Church in the Western Ukraine. It was Peter Shtekher, the original architect, who began what was to be a very long and drawn out process of construction. It took until 1368 for the foundation to be laid and it was another thirty years before the church tower was completed. Nicholas Gonzago of Wroclaw raised a vaulted ceiling over the altar in 1404, and in 1405 the cathedral was dedicated. Completion finally came in 1479–81 under the guidance of architects Joakim Grom and Ambrosius Rabisz of Wroclaw (a gallery topped by a vaulted ceiling was added by Hans Blekher in 1493).

Like the Armenian Cathedral, the Gothic Cathedral underwent numerous structural, sculptural, and artistic changes between the fourteenth and the twentieth century. The sixteenth century saw drastic alterations due to the fire of 1527 which caused extensive damage to the building, the tower, and the vaults of the gallery. Several chapels were added in the sixteenth and early seventeenth centuries because wealthy magnates and merchants sought to have private chapel tombs of their own inside or nearby the cathedral.

In 1619 Martin Campiano, a wealthy merchant, arranged for the services of architects Paolo Dominici Romano and Wojciech Kapinos for the purpose of adding the Campiano Chapel (Kaplitsa Kampianov) to the northern wall of the cathedral. The interior of Campiano Chapel was later used as a burial place and was altered and widened in the seventeenth and eighteenth centuries.

As beautiful as the interior is, the exterior is considered by many to have more artistic value. Tuscan-style pilasters rise from the ground floor and divide the façade into vertical partitions topped by a frieze and an attic with three oval-shaped medallions. Examples of Renaissance plastic art are the reliefs by Jan Pfister which portray the burial of Christ, his ascension, and his appearance before Mary Magdalene (these are located in a space between the pilasters).

Between 1609 and 1617 a chapel was built in the Renaissance style near the Gothic Cathedral. The beautiful Boimi Chapel was designed by architect Jan Pfister and was erected as a tomb for a prominent Lvov merchant of Hungarian descent, Yuri Boimi, his wife Jadwiga, and his son Paul. Portraits of Yuri and Jadwiga, credited to painter Jan Dziani, are still on the back façade of the chapel.

The façade is entirely covered with pieces of sculpture, reliefs, and stone carvings. The basic architectural design of the chapel is cubiform, with a cupola on an octagonal drum, double tiers and semicolumns on an arched portal. The sculptures of the interior are primarily the works of Jan Pfister and Lvov artists of the Renaissance.

The alabaster altar of the nearby Samoisky Chapel (Kaplitsa Zamoiskykh), built in 1592 and attributed to Jan Bely, is quite interesting. A relief with a portrait of the founder of the chapel depicting the Crucifixion is the main attraction but one should also appreciate the general design and exquisite taste of the small details of this lovely altar.

Significant changes in the architectural design and decoration of the Gothic Cathedral began in the eighteenth century. In 1765 many of the chapels located near the Gothic Cathedral were removed with the exception of the Boimi Chapel. Also, beginning in the same year, burials in the town were forbidden, hence the removal of the cathedral burial grounds. The beautiful walls of two-colored brick were plastered, badly damaging the original decorations. The belfry with the Gothic spire was replaced with a 65-meter-high (20 feet) tower topped by a rococo dome in 1767.

The interior also underwent major changes. A new, highly ornamented altar was installed as well as many new statues, most of them the work of sculptors Jan Obroczki and Matsei Palejowski. Stanislaw Stroinsky, a famous Lvov monumental painter, executed a series of murals on the walls and vaults. Other additions were made in the late eighteenth, nineteenth, and twentieth centuries. Many of the icons were painted by Yusef Hoinitski and Alois Reihan. The stained-glass windows were designed at the end of the nineteenth century by Jan Matejko and his pupils, Yusef Mekhkhoffer, Stanislaw Kachor-Batowski, and others. The marble statue of the bishop was executed by Peter Voitovich. The Gothic Cathedral underwent changes in construction and ornamentation for 550 years before it was finally completed.

Church of the Assumption

The earliest building of the Church of the Assumption (Uspenskaya Tserkov) dates back to the fourteenth century when Lvov was under the rule of the Galician princes. Two more churches followed the collapse of the first and the third burned down in 1571. The Stauropegia Fraternity raised the fourth Church of the Assumption in 1591. Completed in 1629 and consecrated two years later, the beautiful structure has survived to the present day.

The Stauropegia Fraternity was one of the strongest and most influential Orthodox communities and had many merchants and craftsmen among its members. So powerful was the fraternity that in the sixteenth and seventeenth centuries it had attained the privilege of a Stauropegion (this meant that it was not under the jurisdiction of the local bishops and was answerable only to the Holy Patriarch in Constantinople). Not only did the fraternity rule the church, it also carried on community work by setting up a school of "seven free sciences" for Ukrainians, a hospital, and a printing house.

Much of the building of the church was financed by Hetman Saghaidachny and Pavel, Jeremiah, and Simon Mogila, all wealthy Moldavian noblemen. Despite their generous contributions, work on the church was often interrupted due to lack of funds. In an attempt to solve the problem, the fraternity dispatched envoys to Fyodor Ioanovich, king of Muscovy, in 1592. The king agreed to contribute to the construction in money and furs. The internal wall of the central cupola bears the coats of arms of Russia, Moldavia, and the fraternity, together with the inscription "The Gracious Tsar and the Great Prince of Muscovy-Russia was the benefactor of this church."

The Church of the Assumption was designed and partially built by architect Paolo Cominici Romano. He supervised construction until 1597, when it was taken over by his father-in-law, Wojciech Kapinos. Ambrogio Przykhylny took charge a year later and the church was completed under his direction.

The design of the church, with its three cupolas, is typical of Ukrainian ecclesiastical structures. The main façade unfortunately faces the very narrow Ruthenian Street, which prevents one from viewing it in its full splendor. The huge wall is made of dark gray limestone, and full-length Tuscan-style pilasters contribute to its well-balanced proportions. Between the pilasters are semicircular blind arches with small windows and a Doric frieze above. There are interesting triglyphs and the metopes are filled in with ornate rosettes and reliefs depicting scenes from the Bible. The sculptors whose names are inscribed on the frieze are Yakov and Constantine Kulchitsky.

The bell tower, commonly known as the Kornyakt Tower, was built between 1572 and 1578 by architect Pietro di Barbona. The tower was damaged by Turkish artillery during the siege of 1672 and was later restored by architect Pietro Beber, who surmounted it with a fourth story. Restoration was again needed after the fire of 1779 and in 1783 the huge Kyrill bell (2 meters [6.5 feet] in diameter), cast by F. Polyansky of Lvov, was hung in the belfry.

The Chapel of the Three Saints (Kaplitsa Tryokh Svyatitelei) is difficult to find within the ensemble because it is hemmed in by modern houses. Passing through a small courtyard, you suddenly become aware of this interesting piece of architecture. The chapel is a small edifice styled very much along the lines of the classical Ukrainian three-frame (cruciform) wooden churches and, like the Cathedral of the Assumption, has three cupolas supported by octagonal drums.

The chapel was built between 1578 and 1591 under the supervision of architect Pietro Krasowsky and the financial aid of Kornyakt. Although the structure is typical of national Ukrainian design, it also shows many characteristics of the Renaissance. Low-set windows are joined by semicircular arches, and four pairs of semicolumns with capitals of palm leaves divide the façade into three, the middle part of which has the portal, which is surrounded by columns and graced with stone carvings.

One of the most popular attractions of the ensemble of the Church of the Assumption is the masterpieces of old Ukrainian painters. Alexander Lyanitsky painted the altar icons and the icon of Incarnation on the façade. The present altar is late eighteenth century and the icons at the side altars are seventeenth century. The silver cross (1638) is the work of Lvov silversmith Kasyanovich, and the huge portrait of Constantine Kornyakt is the work of Luka Dolinsky, a well-known West Ukrainian painter of the late eighteenth and early nineteenth centuries. The stained-glass windows, installed in 1930, complete with harmony the ensemble of the Church of the Assumption.

Cathedral of St. George

Bogdan Khmelnitsky Square is the site of one of the most beautiful architectural monuments in Lvov—the Cathedral of St. George (Sobor Svyatogo Yuriya). Erected on a dominant hill, the cathedral is not the first to have been built on that site.

In the late thirteenth century, when Galicia was under the rule of Prince Lev, a small beechwood church stood on the hill. The church was burned down when Casimir III took control of the town in 1340, but it was restored a year later. The groundwork for a new stone church was laid in

1363 and the new structure was completed in 1437. The church suffered the effects of three centuries of decay and deterioration and was demolished in the 1740s.

The Church of St. George was erected for the monks of the Basilian Order between 1746 and 1770. When the monks were transferred to the Monastery of St. Onufry in 1817, the building became a cathedral of the Greek Uniate Rite and the house next to the cathedral became the residence of the archbishop. The church was designed by the famous Lvov architect Bernard Meretyn. After his death in 1759, architect and sculptor Sebastian Fessinger completed the cupola, altar, and the interior. The church is designed in the shape of a Greek cross with a central circular drum supported by high arches. The chapels, situated in the corners of the cruciform design, and the central cupola are similar to the traditional Orthodox five-domed churches.

The stone figures of St. Anastasius and St. Leo on the façade are by the sculptor Pinzel as is the equestrian statue of St. George (Yuri) the Dragon Slayer which embellishes the attic, and the sculptured figures on the gate and main altar.

The cathedral's interior shows a varied style of artistic talent. The icon of Christ is the work of Frantiszek Smuglevich, a painter of the second half of the eighteenth century. His contemporary, Luka Dolinsky, did the series of oval icon paintings, and in 1876 paintings by Stanislaw Fabjanski were added. Finally, paintings by Mikhail Osinchuk joined the cathedral collection in 1933.

The Cathedral of St. George has witnessed several historical events. The basement of the northern block was used as the meeting place of the secretly held Congress of the Communist Party of Eastern Galicia in 1921. The delegates to the congress were arrested and the trial came to be known as the St. George Trial. In 1946 the clergy of the western regions of the Ukraine met in the church and formally proclaimed their break with the Vatican (ties that were bonded in 1596) and their reunion with the Orthodox Church.

Church of the Dominicans

The Church of the Dominicans (Dominikansky Kostyol) was built on part of the site of the former fourteenth-century Gothic Cathedral which was destroyed in 1745 because of its decaying condition (this is part of the same site discussed in the building of the Cathedral of St. George).

The church, designed by Jan de Witte and built between 1748 and 1764, suffered fires in 1766 and 1778. The fires damaged not only the church but also the monastery with its Gothic vaults and arches. The ground plan is that of an elongated Roman cross, adjoined on each of its two sides by three deep-set chapels. Paired columns culminate in gilded sculptures and the large elliptical dome is a prominent feature of Lvov's skyline.

The interior of the church is excessively lavish. An extensive collection of valuable sculpture includes the four figures at the main altar, characteristic of the school of Macey Paleyowsky. When the fourteenth-century Gothic Cathedral was torn down, several tombs dating from the sixteenth and early seventeenth centuries were installed in the Church of the Dominicans.

A most beautiful example of the later works of sculpture is the marble tomb of Dunin-Borkovskaya, dated 1816, the work of Bertol Torwaldsen. Also on display is a monument to the Polish painter Arthur Grottger, the work of Valerian Gadomski (1880).

Church of St. Mary and Church of St. John the Baptist

The Podzamche (which means "under the castle") is one of the oldest sections of Lvov. In this area stand two churches whose history reaches far back to the early days of the town—the Church of St. Mary (Kostyol Marii Snezhnoi) and the Church of St. John the Baptist (Kostyol Ioanna Krestitelyn).

St. Mary's is located on a small hill facing the Square of the 300th Anniversary of the Ukraine's Reunification with Russia, which is the beginning of Bogdan Khemelnitsky Street. The church was probably rebuilt from an ancient Russian church but there is no doubt that it functioned as a Catholic church and was the religious center for the German colony in Lvov. Its design is typically that of Western European ecclesiastical structures. Almost nothing is known of St. Mary's original architectural design. The church has undergone reconstruction over the centuries, the latest of which was at the end of the nineteenth century when architect Yu. Zakharievich remodeled the building in pseudo-Romanesque style.

The Church of St. John the Baptist has an interesting history. Originally a church of the Orthodox Basilian Monks, it was presented as a gift by Prince Lev Daniilovich to his wife Constance. Constance, daughter of the Hungarian King Bela IV, had the building remodeled to suit the needs of the Dominican missionaries. The church acquired forms of the Romanesque style. The small, one-naved structure was simple in design and decoration but little remains of its old style. A major overhaul of the building was carried out by Zakharievich in 1886–87. While its initial charm is forever lost, visitors can still view the church's old icons in the chancel and two male portraits in the vestry which date back to 1637 and 1647.

Church of St. Nicholas

One of the most interesting structures remaining of the old Ukrainian culture is the Church of St. Nicholas (Tserkov Svyatogo Nikolaya). Built in 1292, it existed until the fourteenth century as the family church of the Lvov princes.

Little remains of the original edifice. The general ground plan, the foundation, and the lower parts of the walls were discovered in 1924. The last structure to be erected as the Church of St. Nicholas was built in the seventeenth and early eighteenth centuries. A vestry was remodeled in 1776 and after a fire in 1788 a cupola was added in 1800. A cupola also topped the central apse and the façade was supported by flat pilasters. The interior was of the typical eighteenth-century rococo style. During World War II the church was damaged but has since been restored. Much of the external form was affected but the basic architectural structure and design remained intact.

Church and Monastery of St. Onufry

This church and monastery are of historical interest, having contained the tomb of Ivan Fyodorov, Russia's first printer. Fyodorov left Moscow in 1567 and lived in Zabludov until the end of 1572, when he moved to Lvov. He settled in the Podzamche and set up his printing press in one of the cells of the St. Onufry Monastery. Later, he set up another printing shop near the Church of the Assumption.

Fyodorov spent several years in Ostrog, returning to Lvov toward the end of his life and died there in 1583. He was buried in the monastery cemetery and remained there until it was done away with in the eighteenth century. His tombstone was moved to the church, where in 1883 it was put into the floor of the Trinity Chapel. During reconstruction work in 1902, the tombstone was blocked in by a new wall and unfortunately it has not survived; a replica is on display at the Lvov Museum of History.

Church of St. Parasceva Pjatnisa

Also located in the Podzamche, at 63 Bogdan Khmelnitsky, is the Church of St. Parasceva Pjatnisa (Tserkov Svyato: Praskovii or Pyatnitskaya Tserkov), the last Orthodox church of the district.

In the thirteenth century a church made of quarry stone stood on the site. The old church had an underground passage to Prince's Hill and was heavily fortified. The Church of St. Parasceva Pjatnisa was built on the foundations of the previous church and was completed between 1643 and 1645. Vasily Lupul, a Moldavian nobleman, contributed to its construction and thus was given a place for Moldavian rulers who were later buried on the premises. Their coat of arms—the sun, the moon, and a crown—decorates the southern wall. The church is most famous for its gold-plated wooden iconostasis consisting of more than seventy individual fragments.

Hill of Glory

One of the most sacred grounds in Lvov and indeed all of the Soviet Union is the Hill of Glory (Kholm Slavy). Here Red Army soldiers and partisans are buried. It was first used as a military burial ground during World War I and between 1914 and 1915 more than two thousand soldiers who died in battle in Galicia were buried here. The common grave is marked by a obelisk to the left of the entrance to the cemetery.

The Hill of Glory is also the final resting place of Nikolai Kuznetsov, Hero of the Soviet Union, whose remains were transferred there in 1960. In the center are the graves of others who have earned the title of Hero of the Soviet Union—twenty-six in all.

Three times a year (on February 23—Soviet Army Day; May 29— Victory Day; July 27—Lvov Liberation Day) thousands of people come to the Hill of Glory to pay tribute to those who gave their lives for their country.

THEATER, OPERA, AND BALLET

Maria Zankowieczka Ukrainian Drama Theater

Lvov is a city rich in appreciation of the performing arts. The Ukrainian Drama Theater, at 1 Lesi Ukrainki Street, is named after Maria Zankowieczka. The theater stands on what was the site of the Lower Castle, a complex of Gothic buildings that were built in the fourteenth and fifteenth centuries. Fire destroyed the Lower Castle in 1564. Several restorations were attempted but it fell into decay and was torn down in the early nineteenth century. In the years 1836–42 the theater was built in late Viennese Empire style by architects L. Pikhl and I. Zaltsman. The theater was used for opera and drama until 1900. The building was later redesigned to show films and it was not until 1940, following another restoration, that it resumed its original purpose as a theater of the performing arts.

Lvov Academic Opera and Ballet Theater

Dedicated to Ivan Franko, the Lvov Academic Opera and Ballet Theater, located on Lenin Prospect, is architecturally characteristic of the late nineteenth century. It was built by architect J. Gorgolewsky between 1897 and 1900. The façade is quite beautiful with several niches, columns, pilasters, garlands, statues, and reliefs. Figures of Life and Art, executed by the sculptor A. Popel, are topped by a relief of the nine Muses and the entire structure is surmounted by large bronze statues of Glory, Victory, and Love, the work of Ukrainian sculptor Peter Voitovich.

USEFUL INFORMATION

Hotels

Intourist, 1 Mitskevicha Square
Ukraina, 4 Mitskevicha Square
Verkhovina, 13 Lenin Prospect
Pervomaiskaya, 21 Lenin Prospect
Dnieper, 45 Lenin Prospect
Lvov, 3 Semisotletiya Lvova Square
Varshavskaya, 4 Vossoyedinenia Square

Restaurants

Intourist (Hotel Intourist), 1 Mitskevicha Square, Tel: 2–67–52
Moskva, 6/7 Mitskevicha Square, Tel: 2–66–35
Pervomaisky (Hotel Pervomaiskaya), 19 Lenin Prospect, Tel: 2–85–21;
    4–20–61
Lvov (Hotel Lvov), 3 Semisotletiya Lvova Square, Tel: 49–15–92
Visoky Zamok, Visoky Zamok Park

Museums

Lvov Branch of the Central Lenin Museum, 20 Lenin Prospect: Open daily
    except Mondays from 11 A.M. to 7 P.M.
Museum of History, 4/6 Rynok Square. Open daily except Wednesdays
    from 10 A.M. to 6 P.M.
Ukrainian Art Museum, 42 Dragomanova Street. Open daily, except Fri-
    days, from 11 A.M. to 6 P.M.; Thursdays from 11 A.M. to 5 P.M.
Museum of Ethnography and Crafts, 15 Lenin Prospect. Open daily,
    except Mondays, from 11 A.M. to 6 P.M.
Art Gallery, 3 Stefanika Street. Open daily, except Mondays and the last
    day of each month, from 11 A.M. to 6 P.M.; Tuesdays from 12 noon
    to 6 P.M.
Literary Museum of Ivan Franko, 152 Ivan Franko Street. Open daily,
    except Tuesdays, from 11 A.M. to 7 P.M.; Mondays from 11 A.M. to
    3 P.M.

Theaters and Circus

Ivan Franko Theater of Opera and Ballet, Lenin Prospect
Ukrainian Drama Theater, 1 Lesi Ukrainki Street
Russian Drama Theater of the Soviet Army, 36 Pervogo Maya Street
Ukrainian Youth Theater, 11 Gorky Street
Circus, 83 Pervogo Maya Street

Cinemas

Imeni Lesi Ukrainka, 6 Mitskevicha Square
Ukraina, 1 Lenin Prospect
Dnepr, 5 Lenin Prospect
Imeni Y. Galana, 131 Lenin Street
Spartak, 5 Lenin Prospect
Mir, Semisotletiya Lvova Square
Imeni Kopernika, 9 Kopernika Street.
Kiev, 8 Shevchenko Prospect
Lvov, 8 Parkhomenko Street (Stryisk Park)
Druzhba, 43a Dzerzhinskogo (Cinema in the Park)

Shops

Central Department Store, 6 1st May Street
Salon of Ukrainian Art, Mitskevicha Square
Souvenir Kiosk "Kashtan" (foreign currency only), Hotel Intourist, 1 Mitskevicha Square
Children's Shop, 5 Mitskevicha Square
House of Books, 8 Mitskevicha Square
Bookshop of Literature from Socialist Countries, 16 Shevchenko Prospect

Transportation and Communications

Airport Agency, 2 Pobedy Square, Tel: 4–13–40
Railway Station, Privoknalnaya Square, Tel: 4–99–11
Central Post Office, 1 Slovatsky Street, Tel: 3–32–21

KISHINEV

GENERAL INFORMATION

Kishinev, the capital of the Moldavian Soviet Socialist Republic, is located along the eastern foothills of the Kodry Mountains in the Bik River Valley. Like many major cities of the Soviet Union, Kishinev has been almost totally reconstructed since the end of World War II. Although Moldavia's agricultural products are world famous, the republic is also important industrially. Kishinev is the center of industrial, cultural, and scientific life in the republic. Moldavians pride themselves not only on their tradition of agriculture and industry, but on their well-preserved folkways which are still apparent in the costumes and handcrafts of the rural areas. Kishinev provides many opportunities for Moldavians to carry on the traditional art and music of the culture. Visitors to the capital will see numerous exhibits of folk art and handcrafts. Frequent folk song and dance festivals are also held in Kishinev. One might expect a modern city of 300,000 inhabitants to be a hurried place. This, however, is not the case in Kishinev. The atmosphere is relaxed and extremely congenial, as is typical of the southern republics. In addition to the interesting sites in and around Kishinev, the visitor will enjoy the abundant food and wines which are very much part of Moldavian hospitality.

HISTORY IN BRIEF

The first historical documents concerning Kishinev date back to 1420. However, the history of the city is inextricable from the history of Moldavia. Legends corroborate history with the saying that "Moldavia lay in the path of all misfortunes." For centuries foreigners invaded Moldavian lands. From the sixteenth to eighteenth centuries Moldavia, better known as Bessarabia, was part of the Ottoman Empire. Tied through culture, economics, and military defense with the Russians and Ukrainians, it is not strange that the Russo-Turkish War of 1806–12 was the turning point in Moldavian history, for it signaled the expulsion of the Turkish sultans.

During the nineteenth century, following annexation to Russia in 1812, the Moldavian population grew, towns proliferated, and agriculture increased along with the development of trade and crafts. Many newly liberated serfs migrated to the southern portions of the territory because of the abundance of agricultural lands and the mild climate. Nevertheless, a cruel autocracy under the tsars adversely affected the people. The social climate was ripe for revolutionary activity by the end of the nineteenth century.

In 1901 the first underground publication of *Iskra* was organized in Kishinev with several issues to follow along with other works written by Lenin. Not only was there revolutionary sympathy in Kishinev, but the city was strategically located near the Rumanian border, so that publications could be circulated abroad. In December 1902, a committee of the Russian Social Democratic Labor Party was founded in Kishinev. Its function was to organize mass movements among Moldavian workers during the 1905 Revolution. Despite the failure of the uprising, the Kishinev RSDLP remained fairly powerful. When the October Revolution of 1917 succeeded, Soviet power was proclaimed in Moldavia in January 1918. However, the Civil War resulted in the takeover of part of Moldavia, still known as Bessarabia, by the Rumanian throne. The remaining area of Moldavia which had reestablished Soviet power in 1924 was incorporated into the Ukraine under Soviet rule. Thus the situation remained for twenty-two years. Numerous Soviet-inspired uprisings in Bessarabia resulted in suppression and persecution. In 1940 the Moldavians were reunited under the Soviet system. The reunion was interrupted from 1941 to 1944 during World War II when Moldavia was occupied by German troops. During this time all industrial and agricultural enterprise was demolished. A totally rebuilt economy has been effected since 1944. Equally rebuilt and decidedly modernized have been the cities, towns, and rural villages of Moldavia.

MUSEUMS AND PLACES OF INTEREST

Victory Square, center city

This is the main square of Kishinev where state holidays are celebrated, and where public proclamations are made. The square is also noted for the monument to Lenin, unveiled on October 12, 1949. The monument was designed by S. D. Mercurov and constructed by A. D. Shusiev and V. D. Turchaninov. At the foot of the monument young people joining Pioneer or Komsomol organizations take their oath of allegiance. The western side of Victory Square houses the historic Victory Arch. Erected in 1840, the arch was designed by Zaushtkevitch and paid for by donations from the people of Kishinev. Behind the arch is a small park, at the center of which is a nineteenth-century cathedral designed by Melnikov, now the Museum of Fine Art Exhibition Hall.

Pushkin Park, corner of Lenin Prospect and Gogol Street

Pushkin Park is dedicated to the memory of the poet, who spent three years in exile in Kishinev (September 1820–June 1823). A monument to Pushkin is located on the west side of the park. Erected in 1885, it was designed by A. Opekushin and paid for by citizens' donations. The monument is a bronze bust set upon a granite column of Corinthian style. At the Gogol Street entrance to the park is a statue of Stephan the Great, ruler of Moldavia from 1457 to 1504. During the period of his reign many victories were wrested from the Turks and Tatars. Stephan is also known for promoting friendly relations with Russia. At the northeastern border of the park is a statue of Karl Marx. Within Pushkin Park is a row of statues called the Alley of Classics. Twelve bronze busts mounted on red granite bases represent the most prominent Moldavian military and cultural heroes. The Alley of Classics was officially opened in April 1958. In the eastern section of the park near Lenin Avenue is the Burial Ground of Soviet Soldiers who died during the liberation of Moldavia in 1944.

Avenue of Youth, northeast of Pushkin Park

A sculptural ensemble greets the visitor upon arrival in this area bordering the Bik River. A large monument to the heroes of the Lenin Komsomol is dramatically designed with the bronze figure of a young girl holding a torch. The girl is mounted on a granite base. The foot of the granite pedestal is encircled by sculptural representations of Civil War heroes, Bessarabian workers, and Soviet soldiers. The ensemble was completed in June 1959 under the direction of L. Dubinovsky and F. Naumov.

Mazaraki Church, on the banks of the Bik River, northeast of Frunze Street

This church was built in the latter half of the eighteenth century by Sardar Vasili Mazaraki, and has been preserved as an architectural relic. Its historical function provides ethnographic information concerning Moldavia during the Ottoman period of rule. "Sardar" was a title granted to distinguished raiders of the Turkman tribes whose genealogy and social structure were characteristic of the tribes found in Central Asia. "Mazar" was a term used to indicate a shrine of the Islamic religion, generally built as a memorial at the grave of an *ishan,* the head of a dervish order. Islamic worshipers could visit a number of mazars as the equivalent of a pilgrimage to Mecca. Many mazars became the objects of local cults, thus attracting pilgrims with their monetary offerings who hoped to partake of the magic housed in the shrine.

Monument to Bulgarian Volunteers, opposite Shipka cinema, northeast of Mazaraki Church

The tall obelisk built on the site of the former Kishinev racetrack marks the spot where Kishinev and Bulgarian volunteer detachments were formed at the announcement of the Russo-Turkish War of 1877. Nearby is a chapel built in 1882 to commemorate the liberation of Bulgaria, Serbia, and Montenegro from Turkish rule.

Lenin Komsomol Park of Culture and Recreation, southwest of Sadovaya Street

From Sadovaya Street (which can be reached by trolley #6 or #10) a flight of stone stairs leads into the park. At the center of the park is a lake for boating, fishing, and swimming. In addition to the lake the park offers many recreational facilities including a 7,000-seat amphitheater, cinema, dance platform, indoor gymnasium, restaurant, and café. There is also a motorcycle race course used for international and Soviet competition. An important feature of the park is the Moldavian Exhibition of Economic Achievements. It is located on the southwest side of the lake and can be reached by foot or microtrain.

Lenin Prospect

This is the main street of Kishinev, intersected by Gogol, Pushkin, Kotovsky, and Ismailovskaya streets. The latter two feed the Kotovsky Highway, which goes southwest toward Lensheny, a town on the Rumanian-Moldavian border. Proceeding southwest on Lenin Prospect from Pushkin Park at Gogol Street, one will find the Planetarium on the north side and the Art Museum on the south side of the avenue. Here are exhibits of Revolutionary, Russian, Moldavian, and Western European art. Turning south on Gogol Street one will find the Krupskaya Library of the Republic, named for Lenin's wife, and the Puppet Theater. Once again on Lenin Prospect, past the Central Square and across Pushkin Street is a cluster of important buildings. These include the Central Telephone and Post Office, the Moldavian Philharmonic, and Chekhov Russian Drama Theater on the north side; the State Bank and Pushkin Moldavian Music and Drama Theater. Where Lenin Prospect merges with Negrutzy Boulevard, one will come upon Liberation Square. In the center is a tall obelisk with a palm branch on top. This is the Monument of Liberation, erected in May 1965, to commemorate the Soviet Army Liberation of Moldavia from the German occupation. At the eastern end of the square is the monument to Grigory Ivanovich Kotovsky, a bronze equestrian statue, erected in February 1954. Kotovsky is a favorite hero of the Moldavian people, a revolutionary legend in his own time. The monument is located near the old branch office of the Kishinev-Odessa Railway where Kotovsky was arrested in 1906 and sentenced to a dozen years' hard labor for revolutionary activity. Where Negrutzy Boulevard becomes Muncheskaya Street one will find the present Kishinev Railway Terminal. Reconstructed in 1948, the terminal stands on the square that formerly was a meeting place for revolutionaries and workers involved in the general strike in 1905, and the scene of victory for the Kishinev Soviet troops who thwarted an attack by the Transylvanian Guard in 1918.

USEFUL INFORMATION

Hotel Kishinev, 7 Negrutzy Boulevard
Hotel Moldova, 8a Lenin Prospect
Motel Strugurash, Kotovsky Highway, on the outskirts of Lenin Komsomol
    Park
Campsite, Chernovtsy Highway, 30 kilometers (19 miles) north of Kishinev
Restaurant Kishinev, Hotel Kishinev
Restaurant Moldova, Hotel Moldova
Restaurant Strugurash, Motel Strugurash

CITIES ALONG
THE WESTERN FRONTIER
Brest, Uzhgorod, Chop, Chernovtsy

BREST—General Information

Brest is the point of entry for motorists and railway passengers entering the Soviet Union via Poland. A bridge spanning the West Bug River forms the entry zone. At the border is a checkpoint where documents are inspected and where the traveler may obtain information and exchange currency. During high travel season (July and August) these procedures may take as long as ten hours because of the volume of tourists.

In addition to Brest's fame as a World War II memorial, the city is the administrative and cultural center of the Brest Region of the Byelorussian S.S.R. Not only is Brest a vital trade and transportation center, owing to its strategic location along major highways, railroad, and inland water routes, it is also a highly industrialized city. Among the chief industries are dairy processing, meat packing, flour milling, and bread baking, along with factories for the production of carpets, clothing, knitwear, and forced concrete. Culturally, Brest is known for its pedagogical institute, railway vocational school, medical and musical training facilities, along with a drama theater, local museum, and numerous cinemas, public libraries, and cultural associations.

HISTORY IN BRIEF

Brest is a very old Byelorussian city; in 1017 it was a fortress on the border between Poland and Lithuania. The city grew as east-west trade routes developed. The town enjoyed only a brief period of uninterrupted growth. In 1240 Brest and its environs were demolished by the Tatars. In 1275 Prince Vladimir of Volinsk ordered the rebuilding of the town. In 1379 Brest was again devastated by invading knights of the Teutonic Order. The only structures to survive were Prince Vladimir's stone tower and pentagonal castle, which remained intact until the Brest Fortress was erected in 1836. From the end of the fourteenth century to the end of the eighteenth century, Brest languished as a feudal backwash. In 1795 the area was reunited with Russia, and Brest was designated as the provincial center. As the town grew in importance as a trade and strategic military location, Russian military engineers recommended the building of a new fortress. However, the war with Napoleon interrupted the plan. It was not until 1836 that the cornerstone was laid for the new fortress, which was completed in 1842. The Brest Fortress was a carefully engineered project which has been continuously reconstructed and improved ever since. Brest continued to occupy a position of administrative, cultural, and military importance until its seizure and occupation by the Germans from 1941 to 1944. Since the end of the war, Brest has been completely rebuilt.

BREST FORTRESS AND DEFENSE MUSEUM

The Brest Fortress is the principal attraction of the city. It is located on the southwestern outskirts on the Street of the Brest Fortress Heroes. The saga of the Brest Fortress is perceived through the numerous exhibits of the Defense Museum and the memorabilia on display within the fortress itself, as well as through the story of the attack on the fortress and the ensuing struggle of the city.

In June 1941 most servicemen stationed at the Brest Fortress actually resided in summer camps outside the city. Only two partially complete infantry regiments were inside the fortress. West of Brest, along the Polish border, twenty-nine German High Command Divisions were poised for attack. At dawn on June 22 the onslaught was launched on the sleeping town. Soviet troops repulsed the enemy at the Terepolsky Gate and forced them back to the river. A second assault was launched on June 29. This time nearly all of the Soviet defenders were killed or captured. By late July the occupation of the fortress was complete. The devastation of the city followed. Brest was liberated on July 28, 1944. The fortress was virtually in ruins. Certain inscriptions scratched by the defenders on the remaining walls have been preserved.

The Brest Fortress Defense Museum was opened on November 8, 1956. It is located in a building reconstructed from the engineers' barracks in the citadel. Today the museum consists of ten exhibit halls divided into the following four departments: History of Brest and the Brest Fortress; the German Attack on the U.S.S.R., Border Fighting, and Fortress Defense June-July 1941; Participation of Fortress Defenders and Battles of the Great Patriotic War 1941–1945; War Veterans.

USEFUL INFORMATION

Hotel

Hotel Bug, 2 Lenin Street

Restaurant

Restaurant Bug, Hotel Bug, 2 Lenin Street

Museums and Theaters

Brest Regional Museum of Local Lore, 34 Lenin Street
Museum of the Brest Fortress Defense, Geroyev Brestkoy Kreposti Street
House of Engineering, 1 Pushkin Street
Brest Drama Theater, 21 Lenin Street

Communications

General Post Office, 10 Moskovskaya Street, Tel: 20–52
International Telephone Office, 32 Lenin Street

UZHGOROD—General Information and History in Brief

Uzhgorod is located at the foot of the Carpathian Mountains on the banks of the Uzh River. It is situated amid the forests, orchards, and vineyards of the Ukraine. The town serves as the checkpoint for motorists and railway passengers entering the Soviet Union from Czechoslovakia.

Uzhgorod is an old Slavic town which separated from Kiev Rus during the eleventh century and was for a long time under Hungarian rule. At numerous times throughout history the peoples of Transcarpathia rebelled against their assorted rulers, but met with defeat and increased suppression. The Hungarian Revolt in 1919 led to the establishment of Soviet rule in Transcarpathia. After several months, however, Soviet rule was disrupted by counter-revolutionary forces, and Transcarpathia was incorporated into Czechoslovakia. In 1938 the territory was annexed to Hungary. Following World War II, the Transcarpathian Ukraine was reunited with the Ukrainian S.S.R. Uzhgorod was then designated as the administrative center of the Transcarpathian Region of the Ukraine.

The main economic resource of Uzhgorod, and indeed of all of Transcarpathia, is forestland. Thus, the primary industries are timbering, woodworking, and furniture making. Uzhgorod boasts such cultural and educational facilities as the Transcarpathian School of Applied Arts, School of Music, the Uzhgorod State University, and various primary, secondary, and specialized schools. A rapidly growing feature of Transcarpathia is the development of its three hundred mineral water springs which provide carbon dioxide, sulfur, methane, and salts with curative properties. The healthful environment of mountain air, mild climate, and mineral water springs has led to the burgeoning of Transcarpathia as a resort area. Sanitaria, hotels, vacation homes, and boarding houses have been constructed with more planned for the near future.

PLACES OF INTEREST

The most important sites are the Hungarian Castle, a relic of ninth-century feudalism which is now the Transcarpathian History and Geography Museum; the Uzhgorod Picture Gallery; and the House of Folk Art. These museums are in center city along Kalinin Street and the Leningradskaya Embankment. One will also find here along the main thoroughfares the Philharmonic Society, State University, and Ukrainian Drama Theater.

USEFUL INFORMATION

Hotels

Hotel Kiev, 1 Koryatovich Street
Hotel Verkhovina, 5 Theater Square
Hotel Uzhgorod, 2 Bogdana Square

Restaurants

Kiev, Hotel Kiev, 1 Koryatovich Street
Verkhovina, Hotel Verkhovina, 5 Theater Square
Uzhgorod, Hotel Uzhgorod, 2 Bogdana Square

CHOP

The principal importance of Chop to the traveler is its function as a checkpoint for those entering the Soviet Union by automobile or railway from Hungary or Czechoslovakia. Chop is a rather new Transcarpathian town located at the foot of the Carpathian Mountains. It is essentially a border town where railway and highway facilities converge between the Soviet Union and Eastern Europe. The city has no tourist facilities.

CHERNOVTSY—General Information and History in Brief

After crossing the border checkpoint between Rumania and the Ukraine at Vadul-Siret en route north, Chernovtsy is the first major Soviet city the visitor will reach, about 37 kilometers (22 miles) from the frontier. On the Prut River, the city functions as the administrative center of the Chernovtsy Region of the Ukrainian S.S.R. The primary industries are food growing and food processing, although a great deal of manufacturing has been introduced as a result of the postwar reconstruction. Chernovtsy has numerous educational facilities, including a State University, medical institute, and postsecondary technical schools, along with the customary primary and secondary schools. Chernovtsy is also noted for its Bukovina Song and Dance Ensemble, a group dedicated to the preservation and popularization of the rich Bukovina folk heritage.

The site of present-day Chernovtsy was a part of Kiev Rus during the eleventh century and later, during the twelfth and thirteenth centuries, it became part of the Galtis-Volin principality. Numerous invasions disrupted the settlement, starting with the Mongol-Tatars in the thirteenth century. Then followed the Hungarian feudal lords in 1352. A period of Turkish rule was later established, only to be succeeded by the Austro-German occupation. What particularly attracted foreigners to the area was the abundance of arable farmland and the plentiful beech forests. The latter, called *buk* in Russian, lent the name Bukovina to the region. Following the withdrawal of the Austrians, Hungarians, and Germans after World War I, Chernovtsy was the site of a popular assembly which proclaimed the merger of Bukovina with the Soviet Ukraine. This event took place in October 1918. That same month, however, Rumania invaded Bukovina and annexed the territory. In June 1940 Northern Bukovina was reunited with the Soviet Ukraine after a diplomatic agreement between the Soviet and Rumanian governments. In July 1941 Chernovtsy was captured by German and Rumanian troops. Most of the industry was destroyed, and the town was left in economic ruins. In March 1944 Chernovtsy was liberated. Since that time the devastated areas of Bukovina have been reconstructed, new industrial plants built and old ones rebuilt. New housing, cultural, and educational facilities have enhanced the region.

MUSEUMS AND PLACES OF INTEREST

Among the most picturesque areas of Chernovtsy is Central Square, flanked by its original (and reconstructed) eighteenth-century buildings. One can visit the Chernovtsy State University, which was formerly the residence of the Bukovina Metropolitan. Other structures include the Church of St. Barbara, Town Hall, Musical Drama Theater, National Theater, and Palace of Young Pioneers. The Museum of History and Geography contains exhibits collected from all over the Bukovina region.

Driving north from Chernovtsy about 37 kilometers (22 miles) one will come to the town of Novoselitsa. It is approximately the same distance between Novoselitsa and the small town of Khotin. Situated along the craggy embankment of the Dniester River, Khotin is the site of a fourteenth-century fortress which can be observed from the highway. Continuing north, about 67 kilometers (40 miles) from Novoselitsa is Kamenets-Podolski, one of the most picturesque towns in the Ukraine. The town was built during the twelfth century and many of the ancient sites have been preserved. The section of Kamenets-Podolski where the old monuments are located is especially dramatic as it is situated among the stark, rocky riverbanks. The fourteenth-century fortress rests on one of these hillocks and has been made into a history museum. The central portion of the town is steeped in the greenery of a seemingly timeless pastoral painting. Here one will find the Dominican Church, the sixteenth-century Peter and Paul Church, an old Catholic church, and the "Turkish Bridge" which crosses the Smotrich River.

USEFUL INFORMATION

Hotels

Hotel Chervona-Bukovina, 1 Central Square
Hotel Intourist, 141 Lenin Street
Hotel Kiev, 46 Lenin Street

Campsite

The Chernovtsy camping facility is located on the eastern outskirts of the city along the Chernovtsy-Novoselitsa Road, approximately 2 kilometers (1.2 miles) from the city limit.

Restaurants

Bukovina, Hotel Intourist, 141 Lenin Street
Kiev, Hotel Kiev, 46 Lenin Street

Café

Chervona, Hotel Chervona-Bukovina, 1 Central Square

SOVIET CENTRAL ASIA
Tashkent, Samarkand

TASHKENT—General Information

Tashkent is the capital of the Uzbek Soviet Socialist Republic and is probably the most heavily traveled tourist city in Soviet Asia. Located in the Chirchik River valley in the foothills of the Tien-Sien mountains, at an altitude of 525 meters (1,575 feet) above sea level, the city covers an area of 240 square kilometers (150 square miles) and has a population of 1,385,000. It is the fourth largest city in the U.S.S.R., ranking after Moscow, Leningrad and Kiev, representing over one hundred nationalities. In terms of area, it is the third largest after Moscow and Leningrad.

The climate in Tashkent is fairly representative of the climate throughout the entire republic of Uzbekistan. Summers are usually long and hot, with an average temperature of 30 degrees C. (86 degrees F.) and often reaching 42 degrees C. (108 degrees F.) in July. Winter temperatures sometimes fall below 0 degrees C. (32 degrees F.) to − 10 degrees to − 15 degrees C. (5 to 10 degrees F.). The city rarely sees snow although the mountains have a heavy snowcap.

Today Tashkent is one of the largest industrial centers of the Soviet Union. The major industry is mechanical engineering, which covers the production of agricultural machinery, mining equipment, excavators, cranes, and textile machinery. As an educational center Tashkent ranks high, with seventeen institutions of higher education including the Lenin State University which was founded in 1920.

HISTORY IN BRIEF

The seventh century A.D. saw Tashkent emerge as a major center of trade and an important intermediary between the tribes of Central Asia. Its wealth was to attract many foreign invaders and the city was often under siege. By 700 A.D. Tashkent had established economic and cultural ties with Siberia, Eastern Europe, China, and the Byzantine Empire. The eighth century was one of turmoil for Tashkent as Arab invaders captured the city and spread Islam throughout the whole of Central Asia. Consolidating their gains during the ninth and early tenth centuries, the Arab conquerors founded the state of Samanides with its capital in Bukhara. Tashkent became part of the newly formed state and again flourished as a center of trade and culture.

At this time the city was moderate in size. The center, called *ark*, was surrounded by a fortified wall. The inner city, or *shahristan*, adjoined the *ark*.

As Genghis Khan swept across Central Asia in the early thirteenth century, Tashkent fell under the control of the Mongol invaders and became part of the Mongol Empire. The city again underwent change in the fourteenth century with the creation of the empire of Tamerlane (Timur). After the death of Tamerlane and especially after the assassination of Ulugh Beg in 1449, a fifty-year period of feudal strife began. By the beginning of the sixteenth century, Tashkent had become part of the large feudal kingdom of the Shaibani dynasty.

In the mid-sixteenth century Russia (Muscovy) decided to establish relations with the cities of Central Asia, and in 1561 and 1575 the ruler of Tashkent, Derwish Khan, sent diplomatic missions to Moscow. Economic and cultural links with the Eastern nations, Europe, and Russia developed so rapidly that by the eighteenth century Tashkent had eighteen caravansaries, some 4,548 stalls, and was developing crafts such as weaving, tanning, and casting. Aside from trade, Tashkent approached the Russian tsar for technical and military aid, and in 1800 word was received that the request would be honored.

While these agreements were being secured with Russia, a powerful neighbor, the Kokand khanate, was conspiring to take control of Tashkent; and in 1814 the Kokand ruler, Alim Khan, seized the city. Tashkent was made into a stronghold, and a new citadel, the *urda*, was erected on the left bank of the Ankhor Canal. Four gates were added to the city wall to supplement the existing eight and the city was divided into four administrative units: Besh Agach, Kukcha, Sheikantaur, and Sibzar.

By 1847 the population had reached 70,000 and signs of internal discontent with the feudal regime were becoming apparent. Mohammed Yusup, a weaver, led a popular revolt which lasted for fourteen days before it was suppressed. However, Kokand rule was ended a short time later when, in 1865, Russia annexed Turkestan. A new era of economic development began for Tashkent and with the newly built Transcaspian and Orenburg railways connecting Central Asia and the industrial centers of Russia, the city as well as the entire Turkestan province entered the Russian market. In 1866 the very lucrative slave market in Tashkent was closed down, slavery was abolished, and all slaves in the city were freed.

In 1867 Tashkent emerged as the political and administrative center of Turkestan, and with its growing importance the city saw the establishment of industrial enterprises such as cotton ginneries, tanneries, oil extracting factories, and breweries. During the 1870s Tashkent was recognized as an influential cultural and scientific center. The Central Asian Polytechnical Society was founded, an astronomical observatory began functioning in 1873, and the first secondary schools and medical institutions were opened in the 1890s.

With the increase of industry and trade a working class began to emerge. Sanitary conditions were poor and disease was a major problem. Running water was nonexistent and there was no sewage system to speak of. The streets remained dark at night and no plans were made for illuminating them.

In 1903 the first Social Democratic organization was established in Tashkent and soon after other similar-type groups were formed. The Russian Revolution of 1905 was strongly felt in Tashkent as numerous labor strikes spread and political demonstrations were organized. The relative failure of the 1905 Revolution did not, by any means, put an end to the movement and by 1910 numerous Social Democratic organizations were once again active. In March 1917 the Tashkent Soviet of Soldiers' and Workers' Deputies was formed and soon afterward the Soviet of Moslem Workers' Deputies and the Soviet of Peasants' Deputies were organized. The governor-general representing the tsarist government was deposed and arrested and a dual power structure was set up on April 7 when a Committee of Russia's Provisional Government was formed in Tashkent.

As a result of the national demarcation of Central Asia, the Uzbek Soviet Socialist Republic was formed in October 1924. In May 1925 it joined the Soviet Union, and Yuldash Akhunbabayev, a leading public figure and statesman, was elected president of the republic. Tashkent was named the capital of Uzbekistan and has remained to this day the leading industrial and cultural center of the republic.

MUSEUMS AND PLACES OF INTEREST

Alisher Navoi Opera House and Theater Square

The Alisher Navoi Opera House is located in Theater Square at 31 Pravdy Vostoka Street, the customary starting point for excursions.

Designed by and constructed under the supervision of architect A. Shchyusev, the Opera House opened in 1947. The interior design of the six foyers is a display of Uzbek folk art with the frescoes and carvings based on folklore from various parts of the republic. The murals are designs based on works by the poet and founder of the Uzbek literary language Alisher Navoi.

The main hall of the theater has a seating capacity of 1,400. The local company performs national operas and ballets by composers from all parts of the U.S.S.R.

Theater Square, once a noisy bazaar, is now a lovely area for spending a relaxing moment or taking a pleasant stroll. In the center of the square is a large, multitiered fountain in the shape of a cotton boll surrounded by rose bushes. The illuminated fountain is quite splendid at night.

Occupying a large outer area of the square is the United Publishing House, which houses the offices of the newspapers *Kyzyl Uzbekistan* (Red Uzbekistan), an Uzbek-language publication; *Pravda Vostoka* (Truth of the East), a Russian-language publication; and *Uzbekistoni Surkh* (also Red Uzbekistan), a publication in the Tajik language.

Near the Publishing House and across the square from the Opera House is the five-story Hotel Tashkent. Built in 1958, the hotel was designed by architects M. Bulatov and V. Levchenko. A new Intourist Hotel, the Rossiya, was opened in 1967 to accommodate the increasing number of visitors to the city.

Lenin Memorial Museum

The Lenin Memorial Museum is located at the side of the Hotel Tashkent and is the most beautiful modern structure in Tashkent. Built in 1970 in observance of the one hundredth anniversary of the birth of Vladimir Lenin, this museum, like the other branches of the Lenin Museum throughout the U.S.S.R., deals with the life and work of the founder of the Soviet state. Inside, one is immediately met by a larger-than-life statue of Lenin. The exhibits are generally interesting but one should look primarily for those having to do with Lenin's work concerning Tashkent and Central Asia.

Hotel Shark

The Hotel Shark, located at 16 Pravdy Vostoka Street, is one of several interesting buildings along this street. The hotel has historical significance for the people of Tashkent for it was here that the Turkestan front had its headquarters in 1920 when the struggle for the establishment of Soviet power in the province was at its height. The strategic plans of Soviet general Mikhail Frunze and revolutionary leader Valerian Kuibischev were drawn up at this hotel and visitors can see the memorial plaques at the entrance which commemorate the struggle.

Uzbek State Philharmonic Society

Built in 1913, the building of the Uzbek State Philharmonic Society was used during the Civil War for meetings of the Communist Party of Turkestan and congresses of Soviets to discuss matters concerning the economic development of the province.

Today the Philharmonic Society presents concerts by well-known Uzbek artists, the Uzbek Symphony Orchestra, and the Orchestra of Folk Instruments. The society also invites foreign artists and orchestras to perform.

The domed concert hall of the State Philharmonic Society is located at 10 Pravdy Vostoka Street.

Common Grave

Proletarskaya Street leads to a green square which was once used as a bazaar but is now the site of a common grave for fourteen people killed during the counter-revolution of 1919. The grave is marked by an obelisk with the inscription "In this common grave rest the remains of fourteen leading Communists of Turkestan, treacherously seized and savagely tortured to death during the counter-revolutionary uprising in January 1919."

Next to the common grave are the gravesites of Yuldash Akhunbabayev, the first president of the Uzbek Republic; Khamid Alimdjan, an Uzbek poet; and Sabir Rakhimov, the first Uzbek general killed in World War II.

Museum of Arts of the Uzbek S.S.R.

The Museum of Arts was founded in 1918 and houses a rich collection of fine, applied, and folk art. Most of the museum's twenty halls are devoted to Uzbek national art. Wood and *ganch* (a soft stone of local origin) carvings and paintings, prints, woven fabrics, silk, embroidery, carpets, metalwork, and ceramics are on display as well as fine oil paintings, drawings, works of sculpture, furniture, and porcelain.

While the Museum of Arts is primarily devoted to national art, there are halls with exhibits from France, Italy, England, Flanders, Holland, China, India, Burma, and Japan.

The museum is located at 101 Gogol Street.

Museum of the History of Uzbekistan and Other Museums of the Academy of Sciences

Both the Museum of the History of Uzbekistan and the Fine Arts Museum are located on Kuibysheva Street and are essentially similar to the other historical and scientific museums of the U.S.S.R. The Museum of the History of Uzbekistan offers exhibits dealing with the history of the peoples of the republic from their early beginnings to the present day as well as with the political and economic history of Uzbekistan.

The Fine Arts Museum has an interesting display of works by Uzbek artists and artists from outside the republic. Both of these museums, like the Museum of Literature (69a Navoi Street), the Museum of Nature (16 Sagban Street), and the Botanical Gardens, are affiliated with the Academy of Sciences of the Uzbek S.S.R.

The Museum of Nature will be informative to those interested in the flora and fauna of the republic as well as the agricultural characteristics of its different regions.

The Navoi Museum of Literature was opened in 1967 in observance of the 525th anniversary of the birth of the beloved Uzbek poet. The museum is of fair interest and deals primarily with the life and work of Alisher Navoi. A bronze monument to Navoi stands in front of the museum together with sculptured busts of other writers and poets of different eras.

A museum of highly specialized interest (and not affiliated with the Academy of Sciences) is the Museum of Atheistic Propaganda of the Ministry of Culture of the Uzbek S.S.R. which is located at 1 Besh-Agach Street.

Tashkent State University

Tashkent State University was founded in 1920 and was the first modern institution of higher education in Central Asia. The old buildings of the university are located at Revolution Square and one of the structures bears a memorial plaque with an inscripted excerpt from Lenin's decree which opened the university. This building houses but one of the university's twelve faculties while the others, along with the administration, have moved to the university township on the outskirts of the city.

Aside from its twelve faculties, the university has eighty-five chairs, ten highly equipped laboratories, a computer center, and an enrollment of eleven thousand students.

Revolution Square

In the heart of the city, where Marx, Engels, Proletarskaya, Kuibischev, Pushkin, and Leningrad streets converge is Revolution Square. The square is dominated by the huge Karl Marx Monument.

One side of the square is now occupied by the site of the new Hotel Intourist. Opposite are the old buildings of the Tashkent State University.

Karl Marx Street

Along Karl Marx Street, Tashkent's main street and the liveliest area of the city, one will find many interesting shops and entertainment facilities. The Gorky Russian Drama Theater is located here. The theater was founded over thirty years ago and the works of Russian playwrights as well as world drama classics have been staged here.

Continuing along, one will find a department store, a bookshop, and a movie theater. Lenin Square is at the end of the street and here one can see the Government House of Uzbekistan. A monument to Lenin stands in front of the building, the work of sculptor B. Korolyov (1935).

Alisher Navoi Public Library

Upon leaving Lenin Square you will see the Alisher Navoi Public Library. Founded in 1870 with the aid of the scientific institutions of Russia, the library has developed into a major educational and cultural institution having the largest collection of books in Central Asia. The library receives at least one copy of every book and periodical published in the Soviet Union and 450 periodicals from other nations; there are now well over two million publications in its collection.

One of the most interesting sections of the library is that of "rare books" where the only edition of the *Turkestan Collection* (a collection of material on Central Asia consisting of 591 volumes) is located.

Alisher Navoi Prospect

Alisher Navoi Prospect is interesting in that it was once the main street of old Tashkent. Along the prospect one can see the building of the Ministry of Agricultural Production and Purveyance of the Uzbek S.S.R., the Pakhtakor Stadium (the name is Uzbek for "cotton grower"), the Ministry of Culture of the Uzbek S.S.R., and the Eastern Department of the university. Navoi Prospect ends at Akhunbabayev Square, the center of the old town. The site of the square was at one time the crossroads of several ancient trade routes.

Biruni Square

Situated on the shores of Komsomol Lake is Biruni Square, one of the most beautiful squares in the city. The square is always crowded with people who are enjoying a pleasant walk, a show at the Mukimi Uzbek Theater of Musical Drama, or the movie theater. For those who simply want to take advantage of the sunny summer days, there are beaches and swimming facilities.

Ancient Structures

While Tashkent is in the process of growing and modernizing, several old structures still remind one of times past. The remains of an ancient settlement—Mingouryuk Hill—can be seen on Proletarskaya Street near the Salar irrigation canal. Another site is a hill named Ak-Tepe which is on Younus-Abad Street. The hill is the ruin of a feudal castle that was destroyed and burned at the end of the seventh century.

In Kukeldash Square stands a magnificently tiled madrasah (Moslem school) of the sixteenth century. The square itself was used for executions in ancient Tashkent.

Perhaps the best known and most famous ensemble of sixteenth-century architecture in Tashkent is located at the end of Hamza Street. One of the most well preserved structures there is the *mazar* (tomb), which was built by Gulian Khusein, a court architect in 1541. Next to the *mazar* is the Barak Khan Madrasah, part of which is Goumbazi Barak Khan; this tomb is considered to be one of the finest examples of early-sixteenth-century Central Asian architecture. Of great interest is the underground tomb chapel (Khorkhana) of Sheikh Zein-ad-Din, also built in the early sixteenth century.

An earlier structure in the same ensemble is the mausoleum of the Mongolian ruler of Tashkent, Younus Khan, built by his son Alacha Khan at the end of the fifteenth century. Adjoining the mausoleum is a madrasah bearing the same name. Another fifteenth-century structure is the Koldyr-gatch-biy Mausoleum with its pyramid-shaped cupola. The Ziyaratkhana (house of worship) which is situated next to the mausoleum of Sheikh an-Tauri should not be overlooked.

USEFUL INFORMATION

Hotels

Intourist, 50 Lenin Street, at Revolution Square
Oktyabr, 14 Shevchenko Street
Pakhtakor Stadium Hotel, 91 Jar-Kucha Street

Pushkinskaya, 18 Pushkin Street
Rossiya, Rustaveli Prospect
Shark, 16 Pravdy Vostoka Street
Tashkent, 50 Lenin Street. This is currently the major tourist hotel.
Uzbekistan, 17 Dzerzhinskovo Street
Zeravshan, 15a Akhunbabayeva Street

Restaurants

Bakhor, 15 Kuibysheva Street
Gulistan, 25 Mahkama Street
Shark, 16 Pravdy Vostoka Street
Tashkent, 50 Lenin Street
Zeravshan, 9 Leningrad Street

Cafés

Ankhor, 33 Tukayeva Street
Moskva, 29 Karl Marx Street
Café Morozhenoye (ice cream parlor), 48 Lenin Street

Museums

Museum of Atheistic Propaganda of the Ministry of Culture of the
    Uzbek S.S.R., 1 Besh-Agach Street
Museum of Arts of the Uzbek S.S.R., 101 Gogol Street
Lenin Memorial Museum, located on the side of the Hotel Tashkent
Museum of Literature of the Uzbek Academy of Sciences, 69a Navoi Street
Museum of Nature of the Uzbek Academy of Sciences, 16 Sagban Street
Botanical Gardens of the Uzbek Academy of Sciences, Karamurtskaya
    Street
Zoo, 23 Alimjana Street

Cinemas

Festival, 7 Proletarskaya Street
Iskra, 40 Lenin Street
Khiva, 7 Proletarskaya Street
Mir, 55 Bakinskaya Street
Molodaya Gvardia, 25 Lenin Street
Moskva, 22 Novo-Moskovskaya Street
Navoi, Besh-Agach Street
Pobeda, 7 Uritskovo Street
Rakhimov, 327 Rakhimova Street
Shuhrat, Kislovodskaya Street
Sputnik, 87 Engels Street

Uzbekistan, 74 Poltoratskovo Street
Vatan, 35 Navoi Street

Theaters, Concert Halls, and Circus

Akhunbabayev Theater for Young Spectators, 8 Hamza Street
Conservatoire, 31 Pushkin Street
Gorky Russian Drama Theater, 28 Karl Marx Street
Hamza Uzbek Drama Theater, 2 Uigura Street
Mukimi Theater of Musical Drama, 189 Almazar Street
Navoi Opera and Ballet Theater, 31 Pravdy Vostoka Street
Philharmonic Concert Hall, 10 Pravdy Vostoka Street
Puppet Show Theater, 6 Karl Marx Street
Circus, 46 Lenin Street

Shops

Department Store, 35 Karl Marx Street
Clothing Store, 29 Pravdy Vostoka Street
Detsky Mir (Children's Store), 43 Shota Rusthaveli Street
Commission Store, 25 Karl Marx Street
Akademicheskaya Kniga (bookshop), 29 Karl Marx Street
Voyennaya Kniga (bookshop), 28 Karl Marx Street
Knigi (bookshop), 31 Karl Marx Street
Knigi (bookshop), 14 Navoi Street

SAMARKAND—General Information

Situated on the left bank of the Zarafshan River, between the Dargom and Siab irrigation canals, is Samarkand. Resting 727 meters (2,385 feet) above sea level, the city lies almost exactly in the center of Central Asia and covers an area of 40 square kilometers (15 square miles). With a population of over 270,000, Samarkand ranks second only to Tashkent in the Uzbek S.S.R. The climate ranges from fairly cold, 0 degrees C. (32 degrees F.), in the winter to very hot in the summer, with temperatures often reaching over 40 degrees C. (104 degrees F.).

Visitors will be intrigued by the city's ancient architecture and ornamental decorations. A rich past boasts names such as Omar Khayyam, Rudagi, Firdausi, Avicenna, Jami, Babur, and Ulugh Beg. Alisher Navoi lived and worked in Samarkand in the late 1460s.

Famous over the centuries for its crafts, Samarkand's embroidery, carpets, jewelry, and ceramics are known throughout the world. It is also interesting to note that Samarkand introduced paper and paper manufacturing to Western Europe. Today Samarkand is one of the ma-

jor industrial and cultural centers of the Uzbek Republic and the entire
Soviet Union.

HISTORY IN BRIEF

Samarkand is a city of mystery and intrigue for it is one of the oldest cities
of civilization. Archaeological finds have shown that man lived in this
region long before the establishment of a formal urban society. One of the
most important finds in Central Asian archaeological history came in 1962
with the discovery of the bones of an Upper Paleolithic Cro-Magnon man.
In 1964 a female grave of the Bronze Age was found in the village of
Muminabad, which lies about 50 kilometers (30 miles) to the southeast of
Samarkand. The grave was dated at approximately 3500 B.C.

Turkic invaders took control of the town in the sixth century and by the
seventh century the rulers of Samarkand had complete control of the
Zarafshan valley. This century was a turning point in the history of the
town because it was at this time that Samarkand became an important
trading center. The eighth century was one of great hardship for the people
of Samarkand as an Arab army led by Qutaiba ibn Muslim seized the town
in 712. Samarkand became part of the Arab caliphate and following a
popular revolt the invaders forced the people out of the town and resettled
it with Arabs.

As the Arab caliphate declined in the ninth century and power was
assumed by local dynasties, Samarkand embarked on a new period of
prosperity and growth. The tenth century saw the establishment of a large
population center to the south of the territory of Afrasiab and the increased
manufacture of pottery, glass, paper, and silk. History, however, again
repeated itself for the people of the region as invasion after invasion swept
across the land in the eleventh and twelfth centuries.

The first half of the thirteenth century marked total disaster for Samarkand as Genghis Khan led his Mongol armies into Central Asia in 1219.
Samarkand was seized and destroyed in 1220, and the people were once
again forced to flee. The town recovered and while Samarkand became one
of the territories to be ruled by Jagatai, Genghis Khan's second son, it was
fairly well rebuilt by the end of the century.

The most famous ruler of Samarkand was Timur (Tamerlane), who ruled
from the time of his crowning as emperor in 1369 to his death in 1405.
His military campaigns established a great empire and he made Samarkand
its capital. The city now underwent a period of extensive building which
saw the rebuilding of the city walls in 1371–72. A citadel was built and new
settlements sprang up on the outskirts of the city. Great palaces were built
and gardens were landscaped.

The empire flourished as Timur established diplomatic relations with foreign courts, but its glory was to be short-lived. While preparing an offensive against China in February 1405 Timur died. His youngest son, Shahrukh, assumed power and immediately moved his capital to Herat. The region between the Syr Darya and Amu Darya was given to Shahrukh's eldest son, Ulugh Beg.

Samarkand was ruled for a brief period at the end of the fifteenth century by the Timurid Zahir ud-Din Babur. The capital was moved at the beginning of the sixteenth century from Samarkand to Bukhara. The seventeenth century was another turning point in the history of Samarkand, for it was early in this century that it became a separate principality in the Uzbek state. The organization of rule in the capital city of Bukhara was weak and disorganized and the Emir Yalangtush-Bahadur, an influential member of the feudal aristocracy, took full advantage of it. By the end of the seventeenth century and the first half of the eighteenth, a total collapse of power was imminent in Bukhara and feudal wars raged throughout the state. Nomadic tribes, making full use of internal strife, swept across the region causing great destruction. Samarkand remained in a state of severe decline until the 1770s, when the town walls were repaired and rebuilt and twenty-four new districts were built. By the nineteenth century the population numbered approximately 25,000.

Russian troops took control of Samarkand on May 2, 1868 with the surrender of the emir. A treaty was signed whereby Russia obtained the Samarkand and Kattakurgan regions and the newly formed Zarafshan district was annexed to the Turkestan governor-generalship. In 1868 Samarkand was the administrative and commercial center of the Zarafshan district and by 1887, of the entire Samarkand region.

The year 1888 marked the beginning of one of the most important and influential undertakings in the history of Samarkand and the whole of Central Asia—the building of the Transcaspian railway. The new railway would provide a direct link from Samarkand to the coastal areas of the Caspian Sea. It was the intention of the Russian Imperial government to connect Central Asia with the industrial centers of Russia via the Caspian and by 1899 tracks had been extended to Margilan, Andizhan, and Tashkent. The entire 1,818 kilometers (1,090 miles) of track from Krasnovodsk to Samarkand were completed in less than eight years. On May 20, 1888 the first train arrived in Samarkand and in 1899 Samarkand and Tashkent were linked. In 1906, eighteen years after the building of the Transcaspian railway began, Samarkand was connected with the railway network of the entire country.

The effects of the Revolution in Russia were widespread in Samarkand and the whole of Turkestan. In February and March of 1905 strikes broke out in Samarkand, Tashkent, Chardzhou, and Kizil-Arvat, and the peasants rose up against the local feudal lords.

The nationwide strike of 1905 forced Nicholas II to agree to the Manifesto of October 17 which guaranteed civil rights to all those under his rule but this only served to increase the fervor of the Revolution. In Samarkand railway workers and workers from the Demurov printing press and numerous other enterprises called a strike on October 18. *Samarkand*, the daily newspaper, called for the taking up of arms by the people.

When the tsarist government crumbled with the abdication of Nicholas II in March 1917 a dual administration was established in Samarkand, as it was throughout the entire country. During the same month the Soviet of Workers' and Soldiers' Deputies was elected along with the Committee of Public Security which represented the Provisional Government.

The dual government was relatively short-lived for on October 25, 1917 the Bolsheviks gained control of the government in Petrograd. On November 28 the Samarkand Soviet of Workers', Soldiers' and Peasants' Deputies decided to take complete control of the local government. On December 4 an independent Bolshevik organization was officially established in Samarkand.

In April 1918 the Fifth Congress of the Soviets of Turkestan decreed the foundation of the Turkestan Autonomous Soviet Socialist Republic within the Russian Federation. Samarkand became the capital of the Uzbek Soviet Socialist Republic in 1925 and retained its position until 1930. The city was once again the Central Asian center of politics, economics, and culture. Today, Tashkent is the capital city of the republic but Samarkand has secured its position as one of the most important and influential cities in Central Asia.

MUSEUMS AND PLACES OF INTEREST

While the museums of Samarkand have a specialized interest, they should certainly not be the tourist's first priority. Rather, one should be sure to visit the architectural structures (Gur Emir Mausoleum, Ulugh Beg Madrasah, Shir Dor Madrasah, Shah Zindeh), Ulugh Beg's Observatory, and, if possible, the ancient site of Afrasiab.

Afrasiab

The ancient ruins of Afrasiab lie to the north of Samarkand. Preliminary excavations were undertaken in 1874 and 1883 but it was not until 1885 that the first major discovery was made by N. I. Veselovsky. He discovered, in addition to the outer wall, two inner walls and several communal watering places. In 1904 serious excavation of the site was resumed. The Great Mosque which the Mongols had burned down was uncovered. Also found were baths made of baked brick, a pottery shop, and, near the Naubehar Gates, a *zindan* (underground prison).

The Institute of History and Archaeology of the Uzbek Academy of Sciences began an extensive project in 1945 which was designed to study the topography and stratigraphy of the cultural layers. Work continued until 1948 and resulted in the conclusion that some of the layers dated back to approximately the middle of the first millennium B.C.

The fact that Afrasiab was much older than was once thought prompted the establishment of the Samarkand Archaeological Branch of the Institute of History and Archaeology of the Uzbek Academy of Sciences for the purpose of conducting extensive studies of the town. The oldest pottery findings do indeed date back to the middle of the first millennium B.C. The human dwellings, which were found mostly in the northern region, are not quite as old and have been dated to approximately the second and third centuries A.D. It has also been concluded that Afrasiab enjoyed its most prosperous era during the rule of the Samanid dynasty in the tenth century and that life ceased to exist in the town after its destruction by the Mongols.

Ulugh Beg's Observatory

At the foot of the Chupan Ata Hill are the ruins of the astronomical observatory built by Ulugh Beg, grandson of Timur and one of history's most gifted scientists. Little is known of the actual building of the observatory but some sources date its construction to 1428–29.

Ulugh Beg's "New Astronomical Tables" contains a fairly comprehensive account of the different chronological systems used by the peoples of Asia as well as astronomical problems and theoretical answers concerning the planets and the universe. Although Ulugh Beg's work was based on the firm belief that the earth was the center of the universe, he was able successfully to catalog 1,019 stars and divide them according to their respective constellations. The catalog is complete to the point that each star is numbered and a description is given concerning its position in a given constellation, its latitude, longitude, and size.

For many years the location of the observatory was unknown but with the aid of a seventeenth-century document which gave an accurate description of where it was situated, V. L. Vyatkin discovered the remains in 1908. He found traces of a round wall and part of a sextant but it was not until Soviet times that the architectural design of the observatory was determined. I. A. Sukharev conducted an excavation under the supervision of Professor M. Y. Masson in 1941 and Professor V. A. Shiskin led a team in 1948. Both digs were revealing, but the 1948 excavation proved that the existing ruins were once part of a large architectural unit and that the round wall was actually the remains of the outer wall of a large cylindrical three-story building. The top of the building was flat and astronomical equipment was kept there. The interior consisted of large halls and long corridors which were linked by several passages. The sextant occupied the central part of the building.

The Ulugh Beg Memorial Museum, located near the observatory on Kuhak Hill at the foot of Chupan Ata, was opened in 1964. It contains many of the objects found during excavations and copies of scientific manuscripts. There is a large wall panel bearing a portrait of Ulugh Beg and other exhibits portraying his life and times.

Ulugh Beg Madrasah

The Ulugh Beg Madrasah, which is located on the Registan central square, was built between 1417 and 1420 and was one of the finest schools in the Moslem world. Ulugh Beg was responsible for the construction of the first public buildings on the Registan (which literally means "sandy place"), the square around which life centered in old Samarkand. The madrasah was a two-story building with a dome on each of the four corner lecture rooms (known as *darskhana*), and four minarets, one on each corner. Two-thirds of the main façade which faces the Registan consist of a large portal with a wide pointed arch. During the hostilities of the 1720s the outer domes and most of the rooms on the first floor were destroyed.

An ambitious project for the complete restoration of the madrasah began in 1952. The initial problem was the fact that the level of the square had risen since its construction over five hundred years earlier. In 1958–59 some of the layer around the northern, eastern, southern, and western façades was removed. Also, the marble paneling on the southern and western façades was restored as well as the western, southeastern, and northeastern minarets.

Shir Dor Madrasah

Directly opposite the Ulugh Beg Madrasah on the Registan is the Shir Dor Madrasah. The madrasah was built on the site of Ulugh Beg's *khanaka* (a place where important guests were accommodated and sometimes a place of residence for the crown prince), which collapsed in the early part of the seventeenth century. It was Yalangtush-Bahadur, the ruler of Samarkand at the time, who decided to erect the madrasah. Designed by the architect Abdul Jabbar, the structure took seventeen years to complete (1619–36). Later, the madrasah became known as the Shir Dor, which literally means "decorated with lions" (the name apparently originated from the decorations on the portal which depict two animals resembling lions).

A productive excavation took place in the summer of 1956 when, under the directorship of S. N. Yurenev, the foundations were reached and shown to be in good condition. They are believed to have been constructed from the wall bricks of the Ulugh Beg *khanaka*. The excavation also produced fragments of ceramics that were used to decorate the *khanaka* as well as a structure which occupied the site before the building of the *khanaka*.

Tilla Kari Madrasah

Yalangtush-Bahadur ordered the construction of a building on the north side of the Registan to occupy the site where Ulugh Beg's Mirzoi caravanserai once stood. The ruler wanted the structure to include a madrasah and a mosque and work began on it in 1646–47. The madrasah later came to be known as Tilla Kari ("decorated with gold"). The interior is beautifully decorated with murals and gold ornament.

Chor Su

The building on the northeast corner of the Shir Dor Madrasah was built over 150 years ago by Shah Murad, the ruler of Bukhara. Known as the building of the Chor Su, it was made from the bricks of the ruins of the Bibi Khanum Mosque and was intended primarily for trade, particularly the selling of headwear.

Bibi Khanum Mosque

The ruins of one of the largest mosques in the whole of Central Asia and indeed the entire Moslem world stand east of the Registan at the end of Tashkent Street. The mosque was built by Timur himself between 1399 and 1404, following a victorious campaign in India. Originally consisting of several buildings surrounded by an outer wall with a minaret at each corner, the ensemble covered a rectangular area 167 meters (548 feet) long and 109 meters (358 feet) wide. Of the outer wall and minarets all that remains is half of the minaret on the northwest side, which now stands 18.2 meters (60 feet) high.

The main entrance portal *(peshtak)* is located on the east side of the inner courtyard. The ruins of the building of the main mosque are located opposite the entrance. The mosque had a tremendous turquoise dome (only part of which has survived). The courtyard was paved with marble and ceramic mosaics. A marble stand which was used for reading from the Koran stands in the center of the courtyard (Ulugh Beg placed it inside the main mosque but it was moved to the courtyard in 1875).

The mosque began to suffer structural cracks shortly after its construction and additional damage was caused by earthquakes. During the earthquake of 1897 a large portion of the portal of the main entrance collapsed. The marble slabs are currently being kept in the courtyard.

Bibi Khanum Mausoleum

The ruins of the Bibi Khanum Mausoleum are all that remain of the Khanum Madrasah which stood opposite the Bibi Khanum Mosque. The madrasah was erected in honor of the mother of Timur's wife, Sarai-Mulk Khanum (Bibi Khanum). The Bibi Khanum Mausoleum was used for burials of female members of the Timurid dynasty.

Gur Emir Mausoleum

One of the most magnificent structures in all of Samarkand is the Gur Emir Mausoleum, a burial vault of the Timurids. Built at the end of the fourteenth and beginning of the fifteenth centuries, the mausoleum is part of an ensemble which consisted of a madrasah and *khanaka* which faced out onto a square courtyard. High walls surrounded the other two sides. Four minarets (which have collapsed) and an entrance gate (which is still standing) complemented the walls.

The history of the Gur Emir ensemble is closely related to the Crown Prince Muhammed Sultan, Timur's favorite grandson. When Muhammed Sultan was killed in 1403 during a military campaign in Persia, his body was brought to Samarkand and was temporarily laid in the *khanaka*. A mausoleum with a burial vault was ordered built by Timur in the southern wall of the courtyard. Timur did not live to see the mausoleum's completion and his remains were temporarily laid in the *khanaka* next to his grandson's.

When the mausoleum was finished Timur's remains were placed inside and buried at the feet of his spiritual advisor, Mir Sa'id Bereke, whose remains were brought from Andkhui in Afghanistan (Timur had commanded this arrangement before his death). The Crown Prince Muhammed Sultan is buried next to Timur on the eastern side.

A blue marble trellis was ordered built around the graves by Ulugh Beg during his rule of Samarkand. Also, an entrance to the mausoleum was built through the gallery on the east side. In addition to the architectural work Ulugh Beg also had a tombstone made for Timur out of a block of dark green jade which he brought back from Mongolistan in 1425 after completing a campaign there. The tombstone was placed in the upper part of the mausoleum and bears an inscription in Arabic which states that Timur was descended from the same line as Genghis Khan.

The entire ensemble deteriorated by the middle of the seventeenth century due to extreme neglect, and since the name of Timur was not as respected as it had been a few centuries earlier, the mausoleum came to be called the Gur Mir after Mir Sa'id Bereke.

In 1924, following a historical and archaeological study of the Gur Emir, a project of extensive restoration was undertaken. In 1941 a government excavation team opened the graves of Timur, Shahrukh, Miranshah, Muhammed Sultan, and Ulugh Beg and determined that the burials had been performed in accordance with Moslem religious rites. Another discovery, and perhaps the most exciting one, is that a study of the skeletons of Timur and Ulugh Beg confirmed the historical beliefs that Timur was lame and had a withered arm and that Ulugh Beg was assassinated.

Ruhabad Mausoleum

The mausoleum known as the Ruhabad ("Abode of the Spirit") was erected over the grave of the mystic Burkhaneddin Sagardzhi. The exact date of its construction is unknown although it is known that the mystic died in the fourteenth century. The Ruhabad Mausoleum is located to the north of the Gur Emir, and while it is not one of the more important structures in Samarkand it should be seen if time allows.

Ak Sarai Mausoleum

The exact date of the construction of the Ak Sarai Mausoleum is unknown but it is believed that it was built in the second half of the fifteenth century. The structure, thought to be a family burial vault for the male descendants of the Timurid dynasty, is located a short distance to the southeast of the Gur Emir.

The central grave of the mausoleum was found to contain a headless skeleton which most scholars agree are the remains of Ulugh Beg's son Abd-al-Latif. Perhaps the most interesting aspect of the Ak Sarai is the interior of the dome whose beautiful decoration was done in *kundal*, a specialized process of painting and gilding ornamental relief.

Shah Zindeh

Located on the southern outskirts of the region called Afrasiab is a group of mausoleums known as the Shah Zindeh. The name of this ensemble originated with the legendary grave of Kusam, the cousin of the prophet Mohammed. Arab sources relate that Kusam came to Samarkand with Arab armies to introduce and spread the religion of Islam. The zealous missionary was killed during the campaign, and legend tells us that after being decapitated Kusam picked up his head and entered a deep well which led to an underground garden where to this day he still lives. Thus, the name Shah Zindeh, which means "Living King."

The visitor best starts his tour of the Shah Zindeh by ascending the steps that lead to the most recently built mausoleums. The portal which is atop this group was built in 1434–35 by Ulugh Beg for his son Abda Laziz. The wooden gates at the entrance were carved by Uzbek craftsmen in 1911 and as one enters the gates one will see a small *chartak* (a domed porch which rests on four arches). To the left of the *chartak* is the entrance to a mosque which was erected at the same time as the portal over the main entrance (1434–35) and is in use today as the Museum of Atheism. The right side of the *chartak* is occupied by several administrative buildings adjoined on the north by a madrasah which dates to 1812–13.

The *aiwan* (a building on wooden columns) of the summer mosque was built by Sadyk in 1911 and can be seen to the left upon leaving the *chartak*. Next to the *aiwan*, and to the left at the foot of a large flight of steps, is a two-tiered mausoleum.

Upon reaching the top of the eighteenth-century staircase one will come upon another *chartak* (built in the eighteenth century) and a group of mausoleums which date back to the second half of the fourteenth century. The first structure on the right of the corridor which adjoins the *chartak* is a mausoleum whose inscription states it was built in 1375–76 in memory of Tuglu Tekin, daughter of the Emir Khoja and mother of Emir Husain, a general in Timur's military.

The mausoleum of Timur's sister, Shirin Bika Aka, stands next to the Tuglu Tekin structure. Although the inscription on the inside of the portal reveals that she died in 1385, the mausoleum was probably built later. It was the first structure in the ensemble to show mosaics on the exterior, and the interior is graced with an upper section of light blue and gold.

Standing opposite the mausoleum of Shirin Bika Aka is a tomb built by Turkan Aka, also a sister of Timur, for her daughter, Shadi Mulk Aka, who died in 1370. The mausoleum was the first structure to be built (1372) in the Shah Zindeh and indeed the whole of Samarkand during Timur's rule. Turkan Aka was buried in the mausoleum near her daughter in 1383.

Built by Shamseddin and Bareddin of Samarkand and Zainuddin of Bukhara, the Shadi Mulk Aka is one of the most beautiful structures in the Shah Zindeh ensemble. The portal is lavishly decorated, and the corner columns, whose designs are finely carved, stand on intricately shaped bases. The interior boasts a decor of majolica tiling set within clearly defined inscriptions.

The open octagonal mausoleum which stands next to the tomb of Shirin Bika Aka is thought to have been built during the time of Ulugh Beg's rule.

The steps to the north of this mausoleum led to an earlier tomb, the remains of which suggest the existence of a mausoleum on that site in the fourteenth century. To the east is a mausoleum which also dates to the fourteenth century whose only remains consist of the burial vault and several marble tombstones.

On the left is the mausoleum of Usto Ali, a master from Nesef (his name appears in one of the inscriptions), but the name of the person for whom the tomb was built is unknown. While the date of its construction is not known, the majolica decoration of the main portal and the interior and the terra-cotta decor of the outer walls suggests that it was erected toward the end of the fourteenth century.

Farther on the left are several structures built by Tuman Aka, Timur's young wife. This ensemble within the Shah Zindeh includes a third *chartak*, a mosque, and Tuman Aka's mausoleum, which stands on the left side of the north courtyard and is dated 1405-06. Immediately noticeable are the mosaics on the portal, the work of the Azerbaijan master Sheikh Mohammed ibn Hojabeg Tebrizi. The mosaics were secured during restoration work carried out in the 1920s.

Two of the oldest mausoleums of the fourteenth century, the Khoja Ahmad mausoleum which was built by Fahri Ali, and a "nameless" mausoleum were in a state of near total ruin at the beginning of the nineteenth century. A project of restoration was undertaken and extensive repairs were successfully performed.

The oldest structure in the Shah Zindeh is the eleventh- to twelfth-century minaret which is the only structure of that time to have survived in its original form in the whole of Samarkand. The interior has a spiral staircase which leads to an upper platform.

The Kusam Mausoleum, also an eleventh-century structure, can be seen by going through the mosque which is located to the left of the minaret. The mausoleum, however, has undergone so many rebuildings (mostly in 1334-35) that its original form has been lost. The tomb has two sections —the burial vault and a mosque, beneath which is an underground chamber which was used during the forty-day fasts.

A new tombstone was built on the grave of Kusam during Timur's rule. Brightly colored with tiles of white, yellow, blue, and green, and ornamented with gold, the bottom two tiers of the four-tiered stone contain gold inscriptions from the Koran; the upper tiers have inscribed the fact that Kusam is buried here. The date of his death is given as 676-677.

The Shah Zindeh provides the most extensive collection of early architecture in Samarkand and to miss seeing it would be to leave a large gap in one's understanding and appreciation of its past.

Ishrat Khan

The name Ishrat Khan ("house of amusement") is paradoxical because a document dated 1464 states that the structure was built by Abu Sa'id's wife, Habibi Sultan Bigim, for their deceased daughter, Sultan Havend Bika. The exact date of its construction is not known but the building does date back to the reign of the Timurid Abu Sa'id (1451-69). In 1940 archaeological investigations revealed thirty graves of women and children.

The once architecturally intricate Ishrat Khan had a tall entrance portal on the west side and a vaulted gallery adjacent to the south wall with another entrance. The north side had a mosque and the structure itself was topped by a dome. In 1903 an earthquake shook the area and the dome collapsed. Despite some repair work in the 1940s the Ishrat Khan consists of a few ruins.

Khoja Abdu Darun Mausoleum

An old cemetery, not too far from the Ishrat Khan, on the southeast outskirts of Samarkand contains the tomb of a ninth-century ruler of Samarkand who is said to be descended from the Arabic Abdu line and is thought to be related to the caliph Osman. Because his grave was situated on land surrounded by a wall (known as the Wall of the Last Judgment) the ruler was nicknamed Khoja Abdu Darun, which means "Abdu the Inside One" (remains of the wall still exist). The mausoleum of the "Inside One" was rebuilt in the fifteenth century.

Khoja Abdu Birun Mausoleum

Khoja Abdu Birun, or "Abdu the Outside One," is buried on the southern outskirts of the city in a mausoleum built in 1633 by the feudal lord Nadir Divanbegi. Abdu Birun was supposedly the son of Abdu Darun.

Museum of the History of Culture and Art, 51 Sovietskaya Street

The first articles placed in the museum's collection were glass, water jugs, pottery, pipes, and other finds from an excavation in Afrasiab which went on public exhibition in 1874. Within a year, more than thirty Oriental manuscripts, seven hundred coins of gold, silver, and copper, and other valuable finds were added to the collection.

Today the museum offers 100,000 exhibits consisting of more than 40,000 archaeological treasures, 11,000 coins, and approximately 14,000 samples of flora and fauna. Of particular value are vessels bearing inscriptions in Old Sogdian as well as a rare collection of mollusks, precious stones, and carved signets. Exhibits of embroidery, metalwork, woodcarvings, and work of marble and *ganch* (a stone of Central Asia), some of which date from as early as the fourth century B.C., help one's understanding of the history of the region and its people throughout the ages.

During the Soviet period in Samarkand, the museum has acquired a collection of material concerning the history of the Revolution in Central Asia. The most interesting exhibits in this section are the documents, pamphlets, and newspapers which relate to Lenin's work.

The museum can be reached via #1 bus, trolley bus, and tram.

Freedom Monument

In 1918 White Cossack forces and soldiers of the Red Guards fought a savage battle near the station of Rostovtsevo (later renamed Krasnogvardeiskaya—Red Guard), 30 kilometers (19 miles) from Samarkand. The fallen Communists were buried in a common grave in Georgievskaya Square (today it is Red Square), and other revolutionaries were later buried there.

In April 1918 Lenin signed a decree concerning the building of monuments for those who lost their lives for the cause of the Revolution, and the workers of Samarkand decided to erect a monument over the common grave. Designed by the Austrian and ex-prisoner of war E. Rusch, the structure was built by peoples of different nationalities—Uzbeks, Tajiks, Russians, and former prisoners of war from Czechoslovakia, Hungary, Austria, and Germany.

A great deal of symbolism is embodied in the Freedom Monument. The cast-iron bas-relief on the west side of the base shows a worker standing near an anvil with a hammer in his right hand and his left arm linked with a peasant in a soldier's uniform in an apparent show of unity and friendship. The east side also has a cast-iron bas-relief depicting an Uzbek peasant in a field, arms raised to the rising sun in the background, which probably symbolizes freedom. The remaining two sides of the base bear the words "Comrades, remember that we perished for the cause of freedom and the revolution" and a verse from a revolutionary song said to be one of Lenin's favorites:

> You fell in the fatal struggle
> A victim of your great love for the people.
> You sacrificed all that you had
> For their honor, life and freedom.

Each corner of the base contains the standing figure of a child with upstretched arms, a proclamation that the future of the country is with the young.

A domed rotunda stands on the base, topped with a statue of a young woman with her right arm raised high. She, of course, symbolizes Russia, the motherland. The Freedom Monument was officially unveiled on May 19, 1919. An eternal flame burns over the grave.

Underground Printing Press

Of some interest, but certainly not priority, is the site of the "Underground Printing Press" on the corner of Respublikanskaya and Pushkinskaya streets.

USEFUL INFORMATION

Hotels

Registan, 36 Lenin Street
Samarkand, 55 Sovetskaya Street
Shark, 1 Tashkent Street

Restaurants

Registan, 36 Lenin Street
Samarkand, 55 Sovetskaya Street
Shark, 1 Tashkent Street
Uzbekistan, 52 Lenin Street
Zarafshan, 79 Karl Marx Street

Museums and Historic Sites

Museum of the History of Culture and Art, 51 Sovetskaya Street. Transportation: Bus 1, Tram, Trolley bus
Ulugh Beg Memorial Museum, Kuhak Hill at the foot of Chupan Ata, Tashkent Highway
Chor Su, Tashkent Street (in the Registan Central Square)
Shir Dor, Tilla Kari, Ulugh Beg Madrasahs, Registanskaya Street (in the Registan Central Square). Transportation: Trolley bus 1 and 2; Bus 1, 3, 10, 12, 13
Bibi Khanum Mosque and Mausoleum, corner of Tashkent Highway and 8 March Street
Gur Emir Mausoleum, Ruhabad quarter. Transportation: Trolley bus 1 and 2; Bus 1 and 10
Shah Zindeh Ensemble, Kozhevennaya Street
Ulugh Beg Observatory, Kuhak Hill at the foot of Chupan Ata, Tashkent Highway

Theaters

Hamid Alimjan Uzbek Drama Theater, Maxim Gorky Central Recreation Park. Transportation: Trolley bus 1, Bus 1
Russian Drama Theater, 51 Lenin Street. Transportation: Trolley bus 1, Bus 1
Opera and Ballet Theater, Gorky Boulevard

Stores and Souvenir Shops

Tsum Central Department Store, 2 Gazovaya Street
Hotel Registan, 36 Lenin Street
Hotel Shark, 1 Tashkent Street
Hotel Samarkand, 55 Sovetskaya Street

Bookshops

48 Lenin Street
75 Tashkent Street
35 Kooperativnaya Street
13 Karl Marx Street
32 Karl Marx Street

Transportation and Communications

Airport Office, 37 Lenin Street, Tel: 3–10–04 (or at any hotel)
Train Information (Ticket Office), corner of Uzbekistanskaya Street and
    Engels Street (or at any hotel)
Central Post Office, 9 Pochtovaya Street

OTHER CITIES OF CENTRAL ASIA

Alma Ata, Ashkhabad,
Bukhara, Dushanbe, Frunze

ALMA ATA—General Information

Alma Ata, which means "father apple" in Kazakh, is the capital of the Kazakhstan Soviet Socialist Republic and is located in the southeastern part of the republic. The city, whose population is 636,000, rests in the northern foothills of the Zailiisky Ala Tau range of the Tien-Sien mountains, approximately 732 meters (2,400 feet) above sea level (only Yerevan, capital of the Armenian S.S.R., is situated on a higher level among republic capitals).

Alma Ata's climate is basically continental. The July mean temperature is generally 38 degrees C. (71 degrees F.) while August days sometimes reach as high as 38 degrees C. (100 degrees F.). Winter months can get as cold as −8 degrees C. (18 degrees F.). The temperature characteristic that visitors most enjoy is the extreme difference between day and night. Even on very hot, sunny days, the nights are always a good deal cooler and very comfortable. Rainfall averages about 61 centimeters (24 inches) a year and generally occurs toward the end of spring and early summer and sudden short, heavy showers are not uncommon. In spring and summer Alma Ata is blessed with profuse greenery, which gives it the appearance of being one tremendous park.

Today Alma Ata is a large industrial center whose major industries include machine building, fruit processing, meat packing, and milk and tobacco processing. Alma Ata, with its eleven institutes of higher learning, is also a city dedicated to education.

HISTORY IN BRIEF

Data organized from archaeological finds indicate that in ancient times the region that Alma Ata now occupies was inhabited by nomadic and seminomadic tribes. The area, then known as the Semirechie, suffered great losses and damage from Mongolian invasions and Timur's (Tamerlane's) military campaigns. The area was part of the Dzhungar khanate from the sixteenth to the eighteenth century; it became part of the Kokand khanate in the nineteenth century.

During the years 1850–53, units of the Russian military made several crossings of the Ili River from the north with orders to protect the caravan routes from aggression by the Kokand khanate. The area began to advance rapidly and in 1853 the Zailiisky territory was incorporated in the Russian Empire. In 1854 a small fortress named Verny was founded on the left bank of the Alma Atinka River and the population of the new town near the fortress rapidly increased, mostly due to the migration of Cossack peasants. The town was known as Verny from 1854 to 1921, when it was renamed Alma Ata, its proper Kazakh name.

The town was almost completely destroyed in 1887 when a powerful earthquake leveled the houses which were made of unbaked brick. After the disaster brick structures were forbidden and Verny literally became a town made of wood.

The Kazakh Republic was so named in 1925 (this is the historically correct name of the people) and in 1936 it became a Union Republic (it was formerly an Autonomous Soviet Socialist Republic).

Kazakhstan occupies approximately one-eighth of the territory of the U.S.S.R. and has a population of 12.5 million. Its borders stretch from the Caspian Sea in the west to the Ala Tau mountain range in the east.

MUSEUMS AND PLACES OF INTEREST

State Museum of the History of Kazakhstan

Your tour of Alma Ata will almost certainly begin with a visit to the wooden cathedral that was built at the beginning of the twentieth century by architect A. Zenkov. The structure, which stands 55 meters (180 feet) high, is constructed solely of wood—there is not a single nail in the structure.

The cathedral, which is located in the Park of the 28 Panfilov Guards, was once the only decorative structure in Alma Ata and houses the State Museum of the History of Kazakhstan. Exhibits help one better understand the rich cultural history of the Kazakh Republic and the Kazakh people as well as present trends in national customs and art.

Shevchenko Art Gallery

The Art Gallery in Alma Ata is named for the Ukrainian poet Taras Shevchenko, who was exiled to Kazakhstan by the tsarist government. The "Taras Willow" tree that Shevchenko planted over a hundred years ago still stands.

The gallery offers an exhibit of paintings by Kazakh artists; this is indeed progress in the field in view of the fact that the Kazakhs had no painters of mention during Shevchenko's time. The most interesting collection is probably that of the works of Khludov, considered to be the founder of the Kazakh fine arts.

Russian and Soviet artists are represented in a special section of the gallery and paintings by Nesterov and Vrubel are of particular interest. Visitors should be sure to see the section of fine seventeenth-century Dutch paintings as well as representative works by French and Italian artists. The exhibits of applied art of medieval China and Japan are rare treats and should not be missed.

Memorial Museums of Mukhtar Auezov and Djambul Djabayev

For those interested in historical trends in Kazakh literature, a visit to the museums of Mukhtar Auezov and Djambul Djabayev is certainly worthwhile. The Auezov Museum offers exhibits depicting the life and work of the Kazakh novelist and playwright as well as the influence of his work on Kazakh literary thought.

The museum of the famous *akyn* (folk poet and singer) Djabayev is particularly interesting because of the relationship that the *akyns* had with the people who listened in what sometimes seemed to be a state of trance to their poetic folk tales. The *akyn* usually accompanied his recitation with the playing of the *dombra,* a Kazakh string instrument. *Aitys,* or lyrical-poetic contests between *akyns* (the people referred to the finest *akyns* as *Salami*), were common.

Theaters of the Performing Arts

Alma Ata offers a good variety of theaters and concert halls. The Abai Academic Opera and Ballet Theater enjoys great patronage as a result of its very fine Kazakh and Russian companies. Productions of ballets and operas by Kazakh, Russian, and foreign classical composers can be enjoyed at this theater.

The Kazakh Song and Dance Company is certainly a treat worth seeing, especially by those unfamiliar with the customs of the people of Kazakhstan. The combination of beautiful song and dramatic dance is quite thrilling.

Other theaters that are highly recommended for their fine companies and unusual productions are the Kurmangazy Folk Instruments Orchestra, Choir and Symphony Orchestra; the Kazakh Academic Drama Theater, which is dedicated to Mukhtar Auezov; and the Uigur Musical and Drama Theater, where the art and customs of the Uigurs (a national minority living in the Kazakh S.S.R.) can be enjoyed and appreciated. Visitors who are interested in stage productions of a more classical nature by Russian, Soviet, and Western European playwrights can attend performances of the Republican Russian Drama Theater dedicated to Lermontov.

Republican Exhibition of Economic Achievements

The exhibition grounds of the economic achievements of the Kazakh Republic are generally the last stop of the guided sightseeing tour. Here you have an opportunity to see and appreciate the vast progress made by the people of the republic in this century and especially in Soviet times. Exhibits such as samples of very fine fleece wool, wire drawing machines, beautifully colored Kazakh carpets, and many samples of the products manufactured at the Alma Ata House Building Plant are among the items in which the people of Kazakhstan take great pride.

Parks of Alma Ata

There is nothing that compares to a simple walk through the streets of this fantastically beautiful city. Alma Ata is indeed blessed by nature, and to stroll through its streets is to feel that the city itself is one enormous park. Of course, there are formally designated parks in Alma Ata, the most popular being the Gorky Recreation Park. On the banks of the Malaya Almatinka Abai, the park has a large swimming pool and a theater; for children's enjoyment, there are a small zoo and the Children's Railway known as Maly Turksib.

The Park of the 28 Panfilov Guards (named for the twenty-eight who distinguished themselves in a battle near Moscow during World War II) is a large and very beautiful area for recreation or a leisurely stroll. The park is best known for its ornamental flowerbeds, numerous fountains, and well-executed pieces of sculpture. Located here is the Museum of the History of Kazakhstan (the old wooden cathedral) and a common grave for those who died fighting for the establishment of Soviet power in the region. There is also an enjoyable summer theater within the boundaries of the park.

In the spring and summer a visit to the Square of Flowers may be worthwhile.

Some Monuments of Alma Ata

Because Alma Ata is a city that invites a great deal of walking, it may be valuable to know of the monuments and statues along the city's streets.

The monument on Vinogradov Boulevard is to Major General Ivan Panfilov, a prominent military figure during World War II. Standing in the square between the old and new buildings of the Government House is a huge statue of Lenin. The 7-meter (23-foot) high bronze figure which stands on a dark brown granite pedestal is the work of Ye. Vuchetich.

The most impressive monument in the city is the equestrian statue of Amangeldy Imanov which stands in Oktyabrskaya Square. An influential leader of the uprising of 1916, Imanov is a national hero to the Kazakh people.

A bronze monument to Abai Kunanbaev, a Kazakh poet, stands on the street of the same name. It is here that a ropeway to the Kok Tobe mountain peak begins.

Excursion to the Mountains

The snow-capped Ala Tau mountain range is one of the most breathtaking natural sites in all of Central Asia and visitors to Alma Ata should certainly not miss the opportunity to take a trip to the mountains. There are usually several excursions available, ranging from a few hours to an entire day. Arrangements can be made through the Service Bureau of the Intourist office and prices range from moderate to moderately high. The usual rate policy is to charge for the rental of a car and guide, rather than per person, so it is advisable to have between two and five people along on the same tour.

The ride to the destination point in the mountains from the center of the city is approximately 1 1/2 hours, making the transportation alone some three hours round trip. Therefore, it might be advisable to eat a late breakfast just before departing. Some visitors might want to take lunch along. Most of the excursion through the mountains is on foot (the car can go only to a certain point) so one should be sure to dress comfortably and wear suitable walking shoes.

Accommodations

Visitors to Alma Ata generally stay in the newly built Hotel Alma Ata or the Hotel Kazakhstan. Both facilities offer complete Intourist services, have comfortable accommodations, and good food.

ASHKHABAD—General Information

Ashkhabad is the capital of the Turkmen Soviet Socialist Republic and the southernmost capital of all the Union Republics. The city derives its name from a combination of the Arabic *ashk,* meaning "love," and the Persian *abad,* meaning "city." Ashkhabad is located within 40 kilometers (25 miles) of the Iranian border in the Kopet Dagh foothill plain.

The city, with a population of 253,000, is in the process of making great advances in agriculture, industry, and housing. Among its growing enterprises are a mechanized glass factory, a large metalworking plant (the Krasny Molot), a factory which manufactures machinery for the oil industry, a carpet-weaving mill, a silk-winding mill, and a meat-packing plant.

Ashkhabad ranks first in the republic as a cultural center with four theaters, a state philharmonic society, and several museums. It is also the site of the Academy of Sciences of the Turkmen S.S.R. and has over thirty scientific institutions, four institutions of higher education (including the State University), and a fine Central Library which houses 1,500,000 volumes.

In 1948 a terrible natural disaster struck Ashkhabad—an earthquake which destroyed almost every structure in the city proper within one minute. With the aid of large sums of money allocated by the government and the peoples of the Soviet republics, Ashkhabad was completely rebuilt within a few years. The city's civic center, which consists of the Academy of Sciences, the State University, the Drama Theater, and the buildings of the Council of Ministers of the Turkmen S.S.R. and the Central Committee of the Turkmen Communist Party, was built after the earthquake.

Today, Ashkhabad is a modern city that, like Alma Ata (although not to the same extent), is blessed with natural beauty. The average mean temperature in Ashkhabad is high and often uncomfortable during the peak tourist months of July and August. The Republic of Turkmenistan is the hottest of all the Central Asian republics with summer temperatures rarely dropping below 29 degrees C (86 degrees F) and sometimes reaching as high as 49.9 degrees C (122 degrees F) in areas near the Kara Kum Desert.

The Turkmen S.S.R. is located in the southwest of Central Asia and is the southernmost of all Union Republics. Its boundaries consist of the Kazakh S.S.R. on the north, the Uzbek S.S.R. on the northeast, Iran on the south, Afghanistan on the southeast, and the Caspian Sea on the west. The population of Turkmenistan is approximately 3 million.

HISTORY IN BRIEF

Sometime during the fourteenth century a Turkmen nationality with one common language emerged. The newly established Turkmens generally lived in tribal communities (although many continued to survive as nomadic tribes) which were usually self-supporting. While some of the tribal population tilled irrigated lands, others used primitive instruments to farm—the *ketman*, or wooden plow, was an invaluable tool. Wheat, barley, melons, and grapes were among the main crops. Crafts also developed in the communities, among them weaving, carpet making, felt rug making, and harness making.

The second half of the eighteenth century found the feudal states of Central Asia in the midst of serious armed conflicts. Fighting continued for more than a century and Turkmenia was involved in constant warfare until the last quarter of the nineteenth century. Ashkhabad was originally founded as a military stronghold in 1881. When hostilities finally ended, Turkmenia, of which Ashkhabad was now a part, found itself in a state of complete economic ruin.

The terrible condition of the Turkmen state prompted it to consider an economic and political alliance with Russia (the region of Turkmenia originally established trade relations with Russia as far back as the ninth to twelfth centuries). The period between the 1860s and 1880s saw 115,000 Caspian Turkmens and Tekins accept Russian citizenship. Soon to follow were the Saryks, Solors, and the Yomuds. By the beginning of the twentieth century, however, the Turkmen nationality was divided between the central government of Turkestan (which by this time was incorporated into the Russian Empire), the emirate of Bukhara, and the khanate of Khiva (which accepted vassalage from the tsar). The people, however, did not immediately benefit from the new Russian-Turkmen ties because the old feudal privileges were essentially upheld.

In time, however, advantages of the economic and political alliance became apparent. Internal feudal wars virtually stopped while the danger of invasion was almost nonexistent. Also, slavery and the slave trade were abolished. As the situation became more stable and irrigated farming produced higher yields, many of the nomadic tribes were able to settle. This, of course, led to the development of towns and with towns came the beginnings of industry. A railway was built, thus improving travel and communication with Russia.

Labor strikes began slowing the economy in 1913, and in 1916, one year before the Revolution in Petrograd, the *daikhans* (whose existence was hampered due to very minimal shares of land and water) rose against the local *bais* and Russian colonial rule. The representative administration of tsarist Russia was removed when, in March 1917, the *daikhans*, workers, and soldiers of Turkmenistan rose as a united force against Russian rule. However, while Soviets of Workers' and Soldiers' Deputies were organized throughout the region, the Committee of the Provisional Government, which was set up in April 1917, was sympathetic to the old system.

Soviet rule was finally established in the Transcaspian region after the success of the Revolution in 1917. The Turkestan Autonomous Soviet Socialist Republic was founded in April 1918 by the Fifth Congress of Soviets of Turkestan and incorporated into the Russian Federation. By mid-1918, however, the local feudal nobility, together with anti-Soviet nationalists and British interventionists (who saw the region as a possible colony), came down upon the Transcaspian region.

Following a struggle, the region was again in the hands of Soviet rule. The First Constituent Congress of Soviets of Turkmenistan founded the Turkmen Soviet Socialist Republic in February 1925 and in May of the same year Turkmenia became a constituent republic, thus giving the Turk-mens statehood. With its newfound place among the republics of the U.S.S.R., Turkmenia immediately began to implement social and economic reforms.

During World War II Turkmenia was instrumental in providing the Soviet Union with necessary materials and products such as cotton, wool, sulfur, sulfate, ozokerite, oil, and meat.

The people of Turkmenia have indeed come a long way from the time they were simple tillers, cattle breeders, and nomadic tribes. The republic, once considered to be the poorest and most backward in the Soviet Union, is now a recognized social and economic entity within the U.S.S.R.

MUSEUMS AND PLACES OF INTEREST

Ashkhabad is still involved in a period of restoration, the plan for which was formulated after the disastrous earthquake of 1948. It is perhaps for this reason that the city does not attract most tourists. There are, of course, museums, the two most interesting of which are the Ashkhabad Regional Lore Museum and the Fine Arts Museum. The Regional Lore Museum contains exhibits concerning the history of the Turkmenian people and the geography, flora, and fauna of Turkmenia. The Fine Arts Museum offers a collection of carpets, among which is the largest ornamental carpet in the world, measuring 192 square meters (230 square feet).

If time permits, Ashkhabad should be used as a base for visiting some of the outlying areas of the city and other interesting sights in Turkmenis-tan.

The summer resort town of Firyuza is not far from Ashkhabad. Aside from being a very pleasant town to visit, it is also the home of the well-known Silk Worm Breeding Farms. Arrangements to visit the farms can probably be made through the Intourist office in Ashkhabad. Some 8 kilometers (5 miles) southeast of the city is the town of Annau. There are several archaeological sites here among which are the ruins of the mausoleum of Khan Abul Kasim Babur built in 1455 and the ruins of Nessa, believed to have been built some 2,500 years ago by Alexander the Great. The site is located about 14.5 kilometers (9 miles) from Ashkhabad.

Merv, one of the most ancient towns in the republic, is the most interesting town in Turkmenia. Located at the crossroads leading to the oases in the Kopet Dagh foothills, Merv was "fair game" for terrible and devastating raids. Indeed, the town has suffered a cruel history as raids came from the nomadic tribes in the north; Greek, Roman, and Arab armies from the west; Mongolian invaders from the east; and Persians from the south.

Most visitors to Merv come to see the twelfth-century mausoleums of Mohammed ibn Said and Sultan Sandzhar. Mohammed ibn Said is, according to legend, a descendant of the Prophet Ali. The mausoleum of Sultan Sandzhar is by far the more lavish. The sultan was the ruler of the Seljuk Empire and the structure was built during his lifetime by a Turkmenian medieval architect known as the son of Atsyz from Serakhs. The main structure is in the shape of a cube while a double sphero-conic dome (one inside the other), fixed on an octagon, tops a large cylindrical dome which stands high over the main structure.

The Khamedani Mosque, which was built in the ninth century, stands near the town of Merv. Its particular attraction is the fact that services are still conducted there.

Another excursion that can probably be arranged through Intourist is to the foothills of the Kopet Dagh mountains, southwest of Kizyl-Arvat. Here one will have the opportunity to see the remains of a *chillekhan*, a structure used during the observance of the forty-day fasts. Built of baked brick in the ninth and tenth centuries, the structure is known among the local people as the Mausoleum of Paravbibi, who, according to legend, was a poor woman who bricked herself up in the mountain to escape captivity.

Also in the Kopet Dagh mountains, 20 kilometers (12 1/2 miles) southeast of the Bakharden settlement, is the Bakharden Cave, the entrance of which is on a sheer slope of limestone. From this point, one descends 10 meters (33 feet), coming upon a large hall with a vaulted ceiling. Following the guide down to another hall and eventually to a depth of 52 meters (170 feet), one reaches the Kau Ata Lake whose depth is 13 meters (42 feet) and whose area is 2,500 square meters (249 square feet). The Kau Ata is the largest underground lake in the Soviet Union.

The Bakharden Cave is inhabited by thousands of bats (which are inactive in the daytime). For this reason, it would be wise to inquire at the Intourist office in Ashkhabad whether or not an excursion to the cave is possible.

A very pleasant day can be spent visiting the Repetek Desert Preserve. On an area of 34,600 hectares (76,500 acres) are some of the most beautiful natural exhibits of desert terrain. Here one can see white saksaul trees, black saksaul groves, and desert sedge. Also, there are thirty species of mammals, twenty-five species of birds, twenty species of reptiles, and thousands of species of insects.

So, while Ashkhabad proper does offer a few museums and an opera and ballet theater as well as theaters for drama, the visitor would do well to use the time to visit the outlying areas of the city and, if time allows, other areas of the republic.

ACCOMMODATIONS

Visitors to Ashkhabad usually stay at the Hotel Turkmenistan, which offers a good restaurant, an Intourist Service Bureau, a newspaper and magazine stand, as well as a modest souvenir stand.

BUKHARA—General Information

Bukhara is located in the republic of Uzbekistan 193 kilometers (120 miles) from Samarkand and is one of the most primitive cities in the U.S.S.R. While Bukhara has made advances over the last decade as a result of the discovery of large resources of oil, gas, and iron ore, it is still, in many ways, the same as it was when the last emir ruled in 1920 and in some ways the same as in the nineteenth century when the slave trade was active. Indeed, much of Bukhara's fascination lies in the fact that it seems lost in the past.

Although most tourists visit the cities of Central Asia during the summer months, it is advisable to avoid Bukhara during July and August when the temperature often rises to an unbearable 55 degrees C. (130 degrees F.) or higher (air-conditioning, as in the other cities of the U.S.S.R., is not usually available).

With a population of about 70,000, Bukhara presently has three colleges, several secondary schools, and a music school. Also, the city is very proud of the Avicenna Public Library, wheere several manuscripts of Navoi, Firdausi, and other well-known poets and philosophers are kept.

HISTORY IN BRIEF

The history of Bukhara is very closely akin to that of the rest of Central Asia and the republic of Turkestan. Archaeological evidence has established that very early civilizations thrived in the region. In fact, traces of irrigation canals, dating to the second and first millennia B.C., have been discovered along with tools, bronze articles, and pottery in the regions of Andizhan, Sukhan-Darya, and Bukhara.

As with the whole of Central Asia, Bukhara's past is one of many wars and conquests. Cyrus the Great, founder of the Persian Empire, conquered the territory in the sixth century B.C. The Persian Empire was supreme until its destruction at the hands of Alexander the Great in 330 B.C. The centuries that followed brought little peace for Bukhara and the rest of Central Asia.

By the sixth century A.D. the entire region was ruled by the Turks. In the seventh and eighth centuries the Arab invaders were victorious and their control, while interrupted in the ninth century, was again supreme in the tenth to twelfth centuries. The most terrible invasion of Bukhara (and Central Asia) came in 1219–21 when the forces of Genghis Khan plundered the land, destroyed the economy and life-style of the people, and murdered much of the population.

It was not until Timur (Tamerlane) established his empire (whose capital was Samarkand) in the fourteenth century that much of the land and regional economy was revived.

By the early sixteenth century, the Uzbek nationality was almost completely formed and Russia took over the area. The Kokand and Bukhara khanates recognized and accepted their vassalage to the Russian Empire in 1868 (it is important to note that no distinction was made between the peoples of Central Asia; therefore the tsarist government simply referred to all of the established nationalities as Turkestanis or "natives" and the entire region as Turkestan).

Although land, water, and all industrial enterprises were nationalized in Turkestan after the Socialist victory in Petrograd in 1917, popular revolutions did not occur in Bukhara (and Khiva) until 1920. Thus, it was nearly three years after the Bolsheviks gained power in Russia (and most of Turkestan) that the rule of the emir of Bukhara (and the khan of Khiva) ended. The emir fled to Afghanistan and the Bukhara (and Khorezm) People's Soviet Republics were formed.

While Bukhara has not advanced as far or as quickly as other Uzbek cities like Tashkent (the capital of the republic) and Samarkand, it is beginning to reach into the twentieth century and has recently begun construction of new and modern buildings.

MUSEUMS AND PLACES OF INTEREST

Like most of the other cities of Central Asia, the interest and beauty of Bukhara lies not in the rooms of museums but in the architecture of the past. Therefore, if time is limited (and with present hotel facilities that is likely), it should not be wasted in museums.

Kalyan Minaret (also known as the Great Minaret and the Tower of Death) and Mosque

The Kalyan Minaret is one of the most popular attractions in Bukhara. Built in 1127, the structure, which is located in the center of the city, stands 45 meters (148 feet) high. Originally used for calling the Moslem faithful to prayer, the Kalyan is the tallest of Bukhara's minarets. The construction of the minaret is quite interesting; it is made only of brown bricks but the pieces are laid so intricately as to make the structure appear to be covered with ornaments.

Aside from its religious use, the Kalyan Minaret also served as a watch-tower to sight tribal invaders. Its cruelest implementation came toward the latter part of the seventeenth and the early eighteenth centuries when the minaret was used for purposes of execution—those who were condemned to death were taken to the top of the "Tower of Death" and were forced to jump.

The Kalyan Mosque is connected to the minaret by an arched stone bridge. The largest mosque in all of Central Asia, its huge cupola reaches such a great height that it can be seen from most parts of the city.

Miri-Arab Madrasah

Situated opposite the Kalyan Mosque is the Miri-Arab Madrasah. Originally constructed in the sixteenth century as a religious school for the training of Moslem clergy, the madrasah was reopened in 1946, the first Moslem religious school to be given permission to operate by the Soviet government since 1917 (this permission was in gratitude for the efforts on the part of the Moslem church to rally support for the Soviet cause in World War II). The madrasah is a two-story structure built around a courtyard. Today it houses the Spiritual Board of the Moslems of Central Asia and Kazakhstan.

Ismail Samani Mausoleum

The Ismail Samani Mausoleum, which dates back to the ninth or tenth century, is one of the oldest existing structures in Bukhara. Built of yellow bricks which are laid vertically, flat, and at an angle, the design has the appearance of intricate lace which seems to change in the morning, afternoon, and evening, depending on the light.

The entrance is made of lancet arches and the mausoleum structure is surrounded by lovely trees, which make for a very calm and peaceful atmosphere. (The Ismail Samani Mausoleum was one of the ancient structures that survived the invasion of Genghis Khan.)

Summer Palace of the Emir

Twenty-four kilometers (13 miles) from the center of the city is the summer palace of the last emir of Bukhara, the most sadistic and cruel of all the rulers of the Bukhara emirate. The inventory of the emir's harem is said to have ranged from 100 to 450 wives. It is with his harem and any other woman who did not satisfy him that the emir employed what came to be known as the "sweet death"—a punishment by which a woman was forced to swallow a lethal boiling, sugar-based concoction. When Communist revolutionaries took control of Bukhara in 1920, the emir fled to Kabul, Afghanistan, where he is said to have become a tea merchant.

A visit to the summer palace is interesting not only from a historical view but also from a natural one. The grounds are surrounded by magnificent foliage and it is not uncommon to see peacocks, their tails fanned in splendor, perched high in the trees.

Citadel (Fortress of Ark)

The ancient fortress from which the emirs of Bukhara ruled dates from the seventh and eighth centuries. The walls of the fortress seem massive and they did indeed thwart many invading enemies until the successful attack of the Communist forces led by General Mikhail Frunze.

The fortress is now a museum which offers exhibits concerning the flora and fauna of the Bukhara region. Displays depict life in Bukhara under the rule of the emir and there are paintings of the slave markets and other dreadful social conditions. Visitors can see dungeons with realistic-looking wax figures in the poses of chained prisoners.

Bug Pit

While the Bug Pit is certainly not one of the more beautiful sights in Bukhara, its gruesome history makes it an unusual tourist attraction. The emirs of Bukhara used the pit as a form of punishment. Prisoners were lowered into the insect-infested pit; there they would be attacked and bitten but would rarely die. The pit was one of the ultimate forms of torture and prisoners would sometimes spend weeks and even months in it.

Other Attractions

There are several additional attractions in Bukhara which might be of interest, among which are the Lyabi Khauz ensemble which dates back to the seventeenth century, the Madrasah of Divan-beghi, the Magoki Attari Mosque, and the Toki-Tilpak Furashon (the dome of the skullcap makers).

Of these, the Toki-Tilpak Furashon may be especially so. Built four hundred years ago, the structure consists of three giant rosettes topped with a central dome. The fascination lies in the fact that the wooden roof was constructed and raised without one nail and to this day does not have a single crack.

Also, a short visit to the marketplaces and bazaars in Bukhara will be an unforgettable experience.

ACCOMMODATIONS

There are two hotels for visitors to Bukhara, the Bukhara and the new Amu-Darya. In the Bukhara, the rooms range from uncomfortable to moderately comfortable. Water pressure in the rooms that have toilet facilities is only fair and there is no escape from the terrible heat of the summer. The restaurant is not particularly good but it is tolerable for a short stay.

The hotel does offer the services of an Intourist Service Bureau, a small souvenir shop (foreign currency only), and a small newsstand. The new Hotel Amu-Darya has 378 rooms and offers music nightly, a bar and barbershop facilities. However, one need spend no more than one night in Bukhara; the most interesting and important sights can be seen and appreciated in a single day.

DUSHANBE—General Information

Dushanbe is the capital of the Tajik Soviet Socialist Republic (Tajikistan is sometimes called the "highland republic" because 93 percent of its territory is taken up by mountains). The city, with a population of 350,000, is situated overlooking the Dushanbe Darya river and is surrounded by the beautiful snow-capped mountains of the Hissar Range of the Pamirs (Communism Peak, 7,495 meters [24,590 feet] above sea level, is the highest point of both the Pamirs and the Soviet Union).

The word "Dushanbe" means "Monday" in the Tajik language. The origin of the name seems to go back several centuries when the village held a weekly bazaar on Mondays.

Once a village of almost complete illiteracy, Dushanbe has, in the past thirty to forty years, put great emphasis on education. Today there are many schools in which children can complete their compulsory education. The city also has thirteen specialized schools as well as a State University, teaching institutes, and institutes for the study of medicine, engineering, agriculture, and foreign languages. Indeed, one out of every seven people in Dushanbe is a student.

The city is also quite proud of its industrial achievements (remember that just forty to fifty years ago, Dushanbe was nothing more than a tiny village under the rule of the emir of Bukhara). Eighty major industrial enterprises are located in Dushanbe, among which are meat packing, tanning, textile manufacturing, and the manufacturing of automatic machine tools and equipment for the oil industry.

The climate of Dushanbe is generally the same as most other Central Asian cities, although it is usually not as excruciatingly hot as Bukhara. However, in July and August visitors should be prepared to be uncomfortably warm in Dushanbe—the months of fall, winter (it can get fairly cold during the winter months), and spring are certainly more pleasant.

HISTORY IN BRIEF

The history of the region that is now Dushanbe and the entire republic of Tajikstan is quite old. Bactria (located on what is now the region south of the Hissar Range) and Sogdiana (on what is now the territory north of the Amu Darya river) were densely populated states which thrived in the sixth to fourth centuries B.C. They were highly successful agricultural societies that mastered the technique of building irrigation systems and supplemented their economies by engaging in trade and commerce.

In the fourth century B.C. Alexander the Great invaded Bactria and Sogdiana. Two centuries later, as Greek rule weakened, the state of Tokharistan emerged on what was the territory of Bactria. Later, when the Kushan Empire was at its height, Tokharistan and Sogdiana were incorporated into it.

Although much of the population of Bactria and Sogdiana were annihilated during centuries of invasion and rule, the geographical location of the region allowed for great economic activity as well as for the intermingling of peoples, languages, and customs. It was through this area of Central Asia that the ancient trade routes (sometimes referred to as the "silk routes") from Europe to China and from India to Siberia ran.

The Arabs overran Central Asia (including the region of Tajikstan) in the seventh and eighth centuries and ruled for two centuries until the Tajik state of the Samanides gained control of the territory at the end of the ninth century. It was at this time, in the land that was Bactria and Sogdiana, that the Tajik nation emerged as a state with a common language that did not differ much from modern Tajik. The newly formed state's economy was based largely on agriculture, handicrafts, mining, and trade with other nations.

The continued greatness of the Tajik society was not to be, as internal strife between local feudal lords and raids by nomadic tribes slowly weakened the Samanide state and finally brought its downfall in the tenth century.

The next thousand years saw the Tajik nation incorporated into several feudal states; this was instrumental in the decline of the culture of the people. Probably the most terrible of the feudal systems that the Tajiks were ruled by was that of the khanate of Bukhara, which was formed in the sixteenth century. The oppression that was set upon the people (Uzbeks as well as Tajiks) by the emirs of Bukhara did much to plunge them into a state of ignorance by which their national culture was practically extinguished.

The turning point in this situation came in 1861 when Russian troops entered Central Asia and the people came into closer contact with the Russian Empire. The emir of Bukhara became a vassal state of Russia in 1868 and retained control of the central and southern regions of present-day Tajikistan. The northern areas of the state (and the Pamirs) were incorporated into the Turkestan administration, which was under the direct control of the tsar. The territory held by the emirate of Bukhara did not fall to the Soviets until 1920.

When in October 1924 the decision was made to divide Central Asia into national states, the Tajik people formed the Autonomous Soviet Socialist Republic of Tajikistan within the Uzbek S.S.R. On October 16, 1929, after several years of bolstering the economic and political conditions in the republic, the Third All-Tajik Extraordinary Congress of Soviets adopted a declaration for the transition from the status of Autonomous Republic to Union Republic; and Dushanbe, renamed Stalinabad (since then renamed Dushanbe), was proclaimed the capital of the republic.

As for Dushanbe itself, it was nothing more than a tiny village consisting of five hundred clay houses when the Soviets took power. Schools were virtually nonexistent and in 1926 the population was under six thousand people. Extensive plans for construction and intensive labor brought Dushanbe from an ancient village to a fairly modern city. In 1939 the population numbered close to 85,000 and today the capital of the Tajik S.S.R. is an industrial city with 350,000 inhabitants.

MUSEUMS AND PLACES OF INTEREST

Visitors to Dushanbe should not expect much in the way of tourist attractions. It is, in fact, one of the least interesting cities (from a tourist point of view) in the Soviet Union.

While Dushanbe is certainly a great testimonial to the achievements of Soviet industry and planning, it does not offer any ancient architectural monuments (the oldest structures in the city are thirty to forty years old) and the museums are not very extensive. The only three museums that are recommended are the Regional Lore Museum, where visitors can become better acquainted with the background and customs of the Tajik people; the Museum of History, which offers exhibits concerning the history of the people and the republic; and the Museum of Fine Arts, which displays the works of the Tajik artists.

Other possibilities for those visitors who are interested include visiting a collective farm (the Intourist office in Dushanbe should be given advance notice for this tour because permission from the head of the collective farm is usually required), the textile factory, some of the educational institutions, and the movie studio where films in the Tajik language are made.

For evening entertainment, Dushanbe can be quite enjoyable. The Lenin State Opera and Ballet Theater offers fine performances of both classical and national operas and ballets. This theater is also the house of the State Philharmonic Society. Other worthwhile entertainment can be found at the Tajik Academic Drama Theater and the Russian Drama Theater.

When quiet relaxation is desired, a visit to the Rakhat *chaikhana* (tearoom) is in order. Here, in this lovely shaded structure, visitors can escape the heat of the sun and simply sit and relax.

ACCOMMODATIONS

The Hotel Dushanbe is the only hotel available for tourists. It is comfortable (although the rooms are extremely warm in the summer) and has a very good restaurant attached to it. Other services include an Intourist Service Bureau, a newspaper and magazine stand, and a small souvenir shop.

FRUNZE—General Information

Frunze, the capital of the Kirghiz Soviet Socialist Republic, is located 483 kilometers (300 miles) northeast of Tashkent. The city, with a population of about 400,000, was named for the Soviet military leader Mikhail V. Frunze, who led the victorious Bukhara campaign which resulted in the downfall of the emirate.

Fifty years ago, the city, then called Pishipek, was nothing more than a small provincial town, most of whose population was illiterate. The primary occupation of the Kirghiz people was horse breeding and animal husbandry. Today, major industries of the city include machine production, metalwork, leathercraft, meat processing, clothing manufacturing, vegetable canning, soap manufacturing, and tobacco curing. Also, nonferrous metals, silk, and karakul pelts are exported to other countries.

Like Alma Ata, Frunze is blessed with magnificent greenery and offers the appearance and mood of a large garden or park. And like Alma Ata, visitors have an opportunity to take an excursion to the beautiful snow-capped mountains of the Kirghiz Range.

The climate of Frunze in the summer is hot but fairly pleasant in comparison with the very hot cities of Central Asia—the abundant foliage helps provide areas of shade and shelter from the direct rays of the summer sun.

Cultural life in Frunze is reasonably extensive and visitors can enjoy performances at the Frunze Opera and Ballet Theater as well as concerts by national and classical orchestras and musical ensembles. There are also several museums of interest.

HISTORY IN BRIEF

The history of the territory of which Frunze is the capital is in many ways similar to that of the other Central Asian cities and republics. Nomadic tribes engaged in cattle breeding and some farming two thousand years B.C. Later, as trade and commerce increased, the land inhabited by the ancestors of the Kirghiz people was the site of an active east-west trade route. Trade routes, as history has shown, were prime targets for attacks by foreign tribes and states and the Kirghiz region was no exception. By the time of the Christian era, the territory belonged to the Parkan kingdom, a slave-owning state of Central Asia which later became known as the state of Kushan.

The period during the sixth and seventh centuries saw the Kirghiz lands become part of the West Turkic khanate; from the tenth to twelfth centuries the territory was engulfed by the feudal state of the Karkhanides. When the Mongols and Tatars invaded Central Asia in the thirteenth century, the region that is now Frunze, and indeed all of Kirghizia, suffered the same fate as the lands of the Kazakhs, Turkmens, Tajiks, and Uzbeks—the fields and land were destroyed, villages were razed to the ground, and much of the population was murdered. The rule of the Mongols brought constant war to the region and for seven centuries thereafter the land of Kirghizia was ruled by many nomadic tribes, one following the other, always at war.

The nineteenth century was a turning point in the long history of the Kirghiz people and land. Early in the century, a powerful Kokand khanate was establishing itself in the Ferghana valley. By the early 1830s, the entire Kirghiz region was under its rule. The most fertile lands were seized by the khans and the people were heavily taxed. Also, clan wars were instigated thus weakening the people from within. This assured the khans of limited resistance.

Seeing little hope of being able to free themselves, some Kirghiz tribal chiefs approached Russia for help (the Kirghiz had been trading with Russia for many centuries). In 1855 the Bugu tribe (who lived east of

Issyk-Kul), under the leadership of its chief, Borombei Bekmuratov, became subjects of the Russian tsar. Other tribes quickly followed the example of the Bugu and by 1870 the entire territory of northern and central Kirghizia was part of the Russian Empire. Southern Kirghizia joined the empire six years later.

The Soviets found it difficult to establish power in Kirghizia. Even after the success of the Socialist Revolution of 1917 in Petrograd, the class differences in different parts of Kirghizia presented a problem. The coal-mining regions in the towns of Kyzyl-Kiya and Sulyukta were very receptive to the formation of local Soviets but it was not until the first half of 1918 that the rest of Kirghizia was in Soviet hands and even then control was not firmly established. A fierce civil war erupted between the overthrown forces (who formed highly organized, well-armed units) and the newly established Soviet government. Ultimately, the Soviet forces were victorious and in 1924 the Kirghiz Autonomous Region within the Russian Federation was formed. On February 1, 1926, the Kirghiz Autonomous Soviet Socialist Republic was established.

In 1936 the Eighth Extraordinary All-Union Congress of Soviets adopted a new constitution of the U.S.S.R. and proclaimed Kirghizia a Union Republic, to be known as the Kirghiz Soviet Socialist Republic. Thus for the first time in their history the Kirghiz people had a national state.

Today the Kirghiz Republic is continuing to improve and expand its industrial and agricultural enterprises and, as a result, is improving the standard of living for its people.

MUSEUMS AND PLACES OF INTEREST

The main attraction of Frunze is the city itself, and tourists should not expect to find magnificent ancient architecture here. Rather, a visit to Frunze should be used as a stopover or connection point to another city. Beautiful Frunze is like a botanical garden—three hundred different kinds of trees grow here. A walk along Dzerzhinsky Boulevard is quite enjoyable and here visitors will find twenty rows of interesting trees. The man-made Komsomolsk Lake is surrounded by 200 hectares (494 acres) of karagach elms. An oak grove grows in the heart of the city proper.

There are, of course, museums in Frunze. The Fine Arts Museum exhibits paintings of Kirghiz artists as well as the works of Russian and Soviet masters. The History Museum will be of particular interest to those who wish to learn of the history of the Kirghiz people and republic. The Zoology Museum is educational and probably the best museum to visit with children.

Frunze offers several options where entertainment is concerned. The

Frunze Opera and Ballet Theater is an ideal place to spend a pleasant and fulfilling evening. Here one can enjoy both national and classical operas, ballets, and concerts.

For those who prefer theater, there are some fine drama theaters that perform plays by national as well as Russian, Soviet, and European playwrights. For the children there is a puppet theater.

ACCOMMODATIONS

The hotel for tourists in Frunze is called the Ala Too. It is a small hotel of reasonable comfort and few services. The hotel has an adequate restaurant, newspaper stand, and a small souvenir shop. Also, there are shoe and garment repair services.

INDEX

accommodations. *See* Campsites; Hotels;
  Motels
Adler, 205–6
air travel and airlines, 31
  Batumi, 217
  entry and exit points, 2
  Kiev, 155
  Leningrad, 130
  Lvov, 368
  Minsk, 352
  Moscow, 33–4, 37–8
  Odessa, 192
  Samarkand, 404
  Sochi, 207, 210
  Sukhumi, 215
Alma Ata, 204–6
  hotels and restaurants, 409
  museums and exhibitions, 206–7,
    408
  monuments, 409
  mountain excursion, 409
  parks, 408
  theaters, 407–8
Alphabet, Russian, 6
Alupka, 225–6
arboretums. *See* Gardens, arboretums
art galleries and museums
  Alma Ata, 407
  Arkhangelskoye, 71

art galleries *(cont'd)*
  Ashkhabad, 412
  Frunze, 423
  Kaunas, 343
  Kharkov, 174
  Kiev, 138–42
  Leningrad, 92–111
  Lvov, 356–8
  Minsk, 349
  Moscow, 61–2, 63, 65, 66
  Odessa, 185–6
  Pyatigorsk, 235
  Riga, 332–3
  Rostov-on-Don, 234
  Samarkand, 401
  Smolensk, 167
  Tallinn, 318
  Tashbrent, 385–6
  Vilnius, 337–9, 342
  Zagorsk, 76
Artashat, 258
Ashkhabad, 410–12
  hotels and restaurants, 414
  museums, places of interest, 412, 414
  excursions from, 412–14
automobile travel, 21
  accommodations, *see* Campsites; Hotels;
    Motels
  chauffeur-driven cars, 23

automobile *(cont'd)*
  driver's license, 1–2
  entry and exit points, 2
  gasoline, 22–3
  Georgian Military Highway, 236
  insurance, 30
  Moscow, 38–40
  parking, 21
  rentals, 22–3, 69–70
  Sochi, 207
  traffic regulations, 29–30
  Vladimir and Suzdal, 267

Baku, 260–1
  hotels, 265
  Maiden's Tower (Kyz Kalasy), 261–2
  Metro, 263
  museums, places of interest, 261–3
  restaurants and cafés, 265
  Shirvan Shahs' Palace, 262
  suburbs, 263–4
  theaters and concert halls, 263, 265
ballet. *See* Opera, ballet and concerts
bars *(see also* Restaurants and cafés), 26–7
Batumi, 215–16
  Botanical Garden, 216
  health and resort areas, 217
  hotels, 217
  Intourist office, 217
  Museum of the Revolution, 216
  Palace of Culture, 216
  post office, 217
  theaters and cinema, 217
  transportation offices, 217
Black Sea, 180–1
Bogolyubovo, 301–23
  Intercession, Church of the, on the Nerl, 304–5
  Nativity of Our Lady Cathedral, 302–3
Borodino, 71–2
botanical gardens. *See* Gardens, arboretums
Brest, 374–5
  hotel and restaurant, 376
  museums, 375–6
  telephone and post office, 376
  theater, 376
Bukhara, 414–15
  Bug Pit, 417
  Citadel (Fortress of Ark), 417
  hotels and services, 418
  Ismail Samani Mausoleum, 416–17
  Kalyan Minaret, 416

Bukhara *(cont'd)*
  madrasah (religious schools), 416, 417
  mosques, 416, 417
  museums, 415–16, 417
  Summer Palace of the Emir, 417
  Toki-Tilpak Furashon, 417–18

cafés. *See* Restaurants and cafés
campsites, 21
  Adler, 206
  Chernovtsy, 379
  Kharkov, 176
  Kishiven, 373
  Moscow, 47
  Novgorod, 160
  Odessa, 191
  Ordzhonikidze, 237
  Pyatigorsk, 235
  Rostov-on-Don, 234
  Smolensk, 170
  Tbilisi, 249
cathedrals, churches, monasteries
  Bogolyubova, 31–5
  Chernovtsky region, 379
  Echmiadzen, 256–7
  Kharkov, 175
  Kideksha, 300–1
  Kiev, 142–6
  Kishinev, 372
  Leningrad, 88–9, 90–2, 111, 116, 121
  Lvov, 358–65
  Moscow, 53–5, 57
  Novgorod, 157, 158–60
  Pereslavl-Zaleski, 163–4
  Riga, 327–30
  Rostov, 163
  Smolensk, 167–8, 169
  Sukhumi area, 214
  Suzdal, 284–300
  Tallinn, 312–17, 321
  Tbilisi and suburbs, 241–2, 244, 246, 248–9
  Tula, 74
  Vilnius, 340–1
  Vladimir, 270–81
  Yaroslavl and environs, 162–4
  Yuryev-Polskoi, 306–8
  Zagorsk, 76
caves
  Bakharden, 413
  Pyatigorsk, 235
  Sigulda, 335
  Sochi, 204

Chernovtsy, 378–9
  hotels, campsite, 379
  museums, places of interest, 379
  restaurants and cafés, 380
Chop, 378
churches. See Cathedrals, churches and
    monasteries
cinemas, 26
  Batumi, 217
  Kiev, 154
  Lvov, 368
  Minsk, 351
  Moscow, 77, 79–80
  Odessa, 191
  Sochi, 209
  Tallinn, 323
  Tashkent, 389–90
  Yerevan, 259
circus
  Kiev, 154
  Lvov, 367
  Minsk, 351
  Moscow, 77, 78
  Odessa, 191
  Rostov-on-Don, 233, 234
  Sochi, 209
  Tashkent, 390
clothing, 23
concerts. See Opera, ballet, concerts
costs, 4–5
Crimea, 218–20
Cruiser Aurora Museum, 113–14
cruises, 32
  Sochi, 207
currency, 5
  customs regulations, 18, 19, 20
  denominations, 22
  exchanging, 21–22
Customs, 18
  declaration, 19
  items, permitted and forbidden entry or
      exit, 18–20
  purchase receipts, 25

driving. See Automobile travel
Dushanbe, 418–20
  hotel and services, 421
  museums, places of interest, 420–1
Dvin, 258

Echmiadzin, 256–7
entertainment (see also cities, specific
    forms), 26–7

Firyuza, 412–13
food (see also Restaurants and cafés), 4–5,
    24–5
Frunze, 421–3
  museums, places of interest, 423–4
  hotel and services, 424

game preserves
  Crimean, 226–7
  Repetek Desert, 414
  Sochi, 203
gardens
  Alma Ata, 408
  Batumi, 216
  Kiev, 150
  Leningrad, 119, 122–3
  Minsk, 347
  Moscow, 60, 61, 65
  Pavlovsk, 125–6
  Peterhof (Pedrodvorets), 124
  Pushkin (Tsarskoye Selo), 125
  Riga, 332
  Rustavi, 248
  Sochi, 200–2, 203
  Sukhumi, 212
  Tashkent, 389
  Tbilisi, 243
  Yalta, 227
Garni, 258
Gatchina, 126–7

health care, 27
health resorts
  Batumi, 217
  Jurmala, 335
  Kiev, 151–2
  Odessa, 190
  Sochi, 194, 206–7
  Sukhumi, 211
  Yalta area, 224
hiking, Sochi area, 206, 207
hotels, 3–4
  Alma Ata, 409
  Ashkhabad, 414
  Baku, 265
  Batumi, 217
  Brest, 376
  Bukhara, 418
  cities with overnight accommodations,
      17–18
  Chernovtsy, 379
  Dushanbe, 421
  Frunze, 424
  Kharkov, 175

hotels *(cont'd)*
  Kiev, 152
  Kishinev, 373
  Leningrad, 127
  Lvov, 367
  meals, 4-5, 24-5
  Minsk, 350
  Moscow, 40-7
  Odessa, 191
  Ordzhonikidze, 237
  Orel, 173
  Pyatigorsk, 235
  registration, 20-1
  Rostov-on-Don, 233-4
  Simferopol, 230
  Smolensk, 170
  Sochi, 208
  Sukhumi, 214
  Tallinn, 322
  Tashkent, 384, 385, 388-9
  Tbilisi, 249
  tipping, 26
  transfers, 20
  Uzhgorod, 377
  Vilnius, 343
  Volgograd, 179
  Yaroslavl, 164
  Yerevan, 259

insurance, 30
Intourist services and offices, 20, 26
  Batumi, 217
  Dushanbe, 421
  Moscow, 39-40
  Odessa, 191
  Simferopol, 230
  Sukhumi, 214
  travel agencies accredited by, 7-15
  Vilnius, 343
  See also Travel arrangements

Kamenets-Podolski, 379
Kaunas, 343
Kharkov, 173-4
  campsite, 175
  cathedrals, 175
  Dzerzhinsky Square, 175
  hotels, 175
  museums, 174
  Post and Telegraph Offices, 176
  Railway Terminal, 176
  restaurants, 176
  Sumskaya Street, 175
  theaters and concert halls, 176

Khatyn, 349-50
Khosta, 206
Kideksha, 300-1
Kiev, 131-6
  art museums, 138-42
  ballet, 149
  cathedrals, churches and monasteries,
    142-6
  circus, 154
  concerts, 149, 154
  Fomin Botanical Gardens, 150
  Golden Gate, 142
  Goloseyevsky Forest Park, 151
  hotels, 152
  Kiev-Pechersky Monastery, 144-45
  Kiev University, 146-7
  Lenin Museum, 138
  museums and exhibitions, 136-8, 140-1,
    147-8, 153-4
  opera, 149
  parks and recreational areas, 150-2
  Post Office, 155
  places of interest, 136-54
  Pushche-Voditsa, 151-2
  restaurants and cafés, 152-3
  Russian Art Museum, 139
  St. Sophia's Cathedral, 142-3
  St. Vladimir's Cathedral, 145-6
  Shevchenko Memorial Museum, 141-2
  Shevchenko Museum, 140-1
  State Museum of History, 136-8
  stores and shops, 154
  telegraph office, 155
  theaters, cinemas, 149-50, 154
  transportation offices, 155
  Trukhanov Island, 151
  Ukrainian Art Museum, 138-9
  Ukrainian Industry and Agriculture,
    Exhibition of Advances Methods in,
    147-8
  Vladimirskaya Hill, 150-1
  Western and Oriental Art Museum,
    139-40
Kishinev, 369-70
  Avenue of Youth, 371
  Bulgarian Volunteers Monument, 372
  Lenin Prospect, 372-3
  hotels, motel, campsite, 373
  Mazaraki Church, 372
  parks, 372, 372
  restaurants, 373
  Victory Square, 371
Klin, 76-7
Kobystan, 264

Lake Preshcheevo, 163
Lazarevskoye, 206–7
Leningrad, 83–8
  Admiralty, 118
  airline office, 130
  Alexander Nevsky Monastery, 90–1
  Alexander's Column, 118
  Annunciation Cathedral
    (Blagoveshchensky Sobor), 90
  Anthropology and Ethnography, Peter I
    Museum of, 112
  area, country palaces, 124–7
  art galleries, 92–111
  ballet, 121
  cathedrals, churches and monasteries,
    88–9, 90–2, 111, 116, 121
  cemeteries, 91
  Central Naval Museum, 113
  country palaces, 124–7
  Coffee House, 123
  concert halls, 129
  Cruiser *Aurora* Museum, 113–14
  Decembrists' Square, 119
  Educational Workers' Palace of Culture,
    121
  Engineer's Castle (Paul's Castle), 123
  Ethnography of the Peoples of the
    U.S.S.R. Museum, 112
  Field of Mars (Marsovo Polye), 122–3
  Finland Railway Station, 114
  Fortress of St. Peter and St. Paul
    (Petropavlovskaya Krepost), 88–90
  gardens, 119, 122–3
  Goddess of Glory Columns, 119
  Great October Socialist Revolution
    Museum, 112
  Hermitage, 92–111
  Heroes of the Revolution and Civil War
    Monument, 122
  History of Leningrad Museum, 113
  Holy Trinity Cathedral (Troitsky Sobor),
    91
  Horse Guards Riding School, 119
  hotels, 127
  Kazan Cathedral, 91
  Korov Opera and Ballet Theater, 121
  Lazarevskoye Cemetery, 91
  Lenenegro Building, 123
  Lenin Museum, 112
  Literary Museum, 113
  Marble Palace, 123
  Maryinsky Palace, 120
  Maxim Gorky Garden, 119
  museums, 88–115, 128–9

Leningrad *(cont'd)*
  Naval Cathedral of St. Nicholas, 121
  Nevsky Prospect, 116–17
  New Holland Arch, 121
  opera, 121
  Palace Square, 117–18
  palaces, 118, 120, 121, 123–7
  Peter I, Cottage of, 115
  Peter I Monument, 119
  places of interest, 88–123
  Post Office, 120, 130
  Puskin Memorial Museum, 113
  Restaurants and cafés, 128
  Rimsky-Korsakov State Conservatory,
    121
  Rostral Columns, 122
  St. Isaac's Cathedral, 92
  St. Isaac's Square, 120
  St. Nicholas Cathedral, 111
  Senate and Synod Buildings, 119
  Smolny area, 114–15
  State Russian Museum, 111–12
  stores and souvenir shops, 129–30
  Strelka of Vasilievsky Island, 122
  Summer Garden (Letny Sad), 122–3
  Summer Palace (Letny Dvorets), 123
  telegraph office, 130
  Theater Square, 120–1
  theaters, 117, 121, 129
  Tikhvinskoye Cemetery, 91
  University, 115–16
  Winter Palace, 92–3, 96, 118
  Zoological Museum, 114
Leninskye-Gorki, 72–3
Livadia, 223–4
Lomonosov, 127
Lvov, 353–5
  Armenian Cathedral, 358–9
  Art Gallery, 357
  Assumption, Church of the, 361–2
  cinemas, 368
  circus, 367
  Dominicans, Church of, 363–4
  Ethnography and Crafts Museum,
    356–57
  Gothic Cathedral (Latinsky Sobor),
    359–61
  Hill of Glory, 366
  History Museum, 355–6
  hotels, 367
  Ivan Franko Memorial Museum, 357–8
  Lenin Museum, 355
  post office, 368
  restaurants, 367

Lvov *(cont'd)*
    St. George Cathedral, 362–3
    St. John the Baptist Church, 364
    St. Mary's Church, 364
    St. Nicholas Church, 364–5
    St. Onufry Church and Monastery, 365
    St. Parasceva Pjatnisa Church, 365
    stores and shops, 368
    theater, opera and ballet, 366, 367
    transportation offices, 368
    Ukrainian Art Museum, 356

Mardaakyany, 264
Massandra, 226
mausoleums
    Bukhara, 416–17
    Samarkand, 397–401
meals (*see also* Restaurants and cafés),
    4–5, 24–5
medical and dental care, 27
medications, 9
medieval towns (*see also* names), 266–7
Melikhovo, 73–4
Merv, 413
Minsk, 344–6
    airline office, 352
    Chelyuskintsky Park, 347
    cinemas, 351
    circus, 351
    excursions, 349–50
    hotels, 350
    Geophysical Observatory, 348
    museums, 348–9, 351
    places of interest, 346–8
    Post and Telegraph Offices, 352
    restaurants and cafés, 350
    stores and shops, 351–2
    theaters and concert halls, 351
monasteries. *See* Cathedrals, churches and
    monasteries
Moscow, 35–7
    air travel, 33–4, 37–8
    Annunciation (Blagoveshchensky)
        Cathedral, 54–5
    area, places of interest, 70–7
    arriving in, 37–40
    art galleries and museums, 61–2, 63, 65,
        66
    automobile, arriving by, 38–40
    automobile travel in, 69–70
    Assumption (Uspensky) Cathedral, 53–4
    ballet, 77, 78
    Bell Tower, 53
    Bolshoi Theater, 60, 61

Moscow *(cont'd)*
    campsite, 47
    car rental, 69–70
    cathedrals and churches, 53–5, 57
    circus, 77, 78
    concerts, 77, 78, 79
    entertainment, 77–80
    gardens, 60, 61, 65
    getting around, 67–71, 77
    Granovitaya Palata, 54
    Great Kremlin Palace, 55–6
    guided tours, 67–9
    GUM (department store), 59
    hotels, motels, 40–7
    Intourist office, 39–40
    Kremlin, 50–6
    Kropotkinskaya Square and vicinity,
        62–4
    Lenin Mausoleum, 29, 58–9
    metro, 69, 70–1
    museums and exhibitions, 52, 58, 63,
        64–7
    National Economic Achievements
        exhibition, 64–5
    opera, 77, 78
    Ostankino Palace, 65
    Palace of Congresses, 52
    palaces, 55–6, 65
    places of interest, 50–71
    public transportation, 69, 70–1
    Red Square, 56–9
    restaurants and cafés, 47–50
    Revolution Square, 59–61
    St. Basil's (Pokrovsky) Cathedral, 57
    shopping and stores, 59, 80–2
    Spasskaya Tower, 57–8
    State History Museum, 58
    Sverdlov Square, 59–61
    taxis, 69, 77
    theaters, cinemas, 60–1, 77–80
    train, arriving by, 38
    transportation in, 69–71, 77
    transportation to, 37–40
    Tretyakov Art Gallery, 61–2
    University, 66
    Vladimir region excursion, 266–7
mosques
    Bukhara, 416, 417
    Merv, 413
    Samarkand, 396
motels, 21
    Kisinev, 373
    Moscow, 41, 47
    Odessa, 191

motels *(cont'd)*
  Rostov-on-Don, 234
  Tbilisi, 249
motion picture theaters. *See* Cinemas;
  names of cities
mountains
  Alma Ata, 409
  Caucasus Range, 231
  Kopet Dagh, 413
  Sochi area, 202–3, 207
  Sukhumi, 213
  Tbilisi, 245–6
Mtskheta, 247–8
museums and exhibitions
  Alma Ata, 406–7, 408
  art, *see* Art galleries and museums
  Ashkhabad, 412, 414
  Baku area, 262–3, 264
  Batumi, 216
  Brest, 375–6
  Bukhara, 415–16, 417
  Chernovtsy region, 379
  Dushanbe, 421
  Kaunas, 343
  Kharkov, 174
  Kiev, 136–8, 140–1, 147–8, 153–4
  Klin, 77
  Leningrad, 88–115, 128–9
  Leninskye-Gorki, 72–3
  Lvov, 355–8, 367
  Melikhovo, 73–4
  Minsk, 348–9, 351
  Moscow, 52, 58, 63, 64–7
  Odessa, 184–6
  Orel, 171–2, 173
  Pereslavl-Zaleski, 164
  Podolsk, 73
  Pyatigorsk, 235
  Riga, 332–4
  Rostov-on-Don, 233, 234
  Samarkand, 393, 395, 401
  Smolensk, 166–7, 170
  Sochi, 198–200, 209
  Sukhumi, 212
  Tallinn, 318–19
  Tashkent, 384, 385–6, 389
  Uzhgorod, 377
  Vilnius, 342
  Volgograd, 178–9, 179
  Yalta, 222–3
  Yasnaya Polyana, 75–6
  Yaroslavl, 162
  Yerevan, 255–6, 259
  Zagorsk, 76

Nalchik, 236
Neftyanye Kamny, 264
night life (*see also* names of cities, specific
  forms of entertainment), 26–7
Novgorod, 156–7
  campsite, 160
  cathedrals and churches, 157, 158–60
  Gorodische, 160
  hotels, 160
  Kremlin, 157–9
  museums and places of interest, 157–60
  restaurants, 160
Novoselitsa, 379

Odessa, 182–4
  Arcadia Resorts, 190
  Archeological Museum, 184
  art museums, 185, 186
  bookshops, 192
  campsite, 191
  circus, 191
  concerts, 188
  Deribassovskaya Street, 189
  Filatov Research Institute, 190
  History and Regional Studies Museum,
    185–6
  hotels, motel, 191
  Intourist office, 191
  Maritime Museums, 185
  museums, 184–6
  October Revolution Square, 188
  Opera and Ballet Theater, 187–8
  places of interest, 184–91
  port, 190–1
  Post and Telegraph Offices, 192
  Potemkin Stairs, 186
  recreational facilities, 189
  restaurants, 191
  Seaside Boulevard, 186–7
  Tairov Institute, 190
  theaters and cinemas, 191
  transportation offices, 192
  Western and Oriental Art Museum, 185
opera, ballet, concerts
  Baku, 265
  Dushanbe, 421
  Frunze, 423
  Kharkov, 176
  Kiev, 149, 154
  Leningrad, 121, 129
  Lvov, 366, 367
  Minsk, 351
  Moscow, 77, 78, 79
  Odessa, 187–8, 191

opera *(cont'd)*
  Riga, 336
  Samarkand, 403
  Smolensk, 170
  Tallinn, 323
  Tashkent, 384, 385, 390
  Tbilisi, 244, 250
  Yerevan, 259
Ordzhonikidze, 236
  hotels, campsites, 237
  restaurants, 237
Oreanda, 224
Orel, 171
  hotels, 173
  Intourist office, 173
  Lenin Square, 172
  monuments, 172
  museums, 171–2
  Post Office, 173
  restaurants, 173
  theaters, 173

palaces
  Arkhangelskoye, 71
  Baku, 262
  Bukhara, 417
  Leningrad, 118, 120, 121, 123–7
  Moscow, 55–6, 65
  Novgorod, 160
  Suzdal, 287
  Yalta area, 223–5
passports, other documents, 1–2,
Pavlovsk, 125–6
Pereslavl-Zaleski, 163–4
photography, 5, 19, 27–9
Pirciupius, 343
Podolsk, 73
Postal Service *(see also* cities), 33
prices and methods of payment, 4–5
Primate Breeding Station (Sukhumi), 213
Pushkin (Tsarskoye Selo), 125
Pyatigorsk, 234–5
  hotels, campsite, 235
  museums, places of interest, 235
  restaurants, 235

rail travel and railways, 31–2
  Batumi, 217
  entry and exit points, 2
  Kharkhov, 176
  Kiev, 155
  Lvov, 368
  Moscow, 38
  Odessa, 192

rail *(cont'd)*
  Riga, 336
  Samarkand, 404
  Smolensk, 170
  Sochi, 207, 210
  Sukhumi, 215
  Suzdal, 267
  Vladimir, 267
  Volgograd, 179
  Yerevan, 259
Ramany, 264
recreational areas and parks
  Alma Ata, 408
  Kiev, 150–2
  Kishinev, 372
  Minsk, 347
  Odessa, 189
  Riga, 332
regions and Republics of U.S.S.R., 16–
  17
restaurants and cafés, 24–5, 26
  Ashkahabad, 414
  Baku, 265
  Brest, 376
  Chernovtsy, 380
  Jurmala, 335
  Kharkov, 176
  Kiev, 152–3
  Kishinev, 373
  Leningrad, 128
  Lvov, 367
  Minsk, 350
  Moscow, 47–50
  Novgorod, 160
  Odessa, 191
  Ordzhonikidze, 237
  Orel, 173
  Pereslavl-Zaleski, 164
  Pyatigorsk, 235
  Riga, 335
  Rostov, 164
  Samarkand, 403
  Simferopol, 230
  Smolensk, 170
  Sochi, 208–9
  Sukhumi, 214
  Tallinn, 321, 322
  Tashkent, 389
  Tbilisi, 249–50
  tipping, 26
  Uzhgorod, 377
  Volgogrod, 179
  Yaroslavl, 164
  Yerevan, 259

Riga, 324–6
City Hall Square, 331
Dom Cathedral, 327
farm market, 334
Forest Park (Mezapark), 332
Guild Halls, 330
homes, old, 331
hotels, 335
museums, 332–4
Old Riga, 326–7
Peter's Castle, 330
Post Office, 336
recreation park, 332
Reformed Church, 329
restaurants and cafés, 335
Riga Castle, 329
Russian courtyard, 330
St. Catherine's (Katrinas) Church, 329
St. Jacob's (Jekaba) Church, 328
Skarnu Street churches, 328
stores and shops, 334, 336
suburbs, 324–5
Swedish Gates, 329–30
theaters and concert halls, 336
transportation offices, 336
warehouses, 331–2
Rostov, 162–3
Rostov-on-Don, 231–2
circus, 233, 234
hotels, motel, campsite, 233–4
museums, places of interest, 232–3, 234
shopping, 234
theaters, 233, 234
Rustavi, 248–9

Salaspils, 334–5
Samarkand, 390–3
Afrasiab, 393–4
Bibi Khanum Mosque, 396
Freedom Monument, 402
hotels, 403
madrasah (religious schools), 395–6
mausoleums, 397–401
museums, 393, 395, 401
Post Office, 404
restaurants, 403
stores and shops, 404
theaters, 403
transportation offices, 404
Ulugh Beg's Observatory, 394–5
shopping and stores, 22, 25
Kiev, 154
Leningrad, 129–30
Lvov, 368

shopping (cont'd)
Minsk, 351–2
Moscow, 59, 80–2
Odessa, 192
purchase receipts, 25
Riga, 334, 336
Rostov-on-Don, 234
Samarkand, 404
Smolensk, 170
Sochi, 195, 209–10
Tallinn, 323
Tashkent, 390
Sigulda, 335
Simferopol, 229–30
hotels, 230
Intourist office, 230
museums, 230
Post and Telegraph Offices, 230
restaurants, 230
Smolensk, 164–6
Assumption Cathedral, 169
campsite, 170
Ioann Bogoslav Church, 167
hotels, 170
Kremlin, 168–9
Michael Archangel (Svirskaya) Church,
168
Petropavlovskaya Church, 168
Post Office, 170
railway station, 170
Regional Museum of Local Lore, 166–7,
170
restaurants and cafés, 170
stores and shops, 170
telephone office, 170
theaters and concert hall, 170
Sochi, 193–7
Arboretum Park, 200–1
areas, nearby, 205–7
beaches, 195
caves, 204
circus, 209
health facilities, 194, 206–7
hotels, 208
Kurortny Prospect, 194–6
Mt. Bolshoi Akhun, 202–3
Nikolai Ostrovsky Museum, 199–200
Park Riviera, 193–4
Post Office, 210
Regional Studies Museum, 198–9
restaurants and cafés, 208–9
stores and shops, 195, 209–10
tea plantations, 203
telephone office, 210

Sochi (cont'd)
  theaters and cinemas, 195
  transportation, 207, 210
  Tree of Friendship, 202
  Yew and Boxtree Grove, 203
steamship travel
  entry and exit points, 2
  Riga, 336
  Sochi, 207
Sukhumi, 211–12
  Botanical Gardens, 212
  historical sites nearby, 214
  hotels, 214
  Intourist office, 214
  monkey nursery, 213
  Mt. Sukhumi, 213
  museum, 212
  Post Office, 215
  restaurants, 214
  theaters, 213, 215
  transportation offices, 215
Sumgait, 263–4
Surakhany, 264
Suzdal, 266, 281–3
  Archbishop's Palace, 287
  Deposition of the Robe Convent, 293
  Entry into Jerusalem and St. Paraskeva,
    Churches of, 290
  Emperor Constantine Church, 291–1
  Gostiny Dvor, 290–1
  Intercession, Convent of the, 295–7
  Kremlin, 284
  Nativity and the Epiphany, Churches of
    the, 294–5
  Nativity, Cathedral of, 284–7
  Our Lady of Kazan Church, 291
  Our Lady of the Sorrows Church, 292
  Psad Marketplace and Central Square,
    289–90
  Resurrection, Church of the, 291
  St. Alexander Monastery, 294
  St. Antipus Church, 292–3
  St. Boris and St. Gelb Church, 288
  St. Cosmas and St. Damian Church,
    288–9
  St. John the Baptist Church, 290
  St. Lazarus Church, 292
  St. Nicholas churches, 287–8, 288
  Sign, Church of the, 389
  Spaso-Yevfimiev Monastery, 297–300
  transportation to, 267

Talashkino, 167
Tallinn, 209–12

Tallinn (cont'd)
  Brotherhood of the Blackheads, House
    of, 316–17
  cafés (kohviks), 321, 322
  cinemas, 323
  Dom Church, 313
  Dominican Monastery, 317
  Fortress Wall, 313–14
  Great Guild Building, 316
  Guild of St. Olaf, 317
  Holy Ghost Church, 315
  homes, medieval, 317–18
  hotels, 322
  museums, 318–19
  Niguliste Church, 314–15
  Oleviste Church, 316
  Peter the Great's Cottage, 319
  Pikk Jalg Street, 314
  Pirita suburb, 321
  Post and Telegraph Offices, 323
  restaurants, 322
  St. Michael Convent, 317
  souvenir shops, 323
  theaters and concert halls, 323
  Toompea castle, 312–13
  Town Hall, 315
  weather vanes, 319–21
Tashkent, 381–03
  Alisher Navoi Public Library, 387
  cinemas, 389–90
  circus, 390
  hotels, 384, 385, 388–9
  museums, 384, 385–6, 389
  places of interest, 384–8
  restaurants and cafés, 389
  stores and shops, 390
  theaters, 384, 388, 390
  university, 386
Tbilisi, 238–41
  Anchiskati Church, 242
  Botanical Gardens, 243
  campsites, 249
  hotels, motels, 249
  hydroelectric station, 242
  Isani (Avlabari) District, 246–7
  Janashi State Museum, 243–4
  Lenin Square, 243
  Maidan, 242
  Metekhi Fortress, 247
  modern city, 243–7
  Mt. Mtatsminda, 245–6
  museums, 241, 250
  Narikala Fortress, 241
  Navtlugi District, 247

Tbilisi *(cont'd)*
  Northern District, 246
  Old City, 241–3
  Post and Telegraph Offices, 250
  places of interest, 241–9
  Pantheon, 246
  Pushkin Square, 243
  Railway Terminal, 250
  restaurants and cafés, 249–50
  St. David Church, 246
  St. George of Kashveti Church, 244
  Sioni Cathedral, 241
  Square of Heroes, 245
  suburbs, 247–9
  theaters and concert halls, 244, 250
tea plantations (Sochi), 203
telephone and telegraph, 33
temperatures (chart), 28
theaters *(see also* Cinemas)
  Alma Ata, 407–8
  Baku, 263, 265
  Batumi, 217
  Brest, 376
  Dushanbe, 422
  Frunze, 424
  Kharkov, 176
  Kiev, 145–50, 154
  Leningrad, 117, 121, 129
  Lvov, 366, 367
  Minsk, 351
  Moscow, 60–1, 77–9
  Odessa, 191
  Orel, 173
  Riga, 336
  Rostov-on-Don, 233, 234
  Samarkand, 403
  Smolensk, 170
  Sochi, 195, 209
  Tallinn, 323
  Tbilisi, 244, 250
  Tashkent, 384, 388, 390
  time of performance, 26
  tickets, 26
  Yerevan, 259
tipping, 26
tours, 2–3
  group, 3, 4
  health treatment, 27
  special interest, 3
traffic regulations, 29–30
trains. *See* Rail travel and railways
Trakai, 342–3
transportation
  airlines *(see also* Air travel), 31, 33–4

transportation *(cont'd)*
  on arrival, 20
  automobile *(see also* Automobile travel),
    1–2, 21, 22–3, 29–30
  costs, and methods of payment, 4–5
  cruises, 32
  driver's license, international, 1
  entry and exit points, 2
  to and from Soviet Union, 2
  trains *(see also* Rail travel and railways),
    31–2
  See also names of cities
travel agencies, 2
  abroad, 9–15
  tours, 4
  United States, 7–9
travel arrangements
  accommodations *(see also* Campsites;
    Hotels; Motels), 3–5, 17–18, 20–1
  automobile travel, 1–2, 21, 22–3, 39–30
  cities open to foreign tourists, 17–18
  classes of service, 3–4
  Customs, Soviet, 18–20
  documents, 1–2
  driver's license, international, 1–2
  entry and exit points, 2
  independent travel, 3–4
  Intourist *(see also* Intourist; specific
    subjects), 20
  meals, 4–5, 24–5
  prices and methods of payment, 4–5
  tours, 2–3, 4
  transportation to and from Soviet
    Union, 2
  transportation in Soviet Union, *see*
    Transportation; specific forms
  travel agencies, 2, 7–15
  what to take and not take with, 5–7
Trukhanov Island (Kiev), 151
Tsarskoye Selo (Pushkin), 125
Tula, 74–5

universities
  Kiev, 146–7
  Leningrad, 115–16
  Moscow, 66
  Tashkent, 386
  Vilnius, 341
Uzhgorod, 376–7

vaccination certificate, 1
visas, other documents, 1–2
Vilnius, 337–9
  Art Gallery, 340

Vilnius *(cont'd)*
  Gediminas Square, 339–40
  hotels, 343
  Intourist office, 343
  museums, 342
  Peter and Paul Cathedral, 341
  places of interest, 339–43
  St. Anna and Bernadine Churches, 340
  St. Mikhail Church, 341
  suburbs, 342–3
  University, 341
Vladimir, 266–9
  Assumption, Cathedral of, 271–5
  Assumption of Our Lady, Cathedral of, 277–8
  Golden Gates, 269–70
  Nativity, Monastery and Cathedral of, 276–7
  Princess's Convent and Cathedral of the Assumption, 278–80
  St. Dimitri Cathedral, 275–6
  St. George Church, 271–2
  St. Nicetas the Martyr Church, 280–1
  St. Nicholas Church, 271
  St. Nicholas at the Galleys Church, 270–1
  Our Savior Church, 271
  transportation to, 266–7
Volgograd, 176–7
  Defense of Stalingrad Museum, 178–9
  hotels, 179
  Lenin Avenue, 178
  Mamayev Hill, 177–8
  Post and Telegraph Office, 179
  railway and port terminals, 179
  restaurants, 179

weather, 27
  temperature chart, 28
wine industry
  Odessa, 190
  Yalta area, 226, 227

Yalta area, 221–2
  Alupka, 225–6
  Chekhov Memorial Museum, 222–3
  Crimean Game Preserve, 226–7
  health facilities, 224
  Livadia, 223–4
  Massandra, 226
  Nikitsky Botanical Garden, 227–8
  Oreanda, 224
Yaroslavl and environs, 161
  hotels, restaurants, cafés, 164
  museums and places of interest, 162
  Pereslavl-Zaleski, 163–4
  Rostov, 162–3
Yasnaya Polyana, 75–6
Yerevan, 251–4
  hotels, 259
  museums, places of interest, 255–6, 259
  Post and Telegraph Office, 259
  Railway Terminal, 259
  restaurants, 259
  suburbs, 256–8
  theaters, concert halls, cinemas, 259
Yuryev-Polskoi, 306
  John Theologos Church, 306–7
  St. George Cathedral, 307–8

Zagorsk, 76